More Praise for *American Film Comedy:*

"Rodney Dangerfield finally gets some respect, as does every comedy writer, director and star included in Scott and Barbara Siegel's thorough and affectionate look at the people who brought laughter to the movies."
—Jack Mathews, film critic, *Newsday*

"A no–nonsense guide to the nonsensical side of film, with clear and concise entries on an impressively wide range of topics. A boon for everyone from hardworking critics to people who just enjoy laughing."
—David Sterritt, film critic, *Christian Science Monitor*

"Thank you Siegels. Every serious laugh buff should find *American Film Comedy* a unique treasure chest of information and insight, from who threw the first movie pie-in-the-face to profiles of the screen's greatest comic actors, directors, and writers. Make room for it immediately on your bookshelf."
—William Wolf, critic and author

"A serious collection of facts on humor. The joke is on movie buffs who don't add this to their library."
—Jeff Strickler, *Minneapolis Star Tribune*

"Movie lovers will treasure this well-researched and brightly written book for its ability to settle arguments, provide insights and inspire nostalgia. Concise, lucid and frankly opinionated, it deserves a prominent place on the reference shelf of any self-respecting film buff."
—Joe Leydon, film critic, *Houston Post*

# American Film Comedy

# American Film Comedy

## Scott and Barbara Siegel

PRENTICE HALL GENERAL REFERENCE

*New York   London   Toronto   Sydney   Tokyo   Singapore*

**PRENTICE HALL GENERAL REFERENCE**
15 Columbus Circle
New York, New York, 10023

Library of Congress Cataloging in Publication Data

Siegel, Scott.
    American film comedy / Scott Siegel and Barbara
Siegel.
        p.       cm.
    Includes bibliographical references and index.
    1. Comedy films—Encyclopedias.    I. Siegel,
Barbara.    II. Title.
PN1995.9.C55S48    1994
791.43′617—dc20                        93-48087

ISBN 0-671-89203-7

Designed by Irving Perkins Associates, Inc.

Manufactured in the United States of America

First Edition

# Dedication

## For Jami Bernard—

With whom we spent more time talking on the phone than we
did writing this book.

In our lengthy nightly phone calls, we solved many of the
world's problems.

Perhaps you noticed?

She, alone, has unravelled the secrets of napping, home repair,
and communicating with taxi drivers.

Together, we have made great headway on the general decline
of the human intellect. As an example of that decline, we chose to
dedicate this book to her even though it precluded us from asking
her for a blurb that might have graced its cover.

So, here we are, getting off the phone (again) at 4 A.M.,
knowing what finally matters most: that we always find the time
for each other.

# Acknowledgments

This is a book that could not have been written without a great many helping hands—and minds. We acknowledge our debt to those who helped us both directly and indirectly in making this book possible.

First and foremost, our thanks go to our editor, Susan Lauzau, who shepherded this volume through the long trek from concept to printed page. Her patient and thoughtful guidance is much appreciated.

Among our friends, we want to single out Kathleen Carroll, who has been supportive of us in countless ways. She sets a high standard for graciousness and charm. In addition, we want to thank Peter Drew, a generous and thoughtful man who also happens to be an immensely knowledgeable film teacher.

The writing of this book also affords us the opportunity to thank the many people who have been helpful to us at various film festivals, where many of the fresh comic talents are found. In particular, we are very grateful for our yearly warm reception from the folks at Toronto's Festival of Festivals, among them Helga Stephenson, Piers Handling, Michèle Maheux, Susan Norget, Nuria Bronfman, Noah Cowan, Dorina Fugiuele, Julie Rekai Rickerd, Karen Tyrell, Jacqueline Brody, Catherine Hayos, and, of course, our friend David Nancoff. From the New York Film Festival and the New Directors/New Films Festival, many thanks to Richard Pena, Wendy Keyes, Joanna Ney, Steve

Grenyo, Genevieve Villaflor, Denise Iullo, and Lara Shapiro. From the Montreal Film Festival, our appreciation goes to Serge Losique, Lorraine Jamison, and (via New York) Samathana Dean and Undine Marshfield. From The Hampton's International Film Festival, thanks go (again) to Lorraine Jamison. From the Israeli Film Festival, we wish to thank Pat Story and her staff. Thanks are also to Peter Chow of the Hong Kong Film Festival and Minnie Hong of the Asian Film Festival.

When it comes to theatrical releases, we greatly appreciate the work of a great many industry publicists and programmers who make screening their films especially pleasurable. We'd like to thank the following for all their efforts on our behalf: Annette Alvarez, Betsy Boesel, Fabiano Canosa, Gerard Depena, Donna Dickman, Howard Feinstein, Paola Freccero, Frank Gafney, Sophie Gluck, Bruce Goldstein, Terry Greenberg, Mary Alice Greene, Dennis Higgins, Jeff Hill, Andrea Hirshon, Lauren Hyman, Susan Jacobs, Sharon Kahn, Teri Kane, John Kelley, Steve Klain, Vivian Lau, Nancy Lefkowitz, Scott Levine, Mark Lipsky, Mary Lugo, Loretta Milana, Debbie Nathin, Catherine Ortiz, Mark Reina, Reid Roosevelt, Rachel Rosen, Peggy Siegal, Jackie Sigmund, Louise Stanton, Anne Stavola, Sandy Thompson, Jeremy Walker, Norman Wang, Cara White, and for their non-film festival efforts, as well, Peter Chow, Samantha Dean, Minnie Hong, Undine Marshfield, Joanna Ney, Pat Story, and Genevieve Villaflor.

# Contents

# Introduction

It's said that humor is idiosyncratic—one person's guffaw is another person's groaner. But Hollywood movies have ultimately made everyone laugh, all over the world. This book is a celebration of the artists and artisans who created that laughter—and who continue to create it today.

From the outset, our intention was to write as comprehensive and as thorough a volume on American film comedy as reasonably possible. That's not to say that every actor, director, and screenwriter who was ever involved in making a comedy is profiled here. To write a book as all-inclusive as *that* would mean we'd never have time to go to the movies again. We approached this project as if we were its audience, instead of its writers. What kind of book did we want for our reference shelf?

This book.

We made sure to include every major Hollywood figure whose work was either exclusively or largely in the field of comedy. However, that wasn't enough to satisfy us. We also included an exhaustive number of comic supporting players, comic film terms, comedy subgenres (like musical comedy), speciality studio histories, examinations of landmark comedies, filmographies, and more.

We cover the history of film comedy, from John Bunny, the first American comedy star, to potential new stars such as Mike Myers. Comedy directors range from Leo McCarey to Hal Hartley; producers range from Mack Sennett to John Hughes. From animal comics to child comics, and from comedy couples to comic chases, we have encompassed the full film comedy experience.

Because, like you, we are movie-lovers, we could not find it in our hearts to write a film book that did not, at least, suggest that we're dealing with a visual medium. Therefore, we are pleased to tell you that we devoted some of the space in this book to pictures, as well as words. This volume is illustrated with approximately seventy-five stills that, we trust, will help you either put a name to a face, or better still, put a smile on your face.

Inevitably someone may ask, "How could you leave so-and-so out of your book?" We had to make tough decisions to keep the length of this volume under control. Plenty of actors, directors, etc., have worked extensively in comedy but are perhaps better known for their work in another genre. Or perhaps someone made several famous comedies, but the bulk of his or her work is in another field. In these gray areas, you can be sure that a lot of agonizing thought went into the process of choosing what (and whom) to include.

Leaf through the following pages and look up favorite actors, discover unusual facts (did you know that Albert Brooks's real name was Albert Einstein?), learn the definition of *pratfall*, or find out what Stanley Kubrick originally intended for the ending of *Dr. Strangelove*. Most of all, however, we hope you read this book in the same spirit in which it was written: to honor and remember those with the gift to make us laugh.

Scott and Barbara Siegel
New York City

# Guide to Abbreviations

To keep the book from being unduly cluttered, we have used abbreviations to describe the various contributions an actor, director, etc., might have made to his or her movies. When an individual is strictly an actor or a director, no identifying symbol is used, as that person's contribution to film comedy is clearly noted in the entry. For instance, Cary Grant will not have the letter *a* next to his films, denoting that he acted in them; we assume you know that.

In any event most of these abbreviations are self-explanatory. The list below includes abbreviations and their meanings:

| | |
|---|---|
| a | actor |
| adapt | adaptation |
| add dial | additional dialogue |
| assoc. p | associate producer |
| chor | choreography |
| co | shared credit |
| co-d | co-director |
| co-dial | co-dialogue |
| co-p | co-producer |
| co-play basis | film is based on co-written play |
| co-sc | co-screenplay |
| d | director |
| d only | directed only |
| dial | dialogue |
| doc | documentary |
| ed | editor |
| exec. p | executive producer |
| mu | music |
| mu perf | musical performance |
| p | producer (generally used interchangeably for producer or executive producer) |
| ph | director of photography |
| sc | screenplay |
| sc adapt | screenplay adaptation |
| UK | United Kingdom production |
| uncred | uncredited |

In most instances we spelled out short words such as *song* and expressions such as *based on play*. These came up rarely enough to allow us the luxury of avoiding a confusing shorthand. Note that some filmographies begin *Films* while others begin with *Films Include*. The former indicates that the filmography is complete through the last noted movie, while the latter indicates a representative filmography. Finally, readers will see certain surnames, film titles, and expressions printed in SMALL CAPITAL letters. This has been done as a cross-referencing guide; the people, movies, and terms (e.g., SATIRE) that appear this way in their first use in an entry have their own entry elsewhere in this volume.

# A

**Abbott and Costello** Although their humor was infantile and their filmic style nonexistent, Abbott and Costello comprised the most popular comedy team of the sound era until supplanted by MARTIN and LEWIS. Slender con man Bud Abbott was the straight man and short, round, and innocent Lou Costello reaped the laughter. The team's silly, escapist humor provided relief from World War II's fearful times, and its success helped Universal Pictures fill its coffers. The team's reign as a top box office draw ended after the war, but the duo briefly regained its ticket-selling clout between 1948 and 1951 before finding a new, young audience on television.

William A. "Bud" Abbott's (1895–1974) parents worked as circus performers, inspiring him to pursue a show business career of his own. It was a long time in coming. When he was just fifteen, he was shanghaied and forced to work as a sailor on a boat heading for Europe. Abbott tried unsuccessfully throughout his twenties and most of his thirties to make a career in the entertainment industry. He had all but given up when, working as a cashier at a Brooklyn VAUDE-VILLE house in 1931, a young comic named Lou Costello reported that his partner was sick. Abbott filled in as Costello's straight man that night, and a long-lasting, if stormy, relationship was born.

Louis Francis Cristillo (1906–1959), later to be known simply as Lou Costello, had an odd assortment of early jobs that included selling newspapers, soda jerking, and working in a hat shop. Later, he became a rather unlikely prizefighter. Yearning to make it into show business, Costello quit the ring in the late 1920s and made his way to Hollywood. The best he could do was to become a stuntman, manag-

ing at one point the unnatural act of doubling for actress Dolores Del Rio.

After joining forces, Abbott and Costello honed their routines on the vaudeville and BURLESQUE circuits for seven years until they had their big break in 1938, appearing on Kate Smith's popular radio show. They quickly became radio favorites, which led to their appearance in the Broadway revue *Streets of Paris* with Carmen MIRANDA.

Hollywood beckoned, and Abbott and Costello were hired by Universal as comic relief in an innocuous musical called *One Night in the Tropics* (1940). Audiences roared at the antics of the two comedians, and Universal promptly signed them to a long-term contract. They starred in their next film, *Buck Privates* (1941). It was a huge hit and was quickly followed by comic romps in two other branches of the military, *In the Navy* (1941) and *Keep 'Em Flying* (1941). Abbott and Costello made a total of five films in 1941, and their combined success put them among Hollywood's top-ten box office draws.

Their early 1940s films, such as *Who Done It?* (1942), *Hit the Ice* (1943), *Lost in a Harem* (1944), and *The Naughty Nineties* (1945), were pleasant, simple comedies without much zaniness. Many of the comic routines in their movies were taken straight from their vaudeville act, such as the immortal "Who's on First?" routine.

Following the war, the poor response to films like *Little Giant* (1946) and *The Wistful Widow of Wagon Gap* (1947) suggested that America's love affair with Abbott and Costello was over. The team tried to recapture past glory by making movies reminiscent

*Bud and Lou in a publicity still from their most enduring comedy,* Abbott and Costello Meet Frankenstein *(1948). With them are Boris Karloff as Frankenstein and Bela Lugosi as Dracula. Lon Chaney, Jr., also starred as the Wolf Man.*
PHOTO COURTESY OF MOVIE STAR NEWS.

of its earlier hits, such as *The Time of Their Lives* (1946), a comic horror story patterned after its 1941 hit *Hold That Ghost*, and *Buck Privates Come Home* (1947), an obvious attempt to remind audiences of its first big hit. It didn't work.

Except for occasionally being loaned to other studios, Abbott and Costello made most of their films at Universal Pictures. Universal's main claim to fame during the 1930s was its horror films. Hoping to revive the popularity of its premier comedy team, the studio combined its two biggest assets in one film, *Abbott and Costello Meet Frankenstein* (1948). The movie boasted supporting performances by Boris Karloff as Frankenstein, Bela Lugosi as Drac-

ula, and Lon Chaney, Jr., as the Wolf Man. The result of Universal's experiment was arguably Abbott and Costello's best, most consistently funny film. It was also, as Universal hoped, a big success at the box office.

The unfortunate result of *Abbott and Costello Meet Frankenstein*, however, was that it spawned a formula that seemed as if it would no sooner die than Dracula himself. With numbing regularity, the team starred in movies with repetitive titles: *Abbott and Costello Meet the Killer* (1949), *Abbott and Costello Meet the Invisible Man* (1950), *Abbott and Costello Meet Captain Kidd* (1952), *Abbott and Costello Meet Dr. Jekyll and Mr. Hyde* (1953), *Abbott and Costello*

*Meet the Keystone Kops* (1955), and *Abbott and Costello Meet the Mummy* (1955).

They made other films during these years, but the comedy was just as uninspired as their horror/comedy film formula movies. In the early 1950s, the duo starred in the TV series "The Abbott and Costello Show," which reprised many of their best vaudeville routines. Even as Abbott and Costello's films were being ignored, a whole new generation of kids grew up on the syndicated reruns of their TV series and then later discovered their movies on television.

The last film that Abbott and Costello made together was *Dance with Me Henry* (1956). They produced the movie themselves and witnessed its painful flop at the box office. Abbott soon thereafter announced his retirement, but Costello went on to make one solo film, *The Thirty-Foot Bride of Candy Rock* (1959). He died of a heart attack, however, before the movie was released to poor reviews and even worse business.

Both Bud Abbott and Lou Costello had run into tax troubles with the government and found themselves in financial difficulties at the end of their lives. Bud Abbott suffered still more, however, when he was crippled by a series of strokes, beginning in 1964. He died in a retirement home ten years later. Their story was made into a TV movie in 1978 titled *Bud and Lou* starring Buddy HACKETT and Harvey Korman.

FILMS: *One Night in the Tropics* (1940); *Buck Privates* (1941); *Hold That Ghost* (1941); *In the Navy* (1941); *Keep 'Em Flying* (1941); *Pardon My Sarong* (1942); *Ride 'Em Cowboy* (1942); *Rio Rita* (1942); *Who Done It?* (1942); *Hit the Ice* (1943); *It Ain't Hay* (1943); *In Society* (1944); *Lost in a Harem* (1944); *Bud Abbott and Lou Costello in Hollywood* (1945); *Here Come the Co-eds* (1945); *The Naughty Nineties* (1945); *Little Giant* (1946); *The Time of Their Lives* (1946); *Buck Privates Come Home* (1947); *The Wistful Widow of Wagon Gap* (1947); *Abbott and Costello Meet Frankenstein* (1948); *Mexican Hayride* (1948); *The Noose Hangs High* (1948); *Abbott and Costello Meet the Killer* (1949); *Africa Screams* (1949); *Abbott and Costello in the Foreign Legion* (1950); *Abbott and Costello Meet the Invisible Man* (1951); *Comin' Round the Mountain* (1951); *Abbott and Costello Meet Captain Kidd* (1952); *Jack and the Beanstalk* (1952); *Lost in Alaska* (1952); *Abbott and Costello Go to Mars* (1953); *Abbott and Costello Meet Dr. Jekyll and Mr. Hyde* (1953); *Abbott and Costello Meet the Keystone Kops* (1954); *Abbott and Costello Meet the Mummy* (1955); *Dance with Me Henry* (1956).

Lou Costello alone: *The Thirty-Foot Bride of Candy Rock* (1959).

## Abrahams, Jim (1944– )

Along with his two partners, David and Jerry ZUCKER, Abrahams helped revolutionize film comedy with the shotgun parody humor of *Airplane!* (1980) and the many similar films he has made since. Like his partners, he brought a full-fledged sense of the ridiculous to his work, taking the kinds of parodies Mel BROOKS had done in the 1970s with *Blazing Saddles* (1974) and *Young Frankenstein* (1974) and ratcheting up the humor an extra notch by casting his films not with comedians, but with well-known former action TV stars. Having those actors say and do the most ludicrous things turned out to be comic magic.

Born in Shorewood, Wisconsin, Abrahams attended the University of Wisconsin at Madison, where he first met and befriended the Zucker brothers. While still in Madison, the three of them created their own version of the Second City comedy troupe, calling themselves the Kentucky Fried Theater. Later, they moved the whole enterprise to Los Angeles, eventually making their first film in 1977, *Kentucky Fried Movie*. Abrahams not only cowrote the film with his two partners, but acted in it as well. The film was a series of often hilarious (and tasteless) sketches that lampooned everything from TV commercials to kung fu movies. *Kentucky Fried Movie* was also one of the most successful independent movies ever made. The film is otherwise noteworthy for being director John LANDIS's first comedy assignment behind the camera.

The group outdid themselves when they wrote, produced, directed, and acted in *Airplane!* (1980). Densely packed with jokes, both verbal and visual, *Airplane!* set the standard for all the genre parodies that have followed, many of them created either by the threesome of Abrahams, Zucker, and Zucker, or individually, as they have gone on to solo careers.

The films Abrahams made in collaboration with the Zucker brothers include *Top Secret!* (1984); *Ruthless People* (1986); *The Naked Gun: From the Files of the Police Squad!* (1988); and *The Naked Gun 2½: The Smell of Fear* (1991). The latter two films were spin-offs of the short-lived "Police Squad" TV show that the group created.

Independent of his college pals, Abrahams directed the more conventional comedy *Big Business* (1988) as well as the engaging, sentimental comedy *Welcome Home, Roxy Carmichael* (1990). After those experiences, however, Abrahams returned to the kind of shotgun comedies he did best, making the *Top Gun* parody *Hot Shots!* (1991) and following it with a Rambo parody via *Hot Shots! Part Deux* (1993).

---

**FILMS:** *The Kentucky Fried Movie* (a, sc, 1977); *Airplane!* (a, sc, p, d, 1980); *Top Secret!* (sc, p, d, 1984); *Ruthless People* (d, 1986); *Big Business* (d, 1988); *The Naked Gun: From the Files of the Police Squad!* (sc, p, 1988); *Cry-Baby* (p, 1990); *Welcome Home, Roxy Carmichael* (d, 1990); *The Naked Gun 2½: The Smell of Fear* (sc, p, 1991); *Hot Shots!* (sc, d, 1991); *Hot Shots! Part Deux* (sc, d, 1993); *Naked Gun 33⅓: The Final Insult* (p, 1994).

---

**Adams, Edie (1927– )** A glamorous blond actress/entertainer/comedian, Adams gained fame largely through her work on television as a regular on the "Ernie Kovacs Show" in the 1950s. She married Ernie KOVACS in 1955. However, Adams was not a one-medium entertainer; she also starred on Broadway, played nightclubs, and added style and

humor to a number of motion pictures, most of them in the 1960s.

Born Elizabeth Edith Enke in Kingston, Pennsylvania, Adams did not drift into a show business career. She graduated from both the Juilliard School of Music and the Columbia School of Drama before taking the beauty contest route. She took the titles Miss New York TV and Miss U.S. TV before making her mark on both the small screen with Kovacs and on Broadway in *Wonderful Town* (1953) and as Daisy Mae in *Li'l Abner* (1956).

Adams was already a seasoned veteran of thirty-three when she appeared in a supporting role in *The Apartment* (1960). Although only approximately half of her films were comedies, she usually played either a comic relief character or a comic second lead throughout the rest of her movie career, making notable contributions to such films as *Lover Come Back* (1961), *Under the Yum Yum Tree* (1963), and *Love with the Proper Stranger* (1964). After *The Honey Pot* (1967), she didn't appear in a feature-length theatrical film again until 1978 when she lent her comic talents to CHEECH AND CHONG in their debut hit movie, *Up in Smoke*. Since then, she has appeared in films of ever-decreasing quality. In more recent years, she has appeared on TV again, starring in, among other projects, a TV movie called *Jake Spanner, Private Eye* (1989).

Adams became a widow when Kovacs died in 1962, leaving her with staggering debts. She paid back every nickel, largely by taking on any kind of work she could, including doing sexy White Owl Cigar TV commercials during the 1960s. Her devotion to Kovacs, however, did not end with either his death or his debts. She participated in two documentaries about her former husband: a theatrical release simply called *Kovacs* (1971) and a made-for-TV film entitled *Ernie Kovacs: Television's Original Genius* (1982).

---

**FILMS:** *The Apartment* (1960); *Lover Come Back* (1961); *Call Me Bwana* (1963); *Under the Yum Yum Tree* (1963); *It's a Mad Mad Mad Mad World* (1963); *Love with the Proper Stranger* (1964); *The Best Man*

(1964); *The Oscar* (1966); *Made in Paris* (1966); *The Honey Pot* (1967); *Kovacs* (doc, 1971); *Up in Smoke* (1978); *Racquet* (1979); *The Happy Hooker Goes to Hollywood* (1980); *Boxoffice* (1981); *Adventures Beyond Belief* (1987).

---

**Alda, Alan (1936—)** The much-beloved Alan Alda, known for his sensitivity as well as his sharp wit, owes most of his fame as a comic actor to TV's popular "M*A*S*H" (1972–1983). While Alda had modest success as a movie actor before his long-running TV series, the show's success allowed him to become, for at least a short while, a considerable force in the film industry, where he eventually became a triple threat actor/writer/director.

The son of actor Robert Alda (who was anything but a comic actor), Alda studied English at Fordham University in New York. He soon followed in the family tradition and began working on the stage, making his breakthrough on Broadway when he starred in *The Owl and the Pussycat*, playing the role George SEGAL would later play in the film.

In 1963 Alda made his film debut in *Purlie Victorious* (later renamed *Gone Are the Days*), but did not appear again on the big screen until he played George Plimpton in *Paper Lion* (1968). Thereafter, he worked steadily in Hollywood, but with little fanfare. It wasn't until "M*A*S*H" was a well-established hit on TV that major film roles started coming his way. For instance, he was one of the stars of Neil SIMON's *California Suite* (1978) and had his biggest movie hit with *Same Time, Next Year* (1978).

After he proved himself to be a capable writer and director by performing both functions on "M*A*S*H", he not only starred in a clever political satire, *The Seduction of Joe Tynan* (1979), he also wrote the screenplay. He went on to write, direct, and star in four films over the next decade, having his greatest success with his first, *The Four Seasons* (1981), and his least success with his last, *Betsy's Wedding* (1990). Most of the films he made during this span dealt with middle-class values and were largely about middle-aged people—a majority of whom, it is generally acknowledged, go to the movies far less often than their children.

In recent years, Alda has begun showing up in supporting roles, playing characters that either gently mock his public image as a sweet, comic everyman (*Crimes and Misdemeanors*, 1989) or make a savage frontal attack on that image (*Whispers in the Dark*, 1992).

---

**FILMS:** *Purlie Victorious/Gone Are the Days* (1963); *Paper Lion* (1968); *The Extraordinary Seaman* (1969); *Jenny* (1969); *The Mephisto Waltz* (1970); *The Moonshine War* (1970); *To Kill a Clown* (1972); *The Glass House* (1972); *California Suite* (1978); *Same Time, Next Year* (1978); *The Seduction of Joe Tynan* (a, sc, 1979); *The Four Seasons* (a, sc, d, 1981); *Sweet Liberty* (a, sc, d, 1986); *A New Life* (a, sc, d, 1988); *Crimes and Misdemeanors* (1989); *Betsy's Wedding* (a, sc, d, 1990); *Whispers in the Dark* (1992); *Manhattan Murder Mystery* (1993).

---

**Allen, Fred (1894—1956)** A celebrated and cerebral radio humorist, Fred Allen did not make a successful transition to the movies like his contemporaries, Will ROGERS, Bob HOPE, and Jack BENNY. Nonetheless, he made occasional film appearances that were noteworthy for his dry, acerbic comic delivery. With his hangdog expression of perpetual misery, coupled with suitcase-sized bags under his eyes, Allen looked and sounded equally irascible.

Born John Florence Sullivan in Cambridge, Massachusetts, Allen went to Boston University, but got his real education in VAUDEVILLE and in the legitimate theater before becoming one of radio's great comic entertainers. Like Jack Benny and George BURNS, Allen often performed with his wife, Portland Hoffa.

Allen appeared in just six feature films, making amusing contributions to such movies as *Thanks a Million* (1935), in which he plays Dick Powell's smart-mouthed manager, and *Love Thy Neighbor* (1940), in which Allen and Jack Benny star, trading barbs in an attempt to cash in on their good-natured radio feud. Curiously, two of his six films, *We're Not Married* and *O. Henry's Full House*, are comic anthologies made in the same year (1952); he stars in a single episode of each of those two movies.

**FILMS: Features:** *Thanks a Million* (1935); *Sally, Irene, and Mary* (1938); *Love Thy Neighbor* (1940); *It's in the Bag* (1945); *We're Not Married* (1952); *O. Henry's Full House* (1952).

**Allen, Gracie** *See* BURNS AND ALLEN

**Allen, Woody (1935—)** One of America's greatest contemporary filmmakers, comic or otherwise, Woody Allen has written, directed, and starred in an impressive body of work that spans four decades. His comic antecedents are many: His New York Jewish humor is in the great tradition of Groucho Marx, while his impeccable comic timing comes from studying Bob HOPE movies. But both as a filmmaker and as a comic personality, Woody Allen is closest to Charlie CHAPLIN. Like Chaplin, he created a character of the little man who triumphs (after a fashion) against all odds. And, like Chaplin, he allowed his meek character to grow and change until that character was no longer needed to express his deepest feelings about the world.

Born Allen Stewart Konigsberg, Woody Allen was brought up in Brooklyn, New York, and lived a life not terribly unlike his young protagonist's in his autobiographical film *Radio Days* (1987). While still in high school, he sold jokes that appeared in Earl Wilson's syndicated newspaper column. After flunking out of New York University (he failed motion picture production), he joined the NBC Writer's Program. At the ripe old age of eighteen, Allen began writing for television, eventually joining such luminaries as Neil SIMON, Mel BROOKS,

*There isn't another contemporary director, let alone writer/actor/ director, who has amassed such a rich and varied body of work as Woody Allen. If he never made another movie, Woody Allen would rank in the pantheon of film artists, comedy or otherwise.* PHOTO COURTESY OF MOVIE STAR NEWS.

and Carl REINER as a writer for the classic 1950s TV series, "Your Show of Shows."

Woody Allen first came to national attention during the early 1960s when he started telling his own jokes as a stand-up comic. His comic persona, developed during those nightclub years, was a brand-new, modern creation—the neurotic everyman.

In 1964 he was paid $35,000 to rewrite the screenplay of *What's New Pussycat?* The film became the most successful comedy of its time, earning a then-staggering $17 million. Although unhappy with the changes made in his work, Allen was suddenly a recognized screenwriter and actor (he had a small part in the movie).

Allen's next film project was *What's Up Tiger Lily?* (1966). This unique comedy was created by taking a low-budget Japanese spy thriller and giving it an entirely new comic soundtrack. With a Japanese superspy named Phil Moscowitz in search of the stolen recipe for the "World's Great Egg Salad," this James Bond spoof became a cult classic.

In 1969 Allen was given a $1.6 million budget to write, direct, and star in his own film. The result was *Take the Money and Run*. It was followed by *Bananas* (1971), a film many fans consider his funniest. Both films were hits, and these two back-to-back money-makers gave Allen the freedom to continue making his own kind of films without studio interference.

When one takes into consideration that Woody Allen writes, directs, and stars in the majority of his movies, his output has been prodigious. Not counting *Tiger Lily*, he has written and directed more than twenty-five films. More important than the quantity, however, is the quality. His 1977 film *ANNIE HALL* was a landmark comedy. It won the Academy Award for best picture, best actress (Diane KEATON), best screenplay (with Marshall BRICKMAN), and best director. Though he didn't win, Allen was also nominated for best actor. It was the most complete sweep of top nominations since Orson Welles's *Citizen Kane* (1941). And it was the first comedy since *Tom Jones* (1963) to be honored as best picture.

However, *Annie Hall* was more than a comedy. Woody Allen had mixed comic human foibles with the sadness of a relationship gone awry and melded those elements into an extremely funny, yet sweet, love story.

It seemed as if Woody Allen had reached the pinnacle of his creative and commercial powers. He could have gone on to make *Annie Hall* clones, but instead chose a whole new direction, writing and directing *Interiors* (1978) in the style of Swedish film director Ingmar Bergman. The film was purposefully lacking in humor; Allen refused to do the expected.

*Interiors* was the most explicit early example of Woody Allen's experimentation in finding a new way to express himself. The remarkable aspect of this search is how often he has managed to create successful movies without seriously repeating himself. *Zelig* (1983); *Broadway Danny Rose* (1984); *The Purple Rose of Cairo* (1985, perhaps his most accomplished film to date and reportedly his personal favorite); and *Hannah and Her Sisters* (1986) firmly established Woody Allen as an independent-minded auteur who has been able to create a vision of the world that is distinctly his own.

While most of Allen's films have not been significant commercial successes, all of them have been provocative and compelling. Even relative failures like *September* (1987) and *Another Woman* (1988) are fascinating for their ambition. Inevitably, however, he learns from his mistakes. Witness, for instance, his artistic triumph with *Crimes and Misdemeanors* (1989) after the aforementioned films.

Woody Allen has almost always worked exclusively in his own films, but on rare occasions he has performed in front of the camera for other filmmakers, most notably in *The Front* (1976) and least notably in *Scenes from a Mall* (1991).

In recent years, his increasingly tenuous box office appeal has diminished still further. Oddly enough, Allen is more popular in Europe than he is in America. Whether critically panned, like *Shadows and Fog* (1992), or highly acclaimed, like *Husbands and Wives* (1992), his movies have not drawn significant crowds in the United States. Even the latter highly publicized film, which seemed like a home movie capturing his breakup with longtime lover Mia FARROW, was a surprising commercial disappointment.

After giving Farrow the leading female role in every movie he directed between 1982 and 1992, Allen cast his former lover/leading lady, Diane Keaton, in *Manhattan Murder Mystery* (1993). Critics were delighted with the light and charming film, enjoying anew the chemistry between Allen and Keaton. Alas, the movie failed to find an audience.

Allen has regularly used his lovers as leading ladies, turning Farrow into a credible actress and Diane Keaton, before her, into a star. Allen was once married to Louise LASSER, who also acted in his early films. His first wife was not in show business, but was immortalized in many of his stand-up comic routines.

FILMS: *What's New, Pussycat?* (a, sc, 1965); *What's Up Tiger Lily?* (assoc. p, a, d, sc, voice dub, 1966); *Casino Royale* (a, sc, 1967); *Don't Drink the Water* (based on his play, 1969); *Take the Money and Run* (a, d, sc, 1969); *Bananas* (a, d, sc, 1971); *Everything You Always Wanted to Know About Sex but Were Afraid to Ask* (a, d, sc, 1972); *Play It Again, Sam* (a, sc, from his play, 1972); *Sleeper* (a, d, mu, mu perf, sc, 1973); *Love and Death* (a, d, sc, 1975); *The Front* (a, 1976); *Annie Hall* (a, d, sc, 1977); *Interiors* (d, sc, 1978); *Manhattan* (a, d, sc, 1979); *Stardust Memories* (a, d, sc, 1980); *A Midsummer Night's Sex Comedy* (a, d, sc, 1982); *Zelig* (a, d, sc, 1983); *Broadway Danny Rose* (a, d, sc, 1984); *The Purple Rose of Cairo* (d, sc, 1985); *Hannah and Her Sisters* (a, d, sc, 1986); *Radio Days* (a, d, sc, 1987); *September* (d, sc, 1987); *Another Woman* (d, sc, 1988); *Crimes and Misdemeanors* (a, d, sc, 1989); *New York Stories* (contributing "Oedipus Wrecks," a, d, sc, 1989); *Alice* (d, sc, 1990); *Scenes from a Mall* (a, 1991); *Shadows and Fog* (a, d, sc, 1992); *Husbands and Wives* (a, d, sc, 1992); *Manhattan Murder Mystery* (a, d, sc, 1993).

## Alley, Kirstie (1955– )

An actress and comedian, Kirstie Alley is best known for her ROMANTIC COMEDY work on the TV sitcom "Cheers," which she joined in 1987. In addition to her TV fame, Alley has made headway in motion pictures as well, starring in the hit comedy *Look Who's Talking* (1989) and the sequels *Look Who's Talking, Too* (1990) and *Look Who's Talking Now* (1993). She has starred in several other comedies, but without the same success.

Born in Wichita, Kansas, she attended both Kansas State University and the University of Kansas before making her way to Hollywood. Long before her stint on "Cheers," Alley came to prominence as Lt. Saavik, a role played with the benefit of Vulcan ears, in *Star Trek II: The Wrath of Khan* (1982).

Alley worked steadily in the movies after that, although with little distinction. She did manage, however, to get major roles in (unfortunately) lesser films, among them *Blind Date* (1984), *Summer School* (1987), as well as *Sibling Rivalry* (1990), which was a better movie that did not find its audience.

With the demise of "Cheers," the question remains whether Kirstie Alley will fulfill her comic potential on the big screen or give the lion's share of her attention to TV, where she has had her greatest success.

FILMS: *Star Trek II: The Wrath of Khan* (1982); *Champions* (1983); *Blind Date* (1984); *Runaway* (1984); *Summer School* (1987); *Shoot to Kill* (1988); *Look Who's Talking* (1989); *Loverboy* (1989); *Look Who's Talking, Too* (1990); *Madhouse* (1990); *Sibling Rivalry* (1990); *Look Who's Talking Now* (1993).

## Anderson, Eddie "Rochester" (1905–1977)

A black actor and comedian, Eddie Anderson became a household name when Jack BENNY hired him to play his servant on his long-running radio and TV shows as well as in many of his movies. With huge eyes and a memorably raspy voice, Anderson was able to make a quick and indelible comic mark.

Born in Oakland, California, Anderson had show business in his blood. His mother was a tightrope walker in the circus, and his father worked the minstrel show circuit. The youngster started performing when he was fourteen, eventually working in VAUDEVILLE as part of a trio that included his brother.

Opportunities for black actors in Hollywood were rare, but Anderson had small roles (porters, handymen, etc.) in a handful of films before connecting with Benny. His first film was *What Price Hollywood?* (1932). Like other black actors, he picked up work in Southern period pieces like *Gone with the Wind* (1939). Anderson's most noteworthy non-Benny film was Vincente Minnelli's *Cabin in the Sky* (1943); Anderson had the lead role in the all-black cast.

Benny hired Anderson in 1937 after a hilarious guest appearance on an Easter Sunday radio broadcast. They continued to work together for the rest of their lives, appearing together in such comedies as *Man About Town* (1939); *Love Thy Neighbor* (1940); *Buck Benny Rides Again* (1940); and *The Meanest Man in the World* (1943).

Anderson's last movie appearance was in the slapstick *IT'S A MAD MAD MAD MAD WORLD* (1963).

---

**FILMS INCLUDE:** *What Price Hollywood?* (1932); *The Green Pastures* (1936); *It Happened in New Orleans/ Rainbow on the River* (1936); *Three Men on a Horse* (1936); *Melody for Two* (1937); *Jezebel* (1938); *Kentucky* (1938); *Thanks for the Memory* (1938); *Gold Diggers in Paris* (1938); *You Can't Take It with You* (1938); *Honolulu* (1939); *You Can't Cheat an Honest Man* (1939); *Man About Town* (1939); *Gone with the Wind* (1939); *Love Thy Neighbor* (1940); *Buck Benny Rides Again* (1940); *Topper Returns* (1941); *Birth of the Blues* (1941); *Kiss the Boys Goodbye* (1941); *Star Spangled Rhythm* (1942); *Tales of Manhattan* (1942); *The Meanest Man in the World* (1943); *Cabin in the Sky* (1943); *Broadway Rhythm* (1944); *Brewster's Millions* (1945); *The Sailor Takes a Wife* (1946); *The Show-Off* (1946); *It's a Mad Mad Mad Mad World* (1963).

---

**animal comics** Audiences have enjoyed the comic antics of animals on film for almost as long as they've laughed at movie SLAPSTICK. The tradition of animal comedians goes back at least as far as Mack SENNETT's Keystone Studio in the 1910s, where Pepper (a cat), Butterfly (a horse), and Teddy (a dog) competed with the other comics on the lot for audience laughter. Over at the Hal ROACH studio in the 1920s, the OUR GANG kids had a comic relief "character" in Petey, the dog. He was the one with the painted-on circle around one eye.

Most animal comedians were supporting characters, like Cheetah (the chimp) in the Tarzan films and Asta (the dog) in the Thin Man movies, but animal comics certainly have also purred, barked, and roared their way to leading roles. Rhubarb the cat owned a baseball team in a comedy of the same name made in 1951. *Clarence, the Cross-Eyed Lion* (1965) provided comedy from a somewhat larger cat, while Clyde the orangutan stole two comedies, *Every Which Way but Loose* (1978) and *Any Which Way You Can* (1980), from co-star Clint Eastwood.

Very few animals have pulled off long comedy careers. The one that hung on the most stubbornly was Francis, The Talking Mule. Between 1950 and 1956, seven talking mule films were made, six of them co-starring the affable Donald O'CONNOR. The last one had Mickey ROONEY as the mule's best friend and confidant. As for Francis, his voice was supplied by actor Chill Wills.

The premier director of such fare was Arthur Lubin, who not only made *Rhubarb* and the first six Francis films, he also created the talking horse TV sitcom, "Mr. Ed."

**animation** The first truly animated movie was made in 1906 by J. Stuart Blackton. It was a one-reeler called *Humorous Phases of Funny Faces*, and it immediately established the cartoon as a vehicle for comedy.

The first major American cartoon character to emerge from the primitive beginnings of animation was, appropriately, a dinosaur. Winsor McCay created *Gertie the Dinosaur* in 1909 and went on to make the very first feature-length animated film in the history of the movies in 1918, *The Sinking of the Lusitania*, which was anything but funny. Nonetheless, comedy remained the focus of animation, with an ever-increasing number of popular characters including Coco the Clown, Felix the Cat, and Krazy Kat.

The success of comic animation brought the young Walt DISNEY to Hollywood in 1923. He created a combination live action and animated series called *Alice in Cartoonland* and then tried another character called Oswald the Rabbit. It wasn't until 1928 that Disney finally emerged from the

*Film animation has been dominated by the Disney studio, but there have been others with different visions and styles who have also had an impact, among them Ralph Bakshi, whose live action/animated feature* Cool World *(1992) is shown here.*
PHOTO BY MERRICK MORTON, © PARAMOUNT PICTURES.

pack with his new creation, Mickey Mouse. However, even Mickey didn't fully catch on until Disney broke the sound barrier in 1929 with *Steamboat Willie*, synchronizing the visuals with a musical soundtrack.

The combination of sound, music, and animation proved to be electric. Disney's "Silly Symphony" series capitalized on this discovery, and virtually every other animation house in Hollywood belatedly tried to copy this success, the most notable example being the WARNER BROS. CARTOONS, which went by the brand names of Merrie Melodies and Looney Tunes. From the latter 1930s to the 1950s, Warner's stable of cartoon characters, including Bugs Bunny, Daffy Duck, and Tweetie Pie, vied with Disney for the allegiance of cartoon-crazy kids.

While others such as Max Fleischer (creator of Popeye) and Tex AVERY (creator of Chilly-Willy the penguin) made successful cartoons, in most respects Disney and Warner Bros. left the competition in the dust. Warner Bros. did it with the wit of its cartoons, while Disney did it by moving forward with innova-

tion after innovation, bringing three-color Technicolor to his animated shorts as early as 1933 and inventing the multi-plane camera for greater clarity, depth, and detail. Early on he pushed forward to make ambitious and critically and commercially successful animated features, including *Snow White and the Seven Dwarfs* (1938), *Pinnochio* (1940), and his belatedly appreciated masterpiece *Fantasia* (1940).

Disney's success was nearly his undoing. A bitter strike against the thriving company led in 1943 to a brigade of top-flight animators setting up shop in competition with their old employer. The new firm, UPA (United Productions of America), went on to create characters such as Gerald McBoing Boing and Mr. Magoo. Because of limited resources, they developed a far more spare and economical visual style, but they made up for that with a more sophisticated, wittier content than the increasingly saccharine Disney product.

The rise of television, particularly Saturday morning television, was the death knell for animated short subjects. Cartoons were available in great quantities on TV, and there was less and less appeal to theater owners to show them on their bills. Animated movies, however, made solely by Disney, held their own during the 1950s and 1960s but were made less frequently.

Animation, at least for theatrical distribution, seemed like a dying art form until the Beatles made *Yellow Submarine* (1968), indicating for the first time that a feature-length animated movie need not be geared strictly for very young children. That lesson was taught yet again with a vengeance by Ralph BAKSHI who made the first X-rated animated feature, *Fritz the Cat* (1971). The film caused a storm of controversy, but its iconoclastic style, energy, and undeniable creativity made it a hit. Bakshi continued to make often angry, idiosyncratic animated features throughout the 1970s and into the 1990s, but his approach became less popular with mass audiences over time.

The animated feature was finally returned to its full glory in the mid-1980s. It started relatively inconspicuously with the release of producer Steven

Spielberg's *An American Tale* (1986), a moderately successful film. However, the revival was in full bloom with the Steven Spielberg and Walt Disney Studio collaborative effort, *Who Framed Roger Rabbit?* (1988). This combination live action and animated feature, made with the latest advances in computer animation, was a colossal hit both with critics and audiences. The resurgence of interest in animated features has continued at a breakneck pace with Disney's return to wholly animated films such as *Oliver and Company* (1988) and the Lucas/Spielberg production of *The Land Before Time* (1988), a film about baby dinosaurs.

In more recent years, Disney's animated features such as *Beauty and the Beast* (1991) and *Aladdin* (1992) became huge box office hits, while also being accorded serious critical attention. Their success has spawned innumerable attempts by other studios and filmmakers in the animated arena. In other words, we are now in a new golden age of animation.

**Annie Hall** The working title of this 1977 comedy classic from Woody ALLEN had been *Anhedonia*, which means an inability to enjoy oneself. Well, maybe Allen didn't enjoy himself, but audiences certainly did, flocking to see his hilarious, yet sadly poignant, ROMANTIC COMEDY. Allen wrote, directed, and starred in what would become the first (of many) of his autobiographical movies. In this film, based on his relationship and breakup with Diane KEATON, he even used Keaton's family name, Hall, in the movie's final title.

*Annie Hall* was a landmark comedy for several reasons. First, it marked a turning point in Woody Allen's career; he blossomed in this film as a mature artist able to combine riotous laughs with emotional truths. Second, in terms of pure filmmaking, it was an audacious movie, full of boldly conceived scenes including subtitled thoughts (while Allen and Keaton jabber meaninglessly on her terrace, the audience can read what they're really thinking about each other), an animated sequence with a cartoon Woody Allen, and even instances where characters could see themselves at earlier points in their lives and comment on the action as they watched. Third, in regard to Hollywood history, Allen made the record books as the first person to be nominated for best director, best screenplay (co-scripted with Marshall BRICKMAN), and best actor Oscars since Orson Welles did for *Citizen Kane* (1941). In addition, Diane Keaton was nominated for best actress. When the dust settled, *Annie Hall* won every one of the awards except best actor, nearly equalling Frank CAPRA's 1934 winning sweep with IT HAPPENED ONE NIGHT. In any event, by winning the Oscar for best picture, the film became the first comedy since *Tom Jones* (1963) to win the Academy Award. Finally, the movie's success even spawned a fashion trend, the "Annie Hall" look, which was based on Keaton's funky wardrobe of baggy pants, loose-fitting shirts, vests, men's ties, and floppy hats.

In addition to Allen and Keaton, the movie featured Tony ROBERTS, Shelley Duvall, Carol KANE, Colleen Dewhurst, Paul Simon, Janet Margolin, and Christopher Walken. In tiny roles, future stars Beverly D'Angelo, Jeff Goldblum, Shelley Hack, and Sigourney Weaver can be seen.

## Arbuckle, Roscoe "Fatty" (1887–1933)

More than simply a fat man mugging for the camera, "Fatty" Arbuckle was a seasoned vaudevillian with remarkable physical dexterity. Arbuckle had tremendous running speed (he reportedly outran a matador in Tijuana) and the toughness of a bull (he was famous for taking extraordinary falls for the sake of a gag). It was the contrast between his immense size and his nimbleness, coupled with his baby face, that elicited laughter from his sizeable silent film audience.

This genial, overweight clown rose to fame during the golden era of Mack SENNETT's Keystone Studio (1912–1915). He was originally one of the KEYSTONE KOPS, but emerged from that anonymity to become one of Mack Sennett's biggest stars along with Mabel NORMAND, Ford STERLING, and, later, Charlie CHAPLIN.

There was nothing sophisticated about Arbuckle's films. While other comic talents experimented and grew, he was satisfied to keep churning out crude, low-budget two-reelers. This remained true even after he left Sennett to form his own company, Comicque Studios, in 1917. It wasn't until 1920 that he began making feature-length comedies. Nonetheless, his popularity remained constant until his career and life were shattered by the famous Virginia Rappe rape case in 1921.

At a Labor Day party, a young woman named Virginia Rappe took ill and died. Arbuckle was accused of rape and manslaughter. The scandal rocked Hollywood and destroyed Arbuckle's career, despite the fact that after three trials Arbuckle was acquitted of all charges. (The 1974 movie *The Wild Party*, directed by James Ivory, was loosely based on this pivotal moment in Arbuckle's life.)

Intense coverage of the sordid details of the case turned audiences away from Arbuckle. Fans could no longer envision "Fatty" as a jovial, simple man. Despite his innocence, the rape case followed him everywhere. His films were pulled from theaters, and many were subsequently lost. He tried an acting comeback on Broadway as well as in Europe, but these also failed. Under the name of William B. Goodrich (an inside joke on the name "Will B. Good"), he continued working as a director, making mostly shorts of no special note. He died virtually forgotten in 1933.

Arbuckle's significance to Hollywood goes far beyond the relative merits of his own films. He made three enormous contributions to movie comedy. The first was that Arbuckle's pants were borrowed by Charlie Chaplin when he created his legendary character of the Little Tramp. The second was that Arbuckle gave Buster KEATON his start in films in 1917 (Keaton, incidentally, remained loyal to Arbuckle to the very end). And the third was that Arbuckle was the very first person on film to be struck in the face with a custard pie. Mabel Normand tossed it at Arbuckle in *A Noise from the Deep* (1913).

**FILMS INCLUDE:** *The Sanitarium* (a, 1910); *Help! Help! Hydrophobia!, A Bandit, Passions He Had Three, The Gangster, The Noise from the Deep, Love and Courage, Mabel's New Hero, Mother's Boy, The Gypsy Queen, A Quiet Little Wedding, Fatty's Day Off, Fatty's Flirtation* (a, 1913); *In the Clutches of the Gang, A Rural Demon, A Film Johnnie, Tango Tangles, His Favorite Pastime, A Suspended Ordeal, The Masquerader, The Rounders, The Knockout, The Sea Nymphs,* (a, 1914); *The Alarm, The Sky Pirate, Fatty and the Heiress, Fatty's Gift, A Brand New Hero, Fatty's Debut, Leading Lizzie Astray, Fatty's Jonah Day, Fatty's Magic Pants, Fatty's Wine Party* (a, co-d, 1914); *Fatty Again* (a, d, 1914); *Mabel and Fatty's Wash Day, The Little Teacher, Mabel and Fatty's Married Life* (a, 1915); *Fatty and the Minnie He-Haw, Fatty's Faithful Fido, Fatty's New Role, Fatty and the Broadway Stars* (a, co-d, 1915); *That Little Band of Gold, When Love Took Wings, Fickle Fatty's Fall, The Village Scandal* (a, d, 1915); *Fatty and Mable Adrift, He Did and He Didn't/Love and Lobsters, Bright Lights/The Lure of Broadway, His Wife's Mistake, The Other Man, The Waiter's Ball, His Alibi, A Cream Puff Romance/A Reckless Romeo* (a, d, 1916); *The Moonshiners* (d only, 1916); *The Butcher Boy, The Rough House, His Wedding Night, Oh Doctor!, Fatty at Coney Island, A Country Hero* (a, d, 1917); *Out West, The Bell Boy, Moonshine, Good Night Nurse, The Cook* (a, d, 1918); *Love, A Desert Hero, Backstage, The Hayseed* (a, d, 1919); *The Life of the Party* (a, 1920); *The Garage* (a, d, 1920); *Brewster's Millions; Gasoline Gus* (a, 1921).

Directed only, as William B. Goodrich: *The Movies, The Tourist, The Fighting Dude* (1925); *Cleaning Up, My Stars, Fool's Luck, His Private Life* (1926); *The Red Mill* (feature); *Special Delivery* (feature, 1927); *Won by a Neck, Up a Tree* (1930); *Smart Work, The Tamale Vendor, The Lure of Hollywood, Honeymoon Trio, Up Pops the Duke, The Back Page, Marriage Rows, Beach Pajamas* (1931); *Bridge Wives, It's a Cinch, Keep Laughing, Moonlight and Cactus, Niagara Falls, Gigolettes, Hollywood Luck, Anybody's Goat* (1932).

## Arden, Eve (1912—1990)

The tart-tongued comic relief in dozens of films, Eve Arden usually played the heroine's sympathetic, yet sarcastic buddy. She put her sardonic style to its best and most memorable use when she created the title character of the radio, TV, and finally film versions of *Our Miss Brooks*. Whether playing in film comedies or dramas, she was usually called upon to make the snappy wisecrack and did so to such good effect in *Mildred Pierce* (1945) that she received a best supporting actress Academy Award nomination.

Born Eunice Quedens in Mill Valley, California, Arden began acting in stock at the age of sixteen. A year later she got her first taste of Hollywood, making her debut (using her real name) in *The Song of Love* (1929). Except for a small role in *Dancing Lady* (1933), she spent the bulk of the 1930s on the stage, learning her craft and making a name for herself as a brittle comedian. By 1934 she had made it to Broadway in *The Ziegfeld Follies*.

Arden returned to Hollywood in 1937, and this time she found plenty of work. She usually had only a few scenes per film, but she appeared in so many movies over the next several years that her sarcastic image was forever cast in celluloid. In movies as disparate as the classy *Stage Door* (1937), the melodramatic *Big Town Czar* (1939), and the zany MARX BROTHERS movie *At the Circus* (1939), she was as tough as nails and hilariously funny.

Concerned about being typecast, however, she briefly left the movie business to star in a light Broadway musical, *Very Warm for May*, in 1939 and in a musical revue, *Two for the Show*, in 1940. It didn't help. She was soon back in Hollywood, wisecracking in such films as *Manpower* (1941) and *She Knew All the Answers* (1941).

Arden worked steadily throughout the 1940s, getting comic relief laughs in dramas as dark as *The Unfaithful* (1947) and in films as frothy as the Danny Kaye comedy *The Kid from Brooklyn* (1946). In 1948, however, her career took a fateful turn when she began a radio show called "Our Miss Brooks" in which she played a warm-hearted, yet smart-alecky English teacher. The success of the radio show led to the TV series (1952–1957), which culminated in a 1956 theatrical film based on the show.

When "Our Miss Brooks" went off the air, Arden slowed down, giving her talents only to a modest number of movies, among them *Anatomy of a Murder* (1959), *The Dark at the Top of the Stairs* (1960), and *Sergeant Deadhead* (1965). Then she was off the big screen for ten years before returning in *The Strongest Man in the World* (1975). Happily, that was not the last that was heard from her; she came back again in grand style (in a role reminiscent of "Our Miss Brooks") as the school principal in the musical comedy hit *Grease* (1978). She reprised her role in *Grease 2* (1982); it was her last film.

FILMS INCLUDE: As Eunice Quedens: *The Song of Love* (1929); *Dancing Lady* (1933).

As Eve Arden: *Oh, Doctor!* (1937); *Stage Door* (1937); *Having Wonderful Time* (1938); *Letter of Introduction* (1938); *Cocoanut Grove* (1938); *Eternally Yours* (1939); *At the Circus* (1939); *Big Town Czar* (1939); *Women in the Wind* (1939); *She Couldn't Say No* (1940); *A Child Is Born* (1940); *Slightly Honorable* (1940); *No, No, Nanette* (1940); *Comrade X* (1940); *Ziegfeld Girl* (1941); *Manpower* (1941); *Whistling in the Dark* (1941); *That Uncertain Feeling* (1941); *Obliging Young Lady* (1941); *She Knew All the Answers* (1941); *Bedtime Story* (1942); *Let's Face It* (1943); *Cover Girl* (1944); *The Doughgirls* (1944); *Earl Carroll Vanities* (1945); *Mildred Pierce* (1945); *Patrick the Great* (1945); *My Reputation* (1946); *The Kid from Brooklyn* (1946); *Night and Day* (1946); *Song of Scheherazade* (1947); *The Unfaithful* (1947); *The Voice of the Turtle* (1947); *One Touch of Venus* (1948); *My Dream Is Yours* (1949); *The Lady Takes a Sailor* (1949); *Paid in Full* (1949); *Tea for Two* (1950); *Goodbye, My Fancy* (1951); *Three Husbands* (1951); *We're Not Married* (1952); *The Lady Wants Mink* (1953); *Our Miss Brooks* (theatrical release of TV series episodes, 1956); *Anatomy of a Murder* (1959); *The Dark at the Top of the Stairs* (1960); *Sergeant Deadhead* (1965); *The Strongest Man in the World* (1975); *Grease* (1978); *Pandemonium* (1981); *Under the Rainbow* (1981); *Grease 2* (1982).

**Arkin, Alan (1934—)** An actor and sometime director, Alan Arkin is best known for eliciting humor from complicated characters. By no means strictly a comic actor, Arkin has made his mark as a dramatic performer as well. Often cast in ethnic roles, he has played both aggressive, loud comic personalities as well as sensitive, introspective types. In either instance, he has been equally effective.

Born in Brooklyn, New York, Arkin went to Chicago to break into show business, gaining attention as a member of Second City, the celebrated improvisational troupe. Not long after, he went to Broadway in the stage version of Carl REINER's *Enter Laughing*, winning a Tony Award for his work.

In his film debut, he joined Carl Reiner on screen in *The Russians Are Coming! The Russians Are Coming!* (1966), playing a confused Soviet submariner. His performance brought him the first of his two Oscar nominations. The second nomination was for his straight dramatic portrayal of a deaf and mute man in *The Heart Is a Lonely Hunter* (1968).

Dark and short with expressive eyes, Arkin has been cast in a wide variety of roles that have taken advantage of both his malleable physicality and his actor's versatility. For instance, he was chilling as the villain in *Wait Until Dark* (1967), warm and vulnerable as the Latin father in *Popi* (1969), wonderfully paranoid as Yossarian in *Catch 22* (1970), comically pathetic in *The Last of the Red Hot Lovers* (1972), loud and bombastic in *Freebie and the Bean* (1974), comically manic in *The In-Laws* (1979), believably graspy and ambitious in *Joshua Then and Now* (1985), and cautiously greedy in *Glengarry Glen Ross* (1992).

Arkin's directorial talent is less well known than his obvious acting skills. He began directing off Broadway with *Eh?*, which introduced Dustin Hoffman (the man knows how to pick 'em). Among other stage productions, he directed Neil SIMON's *The Sunshine Boys* and won an Obie for Jules Feiffer's *Little Murders*, also directing and starring in the latter when it was turned into a movie in 1971. His other film director credits include *Fire Sale* (1977), a black comedy that he starred in as well, and two shorts that he also wrote, *T.G.I.F* and *People Soup*, the latter receiving an Oscar nomination for best short subject.

Arkin was the star (or a lead) in virtually all of his films from the mid-1960s into the mid-1980s. Unfortunately, few of his films of the 1980s were commercially successful. After an absence of nearly five years, he returned to the big screen in the 1990s in supporting character roles.

A multi-talented individual, Arkin is also an author, a songwriter, and has been a musical performer with the folk group The Tarriers. He plays the guitar and flute, not to mention the nose whistle.

His son, Adam Arkin, is also an actor of some considerable comic skill and is best known for his work on the stage and TV.

FILMS: All as actor unless otherwise noted: *The Last Mohican* (short, 1966); *The Russians Are Coming! The Russians Are Coming!* (1966); *Wait Until Dark* (1967); *Woman Times Seven* (1967); *The Heart Is a Lonely Hunter* (1968); *Inspector Closeau* (1968); *T.G.I.F.* (short, d only, 1968); *The Monitors* (1969); *Popi* (1969); *Catch-22* (1970); *Little Murders* (d, a, 1971); *Last of the Red Hot Lovers* (1972); *Freebie and the Bean* (1974); *Rafferty and the Gold Dust Twins* (1974); *Hearts of the West* (1975); *The Seven Per-Cent Solution* (1976); *Fire Sale* (a, d, 1977); *Improper Channels* (1979); *The In-Laws* (a, exec. p, 1979); *The Magician of Lublin* (1979); *Simon* (1980); *Chu Chu and the Philly Flash* (1981); *Full Moon High* (1981); *Deadhead Miles* (1982); *The Last Unicorn* (1982); *The Return of Captain Invincible* (1982); *Bad Medicine* (1985); *Big Trouble* (1985); *Joshua Then and Now* (1985); *Coupe de Ville* (1990); *Edward Scissorhands* (1990); *Havana* (1990); *The Rocketeer* (1991); *Glengarry Glen Ross* (1992).

**Astin, John (1930—)** A strong-featured comic character actor, John Astin is known for getting laughs by playing his scenes big and broad. There is rarely anything subtle about Astin's work, but with his big pop eyes and deep, sonorous voice, he commands the screen and dares you not to laugh. An over-the-top kind of actor, he gained his greatest fame as the patriarch in the commensurately over-the-top 1960s TV sitcom "The Addams Family."

Born in Baltimore, Astin studied acting at the Washington, D.C., Drama School. He also attended Johns Hopkins and the University of Minnesota Graduate School. He worked largely on the stage until he made his film debut in a small role in *West Side Story* (1961). His film career wasn't much to speak of until he made his mark with "The Addams Family." After that, he often had featured roles in such off-kilter comedies as *Candy* (1968), *Viva Max!* (1969), and *Get to Know Your Rabbit* (1972).

By the late 1970s, Astin's movie career petered out. A failed marriage to actress Patty Duke did not help matters. In the mid-1980s, however, he made a modest comeback, first in a small role in *National Lampoon's European Vacation* (1985), and later in larger roles in several low-budget comedy horror films, among them *Teen Wolf, Too* (1987), *Return of the Killer Tomatoes* (1988), and *Killer Tomatoes Strike Back* (1990).

FILMS INCLUDE: *West Side Story* (1961); *That Touch of Mink* (1962); *The Wheeler Dealers* (1963); *The Spirit Is Willing* (1967); *Candy* (1968); *Viva Max!* (1969); *Bunny O'Hare* (1971); *Every Little Crook and Nanny* (1972); *Get to Know Your Rabbit* (1972); *The Brothers O'Toole* (1973); *Freaky Friday* (1977); *National Lampoon's European Vacation* (1985); *Adventures Beyond Belief* (1987); *Teen Wolf, Too* (1987); *Return of the Killer Tomatoes* (1988); *Killer Tomatoes Strike Back* (1990); *Night Life* (1990).

## Auer, Mischa (1905—1967)

With his comically overdrawn sad face, large round eyes, and amusing accent, Mischa Auer added his special brand of humor and eccentric presence to many Hollywood and (later) European productions. It took Auer eight years in Hollywood to find his comic persona, but after that discovery he went on

*Comic character actor Mischa Auer, in costume, is seen here pedaling through the Universal studio lot during a break in filming.* PHOTO COURTESY OF THE SIEGEL COLLECTION.

to refine and polish it for an additional three decades.

Born Mischa Ounskowski in St. Petersburg, Russia, he was fifteen when he was brought to America by his mother's father, Leopold Auer, a well-known concert violinist. It was from his grandfather that he eventually took his stage name.

Young Mischa had little difficulty with his new language. He was already on Broadway when he was still in his early twenties, appearing in *Magda*, when the talkies arrived and Hollywood's mad dash for stage actors began. He went West, like so many others, and stayed. His first film was *Something Always Happens* (1928), in which he played a villain. With his accent and continental style, he continued, for the most part, to play heavies until a comic role came his way in 1936. The film was *My Man God-*

*frey*, and Auer made the most of his opportunity; he received a best supporting actor Academy Award nomination for his work in the film.

From that point on, he played predominantly comic character roles, although he did have the lead in *Unexpected Father* (1939). Some of his most memorable performances are in *Three Smart Girls* (1937); *You Can't Take It with You* (1938); *Spring Parade* (1940); *Hellzapoppin* (1941); *Up in Mabel's Room* (1944); and *Brewster's Millions* (1948).

Auer left Hollywood in the late 1940s, settling in Europe, where he steadily continued to appear in movies. In his first film overseas, *Al Diavolo la Celebrita* (Italy, 1949) he had the lead role, but after that he settled back into character parts, again usually in comedies. He can be seen in movies as varied as *Frou-Frou* (France, 1955), Orson Welles's Spanish/ Swiss co-production, *Mr. Arkadin* (aka *Confidential Report*, 1955), and his last film, an English comedy called *Drop Dead Darling!* (aka *Arrivederci Baby!*, 1966).

---

FILMS INCLUDE: U.S. only: *Something Always Happens* (1928); *Marquis Preferred* (1929); *The Benson Murder Case* (1930); *The Yellow Ticket* (1931); *The Unholy Garden* (1931); *Delicious* (1931); *The Midnight Patrol* (1932); *Scarlet Dawn* (1932); *Tarzan the Fearless* (1933); *Sucker Money* (1933); *Cradle Song* (1933); *Stamboul Quest* (1934); *Viva Villa!* (1934); *The Lives of a Bengal Lancer* (1935); *The Crusades* (1935); *Clive of India* (1935); *My Man Godfrey* (1936); *The Princess Comes Across* (1936); *Winterset* (1936); *Three Smart Girls* (1937); *Vogues of 1938* (1937); *100 Men and a Girl* (1937); *Top of the Town* (1937); *It's All Yours* (1937); *Rage of Paris* (1938); *You Can't Take It with You* (1938); *Sweethearts* (1938); *East Side of Heaven* (1939); *Destry Rides Again* (1939); *Unexpected Father* (1939); *Seven Sinners* (1940); *Alias the Deacon* (1940); *Spring Parade* (1940); *The Flame of New Orleans* (1941); *Hold That Ghost* (1941); *Hellzapoppin* (1941); *Around the World* (1943); *Lady in the Dark* (1944); *Up in Mabel's Room* (1944); *A Royal Scandal* (1945); *And Then There Were None* (1945); *Brewster's Millions* (1945); *Sentimental Journey* (1946); *Sofie* (1948).

---

## Avery, Tex (1907–1980)

He was an influential director of cartoons, especially during the 1940s and 1950s. In addition to being among the crew at Warner Bros. that brought Bugs Bunny to life in the 1930s, Tex Avery explored fresh new approaches and styles of animation.

He was born Fred B. Avery in Dallas, Texas; hence the nickname "Tex." At the age of twenty-three he began his long and varied career in animation. He got his start working on the "Aesop's Fables" cartoons in the early 1930s before going on to direct "Oswald the Rabbit." From Oswald, it was an easy jump to Bugs Bunny at Warner Bros.

By the early 1940s, however, Avery bolted the safe harbor at Warner Bros. to create cartoons of a far more anarchic nature. His increasingly surrealistic style and often violent, freewheeling content was exemplified by his animated penguin named Chilly-Willy, a dog called Droopy, and a duck called Lucky Ducky. He had a considerable effect on his contemporaries, most notably Chuck Jones, who took Avery's style very much to heart when he later made the Road Runner cartoons.

When the market for theatrically released animation dried up in the late 1950s, Avery turned to making commercials.

---

CARTOONS INCLUDE: *Henpecked Hoboes* (1941); *Happy-Go-Nutty* (1944); *Screwball Squirrel* (1944); *The Shooting of Dan MacGoo* (1945); *King Siz Canary* (1947); *Lucky Ducky* (1948); *The Cat That Hated People* (1949); *Little Rural Riding Hood* (1949); *Symphony in Slang* (1951); *Car of Tomorrow* (1952); *TV of Tomorrow* (1953); *Flea Circus* (1953); *The Three Little Pups* (1953); *Deputy Droopy* (1954); *Cat's Meow* (1957); *Polar Pests* (1958).

---

## Axelrod, George (1922– )

A playwright, screenwriter, producer, and director of largely comic material, George Axelrod had his greatest successes in Hollywood during the latter 1950s and throughout the 1960s. In films like *The Seven Year*

*Itch* (1955), *Will Success Spoil Rock Hunter?* (1957), and *How to Murder Your Wife* (1965), he presaged the coming of Paul MAZURSKY, another filmmaker with a similar penchant for comically observing American middle-class values.

A New York boy, Axelrod grew up during the Great Depression, took a fling at acting, and ended up in the service during World War II. When he returned to New York in the latter 1940s, he became a prolific writer for both radio and TV, penning two hit Broadway comedies, *The Seven Year Itch* (1953) and *Will Success Spoil Rock Hunter?* (1955). Success obviously did not spoil Axelrod; he quickly shuttled out to Hollywood and made his screenwriting debut with *Phfft!* (1954).

While Axelrod continued to work in the theater from time to time, most notably writing the highly regarded hit play *Goodbye Charlie* (filmed in 1964), he spent the bulk of the next fifteen years working in Hollywood. While not all of his films were comedies during this period (for instance, he wrote the screenplay and co-produced *The Manchurian Candidate*, 1962), his reputation for creating endearing and amusing characters was much on display in *Breakfast at Tiffany's* (1961), for which he received a best screenplay Academy Award nomination.

Axelrod left filmmaking at the end of the 1960s and didn't return again for a full decade. When he got behind the camera again, he did not make comedies. Instead, he made several thrillers, none of which were either critically or commercially successful.

FILMS: *Phfft* (story, sc, 1954); *The Seven Year Itch* (play, sc, 1955); *Bus Stop* (sc, 1956); *Will Success Spoil Rock Hunter?* (based on play, 1957); *Breakfast at Tiffany's* (sc, 1961); *The Manchurian Candidate* (sc, p, 1962); *Paris When It Sizzles* (sc, p, 1963); *Goodbye, Charlie* (based on play, 1964); *How to Murder Your Wife* (sc, p, 1965); *Lord Love a Duck* (story, sc, p, d, 1966); *The Secret Life of an American Wife* (sc, p, d, 1968); *The Lady Vanishes* (sc, 1979); *The Holcroft Covenant* (sc, 1985); *The Fourth Protocol* (sc adapt, 1987).

**Aykroyd, Dan (1954—)** Arguably the most talented alumnus to graduate to Hollywood from "SATURDAY NIGHT LIVE," Dan Aykroyd has nonetheless been commercially unsuccessful as a solo comic movie star. Unlike fellow comic actors such as Eddie MURPHY, Bill MURRAY, Chevy CHASE, and Tom HANKS, Dan Aykroyd appears to lack a dedicated following.

A writer and chameleonlike comic actor, Aykroyd has successfully played everything from good-natured goofballs to hard-nosed idiots, with several innocent Danny KAYE types in between. At a time when many actors, comic or otherwise, tend to show themselves sparingly on the screen, Aykroyd has been unusually prolific, appearing in nearly two films per year (on average).

*Dan Aykroyd has proven himself a versatile comic actor, whether playing leads or in supporting roles. Here he stuffs paper in his mouth in a bit of character business in Nora Ephron's* This Is My Life *(1992).*  PHOTO BY KERRY HAYES, © 20TH CENTURY-FOX.

Born in Canada, Aykroyd honed his comic talents as a member of Chicago's famous Second City improvisational comedy group. His big break came when he was hired as an original cast member of TV's "Saturday Night Live." It was on "Saturday Night Live" that he and fellow cast member John BELUSHI introduced the characters of the Blues Brothers. It started out as a hip, comic singing act. It caught on and the two of them began performing as Elwood and Jake Blues in sold-out concerts, eventually leading them to star in the classic movie comedy *The Blues Brothers* (1980), which Aykroyd co-scripted. It was Hollywood's first truly big-budget comedy, costing $30 million to produce and miraculously still turning a profit.

*The Blues Brothers*, however, was not Aykroyd's movie debut. He had earlier appeared in the little-known Canadian movie *Love at First Sight* (1974) and in a small role in Steven Spielberg's mega-bomb, *1941* (1979). With the success of *The Blues Brothers*, however, Aykroyd's career was truly launched and was followed by a scattershot variety of performances from the weirdly entertaining *Neighbors* (1981) to the more traditionally comic *Dr. Detroit* (1983). Major box office success eluded him, however, until he played the stuffy stockbroker in the critically admired and commercially successful *Trading Places* (1983). Here, as in *The Blues Brothers*, he was teamed with another strong comic performer, in this case, Eddie Murphy.

It wasn't until the following year, when he co-wrote and starred in the huge comedy hit *Ghostbusters* (1984) that Aykroyd was finally perceived by many as a brilliant comic force, albeit as much for his writing as for his acting. He has co-scripted seven of his films, the majority of them critical and commercial hits. He directed one of those films, *Nothing but Trouble* (1991), which was not a hit.

Since *Ghostbusters*, Aykroyd's career has been richly uneven. While *The Couch Trip* (1988), in which he played an escaped lunatic posing as a radio talk show psychologist, showed an adventurous comic spirit, fans did not come out to see it. On the other hand, he had a hit with his savagely funny version of *Dragnet* (1987), in which he was partnered with the hot comic actor Tom Hanks.

In recent years, Aykroyd has more aggressively branched out of comedy into serious character parts, receiving a best supporting actor Oscar nomination for his work in *Driving Miss Daisy* (1989).

---

**FILMS:** As actor only except where noted: *Love at First Sight* (1974); *1941* (1979); *Mr. Mike's Mondo Video* (1979); *The Blues Brothers* (a, co-sc, 1980); *Neighbors* (1981); *It Came from Hollywood* (1982); *Doctor Detroit* (1983); *Trading Places* (1983); *Twilight Zone—The Movie* (1983); *Indiana Jones and the Temple of Doom* (cameo, 1984); *Ghostbusters* (a, co-sc, 1984); *Nothing Lasts Forever* (1984); *Into the Night* (cameo, 1985); *Spies Like Us* (a, co-sc, 1985); *One More Saturday Night* (exec. p only, 1986); *Dragnet* (a, co-sc, songs, 1987); *The Couch Trip* (1988); *The Great Outdoors* (1988); *Caddyshack II* (1988); *My Stepmother Is an Alien* (1988); *Ghostbusters II* (a, co-sc, 1989); *Driving Miss Daisy* (1989); *Loose Cannons* (1990); *Nothing But Trouble* (a, d, co-sc, 1991); *My Girl* (1991); *This Is My Life* (1992); *The Coneheads* (a, co-sc, 1993); *My Girl 2* (1994).

---

# B

**Baby Leroy**  *See* CHILD COMEDIANS

**Baby Peggy**  *See* CHILD COMEDIANS

**Baby Sandy**  *See* CHILD COMEDIANS

**Bakshi, Ralph (1939—)**   A writer and director of adult animated movies with a dark comic edge, Ralph Bakshi was the first filmmaker to break free of the idea that cartoons were solely for children. If Disney's animated films were essentially for children, Bakshi's movies were ultimately aimed at college-age audiences. From his groundbreaking *Fritz the Cat* (1972) to his ambitious *American Pop* (1981), Bakshi's films tended to be hip rejections of a safe, middle-class America.

Bakshi was born in Palestine but grew up in Brooklyn, New York. After surviving a difficult, poverty-stricken childhood, he found work with Terrytoons, drawing cells for cartoon characters such as Mighty Mouse and Hekyll and Jekyll. Eventually, he would pioneer the use of rotoscoping, an animation procedure that involves the tracing of live-action figures.

Bakshi found his way to prominence in 1972 when, working from his own original script, he created the comic, foul-mouthed, sex-crazed characters in *Fritz the Cat*. This X-rated feature-length movie was a commercial and critical hit that served as a landmark in the development of ANIMATION as an art form. While many hailed him as a new force in

animated film, others derided him as nothing less than a clever pornographer.

The success of *Fritz the Cat* gave the writer/ director the clout to make a still more raunchy film called *Heavy Traffic* (1973), which intercut live-action sequences and animation in imaginative, revolutionary new ways.

He faltered with his next film, *Coonskin* (1975), another movie (similar to his first two) that depicted the bizarre, violent years of his youth in phantasmagoric images.

Bakshi finally changed his milieu, if not his themes and imagery, when he turned to the fantasy genre and made *Wizards* (1977), a film he produced as well as wrote and directed. A message movie about war set in a fantastic future, *Wizards* was a critical and commercial flop. However, fantasy seemed to be a fruitful area for animation, and Bakshi tried again, directing a lively version of *The Lord of the Rings* (1978).

In 1981 Bakshi made his most ambitious movie to date, a multi-generational animated saga that followed the growth and change of popular American music. The film, *American Pop*, was a moderate success with critics but was not up to the quality of Disney's classic *Fantasia*.

In the early 1980s, after directing *Fire and Ice* (1983), an animated fantasy about war that came and went with little fanfare, Bakshi left Hollywood to pursue a career as an artist working in paint and wood. He did not, however, turn his back on animation forever, saying that he would someday return to filmmaking. And, indeed he did, with *Cool World* (1992). Unfortunately, it was not a trium-

*Ralph Bakshi, shown here on the set of his* Cool World *(1992), has had a liberating effect on the art of animation.*

phant return. The film was a poorly conceived, dark version of *Who Framed Roger Rabbit?*, complete with Kim Basinger as the voice of the sexy siren. It was a critical and commercial bomb.

---

**FILMS:** *Fritz the Cat* (1972); *Heavy Traffic* (1973); *Coonskin* (1975); *Wizards* (1977); *The Lord of the Rings* (1978); *American Pop* (1981); *Hey, Good Lookin'* (1982); *Cannonball Run II* (animation sequences only, 1983); *Fire and Ice* (1983); *Cool World* (1992).

---

**Ball, Lucille (1911—1989)** Considered by many to be America's premier female TV comedian, Lucille Ball has left laughter as her legacy to millions of people around the world. The red-headed actress had a very long, if limited, film career before becoming the clown queen of TV. She was, nonetheless, established enough as a movie comedian to easily make the switch to TV in the early 1950s.

Born Lucille Desiree Ball in Jamestown, New York, she tried to break into show business on the legitimate stage with little success. Tall and statuesque, she eventually became a Goldwyn Girl, breaking into the movies with a bit part in *Roman Scandals* (1933). Having given up on Broadway, Ball appeared in a great many films between 1933 and 1937 in miniscule roles. For instance, she can be fleetingly glimpsed in such well-known movies as *Nana* (1934), *Kid Millions* (1934), *Roberta* (1935), *Top Hat* (1935), and *Winterset* (1937).

Her initial breakthrough came in *Stage Door* (1937), where her featured performance was lauded by the critics. It didn't take long for her comic talents to be recognized; she played a supporting role in the Marx BROTHERS' *Room Service* (1938) and starred in a short-lived, low-budget comedy series with Jack OAKIE that began with *The Affairs of Annabel* (1938).

In 1940, she met Desi Arnaz, a popular Cuban bandleader. The two were wed the following year. It was also during this time that Ball became a full-fledged leading comedian, playing opposite Red SKELTON (*Du Barry Was a Lady*, 1943) and Bob HOPE (*Sorrowful Jones*, 1949). For the most part, however, the films belonged to the male stars and not to her. That changed by the late 1940s with movies that were built around her, such as *Miss*

Here is Lucille Ball as a statuesque actress, the very image Lucy aspired to on her hit TV show, "I Love Lucy." She was a show girl before becoming a comic film star and TV icon.
PHOTO COURTESY OF THE SIEGEL COLLECTION.

*Grant Takes Richmond* (1949) and *The Fuller Brush Girl* (1950).

During this time, Ball and Arnaz had a popular radio show on the CBS network called "My Favorite Husband" (1947–1951). Perhaps sensing that her movie star years were running out, she and Arnaz took the plunge into the new TV medium, adapting their radio show for the small screen.

The original "I Love Lucy" ran from 1951 to 1957. The show, of course, was a mammoth hit. From "I Love Lucy," the two stars spun off a hit comedy film, *The Long, Long Trailer* (1954). There were several other incarnations of her TV show in the decades that followed: "The Lucy-Desi Comedy Hour" (1957–1960) and, after her divorce from Arnaz in 1960, "The Lucy Show" (1962–1968) and "Here's Lucy" (1968–1974). At the height of her TV success with Arnaz, the two of them bought RKO Studio, where they ran their growing TV empire under the banner of Desilu Productions, a combination of their first names.

During her years on TV, Ball occasionally returned to the movies, scoring well in *Yours, Mine and Ours* (1968), for example, but flopping badly in *Mame* (1974). By the end of her life, however, her movie successes and failures were a relative footnote compared with her television triumphs.

Ball's second husband was former comedian Gary Morton. Her children, by her marriage to Arnaz, are Luci Arnaz and Desi Arnaz, Jr.

**FILMS:** Exclusive of roles as extra and cameos: *Men of the Night* (1934); *Carnival* (1935); *Top Hat* (1935); *I Dream Too Much* (1935); *Chatterbox* (1936); *Bunker Bean* (1936); *Follow the Fleet* (1936); *The Farmer in the Dell* (1936); *That Girl from Paris* (1937); *Don't Tell the Wife* (1937); *Stage Door* (1937); *Having Wonderful Time* (1938); *Next Time I Marry* (1938); *Joy of Living* (1938); *Go Chase Yourself* (1938); *The Affairs of Annabel* (1938); *Annabel Takes a Tour* (1938); *Room Service* (1938); *Twelve Crooked Hours* (1939); *Beauty for the Asking* (1939); *Five Came Back* (1939); *That's Right, You're Wrong* (1939); *Panama Lady* (1939); *Dance Girl Dance* (1940); *You Can't Fool Your*

*Wife* (1940); *The Marines Fly High* (1940); *Too Many Girls* (1940); *A Girl, a Guy, and a Gob* (1941); *Look Who's Laughing?* (1941); *The Big Street* (1942); *Valley of the Sun* (1942); *Seven Days' Leave* (1942); *Du Barry Was a Lady* (1943); *Best Foot Forward* (1943); *Meet the People* (1944); *Without Love* (1945); *Ziegfeld Follies* (1946); *Lover Come Back* (1946); *The Dark Corner* (1946); *Easy to Wed* (1946); *Two Smart People* (1946); *Her Husband's Affairs* (1947); *Lured* (1947); *Sorrowful Jones* (1949); *Miss Grant Takes Richmond* (1949); *Fancy Pants* (1950); *The Fuller Brush Girl* (1950); *The Magic Carpet* (1951); *The Long, Long Trailer* (1954); *Forever Darling* (1956); *The Facts of Life* (1960); *Critic's Choice* (1963); *Yours, Mine and Ours* (1968); *Mame* (1974).

## Bartel, Paul (1938– )

A multi-talented actor, screenwriter, producer, and director, Paul Bartel is a filmmaker who has appeared in far more movies than he's made, yet is rightly perceived as a genuine auteur. An iconoaclast, he has written and directed a few utterly off-the-wall comedies that are both hysterically funny and deeply disturbing, the unquestioned best of them being *Eating Raoul* (1982). As an actor, he has given his neatly acerbic comic twist to supporting roles in films such as *Eat My Dust* (1976), *Rock 'n' Roll High School* (1979), and *The Pope Must Die* (1991), which was later retitled *The Pope Must Diet*.

Born in Brooklyn, New York, Bartel was among the earliest crop of UCLA theater arts students to break into filmmaking. Upon graduation, he secured a Fulbright scholarship to study directing in Italy. His first film, a short called *Progetti* (1962), was made while he was overseas. His second short, *The Secret Cinema* (1967), brought him to the attention of famed B-movie maestro Roger Corman. As he had for so many others, Corman gave Bartel his first real opportunity to work and learn his craft in commercial features. Bartel's first directorial effort for Corman was the commercial dud (but very good) *Private Parts* (1972). He followed that with a far more successful Corman-produced effort, *Death Race 2000* (1975). The movie he most wanted to make, however, was *Eating Raoul*, a black comedy he had penned about greed and cannibalism. Corman refused to produce it, as did everybody else in Hollywood. Bartel's parents came up with the money to shoot the film, but then he couldn't find a distributor for the controversial project. In desperation, Bartel entered the film in the Los Angeles Film Festival (Filmex), where it had a sensational response. As a consequence, 20th Century-Fox picked up the movie for distribution, and the film became a cult classic virtually overnight. In 1992, he turned the movie into a delightfully macabre musical comedy stage show that flopped.

Bartel's other notable directorial efforts were *Lust in the Dust* (1974), which was a raunchy sendup of the Western genre, and *Scenes from the Class Struggle in Beverly Hills* (1989), which was neither a commercial nor critical success.

As an actor, Bartel has been consistently busy, making his debut in a small role in Brian De Palma's *Hi, Mom* (1970) before casting himself in *Cannonball* (1976). After that, he worked quite often in front of the camera, though usually in low-budget movies like *Piranha* (1978), *Trick or Treats* (1982), and *Chopping Mall* (1986). On occasion, he can be found in bigger budget, mainstream films like *Gremlins 2: The Next Batch* (1990).

FILMS INCLUDE: *Progetti* (short, d, 1962); *The Secret Cinema* (short, d, 1967); *Hi, Mom!* (a, 1970); *Private Parts* (d, 1972); *Death Race 2000* (d, 1975); *Cannonball* (a, sc, d, 1976); *Eat My Dust* (a, 1976); *Hollywood Boulevard* (a, 1976); *Grand Theft Auto* (a, 1977); *Mr. Billion* (a, 1977); *Piranha* (a, 1978); *Rock 'n' Roll High School* (a, 1979); *Eating Raoul* (a, sc, d, 1982); *Heart Like a Wheel* (a, 1982); *Trick or Treats* (a, 1982); *White Dog* (a, 1982); *Get Crazy* (a, 1983); *Not for Publication* (a, sc, song, d, 1984); *Lust in the Dust* (d, 1984); *Into the Night* (a, 1985); *Chopping Mall* (a, 1986); *The Longshot* (d, 1986); *Killer Party* (a, 1986); *Munchies* (a, 1987); *Amazon Women on the Moon* (a, 1987); *Mortuary Academy* (a, 1988); *Shakedown* (a, 1988); *Scenes from the Class Struggle in Beverly Hills* (a, story, sc, d, 1989); *Pucker Up and Bark Like a Dog* (a, 1989); *Out of the Dark* (a, p, 1989); *Gremlins 2: The New Batch* (a, 1990); *Desire and Hell at Sunset Motel* (a, 1990); *The Pope Must Die/The Pope Must Diet* (a, 1991); *Grief* (1994).

**Bathing Beauties**   They were the other side of the comic coin at Mack SENNETT's Keystone Studio. From the mid-1910s through the early 1920s, the Bathing Beauties were an ever-changing troupe of scantily clad (for their day) young starlets who played, mostly in two-reelers, at a more decorous form of comedy. If Sennett's male SLAPSTICK stars tended toward the grotesque in appearance, his Bathing Beauties were quite the opposite, combining sex appeal with the occasional laugh.

Becoming a Bathing Beauty was a way to start in Hollywood, and more than one hundred women held the title. A small percentage of them managed to further their careers beyond the Keystone lot, the most famous of them being Carole LOMBARD. Among the other standouts were Olive Borden, Julia Faye, Juanita Hansen, and Phyllis Haver.

**Beard, Matthew "Stymie"**   *See* OUR GANG

**Beckett, Scotty**   *See* OUR GANG

**Beery, Wallace (1886—1949)**   While today he is better remembered for his serious roles, Wallace Beery was in fact a highly accomplished comic actor. Beery had a long and varied career, rising and falling from major stardom three separate times. He was anything but the leading man type with his big barrel chest, ugly mug, and gravelly voice. However, there was mischief in his eyes and a vulnerability in his oafishness that made him rather lovable, particularly in his many comedies.

The son of a Kansas City policeman, Beery began his show business career by living the old cliché of running away from home to join the circus. In the early 1900s he made his way to the New York stage, but his success was limited to (believe it or not) working as a female impersonator.

He entered the film business in 1913 as an actor and director for the ESSANAY film studio. Again, he became best known for acting in drag, playing a thick-headed Swedish maid known as "Sweedie" in a number of comic shorts.

Beery worked steadily, first as a comedian, including a short stint at Keystone where he met and married Gloria Swanson (the marriage was short lived). He then worked as a heavy in movies such as *The Unpardonable Sin* (1919) and *The Virgin of Stamboul* (1920). His early big break came when Douglas Fairbanks cast him in the important supporting role of King Richard the Lion-Hearted in the smash hit *Robin Hood* (1922). Seen as an actor of versatility, Beery was given larger, more significant roles in heftier budgeted movies such as the silent version of *The Sea Hawk* (1924), the biggest moneymaker of the year.

In 1925 Paramount signed Beery to a long-term contract. He soon became a major star when he was teamed with actor Raymond Hatton in a military comedy called *Behind the Front* (1926). The film spawned far too many sequels, however, and left Beery with a fading popularity.

By the time of the sound era, it appeared as if Beery were washed up. As it turned out, he was only just beginning. After signing with MGM, he unexpectedly became one of the biggest stars of the early 1930s when he was cast, along with Marie DRESSLER, in the surprise comedy hit of the year, *Min and Bill* (1930). He teamed with Dressler again in *Tugboat Annie* (1933), and the result was the same: a big winner at the box office.

The two Dressler films were a wonderful mix of personalities, and the comic timing between the two old pros was something to behold. Equally effective was his teaming with child star Jackie Cooper in *The Champ* (1931). Despite one of the best scene-stealing performances by a child actor in the history of the movies, Beery's over-the-hill boxer brought him an Oscar in a tie with Fredric March (for his performance in *Dr. Jekyll and Mr. Hyde*) and solidified his image as a gruff but warm-hearted rogue.

Beery proved yet again his versatility when he played the desperate businessman in *Grand Hotel* (1932), the nouveau riche social climber married to Jean HARLOW in the social comedy *Dinner at Eight* (1933), and the Mexican revolutionary Pancho Villa in *Viva Villa!* (1934).

Beery's popularity began to flag, however, in the second half of the 1930s. He had been at his best when paired with strong co-stars such as Marie Dressler, Jackie Cooper, and Jean Harlow. They brought out his personality the way few other co-stars could.

Relegated to B movies—many of them rather fine, such as *Port of Seven Seas* (1938) and *Thunder Afloat* (1939)—Beery chugged along at MGM seemingly on a slow downhill spiral. Then, unexpectedly, Beery caught on with the public all over again, becoming a top box office star for yet a third time. For a short while, he regained a large measure of his popularity when he was teamed with Marjorie MAIN in character comedies such as *Barnacle Bill* (1941). The movies with Main re-created (on a smaller scale) the success of his Marie Dressler collaborations of the early 1930s.

By the mid-1940s, however, Beery's career seriously slowed down. There were long gaps between films. His last movie, *Big Jack* (1949), was released after he died of a heart attack that same year.

Beery was the half-brother of actor Noah Beery (1884–1946), who had a notable career as a silent screen heavy and sound era supporting player. He was also the uncle of Noah Beery, Jr., best known as a TV actor. Among the Beery clan, however, Wallace was clearly the brightest star.

FILMS INCLUDE: *Sweedie the Swatter* (1914); *The Plum Tree* (1914); *Sweedie Learns to Swim* (1914); *Sweedie at the Fair* (1914); *Sweedie's Suicide* (1915); *Sweedie and Her Dog* (1915); *Sweedie's Hopeless Love* (1915); *Sweedie Goes to College* (1915); *Sweedie in Vaudeville* (1915); *The Slim Princess* (1915); *Teddy at the Throttle* (1916); *Timothy Dobbs, That's Me* (d, p, 1916); *The Little American* (1917); *Johanna Enlists* (1918); *Behind the Door* (1919); *The Life Line* (1919); *The Love Burglar* (1919); *Soldiers of Fortune* (1919); *The Unpardonable Sin* (1919); *Victory* (1919); *The Last of the Mohicans* (1920); *The Mollycoddle* (1920); *The Round-Up* (1920); *The Virgin of Stamboul* (1920); *The Four Horsemen of the Apocalypse* (1921); *The Golden Snare* (1921); *The Last Trail* (1921); *Patsy* (1921); *Robin Hood* (1922); *Bavu* (1923); *The Flame of Life* (1923); *Stormswept* (1923); *Three Ages* (1923); *Richard the Lion-Hearted* (1923); *Unseen Hands* (1924); *The Sea Hawk* (1924); *The Red Lily* (1924); *So Big* (1925); *The Lost World* (1925); *The Wanderer* (1925); *The Pony Express* (1925); *Behind the Front* (1926); *We're in the Navy Now* (1926); *Old Ironsides* (1926); *Casey at the Bat* (1927); *Fireman Save My Child* (1927); *Now We're in the Air* (1927); *Wife Savers* (1928); *Partners in Crime* (1928); *The Big Killing* (1928); *Beggars of Life* (1928); *Chinatown Nights* (1929); *The River of Romance* (1929); *Stairs of Sand* (1929); *The Big House* (1930); *Billy the Kid* (1930); *A Lady's Morals* (1930); *Min and Bill* (1930); *Way for a Sailor* (1930); *The Secret Six* (1931); *The Champ* (1931); *Hell Divers* (1931); *Grand Hotel* (1932); *Flesh* (1932); *Tugboat Annie* (1932); *Dinner at Eight* (1933); *The Bowery* (1933); *Viva Villa!* (1934); *Treasure Island* (1934); *The Mighty Barnum* (1934); *West Point of the Air* (1935); *O'Shaughnessy's Boy* (1935); *China Seas* (1935); *Ah, Wilderness!* (1935); *A Message to Garcia* (1936); *Old Hutch* (1936); *Good Old Soak* (1937); *Slave Ship* (1937); *The Bad Man of Brimstone* (1938); *Port of Seven Seas* (1938); *Stablemates* (1938); *Stand Up and Fight* (1939); *Sergeant Madden* (1939); *Thunder Afloat* (1939); *The Man from Dakota* (1940); *Twenty-Mule Team* (1940); *Wyoming* (1940); *The Bad Man* (1941); *Barnacle Bill* (1941); *Jackass Mail* (1942); *The Bugle Sounds* (1942); *Salute to the Marines* (1943); *Rationing* (1944); *Barbary Coast Gent* (1944); *This Man's Navy* (1945); *Bad Bascomb* (1946); *The Mighty McGurk* (1947); *Alias a Gentleman* (1948); *A Date with Judy* (1948); *Big Jack* (1949).

**Belushi, John (1949—1982)** A gifted comic actor, John Belushi had all the makings of a future genre superstar. He was a ferocious talent who, in his meteoric rise and tragic fall, still managed to suggest a wide-ranging comic versatility. He could be wildly and hysterically out of control as a man-child with an awesome appetite for just about everything in *National Lampoon's Animal House* (1978); he could be drily funny as a blues singer "on a mission from God" in *The Blues Brothers* (1990); he could play the victim as the butt of humor in *Neighbors* (1981); and despite his roundish body and rubbery face, he could narrowly pull off playing a romantic lead in *Continental Divide* (1981).

Born in Chicago, Illinois, Belushi came to fame as an original member of NBC-TV's Not Ready for Prime Time Players on "SATURDAY NIGHT LIVE" (1975—1979). He later teamed up with his friend and colleague on the show Dan AYKROYD to make

several films including *1941* (1979), *The Blues Brothers* (1980), and *Neighbors* (1981).

John Belushi died at the age of thirty-three from a drug overdose. His life and death are the subject of *Wired*, a book by Robert Woodward, which was later turned into a movie.

Belushi's actor brother, James, has subsequently appeared in numerous movies, many of them comedies, but he has not had anywhere near the same impact in the genre as his brother, John.

---

**FILMS:** *La Honte de la Jungle* (1975); *Goin' South* (1978); *National Lampoon's Animal House* (also song, 1978); *Old Boyfriends* (1978); *1941* (1979); *The Blues Brothers* (1980); *Neighbors* (1981); *Continental Divide* (1981).

---

**Benchley, Robert (1889—1945)** One of the most beloved humorists of his day, Robert Benchley was admired by the intellectual elite for his irreverent wit and by the average moviegoer for his willingness to mock intellectual pretension. A sort of Andy Rooney of the 1930s, he looked at the world around him and satirized it through the inventive and clever short subjects he wrote and starred in between 1928 and 1945. He was also an asset to a great many feature-length films in which he usually had either supporting or featured comic relief roles.

Born in Worcester, Massachusetts, to a middle-class family, young Benchley had a family friend named Lillian Duryea who paid his way through Exeter and then Harvard, where he was elected president of the *Harvard Lampoon* (a satirical review). He repaid her later by calling the female characters Lillian in many of his stories.

While Lillian was like a godmother to Benchley, Gertrude Darling was his lifelong lover and companion. They met as children and later married in 1914.

Benchley began writing soon after college, and *Vanity Fair* published his first piece with the unusual title "No Matter from What Angle You Look at It,

*John Belushi had an enormous comic talent that did not have a chance to fully flourish. His relative handful of movie performances only began to suggest his range and versatility.*
PHOTO COURTESY OF MOVIE STAR NEWS.

Alice Brookhausen Was a Girl Whom You Would Hesitate to Invite into Your Home." Benchley's career as a humorist was launched. He eventually had thirteen books of short stories published.

His writing matched his personality; while gently mocking, he was never abrasive. Similar in many respects to James Thurber both in subject matter and style, Benchley's writing was always intelligent, whimsical, and altogether engaging. When he later began appearing in movie short subjects, he and Will ROGERS became the only two writers of their era whose faces were familiar to the public through the movies.

Benchley was one of the original members of the famed Algonquin Round Table, joining such luminaries as Dorothy Parker, George S. KAUFMAN, and Alexander Woollcott. Though Benchley never aspired to the stage, he wrote and performed a now-legendary act known as *The Treasurer's Report* when the Round Table decided to put on a revue. The writer's performance was seen by Irving Berlin and Sam Harris, and they asked him to repeat his act in the third edition of the *Music Box Revue* on Broadway. The story goes that Benchley (at that time the theater critic for the *New Yorker*) didn't believe a critic should cross the footlights, so he asked for the then-huge sum of $500 per week, expecting that would end all negotiations. Instead, Harris said, "Okay, but you'd better be good."

Benchley performed *The Treasurer's Report* for nine months on Broadway. In fact, it was such a smash that it became his first movie short in 1928. He would ultimately write and appear in a total of forty-six hysterical short subjects with titles such as *The Life of the Polyp* (1928), *How to Train a Dog* (1936), and *How to Eat* (1939). His work was recognized by his Hollywood peers when he won an Academy Award for his short *How to Sleep* (1935).

FILMS INCLUDE: Shorts, as actor and writer: *The Treasurer's Report* (1928); *The Sex Life of the Polyp* (1928); *Stewed, Fried and Boiled* (1929); *Your Technocracy and Mine* (1933); *How to Sleep* (1935); *How to Behave* (1936); *How to Become a Detective* (1936); *How to Vote* (1936); *A Night at the Movies* (1937); *The Romance of Digestion* (1937); *How to Figure Income Tax* (1938); *The Courtship of a Newt* (1938); *Music Made Simple* (1938); *Mental Poise* (1938); *How to Sublet* (1939); *How to Eat* (1939); *Dark Magic* (1939); *See Your Doctor* (1939); *Home Movies* (1940); *The Trouble with Husbands* (1940); *That Inferior Feeling* (1940); *Crime Control* (1941); *How to Take a Vacation* (1941); *The Forgotten Man* (1941); *Nothing But Nerves* (1942); *Keeping in Shape* (1942); *No News Is Good News* (1943); *My Tomato* (1943); *Boogie Woogie* (1945).

Features, as actor: *The Sport Parade* (1932); *Headline Shooters* (1933); *Dancing Lady* (1933); *Social Register* (1934); *China Seas* (1935); *Murder on a Honeymoon* (co-sc only, 1935); *Picadilly Jim* (1936); *Live, Love and Learn* (1937); *Hired Wife* (1940); *Foreign Correspondent* (also dial, 1940); *You'll Never Get Rich* (1941); *Bedtime Story* (1941); *Nice Girl?* (1941); *The Major and the Minor* (1942); *Take a Letter, Darling* (1942); *I Married a Witch* (1942); *Flesh and Fantasy* (1943); *The Sky's the Limit* (1943); *Song of Russia* (1944); *See Here, Private Hargrove* (1944); *Practically Yours* (1944); *Weekend at the Waldorf* (1945); *It's in the Bag* (1945); *Kiss and Tell* (1945); *The Bride Wore Boots* (1946); *Road to Utopia* (1946); *Janie Gets Married* (1946).

## Benjamin, Richard (1938—)

An actor who appeared almost exclusively in comedies, Richard Benjamin made the decision to work behind the camera as a director. In that capacity, he has also gave himself over to humor. His success, however, in both areas has been uneven. As a performer, he had an edge, playing none-too-likeable characters with a certain zesty, comic glee. For a brief period beginning in the late 1960s, Benjamin was a prospective star, playing leading roles in many critically acclaimed, if little-seen films. By the mid-1970s, though, he had become a supporting player, generally cast as the diffident and/or neurotic friend of the hero. His directorial career, which began in 1982, has tilted wildly between warmly comic and blandly saccharine.

Born and raised in New York City, Benjamin was clear about what he wanted to do from an early age. He was not, however, a child actor. Although some reference books list him in the credits of *Thunder Over the Plains* (1953) and *Crime Wave* (1954), that was another actor. After he finished his education, he worked in the theater until he hit it big on Broadway in *The Star-Spangled Girl* in 1966. Television took notice of his success, and he was cast with his wife, Paula Prentiss, in the sophisticated TV sitcom "He and She" in 1967. The series was well liked by the critics but not a commercial success.

When Philip Roth's bestselling novella *Goodbye Columbus* was turned into a movie in 1969, Benjamin was tapped to play the lead. The film did well, and his movie career was finally launched. Good roles were more important to him than stardom, however, so he took the thankless part of the nasty husband in *Diary of a Mad Housewife* (1970). He made other ambitious movies early in the 1970s, such as *The Marriage of a Young Stockbroker* (1971) and the poorly received *Portnoy's Complaint* (1972). By the time he appeared in the thriller *The Last of Sheila* (1973), Benjamin's ordinary looks and lack of box office pull had finally relegated him to the status of supporting player.

Benjamin was well cast and effective during the rest of the 1970s and early 1980s in films such as *The Sunshine Boys* (1975), *House Calls* (1978), and *The Last Married Couple in America* (1979). When he managed a starring role in *Saturday the 14th* (1981), nobody showed up but the critics, and even they weren't all that pleased with his horror spoof.

Benjamin finally moved behind the camera and, to the industry's delight and surprise, made a breezy transition to his new career as a director with the critically and commercially successful, gentle comedy *My Favorite Year* (1982).

He followed his first hit with another highly regarded film, a teenage dramatic love story set in the early 1940s titled *Racing with the Moon* (1984). His success since then has been tempered by several flops, most notably the period action comedy *City Heat* (1984) starring Clint Eastwood and Burt Reynolds; the Kim Basinger comedy *My Stepmother Is an Alien* (1988); and the commercially disappointing Cher comedy/drama *Mermaids* (1990). Benjamin needed a hit and he finally got it with *Made in America* (1993), a mediocre movie that created a stir due to the onscreen and offscreen romance between stars Whoopie GOLDBERG and Ted DANSON.

---

**FILMS INCLUDE:** As actor: *Goodbye Columbus* (1969); *Catch-22* (1970); *Diary of a Mad Housewife* (1970); *The Marriage of a Young Stockbroker* (1971); *The Steagle* (1971); *Portnoy's Complaint* (1972); *The Last of Sheila* (1973); *Westworld* (1973); *The Sunshine Boys* (1975); *House Calls* (1978); *Witches' Brew* (1978); *The Last Married Couple in America* (1979); *Love at First Bite* (1979); *Scavenger Hunt* (1979); *First Family* (1980); *How to Beat the High Cost of Living* (1980); *Saturday the 14th* (1981).

As director: *My Favorite Year* (1982); *City Heat* (1984); *Racing with the Moon* (1984); *The Money Pit* (1986); *Little Nikita* (1988); *My Stepmother Is an Alien* (1988); *Downtown* (1990); *Mermaids* (1990); *Made in America* (1993).

---

## Bennett, Constance (1904—1965)

Generally playing sharp-tongued, modern women who were quick with a quip, Constance Bennett was at her best in sophisticated comedies. She reached the peak of her popularity playing the delightful ghost Marion Kirby in the hit comedy *Topper* (1937).

Bennett and actress sisters Joan and Barbara were all daughters of theater star Richard Bennett. Constance Bennett was a headstrong young woman who began her film career at the age of twelve appearing in a cameo role in one of her father's few films, *The Valley of Decision* (1916). She was wed at the age of sixteen (the first of five marriages), but had the union annulled not long after. The following year, when she was just seventeen, she became serious about the movies and began acting regularly in films such as *Reckless Youth* (1922) and *The Goose Woman* (1925). Bennett quickly became a star, but she chucked it all in 1926 to marry a wealthy member of what might have been called the jet set, had there been any jets in those days.

The marriage lasted just three years and Bennett, with a husky purr that was ideal for the talkies, successfully made her movie comeback in 1929 in *This Thing Called Love*. While she starred in many comedies during the ensuing two decades, such as *Rich People* (1930), *Merrily We Live* (1938), and *Topper Takes a Trip* (1939), the actress also showed a flair for drama in films as diverse as *What Price Hollywood?* (1932) and *The Unsuspected* (1947).

After making more than fifty films between 1922 and 1954, Bennett retired from the screen and founded the Constance Bennett Cosmetics Company. Later, she returned one last time to the big screen to appear in *Madame X* (1966), but died of a cerebral hemorrhage shortly after filming was completed.

---

FILMS: *The Valley of Decision* (cameo, 1916); *Reckless Youth* (1922); *What's Wrong with Women?* (1922); *Evidence* (1922); *Into the Net* (1924); *Cytherea* (1924); *The Goose Hangs High* (1925); *My Son* (1925); *Wandering Fires* (1925); *Code of the West* (1925); *My Wife and I* (1925); *Sally, Irene and Mary* (1925); *The Pinch Hitter* (1925); *The Goose Woman* (1925); *Married?* (1926); *This Thing Called Love* (1929); *Rich People* (1930); *Sin Takes a Holiday* (1930); *Son of the Gods* (1930); *Common Clay* (1930); *Three Faces East* (1930); *Born to Love* (1931); *The Common Law* (1931); *The Easiest Way* (1931); *Bought* (1931); *Two Against the World* (1932); *Rockabye* (1932); *Lady with a Past* (1932); *What Price Hollywood?* (1932); *After Tonight* (1933); *Our Betters* (1933); *Bed of Roses* (1933); *Moulin Rouge* (1934); *The Affairs of Cellini* (1934); *After Tonight* (1934); *After Office Hours* (1935); *Ladies in Love* (1936); *Everything Is Thunder* (UK, 1936); *Topper* (1937); *Service De Luxe* (1938); *Merrily We Live* (1938); *Topper Takes a Trip* (1939); *Tail Spin* (1939); *Two-Faced Woman* (1940); *Law of the Tropics* (1940); *Submarine Zone/Escape to Glory* (1940); *Sin*

*Town* (1942); *Madame Spy* (1942); *Wild Bill Hickock Rides* (1942); *Paris Underground* (1945); *Centennial Summer* (1946); *The Unsuspected* (1947); *Angel on the Amazon* (1948); *Smart Woman* (1948); *As Young as You Feel* (1951); *It Should Happen to You* (1954); *Madame X* (1966).

---

**Benny, Jack (1894—1974)**  Benny's legendary persona of the cheap, vain, self-absorbed comic was developed and honed over a fifty-year career. With his perfectly timed pauses, slightly effeminate hand gestures, and churlish voice, he was a natural screen comedian. However, he generally worked best as part of an ensemble, which limited his appeal as a comic movie star. As a consequence, his best work was on radio and television, but his Hollywood career is nonetheless noteworthy.

Born Benjamin Kubelsky in Waukeegan, Illinois, the young Benny seriously considered a career as a concert violinist. While in the navy during World War I, however, he found himself entertaining his fellow sailors with the violin and getting big laughs for his efforts; he then realized he had the makings of a comedy act. Entering VAUDEVILLE after the war, Benny worked on stage for more than a decade until his fame was such that MGM hired him to introduce the studio's silent movie stars in an early talkie *The Hollywood Revue of 1929*. He was so engaging in the film that his vaudeville career suddenly skyrocketed. He continued to make film appearances in the early 1930s, but most of them were made on the East Coast to accommodate his stage triumphs, which were soon followed by radio fame.

It wasn't until the mid-1930s that Benny began appearing more regularly in films, splitting his time between guest appearances in movies such as *Broadway Melody of 1936* (1935) and *The Big Broadcast of 1937* (1936) and genuine starring roles in films such as *Artists and Models* (1937) and *Artists and Models Abroad* (1938).

By the early 1940s, it seemed as if Benny was destined for a film career as big as his friend Bob

HOPE's. Over a three-year period, from 1940 to 1942, Benny's comedies were the finest and funniest in Hollywood. Far more sophisticated than ABBOTT AND COSTELLO (who had just become a hot, if infantile, property), livelier than the tiring and aging MARX BROTHERS, and more eccentrically human than Bob Hope, Jack Benny was at the height of his movie career when he made in succession *Buck Benny Rides Again* (1940), *Love Thy Neighbor* (1940), *Charley's Aunt* (1941), *To Be or Not to Be* (1942), and *George Washington Slept Here* (1942).

Among the best of these films was Ernst LUBITSCH's *To Be or Not to Be*, a hysterical black comedy about the Nazi occupation of Poland. The movie was thought to be in bad taste at the time; it suffered a drubbing by the critics and did poor business at the box office. Since then, it has come to be regarded as a classic, and because of that, Benny's career has been more kindly looked upon. Mel BROOKS remade *To Be or Not to Be* in 1983 with himself in Jack Benny's role. Unfortunately, he didn't have any more success with it at the box office than Benny did.

Jack Benny's film career went into a rapid decline in the mid-1940s, finished off by the abysmal *The Horn Blows at Midnight* (1945). He appeared in a mere handful of films after that, mostly in cameo roles, while pursuing his more substantial success on radio and TV. His last movie role was in *A Guide for the Married Man* (1967). He was slated to appear in *The Sunshine Boys* (1975), but died before filming began. His best friend, George Burns, took his place and won an Oscar.

Benny's married life was as successful as his life in show business. He was wed in 1927 to his longtime radio co-star Mary Livingstone, and they remained together until his death from cancer at the age of eighty.

**FILMS:** *Hollywood Revue of 1929* (1929); *Chasing Rainbows* (1930); *The Medicine Man* (1930); *Broadway Melody of 1936* (1935); *Transatlantic Merry-Go-Round* (1935); *It's in the Air* (1935); *The Big Broadcast of 1937* (1936); *College Holiday* (1937); *Artists and Models* (1937); *Artists and Models Abroad* (1938); *Man About Town* (1939); *Buck Benny Rides Again* (1940); *Love Thy Neighbor* (1940); *Charley's Aunt* (1941); *To Be or Not to Be* (1942); *George Washington Slept Here* (1942); *The Meanest Man in the World* (1943); *Hollywood Canteen* (1944); *The Horn Blows at Midnight* (1945); *It's in the Bag* (1945); *A Guide for the Married Man* (1967).

## Bergen, Edgar (1903–1978)

Considered the most successful ventriloquist in movie history, Edgar Bergen rose to fame in VAUDEVILLE, radio, movies, and TV. He provided the voice of dummies Charlie McCarthy (a snooty, upper-class wiseguy) and Mortimer Snerd (a hickish moron of comically gargantuan proportions).

Born Edgar John Bergen in Chicago, Illinois, he came from a poor family, but aspired to higher education. Bergen thus came up with a rather novel approach to working his way through college: He bought a wooden dummy for $35, called him Charlie McCarthy, and worked up an act in which Charlie's lips moved rather than his own. (Well, Bergen's lips moved more than a little bit, too, but nobody ever said he was a *great* ventriloquist.)

His act was such a hit that Bergen took his diploma on the road with him, choosing vaudeville over the regular workaday world. Considering that much of the appeal of ventriloquism comes from the visual trick of speaking without moving one's lips, it was downright bizarre that Bergen had his first major success on radio, where the fact that he was a ventriloquist had not the slightest meaning. In any event, he was a hit on the airwaves, helped along by a famous mock feud on the radio between Charlie McCarthy and W. C. FIELDS, a feud that was resuscitated for its promotional and humorous appeal when Bergen and dummies appeared in the Fields classic *You Can't Cheat an Honest Man* (1939).

Bergen's first encounter with the movies, however, came when he and Charlie McCarthy appeared in twelve two-reel comedies between 1933

*Edgar Bergen and Charlie McCarthy (he's the dummy on the donkey) in the two-reeler,* Donkey Business, *with Christina Grayer and an unidentified actor as the Indian chief. Fittingly, all the actors appear as wooden as McCarthy. Nonetheless, the success of this and eleven other shorts made by Bergen and McCarthy between 1933 and 1935 ensured their status as comic movie stars.*
PHOTO COURTESY OF THE SIEGEL COLLECTION.

and 1935. On that basis alone, before any career in feature films, Bergen won a special Academy Award in 1937 for breathing life and humor into Charlie McCarthy. He could hardly abandon the movies after that. He began appearing regularly in films with both Charlie and his newer dummy Mortimer Snerd, creating laughter in such movies as *The Goldwyn Follies* (1938) and *Stage Door Canteen* (1943). These weren't all mere guest appearances. Bergen also appeared in films that were built around him and his wooden troupe, such as *Charlie McCarthy, Detective* (1939).

Bergen was rarely seen in movies after the 1940s, concentrating instead on nightclub and TV work. He had his own daytime TV show called "Do You Trust Your Wife?" Late in life, he returned for a few cameo appearances in films, his last and most notable in Jim HENSON's *The Muppet Movie* (1979). Charlie McCarthy is on display at the Smithsonian, a gift from Edgar Bergen.

Bergen is the father of successful film and TV actress, Candice Bergen, star of the popular TV series "Murphy Brown."

**FILMS:** Features only: *Letter of Introduction* (1938); *The Goldwyn Follies* (1938); *You Can't Cheat an Honest Man* (1939); *Charlie McCarthy, Detective* (1939); *Look Who's Laughing?* (1941); *Here We Go Again* (1942); *Stage Door Canteen* (1943); *Song of the Open Road* (1944); *Fun and Fancy Free* (1947); *I Re-*

*member Mama* (1948); *Captain China* (1949); *One-Way Wahine* (1965); *Don't Make Waves* (1967); *The Phynx* (cameo, 1970); *Won Ton Ton—The Dog That Saved Hollywood* (cameo, 1976); *The Muppet Movie* (cameo, 1979).

---

**Berkeley, Busby (1895—1976)**   In the world of Hollywood musical comedy, Busby Berkeley stands alone as a choreographer and director with a unique and awesome vision. He revolutionized the movie musical, using the camera not just as a recording device but as an active participant in his wildly creative, often campy musical extravaganzas.

Berkeley was more successful at directing musical sequences than he was at directing entire films, but his musical numbers—boasting such attractions as one hundred dancing pianos, chorus girls dressed in costumes made of coins, and waterfalls dripping with scantily clad women—were the very reason audiences flocked to see his movies.

Berkeley's most famous musical numbers appeared in *42nd Street* (1933), *Gold Diggers of 1933* (1933), and *Footlight Parade* (1933). He directed two films for which he is also well known: *Gold Diggers of 1935* (1935) and *The Gang's All Here* (1943). However, Berkeley's film career encompassed much more than these five films, although they certainly represent the gloriously gaudy height of the Hollywood musical. In all, Berkeley worked on more than fifty movies, providing the inspiration for a great many musical comedy numbers that rank among the film industry's most entertaining.

Born William Berkeley Enos, he was the son of a theatrical family whose footsteps he followed by taking to the stage when he was five. At roughly that same time, he was tagged with the nickname—taken from famous stage actress Amy Busby—that would follow him throughout his life.

While his acting career never took off, his ability as a dance director did, and he became much admired for his work on Broadway during the latter half of the 1920s. His reputation was such that Sam-uel Goldwyn hired him to stage the musical comedy numbers for the film version of Eddie CANTOR's *Whoopee!* (1930). After coming to Hollywood, Berkeley found his true element. The movie musical was a new form, just a bare three years old, and he set about doing things that no one had ever imagined before.

After feeling his way through films such as Mary Pickford's only musical, *Kiki* (1931), and several other Eddie Cantor films, including *Palmy Days* (1931), and *The Kid from Spain* (1932), Berkeley was hired by Darryl F. Zanuck (then at Warner Bros.) to add some dash to several contemporary (Depression-era) backstage musicals. *42nd Street*, *Gold Diggers of 1933*, and *Footlight Parade* were all made with lavish budgets, and Berkeley made sure that every nickel was in sight. While these movies were not musical comedies, per se, the musical numbers were so over the top that then, as now, audiences laughed in appreciation of their outrageousness.

Unlike the musical numbers in an Astaire/Rogers film, Berkeley's approach was that of mass choreography, with a screen full of blonde beauties lost in a swirl of light, motion, and kaleidoscopic effects. Critics have called his art everything from fascistic dehumanization to kitsch, but what he was really about was just plain escapism.

Berkeley worked steadily at Warner Bros. from 1933 to 1938, until the studio lost interest in musicals and cut their budgets. Berkeley was the Cecil B. DeMille of the musical, and B-movie budgets simply wouldn't do. Thus, he left Warner Bros. and went to MGM just as it entered its golden age of musicals. He contributed to the start of that era by directing such films as *Babes in Arms* (1939), *Strike Up the Band* (1940), *Babes on Broadway* (1941), and *For Me and My Gal* (1942). In the meantime, Berkeley also continued to direct musical numbers in other directors' films at MGM, including *Born to Sing* (1942), *Cabin in the Sky* (1943), and *Girl Crazy* (1943).

Berkeley had the opportunity to direct his first all-color musical at 20th Century-Fox in 1943 and he produced one of Hollywood's most memorable camp classics, *The Gang's All Here*, with Carmen MIRANDA. While the movie was mediocre, the musical numbers were awe inspiring in their outlandishness.

Berkeley's health failed during the mid-1940s, and he suffered a mental collapse. He finally returned to filming in 1948 with only a modest impact.

Berkeley fell out of fashion for nearly twenty years before he made a triumphant return to the Broadway stage, directing a revival of *No, No, Nanette* in 1970. In the last years of his life he was lionized for work that most agree Hollywood will never duplicate.

---

FILMS: As choreographer only: *Whoopee* (1930); *Kiki* (1931); *Palmy Days* (1931); *Flying High* (1931); *Night World* (1932); *Bird of Paradise* (1932); *The Kid from Spain* (1932); *Roman Scandals* (1933); *42nd Street* (1933); *Gold Diggers of 1933* (1933); *Footlight Parade* (1933); *Wonder Bar* (1934); *Fashions of 1934* (1934); *Twenty Million Sweethearts* (1934); *Dames* (1934); *Go into Your Dance* (1935); *Stars over Broadway* (1935); *In Caliente* (1935); *Gold Diggers of 1937* (1936); *The Singing Marine* (1937); *Varsity Show* (1937); *Gold Diggers of Paris* (1938); *Broadway Serenade* (1939); *Ziegfeld Girl* (1941); *Lady Be Good* (1941); *Born to Sing* (1941); *Girl Crazy* (1943); *Two Weeks with Love* (1950); *Call Me Mister* (1951); *Two Tickets to Broadway* (1951); *Million Dollar Mermaid* (1952); *Small Town Girl* (1953); *Easy to Love* (1953); *Rose Marie* (1954); *Billy Rose's Jumbo* (1962).

As director: *She Had to Say Yes* (co-d, 1933); *Gold Diggers of 1935* (1935); *Bright Lights* (1935); *I Live for Love* (1935); *Stage Struck* (1936); *The Go-Getter* (1937); *Hollywood Hotel* (1937); *Men Are Such Fools* (1938); *Garden of the Moon* (1938); *Comet over Broadway* (1938); *They Made Me a Criminal* (1939); *Babes in Arms* (1939); *Fast and Furious* (1939); *Strike Up the Band* (1940); *Forty Little Mothers* (1940); *Blonde Inspiration* (1941); *Babes on Broadway* (1941); *For Me and My Gal* (1942); *The Gang's All Here* (1943); *Cinderella Jones* (1946); *Take Me Out to the Ballgame* (1949).

---

**black comedy** The term *black comedy* describes a sophisticated form of humor that deals with subject matter that almost always makes an audience uneasy and uncomfortable. Black comedy, or dark humor, often revolves around issues of death and dying, but can also touch upon taboo sexual, social, and political issues. What ultimately separates black comedy from FARCE is that it doesn't undercut or apologize for itself at the end; to be full-blooded black comedy, a film must have the courage of its convictions right through to its comically chilling finale.

The first Hollywood film to edge close to the borders of black comedy was Ernst LUBITSCH's classic 1942 movie about Nazis in Poland, *To Be or Not to Be*. Screamingly funny, the film was dark indeed, with a comic character boastful of his title of "Concentration Camp Erhardt." Despite a happy ending, the film was condemned for its bad taste and bombed when it came out during the early years of World War II.

Another black comedy opened during the war that was a huge hit, although it wasn't about the war. *Arsenic and Old Lace* (1944), based on a hit play of the same name, had two sweet old lady murderers who happily buried their victims in their cellar. Made by Frank CAPRA before he became involved in the war effort and released long after it was made, the film was the first genuine Hollywood black comedy.

Black comedies have rarely been made by Hollywood's studios, which have preferred to simply entertain rather than disturb their audiences. Only an independent filmmaker such as Charlie CHAPLIN could have made such a dark and deeply chilling comedy as *MONSIEUR VERDOUX* (1947), a movie in which he comically murders rich old women for their money. While considered a masterpiece today, the film was reviled at the time it opened.

The 1950s was a time of complacency in America in all manner of things, including black comedy. It wasn't until Stanley Kubrick made *DR. STRANGELOVE OR: HOW I LEARNED TO STOP WORRYING AND LOVE THE BOMB* (1964) that black comedy was reborn both critically and commercially. The film remains one of the most successful black comedies in movie history.

Other black comedies followed, but without the same reception at the box office. *The Loved One* (1965), a film about paying for the burial of a famous Hollywood personality, received a great deal of attention but it didn't draw a large crowd.

The golden age of black comedy began during the 1970s with the low-budget release of two films that quickly became cult classics, *Where's Poppa?* (1970) and *HAROLD AND MAUDE* (1971). By the end of the decade, black comedies were being made with big budgets and major stars, enjoying box office success as evidenced by the popularity of films such as the Burt Reynolds's *The End* (1978).

The boom in black comedies has continued to this day. It's hard to shock American audiences, and bad taste is often seen as a virtue. As a consequence, the dark comic visions of movies such as *Ruthless People* (1986), *Throw Momma from the Train* (1987), and *Death Becomes Her* (1992) have become the normal comic fare of our time.

## Blanc, Mel  *See* WARNER BROS. CARTOONS

## Blondell, Joan (1909—1979)  Every major studio during the 1930s and 1940s had a smart, sassy, wisecracking actress on the lot to play a best friend—there was none better at that role than Joan Blondell. With a large, full face and big eyes, Blondell was not particularly pretty or sexy, but she was a workhorse at Warner Bros., appearing in more than fifty films during the 1930s. She was at home in musicals, crime melodramas, tearjerkers, and even the occasional period piece, but in most cases she was there to provide the sarcastic remark or the cynical jibe.

A member of a successful VAUDEVILLE family, Blondell was one of the original Katzenjammer Kids, touring with her parents virtually from birth. She was a seasoned performer long before she reached Hollywood, having worked in Europe,

China, and Australia before she quit the act and began appearing in stock productions in the United States. Blondell made it to Broadway in 1927, and over the next three years starred in several plays, including two with James Cagney. One of these was *Penny Arcade*, which was bought by Warner Bros. and filmed as *Sinner's Holiday* in 1930 with the original stars.

Blondell and Cagney were often paired together, appearing in films such as *Blonde Crazy* (1931), *Footlight Parade* (1933), and *He Was Her Man* (1934). Other successful pairings were with Pat O'Brien, Glenda Farrell, and Dick Powell (to whom she was married for ten years between 1936 and 1945).

Playing the second banana for the better part of ten years, however, began to wear on Blondell; she wanted bigger, better roles to match her work in *Stage Struck* (1936), but Warner Bros. didn't see her as a serious actress. She left her home studio in 1939 to pursue other opportunities. She would soon be seen in such films as *Model Wife* (1941) and *Topper Returns* (1941).

After World War II began, Blondell took off so much time to entertain the troops that, by virtue of being off the screen for long periods of time, she ultimately crippled her career. She did get her wish, however, to play in more serious fare, joining the cast of *A Tree Grows in Brooklyn* (1945). It was one of her last two great triumphs. The other came long after the war was over, when she made a comeback in *The Blue Veil* (1951), a performance for which she received an Oscar nomination for best supporting actress.

By the late 1950s and 1960s, Blondell was appearing in modest character parts. She stayed busy, finding her way into the TV series *Here Comes the Bride* during the late 1960s. As one would expect of an actress who had worked almost from the day she was born, Joan Blondell worked virtually until the time of her death, appearing in small roles in *Grease* (1978) and *The Champ* (1979). Her last film was a Canadian movie, *The Women Inside* (1981); it was released two years after she died.

FILMS: *The Office Wife* (1930); *Sinner's Holiday* (1930); *Millie* (1931); *Other Men's Women* (1931); *God's Gift to Women* (1931); *Illicit* (1931); *My Past* (1931); *The Public Enemy* (1931); *Night Nurse* (1931); *Big Business Girl* (1931); *The Reckless Hour* (1931); *Blonde Crazy* (1931); *The Crowd Roars* (1932); *Make Me a Star* (1932); *Big City Blues* (1932); *Lawyer Man* (1932); *Union Depot* (1932); *The Greeks Had a Word for Them* (1932); *The Famous Ferguson Case* (1932); *Miss Pinkerton* (1932); *Three on a Match* (1932); *Central Park* (1932); *Blondie Johnson* (1933); *Broadway Bad* (1933); *Gold Diggers of 1933* (1933); *Havana Windows* (1933); *Convention City* (1933); *Goodbye Again* (1933); *Footlight Parade* (1933); *Smarty* (1934); *Dames* (1934); *Kansas City Princess* (1934); *He Was Her Man* (1934); *I've Got Your Number* (1934); *We're in the Money* (1935); *Traveling Saleslady* (1935); *Broadway Gondolier* (1935); *Miss Pacific Fleet* (1935); *Sons o' Guns* (1936); *Colleen* (1936); *Stage Struck* (1936); *Three Men on a Horse* (1936); *Bullets or Ballots* (1936); *Gold Diggers of 1937* (1936); *The King and the Chorus Girl* (1937); *The Perfect Specimen* (1937); *Stand-In* (1937); *Back in Circulation* (1937); *There's Always a Woman* (1938); *East Side of Heaven* (1939); *Off the Record* (1939); *Good Girls Go to Paris* (1939); *The Amazing Mr. Williams* (1939); *The Kid from Kokomo* (1939); *Two Girls on Broadway* (1940); *I Want a Divorce* (1940); *Model Wife* (1941); *Topper Returns* (1941); *Three Girls About Town* (1941); *Lady for a Night* (1942); *Cry Havoc* (1943); *A Tree Grows in Brooklyn* (1944); *Don Juan Quilligan* (1944); *Adventure* (1946); *Nightmare Alley* (1947); *The Corpse Came C.O.D.* (1947); *Christmas Eve* (1947); *For Heaven's Sake* (1950); *The Blue Veil* (1951); *The Opposite Sex* (1956); *This Could Be the Night* (1957); *Lizzie* (1957); *Desk Set* (1957); *Will Success Spoil Rock Hunter?* (1957); *Angel Baby* (1961); *Advance to the Rear* (1964); *The Cincinnati Kid* (1965); *Ride Beyond Vengeance* (1966); *Waterhole #3* (1967); *Kona Coast* (1968); *Stay Away, Joe* (1968); *Big Daddy* (1969); *The Phynx* (cameo, 1970); *Support Your Local Gunfighter* (1971); *Grease* (1978); *The Glove* (1978); *Opening Night* (1978); *The Champ* (1979); *The Woman Inside* (1981).

**Blondie**   *See* SERIES COMEDIES

**Blore, Eric (1887—1959)**   Short and round, with a face that could change from comically cherublike to hysterically haughty, Eric Blore ruled the roost during the 1930s and 1940s as the funniest butler/waiter/valet in Hollywood. With his perfect timing, coupled with a slow, withering delivery of his ever-so-slightly lisping British accent, he could always be counted upon for effective comic relief.

Blore is best remembered for his appearances in five Fred Astaire/Ginger Rogers musicals during the 1930s (usually having comically inspired verbal battles with co-star Edward Everett HORTON). Much admired by his peers, he also worked with LAUREL AND HARDY in *Swiss Miss* (1938), Bob

*There were few comic relief actors who could milk as much laughter out of a few short scenes as Eric Blore. He is best remembered for his exquisitely unctuous butlers, waiters, and valets in a number of Astaire/Rogers musicals, most memorably,* The Gay Divorcee *(1934),* Top Hat *(1935),* Swing Time *(1936), and* Shall We Dance? *(1937).*
PHOTO COURTESY OF THE SIEGEL COLLECTION.

HOPE and Bing CROSBY in *The Road to Zanzibar* (1941), Preston STURGES in *Sullivan's Travels* (1941), and the MARX BROTHERS in *Love Happy* (1949). In addition, Blore had a recurring comic relief role in many of the low-budget, but popular, "Lone Wolf" mysteries during the 1940s.

Born in London, Blore first worked on the stage in Australia before gaining prominence in England as a stage and music hall performer. He arrived in the United States in 1923, working on Broadway before making his way to Hollywood. He had little success in movies during the silent era, but after his hilariously petulant voice could be heard, he worked steadily in the talkies.

FILMS INCLUDE: *The Great Gatsby* (1926); *Laughter* (1930); *Tarnished Lady* (1931); *Flying Down to Rio* (1933); *The Gay Divorcee* (1934); *Top Hat* (1935); *Diamond Jim* (1935); *Swing Time* (1936); *The Ex-Mrs. Bradford* (1936); *Shall We Dance?* (1937); *Quality Street* (1937); *Swiss Miss* (1938); *Island of Lost Men* (1939); *The Lone Wolf Meets a Lady* (1940); *The Lone Wolf Strike* (1940); *The Road to Zanzibar* (1941); *Sullivan's Travels* (1941); *The Lone Wolf Keeps a Date* (1941); *The Lady Eve* (1941); *The Moon and Sixpence* (1942); *Holy Matrimony* (1943); *San Diego, I Love You* (1944); *Kitty* (1945); *Abie's Irish Rose* (1946); *The Lone Wolf in London* (1947); *The Lone Wolf in Mexico* (1947); *Romance on the High Seas* (1948); *Love Happy* (1949); *Fancy Pants* (1950); *Bowery to Bagdad* (1955).

**Blue, Ben (1901—1975)** With a name like Ben Blue, he had to be a sad-faced comic. He was also a novelty dancer and a clown of the first order. Blue starred in comedy shorts before becoming a featured comic personality in full-length movies.

Born Benjamin Bernstein in Montreal, Canada, Blue started in VAUDEVILLE at fifteen. After making it to Broadway, he arrived in Hollywood in 1926, where he starred in several series of popular comedy shorts. He appeared in feature films beginning in 1934, often in backstage musical comedies or films with a revue format, both of which gave him comic turns without being intricately involved in the plots.

Blue disappeared from the movies after 1948, working instead in nightclubs and later in TV. He returned to the big screen in IT'S A MAD MAD MAD MAD WORLD (1963) as did so many other comedy standouts. After being rediscovered in that film, he showed up in cameo roles in a rash of comedies during the rest of the 1960s. His last film was *Where Were You When the Lights Went Out?* (1968).

FILMS INCLUDE: Features: *College Rhythm* (1934); *Follow Your Heart* (1936); *College Holiday* (1936); *Turn Off the Moon* (1937); *Thrill of a Lifetime* (1937); *Top of the Town* (1937); *High, Wide and Handsome* (1937); *Artists and Models* (1937); *The Big Broadcast of 1938* (1938); *Cocoanut Grove* (1938); *College Swing* (1938); *Paris Honeymoon* (1939); *Panama Hattie* (1942); *For Me and My Gal* (1942); *Thousands Cheer* (1943); *Two Girls and a Sailor* (1944); *Broadway Rhythm* (1944); *Two Sisters from Boston* (1946); *Easy to Wed* (1946); *My Wild Irish Rose* (1947); *One Sunday Afternoon* (1948); *It's a Mad Mad Mad Mad World* (1963); *The Russians Are Coming! The Russians Are Coming!* (1966); *A Guide for the Married Man* (1967); *The Busy Body* (1967); *Where Were You When the Lights Went Out?* (1968).

**Bowery Boys**   *See* DEAD END KIDS, THE

**Bracken, Eddie (1920—)**   A comic performer for the better part of seventy years, Eddie Bracken had a fickle relationship with the movies. A former child actor in comedy shorts in the early 1930s, he had a relatively brief period of genuine stardom during the 1940s, highlighted by two brilliant comic performances in the Preston STURGES classics *Hail the Conquering Hero* (1944) and *The Miracle of Morgan's Creek* (1944). Both films took advantage of what Bracken did best, playing the shy, yet manic, good-hearted bumbler.

*Eddie Bracken, in a reluctant clinch with Ella Raines, had his heyday in the early 1940s, gaining lasting fame as the star of two of Preston Sturges's greatest comedies,* The Miracle of Morgan's Creek *(1944) and* Hail the Conquering Hero *(1944). A publicity still from the latter features veteran character actor William Demarest barking at the two lovers.* PHOTO COURTESY OF MOVIE STAR NEWS.

Born Edward Vincent Bracken in Astoria, Queens, New York, Bracken was set for show business at an early age thanks to his education at New York's Professional Children's School. He spent his childhood years in VAUDEVILLE before appearing in a string of comedy shorts featuring kids, most notably in four OUR GANG two-reelers.

Bracken graduated to features when he was twenty. He shined in a number of light romantic comedies in the early 1940s, reaching genuine, if fleeting, stardom before the middle of the decade.

Bracken's popularity began to fade by the end of the 1940s. He hung on into the early 1950s, before retiring from the screen and working instead on TV and stage and later as a theatrical producer. His returns to the big screen have been extremely rare, but in recent years he has been much more visible, most charmingly as the avuncular toy store owner in *Home Alone II: Lost in New York* (1992) and the goofy owner of the Chicago Cubs baseball team in *Rookie of the Year* (1993).

**FILMS INCLUDE:** *Too Many Girls* (1940); *Reaching for the Sun* (1941); *Caught in the Draft* (1941); *Life with Henry* (1941); *Sweater Girl* (1942); *The Fleet's In* (1942); *Star Spangled Rhythm* (1942); *Young and Willing* (1943); *Happy Go Lucky* (1943); *Rainbow Island* (1944); *Hail the Conquering Hero* (1944); *The*

Miracle of Morgan's Creek (1944); Out of This World (1945); Duffy's Tavern (1945); Bring on the Girls (1945); Hold That Blonde (1945); Fun on a Weekend (1947); Ladies' Man (1947); The Girl from Jones Beach (1949); Summer Stock (1950); Two Tickets to Broadway (1951); We're Not Married (1952); About Face (1952); A Slight Case of Larceny (1953); Una Domenica d'Estate (cameo, Italy, 1961); Wild, Wild World (narrator, Italy, 1961); Shinbone Alley (voice only, 1971); National Lampoon's Vacation (1983); Oscar (1991); Home Alone II: Lost in New York (1992); Rookie of the Year (1993).

---

**Bressart, Felix (1892—1949)**  A comically appealing character actor with a sad face, Felix Bressart got laughs by playing his put-upon supporting characters with a touch of cleverness. What

*Warm and avuncular, comic character actor Felix Bressart graced many of Hollywood's most beloved comedies, among them,* Ninotchka *(1939),* The Shop Around the Corner *(1940), and* To Be or Not to Be *(1942).*
PHOTO COURTESY OF MOVIE STAR NEWS.

made him stand out was his ability to find the humor in his characters as well as a certain wistful poignancy. An Ernst LUBITSCH favorite, Bressart can be seen to best effect in the director's *Ninotchka* (1939), *The Shop Around the Corner* (1940), and *To Be or Not to Be* (1942).

Born in East Prussia, Bressart was a successful comic actor in the theater and the movies in Germany. Like so many others, he fled his homeland when Hitler came to power in 1933. He spent several years in Switzerland before finally arriving in the United States in 1937. A haven for talented refugees, Hollywood embraced him and gave him work. Bressart thrived in comedies and dramas, charming his way through a decade's worth of films before dying at the age of fifty-seven.

---

FILMS INCLUDE: U.S. only: *Three Smart Girls Grow Up* (1939); *Ninotchka* (1939); *The Shop Around the Corner* (1940); *Swanee River* (1940); *Edison the Man* (1940); *Bitter Sweet* (1940); *Escape* (1940); *Comrade X* (1940); *Blossoms in the Dust* (1941); *Ziegfeld Girl* (1941); *To Be or Not to Be* (1942); *Crossroads* (1942); *Iceland* (1942); *Above Suspicion* (1943); *Song of Russia* (1944); *The Seventh Cross* (1944); *Greenwich Village* (1944); *Without Love* (1945); *I've Always Loved You* (1946); *A Song Is Born* (1948); *Take One False Step* (1949); *Portrait of Jennie* (1949).

---

**Brice, Fanny (1891—1951)**  A stage and radio comedian of the first order, Fanny Brice nonetheless appeared in only seven films. With somewhat unconventional looks, and famous for her ethnic, Brooklyn-accented comedy, Hollywood's studio chiefs feared she would not play well in the hinterlands.

Born Fanny Borach in New York City, she began her career as an actress in Brooklyn. At nineteen she was already a veteran of VAUDEVILLE and BURLESQUE when Florenz Ziegfeld provided her big chance in his *1910 Follies*. Brice became a star overnight. Her fame was such that she would later star in

*Fanny*, a Broadway show both written and named for her. She became nationally known as "Baby Snooks" through her long-running radio program. Her fame and talent might have been largely forgotten had not Barbra Streisand brought her back to life in the musical comedy show, and later the movie, *Funny Girl* (1968) and sequel *Funny Lady* (1975).

**FILMS:** *Night Club* (1928); *My Man* (1928); *Be Yourself* (1930); *The Man from Blankley's* (1930); *The Great Ziegfeld* (1936); *Everybody Sing* (1938); *Ziegfeld Follies* (1946).

## Brickman, Marshall (1941–)

A screenwriter, director, and sometime producer of a comedic bent, Marshall Brickman is best known for his earlier collaborations with Woody ALLEN. With Allen, he co-scripted three classic comedies—*Sleeper* (1973), *ANNIE HALL* (1977), and *Manhattan* (1979)—winning a best screenplay Oscar for the second of the three. He graduated from his work with Allen to write and direct a satiric comedy gem, *Simon* (1980), that did not get near the attention it deserved. He went off on his own to make a mediocre romantic comedy, *Lovesick* (1983), and a teen protest film, *The Manhattan Project* (1986). After a long time away from his most successful collaborator Brickman finally returned to work with Woody Allen, co-scripting *Manhattan Murder Mystery* (1993).

Born in Rio de Janeiro, Brazil, Brickman had TV comedy experience going back to the mid-1960s when he wrote for "Candid Camera" (1966) and "The Tonight Show" (1966–1970). Woody Allen, who also got his start writing for TV, found a kindred soul in Brickman, each of them bringing out the best in the other's work.

**FILMS INCLUDE:** *Sleeper* (co-sc, 1973); *Annie Hall* (co-sc, 1977); *Manhattan* (co-sc, 1979); *Simon* (sc, d, 1980); *Lovesick* (sc, d, 1983); *The Manhattan Project* (sc, p, d, 1986); *Funny* (a, 1988); *That's Adequate* (a, 1989); *Manhattan Murder Mystery* (co-sc, 1993).

## Broderick, Helen (1891–1959)

In the movies, Helen Broderick was the wisecracking supporting player—usually the heroine's girlfriend, the boss's knowing secretary, or the married woman who knows the score. In any event, whether in a straight comedy, a musical, or a drama, she could be counted upon for brittle and brutally honest quips.

Broderick started in show business as a dancer, but came to fame on Broadway as a singer and actress, appearing in Florenz Ziegfeld's first Broadway show in 1907. Ultimately, she was a much bigger star on Broadway than she ever was in the movies, but this talented singer and comedian did have her moments in Hollywood.

Broderick made a couple of silent films in the 1920s that did not show her off to best advantage. She returned, however, when sound came to the movies and added comic spice to a number of movies, most notably the Fred Astaire and Ginger Rogers classics *Top Hat* (1935) and *Swing Time* (1936).

Helen Broderick was also the mother of film and TV actor Broderick Crawford, who won the Oscar for his performance in *All the King's Men* (1949).

**FILMS INCLUDE:** *High Speed* (1924); *The Mystery Club* (1926); *Fifty Million Frenchmen* (1931); *Top Hat* (1935); *To Beat the Band* (1935); *Swing Time* (1936); *Murder on the Bridle Path* (1936); *Love on a Bet* (1936); *The Life of the Party* (1937); *Meet the Missus* (1937); *Radio City Revels* (1938); *Service de Luxe* (1938); *Naughty but Nice* (1939); *Honeymoon in Bali* (1939); *No, No Nanette* (1940); *Nice Girl?* (1941); *Three Is a Family* (1944); *Love, Honor and Goodbye* (1945); *Because of Him* (1946).

## Broderick, Matthew (1962–)

More boyish than handsome, Matthew Broderick established himself in the 1980s as a star of youth-oriented movies, with the accent on comedy. On stage and in films, he was closely identified with two of Neil SIMON's most compelling personal comedies, as well as with one of the most high-spirited youth

*Moving from teen comedy to romantic comedy, Matthew Broderick, seen here with Heidi Kling, is literally* Out on a Limb *(1992).*
PHOTO BY ELLIOTT MARKS, © UNIVERSAL PICTURES.

movies of the decade. In the 1990s, he has emerged as an adult star of romantic comedies as well as a leading actor in serious dramas.

The son of the late actor James Broderick (most well known as the father in the TV series "Family"), Matthew Broderick grew up among actors and understood the demands of his craft. He made his film debut in a modest part in Neil Simon's *Max Dugan Returns* (1983), one of the playwright/screenwriter's few flops. In that same year, however, Broderick had the lead role in a surprise adventure hit, *WarGames* (1983), which launched the young actor into early stardom.

He followed that success with *Ladyhawke* (1984), before surprising a great many people by choosing to star in the clearly uncommercial, low-budget Horton Foote film *1918* (1984). He was well received by the critics in this otherwise quiet

movie, although the movie came and went rather quickly.

Broderick spent a great deal of his time during the 1980s acting on stage, starring on Broadway in two of Neil Simon's autobiographical plays, *Brighton Beach Memoirs* and *Biloxi Blues*. He also trod the boards off Broadway, starring in several Horton Foote's projects, including *The Widow Claire*.

If Broderick didn't star in a lot of movies, he generally made the ones he did appear in count. He scored big with John HUGHES's boisterous comedy *Ferris Bueller's Day Off* (1986).

His career was nearly cut short by tragedy in 1987 when he was involved in a traffic accident while on vacation in Ireland that killed two people. The actor reportedly caused the accident by driving his vehicle on the wrong side of the road. Broderick was later fined for being at fault but was not imprisoned.

After recovering from his own injury (he broke a leg), Broderick eventually resumed his work. He patched up a quarrel with Neil Simon and starred in the hit film version of *Biloxi Blues* (1988) before co-starring in the seriocomic *Torch Song Trilogy* (1988). He followed that with the much-praised Civil War epic *Glory* (1989). Comedy continued to have its pull on him, though, and he also co-starred in the poorly received *Family Business* (1989) as well as in the jovially good-natured spoof *The Freshman* (1990). Broderick finally came in to his own as an adult—even if he had to wear a beard to do it—in the breezy romantic comedy *The Night We Never Met* (1993).

FILMS INCLUDE: *Max Dugan Returns* (1983); *War-Games* (1983); *Ladyhawke* (1984); *1918* (1984); *Ferris Bueller's Day Off* (1986); *On Valentine's Day* (1986); *Project X* (1987); *Biloxi Blues* (1988); *Torch Song Trilogy* (1988); *Glory* (1989); *Family Business* (1989); *The Freshman* (1990); *The Night We Never Met* (1993).

**Brooks, Albert (1947—)** An iconoclastic comedic filmmaker and actor, Albert Brooks is just as likely to appear in another director's comedies as he is in his own, although his contribution to modern screen comedy is most assuredly in the movies he has scripted, directed, and starred in himself. Brooks's comedies tend toward social satire, often with himself as the butt of the humor. His films have not been hugely popular with the public, but critics generally think highly of his work. While he stars in his own films, he usually plays supporting roles in the movies of others. For instance, he was nominated for a best supporting actor Academy Award for his performance in *Broadcast News* (1987).

There can be no doubt that Albert Brooks is the son of comedian Harry Einstein; who else but a comedian with the name Einstein would name his son Albert? Or maybe the name was appropriate. After all, young Albert Einstein matriculated at Car-

negie Institute of Technology. The call of laughter was stronger than that of science, however, and he shot into the limelight in 1976 with a comedy album called "A Star Is Bought." That same year, he made his film debut in a supporting role in Martin Scorsese's *Taxi Driver* (1976). It was his first and last dramatic role; everything since has been comedy.

Brooks received a certain level of fame for creating amusing short films for TV's "SATURDAY NIGHT LIVE." Building off that modest foundation as a filmmaker, he wrote, directed, and starred in *Real Life* (1978), a documentary spoof of the famous PBS examination of the Loud family (a "typical" American family). He went on to wreak his own form of comic havoc on dating relationships in *Modern Romance* (1981), contemporary values in *Lost in America* (1985), and personal courage in *Defending Your Life* (1991). The latter two are considered his best efforts.

FILMS: *Taxi Driver* (a, 1976); *Real Life* (a, sc, d, 1978); *Private Benjamin* (a, 1980); *Modern Romance* (a, sc, d, 1981); *Twilight Zone—The Movie* (a, 1983); *Unfaithfully Yours* (a, 1983); *Lost in America* (a, sc, d, 1985); *Broadcast News* (a, 1987); *Defending Your Life* (a, sc, d, 1991); *I'll Do Anything* (a, 1994).

**Brooks, Mel (1926—)** One of the most outrageously comic film creators of the last twenty-five years, Mel Brooks has stretched the bounds of film humor, creating several comedy classics in the process. Like Woody ALLEN, Brooks shapes his own comic vision with virtually complete artistic control. An actor/comedian, screenwriter, director, and producer, he has pioneered the area of bad-taste humor with excellent results.

Born Melvin Kaminsky, he was the son of a process server who died when Brooks was two and a half. Brooks started his show business career at fourteen, entertaining guests around the pool of a Catskill mountains resort hotel in upstate New

*Mel Brooks returned to comic form with* Robin Hood: Men in Tights *(1993). He is seen here directing the hilarious spoof while still in makeup and costume for his own modest role in the film.*   PHOTO BY ROBERT ISENBERG, © 20TH CENTURY-FOX.

York. After serving in World War II, he began his stand-up comedy routine in earnest, working at several Catskill hotels until he met Sid CAESAR, which led to Brooks's work as a writer on Caesar's influential TV comedy/variety series "Your Show of Shows" during the early 1950s. Brooks was earning $5,000 per week as a writer until the program went off the air. He fell into near oblivion during the rest of the 1950s until he and Carl REINER went public with a record album of their party routine, with Brooks playing "The Two-Thousand-Year-Old Man." The album, *2,000 Years with Carl Reiner and Mel Brooks* (1960), and its sequels resurrected Brooks's career.

In the 1960s Brooks created the hit TV series "Get Smart" and, in the 1970s, the somewhat less successful TV series "When Things Were Rotten." Despite his long association with TV, Brooks's best, most outrageous humor has been exhibited in his movies.

Brooks's first film was not *The Producers*, which he made in 1968, but rather a cartoon he created and narrated called *The Critic* (1964), for which he won an Oscar for best animated short subject. His failed attempts to write for the legitimate stage during the 1950s and early 1960s were the likely inspiration for his first feature-length film, *The Producers*, one many still consider the writer/director's greatest movie. Its inspired lunacy, culminating in the "Springtime for Hitler" musical number (the original title of the film), remains a cinema milestone in hilarious bad taste. Although the film was not an immediate success at the box office, it has flourished as a cult favorite and earned Brooks an Oscar for best screenplay.

Brooks wrote and directed *The Twelve Chairs* (1970), another very funny film that flopped. It took Brooks four years to get the financing to make his next movie, *Blazing Saddles* (1974), but it became the most successful comedy of its time, earning $45.2 million in North America alone.

Brooks played a small role in *The Twelve Chairs* and two parts in *Blazing Saddles*, establishing himself as a screen comedian. However, it wasn't until he took a major role in *Silent Movie* (1976) and the lead role in *High Anxiety* (1977) that Brooks took center stage in his own films.

From the very beginning of his career as a writer/director, most of Brooks's films have been parodies of movie genres. For instance, *The Producers* made fun of backstage musicals; *Young Frankenstein* (1974) was a comic horror film; *Silent Movie* spoofed silent film conventions (even to the point of eschewing dialogue); *High Anxiety* kidded Alfred Hitchcock's movies; *History of the World—Part I* (1981) made fun of just about every kind of movie genre; and *Spaceballs* (1987) had it in for science fiction films like *Star Wars*.

His latter films have not been terribly successful at the box office. *History of the World—Part I*, in particular, was a major flop. *To Be or Not to Be* (1983), a remake of the 1942 Ernst LUBITSCH classic, had mixed results with both critics and ticket-buyers. *Spaceballs* was one of the rare Brooks films to be reasonably well received by the critics, but it wasn't quite the hit its belly laughs would have suggested. He followed that, however, with a film that neither critics nor audiences could stomach, *Life Stinks* (1991), which easily ranks as his worst movie. Happily, he made a comeback with *Robin Hood: Men in Tights* (1993).

Brooks has consistently surrounded himself with fine comic actors, using many of the same people in his films, such as Gene WILDER, Madeline KAHN, the late Marty FELDMAN, Cloris Leachman, and Ron Carey.

In addition to his comic works, Brooks has shown yet another side of his personality through his company, Brooksfilm, producing among others such diverse movies as *The Elephant Man* (1980), *Solarbabies* (1986), and *The Fly* (1986).

Brooks has been married to actress Anne Bancroft since 1964. It is his second marriage.

**FILMS:** As actor unless otherwise indicated: *New Faces* (co-sc only, 1954); *The Critic* (short, d, voice only, 1964); *The Producers* (d, sc, 1968); *Putney Swope* (1969); *The Twelve Chairs* (d, sc, 1970); *Shinbone Alley* (1971); *Blazing Saddles* (d, sc, song, 1974); *Young Frankenstein* (d, sc, 1974); *Silent Movie* (d, sc, 1976); *High Anxiety* (d, p, sc, songs, 1977); *The Muppet Movie* (1979); *The Elephant Man* (p only, 1980); *The Nude Bomb* (based on his "Get Smart" characters, 1980); *History of the World—Part I* (d, p, sc, songs, 1981); *Frances* (p only, 1982); *To Be or Not to Be* (p, sc, songs, 1983); *Sunset People* (1984); *The Doctor and the Devils* (p only, 1985); *84 Charing Cross Road* (p only, 1986); *The Fly* (p only, 1986); *Solarbabies* (p only, 1986); *Spaceballs* (d, p, sc, song, 1987); *Look Who's Talking Too* (voice only, 1990); *Life Stinks* (d, p, sc, story, 1991); *Robin Hood: Men in Tights* (d, p, sc, 1993).

## Brown, Joe E. (1892—1973)

A second-tier comedy star, Joe E. Brown had a famous large mouth (from which came the most hilarious comic howls), mischevious squinting eyes, and distinctive go-getter enthusiasm that made him a favorite of generally youthful male moviegoers. A versatile athlete, many of his best comedies centered around sports, such as baseball in *Elmer the Great* (1933) and football in *$1,000 Touchdown* (1939).

Born Joe Evans Brown in Holgate, Ohio, he performed acrobatics in the circus while he was still a child. A gifted athlete, he played semi-pro baseball but was too small for the major leagues. Brown turned to VAUDEVILLE and BURLESQUE for his living, eventually graduating to Broadway in 1918. With the coming of sound, he heeded the call to Hollywood and immediately put his circus background to good use in *The Circus Kid* (1928).

Brown's films were generally low-budget affairs that were churned out quickly. Few were gems; likewise, few were lumps of coal. He was a consistently engaging performer who held sway on the comedy circuit for the better part of fifteen years,

*One of the most underrated of sound era comics is Joe E. Brown, who flourished in B-movie comedies—often with a sports theme—during the 1930s. Here he is in a scene from* Polo Joe *(1936). Brown is best remembered today for his memorable supporting role in* Some Like It Hot *(1959), in which, upon discovering that Jack Lemmon isn't a woman, he says, "Well, no one's perfect."* PHOTO COURTESY OF THE SIEGEL COLLECTION.

**FILMS INCLUDE:** *The Circus Kid* (1928); *Crooks Can't Win* (1928); *Hit the Show* (1928); *One with the Show* (1929); *Molly and Me* (1929); *Painted Faces* (1929); *Sally* (1929); *My Lady's Past* (1929); *Hold Everything* (1930); *Maybe It's Love* (1930); *The Lottery Bride* (1930); *Song of the West* (1930); *Going Wild* (1930); *Sit Tight* (1931); *Local Boy Makes Good* (1931); *Broad Minded* (1931); *You Said a Mouthful* (1932); *The Tenderfoot* (1932); *Fireman, Save My Child* (1932); *Elmer the Great* (1933); *Son of a Sailor* (1933); *The Circus Clown* (1934); *Alibi Ike* (1935); *A Midsummers' Night Dream* (1935); *Bright Lights* (1935); *Polo Joe* (1936); *Sons o' Guns* (1936); *Riding on Air* (1937); *Fit for a King* (1937); *Flirting with Fate* (1938); *The Gladiator* (1938); *Wide Open Faces* (1938); *Beware Spooks!* (1939); *$1,000 Touchdown* (1939); *So You Won't Talk?* (1940); *Shut My Big Mouth* (1940); *Chatterbox* (1943); *Casanova in Burlesque* (1944); *Pin Up Girl* (1944); *The Tender Years* (1947); *Show Boat* (1951); *Around the World in 80 Days* (1956); *Some Like It Hot* (1959); *It's a Mad Mad Mad Mad World* (1963); *The Comedy of Terrors/The Graveside Story* (1964).

having most of his success in the 1930s. He was a big enough star, in any event, to be counted among the cast of the all-star *A Midsummers' Night Dream* (1935).

When his abilities as a physical comedian faded with age in the early 1940s, Brown retired from the big screen. He returned every so often, though, to appear in featured roles in movies such as *Show Boat* (1951), *Around the World in 80 Days* (1956), and *Some Like It Hot* (1959). He was among the all-star comedy cast of *IT'S A MAD MAD MAD MAD WORLD* (1963). Brown's last movie was the amusing low-budget horror farce *The Comedy of Terrors* (1964).

**Bruckman, Clyde (1894–1955)** A screenwriter and director, Clyde Bruckman lent his talents to a number of comedians, among them W. C. FIELDS, LAUREL AND HARDY, and Harold LLOYD. However, his greatest contribution came as the co-screenwriter of many of Buster KEATON's greatest feature-length comedies, among them *The Three Ages* (1923), *Our Hospitality* (1923), *Sherlock, Jr.* (1924), and *The Navigator* (1924). With Keaton he also co-wrote and co-directed Keaton's most enduring masterpiece, *The General* (1927).

A rare original Californian, Bruckman was born in San Bernardino. He worked as a journalist before breaking into the movie business as a screenwriter. His association with Keaton was the highlight of his career, providing him with the credentials to become a director in his own right. Bruckman had little trouble making the switch to sound comedies, but by the mid-1930s he could not get another directing job despite having made, among other fine films, W. C. Fields's classic short *A Fatal Glass of Beer* (1933) and the amusing Fields feature *The Man on the Flying Trapeze* (1935). In the years after 1935, he had only the sparest success as a screenwriter. Neither comedy nor life comes easily to a desperate man; in 1955 he killed himself in the men's room of a restaurant when he did not have the money to pay his bill.

FILMS INCLUDE: *Rouged Lips* (co-sc, 1923); *The Three Ages* (co-sc, 1923); *Our Hospitality* (co-sc, 1923); *Sherlock, Jr.* (co-sc, 1924); *The Navigator* (co-sc, 1924); *Seven Chances* (co-sc, 1925); *Keep Smiling* (co-sc, 1925); *For Heaven's Sake* (co-sc, 1926); *The General* (co-sc, co-d, 1927); *Horse Shoes* (d, 1927); *Call of the Cuckoos* (short, d, 1927); *Putting Pants on Philip* (short, 1927); *Love 'Em and Feed 'Em* (short, 1927); *The Battle of the Century* (short, d, 1927); *The Cameraman* (co-story, 1928); *A Perfect Gentleman* (d, 1928); *Leave 'Em Laughing* (short, d, 1928); *The Finishing Touch* (short, d, 1928); *Welcome Danger* (co-story, d, 1929); *Feet First* (d, 1930); *Everything's Rosie* (d, 1931); *Movie Crazy* (d, 1932); *Too Many Highballs* (short, d, 1933); *The Human Fish* (short, d, 1933); *A Fatal Glass of Beer* (short, d, 1933); *Spring Tonic* (d, 1935); *The Man on the Flying Trapeze* (d, 1935); *Professor Beware* (co-story, 1938); *Swingtime Johnny* (sc, 1943); *She Gets Her Man* (co-sc, 1945).

**Bugs Bunny**   *See* WARNER BROS. CARTOONS

**Bunny, John (1863—1915)**   The first movie comedy star in the history of the American cinema, John Bunny became an international star almost as soon as he began making movie shorts in 1910 for Vitagraph.

Bunny was born to an English naval officer who later took up residence in Brooklyn, New York. While still a youth, the future comedian joined a minstrel show and eventually became an actor in the theater of his day.

A 300-pound ball of comic energy, Bunny developed the art of humorous pantomime. He made more than two hundred hugely successful one-reelers before his untimely death at the age of fifty-two. His humor was reportedly based upon his substantial size, much like the comedy of Fatty AR-BUCKLE, who followed in his immense footsteps.

While most of Bunny's work was comedic, he did occasionally appear in dramatic films, demonstrating his versatility as a performer.

Unfortunately, none of his movies have survived. All that remains are written records of his work.

FILMS INCLUDE: *In Neighboring Kingdoms* (1910); *The New Stenographer* (1911); *Her Hero* (1911); *Subduing Mrs. Nag* (1911); *The Leading Lady* (1911); *A Tale of Two Cities* (1911); *Vanity Fair* (1911); *The First Violin* (1912); *Stenographers Wanted* (1912); *The Troublesome Step-Daughters* (1912); *Chumps* (1912); *Leap Year Proposals* (1912); *Bunny All at Sea* (1912); *Bunny's Suicide* (1912); *Bunny at the Derby* (1912); *Freckles* (1912); *Bunny Blarneyed* (1913); *Bunny as a Reporter* (1913); *Bunny's Honeymoon* (1913); *Bunny's Dilemma* (1913); *The Pickwick Papers* (1913); *John Tobin's Sweetheart* (1913); *Pigs Is Pigs* (1914); *Father's Flirtation* (1914); *The Honeymooners* (1914); *Bunny Buys a Harem* (1914); *Bunny's Mistake* (1914); *Bunny in Disguise* (1914); *Bunny's Birthday* (1914); *Love, Luck, and Gasoline* (1914); *Bunny in Bunnyland* (1915).

**Burke, Billie (1885—1970)**   Although she is remembered today as Glinda, The Good Witch, in *The Wizard of Oz* (1939), Billie Burke projected a very different image in most of her other films during the 1930s and 1940s. After playing leads in a variety of movies during the silent era, she emerged in the talkies as the ultimate scatterbrained socialite. In that guise, she appeared in scores of fondly remembered movies, including *Dinner at Eight* (1933),

*Topper* (1937), and *The Man Who Came to Dinner* (1942).

Born Mary William Ethelbert Appleton Burke in Washington, D.C., she was the daughter of a circus clown whose nickname was "Billy." She not only took his clowning sensibility, but also his name when she entered show business—which she did at the age of eight on a London stage.

Long after Burke became a Broadway star, she met and married the legendary showman Florenz Ziegfeld. It was a union of great devotion that lasted from 1914 until the impressario's death in 1932. During that time, Ziegfeld struck a deal with the famed film producer Thomas Ince for his wife's services in Hollywood. She was paid the astronomical sum of $300,000 to make her motion picture debut in *Peggy* (1916). Burke went on to make eleven more films over the next five years, many of them sophisticated comedies.

She went back to Broadway and didn't return to Hollywood for more than a decade, and when she did, it was to help her financially strapped husband who had gone broke in the ever-deepening Great Depression. After Ziegfeld died, she stayed in the film capital and continued to build a brand-new career for herself as a ditzy comedian.

By the mid-1940s she eased into warm, motherly roles, culminating in her performance as Elizabeth Taylor's mother and Spencer Tracy's wife in *Father of the Bride* (1950) and its sequel *Father's Little Dividend* (1951).

Burke was portrayed by Myrna Loy in the biopic *The Great Ziegfeld* (1936), a movie for which the widow served as a consultant.

FILMS: *Peggy* (1916); *Gloria's Romance* (1916); *The Mysterious Miss Terry* (1917); *Arms and the Girl* (1917); *The Land of Promise* (1917); *In Pursuit of Polly* (1918); *Let's Get a Divorce* (1918); *The Make-Believe Wife* (1918); *Eve's Daughter* (1918); *The Misleading Widow* (1919); *Good Gracious, Annabelle!* (1919); *Sadie Love* (1919); *Wanted—A Husband* (1919); *The Frisky Mrs. Johnson* (1920); *Away Goes Prudence* (1920); *The Education of Elizabeth* (1921); *A Bill of Divorcement* (1932); *Christopher Strong* (1933); *Only Yesterday* (1933); *Dinner at Eight* (1933); *Where Sinners Meet* (1934); *Finishing School* (1934); *We're Rich Again* (1934); *Forsaking All Others* (1934); *Society Doctor* (1935); *Becky Sharp* (1935); *After Office Hours* (1935); *Only Eight Hours* (1935); *She Couldn't Take It* (1935); *Splendor* (1935); *A Feather in Her Hat* (1935); *Doubting Thomas* (1935); *Piccadilly Jim* (1936); *My American Wife* (1936); *Craig's Wife* (1936); *Parnell* (1937); *The Bride Wore Red* (1937); *Topper* (1937); *Navy, Blue and Gold* (1937); *Merrily We Live* (1938); *Everybody Sing* (1938); *The Young in Heart* (1938); *Zenobia* (1939); *Topper Takes a Trip* (1939); *Bridal Suite* (1939); *Eternally Yours* (1939); *Remember?* (1939); *The Wizard of Oz* (1939); *And One Was Beautiful* (1940); *The Ghost Comes Home* (1940); *Irene* (1940); *The Captain Is a Lady* (1940); *Dulcy* (1940); *Hullabaloo* (1940); *Topper Returns* (1941); *One Night in Lisbon* (1941); *The Wild Man of Borneo* (1941); *In This Our Life* (1942); *The Man Who Came to Dinner* (1942); *What's Cookin'?* (1942); *Girl Trouble* (1942); *They All Kissed the Bride* (1942); *Hi Diddle Diddle* (1943); *You're a Lucky Fellow, Mr. Smith* (1943); *Gildersleeve on Broadway* (1943); *So's Your Uncle* (1943); *The Laramie Trail* (1944); *Swing Out, Sister* (1945); *The Cheaters* (1945); *Breakfast in Hollywood* (1946); *The Bachelor's Daughters* (1946); *And Baby Makes Three* (1949); *The Barkleys of Broadway* (1949); *Father of the Bride* (1950); *Three Husbands* (1950); *Boy from Indiana* (1950); *Father's Little Dividend* (1951); *Small Town Girl* (1953); *The Young Philadelphians* (1959); *Sergeant Rutledge* (1960); *Pepe* (1960).

**burlesque** The risque sibling of VAUDEVILLE, burlesque is generally remembered for its striptease artists. However, the burlesque houses that thrived during the early decades of the twentieth century also featured comedians who made their livelihoods with a good line of patter and a fair helping of lowbrow comic antics.

Burlesque, like vaudeville, had its roots in the

English music hall tradition. Among the many famous comedians who played in burlesque were ABBOTT AND COSTELLO, Fanny BRICE, Eddie CANTOR, Phil SILVERS, and Mae WEST.

The word *burlesque*, of course, means to spoof something that is otherwise serious. The word was used in that context in an early 1930s series of Shirley Temple comedy shorts called "Baby Burlesks." They were one-reel sendups of current popular hits. The name of the series was purposefully misspelled to suggest the comedy of the burlesque tradition without the sexual connotation.

Movies either set in the burlesque milieu or incorporating scenes from burlesque include *Applause* (1929), *Lady of Burlesque* (1943), *Gypsy* (1962), *The Night They Raided Minsky's* (1968), and *Funny Girl* (1968).

Burlesque, like vaudeville, began losing its popularity in the 1930s. This was partly due to the talkies siphoning off their audiences but also to the rise of a more strict societal moral code.

## Burnett, Carol (1933—)

A TV comedian who has occasionally ventured into feature films, Carol Burnett has starred in only a handful of movies, most of them seriocomic in nature, such as the wryly perceptive *The Four Seasons* (1981). She has also taken a modest number of supporting parts, and these have generally been more out-and-out comedic, such as the role of Miss Hannigan in *Annie* (1982).

Born in San Antonio, Texas, Burnett had early access to films: Her father owned a movie theater. Rather than head for Hollywood, though, the aspiring performer went to New York, singing and acting in off-Broadway revues before Garry Moore discovered her and put her on his TV show in the late 1950s. One show business success after another followed, taking her from Broadway to her own highly acclaimed and long-running TV series, "The Carol Burnett Show."

Burnett had her first stab at the movies in the Dean Martin comedy *Who's Been Sleeping in My Bed?* (1963), in which she had a leading role. Her burgeoning TV career kept her away from the big screen for nearly ten years before she scored a surprise hit with Walter MATTHAU in the touching *Pete 'n' Tillie*. Later, she joined with director Robert Altman during his "ensemble period" and distinguished herself in two of his hip, satirical movies, *A Wedding* (1978) and *Health* (1979).

An actress and comedian of considerable range and skill, Burnett was again off the big screen for a decade between *Annie* and the FARCE *Noises Off* (1992).

---

**FILMS INCLUDE:** *Who's Been Sleeping in My Bed?* (1963); *Pete 'n' Tillie* (1972); *The Front Page* (1974); *A Wedding* (1978); *Health* (1979); *Chu Chu and the Philly Flash* (1981); *The Four Seasons* (1981); *Annie* (1982); *Noises Off* (1992).

---

## Burnette, Smiley (1911—1967)

When it comes to comic Western sidekicks, there is hardly anyone more amusing than Smiley Burnette. He tagged along with Gene Autry in an astounding eighty-one of the singing cowboy's motion pictures. Even so, that was but a fraction of the more than two hundred Westerns to which Burnette added his droll presence—and that doesn't count his occasional appearances in such other fare as murder mysteries and Dick Tracy serials.

Born Lester Alvin Burnette in Summum, Illinois, he got his flair for performing from his preacher father. Burnette and his longtime pal Gene Autry worked together on stage and on the radio long before they arrived in Hollywood in 1934.

By turns comically crotchety and farcially dense, Burnette got most of his laughs from his acting, rather than from his thin scripts. Much beloved by Western fans, he went on to become a drawing card in his own right (despite the fact that he never had a starring role), earning a place on the top-ten box office list of Western actors between the years 1940 and 1952.

In addition to his acting, Burnette was also a prolific songwriter, penning in excess of three hundred Western tunes, a considerable number of which can be heard in his movies.

Burnette's last film appearance was in 1953, but he returned from retirement eleven years later to play the railroad engineer in the "Petticoat Junction" TV series from 1964 until his death in 1967.

**FILMS INCLUDE:** *In Old Santa Fe* (1934); *The Phantom Empire* (serial, 1935); *Tumblin' Tumbleweeds* (1935); *The Singing Cowboy* (1936); *Dick Tracy* (serial, 1937); *The Stadium Murders* (1938); *Rhythm of the Saddle* (1938); *Under Western Stars* (1938); *South of the Border* (1939); *Rancho Grande* (1940); *Down Mexico Way* (1941); *Cowboy Serenade* (1942); *Terror Trail* (1947); *Last Days of Boot Hill* (1948); *Laramie* (1949); *Across the Badlands* (1950); *Bonanza Town* (1951); *Smoky Canyon* (1952); *Winning of the West* (1953).

## Burns, "Bazooka" Bob (1893—1956) A

humorist who specialized in rural comedy, "Bazooka" Bob Burns played naive hayseeds who persevered and ultimately triumphed by relying on their down-home country values. It was no wonder, then, that the Arkansas-born comic picked up a second nickname of "The Arkansas Philosopher." He had earlier earned the moniker "Bazooka," thanks to his invention of a comic musical instrument of the same name.

In the 1930s, when he had his vogue in Hollywood, a large percentage of the moviegoing public either still lived outside of the large cities or had recently come from the country. Burns appealed to this audience in radio, VAUDEVILLE, and films such as *Mountain Music* (1937), *I'm from Missouri* (1939), and *Comin' Round the Mountain* (1940).

**FILMS INCLUDE:** *Quick Millions* (1931); *The Singing Vagabond* (1935); *Rhythm on the Range* (1936); *The Big Broadcast of 1937* (1936); *Waikiki Wedding* (1937); *Mountain Music* (1937); *Radio City Revels* (1938); *Tropic Holiday* (1938); *I'm from Missouri* (1939); *Comin' Round the Mountain* (1940); *Belle of the Yukon* (1944).

**Burns, George** *See* BURNS AND ALLEN

**Burns and Allen** Gracie Allen played a ditsy woman who thought she was smart, while George Burns, the straight man, patiently asked her questions to which she gave hilarious answers. Their humor came out of absurd interpretations of language and common experiences that Allen saw with a comically inspired logic of her own. The husband and wife comedy team had its greatest success on VAUDEVILLE, radio, and TV, although they also had a notable film career together during the 1930s. A longtime comedy legend, Burns suddenly, and unexpectedly, became a genuine movie star in his own right (as a solo) when he was seventy-nine years old.

Born Grace Ethel Cecile Rosalie Allen in San Francisco (1902–1964), the young comedian was the daughter of show business parents and joined their act at a young age. George Burns (1896–), born Nathan Birnbaum in New York City, was one of fourteen children. He quit school at thirteen to help support his family. He sang in the streets of New York for pennies with his group, The Peewee Quartet, eventually working his way into vaudeville.

Burns and Allen met on the vaudeville circuit and formed an act in 1923, marrying in 1926. Originally, Burns was the comic and Allen was the straight one. When Allen received laughs just by asking Burns questions, however, they decided to switch roles. By the time they were married, Burns and Allen had hit the big time in vaudeville with their "Lamb Chop" routine.

Their success in vaudeville led them to Hollywood where they made fourteen comedy shorts during the 1930s. Their first feature film appearance was in *The Big Broadcast* (1932). They played impor-

*The beloved Burns and Allen comedy team were hits in all media, gaining fame in vaudeville, radio, movies, and TV. George Burns was the ultimate straight man to Gracie's scatterbrained wit.*   PHOTO COURTESY OF THE SIEGEL COLLECTION.

tant supporting characters in virtually all of their twenty feature films. Their most noteworthy roles were in *We're Not Dressing* (1934), *Big Broadcast of 1936* (1935), and *Damsel in Distress* (1937), the last of which was in support of Fred Astaire. They not only provided comic relief, they also did a splendid dance routine!

Allen performed in three films without her husband: *The Gracie Allen Murder Case* (1939), *Mr. and Mrs. North* (1942), and *Two Girls and a Sailor* (1944). In the meantime, Burns and Allen had an enormously popular radio show that ran from 1933 to 1950, when the program made the move to television. "The Burns and Allen Show" continued on TV until Allen retired in 1958.

Burns, who had been in charge of their act and who oversaw their radio and TV show, went on working solo, starring in two other TV series. Then, after a thirty-five-year absence from the big screen and more than a decade after Allen's death,

Burns emerged in 1975 as a movie star in Neil SIMON's *The Sunshine Boys*. Stepping into the role originally intended for his best friend, Jack BENNY (who had suddenly died), Burns won an Oscar. He went on to star in a surprisingly large number of films, receiving his greatest acclaim for *Oh, God!* (1977), in which he played God with endearing comic aplomb. Unfortunately, the many sequels have not been up to Burns's talents. In addition to his latter-day film work, he has also written best-selling books, recorded country western albums, and hosted TV specials.

**FILMS:** *The Big Broadcast* (1932); *College Humor* (1933); *International House* (1933); *Six of a Kind* (1934); *We're Not Dressing* (1934); *Many Happy Returns* (1934); *Love in Bloom* (1935); *Big Broadcast of 1936* (1935); *Here Comes Cookie* (1935); *The Big Broadcast of 1937* (1936); *College Holiday* (1936); *A Damsel in Distress* (1937); *College Swing* (1938); *Honolulu* (1939); *The Solid Gold Cadillac* (1956).

Allen only: *The Gracie Allen Murder Mystery* (1939); *Mr. and Mrs. North* (1942); *Two Girls and a Sailor* (1944).

Burns only: *The Sunshine Boys* (1975); *Oh, God!* (1977); *Movie Movie* (1978); *Sgt. Pepper's Lonely Hearts Club Band* (1978); *Going in Style* (1979); *Just You and Me, Kid* (1979); *Oh, God! Book II* (1980); *Oh, God! You Devil* (1984); *18 Again!* (1988).

**Burton, Tim (1960—)**   In the second half of the 1980s and the early 1990s, director Tim Burton emerged as the dark prince of the comically surreal. Schooled in ANIMATION, he became a live-action creator of bizarre comic (and comic book) grotesques, from Pee-wee HERMAN's first feature film to the grim black humor of the first two Batman movies.

Growing up in Burbank, California, Burton lived in the shadow of the make-believe world of Hollywood. He attended the California Institute of the Arts on a Disney fellowship and upon graduation went to work at the Disney studio, helping animate such films as *The Fox and the Hound* (1983) and *The Black Cauldron* (1985).

Burton's initial directorial effort was the animated short *Vincent*, a six-minute film about a young boy's fascination with Vincent Price (the movie was also narrated by Price). *Vincent* won a number of awards, which led to a live-action project, the twenty-nine-minute *Frankenweenie* (1982). This film was considered both brilliant and unreleasable. Burton's undeniable talent, however, brought him a shot at directing his first feature-length comedy, *Pee-wee's Big Adventure*, starring Paul Reubens (Pee-wee Herman). Burton was just twenty-five years old at the time, but he turned in an impressive, original, and visually stimulating film that began an impressive string of critically and commercially successful comedies.

After the success of his second cartoonish, dark burlesque, *Beetlejuice* (1988), Burton seemed the logical choice to direct yet another bleak comic vision, *Batman* (1988). Ominous and hilarious, just like the film's central villain, Jack Nicholson's Joker, *Batman* was a megahit with both the critics and the moviegoing public. It led to a sequel, with Burton once again at the helm. Before that movie came into being, the director created yet another original motion picture, *Edward Scissorhands* (1990), a quirky, poignant comedy about a young man with scissors for hands. It, too, was a hit.

It seemed like Burton could do no wrong until *Batman Returns* arrived in movie theaters in 1992. The movie made a ton of money, but not as much as Warner Bros. expected; the film's horrific comedy was often repellant. While visually stunning, the movie was an artistic miss.

FILMS: *Pee-wee's Big Adventure* (1985); *Beetlejuice* (1988); *Batman* (1989); *Edward Scissorhands* (also story, p, 1990); *Batman Returns* (1992); *Tim Burton's The Nightmare Before Christmas* (story, p only, 1993).

## Butterworth, Charles (1896—1946)
Usually in supporting roles, Charles Butterworth was a consistently amusing player in light comedies. He was untouchable playing eccentric, often drunken stuffed shirts.

Born in South Bend, Indiana, Butterworth was a bright, but unfocused young man. Attending Notre Dame, he flitted from law to journalism. He then took a fling at acting, where he found his home. After some success on Broadway, Butterworth went to Hollywood. He appeared in films beginning with *The Life of the Party* in 1930 and continued on the big screen until his sudden death in a traffic accident in 1946. Among his memorable performances were those in *Love Me Tonight* (1932), *Swing High, Swing Low* (1937), and *Every Day's a Holiday* (1937).

FILMS INCLUDE: *The Life of the Party* (1930); *Side Show* (1931); *Manhattan Parade* (1932); *Love Me Tonight* (1932); *My Weakness* (1933); *The Nuisance* (1933); *The Cat and the Fiddle* (1934); *Hollywood Party* (1934); *Orchids to You* (1935); *The Night Is Young* (1935); *Magnificent Obsession* (1936); *Half Angel* (1936); *Rainbow on the River* (1936); *Swing High, Swing Low* (1937); *Every Day's a Holiday* (1937); *Thanks for the Memory* (1938); *Let Freedom Ring* (1939); *The Boys from Syracuse* (1940); *Sis Hopkins* (1941); *What's Cooking?* (1942); *This Is the Army* (1943); *Bermuda Mystery* (1944).

# C

**Caesar, Sid (1922—)** A brilliant comic actor, Sid Caesar achieved his greatest fame in the 1950s with his TV program "Your Show of Shows." A comedian who seemed larger than life on TV, he did not loom large on the big screen. A sketch comedian, Caesar did not develop a distinct persona around which to build a movie career. He did, however, provide the venue (by way of his TV show) for future comic giants to learn their craft, among them Woody ALLEN, Mel BROOKS, and Neil SIMON.

Born in Yonkers, New York, Caesar had ambitions to be a serious musician. He studied both the saxophone and the clarinet at the prestigious Juilliard School in New York City. He didn't get very far with his studies before World War II changed the course of his life. While in the Coast Guard he switched from music to comedy and wound up in the armed forces show *Tars and Spars*. When the show was put on film in 1946, his career was launched.

Caesar further built his reputation for comedy on the nightclub circuit and later on Broadway, where he scored a hit in *Make Mine Manhattan*. A young star on the rise, he took a gamble on the fledgling TV medium and it paid off handsomely with the fondly remembered "Your Show of Shows." A recreation of that era and of Caesar himself can be seen in Joseph Bologna's performance in *My Favorite Year* (1982).

After Caesar's long-running TV show went off the air, the comedian went into a steep and rapid decline. He made a modest comeback in the late 1960s and resurfaced again in the latter half of the 1970s in featured roles. In more recent years he has made TV guest appearances.

---

**FILMS INCLUDE:** *Tars and Spars* (1946); *The Guilt of Janet Ames* (1947); *It's a Mad Mad Mad Mad World* (1963); *A Guide for the Married Man* (1967); *The Busy Body* (1967); *The Spirit Is Willing* (1967); *Ten from Your Show of Shows* (compilation of TV skits, 1973); *Airport 1975* (1974); *Silent Movie* (1976); *Fire Sale* (1977); *Barnaby and Me* (1977); *The Cheap Detective* (1978); *Grease* (cameo, 1978); *The Fiendish Plot of Dr. Fu Manchu* (1980); *The Munsters' Revenge* (1981); *Over the Brooklyn Bridge* (1983); *Stoogemania* (1985).

---

**Cambridge, Godfrey (1933—1976)** A black stand-up comic, Godfrey Cambridge's motion picture success in a number of race-conscious comedies in the early 1970s helped pave the way for the far more substantial careers of Richard PRYOR and Eddie MURPHY. A moonfaced teddy bear of a man, he had a sly, self-deprecating comic style that belied his considerable bite.

Cambridge was born in New York City to parents who had immigrated from British New Guinea. Performing was a stronger lure than the classroom, so Cambridge did not finish college. Instead, he worked off Broadway, learning his craft as an actor while also developing a comedy stand-up act.

There was nothing funny, however, about his film debut; he played a thug in *The Last Angry Man*

*Godfrey Cambridge, in a scene from* The President's Analyst *(1967), parlayed his success as a stand-up comic in the 1960s to become the first black actor to star in his own pointed comedies, most notably* Watermelon Man *(1970).*
PHOTO COURTESY OF MOVIE STAR NEWS.

(1959). It was humor, though, that brought him to public attention when he wowed TV audiences with his fresh and witty comedy routines. Roles in hip comedies like *The President's Analyst* (1967) followed, and by 1970 he had the starring role in what was then a unique vehicle: a comedy about race relations in America called *Watermelon Man* (1970). He had two other memorable seriocomic ventures, *Cotton Comes to Harlem* (1970) and its sequel *Come Back, Charleston Blue* (1972).

Cambridge's film projects were tending toward the more serious when he died suddenly of a heart attack in 1976 while filming the TV movie *Victory at Entebbe* (1976). He was slated to play Uganda dictator Idi Amin, but was replaced by Julius Harris.

**FILMS INCLUDE:** *The Last Angry Man* (1959); *Gone Are the Days!/Purlie Victorious* (1963); *The Troublemaker* (1964); *The Busy Body* (1967); *The President's Analyst* (1967); *The Biggest Bundle of Them All* (1968); *Bye, Bye, Braverman* (1968); *Watermelon Man* (1970); *Cotton Comes to Harlem* (1970); *The Biscuit Eater* (1972); *Come Back, Charleston Blue* (1972); *Whiffs* (1975); *Friday Foster* (1975); *Scott Joplin* (1977).

**Campbell, Eric (1870—1917)** If it appears that the mammoth and fierce-looking Eric Campbell is the ultimate silent comedy villain, it's because he is seen as such in a number of Charlie CHAPLIN's most famous early two-reel comedies, among them *The Pawnshop* (1916), *The Rink* (1916), and *Easy Street* (1917). Unfortunately, Campbell had a short career in the movies, appearing in just eleven comedy shorts in less than two years.

Campbell was a Scot who worked, as Chaplin once did, in Fred Karno's comedy troupe. Looking for a suitable foil, Chaplin hired the imposing actor in 1916 and used him in ten of the eleven films in which Campbell eventually worked. He might have appeared in a great many more Chaplin films had he not died in a traffic accident in 1917.

**FILMS:** *The Floorwalker* (1916); *The Fireman* (1916); *The Vagabond* (1916); *The Count* (1916); *The Pawnshop* (1916); *Behind the Screen* (1916); *The Rink* (1916); *Easy Street* (1917); *The Cure* (1917); *The Immigrant* (1917); *The Adventurer* (1917).

**Candy, John (1950—1994)** A tall, heavyset, good-natured comic talent who came into his own as a star in the mid-1980s, John Candy often

*An engaging comic actor, John Candy is an alumnus of "SCTV." He emerged during the latter half of the 1980s as a major star, even taking a fling at romantic comedy in* Only the Lonely *(1991), shown above.*
PHOTO BY DON SMETZER, © 20TH CENTURY-FOX.

played comically obnoxious types, much in the mode of Jackie GLEASON, to whom he has a passing resemblance. The difference between the two is that Candy's characters are inevitably more sentimental, more vulnerable, and ultimately more lovable, particularly since he became a star; his characters were far more caustic when he was a supporting comic player.

Born John Franklin Candy in Toronto, Canada, he was a journalism major in college. He began working as a comic with Chicago's Second City improvisational group in 1972. He later went back home, where he co-created Toronto's own famed Second City troupe, which became the jumping-off point for his work in the now-legendary Canadian "SCTV" comedy show, for which he both wrote and performed.

Just three years after Candy started in comedy, he had his first movie role, a supporting part as a bumbling cop in the Canadian film *It Seemed Like a Good Idea at the Time* (1975). Other comic relief and/or supporting roles followed; he played minor roles in a couple of John BELUSHI's films, *1941* (1979) and *The Blues Brothers* (1980).

Candy started showing a less strident, richer comic vein of talent in *Stripes* (1981), proving himself a good foil for Bill MURRAY. His recognition factor grew considerably in 1983 when he played significant supporting roles in two very different hit comedies, *National Lampoon's Vacation* and *Splash*. Largely on that basis, Candy got his first starring role in the low-budget hit comedy *Summer Rental* (1985). That same year, he was a co-lead with Tom HANKS in the critically panned, yet commercially successful *Volunteers* (1985).

Except for the occasional cameo, Candy has starred in the rest of his films, showing a marked inclination to work with writer/producer/and sometimes director John HUGHES. He has shared a seven-film association with Hughes, including the previously mentioned *National Lampoon's Vacation* as well as *Planes, Trains and Automobiles* (1987), *The Great Outdoors* (1988), *Uncle Buck* (1989), a small role in *Home Alone* (1990), and *Career Opportunities* (1991). The latter film did not do well at the box office, nor did the Candy/Hughes collaboration on *Only the Lonely* (1991), a valiant attempt by Hughes as producer and Chris COLUMBUS as writer/director to turn Candy into a romantic comedy lead. The film was pretty good, but the audience didn't show up to find out.

Until *Cool Runnings* (1993), Candy had not had a bonafide hit film as a star since 1989 and had taken to showcasing his versatility by doing an increasing number of cameos and unbilled performances. For instance, he put on a thick New Orleans accent, and joined the all-star cast of Oliver Stone's *JFK* (1991), and then showed up as a Chicago Cubs announcer in the amusing baseball fantasy *Rookie of the Year* (1993).

FILMS: *It Seemed Like a Good Idea at the Time* (1975); *The Clown Murders* (1976); *The Silent Partner* (1978); *1941* (1979); *Lost and Found* (1979); *The Blues Brothers* (1980); *Heavy Metal* (1981); *Stripes* (1981); *It Came from Hollywood* (1982); *Going Berserk* (1983); *National Lampoon's Vacation* (1983); *Splash* (1983); *Brewster's Millions* (1985); *Summer Rental* (1985); *Volunteers* (1985); *Armed and Dangerous* (1986); *Find the Lady* (1986); *Little Shop of Horrors* (1986); *Planes, Trains and Automobiles* (1987); *Spaceballs* (1987); *The Great Outdoors* (1988); *Hot to Trot* (1988); *Speed Zone* (1989); *Uncle Buck* (1989); *Who's Harry Crumb?* (also p, 1989); *Home Alone* (1990); *The Rescuers Down Under* (voice only, 1990); *Masters of Menace* (1991); *Nothing but Trouble* (1991); *Career Opportunities* (1991); *Delirious* (1991); *Only the Lonely* (1991); *JFK* (1991); *Once Upon a Crime* (1992); *Rookie of the Year* (uncred, 1993); *Cool Runnings* (1993).

## Canova, Judy (1916—1983)

A forerunner of Minnie Pearl, Judy Canova was famous for her rural humor, highlighted by her famous, earsplitting comic yodel. The most significant part of her film career was in the latter half of the 1930s and early 1940s.

Born Juliet Canova in Jacksonville, Florida, she came to prominence as a singing comedian in VAUDEVILLE. As did so many performers, she reached the apex of her stage career by performing in a Ziegfeld show, *Calling All Stars*, in the mid-1930s. Her success on Broadway led to her debut in the Warner Bros. musical comedy *In Caliente* (1935). With her movie career launched, Canova began appearing in films with increasing regularity until she hit her stride in the early 1940s in films such as *Joan of Ozark* (1942) and *Louisiana Hayride* (1944). She had equal, if not greater fame, on radio, with a ten-year run as a popular broadcast comedy star.

Canova's movie career trailed off during the early

1950s; she made only two films after 1955, her last appearance in *Cannonball* (1976).

FILMS: *In Caliente* (1935); *Going Highbrow* (1935); *Thrill of a Lifetime* (1937); *Artists and Models* (1937); *Scatterbrain* (1940); *Puddin' Head* (1941); *Sis Hopkins* (1941); *Joan of Ozark* (1942); *Sleepytime Gal* (1942); *True to the Army* (1942); *Sleepy Lagoon* (1943); *Chatterbox* (1943); *Louisiana Hayride* (1944); *Hit the Hay* (1945); *Singing in the Corn* (1946); *Honeychile* (1951); *Oklahoma Annie* (1952); *The WAC from Walla Walla* (1952); *Untamed Heiress* (1954); *Lay That Rifle Down* (1955); *Carolina Cannonball* (1955); *The Adventures of Huckleberry Finn* (1960); *Cannonball* (1976).

## Cantor, Eddie (1892—1964)

A musical comedy star with an enormous energy level, Eddie Cantor could put over a song like Jolson and throw off comic one-liners like Groucho. It is less well known that he also sometimes wrote his work. Most of his career was spent in radio, but with his pop eyes, optimistic attitude, and willingness to do anything for a laugh, Cantor gained a popularity in films that defied the box office doom visited upon so many other film stars during the worst of the Great Depression.

Born Edward Israel Iskowitz in New York City, he became an orphan at an early age, supporting himself any way he could, including as a singing waiter before making his mark in VAUDEVILLE. Cantor rose to fame on Broadway in *The Midnight Frolics* (1916) and joined the ranks of popular show business entertainers during the 1920s when he starred in the *Ziegfeld Follies* and later in hit shows including *Kid Boots* (1926) and *Whoopee* (1930).

Cantor made a silent film version of *Kid Boots* in 1926, but he didn't become a film star until talkies enabled him to show off his unique musical comedy style. By and large, he played cowardly, ineffectual types who, nonetheless, became heroes by the end of the film.

Samuel Goldwyn signed up Cantor, who made a

number of wonderfully silly musical comedies, including *Whoopee* (1930), *Palmy Days* (1931), *The Kid from Spain* (1932), *Roman Scandals* (1933), and *Kid Millions* (1934).

Cantor continued acting in films in the latter half of the 1930s and in the 1940s, but considerably less frequently. The movies took a back seat to his immensely popular radio show.

The last two films he starred in were *Show Business* (1944) and *If You Knew Susie* (1948), a film based on his most famous hit song. He produced both movies and, except for a brief appearance playing himself in the 1952 *The Story of Will Rogers*, he did not appear on film again due to a disabling heart attack that same year. His life story, however, was told in a poorly done biopic called *The Eddie Cantor Story* (1953), for which the famous entertainer dubbed his own songs.

Cantor was given a special Academy Award in 1956.

FILMS: *Kid Boots* (1926); *Special Delivery* (plus story, 1927); *Glorifying the American Girl* (1929); *Whoopee* (1930); *Mr. Lemon of Orange* (co-sc only, 1931); *Palmy Days* (also story, sc, 1931); *The Kid from Spain* (1932); *Roman Scandals* (1933); *Kid Millions* (1934); *Strike Me Pink* (1936); *Ali Baba Goes to Town* (1937); *Forty Little Mothers* (1940); *Thank Your Lucky Stars* (1943); *Hollywood Canteen* (1944); *Show Business* (also p, 1944); *If You Knew Susie* (also p, 1948); *The Story of Will Rogers* (1952); *The Eddie Cantor Story* (1953).

## Capra, Frank (1897—1991)

There is no mistaking Frank Capra's best films for those of any other director; his good humor, proletarian point of view, sentimentalism, and rollicking fast pace represent a unique signature. One of the leading directors of the 1930s and early 1940s, Capra made light romantic comedies and black comedies, but he is best known for his social comedies, in particular his string of films made between 1936 and 1941. It would have been enough for film lovers if he had only made *It's a Wonderful Life* (1947), but Capra made an astonishing number of excellent films—comedies and dramas alike—even before he became famous with his industry-rocking comedy hit of 1934, IT HAPPENED ONE NIGHT.

Born in Sicily, he immigrated with his poor family to America when he was six, settling in California where his father worked in the fields picking fruit. Young Capra was an extremely bright young man and he struggled to get a college education, graduating with a degree in chemical engineering from the prestigious California Institute of Technology in 1918.

After a short stint in the army at the end of World War I, Capra led a rudderless existence. When he found himself in desperate need of a job, he talked a small film company into letting him direct a short called *Fultah Fisher's Boarding House* (1922). His fascination with the film medium was born, and he spent the next several years learning everything he could about the movie business, working in a film lab and taking on jobs as a propmaster and editor. Perhaps his most important training came when he worked as a gagman, first on the OUR GANG silent comedies for Hal ROACH and then for Harry LANGDON at the Mack SENNETT studio.

Capra's understanding of comedy was put on display in Langdon's first three touching and very funny feature films, *Tramp, Tramp, Tramp* (1926), which Capra both co-scripted and co-directed, *The Strong Man* (1926), and *Long Pants* (1927). Capra's importance to Langdon's career was particularly obvious because the comedian's art deteriorated immediately after the young director was fired.

Capra was at loose ends and went to New York, directing Claudette COLBERT in her movie debut, *For the Love of Mike* (1927), but it was not a success. He went back to work for Sennett for a short while before Harry Cohn made the smartest decision of his long career at Columbia Pictures, hiring Capra in 1928 in what was then a very special arrangement. Capra agreed to be paid the relatively paltry sum of $1,000 per picture in exchange for full control of his movies. While the amount of money Capra earned would ultimately skyrocket, the other terms of the agreement remained in force for thirteen years.

His first film at Columbia was the delightful comedy *That Certain Thing* (1928). He worked quickly during the next several years, directing an astonishing number of movies and easily making the transition to sound. He learned his craft in a number of minor but increasingly popular films, many of them comedies such as *Say It with Sable* (1928), *Platinum Blonde* (1931), and *American Madness* (1932).

Capra was a hitmaker, but his early success at Columbia was nothing compared with what was to come. In 1934 he made the blockbuster hit of the year, *It Happened One Night*, with Claudette Colbert and Clark Gable. It became the first film to sweep all five top Oscars: best picture, best director, best screenplay (Robert RISKIN), best actor, and best actress. Neither Gable (on loan to Columbia as punishment) nor Colbert (who had worked with Capra without success in her movie debut) had wanted to be in the film.

The box office reaction was so strong that this single picture turned the two actors into superstars. Capra became the hottest director in Hollywood, and the film propelled Columbia overnight into the realm of major studio. In fact, it's fair to say that Harry Cohn's Columbia Pictures would have been a mere footnote in Hollywood history had it not been for the thirteen-year association between the studio and its greatest director. Capra was irreplaceable to Columbia and, in retrospect, the reasons are obvious: He made films about people with whom the audience could identify—cynics, idealists, working people, out-of-work John Does, small town folks with unfulfilled dreams, and so on. In other words, his characters were flesh and blood when most other directors made films about bigger-than-life heroes. He also imbued his characters with humor. With rare exceptions, Capra balanced his dramas with heavy doses of comedy, and his comedies with heavy doses of drama.

After *It Happened One Night*, Capra went on to make a series of films for which he is justly best remembered. His social comedies, beginning with *Mr. Deeds Goes to Town* (1936) and continuing with *You Can't Take It with You* (1938), *Mr. Smith Goes to Washington* (1939), and *Meet John Doe* (1941) are sometimes known as "Capracorn" for their strong belief in the goodness of people. Despite their naivete, in their time these films were biting indictments of greed, corruption, and selfishness. In fact, Capra's *Mr. Smith Goes to Washington*, which premiered in the nation's capital with an audience full of congressmen, was roundly booed and criticized by the nation's elected officials for even suggesting that one of their members might be on the take. Nonetheless, *Mr. Smith* was nominated for a best picture Oscar, and Capra was nominated as best director for the film. Capra won the best director Oscar for *Mr. Deeds Goes to Town* and both a best picture and a best director Oscar for *You Can't Take It with You*. In addition, his gentle, romantic fantasy film, *Lost Horizon* (1937), was nominated for best picture.

During World War II, Capra distinguished himself still further when he joined the service and made a documentary series titled *Why We Fight*, a stirring explanation of America's role in the world. He won a best documentary Oscar in 1942 for his efforts and went on to make a number of excellent films for the army. Before he left Hollywood, however, he made *Arsenic and Old Lace*, which was released in 1944 to keep his work in front of the American public. It was yet another huge box office success despite Capra's unexpected detour into BLACK COMEDY.

After the war, however, Capra seemed to lose his touch—not as a filmmaker, but as a hitmaker. *It's a Wonderful Life* (1947), while much loved and revered today as the quintessence of Capracorn, was a box office underachiever when it was released. *State of the Union* (1948) fared somewhat better, but *Riding High* (1950) and *Here Comes the Groom* (1951) were likable Bing Crosby vehicles at best, but hardly on a par with Capra's earlier works.

After a long hiatus, Capra made his last two films, the underrated comedy *A Hole in the Head* (1959) and the overrated comedy *Pocketful of Miracles*

(1961). He subsequently retired from directing, eventually publishing an intriguing and informative autobiography, *Frank Capra: The Name Above the Title*, in 1971.

FILMS: As director: *Fultah Fisher's Boarding House* (short, 1922); *The Strong Man* (1926); *Tramp, Tramp, Tramp* (also story, sc, p, 1926); *For the Love of Mike* (1927); *His First Flame* (sc only, 1927); *Long Pants* (1927); *That Certain Thing* (1928); *The Matinee Idol* (1928); *The Power of the Press* (1928); *Say It with Sables* (also story, 1928); *So This Is Love* (1928); *Submarine* (1928); *The Way of the Strong* (1928); *The Donovan Affair* (1929); *Flight* (also dial, 1929); *The Younger Generation* (1929); *Ladies of Leisure* (1930); *Rain or Shine* (1930); *Dirigible* (1931); *The Miracle Woman* (1931); *Platinum Blonde* (1931); *American Madness* (1932); *The Bitter Tea of General Yen* (1932); *Forbidden* (also story, 1932); *Lady for a Day* (1933); *Broadway Bill* (1934); *It Happened One Night* (1934); *Mr. Deeds Goes to Town* (also p, 1936); *Lost Horizon* (also p, 1937); *You Can't Take It with You* (also p, 1938); *Mr. Smith Goes to Washington* (also p, 1939); *Meet John Doe* (also p, 1941); *Prelude to War* (doc, also p, 1942); *The Nazis Strike* (doc, co-d, 1942); *Divide and Conquer* (doc, co-d, 1943); *Battle of Britain* (doc, co-d, 1943); *Battle of Russia* (doc, p only, 1943); *Battle of China* (doc, co-d, 1943); *The Negro Soldier* (doc, 1944); *War Comes to America* (doc, p only, 1944); *Tunisian Victory* (doc, co-d, 1944); *Arsenic and Old Lace* (1944); *Know Your Enemy: Japan* (doc, co-d, 1945); *Two Down and One to Go* (doc, 1945); *It's a Wonderful Life* (also co-sc, p, 1947); *State of the Union* (also co-p, 1948); *Riding High* (also p, 1950); *Here Comes the Groom* (also p, 1951); *Westward the Women* (story only, 1951); *A Hole in the Head* (also p, 1959); *Pocketful of Miracles* (also p, 1961).

**Carney, Art (1918—)**   Known as a comic actor, Art Carney has also proven himself to be a resourceful dramatic performer. Nonetheless, with his unique voice, rubbery face, and exquisite comic timing, he has made a career out of making people laugh in most media, including, TV, radio, stage, and film. While best known (and considerably beloved) as Jackie GLEASON's upstairs neighbor Ed Norton in the classic 1950s TV sitcom *The Honeymooners*, Carney surprised everyone with his late-blooming career as a movie star in the middle to late 1970s, most notably when he won the best actor Academy Award for his performance in Paul MAZURSKY's *Harry and Tonto* (1974).

Born Arthur William Matthew Carney in Mount Vernon, New York, he got his first major break in show business during the 1930s as a radio sidekick, working with the likes of Fred ALLEN and Edgar BERGEN. His only appearance on film in these early years was a bit part in *Pot o' Gold* (1941).

After returning from World War II service (with a wound that left him with a lifelong limp), he began building his reputation as an actor, particularly on TV. His success as Ed Norton, however, was a mixed blessing because it left him typecast and unable to find challenging work. He found his salvation on the stage where he had several hit shows, including Neil SIMON's *The Odd Couple* and *The Prisoner of Second Avenue*.

Carney did not accept success easily. Bouts of depression and a battle with the bottle hurt his career, but a couple of featured roles in hit comedies of the 1960s kept him in the public mind. TV work also kept him going until *Harry and Tonto*, the sleeper hit of 1974, catapulted him to instant stardom.

There being relatively few major roles for aging character comics, Carney acquitted himself well in the movies that came few and far between. The best of these was certainly *Going in Style* (1979), a geriatric comedy caper in which he shared top billing with George BURNS and Lee Strasberg. Recently, he had a small role in Arnold Schwarzenegger's *Last Action Hero* (1993).

FILMS INCLUDE: *Pot o' Gold* (bit, 1941); *The Yellow Rolls Royce* (1964); *A Guide for the Married Man* (1967); *Harry and Tonto* (1974); *W. W. and the Dixie*

*Dance Kings* (1975); *Won Ton Ton—The Dog Who Saved Hollywood* (1976); *Scott Joplin* (1977); *The Late Show* (1977); *Movie, Movie* (1978); *House Calls* (1978); *Steel* (1979); *Sunburn* (1979); *Going in Style* (1979); *Defiance* (1980); *Take This Job and Shove It* (1981); *The Muppets Take Manhattan* (1984); *The Naked Face* (1984); *Izzy and Moe* (1985); *The Blue Yonder* (1985); *Night Friend* (1987); *Last Action Hero* (1993).

## Chaney, Norman "Chubby"   *See* OUR GANG

## Chaplin, Charlie (1889—1977)   There is a
tendency today to think of Charlie Chaplin as merely that funny-looking fellow with the mustache, peculiar gait, and twirling cane. However, he was so much more. His unique blend of comic invention and pathos gave rise to the one word that described Chaplin best: sublime. Stan Laurel, who understudied Chaplin and saw his rise to fame, said simply, "He's the greatest artist that was ever on the screen." At the height of his popularity, Chaplin was the most beloved film personality in the entire world. Although he lost a great many fans in his later years, his comic genius was never questioned. And for good reason. Chaplin was a writer/director/actor/producer/musician without peer.

Chaplin was born in London, England, and his childhood gave him hands-on training for the character of the Little Tramp. He lived a life of punishing poverty. His father died of alcoholism and his mother was often hospitalized. Chaplin spent two years in an orphanage, and he and his older half-brother frequently lived in the street.

He made his first professional appearance at the age of five, filling in for his mother (who tried to make a living as a musician) and singing one of her numbers. For Chaplin, it was a career made out of desperation. By the age of eight, he was a member of a touring music hall troupe, The Eight Lancashire Lads.

*For the ultimate combination of pathos and humor, no one has ever topped Charlie Chaplin. He is seen here with Virginia Cherrill, the blind flower girl, in his hilarious, yet deeply moving,* City Lights *(1931). Remarkably, except for a musical score and sound effects, this was a silent film released four years after the coming of sound and was one of the biggest hits of the year; such was the popularity of Charlie Chaplin.*
PHOTO COURTESY OF MOVIE STAR NEWS.

Chaplin was seventeen and a seasoned professional when he joined the Fred Karno Pantomime Troupe. He stayed with the Karno company for seven years until he became their star attraction. While on tour with Karno in America in 1913, he was signed up by Mack SENNETT's Keystone Studio.

Chaplin's first one-reeler, in support of Keystone's main players, was *Making a Living* (1913). For his second film, *Kid Auto Races in Venice* (1913), he borrowed Fatty ARBUCKLE's pants, Ford STER-LING's massive shoes (putting them on the opposite feet), a tight-fitting jacket, a tiny derby, and one of Mack SWAIN's mustaches (trimmed down, of course). Thus, the Little Tramp was born. Chaplin didn't always dress as the tramp in his early one-reelers at Keystone, but the character began to slowly evolve. According to Gerald Mast in his book *The Comic Mind*, "The most significant lesson that Chaplin learned at Keystone was . . . . how to relate to objects and how to make objects relate to him." However, Keystone was not a place for detail and finesse. Chaplin needed to move on and grow.

He left Sennett in 1915 and went to the ESSANAY Studio. Chaplin had already become popular, but he now had the time to develop his character. Still, the movies were crude. When he titled one of his fun-niest two-reelers *The Tramp* (1915), however, film comedy was never the same again.

From Essanay, Chaplin moved to Mutual in 1916, and it was with this new company that he made some of his most famous two-reelers, consolidating the artistic breakthroughs he had made at Essanay. Films such as *The Pawnshop* (1916), *The Immigrant* (1916), and *Easy Street* (1916) were so inventive, intimate, and hilariously clever that Chaplin became popular worldwide. He was imitated by all sorts of film comedians, but no one was remotely like him. He was earning $10,000 per week (receiving a $100,000 advance upon his salary) and was still being underpaid in relation to his value to the studio.

His next step took him to First National in 1918 where he was supposed to make eight two-reelers. All of his films for First National were classics, but they weren't all two-reelers. After *A Dog's Life* (1918), *Shoulder Arms* (1919), *Sunnyside* (1919), and *A Day's Pleasure* (1919), Chaplin decided to make his first feature, *The Kid* (1921). It took a year and a half to make, was six reels long, and was made despite the protests of the film company—and it became the biggest hit in movie history up until that time except for *The Birth of a Nation* (1915). Thereafter, Chaplin's other films with First National were of any length he chose.

Chaplin wanted more freedom as an artist, so he joined with the other great lights of the silent era—Mary Pickford, Douglas Fairbanks, and D. W. Griffith—to form a film company called United Artists.

For his first film for his new company, Chaplin wrote and directed (but did not star in) *A Woman of Paris* (1923). His longtime leading lady Edna Pur-viance had the lead. It was a serious film that was disappointing at the box office, but seen today, it shows a great deal of sophistication for its time.

Chaplin then took two years to make his next, and perhaps most famous feature, *The Gold Rush* (1925). This story of the tramp in Alaska was epi-sodic but both moving and very funny. As is the case with most of his work, *The Gold Rush* stands with-out any apologies to the passing of time. When Chaplin, starving to death in a cabin during a snow-storm, eats his shoe as if it were a delicacy, artistry stops all clocks. And his "Oceana Roll," otherwise known as the dance of the buns, is one of the most charming moments in the history of the cinema.

Chaplin's output slowed down even further after *The Gold Rush*. It was three years before *The Circus* (1928) appeared. It was yet another hit. He was nominated for a best actor Academy Award that year, as well as for best comedy director. While he won in neither category, he was nonetheless awarded a special Oscar that year for "versatility and genius in writing, acting, directing, and producing *The Circus*."

When everyone else in Hollywood was making talkies, Chaplin all but ignored the new technology and made another silent film, CITY LIGHTS (1931). Although Chaplin wrote a wonderful musical score for the film and included sound effects, there was no dialogue in the film. The industry thought he was doomed to suffer a terrible disaster. No one, they were convinced, would go see a silent movie. And they wouldn't—unless it was a Charlie Chaplin movie. *City Lights* was the fourth biggest grosser of the year!

And then Chaplin did it again, making yet an-other silent film in 1936, *Modern Times*, although in this movie he did sing a song in gibberish. *Modern Times* was a clear attack on the industrial world and its dehumanizing machinery. It also had a mild left-wing point of view that signaled Chaplin's growing political conviction. Mostly, however, it was both moving and funny. The film was the second biggest money-earner of the year, just behind *San Francisco*.

Chaplin finally decided to make an all-talking movie nearly fifteen years after the end of the silent era. And when he started talking, the world was surprised to find he had such a lovely voice. His next film, *The Great Dictator* (1940), was a savage comic attack on fascism. Chaplin played two roles in the film, a Jewish barber (a character closely akin to the tramp) and Adenoid Hynkel (based on Hitler). The highlight of the film was Chaplin's balletic dance of the globe, as Hynkel dreams of world conquest. Chaplin had put his art on the line, making a striking anti-Nazi film before America entered World War II. And audiences responded, making it the biggest hit of the year. He also received Academy Award nominations for best actor, best screenplay, and best picture.

While Chaplin's artistry continued to flourish in his next two films, his popularity (at least in America) did not. Finally relinquishing the tramp persona, Chaplin played a lady killer (literally) in MONSIEUR VERDOUX (1947), a BLACK COMEDY about murder with a political point of view. At the time, the film received scathing reviews and did poorly with audiences who were both offended by Chaplin's dark humor and upset that the tramp was no more. Nonetheless, he did receive an Oscar nomination for his screenplay.

Chaplin's unequivocal left-wing sentiments brought him under fire during the red-baiting years of the late 1940s and early 1950s. At the same time, some Americans were fuming that Chaplin had never become a U.S. citizen. When the star left for Europe to promote his next film, *Limelight* (1952), he was told that he might not be allowed back into the country. Unwilling to live where he wasn't wanted, Chaplin settled with his young wife, Oona O'Neill, in Switzerland. O'Neill was Chaplin's fourth wife.

He had previously been married to Mildred Harris, Lita Grey, and Paulette Goddard. All four of his wives were teenagers when he married them.

*Limelight* was a hit in Europe but a disaster in the United States. The nostalgic movie recreated London at the turn of the century with Chaplin playing Calvero the Clown, an aging music hall performer who, much like Chaplin, had lost his audience. It was a sweet film about art and redemption that boasted a hit song, "Smile," which Chaplin penned himself.

His last two films, *A King in New York* (1957) and *A Countess from Hong Kong* (1967) were mediocre movies that seemed far more disappointing because expectations ran so high. The latter film was written and directed by Chaplin, and starred Marlon Brando and Sophia Loren, with Chaplin merely making a cameo appearance as a waiter.

In addition to being knighted Sir Charles Chaplin, the most memorable moment of Charlie Chaplin's later career was his triumphant return to Hollywood in 1971. A frail old man of eighty-two, he came back to his adopted home to receive an honorary Academy Award. After a splendid film tribute, he appeared on the stage, and the audience of Hollywood's greatest stood up and gave him a thunderous and almost never-ending ovation. There were tears in Chaplin's eyes. It was sublime.

The great screen comedian's life was the subject of a recent film, *Chaplin* (1992), in which Robert Downey, Jr., played the title role, receiving a best actor Oscar nomination for his performance.

---

**FILMS:** As actor, director, and screenwriter unless otherwise indicated: *Making a Living* (a only, 1914); *Kid Auto Races at Venice* (a, sc only, 1914); *Between Showers* (a, sc only, 1914); *Cruel, Cruel Love* (a, sc only, 1914); *Dough and Dynamite* (a, d only, 1914); *Laughing Gas* (1914); *A Busy Day* (1914); *Caught in a Cabaret* (1914); *Caught in the Rain* (1914); *The Face on the Barroom Floor* (1914); *The Fatal Mallet* (1914); *Getting Acquainted* (1914); *A Film Johnnie* (1914); *The Knockout* (a, sc only, 1914); *Gentlemen of Nerve* (1914); *Her Friend the Bandit* (1914); *His Favorite Pastime* (a, sc only, 1914); *His Musical Career* (1914);

*His Prehistoric Past* (1914); *His Trysting Place* (1914); *His New Profession* (1914); *Mabel at the Wheel* (a, sc only, 1914); *Mabel's Busy Day* (1914); *Mabel's Married Life* (1914); *Mabel's Strange Predicament* (a, sc only, 1914); *Making a Living* (a, sc only, 1914); *The Masquerader* (1914); *The New Janitor* (1914); *The Property Man* (1914); *Recreation* (1914); *The Rounders* (1914); *The Star Boarder* (a, sc only, 1914); *Tango Tangles* (a, sc only, 1914); *Those Love Pangs* (1914); *Tillie's Punctured Romance* (a only, 1914); *His Regeneration* (a only, 1915); *Twenty Minutes of Love* (a, sc only, 1914); *His New Job* (1915); *A Night Out* (1915); *The Champion* (1915); *In the Park* (1915); *A Jitney Elopement* (1915); *The Tramp* (1915); *By the Sea* (1915); *Work* (1915); *A Woman* (1915); *The Bank* (1915); *Shanghaied* (1915); *A Night in the Show* (1915); *Charlie Chaplin's Burlesque on Carmen* (1916); *Police!* (1916); *The Count* (1916); *The Floorwalker* (1916); *The Fireman* (1916); *One A.M.* (also p, 1916); *The Pawnshop* (also p, 1916); *Behind the Screen* (also p, 1916); *The Rink* (also p, 1916); *The Vagabond* (1916); *The Adventurer* (1917); *The Cure* (1917); *Easy Street* (1917); *The Immigrant* (1917); *The Bond* (1918); *A Dog's Life* (1918); *Shoulder Arms* (1918); *A Day's Pleasure* (also p, 1919); *Sunnyside* (also p, 1919); *The Idle Class* (also p, 1921); *The Kid* (also p, 1921); *The Nut* (a only, 1921); *Nice and Friendly* (1922); *Pay Day* (also p, 1922); *The Pilgrim* (also p, 1923); *Souls for Sale* (a only, 1923); *A Woman of Paris* (also p, mu, 1923); *The Gold Rush* (also p, 1925); *A Woman of the Sea* (idea and p only, 1926); *The Circus* (also p, ed, 1928); *Show People* (a only, 1928); *City Lights* (also p, ed, mu, 1931); *Modern Times* (also p, mu, 1936); *The Great Dictator* (also p, 1940); *Monsieur Verdoux* (also p, mu, 1947); *Limelight* (also p, story, mu, chor, 1952); *A King in New York* (also p, mu, 1957); *A Countess from Hong Kong* (also p, mu, song, 1967).

## Chase, Charlie (1893—1940)

Also known as Charley Chase, he had a film career that intersected many of the most famous names in Hollywood comedy. Charlie Chase worked for both Mack SENNETT and Hal ROACH, directed such comic luminaries as Fatty ARBUCKLE and the THREE STOOGES, appeared on screen with Charlie CHAPLIN, and was directed by a young Leo MCCAREY. While Chase was neither a great comic actor nor a brilliant director, he was more than competent in both arenas and showed considerable talent as a screenwriter. In a film comedy career that lasted twenty-five years, Chase proved to be a resourceful and dependable comic craftsman.

Born Charles Parrott, he built his early reputation in VAUDEVILLE before joining up with Mack Sennett's Keystone crew in 1914, where he often played second fiddle to Charlie Chaplin. By the following year, he had learned enough about film comedy techniques that he began directing both himself and others in two-reelers. Despite—or perhaps because—his stage name was so derivative of Charlie Chaplin's, Chase did not seriously rival the major comic talents of the 1910s. In the early 1920s he moved over to Hal Roach's studio and began directing others, most notably Snub POLLARD, with considerable comic flair, this time under his real name (Parrott). He also wrote many of the scripts he filmed.

Emboldened, Chase began directing himself in two-reel comedies in 1924, once more using the name Charlie Chase for his acting persona, while retaining Charles Parrott for his credit behind the camera. This time he caught the public's fancy playing shy characters who persevered through comic trials and tribulations. It was during this period at the Roach studio that he was directed on several occasions by Leo McCarey.

The arrival of talking pictures did not hamper Chase. He demonstrated a rich speaking voice and a surprisingly pleasant singing voice as well. As an actor, he began playing comic supporting and featured roles in the 1930s, while continuing to direct comedy short subjects until alcoholism ultimately curtailed his career and life. He died of a heart attack.

FILMS INCLUDE: As actor only: *The Masquerader* (1914); *The Knockout* (1914); *The Rounders* (1914); *His New Profession* (1914); *His Musical Career* (1914); *Tillie's Punctured Romance* (1914); *All Wet* (1924); *His Wooden Wedding* (1925); *Bad Boy* (1925); *The Rat's Knuckles* (1925); *What Price Goofy?* (1925); *Innocent Husbands* (1925); *Mighty Like a Moose* (1926); *There Ain't No Santa Claus* (1926); *Crazy Like a Fox* (1926); *Movie Night* (1929); *You Can't Buy Love* (1929); *Crazy Feet* (1929); *Whispering Whoopee* (1930); *Fifty Million Husbands* (1930); *The Real McCoy* (1930); *The Pip from Pittsburgh* (1931); *The Tabasco Kid* (1932); *Sons of the Desert* (1933); *Fallen Arches* (1933); *Kelly the Second* (1936); *From Bad to Worse* (1937); *Time Out for Trouble* (1938); *Pie a la Maid* (1939); *South of the Boudoir* (1940); *The Heckler* (1940); *His Bridal Fright* (1940).

As director only: *Dirty Work in a Laundry* (1915); *Only a Messenger Boy* (1915); *All at Sea* (1919); *Live and Learn* (1920); *His Best Girl* (1921); *The Hustler* (1921); *Days of Old* (1922); *The Dumb Bell* (1922); *In the Movies* (1922); *Jack Frost* (1923); *The Courtship of Miles Sandwich* (1923); *The Bargain of the Century* (1933); *Oh, What a Knight!* (1937); *The Old Raid Mule* (1938); *Tassels in the Air* (1938); *Ankles Away* (also sc, 1938); *Halfway to Hollywood* (1938); *Violent Is the Word for Curly* (1938); *Flat Foot Stooges* (1938); *A Nag in the Bag* (1938); *Mutts to You* (1938); *Mutiny on the Body* (1939); *Static in the Attic* (1939); *Boom Goes the Groom* (1939); *Saved by the Belle* (1939).

As actor/director: *The Anglers* (1914); *Do-Re-Mi-Fa* (1915); *A Dash of Courage* (1916); *Chased into Love* (also sc, 1917); *Hello Trouble* (1918); *Ship Ahoy!* (also sc, 1919); *Kids Is Kids* (1920); *Midsummer Mush* (1933); *The Chases of Pimple Street* (1934); *You Said a Hateful!* (1934); *Fate's Fathead* (1934); *I'll Take Vanilla* (co-d, 1934); *Poker at Eight* (1936); *The Four-Star Boarder* (1936); *Manhattan Monkey Business* (co-d, 1936); *Okay, Toots!* (co-d, 1936); *Vamp till Ready* (co-d, 1936); *Neighborhood House* (co-d, 1936).

## Chase, Chevy (1944—)

A sardonic, comically cool leading man, Chevy Chase came to prominence as an original member of the Not Ready for Prime Time Players on NBC-TV's hit television comedy show "SATURDAY NIGHT LIVE."

Born Cornelius Crane Chase, he thought of himself as a writer rather than as a comedian. When pressed into service before the cameras when "Saturday Night Live" first aired, however, he became an instant audience favorite. Tall and good looking, with a whimsically aloof personal style, Chase was the first star of the late-night hit show to head for Hollywood with a lucrative multi-picture deal. Among those who eventually followed his lead were Dan AYKROYD, John BELUSHI, Bill MURRAY, Gilda RADNER, and Eddie MURPHY.

Chase had earlier appeared in two raunchy, low-budget comedies in the mid-1970s, *The Groove Tube* (1974) and *Tunnelvision* (1976). He played his first starring role in the smash comedy *Foul Play* (1978) with Goldie HAWN. He followed that success with an engaging supporting role in *Caddyshack* (1980), only to see his film career go careening off track when he shared top billing with a dog, Benji, in *Oh, Heavenly Dog!* (1980). Except for his successful reteaming with Goldie Hawn in *Seems Like Old Times* (1980), many of the actor's subsequent films were (justifiably) berated by the critics and ignored by his fans. Movies such as *Modern Problems* (1981), *Under the Rainbow* (1981), and *Deal of the Century* (1983) were unmitigated disasters.

Chase's once-promising career was saved by his starring role in *National Lampoon's Vacation* (1983), a film that brought him back to his eccentric comedy roots. Not long after, he starred in *Fletch* (1985), a hit comedy/detective piece that solidified his return to box office credibility.

From the very beginning of his movie years, Chase has not been treated well by critics. His comic persona has a disdainful element to it that puts many people off and, in addition, his throwaway style gives the impression that he doesn't work very hard at his humor. Finally, though, after being panned in films such as *National Lampoon's European Vacation* (1985) and *Three Amigos* (1986), he achieved near unanimous praise for his restrained comic performance in *Funny Farm* (1988), a movie he also produced and that many still consider his best work to date. The complaint against Chase is that he isn't ambitious enough. He seems content to muddle through mediocre sequels, rather than develop original comic creations like *Funny Farm*. His *Memoirs of an Invisible Man* (1992), however, was a more ambitious, if flawed, effort in that direction.

---

**FILMS:** *The Groove Tube* (1974); *Tunnelvision* (1976); *Foul Play* (1978); *Caddyshack* (1980); *Oh, Heavenly Dog!* (1980); *Seems Like Old Times* (1980); *Modern Problems* (1981); *Under the Rainbow* (1981); *Deal of the Century* (1983); *National Lampoon's Vacation* (1983); *Fletch* (1985); *National Lampoon's European Vacation* (1985); *Sesame Street Presents: Follow That Bird* (1985); *Spies Like Us* (1985); *Three Amigos* (also song, 1986); *Caddyshack II* (1988); *The Couch Trip* (1988); *Funny Farm* (also p, 1988); *Fletch Lives* (1989); *National Lampoon's Christmas Vacation* (1989); *L.A. Story* (uncred, 1991); *Nothing but Trouble* (1991); *Memoirs of an Invisible Man* (1992); *Hero* (uncred, 1992).

---

## Chayevsky, Paddy (1923—1981)

In his early career, Paddy Chayevsky built a reputation for writing about the problems of ordinary people with sympathetic humor. Later, he became a firebrand, writing (some said overwriting) with biting wit about "big" issues. Considering that he was associated with just eleven movies, his success ratio in Hollywood was truly stunning; he was nominated for a best screenplay Academy Award four times, winning three Oscars.

Born Sidney Aaron Chayevsky, he made his first stab at show business as a comedian. He turned to writing while recuperating from wounds suffered during his World War II service. Chayevsky contin-

ued writing after the war, penning short stories and eventually breaking into radio and TV as a scriptwriter. One of his early works became the basis of a modest movie called *As Young as You Feel* (1951). His first major success, however, came with his teleplay *Marty*, the story of a middle-aged, unattractive Bronx butcher who falls in love with a plain and shy woman. It was a much-admired TV production that Chayevsky then rewrote for the screen. *Marty* (1955) was the sleeper hit of the year, winning four Oscars, including best screenplay, best actor (Ernest Borgnine as Marty), best direction (Delbert Mann), and best film.

It was a long time before Chayevsky had that kind of film success again. In any event, he didn't work very often in Hollywood, although he seemed to give it his strongest effort in the latter half of the 1950s. He was involved with a handful of projects during that half of the decade, most notably *The Goddess* (1958), for which he received an Oscar nomination for best screenplay.

An acclaimed playwright (*The Tenth Man*, *Gideon*, and *The Latent Heterosexual*), he worked even less in Hollywood in the 1960s, making a strong impression with his script for the cynically brassy, romantic comedy *The Americanization of Emily* (1964), but then stumbling with his flop adaptation of *Paint Your Wagon* (1969), although few blamed the script for the movie's failure.

The 1970s was Chayevsky's decade. Even so, he only wrote three screenplays, but two of them were vivid, powerful works. He wrote the sharply satirical exposé of medical practices, *The Hospital* (1971), winning his second best screenplay Oscar, and then followed that with the screenplay for which he is best remembered, *NETWORK* (1976). He won his third Oscar for this bitterly funny script about the corrupting power of television. His phrase from *Network*, "I'm mad as hell and I'm not going to take it anymore," became a rallying cry even for those who never saw the film. His last script, *Altered States* (1980), was based upon his own novel of the same name. He was so disappointed by director Ken

Russell's approach to the material that he had his screenplay credit changed to Sidney Aaron.

Chayevsky died at the height of his powers at the age of fifty-eight.

---

**FILMS:** *A Double Life* (a, 1947); *As Young as You Feel* (story, 1951); *Marty* (sc, based on teleplay, 1955); *The Catered Affair* (based on teleplay, 1956); *The Bachelor Party* (assoc, p, sc, based on teleplay, 1957); *The Goddess* (story, sc, 1958); *Middle of the Night* (sc, based on play, 1959); *The Americanization of Emily* (sc, 1964); *Paint Your Wagon* (sc adapt, 1969); *The Hospital* (story, sc, 1971); *Network* (sc, 1976); *Altered States* (sc, based on novel, 1980).

---

**Cheech and Chong** A couple of counterculture oddballs, Cheech and Chong stunned the filmmaking world by becoming the hottest comedy team of the late 1970s and early 1980s. Thomas Chong and Richard "Cheech" Marin discovered that the characters they created—of lovable drug-obsessed halfwits—somehow touched a funny bone not just in the radical fringe, but among a vast audience of young people. It didn't matter that their movies had plots that were as much about dope as they were dopey; it didn't matter that the films were often crudely made and full of even cruder language. It was hip to like Cheech and Chong; for about five years, their films made people laugh, and their box office take was often as high as their characters— which were plenty high.

Thomas Chong (1938–) was born in Canada, his mother Scottish-Irish and his father Chinese. He was a high school dropout who dreamed of making it as a rock and roller. And he did. He co-wrote a hit song for The Vancouvers called "Does Your Mama Know About Me." Moving from music to comedy, he formed an improvisational group that played his brother's Vancouver nightclub. It was there that Chong met his future partner, Cheech Marin.

Richard "Cheech" Marin (1946–) grew up in Los Angeles, the son of a policeman. He was a kid when he got his nickname, picking it from his favorite food, a Chicano dish called *cheecharone* ("cracklings"). Although he plays a semi-moron in his films with Chong, he was a very bright student in college, but the Vietnam War drove him out of America. He avoided the draft in 1968 by moving to Canada.

Marin joined Chong's improv group, and the pair worked together for two years before setting off as a twosome on the comedy/nightclub circuit. They did so well that they were signed up to do albums, which eventually led to a wholly unexpected Grammy Award.

They went from making comedy records to making movies. Their first film, *Up in Smoke* (1978), was a low-budget comedy made for a measly $2 million. It grossed $47.5 million, making it the most profitable movie of the year! Were they a fluke? Was it a one-time blip on the comedy radar screen? The appropriately named *Cheech and Chong's Next Movie* (1980) proved that they were for real, plus it had the added allure of being directed by Chong. By this time, critics (and even some admirers) were calling them ABBOTT AND COSTELLO on drugs.

Cheech and Chong's next two movies were also hits: *Cheech and Chong's Nice Dreams* (1981) and *Things Are Tough All Over* (1982), the latter film surprising some by actually having a structured story. However, that essentially ended their string of successes. After *Cheech and Chong's Still Smokin'* (1983) proved that there was little fire or smoke left in their druggie routine, they gave their characters a new set of concerns by making *Cheech and Chong's The Corsican Brothers*, a remake (in their peculiar fashion) of the Alexander Dumas classic. This also failed to find an audience and was not much admired by critics (who never liked the twosome, anyway).

After the failure of *The Corsican Brothers*, Marin and Chong, for the most part, went their separate ways. Except for a "joint" appearance in Martin Scorsese's *After Hours* (1985) and a Chong vehicle with four flat tires called *Far Out Man* (1990) in which Marin only shows up for a cameo, they have not made a film together. Chong has all but dropped out of the movie business completely. He is well represented on the big screen, however, by his daughter actress Rae Dawn Chong.

Marin, on the other hand, continues to work in movies. He wrote, directed, and starred in *Born in East L.A.* (1987), but has otherwise confined himself to acting in such films as *Ghostbusters II* (1989), *Rude Awakening* (1989), and *The Shrimp on the Barbie* (1990).

---

**FILMS:** As team: *Cheech & Chong's Up in Smoke* (a, sc, song, 1978); *Cheech & Chong's Next Movie* (a, sc, Chong—d, 1980); *Cheech & Chong's Nice Dreams* (a, sc, song, Chong—d, 1981); *It Came from Hollywood* (a, 1982); *Things Are Tough All Over* (a, sc, 1982); *Cheech & Chong's Still Smokin'* (a, sc, Chong—d, 1983); *Yellowbeard* (a, 1983); *Cheech & Chong's The Corsican Brothers* (a, sc, Chong—d, 1984); *After Hours* (a, 1985); *Far Out Man* (a, sc, Chong—d, 1990); *FernGully: The Last Rainforest* (voices only, 1992).

Cheech alone: *Echo Park* (a, 1986); *Born in East L.A.* (a, sc, lyrics to title song, d, 1987); *Oliver and Company* (a, 1988); *Ghostbusters II* (a, 1989); *Rude Awakening* (a, 1989); *Troop Beverly Hills* (a, 1989); *The Shrimp on the Barbie* (a, 1990).

---

## Chevalier, Maurice (1888—1972)

In light comedies and hilarious operettas, slyly charming Maurice Chevalier managed to be both amusingly lustful and lustfully amusing. It seemed as if his eyes never stopped twinkling.

A singer, actor, and dancer, Chevalier had two distinct periods of Hollywood stardom, playing a young and then an older version of the same character: a lover with a remarkable combination of suggestiveness and innocence. Chevalier could be earthy, yet unlike Mae WEST, he was never vulgar. Perhaps he got away with it because of that melodious French accent of his. Chevalier also had a pouting lower lip, a trademark straw hat, and an overwhelming desire to please his audiences.

Born to an alcoholic house painter, Chevalier was the ninth of ten children. A year after his father died, the twelve-year-old future star embarked on his first show business venture as an acrobat. He was not a success. He traveled through cafe society, singing in the streets for money until he gained a job as a performer in a trendy cafe in 1906. Next, he entered French VAUDEVILLE and made a modest success, eventually becoming the partner of the famed Folies Bergère dancing star Mistinguett. They were lovers as well as dancing partners; Chevalier's sex appeal was already very much in evidence.

During World War I, Chevalier was wounded and became a prisoner of war for two years, during which time he learned English from a cellmate. His second language served him well when, after nearly a decade of success in France as a popular performer in clubs and on the stage, he was offered a screen test by Irving Thalberg of MGM in 1927. Thalberg faltered, seeing no future for Chevalier as a Hollywood star. After seeing the same screen test, Paramount thought differently.

His first film for Paramount was *Innocents of Paris* (1929), making Chevalier a movie star virtually overnight. He had appeared in a number of French shorts as early as 1908, but his American debut was nothing less than sensational at the box office. And it got better. In the hands of Ernst LUBITSCH, a director whose touch with light bedroom comedy and operettas became legendary, Chevalier had a string of hits that were as well made as they were successful, among them *The Love Parade* (1929), for which he received an Academy Award nomination for best actor; *The Big Pond* (1930), which brought him yet another best actor Oscar nomination; *The Smiling Lieutenant* (1931); and *One Hour with You* (1932). Very much in the Lubitsch mold was *Love Me Tonight* (1932), directed by Rouben Mamoulian and considered by many to be Chevalier's best film.

Teamed with Jeanette MacDonald in many of these early pre-censorship code operettas, Chevalier projected a strong, healthy sex drive that was happily played for laughs. Although he is often remembered for his songs such as "Mimi" and "Every Little

Breeze Seems to Whisper Louise," above all else, Chevalier was a wonderful comedian.

The laughs, however, were growing thin by 1933. This time Thalberg took action and brought Chevalier to MGM. It was a mixed blessing. After the critical success of *The Merry Widow* (1934), again with Lubitsch at the helm, and then loaning Chevalier to 20th Century-Fox for *Folies Bergère* (1935), Thalberg made the mistake of insisting that Chevalier take second billing to actress Grace Moore. Insulted, the actor refused and left Hollywood in a huff. He didn't appear in another Hollywood movie until 1956.

He did, however, star in a number of French and British films throughout the rest of the 1930s and then again in the second half of the 1940s and early 1950s. None of them had the international success of his Hollywood films.

Chevalier ran into trouble during and immediately after World War II. He performed in Vichy France during those years, singing for German soldiers as well as his own countrymen. When the war was over, there was a hue and cry that Chevalier had been a Nazi collaborator. He defended himself, claiming he sang to the Germans to aid Jewish friends; his defense was accepted.

Beginning in the late 1940s, he regained a measure of his earlier fame by putting on one-man shows all over the world. His second career as a Hollywood film star began when Billy WILDER cast him as Audrey Hepburn's father in *Love in the Afternoon* (1956). It opened the door to *Gigi* (1958), his greatest hit as an elder statesman of the cinema. He might well have been nominated for his splendid comic performance as the aging roué in *Gigi*, but instead he was honored with a special Oscar that year for "his contributions to the world of entertainment for more than half a century."

Chevalier worked steadily throughout the rest of the 1950s and into the 1960s, usually giving a comic edge to the ever-so-charming grandfathers he played in films such as *Can-Can* (1959), *Fanny* (1960), and *I'd Rather Be Rich* (1964).

His last screen appearance was in Disney's less than inspired *Monkeys, Go Home!* (1967). His unique voice, however, can be heard singing the title song of Disney's far more charming *The Aristocats* (1970), recorded two years before his death.

FILMS: U.S. only: *Bonjour New York!* (short, 1928); *Innocents of Paris* (1929); *The Love Parade* (1929); *Paramount on Parade* (1930); *The Big Pond* (1930); *Playboy of Paris* (1930); *The Stolen Jools* (short, 1931); *The Smiling Lieutenant* (1931); *One Hour with You* (1932); *Love Me Tonight* (1932); *Make Me a Star* (1932); *A Bedtime Story* (1933); *The Way to Love* (1933); *The Merry Widow* (1934); *Folies Berg`ere* (1934); *Beloved Vagabond* (1936); *Love in the Afternoon* (1957); *Gigi* (1958); *Count Your Blessings* (1959); *Can-Can* (1960); *Pepe* (1960); *A Breath of Scandal* (1960); *Fanny* (1961); *Jessica* (1962); *In Search of the Castaways* (1962); *A New Kind of Love* (1963); *Panic Button* (1964); *I'd Rather Be Rich* (1964); *Monkeys Go Home!* (1967); *The Aristocats* (voice only, 1970).

**Chong, Thomas** See CHEECH AND CHONG

**child comedians** There have been scores of child actors, but very few ever established themselves in comedy. The first child comedy star of note was Jackie Coogan, who became world famous as Charlie CHAPLIN's co-star in *The Kid* (1920). Coogan, himself, was the object of Chaplin's sentimental comedy, rather than the perpetrator of it, and he went on to become a child star of dramas, rather than comedies, during the rest of his adolescence. The success of *The Kid*, however, opened the eyes of producers everywhere to the appeal of child actors—particularly in comedy.

Baby Peggy (Peggy Montgomery, born 1917) started showing up in movies in 1920, becoming a genuine star attraction by the time she was five years old. Her comedies (among them shorts and features) included such titles as *Peggy Behave* (1922), *The Dar-*

*There hasn't been a child star with the box office draw of Macaulay Culkin, seen here in* Home Alone 2: Lost in New York *(1992), since the days of Margaret O'Brien in the early 1940s or perhaps even Shirley Temple in the 1930s.*
PHOTO BY ANDY SCHWARTZ, © 20TH CENTURY-FOX.

ling of New York (1923), and the future Shirley Temple vehicle *Captain January* (1924). Like the vast majority of child actors, her career faded away after adolescence.

By the early 1930s, though, another baby had come to the fore, this one Baby LeRoy (LeRoy Winebrenner, born 1932). Best known as the foil of W. C. FIELDS, Baby LeRoy "signed" a seven-year contract when he was one, only to retire into his golden years when he was four. The amusing tyke appeared with Fields in *Tillie and Gus* (1933), *Alice in Wonderland* (1933), *The Old Fashioned Way* (1934), and *It's a Gift* (1934). He can also be seen in *A Bedtime Story* (1933), *Torch Singer* (1933), *Miss Fane's Baby Is Stolen* (1934), *The Lemon Drop Kid* (1934), and *It's a Great Life* (1936).

The only other "Baby" to gain fame was Baby Sandy (Sandra Lee Henville, born 1938) in the late 1930s and early 1940s. She was "Baby of the Year," according to *Parents Magazine* in 1940; she earned the title by ever-so-briefly grabbing the child star crown from the teenage Shirley Temple. Baby Sandy had several hot years before she was washed up at five. Among her better films are *Sandy Is a Lady* (1940), *Sandy Gets Her Man* (1940), and *Sandy Steps Out* (1941).

As for Miss Curly Top herself, Shirley Temple was less a comedy star than she was a star of sentimental musicals, some of which had comedy, but she isn't generally viewed as a comedy star, per se.

Less talented than Temple, but purely comedy stars, were all the kids from the OUR GANG series. When speaking of child comedy, this is the grandchild of them all. The series, which ran from 1922 to 1944, used an extraordinary number of child actors, wringing laughs out of their singularly childlike actions. The original child actors who starred in the series were Joe Cobb, Mary Kornman, Farina (Allen Clayton Hoskins), Mickey Daniels, Jackie Condon, and Jackie David. Later, cast members included Jackie Cooper, Bobby "Wheezer" Hutchins, Matthew "Stymie" Beard, Norman "Chubby" Chaney, Dickie Moore, and Scotty Beckett in the late 1920s and early 1930s. However, it was the addition of George "Spanky" McFarland, Carl "Alfalfa" Switzer, and Darla Hood that solidified their appeal through the better part of the 1930s.

One of the few child comedy stars to have an adult career was Mickey ROONEY (Joe Yule, Jr., born 1920). Between 1927 and 1933 he starred in a long-running series of comedy shorts based on the comic strip character Mickey McGuire. Rooney began starring in the famous Andy Hardy sentimental family comedies in 1937. From 1939 to 1941, he was the top box office draw in the nation.

The 1950s and 1960s offered little in the way of child comedy stars. TV sitcoms like "Father Knows Best," "The Donna Reed Show," and "The Patty Duke Show" absorbed potential talent. Nonetheless, on a modest level child actors like Billy Chapin, Kevin "Moochie" Corcoran, and George "Foghorn" Winslow garnered a few laughs in the movies, while Hayley Mills and Kurt Russell had considerably more substantial careers in the early 1960s, primarily in Disney films.

The first indication that child comedians might again be in vogue came in the 1970s with *Paper Moon* (1973), co-starring little Tatum O'Neal (born 1962). The film was a hit, and O'Neal won a best supporting actress Academy Award. In her second film, *Bad News Bears* (1976), she became the highest paid child star in movie history, with a salary of $350,000 and 9 percent of the net profit of a very profitable hit film.

There were a number of films starring children in the years that followed, but no one child star emerged a prince or princess of comedy—until Macaulay Culkin (born 1980) threw his hands up to his cheeks in comic surprise in *Home Alone* (1990) and turned the film into a megahit. The sequel, *Home Alone 2: Lost in New York* (1992), proved just as potent at the box office, and Culkin received the astronomical fee of $5 million and 5 percent of the gross to appear in it, easily taking the record for the highest paid child star in Hollywood history—and for a comedy, at that.

The early 1990s have, in fact, been jam-packed with comedies starring children. From *Rookie of the Year* (1993) to *Dennis the Menace* (1993), there are films coming out left and right with child actors, all of whom are hoping they'll be the next Macauley Culkin. Why the rash of films? The echo boom has struck in its full force, with baby boomers having families of their own. With a new, large generation of children, Hollywood is providing them with entertainment that is not only for kids, but starring kids as well.

## Christie, Al (1886—1951)

As both director and producer, Al Christie was responsible for a great many hilarious shorts and feature films during the silent and early sound eras. Like his contemporaries Mack SENNETT and Hal ROACH, Christie had his own production company that churned out popular two-reel comedies and features. Unlike Sennett and Roach, however, he neither created nor nurtured great comedic talents; he did not have the likes of the KEYSTONE KOPS or LAUREL AND HARDY, so most of his movies did not weather the test of time.

"Christie comedies" were known for their unadorned knockabout slapstick; there was nothing sophisticated about any of these films, but they entertained millions during the late 1910s and the better part of the 1920s.

Born Albert Christie in London, Ontario, Canada, he got his start in the movie business at the Nestor company in 1909, doing anything that was needed while he learned the nature of this new moving picture art form. By 1912 he was producing Western shorts, but found his niche directing (and later producing) comedies, first for Nestor, then for Universal, and by 1916 for his own studio. When his business eventually failed, he continued producing comedies in the 1930s for several studios, most notably for another independent comedy house, EDUCATIONAL PICTURES.

FILMS INCLUDE: *All Aboard* (d, 1915); *When the Mummy Cried for Help* (d, 1915); *Little Egypt Malone* (d, 1915); *Eddie's Little Love Affair* (co-sc, d, 1915); *Wanted: A Husband* (d, 1916); *Never Lie to Your Wife* (p, d, 1916); *Seminary Scandal* (p, d, 1916); *Five Little Widows* (p, d, 1917); *Who's Looney Now?* (p, d, 1917); *Reckless Sex* (p, d, 1920); *Wedding Blues* (p, d, 1920); *Kiss and Make Up* (p, d, 1921); *See My Lawyer* (feature, p, d, 1921); *That Son of Sheik* (p, d, 1922); *The Chased Bride* (p, d, 1923); *Bright Lights* (p, d, 1924); *Charley's Aunt* (feature, p, 1925); *Hot Doggie* (p, d, 1925); *The Nervous Wreck* (feature, p, 1926); *Tillie's Punctured Romance* (feature, p, 1928); *Divorce Made Easy* (p, d, 1929); *Sweethearts on Parade* (feature, p, 1930); *Girls Will Be Boys* (p, 1931); *He's a Honey* (p, 1932); *Static* (p, 1933); *Second-Hand Husbands* (p, 1934); *College Capers* (p, 1935); *Spooks* (p, 1936); *The Bashful Ballerina* (p, 1937); *Koo Koo Korrespondence Skool* (p, 1937); *Pardon My Accident* (p, 1938).

## City Lights

Against all advice, Charlie CHAPLIN made and released the silent film *City Lights* in 1931, four years after the advent of sound. There is no spoken dialogue in the film; the only sounds are the comical squeaks emanating from a politician and a musical score composed by Chaplin himself. The result? *City Lights* was justifiably one of the biggest box office hits of the year. This exquisite film is perhaps Charlie Chaplin's greatest achievement. He produced, wrote, directed, and starred in a comedy that is as funny and moving today as it was when it was first released.

The story is about a tramp (Chaplin) who falls in love with a blind flower girl (Virginia Cherrill) and is a perfect blend of humor and pathos. The tramp's on-again, off-again friendship with a drunken millionaire (Harry Myers), who doesn't remember Charlie when he's sober, provides the extra layer of plot that balances the film.

The famous boxing match where Charlie bobs and weaves like a whirling dervish and the restaurant scene where he slips and slides across the dance floor are just a few of the vintage Chaplin comic touches. However, it's the climax of the movie that makes it sublime. When Chaplin and the flower girl meet again (now, with her sight restored, thanks to Charlie, she can see him for what he is), there is a long close-up of Charlie that is one of the most haunting, aching images in all of film history.

**Clark and McCullough**   Adored by both the critics and the moviegoing public, Clark and McCullough made thirty-eight comedy shorts between 1928 and 1935, many of them ranking among the most consistently funny two-reelers of the sound era. Their humor was reminiscent of the MARX BROTHERS in its anarchic spirit, and Bobby Clark even wore greasepaint glasses, just as Groucho Marx wore a greasepaint mustache.

Robert Edwin "Bobby" Clark (1888–1960) was born in Springfield, Ohio, to a train conductor. While still in elementary school, he met Paul McCullough (1892–1936). Despite their four-year age difference, the two boys found common ground in gymnastics and practiced their tumbling routines so

religiously that by 1900, when Bobby was merely twelve and McCullough just sixteen, they formed a tumbling team and entered show business.

The twosome learned the entertainment ropes first in minstrel shows and then in the circus, where they added comedy to their acrobatics. They then moved to VAUDEVILLE, where they dropped the tumbling and added sketch comedy and patter to their routine. In the late 1910s they conquered BURLESQUE and soon found themselves hits on the legitimate stage in London in a show called *Chuckles of 1922*.

They worked almost constantly on Broadway during the rest of the 1920s, rivaling the Marx Brothers in popularity. Like the Marx Brothers, they were tapped for Hollywood as soon as sound arrived. They made comedy shorts for Fox that fell below the duo's standards, so the comedians soon returned to Broadway. They starred in two successive hit shows before giving Hollywood another try, this time making a series of hilarious shorts for RKO, beginning with *False Roomers* (1931). The plots were wildly outrageous (one such plot concerned the 18,000th ammendment to a mythical country's constitution, which outlawed the sale of salami!), and their inspired craziness was backed by verbal and visual gags galore. Among their most memorable comedies were *Kickin' the Crown Around* (1933), *Odor in the Court* (1934), and *Alibi Bye Bye* (1935).

Clark and McCullough never stopped working on Broadway during this time—they filmed their shorts every summer. The pace was literally killing them. Paul McCullough, a victim of nervous exhaustion, was hospitalized in 1936. Within hours of his release, he committed suicide by slashing his throat and wrists in a barber shop. The loss of his partner and childhood friend sent Bobby Clark into seclusion for several months.

Eventually, Clark made one more movie after the death of McCullough, appearing in *The Goldwyn Follies* (1938), in which he suffered the indignity of being forced by the producer to wear *real* glasses. Clark never returned to the big screen; he was content to star in Broadway shows in a successful career that lasted another two decades.

---

**FILMS INCLUDE:** Shorts only: *Clark and McCullough in the Interview* (1928); *Clark and McCullough in the Honor System* (1928); *The Bath Between* (1929); *The Diplomats* (1929); *Waltzing Around* (1929); *In Holland* (1929); *Belle of Samoa* (1929); *Beneath the Law* (1929); *The Medicine Men* (1929); *Music Fiends* (1929); *Knights Out* (1929); *All Steamed Up* (1929); *Hired and Fired* (1929); *Detectives Wanted* (1929); *A Peep on the Deep* (1930); *Chesterfield Celebrities* (1931); *Such Popularity* (1931); *False Roomers* (1931); *A Melon-Drama* (1931); *Scratch as Catch Can* (1931); *The Iceman's Ball* (1932); *The Millionaire Cat* (1932); *Jitters the Butler* (1932); *Hokus Focus* (1933); *The Druggist's Dilemma* (1933); *The Gay Nighties* (1933); *Kickin' the Crown Around* (1933); *Fits in a Fiddle* (1933); *Snug in the Jug* (1933); *Hey Nanny Nanny* (1934); *In the Devil's Doghouse* (1934); *Bedlam of Beards* (1934); *Love and Hisses* (1934); *Odor in the Court* (1934); *Everything's Ducky* (1934); *In a Pig's Eye* (1934); *Flying Down to Zero* (1935); *Alibi Bye Bye* (1935).

Clark alone, feature: *The Goldwyn Follies* (1938).

---

# Cline, Eddie (1892—1961)

A director of comedies for more than thirty years, Eddie Cline had no discernible visual style, nor a particular comic sensibility, but he knew how to construct a gag and make it work on film, and that was no small accomplishment. One of his own film titles aptly describes his career: *Slightly Terrific*.

Born Edward F. Cline in Kenosha, Wisconsin, the comically inclined young man began in the film business as an actor, getting his start as one of the KEYSTONE KOPS in 1913. He soon became Mack SENNETT's assistant and was assigned the job of directing many of the Keystone Studio's BATHING BEAUTIES comedies in the latter half of the 1910s.

In the early 1920s, Cline hooked up with Buster KEATON, co-scripting and co-directing a sizeable number of Keaton's two-reel masterpieces, among them *The Playhouse* (1921), *The Boat* (1921), *Cops* (1922), and *The Balloonatic* (1923), as well as his first feature, *The Three Ages* (1923). Obviously, these films are reflections of Keaton's genius, but Cline's greatest contributions to film comedy have less to do with his own comic vision, than in imparting a certain craftsmanship to the work of far greater talents. Cline also directed W. C. FIELDS's most beloved comedies, *The Bank Dick* (1940), *My Little Chicadee* (1940), and *Never Give a Sucker an Even Break* (1941). He also put OLSEN AND JOHNSON on the big screen in *Crazy House* (1943) and *Ghost Catchers* (1944).

Cline was a workhorse director who made more than two hundred shorts and in excess of sixty features, the vast majority of them comedies. His career petered out in the latter 1940s with the low-budget Jiggs and Maggie comedy series at Monogram Pictures. However, Cline came full circle, returning to his roots as a screen actor, when he appeared in *The Story of Will Rogers* (1952).

---

**FILMS INCLUDE:** As director, shorts: *His Busted Trust* (1916); *The Winning Punch* (1916); *The Dog Catcher's Love* (1917); *A Bedroom Blunder* (1917); *The Pawnbroker's Heart* (1917); *Those Athletic Girls* (1918); *The Kitchen Lady* (1918); *The Summer Girls* (1918); *Whose Little Wife Are You?* (1918); *Hide and Seek Detective* (1918); *When Love Is Blind* (1919); *Cupid's Day Off* (1919); *Hearts and Flowers* (1919).

Shorts as both co-screenwriter and co-director with Keaton: *One Week* (1920); *The Scarecrow* (1920); *Convict 13* (1920); *Neighbors* (1920); *Hard Luck* (1921); *The Haunted House* (1921); *The High Sign* (1921); *The Playhouse* (1921); *The Boat* (1921); *The Paleface* (1922); *Cops* (1922); *The Frozen North* (1922); *The Electric House* (1922); *My Wife's Relations* (1922); *Day Dreams* (1922); *The Balloonatic* (1923); *The Love Nest* (1923).

Shorts as director: *The Plumber* (1924); *Bashful Jim* (1925); *Tee for Two* (1925); *Cold Turkey* (1925); *Love and Kisses* (1925); *Dangerous Curves Behind*

(1925); *Spanking Breezes* (1926); *A Love Sundae* (1926); *The Gosh-Darn Mortgage* (1926); *The Ghost of Folly* (1926); *Smith's Baby* (1926); *Flirty Four Flushers* (1926); *A Blonde's Revenge* (1926); *The Girl from Everywhere* (1927); *The Bullfighters* (1927); *The Jolly Jilter* (1927); *Love at First Sight* (1928); *Man Crazy* (1928); *Hold That Pose* (1928).

Features: *The Three Ages* (co-sc and co-d with Keaton, 1923); *Circus Days* (1923); *The Meanest Man in the World* (1923); *When a Man's a Man* (1924); *Good Bad Boy* (1924); *Along Came Ruth* (1924); *Captain January* (1924); *Little Robinson Crusoe* (1924); *Old Clothes* (1925); *The Rag Man* (1925); *Soft Cushions* (1927); *Let It Rain* (1927); *Ladies' Night in a Turkish Bath* (1928); *The Head Man* (1928); *The Vamping Venus* (1928); *The Crash* (1928); *His Lucky Day* (1929); *Broadway Fever* (1929); *The Forward Pass* (1929); *The Widow from Chicago* (1930); *Leathernecking* (1930); *In the Next Room* (1930); *Sweet Mama* (1930); *Hook, Line and Sinker* (1930); *The Naughty Flirt* (1931); *Cracked Nuts* (1931); *The Girl Habit* (1931); *Million Dollar Legs* (1932); *Parole Girl* (1933); *So This Is Africa* (1933); *Peck's Bad Boy* (1934); *Fighting to Live* (1934); *The Cowboy Millionaire* (1935); *When a Man's a Man* (1935); *It's a Great Life* (1936); *Forty Naughty Girls* (1937); *High Flyers* (1937); *Breaking the Ice* (1938); *Go Chase Yourself* (1938); *Peck's Bad Boy with the Circus* (1938); *The Bank Dick* (1940); *My Little Chickadee* (1940); *The Villain Still Pursued Her* (1940); *Cracked Nuts* (1941); *Meet the Chump* (1941); *Never Give a Sucker an Even Break* (1941); *Private Buckeroo* (1942); *Behind the Eight Ball* (1942); *Give Out, Sisters* (1942); *Snuffy Smith, Yard Bird* (1942); *What's Cooking?* (1942); *Crazy House* (1943); *He's My Guy* (1943); *Ghost Catchers* (1943); *Moonlight and Cactus* (1944); *Hat Check Honey* (1944); *Night Club Girl* (1944); *Swingtime Johnny* (1944); *Slightly Terrific* (1944); *See My Lawyer* (1945); *Penthouse Rhythm* (1945); *Bringing Up Father* (also story, 1946); *Jiggs and Maggie in Court* (also sc, 1948); *Jiggs and Maggie in Society* (also sc, 1948).

**Cobb, Joe**   *See* OUR GANG

## Coco, James (1929—1987)

A round-faced, butterball of a comic character actor, James Coco reached a surprising level of fame when he was middle-aged. He either starred in or had major supporting roles in a modest number of films, reaching his peak on the silver screen between 1971 and 1981.

Coco was a child actor who struggled for a foothold in show business as an adult. He eventually found work in off-Broadway stage productions before making his breakthrough twelve years later in the lead role of Neil SIMON's *Last of the Red Hot Lovers* (1969). By that time he had already appeared in small roles in a couple of films, making his movie debut in *Ensign Pulver* (1964).

Neil Simon proved to be Coco's guardian angel, providing comic film roles for the actor in *Murder by Death* (1976), *The Cheap Detective* (1978), and *Only When I Laugh* (1981), the latter earning Coco a best supporting actor Academy Award nomination. Even so, he might not have had much of a film career had he not been so impressive in *A New Leaf* (1971) and *Such Good Friends* (1971), which were the two films that put him on the movie map.

His failures were sometimes as intriguing as his successes. For instance, he played a credible Sancho Panza in the execrable *Man of La Mancha* (1972) and had the starring role in the ambitious, if flawed, James Ivory-directed drama *The Wild Party* (1975), which was loosely based on the Fatty ARBUCKLE rape case.

Academy Award nominations often send a career to new heights. In Coco's case, his 1981 nomination was his peak. Except for a small role in the amusing *The Muppets Take Manhattan* (1984), he appeared in no other movies of note. He did, however, star in two TV sitcoms, "Carlucci's Department" and "The Dumplings," before his death at the age of fifty-eight.

FILMS: *Ensign Pulver* (1964); *Generation* (1969); *The End of the Road* (1970); *The Strawberry Statement* (1970); *Tell Me That You Love Me, Junie Moon* (1970); *A New Leaf* (1971); *Such Good Friends* (1971); *Man of La Mancha* (1972); *The Wild Party* (1975); *Murder by Death* (1976); *Charleston* (1978); *The Cheap Detective* (1978); *Reve de Singe* (1978); *Scavenger Hunt* (1979); *Wholly Moses!* (1980); *Only When I Laugh* (1981); *The Muppets Take Manhattan* (1984); *The Bradbury Trilogy* (1985); *Hunk* (1987); *The Chair* (1989); *That's Adequate* (1989).

**Colbert, Claudette (1905—)** Considered a great beauty in her early years in Hollywood, Claudette Colbert seemed destined to be the decoration in big-budget epics before she emerged as a sprightly and witty actress in Frank CAPRA'S *IT HAPPENED ONE NIGHT* (1934). Although she starred in more than sixty films, appearing in everything from contemporary dramas to costume epics, she left her mark in Hollywood as a star of sophisticated comedies.

Born Claudette Lily Chauchoin in Paris, she moved with her family to New York City when she was six. Acting had never been her goal in life; instead, she hoped to become a successful fashion designer. It was not to be. Discovered at a party, Colbert was talked into giving the theater a chance and soon made her stage debut in 1923 at eighteen. She worked steadily in modest stage roles during the rest of the 1920s, learning her craft and gaining a growing reputation as a quality player. At one point, she was coaxed into making her film debut in a low-budget silent, *For the Love of Mike* (1927), a film that was rarely shown due to both the poor quality of the production and the new interest in talkies. It was directed by a very green Frank Capra, who later made amends by giving her the biggest hit of her career.

After sound was perfected and Broadway actors became heavily in demand, Colbert tried the movies again, this time with considerably better luck. Her first sound feature was *The Hole in the Wall* (1929). Her ability to speak French came in handy during her early Hollywood stint, as she made both the English and French versions of the same movies. She worked steadily but without any particular distinction, save for the camera's love affair with her photogenic face and shapely legs.

It was Cecil B. DeMille who raised Colbert from leading lady to star when he cast her in one of his early biblical epics, *The Sign of the Cross* (1932). Not long after, he gave her the title role in *Cleopatra* (1934). She was effective in both, as well as in *Three-Cornered Moon* (1933).

Earning $25,000 per picture from Paramount, Colbert was lured to star in Capra's *It Happened One Night* while she was on vacation. With the promise that all of her scenes would be shot in four weeks and that she would be paid twice her usual salary, Colbert agreed to work at Columbia Pictures. *It Happened One Night*, of course, was a staggering hit that put Columbia on the map, earned Colbert her only best actress Oscar, and showed off, for the first time, her considerable flair for comedy, which was put on display in many of her most memorable films during the next fifteen years.

Among her many sophisticated romantic comedies were *The Gilded Lily* (1935), *The Bride Comes Home* (1936), *Bluebeard's Eighth Wife* (1938), *The Palm Beach Story* (1942), and *The Egg and I* (1947).

Colbert was no slouch in the drama department either, starring in such highly regarded films as *Imitation of Life* (1934), *Tovarich* (1937), *Drums Along the Mohawk* (1939), and *Boom Town* (1940). She also received best actress Oscar nominations for *Private Worlds* (1935) and *Since You Went Away* (1944).

After a strong performance in *Three Came Home* (1950), her career began to seriously wither. Colbert was not meant for matronly roles, and audiences no longer found her quite as appealing in her middle age. She made few films thereafter, *Texas Lady* (1955) being the last before she retired from the screen for six years. She returned to make *Parrish* in

1961, gaining good reviews in a supporting role, but it was the last film for theatrical release that she made. Except for touring on stage and making the rare television appearance (she was excellent as the mother in "The Two Mrs. Grenvilles," a 1987 miniseries), Colbert has lived a quiet life of leisure.

---

**FILMS:** *For the Love of Mike* (1927); *A Hole in the Wall* (1929); *The Lady Lies* (1929); *The Big Pond* (1930); *Manslaughter* (1930); *Young Man of Manhattan* (1930); *His Woman* (1931); *Honor Among Lovers* (1931); *Secrets of a Secretary* (1931); *The Smiling Lieutenant* (1931); *The Man from Yesterday* (1932); *The Misleading Lady* (1932); *The Phantom President* (1932); *The Sign of the Cross* (1932); *The Wiser Sex* (1932); *I Cover the Waterfront* (1933); *Three Cornered Moon* (1933); *Tonight Is Ours* (1933); *Torch Singer* (1933); *Cleopatra* (1934); *Four Frightened People* (1934); *Imitation of Life* (1934); *It Happened One Night* (1934); *The Gilded Lily* (1935); *Private Worlds* (1935); *She Married Her Boss* (1935); *The Bride Comes Home* (1936); *Under Two Flags* (1936); *I Met Him in Paris* (1937); *Maid of Salem* (1937); *Tovarich* (1937); *Bluebeard's Eighth Wife* (1938); *Drums Along the Mohawk* (1939); *It's a Wonderful World* (1939); *Midnight* (1939); *ZaZa* (1939); *Arise, My Love* (1940); *Boom Town* (1940); *Remember the Day* (1941); *Skylark* (1941); *The Palm Beach Story* (1942); *No Time for Love* (1943); *So Proudly We Hail* (1943); *Practically Yours* (1944); *Since You Went Away* (1944); *Guest Wife* (1945); *The Secret Heart* (1946); *Tomorrow Is Forever* (1946); *Without Reservations* (1946); *The Egg and I* (1947); *Family Honeymoon* (1948); *Sleep, My Love* (1948); *Bride for Sale* (1949); *The Secret Fury* (1950); *Three Came Home* (1950); *Let's Make It Legal* (1951); *Thunder on the Hill* (1951); *The Planter's Wife* (1952); *Daughters of Destiny* (1953); *Texas Lady* (1955); *Parrish* (1961).

---

## Coleman, Dabney (1932—)

A late-blooming character actor/comedian, Dabney Coleman has come to play comic villains in his later career, showing a special flair for self-important, contemporary bullies. To his credit, he gives these mean-spirited bad guys so much verve that audiences tend to like him—or at least enjoy him. He has acted in films since 1965, but it was TV's tongue-in-cheek soap opera "Mary Hartman, Mary Hartman" (1976–1977) that highlighted Coleman's comic abilities. As a consequence, his career shot up several notches with his casting in the high-profile hit comedy *9 to 5* (1980), playing the lecherous, evil supervisor of secretaries Lily TOMLIN, Dolly Parton, and Jane Fonda. He has been typecast ever since.

Born in Austin, Texas, Coleman studied law at the University of Texas before turning to the stage. When he first began appearing in movies in the latter half of the 1960s, he usually played villains, but without the comic edge. He worked steadily, if in relative obscurity, during the first half of the 1970s until the "Mary Hartman, Mary Hartman" phenomenon struck. He thrived throughout most of the 1980s, turning in good performance in major films like *On Golden Pond* (1981), *Tootsie* (1982), *The Muppets Take Manhattan* (1984), and *Dragnet* (1987).

By the end of the 1980s and early 1990s, however, his films, as well as his tried-and-true characterizations, were beginning to wear thin. While Coleman was still much admired for his comic touch, his films were nonetheless failing at the box office—witness *Amos and Andrew* (1993).

---

**FILMS INCLUDE:** *The Slender Thread* (1965); *This Property Is Condemned* (1966); *The Scalphunters* (1968); *The Trouble with Girls* (1969); *Downhill Racer* (1969); *I Love My Wife* (1970); *The Other Side of the Mountain* (1974); *The Dove* (1974); *Bite the Bullet* (1975); *The Black Streetfighter Black Fist* (1976); *Viva Knievel!* (1977); *Rolling Thunder* (1977); *Nothing Personal* (1979); *North Dallas Forty* (1979); *9 to 5* (1980); *How to Beat the High Cost of Living* (1980); *Melvin and Howard* (1980); *Modern Problems* (1981); *On Golden Pond* (1981); *Young Doctors in Love* (1982); *Tootsie* (1982); *WarGames* (1983); *The Muppets Take Manhattan* (1984); *Cloak and Dagger* (1984); *The Man with One Red Shoe* (1985); *Dragnet*

(1987); *Hot to Trot* (1988); *Short Time* (1990); *Where the Heart Is* (1990); *Meet the Applegates* (1991); *Amos and Andrew* (1993); *Clifford* (1994).

## Columbus, Chris (1959—)

A screenwriter and director, Chris Columbus has built a wildly successful career by specializing in commercial adventure/comedies with child protagonists. Except for *Mrs. Doubtfire* (1993), the only films he's made that have been box office winners have been about children.

He was born (and actually named) Christopher Columbus in Spangler, Pennsylvania, to a family that worked in the coal mines. Growing up outside of Youngstown, Ohio, he began making 8-mm movies in high school. A precocious teenager, he studied film directing at New York University's Tisch School of the Arts, but made his first breakthrough as a screenwriter with the teenage rebellion film *Reckless* (1984).

More important for his career, however, was his early association with Steven Spielberg's Amblin' Entertainment, for whom he wrote three original comedic screenplays, *Gremlins* (1984), *The Goonies* (1985), and *Young Sherlock Holmes* (1985). The success of these movies led to the opportunity to direct *Adventures in Babysitting* (1987), which was yet another hit comedy. He stumbled slightly with his own *Heartbreak Hotel* (1988), but his next directorial effort put him in the stratosphere. He had teamed up with writer/producer John HUGHES to make a modest family comedy with yet another child protagonist, and it turned into the monster hit of 1990: *Home Alone*. He detoured after that to write and direct a sweet romantic comedy with John CANDY, *Only the Lonely* (1991), which died at the box office. Bouncing back quickly, he directed *Home Alone 2: Lost in New York*, and that movie, while seriously inferior to the original, still brought in a bundle, leaving Columbus in the enviable position of being one of the most bankable comedy directors in Hollywood.

**FILMS:** *Reckless* (sc, 1984); *Gremlins* (sc, 1984); *The Goonies* (sc, 1985); *Young Sherlock Holmes* (sc, 1985); *Adventures in Babysitting* (d, 1987); *Heartbreak Hotel* (sc, d, 1988); *Gremlins 2: The New Batch* (based on his characters, 1990); *Home Alone* (d, 1990); *Only the Lonely* (sc, d, 1991); *Home Alone 2: Lost in New York* (d, 1992); *Mrs. Doubtfire* (d, 1993).

## comedy couples

Throughout Hollywood history there have been instances when the pairing of an actor and an actress causes comedic combustion. When that chemistry occurs, the two stars usually are paired again and again until either the box office magic dies or they do. In this instance, we're not talking about comedy teams, but rather "mainstream" performers, at least one of whom isn't necessarily known for humor.

Such pairings happened with greater frequency during the studio era of the 1930s and 1940s when actors were under contract and had to do (more or less) what they were told. It didn't matter if the two stars were sick of looking into each others' eyes; if Jack Warner said they had to work together, then that's what they did.

Speaking of Warner, he paired stars quite regularly, and the one star who seemed to bring out the humor in her fellow actors was Joan BLONDELL. She was known for her long, comedic pairings not with just one star, but two. She came to Hollywood with James Cagney, and they co-starred in a total of six films, beginning with *Sinner's Holiday* (1930). Most of their movies together brimmed with wisecracks and a fresh brew of tough, urban romantic comedy. In her musical comedy phase later in the 1930s, Blondell coupled with Dick Powell for ten films.

The comedy couple with the most films together consisted of William Powell and Myrna Loy, who starred in twelve, six of them Thin Man movies full of sparkle, adult wit, and charm. They were brought together by director W. S. Van Dyke because he

*A comically sophisticated couple, Katharine Hepburn and Spencer Tracy, seen here in* Adam's Rib *(1949), were paired in nine movies, with Tracy always having top billing—it was in his contract. Incidentally, that's David Wayne with his arm around Kate's shoulder, lest anyone be confused.*

PHOTO COURTESY OF MOVIE STAR NEWS.

thought they'd make a wonderful comic team, and he was right.

A team of shorter duration but powerful box office clout during its time was that of Marie DRESSLER and Wallace BEERY. They made three films together, all of them big comedy hits: *Min and Bill* (1930), *Tugboat Annie* (1933), and *Dinner at Eight* (1933). Had Dressler not died in 1934, there would have undoubtedly been more. After all, thanks to her pairing with Beery, Dressler was voted Hollywood's top box office draw in 1933.

Another pairing that ended with the death of one of the stars was that of Jean HARLOW and Clark Gable. Their highly charged romantic (often sexual) combat was often very funny, even when it was in the

service of a drama, such as in their first film together, *Red Dust* (1932). Their four follow-up movies took even greater advantage of their comic verbal sparring; they can be seen together in *Hold Your Man* (1933), *China Seas* (1935), *Wife vs. Secretary* (1936), and *Saratoga* (1937), the last of which was finished after Harlow's tragic death at the age of twenty-six.

A pairing that began in the studio era but was sustained by the relationship between the two stars was that of Spencer Tracy and Katharine Hepburn. In Tracy's long, distinguished career he appeared in precious few comedies, but his pairings with Hepburn brought out his humor. More, but not a majority, of Hepburn's career was spent in comedies. Together, however, they created a special, warm comic couple with whom audiences could both easily identify and admire. The two stars appeared together in nine films, beginning with *Woman of the Year* (1942) and ending with *Guess Who's Coming to Dinner?* (1967). Tracy died immediately after shooting this last film.

In more recent years, the chances of a couple making lots of movies together seems rather remote, if for no other reason than most actors simply don't make that many movies, period. The closest we've come to a comedy couple since the end of the studio era is Rock Hudson and Doris DAY, who teamed for three films, *Pillow Talk* (1959), *Lover Come Back* (1961), and *Send Me No Flowers* (1964). These so-called sophisticated sex farces seem rather tame today, but were considered mildly risqué at the time of their release. In any event, they were funny and they were hits. The films had such an impact that many people believe Hudson and Day starred in far more than just three movies together.

Who are the contenders for the comedy couple of our era? Perhaps Tom HANKS and Meg RYAN; they've been in two comedies together, *Joe versus the Volcano* (1990) and *Sleepless in Seattle* (1993).

**comic chase** The chase is a classic element of screen comedy used in both silent and sound motion pictures, drawing its humor both from the speed of the action and from the unexpected clever twists and turns that keep the protagonist hurtling on his way, just out of reach of his pursuer. The comic chase is far less important in literature and theater because it isn't cerebral or verbal; the chase is a visual form of humor that depends upon seeing the action unfold in a series of edits and against a large canvas.

Chases were a required ingredient in the vast majority of silent comedies. Mack SENNETT quickly discovered the formula and made sure that virtually every one of his KEYSTONE KOPS pictures ended with a chase. In fact, chases were such an integral part of the silent era that one successful comedy star cleverly called himself Charlie CHASE.

Even comedians as sophisticated as Buster KEATON and Charlie CHAPLIN relied upon comic chase scenes. For instance, Buster Keaton, pursued by literally hundreds of policemen in *Cops* (1922), is funny because of his combination of wit and luck in avoiding capture by such an incredible number of nightstick-wielding lawmen.

When talkies came into vogue, the comic chase went into a temporary decline. The microphone kept movies relatively static and studio-bound. However, as sound technology improved throughout the 1930s, the comedy chase flourished yet again with films like Frank CAPRA's *IT HAPPENED ONE NIGHT* (1934) and the MARX BROTHERS' *Go West* (1940), which was lifted from the climax of Buster Keaton's silent masterpiece, *The General* (1926).

Many films have used the chase for comic effect, but only a small handful—such as *IT'S A MAD MAD MAD MAD WORLD* (1963)—have been structured from beginning to end around the chase.

The comic chase hasn't been used very often in recent years, but it has been occasionally brought back to life in films such as *What's Up, Doc?* (1972), *Blazing Saddles* (1974), *The Muppet Movie* (1979), *The Blues Brothers* (1980), and *Honeymoon in Vegas* (1992).

**Condon, Jackie** *See* OUR GANG

### Conklin, Chester (1888–1971)

A comic actor, Chester Conklin made his movie debut alongside Charlie CHAPLIN in *Making a Living* (1914). With his trademark walrus mustache, Conklin never became a big star, but was a working comic actor in movies over a fifty-two-year period. He was best known during the latter half of the 1910s through the 1920s. His arch silent comedy style had no place in talkies, and he worked with decreasing frequency during the decades that followed, usually in either featured or supporting roles.

Born in Oskaloosa, Iowa, Conklin got his start in VAUDEVILLE, worked in the circus, and finally found himself on Mack SENNETT's doorstep in 1913 where he became one of the KEYSTONE KOPS. The following year he worked almost exclusively with Chaplin, and soon after had some additional success in the Ambrose and Walrus two-reelers he made with Mack SWAIN. Most of his work in the movies, however, was done in features. He appeared almost as often in dramas as he did in comedies, but regardless of the movie, he usually played a comic character.

Conklin can be seen in films as diverse as the Lon Chaney version of *Phantom of the Opera* (1925) and Gary Cooper's classic Western, *The Virginian* (1929). However, he is probably best remembered for his work with Chaplin, both in their early silent days as well as in the featured roles Chaplin gave him in his later masterpieces, *Modern Times* (1936) and *The Great Dictator* (1940). Preston STURGES also took the aging comedian under his wing, casting him in *Hail the Conquering Hero* (1944) and *The Beautiful Blonde from Bashful Bend* (1949). Conklin fell off the Hollywood map after the latter Sturges film, surfacing in a 1954 news report that he had become a department store Santa Claus. Two more film roles eventually followed; the last one, *A Big Hand for a Little Lady* (1966), came several years after he entered a Los Angeles nursing home.

FILMS INCLUDE: *Making a Living* (1914); *Between Showers* (1914); *Mabel's Strange Predicament* (1914); *Cruel, Cruel Love* (short, 1914); *Tango Tangles* (1914); *Caught in a Cabaret* (1914); *The Face on the Barroom Floor* (1914); *The Anglers* (1914); *The Masquerader* (1914); *Dough and Dynamite* (1914); *Tillie's Punctured Romance* (1914); *Love, Speed and Thrills* (1915); *A One Night Stand* (1915); *The Cannon Ball* (1915); *Ambrose's Sour Grapes* (1915); *The Best of Enemies* (1915); *A Tugboat Romeo* (1916); *Dizzy Heights and Daring Hearts* (1916); *Cinders of Love* (1916); *A Clever Dummy* (1917); *An International Sneak* (1917); *The Pullman Bride* (1917); *Ladies First* (1918); *It Pays to Exercise* (1918); *The Village Chestnut* (1918); *Yankee Doodle in Berlin* (1919); *Married Life* (1920); *Skirts* (1921); *Anna Christie* (1923); *Greed* (1924); *Galloping Fish* (1924); *The Great Love* (1925); *The Masked Bride* (1925); *The Pleasure Buyers* (1925); *A Woman of the World* (1925); *The Phantom of the Opera* (1925); *A Social Celebrity* (1926); *Say It Again* (1926); *Behind the Front* (1926); *We're in the Navy Now* (1926); *The Duchess of Buffalo* (1926); *The Nervous Wreck* (1926); *McFadden's Flats* (1927); *Two Flaming Youths* (1927); *A Kiss in a Taxi* (1927); *Tell It to Sweeney* (1927); *Tillie's Punctured Romance* (1928); *The Big Noise* (1928); *The Haunted House* (1928); *Gentlemen Prefer Blondes* (1928); *Varsity* (1928); *Taxi 13* (1928); *The Studio Murder Mystery* (1929); *The House of Horror* (1929); *The Virginian* (1929); *Fast Company* (1929); *Swing High* (1930); *Her Majesty Love* (1931); *Hallelujah, I'm a Bum* (1933); *Modern Times* (1936); *Every Day's a Holiday* (1938); *Zenobia* (1939); *Hollywood Cavalcade* (1939); *The Great Dictator* (1940); *Hail the Conquering Hero* (1944); *Goodnight, Sweetheart* (1944); *Knickerbocker Holiday* (1944); *Springtime in the Sierras* (1947); *The Perils of Pauline* (1947); *The Beautiful Blonde from Bashful Bend* (1949); *Jiggs and Maggie in Jackpot Jitters* (1949); *Apache Woman* (1955); *Paradise Alley* (1962); *A Big Hand for the Little Lady* (1966).

**Conway, Tim (1933—)**   A pudgy, balding comedian with a shy, shambling demeanor, Tim Conway has specialized in comedies for children. While he played second fiddle on TV, both in the sitcom version of "McHale's Navy" and on the "Carol Burnett Show," he graduated to starring roles in low-budget family comedies, occasionally teaming with Don KNOTTS. Despite his readily apparent talents, his films have largely been ignored by the critics.

Born in Willoughby, Ohio, Conway got his start in show business in Cleveland, working as a writer/director for a local TV station. His breakthrough came as a stand-up performer on the late-night TV program "The Steve Allen Show." His greatest success in the movies occurred in the mid-1970s through the end of the decade, with *The Apple Dumpling Gang* (1975) becoming one of his bigger hits. He has been rarely seen on the big screen since the mid-1980s.

FILMS INCLUDE: *McHale's Navy* (1964); *The World's Greatest Athlete* (1973); *The Apple Dumpling Gang* (1975); *Gus, The Shaggy D.A.* (1976); *The Billion Dollar Hobo* (1978); *They Went That-A-Way and That-A-Way* (1978); *The Apple Dumpling Gang Rides Again* (1979); *The Prizefighter* (also story, 1979); *The Private Eyes* (1980); *The Longshot* (1985).

**Cooper, Jackie**   *See* OUR GANG

**Cort, Bud (1950—)**   An enigmatic comic character actor, Bud Cort briefly became a cult movie star when he was twenty-one thanks to the success of the wildly eccentric, romantic BLACK COMEDY *HAROLD AND MAUDE* (1972). That film represented the height of his popularity; he was little seen on movie screens during the next decade, and after finally returning to the big screen with greater regularity, his roles have usually been supporting comedic parts.

Born Walter Edward Cox in New Rochelle, New York, Cort attended New York University. He got his real education, however, in the movies, either starring or playing supporting roles in five comedies in 1970, two of which were directed by Robert Altman: *Brewster McCloud* (1970) and *M\*A\*S\*H* (1970).

While hardly a star, Cort was certainly seen as a comer, and he came on quick in the unexpected hit *Harold and Maude*, playing a young man obsessed with death who falls in love with an extremely liberated seventy-nine-year-old woman (Ruth GORDON). This May/December romance caught on, but Cort did not vault to any further cinematic glory. His career has been uneven, at best, marked by low-budget movies that have neither been mainstream successes nor cult favorites.

**FILMS INCLUDE:** *Brewster McCloud* (1970); *Gass-s-s-s!* (1970); *M\*A\*S\*H* (1970); *The Traveling Executioner* (1970); *The Strawberry Statement* (1970); *Harold and Maude* (1972); *Why Shoot the Teacher?* (1976); *Die Laughing* (1980); *She Dances Alone* (1981); *Hysterical* (1983); *Love Letters* (1983); *The Secret Diary of Sigmund Freud* (1984); *Electric Dreams* (1984); *Maria's Lovers* (1985); *Invaders from Mars* (1986); *Love at Stake* (1987); *The Chocolate War* (1988); *Out of the Dark* (1989); *Brain Dead* (1990); *Going Under* (1991); *Ted and Venus* (also d, 1991).

## Cosby, Bill (1937 –)

A powerhouse performer on TV, Bill Cosby has been seen infrequently in the movies. His combination of sturdy masculinity and childlike charm has served him well as a comic performer in nightclubs, concerts, recordings, TV, and film. His most productive period on the big screen took place in the 1970s when he co-starred with Sidney Poitier in three successful action comedies, *Uptown Saturday Night* (1974), *Let's Do It Again* (1975), and *A Piece of the Action* (1977). His other noteworthy film comedies include *Mother, Juggs & Speed* (1976) and Neil SIMON's *California Suite*

(1978). The 1980s and 1990s have been far less kind to Cosby; his rare movies—*Leonard, Part 6* (1987) and *Ghost Dad* (1990)—have been nothing short of awful.

Born William H. Cosby, Jr., he grew up in Philadelphia, Pennsylvania and went to college at Temple University. A stand-up comedy career during the 1960s led to numerous TV appearances, which culminated in his being cast as the co-star (with Robert Culp) in the TV adventure drama "I Spy" (1965–1969). The color-blind casting of Cosby was a breakthrough for television (and America). He later reteamed with Culp to make the action film, *Hickey and Boggs* (1972).

Cosby went on from "I Spy" to become a TV icon as the star of the long-running, top-rated "The Cosby Show" (1984–1992). In the years between, he worked in children's TV with his "Fat Albert and the Cosby Kids" cartoon series (1972–1979). Most recently, he revived Groucho MARX's famous 1950s TV game show "You Bet Your Life" (1992–1993). During most of this time he has been the national TV pitchman for a number of major products, saturating the airwaves with his presence. Reputed to be one of the richest men in show business, Cosby has made serious efforts to acquire the NBC-TV network.

**FILMS INCLUDE:** *Man and Boy* (also p, 1972); *Hickey and Boggs* (1972); *Uptown Saturday Night* (1974); *Let's Do It Again* (1975); *Mother, Juggs & Speed* (1976); *A Piece of the Action* (1977); *California Suite* (1978); *The Devil and Max Devlin* (1981); *Bill Cosby—Himself* (also sc, p, d, 1983); *Leonard, Part 6* (also story, p, 1987); *Ghost Dad* (1990).

## Crosby, Bing (1901 – 1977)

Although he was the leading recording artist of his era with more than 30 million records sold, Bing Crosby was also one of Hollywood's most potent box office attractions. He appeared in more than sixty films (most of them as a star) and won one best actor Oscar. Crosby's

*Bing Crosby, whose close personal and professional relationship with Bob Hope led to the famous "Road" comedy series, is seen here at play with his pal. As usual, Crosby is playing it cool and is in complete charge.*

PHOTO COURTESY OF THE SIEGEL COLLECTION.

specialities were musicals and light comedies, but he also occasionally scored in dramatic roles.

Crosby was one of the most popular entertainers of the 1930s and 1940s. His long film career reflected the great affection his millions of fans held for him. Blessed with a velvet baritone and an easy, affable manner, the term *crooning* seemed invented for Crosby. Although he was hardly a handsome man, with his plain face and large ears, he was so comfortable and natural on film that his looks never seemed to matter. Most of the time, he even got the girl.

Born Harry Lillis Crosby in Tacoma, Washington, he later took the stage name of Bing from a comic strip character. After a stint at Gonzaga University, Crosby pursued his singing career, joining

up with Al Rinker in 1921. They referred to themselves as "Two Boys and a Piano—Singing Songs Their Own Way." Later, he joined the Paul Whiteman Band and became one of "Paul Whiteman's Rhythm Boys." He had already begun recording as a solo act, but was by no means a big star during the 1920s. His modest success as a recording artist, however, did lead to roles in a number of short subjects during the early sound era.

Crosby's first feature film appearance was in *King of Jazz* (1930), but it was not very memorable; he was merely one of the Rhythm Boys. A few other minor film appearances followed that year, but the big breakthrough for Crosby came not in films but in radio. He got his own program, and it was an immediate sensation. His record sales zoomed, and suddenly he was a hot property.

Hollywood pounced on him, much the way it would later go after Frank Sinatra and Elvis Presley. He was signed by Paramount, the studio with which he has always been most closely associated, and immediately embarked on his new career as a movie star. During the 1930s he mostly made light musicals, although many of them might better be described as light comedies with music. Crosby usually sang approximately four songs in these thinly plotted vehicles.

Crosby's career went into overdrive during the 1940s when he teamed with Bob HOPE and Dorothy Lamour for their first "Road" comedy, *The Road to Singapore* (1940). The vehicle was originally intended for Fred MacMurray and George BURNS, but MacMurray backed out. Hope and Crosby seemed like a more suitable duo, and the film was a surprise comedy blockbuster, thanks largely to the perfect chemistry of the two stars. They clearly had fun making the movie and their good cheer, irreverence, and obvious ad-libbing made audiences feel as if they were all in on the joke. Six more "Road" pictures followed during the next twenty-two years, all of them hits.

If Crosby had been popular before, the combination of the "Road" movies, plus his more ambitious, bigger budget hits of the 1940s, kept him in the top ten of male box office performers through-out the decade, often in the top slot. It was during this decade that he made the first of what have become his most beloved, nostalgic classics, starting with *Holiday Inn* (1942), which introduced his trademark hit song, "White Christmas," the most popular recording in music business history.

Not long after, he continued in the same vein when he starred as a priest in Leo McCAREY's warmhearted *Going My Way*, winning his only best actor Academy Award in the bargain. The movie was a monster hit, leading to an even bigger smash sequel, *The Bells of St. Mary's* (1945). Playing the same role, Crosby was nominated yet again for an Oscar, but didn't win. Thanks to Crosby and aided and abetted by Ingrid Bergman and director Mc-Carey, *The Bells of St. Mary's* became one of the few sequels in Hollywood history to do better at the box office than its predecessor. At this point, Crosby was at the top of his career—a role model of warmth, decency, and puckish good humor.

Among Crosby's films during the second half of the 1940s were *Blue Skies* (1946), *The Emperor Waltz* (1948), and *A Connecticut Yankee in King Arthur's Court* (1949). The last of these films was rather charming, but after nearly twenty years, audiences were beginning to cool to him. Sinatra was the hot young singer, although Crosby was still a formidable force in the right vehicles; the "Road" pictures usually came along when he needed a lift and there were several other solid, if unspectacular entries during the early 1950s, the best of them *Riding High* (1950), *Here Comes the Groom* (1951), and *Little Boy Lost* (1953).

Then came one of his biggest hits of the 1950s, *White Christmas* (1954). It might have been his last hurrah, but he surprised audiences when, in a striking bit of casting, he played an alcoholic former entertainer in the film version of Clifford Odets's *The Country Girl* (1954). It was far more demanding than any other dramatic role he had ever played; he had to portray a pathetic character who was essentially unlikable. He showed enormous range and great courage in the part, winning a much deserved

Oscar nomination for his performance. Grace Kelly, his co-star, won an Oscar. She joined him, along with Sinatra, in the musical version of *The Philadelphia Story*, titled *High Society* (1956). This hit was Crosby's last major success.

Crosby made several films during the rest of the 1960s, but none of them were particularly distinguished. His last "Road" picture with Hope and Lamour, *Road to Hong Kong* (1962), was amusing, but it was the least entertaining in the series. He rarely appeared in movies during the rest of the 1960s, although in a small comic role he nearly stole *Robin and the Seven Hoods* (1964) from Sinatra and the rest of the cast. His last film was the ill-conceived remake of *Stagecoach* (1966), in which he played the Thomas Mitchell role of the drunken doctor.

Throughout the 1960s and right up until his death, Crosby continued to appear in TV specials. He was reportedly one of Hollywood's wealthiest individuals, amassing a fortune estimated at well over $200 million. Like his old friend Bob Hope, he was an avid golfer, and it was on the golf course that he died of a heart attack.

---

**FILMS:** *King of Jazz* (1930); *The Big Broadcast* (1932); *College Humor* (1933); *Going Hollywood* (1933); *Too Much Harmony* (1933); *Here Is My Heart* (1934); *She Love Me Not* (1934); *We're Not Dressing* (1934); *The Big Broadcast of 1936* (1935); *Mississippi* (1935); *Two for Tonight* (1935); *Anything Goes* (1936); *Pennies from Heaven* (1936); *Rhythm on the Range* (1936); *Double or Nothing* (1937); *Waikiki Wedding* (1937); *Doctor Rhythm* (1938); *Sing, You Sinners* (1938); *East Side of Heaven* (1939); *Paris Honeymoon* (1939); *The Star Maker* (1939); *If I Had My Way* (1940); *Rhythm on the River* (1940); *Road to Singapore* (1940); *Birth of the Blues* (1941); *Road to Zanzibar* (1941); *Holiday Inn* (1942); *Road to Morocco* (1942); *Star Spangled Rhythm* (1942); *Dixie* (1943); *Going My Way* (1944); *Here Come the Waves* (1944); *The Bells of St. Mary's* (1945); *Duffy's Tavern* (1945); *Blue Skies* (1946); *Road to Utopia* (1946); *Road to Rio* (1947); *Variety Girl* (1947); *Welcome Stranger* (1947); *The Emperor*

*Waltz* (1948); *A Connecticut Yankee in King Arthur's Court* (1949); *Down Memory Lane* (1949); *Top o' the Morning* (1949); *Mr. Music* (1950); *Riding High* (1950); *Here Comes the Groom* (1951); *Just for You* (1952); *Road to Bali* (1952); *Little Boy Lost* (1953); *The Country Girl* (1954); *White Christmas* (1954); *Anything Goes* (1956); *High Society* (1956); *Man on Fire* (1957); *Alias Jesse James* (1959); *Say One for Me* (1959); *High Time* (1960); *Let's Make Love* (1960); *Pepe* (1960); *Road to Hong Kong* (1962); *Robin and the Seven Hoods* (1964); *Stagecoach* (1966); *Ben* (p only, 1972); *That's Entertainment!* (1974).

---

**Crystal, Billy (1947—)**   An all-around comic talent, Billy Crystal has conquered stand-up and TV and evolved into a genuine comedy movie star who not only acts but has begun writing, directing, and producing his own work. A slightly built, curly headed actor with a sharp wit and a baby face, Crystal became almost as famous for emceeing the Academy Award shows in the early 1990s with astonishing originality as he was for his burgeoning movie career.

Born and raised in Long Beach, New York, Crystal was a successful stand-up comedian whose early career in TV and the movies is marked by "firsts" rather than "bests." For instance, he played the first gay character in a prime-time TV series (the comic soap opera, aptly called "Soap," 1977–1981) and the first pregnant man in Joan Rivers's unfortunate directorial debut, *Rabbit Test* (1978).

Earlier in his career, Crystal had chosen not to become an original cast member of "SATURDAY NIGHT LIVE's" Not Ready for Prime Time Players. He did join the hip hit show during the 1984–1985 season, but that exposure was ultimately less important, in the long run, than his long and fruitful association with director Rob REINER. Crystal had a small part in Reiner's rock and roll documentary spoof *This Is Spinal Tap* (1984) and then starred in the director's hit comedies *The Princess Bride* (1987) and *When Harry Met Sally* (1989). In between, Crys-

*Emerging as a major comedy star, Billy Crystal hit the big time in the late 1980s and early 1990s with hits such as* When Harry Met Sally *(1989) and, seen above,* City Slickers *(1991). He made his directorial debut with the ambitious commercial disappointment* Mr. Saturday Night *(1992), a comedy that will surely be rediscovered in the years ahead.*
PHOTO COURTESY OF MOVIE STAR NEWS.

tal co-starred with Danny DeVITO in *Throw Momma from the Train* (1987), giving Crystal three hit films in a row. Crystal had fully hit his stride and proved it with *City Slickers* (1991), a megahit comedy that he also produced.

His next project was the ambitious life story of a nasty, unhappy fictional comedian who had achieved stardom, only to lose it. In many ways a bold and daring comedy, *Mr. Saturday Night* (1992) was met with critical acclaim but a disappointing box office. Crystal had done it all in the movie—writing, directing, producing, and starring—and done it well.

FILMS INCLUDE: *Rabbit Test* (1978); *Animalympics* (1979); *This Is Spinal Tap* (1984); *Running Scared* (1986); *The Princess Bride* (1987); *Throw Momma from the Train* (1987); *Memories of Me* (also sc, p, 1988); *When Harry Met Sally* (1989); *City Slickers* (also p, 1991); *Mr. Saturday Night* (also sc, p, d, 1992); *City Slickers II* (1994).

**Cukor, George (1899—1983)** A director of many of Hollywood's most sophisticated comedies, George Cukor was often called a "woman's director" because he elicited top-notch performances from many of Hollywood's most famous actresses. Cukor was simply a sensitive filmmaker who understood women in an industry that lacked female directors. It was no wonder, then, that after he demonstrated his ability to work with strong actresses—many of whom excelled at comedy—he was usually the first to be called upon to direct them.

The actresses whose careers he influenced are legion. Prominent among them are Katharine Hepburn, whom he introduced to movie audiences in *A Bill of Divorcement* (1932) and then the wonderfully brittle comedy *The Philadelphia Story* (1940). Along the way he directed her in some of her best ROMANTIC COMEDY movies, just a few of which are *Sylvia Scarlett* (1935), *Holiday* (1938), *Adam's Rib* (1949), and *Pat and Mike* (1952).

It is perhaps with Katharine Hepburn that Cukor is most closely associated, but he also directed an enormous number of other actresses in some of their best roles, including Greta Garbo in *Camille* (1937); Ingrid Bergman in *Gaslight* (1944); Judy HOLLIDAY in *Born Yesterday* (1950); Jean Simmons in *The Actress* (1952); Judy Garland in *A Star Is Born* (1954); Ava Gardner in *Bhowani Junction* (1956); and Audrey Hepburn in *My Fair Lady* (1964).

In addition to his reputation as a woman's director, Cukor is also known as Hollywood's most successful adapter of books and plays for the screen. From *Dinner at Eight* (1933) to *Travels with My Aunt* (1972), he demonstrated his ability to capture the essence of his sources without being slavishly devoted to the original material.

Above all else, Cukor's movies are about imagination. The characters in his best films are generally vulnerable souls caught up in their own rendition of the truth. It is a theme that he always handled with touching grace, sympathy, and style—and always with a lively sense of humor.

FILMS: *Grumpy* (1930); *The Royal Family of Broadway* (1930); *The Virtuous Sin* (1930); *Girls About Town* (1931); *Tarnished Lady* (1931); *A Bill of Divorcement* (1932); *Rockabye* (1932); *What Price Hollywood?* (1932); *Dinner at Eight* (1933); *Little Women* (1933); *Our Betters* (1933); *David Copperfield* (1935); *Sylvia Scarlett* (1935); *Romeo and Juliet* (1936); *Camille* (1937); *Holiday* (1938); *The Women* (1939); *Zaza* (1939); *The Philadelphia Story* (1940); *Susan and God* (1940); *Two-Faced Woman* (1941); *A Woman's Face* (1941); *Her Cardboard Lover* (1942); *Keeper of the Flame* (1942); *Gaslight* (1944); *Winged Victory* (1944); *Desire Me* (1947); *A Double Life* (1947); *Edward, My Son* (1948); *Adam's Rib* (1949); *Born Yesterday* (1950); *A Life of Her Own* (1950); *The Model and the Marriage Broker* (1951); *The Marrying Kind* (1952); *Pat and Mike* (1952); *The Actress* (1953); *It Should Happen to You* (1954); *A Star Is Born* (1954); *Bhowani Junction* (1956); *Les Girls* (1957); *Wild Is the Wind* (1957); *Heller in Pink Tights* (1960); *Let's Make Love* (1960); *Song Without End* (1960); *The Chapman Report* (1962); *My Fair Lady* (1964); *Justine* (1969); *Travels with My Aunt* (also p, 1972); *The Blue Bird* (1976); *Rich and Famous* (1981).

# D

**Daffy Duck**  *See* WARNER BROS. CARTOONS

**Dangerfield, Rodney (1921–)**  Bulging eyes
flashing left and right, head bobbing, with sweat
pouring down his face as he tugs at his shirt collar,
Rodney Dangerfield is the comedian who "gets no
respect." He created a comic character on nightclub
stages and on television that was strangely at odds
with his movie persona. On film, he became the
fast-talking, loud, obnoxious yet somehow lovable
bumbler who says all the rude things we often think
but are afraid to speak. He's made only six movies,
starring in only a few of them, but his comic presence is such that he cannot be ignored.

Dangerfield grew up during the Great Depression on New York's Long Island. At the age of
nineteen, using the pseudonym Jack Roy, he began
performing a stand-up routine in nightclubs that
were off the beaten track. One of his friends during
this period was future comedy legend Lenny Bruce.
Nonetheless, Dangerfield's first attempt at show
business was a flop. He quit at the age of twenty-
eight, finally returning to the nightclub scene a
dozen years later to try again.

He got his big break when he was booked on
TV's "Ed Sullivan Show" and did the unimaginable:
He made Sullivan laugh. He became a TV talk show
regular, appearing more than sixty times on "The
Tonight Show, Starring Johnny Carson."

Dangerfield appeared in one movie during his
early years of success, playing a comical villain in the
cult favorite *The Projectionist* (1971). By the time he
was seen in his second film, playing a riotously

*A longtime stand-up comedian, Rodney Dangerfield became a
surprise movie star in the 1980s. Unfortunately, he hasn't made
nearly so many films as his fans would have liked. He is seen here
in a publicity still from one of his lesser efforts,* Ladybugs *(1992).*
PHOTO BY STEVE SCHAPIRO, © PARAMOUNT PICTURES.

funny supporting role in *Caddyshack* (1980), he had
become a major stand-up comedy star. *Easy Money*
(1983), which Dangerfield also wrote, was his first
starring role in a comedy, and it received a fair
degree of positive recognition. His best film, by far,
was *Back to School* (1986). It was a deservedly big hit,
and Dangerfield was at the top of his comedy game.
But it was downhill after that. Both *Moving* (1988)
and *Ladybugs* (1992) were pale imitations of his ear-

lier success, the latter film thoroughly bombing both critically and commercially.

---

FILMS: *The Projectionist* (1971); *Caddyshack* (1980); *Easy Money* (also sc, 1983); *Back to School* (also story, sc, song, 1986); *Moving* (1988); *Ladybugs* (1992).

---

## Daniels, Mickey    *See* OUR GANG

## Danson, Ted (1947—)    A tall, good-looking, comic leading man, Ted Danson distinguished himself in dramatic supporting roles in films such as *The Onion Field* (1979) and *Body Heat* (1981). There was little hint of his comic abilities until they were given the chance to shine in the TV sitcom "Cheers." The long-running hit comedy not only showcased his comedic flair, its success gave him the clout to get starring roles in big-budget films—most of them comedies. He gets most of his humor from playing characters not unlike Sam Malone on "Cheers"; he often plays men who appear overconfident while, at heart, they are insecure. In that conflict, he finds the comedy.

Born in Flagstaff, Arizona, Danson did his undergraduate work at Stanford University before studying drama at Carnegie-Mellon University in Pittsburgh. He worked in the theater and taught acting at the Actors Institute in Los Angeles.

The starring roles started coming in 1985 with *Little Treasure*, but not necessarily the triumphs. Neither that film nor the next two did much for his movie career, despite the fact that one of them, *A Fine Mess* (1986), was directed by Blake EDWARDS. After three disappointments, it may have appeared that Danson was simply one of those TV stars who could not make the transition to movie star. But then came *Three Men and a Baby* (1987), in which he had the choice comic role of the self-absorbed actor. The movie was a surprise critical and box office winner, compelling a sequel, *Three Men and a Little*

*Lady* (1990), in which he also starred and scored a hit. In between, he played the male lead in the ROMANTIC COMEDY *Cousins* (1989), a film that, unlike *Three Men and a Baby*, did not translate well from its French original.

Danson changed gears to co-star in the serio-comic *Dad* (1989) with Jack LEMMON. He later shared top billing and a relationship with another famous comic performer, Whoopi GOLDBERG, in the mediocre comedy *Made in America* (1993).

Now that "Cheers" is off the air (except, of course, for reruns), Danson's movie career will play center stage. He has indicated an interest in playing darker, less comic characters in the future.

---

FILMS: *The Onion Field* (1979); *Spiderman: The Dragon's Challenge* (1980); *Body Heat* (1981); *Creepshow* (1982); *Little Treasure* (1985); *A Fine Mess* (1986); *Just Between Friends* (1986); *Three Men and a Baby* (1987); *Cousins* (1989); *Dad* (1989); *Three Men and a Little Lady* (1990); *Made in America* (1993).

---

## David, Jackie    *See* OUR GANG

## Day, Doris (1924—)    An actress and singer, Doris Day reached her height of popularity when starring in a series of popular romantic comedies in the late 1950s and early 1960s. Curiously, Day often played career woman roles, yet she was the personification of American womanhood at a time when women were expected to stay at home. Film audiences were drawn to her because she was accessible, warm, bubbly, but not quite saccharine; she was the girl next door but with sex appeal.

Born Doris Von Kappelhoff, Day originally intended on a career as a dancer. At the age of fourteen, however, before leaving Cincinnati for Los Angeles to pursue her dream, a car in which she was a passenger was hit by a train. Her right leg was badly injured.

If she could no longer dance, at least she could

still sing. By the time she was seventeen, Day became the featured singer for a big band, Barney Rapp and his New Englanders. Not long after, she sang for the far more well known Bob Crosby and the Bobcats and eventually hit the big time as the lead singer with Les Brown and his Band of Renown.

When a star was needed for a Warner Bros. musical, *Romance on the High Seas* (1948), the studio signed Betty Hutton. When Hutton had to drop out due to pregnancy, Warner tested and signed Day for the role. The film was nothing special, but it was a hit and it turned the brand-new actress into an instant star.

Warner followed that success by putting her in movies similar to her original hit. Most of her early films, such as *My Dream Is Yours* (1949) and *Tea for Two* (1950), were mildly entertaining light musical comedies. The films in which she had supporting roles, such as *Young Man with a Horn* (1950) and *Storm Warning* (1951), usually had better scripts. Nonetheless, she quickly came into her own as a major star very quickly, particularly after her starring role in the hit musical *Calamity Jane* (1953). Among her other notable successes during the 1950s were *Young at Heart* (1954), *The Pajama Game* (1957), and *Teacher's Pet* (1958). In addition, it was during the 1950s that she starred in her only purely dramatic roles, *Love Me or Leave Me* (1955), with James Cagney, and *The Man Who Knew Too Much* (1956), directed by Alfred Hitchcock. She proved her range as an actress in both films, finding her theme song "Que Sera, Sera" in the latter movie.

After a career of more than ten years in which she played a variety of parts, from dramatic to musical to light comedy, Day embarked on a series of so-called sophisticated ROMANTIC COMEDIES that were aimed at the American middle class. *Pillow Talk* (1959), with Rock Hudson, started the hugely popular cycle. The film proved such a sensation, in fact, that Day was actually nominated for a best actress Academy Award. She followed her success in *Pillow Talk* with similar films such as *Lover Come Back* (1961), *That Touch of Mink* (1962), *The Thrill of It All*

(1963), *Move Over Darling* (1963), *Send Me No Flowers* (1964), and *Do Not Disturb* (1965). Along the way, she also starred in several other films, among them the very popular comedy *Please Don't Eat the Daisies* (1960) and the hit musical *Billy Rose's Jumbo* (1962).

After the mildly successful *The Glass Bottom Boat* (1966), she hit the skids in a big way with such light comedy flops as *Caprice* (1967) and *With Six You Get Eggroll* (1968), which was also her last motion picture. Clearly, after the mid–1960s, Day's brand of naive romantic farces had gone out of fashion. After all, *Caprice* came out the same year as THE GRADUATE.

Her film career was fading and her late third husband (Martin Melcher) had mismanaged and/or embezzled her $20 million in earnings. Day found herself in a TV series that Melcher signed her to without her knowledge. "The Doris Day Show" had modest success. Day later won a $22 million judgment against her attorney who had worked with her late husband.

Day has mostly been absent from show business since the early 1970s. She finally returned to television in 1985 with a short-lived series on CBN Cable, "Doris Day's Best Friends." Most of her efforts from the 1970s to the present have gone to the protection of animal rights. She formed the Doris Day Animal League, a lobbying organization designed to bring attention to the use of animals in laboratory testing.

---

**FILMS:** *Romance on the High Seas* (1948); *It's a Great Feeling* (1949); *My Dream Is Yours* (1949); *Tea for Two* (1950); *The West Point Story* (1950); *Young Man with a Horn* (1950); *The Lullaby of Broadway* (1951); *On Moonlight Bay* (1951); *Starlift* (1951); *Storm Warning* (1951); *April in Paris* (1952); *I'll See You in My Dreams* (1952); *The Winning Team* (1952); *By the Light of the Silvery Moon* (1953); *Calamity Jane* (1953); *Lucky Me* (1954); *Love Me or Leave Me* (1955); *Young at Heart* (1955); *Julie* (1956); *The Man Who Knew Too Much* (1956); *The Pajama Game* (1957); *Teacher's Pet* (1958); *The Tunnel of Love*

(1958); *It Happened to Jane* (1959); *Pillow Talk* (1959); *Midnight Lace* (1960); *Please Don't Eat the Daisies* (1960); *Billy Rose's Jumbo* (1962); *Lover Come Back* (1962); *That Touch of Mink* (1962); *Move Over, Darling* (1963); *The Thrill of It All* (1963); *Send Me No Flowers* (1964); *Do Not Disturb* (1965); *The Glass Bottom Boat* (1966); *Caprice* (1967); *The Ballad of Josie* (1967); *Where Were You When the Lights Went Out* (1968); *With Six You Get Eggroll* (1968).

---

**Dead End Kids, The** Although they didn't start out as a comedy team, many of the core members of this tough-guy ensemble, principally Leo Gorcey (1915–1969) and Huntz Hall (1920–), realized where their futures lay and then shaped and refined their personalities until they had evolved into a comedy troupe specializing in lowbrow, juvenile humor. Perhaps the funniest aspect of their appeal, particularly in their later films, was the fact that they were clearly middle-aged men pretending to be teenagers. In all, the group that began as The Dead End Kids and ended up as the Bowery Boys made a total of eighty-six movies between 1937 and 1958, the vast majority of them comedies.

The Dead End Kids got their name from the play they had starred in on Broadway, Sidney Kingsley's powerful drama *Dead End*, in which they played a gang of incorrigible juvenile delinquents. When the play was turned into a film in 1937, the young actors were hired to re-create their roles. The original group consisted of Billy Halop, Leo Gorcey, Huntz Hall, Bobby Jordan, Gabriel Dell, and Bernard Punsley. They were such a hit in the movie that Warner Bros. signed them up to play much the same kinds of characters in six follow-up films, one of which, *Angels with Dirty Faces* (1938), is a genuine gangster classic starring James Cagney. All six were dramas, although there were comedic elements in the interactions between the kids themselves.

Humor crept into their act still further when the group splintered and some of them began working at Universal Pictures, launching a series of muddled comedies called Dead End Kids and Little Tough Guys. There were nine such films between 1938 and 1943. Meanwhile, another series, this one called East Side Kids, featured the remaining members of the troupe. Twenty-two of these low-budget action comedies were made between 1940 and 1945. Neither series solely focused on comedy.

Everything changed in 1946 when Leo Gorcey took charge of the group, created a formula for their movies, and changed their name to the Bowery Boys. By this point, Huntz Hall had rejoined Gorcey, and the two of them became the main comedic players. Gorcey was the head of the gang, taking the name of Slip Mahoney, while Hall played his moronic sidekick, Sach Jones. Gorcey also hired his father, veteran stage and screen actor Bernard Gorcey, to play Louis Dombrowski, the cranky, yet lovable owner of the candy store where the boys always hung out. Between 1946 and 1958, they made forty-eight Bowery Boys comedies. The only major cast changes occurred in 1956 when the elder Gorcey died. Leo Gorcey immediately quit the group, replaced for the final two years (and seven pictures) by Stanley Clements.

Among the original Dead End Kids, only Billy Halop (1920–1976), who was the original leader of the gang (not Leo Gorcey), took a stab at a solo career. He left the group in the early 1940s and had only limited, early success before he fell into near obscurity. He wrote a book about his experience titled *There's No Dead End*.

The only other member of the troupe to have any genuine success outside the confines of the gang was Huntz Hall, who played comic relief characters in a number of movies and on TV.

As for Leo Gorcey, he only came out of retirement to make cameo appearances in a couple of comedies, most appropriately in the all-star comedy hit *IT'S A MAD MAD MAD MAD WORLD* (1963).

---

**FILMS: As The Dead End Kids:** *Dead End* (1937); *Crime School* (1938); *Angels with Dirty Faces* (1938); *They Made Me a Criminal* (1939); *Hell's Kitchen* (1939);

*Angels Wash Their Faces* (1939); *On Dress Parade* (1939).

As The Dead End Kids and Little Tough Guys: *Little Tough Guy* (1938); *Call a Messenger* (1939); *You're Not So Tough* (1940); *Give Us Wings* (1940); *Mob Town* (1941); *Hit the Road* (1941); *Tough as They Come* (1942); *Mug Town* (1943); *Keep 'em Slugging* (1943).

As East Side Kids: *East Side Kids* (1940); *That Gang of Mine* (1940); *Boys of the City* (1940); *Bowery Blitzkrieg* (1941); *Pride of the Bowery* (1941); *Flying Wild* (1941); *Spooks Run Wild* (1941); *Let's Get Tough* (1942); *Smart Alecks* (1942); *Mr. Wise Guy* (1942); *'Neath Brooklyn Bridge* (1942); *Kid Dynamite* (1943); *Ghosts on the Loose* (1943); *Clancy Street Boys* (1943); *Mr. Muggs Steps Out* (1943); *Follow the Leader* (1944); *Bowery Champs* (1944); *Block Busters* (1944); *Million Dollar Kid* (1944); *Mr. Muggs Rides Again* (1945); *Come Out Fighting* (1945); *Docks of New York* (1945).

As Bowery Boys: *Bowery Bombshell* (1946); *In Fast Company* (1946); *Live Wires* (1946); *Mr. Hex* (1946); *Spook Busters* (1946); *Bowery Buckaroos* (1947); *Hardboiled Mahoney* (1947); *News Hounds* (1947); *Angels' Alley* (1948); *Smuggler's Cove* (1948); *Jinx Money* (1948); *Trouble Makers* (1948); *Angels in Disguise* (1949); *Fighting Fools* (1949); *Hold That Baby!* (1949); *Master Minds* (1949); *Blond Dynamite* (1950); *Blues Busters* (1950); *Lucky Losers* (1950); *Triple Trouble* (1950); *Bowery Battalion* (1951); *Crazy Over Horses* (1951); *Ghost Chasers* (1951); *Let's Go Navy* (1951); *Feudin' Fools* (1952); *Here Come the Marines* (1952); *Hold That Line* (1952); *No Holds Barred* (1952); *Clipped Wings* (1953); *Jalope* (1953); *Loose in London* (1953); *Private Eyes* (1953); *Bowery Boys Meet the Monsters* (1954); *Jungle Gents* (1954); *Paris Playboys* (1954); *Bowery to Bagdad* (1955); *High Society* (1955); *Jail Busters* (1955); *Spy Chasers* (1955); *Crashing Las Vegas* (1956); *Dig That Uranium* (1956); *Hot Shots* (1956); *Fighting Trouble* (1956); *Hold That Hypnotist* (1957); *Looking for Danger* (1957); *Spook Chasers* (1957); *Up in Smoke* (1957); *In the Money* (1958).

## Dee, Sandra (1942—)

A wholesome blonde beauty, Sandra Dee starred in a long string of light romantic comedies aimed at teenagers during the late 1950s and early 1960s. She remains, in the minds of many, the last example of unaffected romantic innocence in American movies.

Born Alexandra Zuck in Bayonne, New Jersey, Dee was a child model, an adolescent TV actress, and, after just her second movie, *The Reluctant Debutante* (1958), a teenage star at sixteen. The hits came fast and furious in the years that followed, and she made her mark in the title role of *Gidget* (1959) as well as in the already popular teenage series of Tammy films. By the mid-1960s, however, as the next generation began to protest racial discrimination, the Vietnam War, and so on, Sandra Dee soon came to be seen as terribly unhip. Nonetheless, she

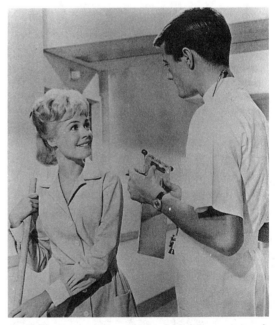

*Sandra Dee was an enormously popular light romantic comedy lead during the late 1950s and early 1960s. She was so influential among teenagers of her day that her name ended up in the lyrics of a song in the Broadway musical* Grease *and its 1978 film version. Dee is seen here with Peter Fonda in* Tammy and the Doctor *(1963).* PHOTO COURTESY OF MOVIE STAR NEWS.

remained a nostalgic icon and continued to be lionized, even to the point of her name being used in the lyrics of a song in the hit Broadway show and movie *Grease* (1978).

Dee was married to pop star/actor Bobby Darin from 1960 to 1967. After virtually disappearing from public view in the 1970s and 1980s, Dee reemerged in the early 1990s in a revealing *People* magazine cover story. She indicated an interest in returning to work in the movies.

FILMS INCLUDE: *Until They Sail* (1957); *The Reluctant Debutante* (1958); *The Restless Years* (1958); *Imitation of Life* (1959); *A Summer Place* (1959); *Gidget* (1959); *A Portrait in Black* (1960); *Romanoff and Juliet* (1961); *Tammy Tell Me True* (1961); *Come September* (1961); *If a Man Answers* (1962); *Take Her, She's Mine* (1963); *Tammy and the Doctor* (1963); *I'd Rather Be Rich* (1964); *That Funny Feeling* (1965); *A Man Could Get Killed* (1966); *Rosie!* (1968); *The Dunwich Horror* (1970).

## De Luise, Dom (1933—)

A big, balding, rotund comedian with a high energy level and a nervously effervescent voice, Dom De Luise has been a consistent comic presence in movies since the mid-1960s. Part of the Mel BROOKS informal stock company, he has graced six of Brooks's comedies over a twenty-three year period, most recently in *Robin Hood: Men in Tights* (1993). He has also been a regular provider of comic relief in many Burt Reynolds films, most memorably in *The End* (1978). De Luise has occasionally had top billing, such as the Anne Bancroft-directed *Fatso* (1979), and has also directed himself in one movie, *Hot Stuff* (1979). Most of the time, however, he plays supporting comic characters with relish. Since the early 1980s, he has also been regularly providing voices for animated characters in feature films.

Born in Brooklyn, New York, De Luise knew he was destined for a career in show business. He went to the High School for the Performing Arts (made famous by the movie *Fame*, 1980) in Manhattan and then went on to Tufts University. He later returned to New York where he developed a reputation as a fine comic actor on the stage. He eventually moved on to conquer TV as Dominick the Great, an incompetent magician, on "The Garry Moore Show." He has been a regular performer/guest on TV since then.

De Luise's movie career began rather unexpectedly with a drama, *Fail Safe* (1964), but it's been comedies for him ever since. He's worked with talents as diverse as Doris DAY in *The Glass Bottom Boat* (1966) and Dustin Hoffman in *Who Is Harry Kellerman, and Why Is He Saying Those Terrible Things About Me?* (1971). His fellow comics have used him in a number of films. For instance, Gene WILDER directed him in *The Adventure of Sherlock Holmes' Smarter Brother* (1975) and *The World's Greatest Lover* (1977). Neil SIMON used him in *The Cheap Detective* (1978), and even Mae WEST used him in her last film, *Sextette* (1978).

FILMS INCLUDE: *Fail Safe* (1964); *The Glass Bottom Boat* (1966); *The Busy Body* (1967); *What's So Bad About Feeling Good?* (1968); *Norwood* (1970); *The Twelve Chairs* (1970); *Who Is Harry Kellerman, and Why Is He Saying Those Terrible Things About Me?* (1971); *Every Little Crook and Nanny* (1972); *Blazing Saddles* (1974); *The Adventure of Sherlock Holmes' Smarter Brother* (1975); *Silent Movie* (1976); *The World's Greatest Lover* (1977); *The Cheap Detective* (1978); *Sextette* (1978); *The End* (1978); *Fatso* (1979); *The Last Married Couple in America* (1979); *Hot Stuff* (also d, 1979); *The Muppet Movie* (1979); *Diary of a Young Comic* (1979); *The Cannonball Run* (1980); *Wholly Moses!* (1980); *Smokey and the Bandit II* (1980); *History of the World, Part I* (1981); *The Secret of NIMH* (voice only, 1982); *The Best Little Whorehouse in Texas* (1982); *Cannonball Run II* (1983); *Johnny Dangerously* (1984); *An American Tail* (voice only, 1986); *Haunted Honeymoon* (1986); *Going Bananas* (1987); *Spaceballs* (1987); *Oliver and Company* (voice only, 1988); *Loose Cannons* (1989); *All Dogs Go to Heaven* (voice only, 1989); *Driving Me*

Crazy (1991); *Almost Pregnant* (1991); *Happily Ever After* (voice only, 1993); *Robin Hood: Men in Tights* (1993).

---

## Devine, Andy (1905—1977)

Baby boomers probably remember Andy Devine as either the host of the Saturday morning TV show "Andy's Gang" or as the comic sidekick Jingles to Wild Bill Hickok in the TV series of the same name (crying out at the end of each episode, "Hey, Wild Bill, wait for me!"). To generations of older fans, however, Devine was a venerable comic presence in movies for nearly fifty years, usually playing the simple-minded buddy of a whole corral full of Western heroes. With his trademark gravelly voice and his big, bulky frame, Devine was an unmistakable presence in the movies.

Born Jeremiah Schwartz in Flagstaff, Arizona, Devine suffered a throat injury when he was a kid that left him with his unique sound. It proved no impediment, however, to his career when talkies came in. He worked steadily, though not exclusively, in Westerns. For instance, he can be seen in, of all things, *Romeo and Juliet* (1936) and *A Star Is Born* (1937), not to mention *Ali Baba and the Forty Thieves* (1944). Even so, the movie role most people associate with him is that of the stagecoach driver in John Ford's classic *Stagecoach* (1939). His reputation for comedy, however, was recognized when he was invited to join the all-star comedy cast of IT's A MAD MAD MAD MAD WORLD (1963).

---

FILMS INCLUDE: *Red Lips* (1928); *Hot Stuff* (1929); *The Spirit of Notre Dame* (1931); *Destry Rides Again* (1932); *The Man from Yesterday* (1932); *Doctor Bull* (1933); *The President Vanishes* (1934); *The Farmer Takes a Wife* (1935); *Way Down East* (1935); *Romeo and Juliet* (1936); *A Star Is Born* (1937); *In Old Chicago* (1938); *Yellow Jack* (1938); *Stagecoach* (1939); *When the Daltons Rode* (1940); *The Flame of New Orleans* (1941); *Raiders of the Desert* (1941); *Crazy House* (1943); *Ali Baba and the Forty Thieves* (1944); *Canyon Passage* (1946); *Eyes of Texas* (1948); *New Mexico* (1951); *Montana Belle* (1952); *Pete Kelly's Blues* (1955); *Around the World in 80 Days* (1956); *The Adventures of Huckleberry Finn* (1960); *Two Rode Together* (1961); *The Man Who Shot Liberty Valance* (1962); *How the West Was Won* (1962); *It's a Mad Mad Mad Mad World* (1963); *The Ballad of Josie* (1968); *Myra Breckinridge* (1970); *A Whale of a Tale* (1977); *The Mouse and His Child* (voice only, 1977).

---

## DeVito, Danny (1944—)

A pint-size powerhouse, Danny DeVito has become a star actor/director with a string of hits from the mid-1980s to the early 1990s. An unlikely star, he is not only extremely short, he is bald, pudgy, and hardly good looking. However, he has a mischievous glint in his eyes that lights up at the slightest hint of comic revenge and a gleefully evil laugh that rocks with power despite his small stature.

Born in Asbury Park, New Jersey, DeVito's first role was as St. Francis of Assisi in a school play at Oratory Prep School in Summit, New Jersey. He would never play a role nearly so saintly again. After high school, he showed an interest in the theater, but it wasn't acting that he intended to pursue; he enrolled in the prestigious American Academy of Dramatic Arts to learn stage makeup. During his two-year stay there, however, he began taking acting lessons.

The young DeVito began working off-off-Broadway and off-Broadway in a number of plays, culminating in his memorable performance as Martini in *One Flew Over the Cuckoo's Nest*, the same role he would eventually play in the 1975 film adaptation of Ken Kesey's famous novel, a part that came to him after a number of appearances in less memorable movies.

It should be noted that Michael Douglas produced *Cuckoo's Nest*; he and DeVito were already longtime friends at this point, having met during the mid-1960s when they were both working at the Eugene O'Neill Foundation. Their careers would

*Comedies with Danny DeVito have often been a feast of laughter. He served up* Jack the Bear *in 1993, one of his more seriocomic efforts, shown above. From left to right are Reese Witherspoon, Robert J. Steinmiller, Jr., Julia Louis-Dreyfuss, Miko Hughes, and Danny DeVito.*

PHOTO BY MELINDA SUE GORDON, © 20TH CENTURY-FOX.

be inextricably intertwined during the years ahead, much to their mutual benefit. For instance, DeVito co-starred with Douglas and Kathleen Turner in the two hit adventure comedies *Romancing the Stone* (1984) and *The Jewel of the Nile* (1985). He also directed Douglas and Turner in the bitter comedy hit *War of the Roses* (1989).

DeVito originally established himself as a comic presence on TV in the hit sitcom "Taxi" (1978–1982), playing the hysterically vicious dispatcher Louis DePalma. It was his success in "Taxi" that launched him into significant supporting roles in such high-profile movies as *Terms of Endearment* (1983).

In 1986 DeVito made his bid for stardom by sharing top billing with Bette MIDLER in *Ruthless People*. He was perfectly cast, delighting in the savage humor of this BLACK COMEDY, and his happily demonic performance helped turn the movie into a major hit. He followed it with similar roles in movies such as *Tin Men* (1987), *Twins* (1988), and *Other People's Money* (1991).

Something subtly different, however, crept into DeVito's work in the early 1990s. On the one hand, the character of The Penguin he played in *Batman Returns* (1992) was so disgusting that it turned many people off (although this miscue must be placed at the feet of the film's director, Tim BURTON). On the other hand, his overwrought direction of the ambitious biopic *Hoffa* (1992) was misguided at best, and the casting of himself in a supporting role in the film only made matters worse. The film was a notable flop. So was his sentimental family comedy *Jack the Bear* (1993). It would seem that audiences respond to DeVito within relatively narrow parameters. They love him as a cackling, comic vulgarian and appreciate his need for comic retribution; what they don't appear to accept is DeVito as someone who is too vicious, too sweet, or too serious.

FILMS: *Dreams of Glass* (1968); *Lady Liberty* (1972); *Hurry Up, or I'll Be 30* (1973); *Scalawag* (1973); *One Flew Over the Cuckoo's Nest* (1975); *The Van* (1977); *The World's Greatest Lover* (1977); *Goin' South* (1978); *Going Ape!* (1981); *Terms of Endearment* (1983); *Johnny Dangerously* (1984); *Romancing the Stone* (1984); *The Jewel of the Nile* (1985); *Head Office* (1985); *My Little Pony* (voice only, 1986); *Ruthless People* (1986); *Wise Guys* (1986); *Throw Momma from the Train* (also d, 1987); *Tin Men* (1987); *Twins* (1988); *The War of the Roses* (also d, 1989); *Other People's Money* (1991); *Batman Returns* (1992); *Hoffa* (also d, 1992); *Jack the Bear* (a, 1993); *Reality Bites* (p only, 1994).

## De Wolfe, Billy (1907—1974)

A comic supporting player, Billy De Wolfe appeared in more than a dozen films, mostly during the 1940s and 1950s. While he rarely had much screen time, he still managed a memorable presence by virtue of his usually unctuous behavior, coupled with a thousand-kilowatt smile that was purposefully insincere. An affected speech pattern, which sounded like a lisp, added to the comic image of the maitre d', concierge, and so on, that he was often asked to play.

Born William Andrew Jones in Wollaston, Massachusetts, De Wolfe began in VAUDEVILLE as a comic dancer. He had some success as a nightclub entertainer, as well, by the time the movies tapped him for his comic character work.

FILMS: *Dixie* (1943); *Duffy's Tavern* (1945); *Our Hearts Were Growing Up* (1946); *Miss Susie Slagle's* (1946); *Blue Skies* (1946); *Dear Ruth* (1947); *The Perils of Pauline* (1947); *Variety Girl* (1947); *Isn't It Romantic?* (1948); *Tea for Two* (1950); *Dear Wife* (1950); *Lullaby of Broadway* (1951); *Dear Brat* (1951); *Call Me Madam* (1953); *Billie* (1965); *The World's Greatest Athlete* (1973).

## Diamond, I. A. L. (1920—1988)

A screenwriter and producer, I. A. L. Diamond is best known for creating morally complex comedies in collaboration with director Billy WILDER. These films were the apex of both of their careers. Diamond's work before teaming up with Wilder was rarely special, but the key to what he offered Wilder might be found in the witty SCREWBALL COMEDY he wrote for Howard HAWKS, *Monkey Business* (1952). It was hysterically observant about sex and society, both of which have always been themes close to Wilder's heart. In any event, there was something comedically combustible in their work together, and it produced a best screenplay Academy Award for *The Apartment* (1960) as well as best screenplay Oscar nominations for *Some Like It Hot* (1959) and *The Fortune Cookie* (1966).

Born Itek Dommnici in Rumania, Diamond came to the United States when he was nine. Known alternatively as Isadore and Izzy Diamond, he added the initials A. and L. for effect. After graduating from Columbia University, where he became deeply involved in college theatrics, he went to Hollywood and quickly broke into the movie game as a screenwriter, his first being *Murder in the Blue Room* (1944).

Diamond usually wrote his screenplays in collaboration, so it was not unnatural for him to consider working with writer/director Wilder when the latter was in the market for a replacement for his longtime partner Charles Brackett. Their first joint project was *Love in the Afternoon* (1957). Eventually,

Diamond not only co-wrote with Wilder, he also produced their films together.

If their movies were comedy firecrackers in the late 1950s and 1960s, they were just plain bombs in the 1970s and early 1980s. The team seemed to lose touch with its audience, making such latter-day flops as *Fedora* (1978) and *Buddy, Buddy* (1981), which was their final film.

---

**FILMS:** *Murder in the Blue Room* (1944); *Never Say Goodbye* (1946); *Two Guys from Milwaukee* (also story, 1946); *Always Together* (dial only, 1947); *Love and Learn* (1947); *Romance on the High Seas* (dial only, 1948); *Two Guys from Texas* (1948); *It's a Great Feeling* (story only, 1949); *The Girl from Jones Beach* (1949); *Love Nest* (1951); *Let's Make It Legal* (1951); *Monkey Business* (1952); *Something for the Birds* (1952); *That Certain Feeling* (1956); *Love in the Afternoon* (1957); *Merry Andrew* (1958); *Some Like It Hot* (1959); *The Apartment* (1960); *One, Two, Three* (1961); *Irma La Douce* (1963); *Kiss Me, Stupid* (1964); *The Fortune Cookie* (1966); *Cactus Flower* (1969); *The Private Life of Sherlock Holmes* (1970); *Avanti!* (1972); *The Front Page* (1974); *Fedora* (also p, 1978); *Buddy, Buddy* (1981).

---

**Diller, Phyllis (1917– )** Generally thought of today as strictly a TV and nightclub comedian, Phyllis Diller appeared with considerable regularity in the movies during the late 1960s, most notably as a comic leading lady for Bob HOPE in *Boy, Did I Get a Wrong Number* (1966), *Eight on the Lam* (1967), and *The Private Navy of Sgt. O'Farrell* (1968). Unfortunately for both Hope and Diller, there was nothing distinguished about any of those films. She disappeared from the movies during the 1970s, returning briefly in a few low-budget movies in more recent years, also without much distinction.

Born Phyllis Driver in Lima, Ohio, she came to professional comedy rather late in life. She was a middle-aged housewife and mother of five when she became a hit standup comic at the famed Purple

Onion in San Francisco. However, her big break came when she appeared on Groucho Marx's TV quiz show, "You Bet Your Life." The response to her comically exaggerated laugh, electric-socket hairdo, and daggerlike quips propelled her to national prominence.

Quite unexpectedly, Diller made her movie debut in support of Natalie Wood and Warren Beatty in the lushly romantic *Splendor in the Grass* (1961). As of late, she has been extolling the virtues of plastic surgery on TV talk shows.

---

**FILMS INCLUDE:** *Splendor in the Grass* (1961); *Boy, Did I Get a Wrong Number* (1966); *The Fat Spy* (1966); *Eight on the Lam* (1967); *Mad Monster Party* (voice only, 1967); *Did You Hear the One About the Traveling Saleslady?* (1968); *The Private Navy of Sgt. O'Farrell* (1968); *The Adding Machine* (1969); *Pink Motel* (1982); *Pucker Up and Bark Like a Dog* (1989); *The Boneyard* (1990); *The Perfect Man* (1993).

---

**Disney, Walt (1901–1966)** The comic animated creations of Walt Disney—most notably Mickey Mouse and Donald Duck—are known to billions of people all over the world. A visionary creative force as an animator, producer, and businessman, he built theme parks based on the power and appeal of his cartoon characters and found a niche in Hollywood as *the* provider of family entertainment.

Born Walter Elias Disney to a middle-class family in Chicago, Illinois, he studied his chosen craft of drawing at the Kansas City Art Institute when he was fourteen. After driving an ambulance for the Red Cross in France during World War I, he returned to Kansas City to work as a commercial artist. With his lifelong friend, Ub Iwerks, Disney eventually began making crude animated shorts, called Laugh-O-Grams, for local Kansas City theaters.

In 1923 Disney gambled on a trip to Hollywood, establishing an ANIMATION company with his brother, Roy Disney. They produced a combination live-action/animated cartoon called *Alice in Cartoonland*. It was a flop. So was the 1927 *Oswald the Rabbit* cartoon series. Meanwhile, Ub Iwerks had finally joined Disney in Los Angeles, and together they took another try at creating a cartoon character. This time they hit paydirt with Mickey Mouse in *Plane Crazy* (1928). It was a silent animated short, as was the second Mickey Mouse venture, *Gallopin' Gaucho* (1928). In an effort to stay ahead of the animated competition, Disney quickly turned to sound and made what became his watershed cartoon starring Mickey Mouse, *Steamboat Willie* (1929), with Disney himself supplying the little rodent's squeaky voice.

As shown in *Steamboat Willie*, music and animation made a potent combination, and Disney created a series of shorts called "Silly Symphonies," the most famous of which was *The Three Little Pigs* (1933), which introduced the hit tune "Who's Afraid of the Big Bad Wolf?" The cartoon won the best animated short subject Academy Award. During his lifetime, Disney would garner twenty-nine Oscars, all of them for his short subjects, except for several special Academy Awards honoring his features.

Ever the innovator, Disney created not only new characters such as Minnie Mouse, Dippy Dawg (later changed to Goofy), and Pluto, he also improved the technology of animation, incorporating the use of Ub Iwerk's multi-plane camera, a device that enabled greater clarity, depth, and detail in animated filmmaking.

Not content to remain in the relative backwater of short subjects, Disney decided to test the appeal of animation in the feature-length format. Putting his new-found prosperity on the line, he plunged into the making of *Snow White and the Seven Dwarfs* (1937), which was not only a big hit but was also given an honorary Academy Award. *Pinocchio* (1940) followed and was another hit. However, *Fantasia* (1940), his most ambitious animated feature, flopped at the time of its release; it is now considered his greatest achievement. In fairness, it was appreciated in its day by Disney's peers, who

gave him yet another honorary Oscar for his work on the film.

Disney continued making animated movies throughout the rest of his lifetime, although he did diversify into live-action films, beginning in 1950 with *Treasure Island*. In the 1960s, he combined animation and live action to excellent effect in his last great hit, *Mary Poppins* (1964), which was also nominated for a best picture Oscar. In the meantime, he also became a force on TV by hosting a one-hour show every Sunday night during prime time.

He died during lung surgery in 1966. After Disney's death, the Disney empire continued to thrive by merely feeding off its founder's original success formula. The gravy train derailed, however, in the 1970s when the studio turned away from filmmaking to concentrate on real estate development. In the early 1980s, the company was on the verge of being dismantled and sold for its parts. Instead, Michael Eisner was brought in as chairman in 1984 and turned the company around, building on the success of the company's first hit film, *Splash* (1984), since *The Love Bug* (1969).

More adult live-action comedies followed, released through its Touchstone Pictures subsidiary, among them *Down and Out in Beverly Hills* (1986), *Ruthless People* (1986), *Outrageous Fortune* (1987), *Good Morning, Vietnam* (1987), and *Three Men and a Baby* (1988). The concept the company followed was simple and effective: Use actors with stalled careers (to get their services more cheaply), and make relatively inexpensive comedies. Although the films hardly could be construed as family entertainment, the approach worked beyond anyone's wildest dreams, making Disney one of Hollywood's most successful companies during the latter half of the 1980s and early 1990s.

Finally, after being dormant in the field of animated features, Disney returned to its former place of leadership after joining with Steven Spielberg to make *Who Framed Roger Rabbit?* (1988). Disney followed with such highly regarded animated hits as *Oliver and Company* (1988), *The Little Mermaid* (1989), *Beauty and the Beast* (1991), and *Aladdin*

(1992), which became the biggest commercial hit in animated movie history, earning more than $200 million at the box office.

In other words, Disney's legacy of animated excellence and success continues.

---

**FILMS INCLUDE:** Features produced by Walt Disney only: *Snow White and the Seven Dwarfs* (1937); *Pinocchio* (1940); *Fantasia* (1940); *Dumbo* (1941); *The Reluctant Dragon* (1941); *Bambi* (1942); *The Three Caballeros* (1944); *Make Mine Music* (1946); *Song of the South* (1946); *Fun and Fancy Free* (1947); *Melody Time* (1948); *So Dear to My Heart* (1948); *Ichabod and Mr. Toad* (1949); *Cinderella* (1950); *Treasure Island* (1950); *Alice in Wonderland* (1951); *The Story of Robin Hood* (1952); *Peter Pan* (1953); *The Sword and the Rose* (1953); *The Living Desert* (1953); *20,000 Leagues under the Sea* (1954); *Davy Crockett—King of the Wild Frontier* (1955); *Lady and the Tramp* (1955); *The Littlest Outlaw* (1955); *Davy Crockett and the River Pirates* (1956); *Johnny Tremain* (1957); *Old Yeller* (1957); *Tonka* (1958); *The Light in the Forest* (1958); *Sleeping Beauty* (1959); *The Shaggy Dog* (1959); *Kidnapped* (1960); *Jungle Cat* (1960); *The Swiss Family Robinson* (1960); *The Sign of Zorro* (1960); *101 Dalmations* (1961); *The Absent-Minded Professor* (1961); *Big Red* (1962); *In Search of the Castaways* (1962); *Son of Flubber* (1963); *The Sword in the Stone* (1963); *The Misadventures of Merlin Jones* (1964); *The Moon-Spinners* (1964); *Emil and the Detectives* (1964); *Mary Poppins* (1964); *Those Calloways* (1965); *That Darn Cat* (1965); *The Ugly Dachshund* (1966); *Follow Me Boys* (1966); *The Gnome-Mobile* (1967); *Monkeys Go Home* (1967); *The Jungle Book* (1967); *The Happiest Millionaire* (1967).

---

## Divine (1947—1989)

A female impersonator, Divine gained fame as a cult figure thanks to his outrageously comic work in the underground cinema of writer/director John WATERS, his childhood friend. Divine appeared in one dozen films,

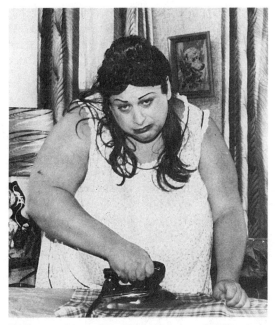

*Divine, seen here in John Waters'* Hairspray *(1988), was the creation of Harris Glenn Milstead, who never did iron out his/her problems. Milstead hoped to become a mainstream actor, but he was trapped by his fame as Divine.*
PHOTO COURTESY OF MOVIE STAR NEWS.

half of which were made by Waters. The movie that launched both actor and director to prominence was the gross-out movie hit *Pink Flamingos* (1972).

Born Harris Glenn Milstead, he grew up to be a rather sweet-looking, overstuffed man who, when he dressed and made himself up as Divine, became an earthy, vulgar, and menacing-looking female with a distinct comic edge. As Divine became more famous, he yearned for greater recognition and the opportunity to act in more mainstream films. Neither came to be. He died at forty-two, having made a number of memorable (if exceedingly eccentric) comedies over a twenty-year period. In addition to *Pink Flamingos*, his most important roles were in *Female Trouble* (1975), *Polyester* (1981), *Lust in the Dust* (1984), and *Hairspray* (1988).

---

**FILMS:** *Mondo Trasho* (1970); *Multiple Maniacs* (1971); *Pink Flamingos* (1972); *Female Trouble* (also song, 1975); *Underground and Emigrants* (1976); *Tally Brown, N.Y.* (1979); *The Alternative Miss World* (1980); *Polyester* (1981); *Lust in the Dust* (1984); *Trouble in Mind* (1985); *Hairspray* (1988); *Out of the Dark* (1989).

---

**Dr. Strangelove**  A film that ends with the start of World War III hardly seems like the stuff of comedy, but it remains the funniest, if not the darkest, political comedy ever made. This 1964 BLACK COMEDY's complete title is *Dr. Strangelove or: How I Learned to Stop Worrying and Love the Bomb*. While technically a British film, the movie is as American as its writer, director, and producer, Bronx-born Stanley Kubrick.

Starring Peter SELLERS in three roles, plus George C. Scott, Sterling Hayden, Keenan Wynn, James Earl Jones, and the inimitable Slim Pickens, the movie boasted an exemplary cast, all of them in service to a brilliant screenplay. Kubrick's original intention was to make a serious film based on the novel *Red Alert*. The more he worked on the script, though, the funnier it became. Eventually, he followed his instincts and turned it into a comedy.

The film is noteworthy as the first openly satirical take on American leadership and values. More than that, it tapped into the beginnings of an American counterculture that turned the film, rather unexpectedly, into a hit. As a consequence, *Dr. Strangelove* opened the way for the black comedies that came in its wake.

The film didn't originally end with Pickens (as Captain King Kong) riding an atomic bomb as if it were a bucking bronco down to the Russian target site below. Originally, the film had a different final scene: a custard pie fight between the Americans and Russians in the U.S. war room. Happily, Kubrick cut it out after the movie's initial previews.

**Dooley, Paul (1928—)**  An accomplished character actor, Paul Dooley has specialized in gently comedic roles, often playing fatherly types who can't quite keep up with the world around them. He's probably best known for playing the father in 1979's sleeper hit *Breaking Away*, although he could not have been better cast than in *Popeye* (1980), in which he played Wimpy, the character who would gladly pay you Tuesday for a hamburger today. *Popeye* is one of the five Robert Altman films with which Dooley has been associated. Most notably, he co-wrote the screenplay and acted in Altman's *Health* (1979).

Born in Parkersburg, West Virginia, Dooley made his debut in the comedy *What's So Bad About Feeling Good?* (1968). His most successful period was in the late 1970s and early 1980s. Except for *Sixteen Candles* (1984), neither hits nor particularly good roles came his way during most of the rest of the 1980s. By the early 1990s, this fine comic actor found himself in the critically and commercially shunned *Shakes, the Clown* (1991).

---

FILMS INCLUDE: *What's So Bad About Feeling Good?* (1968); *The Out-of-Towners* (1970); *Death Wish* (1974); *The Gravy Train* (1974); *Raggedy Ann and Andy* (1976); *Slap Shot* (1977); *A Wedding* (1978); *Breaking Away* (1979); *A Perfect Couple* (1979); *Rich Kids* (1979); *Health* (also sc, 1979); *Popeye* (1980); *Paternity* (1981); *Endangered Species* (1982); *Kiss Me Goodbye* (1982); *Going Berserk* (1983); *Monster in the Closet* (1983); *Strange Brew* (1983); *Sixteen Candles* (1984); *Big Trouble* (1985); *O. C. and Stiggs* (1987); *Last Rites* (1988); *Flashback* (1990); *Shakes, the Clown* (1991).

---

**double take**  When a character pays no attention to something he hears or sees and then suddenly whips his head around realizing the importance of what has just transpired, he has done a double take. More simply put, the first "take" doesn't register with the character, but the second "take" registers with tremendous impact.

The double take is a visual comic device often

used in movies, theater, and TV. The double take elicits laughter because the audience knows that a character allowed important information to slip past him and then waits with comic anticipation for the reaction. In essence the audience is in on the joke before the visual punch line.

Actors and comedians who have used the double take with hilarious results are legion, but one of the better double-take artists was Cary GRANT, who milked sudden, stunned surprise to hilarious effect in movies like *Bringing Up Baby* (1938), *Arsenic and Old Lace* (1944), and *I Was a Male War Bride* (1949). Another master of the double take was Oliver Hardy, who never failed to be startled at a second look at Stan Laurel's antics. However, the two greatest double-take artists of them all were film actors James FINLAYSON and Jack OAKIE.

Finlayson, active in both the silent and sound era, was a slightly built man with a bald head and mustache. He perfected the double take by exaggerating his reactions to a comic extreme and then adding another twist by slowly retreating his head. He dubbed this new variation the "double take and fade away."

Jack Oakie was a portly star of B-movie comedies who also offered comic relief in larger films. With his round and rubbery face, his double takes—which he perfected into triple takes—were a marvel to behold.

Unfortunately, due to overuse, the double take has become such a theatrical cliché that it is rarely used today in anything but the broadest of comedy scenes.

## Downey, Robert (1936–)

He has been an actor, screenwriter, producer, and director, and in the latter three categories, Robert Downey has made his mark as an iconoclastic, irreverent, and bitingly humorous filmmaker. Working with low budgets, long before independent movies came into vogue, Downey blazed a unique and hysterically incisive path with a number of underground films that ultimately found a cult following. His most successful film in that regard was *Putney Swope* (1969), a comedy about a hip black man who accidentally becomes the head of a major, all-white advertising agency.

Downey did not have an easy youth. He never finished high school, failed in his attempt to become a professional baseball player, and eventually drifted into acting. A growing fascination with the filmmaking process led him to make his first film in 1963, *Babo 73*. It was his second film, however, *Chafed Elbows* (1965), that put him on the movie map; it was made for a paltry $25,000 and received a surprisingly appreciative critical reaction. After one more film, Downey hit paydirt with *Putney Swope*. It was the high point of his career, but not his only success; he also received attention for his next three films, *Pound* (1970), *You've Got to Walk It Like You Talk It or You'll Lose That Beat* (1971), and *Greaser's Palace* (1972).

Downey's directorial career waned during the rest of the 1970s and then picked up somewhat during the early 1980s. In 1980 he wrote the screenplay for the crassly commercial *The Gong Show Movie* and also directed the teen comedy *Up the Academy*. His filmmaking work since then has been of little consequence. He has, in fact, appeared in as many movies as an actor (in cameos) as he has either written or directed, although in recent years he seems to have worked behind the camera with somewhat greater frequency.

His son Robert Downey, Jr., has become a star in his own right. He made his debut in his father's film *Pound* (he was five years old and played a puppy!) and went on to appear in four others by his dad. Like his father, Robert Downey, Jr., has proven himself at comedy, appearing in such amusing confections as *Weird Science* (1985) and *Back to School* (1986). He emerged as a young star with his performance in *Less Than Zero* (1987). He was recognized with a best actor Academy Award nomination for his brilliant performance in the title role in *Chaplin* (1992).

FILMS: *Babo 73* (sc, p, d, 1964); *Chafed Elbows* (sc, p, d, 1965); *No More Excuses* (a, d, 1968); *Putney Swope* (sc, d, 1969); *Pound* (sc, d, 1970); *Is There Sex after Death?* (a, 1971); *You've Got to Walk It Like You Talk It or You'll Lose That Beat* (a, 1971); *Greaser's Palace* (sc, p, d, 1972); *Two Tons of Turquoise to Taos Tonight* (a, 1976); *Jive* (sc, 1979); *The Gong Show Movie* (sc, 1980); *Up the Academy* (d, 1980); *America* (sc, d, 1982); *To Live and Die in L.A.* (a, 1985); *Johnny Be Good* (a, 1988); *Rented Lips* (d, 1988); *Too Much Sun* (sc, d, 1991).

---

**Dressler, Marie (1869—1934)**  A silent comedy star, Marie Dressler faded into obscurity only to become a major comedy star all over again in the talkie era. Dressler had neither youth nor beauty on her side. Even when she was a hit in silent films, she was well into middle age. When she made her comeback, she was downright old and obese, with a voice that sounded like a foghorn. Dressler's resurrection was due to her inimitable talent, common touch, and personal history. Audiences knew her life story, and it was an inspiration to them in that Depression-era time. It was no wonder that she was once called "The Heart of America."

Named Leila Von Koerber when she was born in 1869 in Canada, Dressler eventually made her way to New York and became a comic actress. At the turn of the century and beyond, Dressler was a major name in VAUDEVILLE, scoring successes in New York and London. In 1914, she joined with Mack SENNETT to make a film version of one of her hit shows. The movie was TILLIE'S PUNCTURED ROMANCE (1914), a six-reel comedy (the first at that length) that was a huge critical and financial success.

Although Dressler continued to make silent comedies, none of them were as commercially successful as her first. The downward slide had begun, and her pro-union activities hurt her vaudeville career as well. By 1927 Dressler was a has-been who was about to take a job as a maid.

During this time MGM screenwriter Frances Marion wrote *The Callahans and the Murphys* (1927) with Dressler in mind and won Irving Thalberg's permission to sign her for the film. The movie was not a hit, but Marion kept trying, for Dressler had been a great help to the screenwriter earlier in her career. Despite Marion's best efforts, none of the new silent film roles helped Dressler's career. Then came sound.

As a stage-trained actress, Dressler finally had her chance to reach the heights again. After a series of small roles that established Dressler as a comic personality, Marion once more stepped in, convincing Thalberg to use her in a straight role in Greta Garbo's *Anna Christie* (1930). The film, and Dressler, were hits. MGM eventually signed her up to a long-term contract. *Min and Bill* (1930), a classic comedy with Wallace BEERY, brought her an Oscar as best actress and was one of the top-grossing films of the year. Two years later she was nominated as best actress for her role in *Emma* (1932). Finally, in 1933, she had two of her best-remembered roles, starring in the rough-and-tumble comedy *Tugboat Annie* (again with Beery), and the all-star movie *Dinner at Eight*. In that year, just like the three that preceded it, Marie Dressler was voted Hollywood's top box office draw.

---

FILMS INCLUDE: *Tillie's Punctured Romance* (1914); *Tillie's Tomato Surprise* (1915); *The Scrublady* (1917); *Tillie Wakes Up* (1917); *The Agonies of Agnes* (1918); *The Cross Red Nurse* (1918); *The Callahans and the Murphys* (1927); *Breakfast at Sunrise* (1927); *The Joy Girl* (1927); *The Patsy* (1927); *Bringing Up Father* (1928); *The Divine Lady* (1929); *The Hollywood Revue of 1929* (1929); *The Vagabond Lover* (1929); *Anna Christie* (1930); *Caught Short* (1930); *Chasing Rainbows* (1930); *The Girl Said No* (1930); *Let Us Be Gay* (1930); *Min and Bill* (1930); *One Romantic Night* (1930); *Politics* (1931); *Reducing* (1931); *Emma* (1932); *Prosperity* (1932); *Tugboat Annie* (1933); *Dinner at Eight* (1933); *Christopher Bean* (1933).

---

**Dreyfuss, Richard (1948—)**  Although he has played a full range of characters, from mobsters to cops to pianists to pornographers, Richard Dreyfuss's true calling has been comedy. Exuding energy and intelligence, along with a rascally charm, he is a character actor star who has become a comic everyman.

Born in Brooklyn, New York, Dreyfuss moved with his well-to-do family (his father was an attorney) to Los Angeles when he was nine. He began acting at the Beverly Hills Jewish Center. His professional debut was in a local Los Angeles production of *In Mama's House* when he was fifteen. An agent spotted him and soon found him work in TV shows such as "Peyton Place" and "The Big Valley." Dreyfuss made his film debut in a bit part in *Valley of the Dolls* (1967). He also had a tiny part in *The* GRADUATE (1967). His first important film part, however, suited his cherubic good looks and manic intensity; it was the supporting, but splashy, role of Baby Face Nelson in *Dillinger* (1969).

After a minor flop in *The Second Coming of Suzanne* (1973), Dreyfuss won the role of Curt in *American Graffiti* (1973), joining a superb cast of future stars. He stood out from the crowd, bringing a thoughtfulness and integrity to the center of this surprise hit coming-of-age film.

In *The Apprenticeship of Duddy Kravitz* (1974), Dreyfuss gave one of the greatest seriocomic performances of the decade. His kinetic, nervous energy was palpable as the pushy, conniving young man who yearns for success but loses his moral bearings along the way. His Duddy was a richly drawn person played with remarkable sensitivity. The small-budget movie wasn't a big popular success, but it marked the arrival of a giant talent.

What soon followed was a giant shark. Dreyfuss had one of the three lead roles (as the marine biologist) in *Jaws* (1975). The film's gargantuan success suddenly put the young actor in the category of potential superstar. Instead of making another obviously commercial feature, though, he chose to star in an artsy, low-budget, X-rated film called *Inserts* (1976). The movie was an intriguing tour de force of anguish and angst, but it bombed at the box office.

After appearing in a small role in an all-star TV movie, *Victory at Entebbe* (1976), Dreyfuss's next two films, both released in 1977, brought him to the first crest of his career. He first starred in Steven Spielberg's uplifting and enchanting *Close Encounters of the Third Kind*. Dreyfuss then easily shifted gears to play a romantic comic lead (for the first time) in Neil Simon's *The Goodbye Girl* (1977); he won the best actor Academy Award for the latter effort, proving himself a superb comedian.

His next string of projects, among them *The Big Fix* (1978), *The Competition* (1980), *Whose Life Is It Anyway?* (1981), and *The Buddy System* (filmed in 1982 but released in 1984) all featured fine performances, but none of them were big winners at the box office—and some of them were major disasters. His shipload of talent was sinking in red ink. Dreyfuss was supposed to have starred in Bob Fosse's *All that Jazz* (1979), but he quit the project at the last minute (replaced by Roy Schieder). Much of what he did (and did not do) during these years was a result of his drug abuse.

When his car hit a tree and overturned one night in late 1982, he not only ended up in the hospital but was also arrested for cocaine possession. It took three years for him to make a comeback in Paul MAZURSKY's hit comedy *Down and Out in Beverly Hills* (1986). When he did, however, it was a changed, more mature Dreyfuss who took hold of the screen and held it. It was no mean feat, considering he shared the film with Bette MIDLER and Mike the Dog.

In *Down and Out in Beverly Hills*, Dreyfuss played a character role, and this role signalled a transformation in his approach to the movies. It was also this film that truly and finally turned Dreyfuss into a comedy star. His next film, the critically acclaimed *Tin Men* (1987) was a splendid, yet touching comedy that was also built on character roles rather than star turns. *Stakeout* (1987) was his third comedy hit in a row. After a short excursion into drama, playing against Barbra Streisand's powerful performance in *Nuts* (1988), Dreyfuss stuck largely to (and had his greatest successes in) comedy, appearing in *Moon over Parador* (1988), *Postcards from the Edge* (1990);

*What About Bob?* (1991), and *Another Stakeout* (1993).

---

**FILMS:** *Valley of the Dolls* (1967); *The Graduate* (1967); *The Young Runaways* (1968); *Hello Down There* (1969); *Dillinger* (1969); *The Second Coming of Suzanne* (1973); *American Graffiti* (1973); *Jaws* (1975); *Inserts* (1976); *Close Encounters of the Third Kind* (1977); *The Goodbye Girl* (1977); *The Big Fix* (1978); *The Competition* (1980); *Whose Life Is It Anyway?* (1981); *The Buddy System* (1984); *Down and Out in Beverly Hills* (1986); *Stand by Me* (1986); *Tin Men* (1987); *Stakeout* (1987); *Nuts* (1988); *Moon over Parador* (1988); *Always* (1989); *Let It Ride* (1989); *Postcards from the Edge* (1990); *Rosencrantz and Guildenstern Are Dead* (1990); *Once Around* (1991); *What About Bob?* (1991); *Lost in Yonkers* (1993); *Another Stakeout* (1993).

---

**Duck Soup** The 1933 MARX BROTHERS movie *Duck Soup* is seventy minutes of pure, unadulterated comic mayhem. Fans and critics alike consider this the team's best, purest comedy. After all, there is no sappy love interest (that would later mar their films at MGM), and there are no interludes where the brothers show off their musical skills. *Duck Soup* is just fast, furious humor, built on an exuberantly anarchic script, verbal and visual gags galore, and the Marx Brothers at the height of their comic abilities. Expertly directed by Leo MC-CAREY, the finest director with whom the boys would ever work, the film is a tight, rollicking piece of comic genius.

The film was originally titled *Cracked Ice*, but Paramount changed the name so that it would follow the "animal" motif that had begun with their second film, *Animal Crackers* (1930), which had then been followed by *Monkey Business* (1931) and *Horsefeathers* (1932).

McCarey was well trained in movie comedy, having worked with Mack SENNETT at the Keystone Studio. The script, music, and lyrics were provided by KALMAR AND RUBY, with Arthur Sheekman and Nat Perrin providing additional dialogue.

The plot, if you can call it that, involves Groucho becoming the dictator of a Ruritanian country called Freedonia. He gets the job because he has apparently wooed the nation's richest widow, naturally played by Margaret DUMONT. Meanwhile, Ambassador Trentino (Louis Calhern) of neighboring Sylvania wants to control Freedonia and, with the hilarious help of his two spies, Chico and Harpo, the two countries go to war (they have to, says Groucho, because he already paid the rent on the battlefield).

*Duck Soup* was a masterful comic send-up of dictators, government, nationalism, war, and politics. Made during the height of the Great Depression and during the same year that Hitler came to power, the film was a welcome and refreshing piece of satire. It's no coincidence that Mussolini banned the film in Italy.

Although the funniest of their films (Groucho thought it was certainly their craziest), *Duck Soup* did poorly with audiences, and Paramount didn't renew the Marx Brothers' contract. Zeppo left the team after this movie to become a theatrical agent, while the three remaining brothers went on to MGM, where Irving Thalberg created a new, more mainstream image for the team with *A Night at the Opera* (1935).

**Dumont, Margaret (1889–1965)** The ultimate comic dowager, Margaret Dumont was the ideal straight woman. Tall, stately, and completely unperturbable (Groucho Marx used to say that she didn't understand any of his jokes), Dumont graced Hollywood with her presence for nearly thirty-five years. Known variously as "The Fourth Marx Brother" and "The Fifth Marx Brother," depending on whether or not Zeppo Marx was still in the act, she became so associated with them—having shared the screen with the boys in seven of their thirteen films—that it is easy to forget that she had a long and vibrant career providing herself as foil to the likes of W. C. Fields, Laurel and Hardy, Danny Kaye, Jack Benny, and Abbott and Costello.

Born Margaret Baker in Brooklyn, New York, Dumont aspired to become a singer. She had some early, modest success, but when she was cast in 1925 in the Broadway smash *The Cocoanuts*, starring the Marx Brothers, her comic fate was sealed. When that play finally finished its run three years later, she found herself in the Marx's next stage hit, *Animal Crackers*. She reprised her roles in both when they were transferred to the screen. Her other five Marx Brothers films were *Duck Soup* (1933), *A Night at the Opera* (1935), *A Day at the Races* (1937), *At the Circus* (1939), and *The Big Store* (1941).

Dumont worked regularly in other films, playing the same stoical, unfazed rich matron (ignoring the craziness all around her) in most of her films of the 1930s and 1940s. She worked far less during the 1950s and early 1960s. Her last film was the comedy *What a Way to Go!* (1964).

---

**Films Include:** *The Cocoanuts* (1929); *Animal Crackers* (1930); *The Girl Habit* (1931); *Duck Soup* (1933); *A Night at the Opera* (1935); *Anything Goes* (1936); *A Day at the Races* (1937); *Dramatic School* (1938); *At the Circus* (1939); *The Big Store* (1941); *Never Give a Sucker an Even Break* (1941); *Born to Sing* (1942); *The Dancing Masters* (1943); *Up in Arms* (1944); *The Horn Blows at Midnight* (1945); *Little Giant* (1946); *Stop, You're Killing Me* (1952); *Auntie Mame* (1958); *Zotz!* (1962); *What a Way to Go!* (1964).

---

## Durante, Jimmy (1893—1980)

In the old-fashioned sense, Jimmy Durante was the consummate entertainer. A comic song and dance man who conquered vaudeville, stage, radio, TV, and film, Durante was a dynamo of energy and good-natured lowbrow charm. Short, wiry, balding, and with a nose that just would not quit, he rarely got the girl, but he always got the laughs.

Born James Francis Durante in New York City,

*"The Schnozzola," Jimmy Durante, was a much admired comic song and dance man who was famous for, among many things, mangling the English language. He once said, "I don't split infinitives. When I get to work on 'em, I break 'em up into little pieces." Here he is in a scene from* Start Cheering *(1938) with Joan Perry.* PHOTO COURTESY OF MOVIE STAR NEWS.

he played the piano in nightclubs as early as age sixteen before joining with Lou Clayton and Eddie Jackson to create a popular vaudeville trio. He was still a member of the group when he made the big time on Broadway, appearing in Ziegfeld's *Show Girl* in 1929.

With the talkie revolution in full swing in Hollywood, the movies were clamoring for actors with voices, and certainly Durante's unique sandpaper sound was appealing. He appeared on the big screen the following year, making his debut in *Roadhouse Nights* (1930).

Although he had a five-year contract with MGM, Durante didn't sit on his laurels. He shuttled back and forth between Hollywood and Broadway, becoming famous in both places. All in all, he worked with considerable steadiness in Hollywood for twenty years. Among his better movies of this era were *The Passionate Plumber* (1932) with Buster Keaton, *The Man Who Came to Dinner* (1942), and *It Happened in Brooklyn* (1947). Like so many great comedians, he appeared in *It's a Mad Mad Mad Mad World* (1963). In that film, he literally "kicks the bucket," sending the movie on its merry way in search of "The Big W." It was his last motion picture, although he continued to work into the 1970s, starring in nightclubs and on TV. His trademark exit—hat in hand, arms extended and quivering back and forth, and head shaking side to side as he strutted off the stage—is perhaps the most copied exit in show business.

---

**FILMS:** *Roadhouse Night* (1930); *The Cuban Love Song* (1931); *New Adventures of Get-Rich-Quick Wallingford* (1931); *The Wet Parade* (1932); *The Passionate Plumber* (1932); *Speak Easily* (1932); *The Phantom President* (1932); *Blondie of the Follies* (1932); *Meet the Baron* (1933); *What! No Beer?* (1933); *Broadway to Hollywood* (1933); *Hell Below* (1933); *George White's Scandals* (1934); *Palooka* (1934); *Strictly Dynamite* (1934); *She Learned About Sailors* (1934); *Student Tour* (1934); *Hollywood Party* (1934); *Carnival* (1935); *Sally, Irene and Mary* (1938); *Little Miss Broadway* (1938); *Start Cheering* (1938); *Forbidden Music* (1938); *Melody Ranch* (1940); *You're in the Army Now* (1941); *The Man Who Came to Dinner* (1942); *Two Girls and a Sailor* (1944); *Music for Millions* (1945); *Two Sisters from Boston* (1946); *It Happened in Brooklyn* (1947); *This Time for Keeps* (1947); *On an Island with You* (1948); *The Milkman* (1950); *The Great Rupert* (1950); *Beau James* (cameo, 1957); *Pepe* (1960); *Jumbo* (1962); *It's a Mad Mad Mad Mad World* (1963).

---

## Durfee, Minta (1897–1975)

Largely forgotten today, Minta Durfee was a major comedy star during the 1910s, playing female leads opposite her one-time husband Fatty ARBUCKLE as well as sharing top billing with Charlie CHAPLIN in his earliest twelve film comedies.

Durfee was born in Los Angeles and found her way into show business as a dancer. The pretty and slim young actress married Fatty Arbuckle long before he became famous. They were wed in 1908, and she didn't begin appearing with him in Keystone comedies until 1913, when they both joined Mack SENNETT's troupe together. His huge body versus her petite frame was the premise for any number of gags.

Durfee's film career spanned just five years, ending when she walked out on Arbuckle in 1918. She made only rare film appearances after that, and always just in cameos. For instance, she can be seen in John Ford's *How Green Was My Valley* (1941) as well as in the all-star comedy film *IT'S A MAD MAD MAD MAD WORLD* (1963).

---

**FILMS INCLUDE:** *Fatty at San Diego* (1913); *Fatty's Flirtation* (1913); *Fatty's Day Off* (1913); *Fatty's Finish* (194); *The Alarm* (1914); *Fatty and the Heiress* (1914); *Fatty's Debut* (1914); *Fatty's Wine Party* (1914); *Fatty and Minnie He-Haw* (1914); *Leading Lizzie Astray* (1914); *Ambrose's First Falsehood* (1914); *Making a Living* (1914); *A Film Johnnie* (1914); *Twenty Minutes of Love* (1914); *Caught in a Cabaret* (1914); *Cruel, Cruel Love* (1914); *The Masquerader* (1914); *His New Profession* (1914); *The Rounders* (1914); *The New Janitor* (1914); *Tillie's Punctured Romance* (1914); *Little Hatchet* (1915); *Love, Speed and Thrills* (1915); *Ambrose's Fury* (1915); *Ambrose's Little Hatchet* (1915); *The Home Breakers* (1915); *Fatty's Reckless Fling* (1915); *Fickle Fatty's Fall* (1915); *When Love Took Wings* (1915); *Tin Type Tangle* (1915); *Dirty Work in a Laundry* (1915); *A Village Scandal* (1915); *His Wife's Mistake* (1916); *The Other Man* (1916); *The Great Pearl Tangle* (1916); *Bright Lights* (1916); *Mickey* (1918); *Naughty Marietta* (cameo, 1935); *How Green Was My Valley* (cameo, 1941); *It's a Mad Mad Mad Mad World* (cameo, 1963); *The Unsinkable Molly Brown* (cameo, 1964).

# E

**East Side Kids**  *See* DEAD END KIDS, THE

**Educational Pictures**  Without doubt, Educational Pictures was the most misnamed company in American movie history. It did start out in 1919 with the intention of making educational films for distribution throughout America's school systems, but that plan barely lasted into the new decade, when the studio abruptly changed direction and began churning out a steady stream of comedy short subjects.

Unlike the companies that moved to Los Angeles during the consolidation of the movie business during the 1910s and early 1920s, Educational Pictures stayed in New York, shooting its two-reelers in Astoria, Queens. Its secret of success was using hot East Coast Broadway and VAUDEVILLE talents, catching them between engagements and getting their acts on film. And it worked. Educational Pictures was a small, but profitable, company, especially in the 1920s and early 1930s. The company caught comedians either at the beginning of their careers, giving them their first exposure in films (as in the case of Danny KAYE, Milton Berle, and the RITZ BROTHERS), or else it caught aging comics on their downslide, milking them for whatever their fading fame might have been worth (as in the case of Buster KEATON and Harry LANGDON).

Educational Pictures, which was never a big operation, finally ran out of cash in the late 1930s and closed its doors.

**Edwards, Blake (1922–)**  A filmmaker who finds humor (as well as suspense) in the commonplace, Blake Edwards has created his own niche in the film business, consistently providing laughter in an area that most modern directors fear to tread, namely SLAPSTICK comedy. He is, in fact, so associated with comedies, such as the *Pink Panther* films (he is responsible for all of them), that it is easy to forget that he has also directed hit thrillers and high dramas such as *The Tamarind Seed* (1974) and *Days of Wine and Roses* (1962).

Born William Blake McEdwards in Tulsa, Oklahoma, he had his first taste of Hollywood when he was only twenty. He appeared in a small role in *Ten Gentlemen from West Point* (1942), but military service cut short his career as a thespian. When Edwards returned to the popular arts, his first important break came not in the movies but in radio. He created the successful "Richard Diamond: Private Detective" series, which later also had a run as a TV series. He went on to create "Dante" and "Peter Gunn" for TV (*Gunn*, based on his TV show, was also made into a movie by Edwards in 1967).

Edwards's success on radio gave him the opportunity to write screenplays. He wrote seven of them, including *Operation Mad Ball* (1957), all of which were directed by Richard Quine. His first directorial effort was in 1955 with *Bring Your Smile Along*. He showed nothing special beyond a solid professionalism in the several films that followed his debut, until he directed *Operation Petticoat* (1959). The film was an inspired submarine comedy with Cary GRANT and Tony Curtis, the success of which

**101**

eventually gave Edwards the chance to direct *Breakfast at Tiffany's* (1961) and *Days of Wine and Roses* (1962). These latter two movies were among the most popular of the early 1960s and established Edwards as a directorial star.

Edwards's glittering career in the early part of the decade shined even brighter when he made the hits *The Pink Panther* (1963), *A Shot in the Dark* (1964), and *The Great Race* (1964). The latter half of the 1960s and the first half of the 1970s were far less golden for the director.

In the midst of his slump in 1969, Edwards married actress Julie Andrews (it was his second marriage), and she subsequently appeared in a great many of his movies. However, it wasn't the presence of his famous wife in his films that saved his career. It was the clever reuniting with Peter SELLERS to make three more Pink Panther movies that did the trick. All of them were hits, and Edwards's revitalized comedy reputation gave him the opportunity in 1979 to direct *10*, which was one of the biggest comedy hits of the year. In addition to proving that Edwards could make a hit film without Peter Sellers, it also made a star out of Dudley MOORE and introduced Bo Derek to the world.

Edwards still pursued a bitter, melancholy sort of humor in films such as *S.O.B.* (1981) and *That's Life* (1986), meeting rather poor results at the box office. However, the director's work was nonetheless seen as worthy of serious discussion, rather than abject dismissal. And between his dour comedies he offered audiences more commercial films such as the cross-dressing comedy *Victor/Victoria* (1982), for which he received his only Oscar nomination (for best screenplay); the slapstick FARCE *Blind Date* (1987), which introduced Bruce Willis to the big screen in his first starring role; and *Skin Deep* (1989), which featured a hysterical scene involving a glowing condom.

FILMS: *Ten Gentlemen from West Point* (a, 1942); *In the Meantime, Darling* (a, 1944); *Marshal of Reno* (a, 1944); *Strangler of the Swamp* (a, 1945); *Tokyo Rose* (a, 1945); *Panhandle* (a, p, sc, 1948); *Stampede* (p, sc, 1949); *Rainbow Round My Shoulder* (sc, 1952); *Sound Off* (sc, story, 1952); *All Ashore* (sc, story, 1953); *Cruisin' Down the River* (sc, story, 1953); *The Atomic Kid* (story, 1954); *Drive a Crooked Road* (sc, 1954); *Bring Your Smile Along* (d, sc, story, song (1955); *My Sister Eileen* (sc, 1955); *He Laughed Last* (d, sc, story, 1956); *Mister Cory* (d, sc, 1957); *Operation Mad Ball* (sc, 1957); *This Happy Feeling* (d, sc, 1958); *Operation Petticoat* (d, 1959); *The Perfect Furlough* (d, 1959); *High Time* (d, 1960); *Breakfast at Tiffany's* (d, 1961); *The Couch* (story, 1962); *Days of Wine and Roses* (d, 1962); *Experiment in Terror* (d, p, 1962); *The Notorious Landlady* (sc, 1962); *Soldier in the Rain* (sc, 1963); *The Pink Panther* (d, sc, 1964); *A Shot in the Dark* (d, p, sc, 1964); *The Great Race* (d, story, 1965); *Waterhole #3* (p, 1967); *What Did You Do in the War, Daddy?* (d, p, story, 1968); *Gunn* (d, sc, story, 1967); *The Party* (d, p, sc, story, 1968); *Darling Lili* (d, p, sc, 1970); *Wild Rovers* (d, p, sc 1971); *The Cary Treatment* (d, 1972); *The Tamarind Seed* (d, sc, 1974); *The Return of the Pink Panther* (d, p, sc, 1975); *The Pink Panther Strikes Again* (d, p, sc, 1976); *Revenge of the Pink Panther* (d, p, sc, story, 1978); *10* (d, p, sc, 1979); *S.O.B.* (d, p, sc, 1981); *Trail of the Pink Panther* (d, p, sc, story, 1982); *Victor/Victoria* (d, p, sc, 1982); *Curse of the Pink Panther* (d, p, sc, 1983); *The Man Who Loved Women* (d, p, sc, 1983); *City Heat* (sc, story, 1984); *Micki and Maude* (d, 1984); *A Fine Mess* (d, sc, 1986); *That's Life!* (d, sc, 1986); *Blind Date* (d, 1987); *Sunset* (d, sc, 1988); *Skin Deep* (d, sc, 1989); *Switch* (d, sc, 1991); *Son of the Pink Panther* (d, sc, 1993).

**Elmer Fudd**   *See* WARNER BROS. CARTOONS

**Ephron and Ephron**   A play- and screenwriting team, Henry (1912–1992) and Phoebe (1914–1971) Ephron also happened to be married. Their works were largely light ROMANTIC COMEDIES; they also adapted stage musicals to the screen. Later in their career, Henry began producing the films

*Writer/director Nora Ephron on location in New York City during the shoot of her film* This Is My Life *(1992).*
PHOTO BY KERRY HAYES, © 20TH CENTURY-FOX.

that were based on their scripts, most notably the sophisticated Hepburn/Tracy comedy *Desk Set* (1957).

The Ephrons were married in 1934. They wrote for the stage before working in Hollywood, scoring on Broadway with *Three's a Family* before penning their first screenplay, *Bride by Mistake* (1944). They went on to write for the big screen for two decades, creating witty dialogue for such films as *John Loves Mary* (1949), *The Jackpot* (1950), and *Daddy Long Legs* (1955).

Screenwriter/director Nora EPHRON is their daughter.

---

**FILMS INCLUDE:** *Bride by Mistake* (1944); *Always Together* (1947); *Wallflower* (1948); *Look for the Silver Lining* (1949); *John Loves Mary* (1949); *The Jackpot*

(1950); *On the Riviera* (1951); *Belles on Their Toes* (1952); *What Price Glory?* (1952); *There's No Business Like Show Business* (1954); *Daddy Long Legs* (1955); *Carousel* (also Henry—p, 1956); *Desk Set* (also Henry—p, 1957); *Take Her, She's Mine* (based on play, 1963); *Captain Newman, M.D.* (1964).

---

**Ephron, Nora (1941—)** Screenwriting, it would seem, is in Nora Ephron's blood; she is the daughter of longtime Hollywood screenwriters and playwrights Henry EPHRON AND Phoebe EPHRON, who also were noted for their comedic gift. Nora, however, has done her parents one better by becoming a comedy director with some considerable early success.

Born in New York City, Nora Ephron grew up in the heady worlds of Broadway and Hollywood, but she went off to school at the more secluded Wellesley College in Massachusetts. Ephron made her early mark in publishing, writing essays that were eventually collected into two best-selling volumes, *Crazy Salad* and *Scribble, Scribble*. She also wrote a novel, *Heartburn*, that was loosely based on her relationship with her former husband, Carl Bernstein (of Watergate fame). She later adapted the book for the screen; it was a somewhat sad human comedy directed by Mike NICHOLS and starring Meryl Streep and Jack Nicholson. The film was one of her few projects that disappointed.

Ephron started out in Hollywood like gangbusters, winning a best screenplay Oscar nomination for her first script (in collaboration with Alice Arlen) for *Silkwood* (1983). After *Heartburn*, she wrote and produced the comedy *Cookie* (1989), which had its supporters, although few of them showed up at the box office. Everyone showed up, however, to see the film based on her next screenplay, *When Harry Met Sally* (1989), a riotously funny and insightful look at modern relationships. Once again, she was nominated for a best screenplay Oscar.

Following the unsuccessful release of *My Blue Heaven* (1990), Ephron decided to try her hand at directing. Her first effort was *This Is My Life* (1992), which she had also written. The amusing and heartfelt comedy received mixed reviews and did not perform well at the box office, yet her skill as a director was very much in evidence.

She decided to direct someone else's work for her next project, choosing a script called *Sleepless in Seattle* (1993). This ROMANTIC COMEDY was both a critical and commercial hit.

FILMS: *Silkwood* (co-sc, 1983); *Heartburn* (novel, sc, 1986); *Cookie* (sc, p, 1989); *Crimes and Misdemeanors* (a, 1989); *When Harry Met Sally* (sc, p, 1989); *My Blue Heaven* (sc, p, 1990); *This Is My Life* (co-sc, d, 1992); *Sleepless in Seattle* (d, 1993).

## Errol, Leon (1881–1951)

A sour-faced, nervous, bald comedian, Leon Errol wisely made himself the butt of his own humor in his popular short subjects. He appeared in approximately 150 films, roughly two-thirds of them two-reel comedies that were made between 1933 and 1951. Errol occasionally had starring roles in features, but usually played in comic support of larger stars. While relatively few of his feature film appearances are in memorable movies, he can be seen in high comic form in the W. C. FIELDS vehicle *Never Give a Sucker an Even Break* (1941).

*Leon Errol, on the witness stand, was a familiar presence in Hollywood films, having appeared in more than 150 movies, starring in approximately 100 two-reelers.*
PHOTO COURTESY OF MOVIE STAR NEWS.

Born in Sydney, Australia, Errol came to the United States when he was a boy. He soon found his way into show business, climbing the ladder from VAUDEVILLE to BURLESQUE to Broadway before heading west to Hollywood. His success in the silents was limited, by the 1930s, in his middle age, he had the looks to match his material, playing put-upon husbands, in particular, with comedic ferocity.

FILMS INCLUDE: Features only: *Yolanda* (1924); *Sally* (1925); *Clothes Make the Pirate* (1925); *The Lunatic at Large* (1927); *Only Saps Work* (1930); *Finn and*

Hattie (1931); *Her Majesty Love* (1931); *Alice in Wonderland* (1933); *We're Not Dressing* (1934); *The Captain Hates the Sea* (1934); *Princess O'Hara* (1935); *Make a Wish* (1937); *The Girl from Mexico* (1939); *Mexican Spitfire* (1940); *Pop Always Pays* (1940); *Six Lessons from Madame La Zonga* (1941); *Never Give a Sucker an Even Break* (1941); *Mexican Spitfire at Sea* (1942); *Higher and Higher* (1943); *Babes on Swing Street* (1944); *The Invisible Man's Revenge* (1944); *She Gets Her Man* (1945); *Mama Loves Papa* (1945); *What a Blonde!* (1945); *Joe Palooka, Champ* (1946); *The Noose Hangs High* (1948); *Footlight Varieties* (1951).

## Erwin, Stuart (1902—1967)

He was an actor who made an art out of playing middle-class characters who tried to be "normal" despite being woefully timid. Most of the time, Stuart Erwin looked entirely miserable on screen, and that was the source of his humor; he suffered so that we might laugh, knowing that it could just as easily be us instead of him.

Born in Squaw Valley, California, Erwin began acting when he was twenty-two. After four years of stage work, he made his first film, *Mother Knows Best* (1928). He played secondary characters in most of his more than 100 film appearances—but he played them well, gaining a best supporting actor Academy Award nomination for his performance in *Pigskin Parade* (1936). Most active on the big screen during the 1930s and 1940s, he became a TV star in the 1950s, appearing with his wife, actress June Collyer, on a sitcom called "The Trouble with Father." His success with the program was such that it was renamed "The Stu Erwin Show." The comic actor's later film appearances were few, but he could be seen in supporting roles in such films as *Son of Flubber* (1963) and *The Adventures of Merlin Jones* (1964).

FILMS INCLUDE: *Mother Knows Best* (1928); *Dangerous Curves* (1929); *The Exalted Flapper* (1929); *Sweetie* (1929); *This Thing Called Love* (1929); *Love Among the Millionaires* (1930); *Only Saps Work* (1930); *Along Came Youth* (1930); *Happy Days* (1930); *Playboy of Paris* (1930); *Dude Ranch* (1931); *Up Pops the Devil* (1931); *No Limit* (1931); *The Magnificent Lie* (1931); *Two Kinds of Women* (1932); *Strangers in Love* (1932); *The Big Broadcast* (1932); *Make Me a Star* (1932); *International House* (1933); *Going Hollywood* (1933); *The Crime of the Century* (1933); *The Band Plays On* (1934); *Viva Villa!* (1934); *After Office Hours* (1935); *All American Chump* (1936); *Women Are Trouble* (1936); *Pigskin Parade* (1936); *Dance, Charlie, Dance* (1937); *I'll Take Romance* (1937); *Second Honeymoon* (1937); *Small Town Boy* (1937); *Three Blind Mice* (1938); *Passport Husband* (1938); *Hollywood Cavalcade* (1939); *It Could Happen to You* (1939); *Our Town* (1940); *Little Bit of Heaven* (1940); *The Bride Came C.O.D.* (1941); *Adventures of Martin Eden* (1942); *He Hired the Boss* (1943); *The Great Mike* (1944); *Heaven Only Knows* (1947); *Father Is a Bachelor* (1950); *Main Street* (1953); *For the Love of Mike* (1960); *Son of Flubber* (1963); *The Adventures of Merlin Jones* (1964).

## Essanay

Between 1907 and 1917, Essanay was a major film production and distribution company that centered on two genres, Westerns and comedies. Billed as "The House of Comedy Hits," Essanay was a specialist in the SLAPSTICK comedy that was so popular in the silent era.

Created by George K. Spoor and G. M. "Broncho Billy" Anderson, Essanay got its name from the first initial of each of its founders' last names. Anderson shot and starred in one- and two-reel Westerns, while comedy stars such as Augustus Carney, Ben TURPIN, France's Max Linder, and a very young Wallace BEERY (in drag) provided the laughs.

Essanay's most famous comedy star, of course, was Charlie CHAPLIN, who came to work for Essanay after he left Mack SENNETT's Keystone studio in 1915. Essanay paid a fortune for Chaplin's services, and they were well worth the price, but the blow to the company when he left them a year later for Mutual was severely damaging. Essanay closed its doors one year later.

## Ewell, Tom (1909—)

A talented character actor, Tom Ewell played average Joes with a comic edge, often in leading roles, especially during the 1950s. His archetypal starring role is also his most famous, as the smitten, shy, and guilt-ridden married neighbor of Marilyn Monroe in *The Seven Year Itch* (1955).

Born Yewell Tompkins in Owensboro, Kentucky, he made his way up north to the University of Wisconsin where he became enamored with performing. Ewell was twenty when he became a professional actor, but it only took him six years to make it to Broadway, where he continued to work with reasonable steadiness between 1934 and 1949. It was in the latter year that he and Judy HOLLIDAY recreated their stage triumphs on film in *Adam's Rib*.

Ewell had appeared in a couple of films during the early 1940s, but this time he stayed in Hollywood, building a reputation as an amusing leading man in such modest comedies as *Up Front* (1951), *The Lieutenant Wore Skirts* (1956), and *The Girl Can't Help It* (1956). Ewell had the good fortune to work with gifted comedy director Frank TASHLIN on the latter two films.

After a failed attempt at television in 1960 ("The Tom Ewell Show"), the actor's fortunes began to fade. Returning to the stage for the bulk of the 1960s, he didn't reappear on film until the early 1970s, when he made four movies, two of them comedies. His last role of note was a modest part in Rodney DANGERFIELD's *Easy Money* (1983).

FILMS INCLUDE: *They Knew What They Wanted* (1940); *Desert Bandit* (1941); *Adam's Rib* (1949); *A Life of Her Own* (1950); *Mr. Music* (1950); *An American Guerilla in the Philippines* (1950); *Up Front* (1951); *Lost in Alaska* (1952); *Finders Keepers* (1952); *The Seven Year Itch* (1955); *The Lieutenant Wore Skirts* (1956); *The Girl Can't Help It* (1956); *State Fair* (1962); *Tender Is the Night* (1962); *Suppose They Gave a War and Nobody Came?* (1970); *They Only Kill Their Masters* (1972); *To Find a Man/Sex and the Teenager* (1972); *The Great Gatsby* (1974); *Easy Money* (1983).

# F

**Falk, Peter (1927—)** A gifted comic actor, Peter Falk is at his best when playing a blue-collar character who is either dumber than he thinks he is or smarter than everyone else thinks he is. In either case, Falk is always playing the subtext, getting comedy out of the clash of perceptions. He is most famous for his portrayal of TV's rumpled police detective Lt. Columbo, but he has also had a long and distinguished career in the movies dating to the late 1950s. His best comic period came in the latter half of the 1970s, although he has made excellent comedies since then.

Born in New York City, Falk suffered an accident when he was three years old, resulting in the loss of an eye. His famous squint is caused by a glass eye. As a young man, Falk worked in the merchant marine before attending various colleges and universities, eventually earning an MBA in public administration from Syracuse. He was an efficiency expert for Connecticut's Budget Bureau before jumping from amateur community theater to the real thing. He worked on the New York stage, both on and off Broadway, which led to further exposure on television during the 1950s.

Falk's first film role was in *Wind Across the Everglades* (1958). He stuck mostly to dramas in those early years, often playing thugs. No wonder, then, that he was featured in films like *Pretty Boy Floyd* (1960) and *Murder, Inc.* (1961). Falk was so impressive in the latter that he was nominated for a best supporting actor Academy Award. He received another Oscar nomination for best supporting actor the following year for his work in *Pocketful of Miracles* (1961). During the mid-1960s, however, Falk's

comic abilities were finally put on display, most notably in *IT's A MAD MAD MAD MAD WORLD* (1963), *The Great Race* (1965), and *Luv* (1967).

The 1970s was his richest decade, by far. In addition to playing the title role in TV's "Columbo" from 1971 to 1977, he also co-starred in two of John Cassavetes's greatest films, the seriocomic *Husbands* (1970) and the shattering *A Woman Under the Influence* (1974). As for comedy, he chewed up the scenery in the Columbo/Humphrey Bogart spoofs written by Neil SIMON: *Murder by Death* (1976) and *The Cheap Detective* (1978). He was also in top form in *The Brink's Job* (1978) and *The In-Laws* (1979).

Falk slowed down in the 1980s and early 1990s, choosing to play more featured roles rather than leading ones. He had also reached the point in his career where he could play himself, which he did in Wim Wenders's *Wings of Desire* (1987). More recently, he turned out a comically expansive performance in the little-seen gem *Tune in Tomorrow* (1990).

---

**FILMS INCLUDE:** *Wind Across the Everglades* (1958); *The Bloody Brood* (1959); *Murder, Inc.* (1960); *Pretty Boy Floyd* (1960); *The Secret of the Purple Reef* (1960); *A Pocketful of Miracles* (1961); *Pressure Point* (1962); *The Balcony* (1963); *It's a Mad Mad Mad Mad World* (1963); *Italiano Brava Gente* (Italy, 1964); *Robin and the Seven Hoods* (1964); *The Great Race* (1965); *Penelope* (1966); *Luv* (1967); *Anzio* (1968); *Castle Keep* (1969); *Machine Gun McCain* (Italy, 1969); *Husbands* (1970); *A Woman Under the Influence* (1974); *Mikey and Nicky* (1976); *Murder by Death* (1976); *Opening Night* (1977); *The Cheap De-*

tective (1978); *The Brink's Job* (1978); *The In-Laws* (1979); *All the Marbles* (1981); *The Great Muppet Caper* (1981); *Big Trouble* (1985); *Happy New Year* (1987); *Wings of Desire* (1987); *The Princess Bride* (1987); *Vibes* (1988); *Cookie* (1989); *In the Spirit* (1990); *Motion and Emotion* (1990); *Tune in Tomorrow* (1990); *Faraway, So Close* (1993).

**farce**  A term describing a certain kind of comedy, a farce has a wildly improbable plot that is usually built around at least one or more cases of mistaken identity. SLAPSTICK humor, split-second timing, and a furiously fast pace are some of the other elements one is likely to find in a farce.

True farce, as practiced in the theater, involves a virtual whirlwind of activity as characters hurtle through the play, missing, by mere nanoseconds, the connections that would otherwise solve the comic confusions. This kind of comic experience is ultimately impossible on the big screen because editing robs film of the giddy immediacy of seeing real-life actors practicing the highwire act of a genuine farce.

Take, for instance, the 1992 film farce *Noises Off*. For all its huffing and puffing, the movie is a pale imitation of the stage show because its cuts between actions inherently reduce the comic tension of scenes that, on stage, take place in real, uninterrupted time. To make an analogy, magic tricks are far more impressive in person than they are on TV or in the movies because we instinctively know that the media can trick us with special effects, edits, and so on. The same is true of farce.

Nonetheless, a sort of bastardized farce has succeeded in the movies, complete with crazy plot twists, mistaken identities, and a fair share of comically missed moments. The filmmakers who have excelled at farce in Hollywood include Ernst LUBITSCH, who made the BLACK COMEDY farce *To Be or Not to Be* (1942), and Preston STURGES, who made such dizzy farces as *Hail the Conquering Hero* (1944) and *The Miracle of Morgan's Creek* (1944).

**Farrow, Mia (1945— )**  Who would have guessed that delicate, vulnerable, waiflike Mia Farrow had comedic potential? Woody ALLEN did, and he became her longtime lover. All of that ended, however, when they both endured a highly publicized and bitter breakup after making a dozen movies together between 1982 and 1992. Allen not only brought out her ability as a comic actress, he also provided her with the best roles of her career in films such as *Broadway Danny Rose* (1984), *The Purple Rose of Cairo* (1985), and *Alice* (1990). In the last of these, she actually played a female version of Allen, complete with his unique vocal rhythms and mannerisms.

Born Maria de Lourdes Villiers Farrow in Hollywood, California, she was the third of seven children of director John Farrow and actress Maureen O'Sullivan. She had a bout with polio when she was nine years old, and was often ill during her childhood. Her poor health accentuated her frail, small-boned appearance.

Farrow made her screen debut at fifteen in a bit part in a film her father directed, *John Paul Jones* (1959). She wouldn't appear in another feature until 1964 when she had a supporting role in the English production of *Guns at Batasi*. Her real fame during the early 1960s was on the prime-time TV soap opera "Peyton Place," in which she played Allison Mackenzie for two years. This role was followed by a real-life soap opera when in 1966 she married show business icon Frank Sinatra. He was a full three decades older than his bride, and the stormy marriage ended in divorce in 1968.

Composer/conductor Andre Previn was the father of twins she bore in 1970, and they married later that year; it was a union that lasted until 1979.

In the meantime, Farrow's film career rose and dipped like a ship on a stormy sea. She did well early on, starring in such high-profile films as *A Dandy in Aspic* (1968), *Rosemary's Baby* (1968), *Secret Ceremony* (1968), and *John and Mary* (1969), but virtually all of the 1970s was a deep trough, highlighted by the disastrous *The Great Gatsby* (1974), in which she played a bloodless Daisy Buchanan.

Farrow was hardly known for comedy after appearing in such movies as *Avalanche* (1978), *Hurricane* (1979), and *The Last Unicorn* (1982). Her personal and professional life took a turn, however, when she and Woody Allen became lovers in 1982. Critics suddenly began lauding her newfound talent for humor in Allen's films. And even if most of his films in this period weren't as commercially successful as his earlier movies with Diane KEATON, Allen did not make a single film without his new companion. Their last movie together, the brilliant *Husbands and Wives* (1992), is an eerie and shockingly intimate examination of their later life together and presaged the end of their relationship. Even so, she was slated to star in Allen's *Manhattan Murder Mystery* (1993), but their vitriolic breakup caused the filmmaker to cast Diane Keaton in her stead.

FILMS INCLUDE: *John Paul Jones* (1959); *The Age of Curiosity* (short, 1963); *Guns at Batasi* (1964); *A Dandy in Aspic* (1968); *Rosemary's Baby* (1968); *Secret Ceremony* (1978); *John and Mary* (1969); *See No Evil* (1971); *High Heels* (1972); *Docteur Popaul* (1972); *Follow Me!* (1972); *The Great Gatsby* (1974); *The Haunting of Julia* (1976); *Full Circle* (1977); *Death on the Nile* (1978); *Avalanche* (1978); *A Wedding* (1978); *Hurricane* (1979); *The Last Unicorn* (1982); *Sarah* (1982); *A Midsummer Night's Sex Comedy* (1982); *Zelig* (1983); *Broadway Danny Rose* (1984); *Supergirl* (1984); *The Purple Rose of Cairo* (1985); *Hannah and Her Sisters* (1986); *Radio Days* (1987); *September* (1987); *Another Woman* (1988); *Crimes and Misdemeanors* (1989); *New York Stories* (in "Oedipus Wrecks," 1989); *Alice* (1990); *Shadows and Fog* (1992); *Husbands and Wives* (1992).

## Feldman, Marty (1933–1982)

A small, wiry, bug-eyed comedian, Marty Feldman came to international prominence in the mid-1970s as a member of Mel BROOKS's cast in both *Young Frankenstein* (1974) and *Silent Movie* (1976). Between those two films, he also starred in *The Adventure of Sherlock*

*Holmes' Smarter Brother* (1975), which was the directorial debut of Mel Brooks's protégé Gene WILDER. Perhaps inspired by both Brooks and Wilder, Feldman (who had previously written the screenplay for *Every Home Should Have One*, 1970), wrote, directed, and starred in the amusing *The Last Remake of Beau Geste* (1977), which was clearly similar to a Brooks film in its comedic style and content.

Born in London, Feldman was active as a musician and performer of music hall-type humor on the British stage before turning to the BBC, where he established himself as a reputable comedy writer during the late 1950s and early 1960s. Later, he began performing on British TV, eventually having his own show called "Marty." His TV fame led to his making movies in England, beginning with a small role in the controversial *The Bed Sitting Room* (1969).

Following his mid-1970s success, Feldman made the religious spoof *In God We Trust* (1980), once again writing, directing, and starring in his own film. The critical and commercial reaction to the project was disastrous. It might have been the inevitable downswing that comes in every filmmaker's career, but neither Feldman nor his audience would ever know; he shot scenes for two other comedies that were released after his death in 1982.

FILMS INCLUDE: *The Bed Sitting Room* (1969); *Every Home Should Have One* (also sc, 1970); *Young Frankenstein* (1974); *The Adventure of Sherlock Holmes' Smarter Brother* (1975); *Silent Movie* (1976); *The Last Remake of Beau Geste* (also story, sc, d, 1977); *In God We Trust* (also sc, d, 1980); *Yellowbeard* (1983); *Slapstick of Another Kind* (1984).

## Fetchit, Stepin (1892–1985)

Throughout the bulk of his career, Stepin Fetchit was cast in comic relief roles that called for him to play slow-talking, slow-thinking, lazy, constantly frightened characters. He ultimately became a symbol of Hollywood's racist attitudes during the studio era of the 1930s and 1940s. Nonetheless, in an industry that offered little hope to black actors, Fetchit managed to become the first African-American to receive featured billing in otherwise all-white Hollywood movies.

Born Lincoln Theordore Monroe Andrew Perry in Key West, Florida, the actor took his stage name from a horse he once bet on that came in a winner. He had kicked around VAUDEVILLE as a young man and found his way to Hollywood at around the time Al Jolson was singing in blackface in *The Jazz Singer* (1927). Some of Fetchit's early appearances on film can be found in *In Old Kentucky* (1927), *The Ghost Talks* (1929), and an early version of *Show Boat* (1929). Although it is not to his credit, director John Ford used Fetchit fairly often in demeaning roles in such films as *Salute* (1929), *Judge Priest* (1934), and *Steamboat 'Round the Bend* (1935).

If a movie was set in the rural deep south, Fetchit was likely to have a part in it. While he usually played minor roles, he did reach the top of the credit list in an all-black film, starring in *Miracle in Harlem* (1947), a movie so full of racial stereotypes that it will not likely be shown on TV. By then, however, his career was already on the wane.

Fetchit was a popular comic actor, at least among whites. He was so much in demand during the 1930s that, in that decade, alone, he may have earned as much as $2 million. With the advent of socially conscious films in the late 1940s such as *Pinky* (1949), racial attitudes in films were finally beginning to change. Fetchit's persona was so deeply ingrained in the public consciousness that, despite his less outlandish performances in films such as *Bend of the River* (1952) and *The Sun Shines Bright* (1953), he was essentially finished as an actor.

Perhaps in reaction to the image his name conjures up among movie fans, he joined the Muslims in the latter half of the 1960s. Then there was a last hurrah, when he made a cameo appearance in his final film, an all-black comedy movie called *Amazing Grace* (1974).

FILMS INCLUDE: *In Old Kentucky* (1927); *The Tragedy of Youth* (1928); *Hearts in Dixie* (1929); *Show Boat* (1929); *The Ghost Talks* (1929); *Follies of 1929* (1929); *Salute* (1929); *Cameo Kirby* (1930); *Swing High* (1930); *The Prodigal* (1931); *Carloine* (1934); *Judge Priest* (1934); *David Harum* (1934); *The County Chairman* (1935); *One More Spring* (1935); *Charlie Chan in Egypt* (1935); *Steamboat 'Round the Bend* (1935); *Dimples* (1936); *On the Avenue* (1937); *Love Is News* (1937); *Zenobia* (1939); *Miracle in Harlem* (1947); *Bend of the River* (1952); *The Sun Shines Bright* (1953); *Amazing Grace* (1974).

## Fields, W. C. (1879–1946)

With his big, bulbous nose, portly body on skinny legs, and inimitable raspy voice, W. C. Fields played victim to a hostile world. Like all great comedians, he knew that the underdog always gets the laughs. The character that Fields created was hilariously put upon by virtually every institution in American society, from marriage to Hollywood itself. The master of the throwaway line, he made his cinematic reputation through the use of nasty comments made slyly under his breath. This misanthrope of the movies said what a great many people were afraid to say, and audiences loved him for it.

Born Williaml Claude Dunkinfeld, Fields came from a poor family in Philadelphia. His childhood was an unhappy one, and he ran away from home when he was eleven. At fourteen he had perfected enough skill to land a job as a juggler in an amusement park. Starting at the bottom of the VAUDEVILLE circuit, Fields's climb to the top took just six short years; by twenty he was a headliner.

The next twenty years of Fields's life were prosperous and productive. He toured the world with his comic juggling and billiard acts and eventually joined the Ziegfeld Follies. His only film during this period was a silent short made of his vaudeville act, *Pool Sharks* (1915).

Fields starred in the Broadway hit *Poppy* in 1923, and the character he played—a con man with good intentions—established his stage, film, and radio persona for the rest of his career. Paramount bought *Poppy*, rewrote it, and gave Fields a much-reduced

*Famous for hating children, W. C. Fields has his wish in a publicity still, stuffing his movie nemesis, Baby LeRoy, into a garbage can.*     PHOTO COURTESY OF THE SIEGEL COLLECTION.

part in the newly named *Sally of the Sawdust* (1925), which incidentally was directed by the master, D. W. Griffith. Fields, nonetheless, was a hit in the movie, finding his film career launched at a mature forty-six.

In most of his subsequent silent films, the critics lauded him, and the public collectively shrugged its

shoulders. Fields was not much of a movie star yet. The tide began to turn in his favor, though, when he made his first sound shorts, the most successful of which were made for Mack SENNETT in 1932 and 1933: *The Dentist, The Fatal Glass of Beer, The Pharmacist,* and *The Barber Shop.*

At Paramount, Fields appeared in a succession of films that were moderately successful. Although they used his talents and he often had top billing, movies such as *Million Dollar Legs* (1932) and *International House* (1933) weren't built around his unique comic personality.

In any event, his cult status was growing among fans, and that was helped along when Fields starred in his most suitable vehicle to date, *It's a Gift* (1934). Finally, Fields had Baby Leroy and a wife to chide; the result was a minor masterpiece. His reputation grew still further thanks to his affecting, restrained performance as Mr. Micawber in MGM's production of *David Copperfield* (1935).

There were only a few more films before illness kept him idle for nearly two years. The hard-drinking screen comic made one of his funniest films, *The Man on the Flying Trapeze* (1935), and then *Poppy* (1936), a version closer to the original play that he had starred in more than a decade earlier.

After leaving Paramount in 1938, Fields entered into his short but most creative period with Universal. Studio heads gave him virtual carte blanche to make any movie he wanted, just so long as it could be done inexpensively. With the freedom to create his own comedies, Fields made four films that are considered among his best. Written under pen names such as Mahatma Kane Jeeves and Otis J. Criblecoblis, Fields penned *You Can't Cheat an Honest Man* (1939), *My Little Chickadee* (1940) with Mae WEST, *The Bank Dick* (1940), and *Never Give a Sucker an Even Break* (1941). Legend has it that the last of these scripts was written on the back of an envelope by Fields while he sat on a toilet.

*Never Give a Sucker an Even Break* was Fields's most outlandish movie. Its threadbare plot concerned the making of a movie by Fields, playing himself, and was surrealism at its most comicly potent, taking a slap at Hollywood, filmmaking, and all sorts of movie clichés. While sometimes more astonishing than funny, the film acutely captures Fields's sour outlook and expresses it in wildly imaginative style.

It was the last great film of his career. He appeared in a few more minor movies in the early to mid-1940s, but his drinking and failing health combined to keep him from being active. He died on Christmas Day in 1946. When asked what he wanted written on his tombstone, Fields reportedly replied, "On the whole, I'd rather be in Philadelphia." *W. C. Fields and Me* (1976), which stars Rod Steiger, offers a fair account of the famous comedian.

FILMS: As actor for all films: *Pool Sharks* (1915); *Janice Meredith* (1924); *Sally of the Sawdust* (1925); *That Royle Girl* (1925); *It's the Old Army Game* (1926); *So's Your Old Man* (1926); *The Potters* (1927); *Running Wild* (1927); *Two Flaming Youths* (1927); *Fools for Luck* (1928); *Tillie's Punctured Romance* (1928); *The Golf Specialist* (story, 1930); *Her Majesty, Love* (1931); *If I Had a Million* (1932); *Million Dollar Legs* (1932); *The Dentist* (story, 1932); *The Barber Shop* (story, 1933); *The Fatal Glass of Beer* (story, 1933); *The Pharmacist* (story, 1933); *Alice in Wonderland* (1933); *Hip Action* (1933); *International House* (1933); *Tillie and Gus* (1933); *It's a Gift* (story, 1934); *Mrs. Wiggs of the Cabbage Patch* (1934); *The Old-Fashioned Way* (story, 1934); *Six of a Kind* (1934); *You're Telling Me* (1934); *David Copperfield* (1935); *Man on the Flying Trapeze* (story, 1935); *Mississippi* (1935); *Poppy* (1936); *The Big Broadcast of 1938* (1938); *You Can't Cheat an Honest Man* (story, 1939); *The Bank Dick* (sc, 1940); *My Little Chickadee* (sc, 1940); *Never Give a Sucker an Even Break* (story, 1941); *Tales of Manhattan* (1942); *Follow the Boys* (1944); *Song of the Open Road* (1944); *Sensations of 1945* (1945).

## Finlayson, James (1887–1953)  A scrawny, bantam-weight comedian, James Finlayson often

got his laughs by acting the bully. With a bald head, a big mustache, and a comically exaggerated "evil eye" squint, he was the perfect nemesis for LAUREL AND HARDY, with whom he is most closely associated. He was their comic foil in many of their most memorable short subjects, including the classic *Big Business* (1929). The better part of his career during the sound era was spent in Laurel and Hardy features, most notably *Pardon Us* (1931), *Way Out West* (1937), and *A Chump at Oxford* (1940).

Born in Falkirk, Scotland, Finlayson's background was different from most of the knockabout comedians who drifted into show business in the early part of the twentieth century—he wasn't poor. He came from a wealthy family, which offered him a college education; he skipped it for the lure of the stage. After working in the theater in Scotland, he toured with a show in the United States that passed through Los Angeles. The show moved on, but he stayed; the year was 1916.

Finlayson worked for several comedy producers during the late 1910s and early 1920s, among them Mack SENNETT, but his career found solid footing when he became a member of Hal ROACH's comedy troupe in 1923. It was there that he eventually began working with Laurel and Hardy.

One of the great practitioners of the DOUBLE TAKE, Finlayson perfected a variation unique unto himself, dubbed "The Double Take and Fade Away," in which, after the second shocked look, he turns his gaze away, ever so slowly, in comic disbelief.

FILMS INCLUDE: *Married Life* (1920); *Home Talent* (1921); *A Small Town Idol* (1921); *Homemade Movies* (1922); *The Crossroads of New York* (1922); *Welcome Home* (1925); *Do Detectives Think?* (1927); *Flying Elephants* (1927); *The Second Hundred Years* (1927); *Sugar Daddies* (1927); *Show Girl* (1928); *Lady Be Good* (1928); *Ladies' Night in a Turkish Bath* (1928); *Big Business* (1929); *Men o' War* (1929); *Wall Street* (1929); *Two Weeks Off* (1929); *Liberty* (1929); *Chickens Come Home* (1930); *The Dawn Patrol* (1930); *Pardon Us* (1931); *Our Wife* (1931); *The Chimp* (1932); *Pack Up Your Troubles* (1932); *The Devil's*

*Brother* (1933); *Bonnie Scotland* (1935); *Our Relations* (1936); *Way Out West* (1937); *Blockheads* (1938); *Hollywood Cavalcade* (1939); *The Great Victor Herbert* (1939); *The Flying Deuces* (1939); *A Chump at Oxford* (1940); *Saps at Sea* (1940); *To Be or Not to Be* (1942); *The Perils of Pauline* (1947); *Royal Wedding* (1951).

---

## Ford, Paul (1901–1976)

Sputtering and stammering his way through a thirty-year movie career, jowly Paul Ford got laughs by playing incompetent authority figures. While his name wasn't always known to the masses who saw him on TV and in the movies, his face—as well as his voice—was instantly recognized by millions.

Born Paul Ford Weaver in Baltimore, Maryland, he came to show business late in life, more out of necessity than by design. He was forty, out of work, and the father of five when he made ends meet by working in a puppet show sponsored by the government's Works Progress Administration (WPA) toward the end of the Great Depression. His experience as a performer, coupled with his easy manner, led first to work on the radio and then on the legitimate stage.

From Broadway, Ford moved to Hollywood in 1945, making his movie debut in the powerful documentary-style drama *The House on 92nd Street*. He continued appearing in major serious films, most notably *All the King's Men* (1949), until he went back to Broadway, scoring a hit as a buffoonish colonel in *The Teahouse of the August Moon*. He recreated his role in the 1956 film version of the play, forever typecasting himself. He spent much of the rest of his life, both on television ("Sergeant Bilko," "The Phil Silvers Show," etc.) and film (*The Russians Are Coming! The Russians Are Coming!*, *The Spy with the Cold Nose*, etc.), playing the same kind of role with considerable comic gusto.

---

**FILMS INCLUDE:** *The House on 92nd Street* (1945); *The Naked City* (1948); *All the King's Men* (1949); *Perfect Strangers* (1950); *The Teahouse of the August Moon* (1956); *The Matchmaker* (1958); *Advise and Consent* (1962); *The Music Man* (1962); *It's a Mad Mad Mad Mad World* (1963); *Never Too Late* (1965); *A Big Hand for a Little Lady* (1966); *The Russians Are Coming! The Russians Are Coming!* (1966); *The Spy with a Cold Nose* (1966); *The Comedians* (1967); *Journey Back to Oz* (voice only, 1974).

---

## Fox, Michael J. (1961–)

Cute and boyish, with a voice that's somewhere between husky and raspy, Michael J. Fox has been among the most commercially successful big-screen comedians of the late 1980s and early 1990s. His three *Back to theFuture* films all made money, as did all of his other

*Michael J. Fox, who made the transition from TV star to movie star with the hugely popular* Back to the Future *(1985) and its two sequels, continues to show his dramatic and comedic range. He is seen here in a publicity still from* The Hard Way *(1991).*

comedies between 1985 and 1991. He has been less successful at the box office in dramas, but he has, nonetheless, proven himself a capable all-around actor.

Born in Edmonton, Alberta, Canada, Fox started acting professionally at fifteen in a Canadian TV series called "Leo and Me." He then left Canada for Los Angeles. Although he became famous for his role of Alex P. Keaton, the comically insufferable, wisecracking future yuppie in the TV sitcom "Family Ties," he had actually started in yet another series, "Palmerstown, USA." Luckily for him, the series folded quickly, and he was free to star in "Family Ties," which he did for seven full seasons.

In the midst of his TV success, movie stardom beckoned. *Back to the Future* (1985), which he shot while on hiatus from the show, became an unexpected monster hit. It wasn't his first film—*Midnight Madness* (1980) has that distinction—but it was certainly his biggest. Two sequels followed, as did the hit comedies *The Secret of My Success* (1987) and *Doc Hollywood* (1991). *The Hard Way* (1991), however, did not perform well at the box office.

Meanwhile, Fox had been impressive in the gritty, Vietnam drama *Casualties of War* (1989), but his fans clearly didn't want to see him in it, just as they had avoided him in the serious *Bright Lights, Big City* (1988).

After marrying actress Tracy Pollan, fathering a baby, and taking two years off, Fox returned with the charming *Life with Mikey* (1993) and *For Love or Money* (1993); this time audiences deserted him even though the films were comedies.

**FILMS INCLUDE:** *Midnight Madness* (1980); *Class of 1984* (1982); *Back to the Future* (1985); *Teen Wolf* (1985); *Dear America* (1987); *Light of Day* (1987); *The Secret of My Success* (1987); *Bright Lights, Big City* (1988); *Back to the Future II* (1989); *Casualties of War* (1989); *Back to the Future III* (1990); *The Hard Way* (1991); *Doc Hollywood* (1991); *Life with Mikey* (1993); *For Love or Money* (1993); *Greedy* (1994).

**Freleng, Friz** *See* WARNER BROS. CARTOONS

# G

**Garner, James (1928—)** Tall and handsome, James Garner has built a long career out of juxtaposing his heroic stature with an irresolute disposition. He connects with the comic side of his audience by desperately trying to avoid confrontations because he's all clever talk and big bluff. He knows it, we know it, only his adversaries are unaware that he's a cynical, cleverly manipulative double-talker. Of course, he hasn't always played such characters, but he's played this combination of Charlton Heston and Bob HOPE to perfection with considerable regularity, both on TV and in the movies, virtually from the beginning of his stardom in the 1950s.

Born James Scott Baumgarner in Norman, Oklahoma, he dropped out of high school at sixteen and went to sea as a young crewman in the merchant marine. Garner gave up sailing for soldiering during the Korean War, taking home a war wound and a Purple Heart to match. The more worldly young man took a stab at college, going to the University of Oklahoma, but soon decided to try his luck in New York. He supported himself with various jobs, including working as a model (swim trunks were a speciality).

Garner was introduced to the possibility of becoming an actor when a producer, who knew him as a child, offered him a bit role in *The Caine Mutiny Court Martial*, a 1954 stage show that proved a hit on Broadway before becoming a film (Garner was not in the movie). Bitten by the acting bug, he studied his craft at the Berghof School and soon picked up guest spots on a variety of TV shows, as well as small roles in movies. The big break came in 1957 when Garner was cast as Brett Maverick in the prime-time TV Western series "Maverick." The show not only made him a star, it also exhibited Garner's talent for light comedy and the self-aware, comic cynicism that would later mark his movie star persona.

Garner was one of the few TV performers of the 1950s to manage a transition to Hollywood movie stardom. In the decades that have followed, he has moved with surprising ease between TV (he was also in the TV shows "Nichols" and "The Rockford Files") and films.

Garner has displayed a penchant for sly humor in dramas and wit and whimsy in his comedies. He could be a light ROMANTIC COMEDY leading man in films like *Boys' Night Out* (1962) and *The Americanization of Emily* (1964) as well as tongue-in-cheek funny in the comedy *Support Your Local Sheriff* (1969). Nor were his talents unappreciated by his peers. He received a surprise best actor Academy Award nomination for his performance as a comic romantic lead in *Murphy's Romance* (1985).

Garner has taken to starring in TV movies during the 1980s and early 1990s, showing up rarely on movie screens in recent years.

**FILMS INCLUDE:** *The Girl He Left Behind* (1956); *Toward the Unknown* (1956); *Sayonara* (1957); *Shootout at Medicine Bend* (1957); *Darby's Rangers* (1958); *Up Periscope* (1959); *Cash McCall* (1959); *The Children's Hour* (1961); *Boys' Night Out* (1962); *The Great Escape* (1963); *The Thrill of It All* (1963); *Move Over, Darling* (1963); *The Wheeler Dealers* (1963); *The Americanization of Emily* (1964); *36 Hours* (1964); *The Art of Love* (1965); *Mister Buddwing* (1965); *Grand Prix* (1966); *Duel at Diablo* (1966); *A Man*

*Could Get Killed* (1966); *Hour of the Gun* (1967); *How Sweet It Is* (1968); *The Pink Jungle* (1968); *Marlowe* (1969); *Support Your Local Sheriff* (1969); *A Man Called Sledge* (1970); *Skin Game* (1971); *Support Your Local Gunfighter* (1971); *They Only Kill Their Masters* (1972); *One Little Indian* (1973); *The Castaway Cowboy* (1974); *Health* (1979); *The Fan* (1981); *Victor/Victoria* (1982); *Tank* (1984); *Murphy's Romance* (1985); *Sunset* (1988); *The Distinguished Gentleman* (1992); *Fire in the Sky* (1993).

## Gilbert, Billy (1894—1971)

In his more than forty years in the movies, Billy Gilbert was the consummate comic relief, doing yeoman work in various dramas and light comedies as various huffy waiters, bemused bartenders, and the like. He also played the foil to numerous comedians, most notably LAUREL AND HARDY, in shorts and feature-length films. The hulking Gilbert, who might have otherwise easily played villains (given his size), had a small, round head and an unusual speaking voice that added to his comic appeal.

Born in Louisville, Kentucky, to professional opera singer parents, Gilbert went into show business at age twelve. Like Edgar KENNEDY, who developed his "slow burn" shtick, Gilbert perfected a comic sneezing routine that served him well in countless films and that led to his perfect (voice/sneeze) casting as Sneezy in Walt Disney's first animated feature, *Snow White and the Seven Dwarfs* (1937). He can be seen (as well as heard) to best effect in such films as the famous Laurel and Hardy short *The Music Box* (1932), the W. C. FIELDS/Jack OAKIE vehicle *Million Dollar Legs* (1932), Laurel and Hardy's *Blockheads* (1938), the famous comic Western *Destry Rides Again* (1939), as "Herring" (alias Hermann Goering) in Charlie CHAPLIN's masterpiece *The Great Dictator* (1940), and in support of OLSEN AND JOHNSON in their merry romp *Crazy House* (1945). In all, Gilbert appeared in more than two hundred features and comedy shorts.

FILMS INCLUDE: *Dynamite Allen* (1921); *Noisy Neighbors* (1929); *Their First Mistake* (short, 1932); *The Music Box* (short, 1932); *Million Dollar Legs* (1932); *Pack Up Your Troubles* (1932); *Sutter's Gold* (1936); *The Outcasts of Poker Flat* (1937); *Broadway Melody of 1938* (1937); *Rosalie* (1937); *The Toast of New York* (1937); *100 Men and a Girl* (1937); *On the Avenue* (1937); *Snow White and the Seven Dwarfs* (voice—Sneezy, 1937); *Blockheads* (1938); *Joy of Living* (1938); *My Lucky Star* (1938); *Happy Landing* (1938); *Destry Rides Again* (1939); *His Girl Friday* (1940); *The Great Dictator* (1940); *No, No Nanette* (1940); *Model Wife* (1941); *One Night in Lisbon* (1941); *Weekend in Havana* (1941); *Arabian Nights* (1942); *New Wine* (1942); *Crazy House* (1945); *Anchors Aweigh* (1945); *The Kissing Bandit* (1948); *Down Among the Sheltering Palms* (1953); *Five Weeks in a Balloon* (1962).

## Gleason, Jackie (1916—1987)

"The Great One" on television, Jackie Gleason was a fat and sometimes overbearing superstar comedian who commanded a large and loyal following. It was a different story, however, in the movies, where Gleason also worked. Although large in physical stature, he never loomed quite so large as a major movie comic. He had a relative handful of starring roles in comedies, ultimately getting his most successful big screen roles near the end of his career.

Born Herbert John Gleason in Brooklyn, New York, he dropped out of school to perform on stage when he was fifteen. He knocked around the fringes of show business, taking jobs in carnivals and saloons until he built a modest reputation in what was left of VAUDEVILLE during the latter half of the 1930s. He broke into Hollywood in 1941 as a low-level character actor, often playing sheepish oafs, dumb gang members, and the like in films such as *Navy Blues* (1941) and the Bogart vehicle *All Through the Night* (1942). He did not distinguish himself and was (temporarily) out of the movies by the end of 1942.

Gleason returned to New York and worked on the stage, including Broadway shows, but his was hardly a household name. A new medium, television, became his saving grace. He starred in TV's original version of "The Life of Riley," but was not right for the role. William Bendix took it over and turned it into a hit series. Gleason had a second chance, however, with another sitcom, the freshly original "The Honeymooners," and this time everything fell into place. The show was a major success, running from 1949 to 1954. He continued to triumph on TV in later years with "The Jackie Gleason Show," as well as with a number of specials. It was during these years of success that he also built a modest reputation as a composer, with several orchestral albums to his credit.

At the height of his TV fame in the 1950s and 1960s, he made relatively few movies. His most notable performance during this era was in *The Hustler* (1961), in which he played pool shark Minnesota Fats. It was a role close to his heart because Gleason was, in his own right, an expert pool player. He also provided the story and starred in the sentimental *Gigot* (1962) and showed his dramatic mettle alongside Steve McQueen in *Soldier in the Rain* (1963). However, comedy was still Gleason's mainstay, and he starred in films such as *Papa's Delicate Condition* (1963), *How to Commit Marriage* (1969), and the film adaptation of Woody ALLEN's play *Don't Drink the Water* (1969), none of which were big box office hits.

Never known for his work ethic, Gleason coasted throughout much of the 1970s, only to reemerge on the big screen in strong performances as Burt Reynolds's nemesis in the hit *Smokey and the Bandit* movies (1977 and 1980). He was so integral to the success of those films that he even starred in the third installment (1983) without Reynolds, but it bombed. His last film, however, is regarded by many to be his best seriocomic work in the movies; he played Tom HANKS's difficult, demanding father in *Nothing in Common* (1986). It was a highly regarded and classy way to go out.

FILMS: *Navy Blues* (1941); *All Through the Night* (1942); *Escape from Crime* (1942); *Larceny, Inc.* (1942); *Springtime in the Rockies* (1942); *Orchestra Wives* (1942); *Lady Gangster* (1942); *Tramp, Tramp, Tramp* (1942); *The Desert Hawk* (1950); *The Hustler* (1961); *Gigot* (also story, music, 1962); *Requiem for a Heavyweight* (1962); *Soldier in the Rain* (1963); *Papa's Delicate Condition* (1963); *Skidoo* (1968); *Don't Drink the Water* (1969); *How to Commit Marriage* (1969); *How Do I Love Thee?* (1970); *Mr. Billion* (1977); *Smokey and the Bandit* (1977); *Smokey and the Bandit II* (1980); *The Toy* (1982); *The Sting II* (1982); *Smokey and the Bandit III* (1983); *Nothing in Common* (1986).

**Goldberg, Whoopi (1949—)** An actress/comedian, Whoopi Goldberg has coupled her cool, sardonic verbal humor with an enormously expressive face to create in her characters a sort of comic confusion. That mix of hot emotions and cool language can be seen in such films as *Ghost* (1990), *Sister Act* (1992), and *Made in America* (1993), which also happen to be her most successful comedies.

Born Karen Johnson in New York City, she began performing when she was eight. In her mid-twenties, Goldberg moved to San Diego, where she appeared in the San Diego Repertory Theatre's productions of Bertold Brecht's *Mother Courage* and Marsha Norman's *Getting Out*. At the same time, she was also a member of a local improvisational group called Spontaneous Combustion.

Her first leap forward came when she created *The Spook Show*, a stage vehicle that toured the United States and Europe. In 1983, director Mike NICHOLS saw the show and "discovered" her. He produced her new one-woman show on Broadway, which was a critical and commercial hit. The HBO version of her show was seen by Steven Spielberg, who was so impressed he hired her to star in his dramatic rendering of Alice Walker's *The Color Purple* (1985), in which Goldberg made her motion picture debut—

and for which she was nominated for a best supporting actress Academy Award.

Goldberg returned to her comedy roots in her second film, the disappointing *Jumpin' Jack Flash* (1986). For the most part, she kept trying to score in comedies throughout the rest of the decade, but whether she went for laughs or tears, neither critics nor the public seemed interested. Her once bright film career seemed seriously in jeopardy until 1990, when she played a comic con artist turned spirit channeler in *Ghost*. She won a best supporting actress Oscar for her performance in the hit film, and her career was back on track. In that same year, she was highly praised for her work in the drama *The Long Walk Home* (1990). Goldberg then went on to a modest supporting role in *Soapdish* (1991), was miscast in *Sarafina!* (1992), and still had yet to break through as a comedy star who could carry her own vehicles.

Then came *Sister Act* (1992), a summer comedy that simply would not quit at the box office. Her next major release, *Made in America* (1993), was at best a mediocre film. She subsequently capitalized on the success of *Sister Act* with *Sister Act II: Back in the Habit* (1993).

---

**FILMS:** *The Color Purple* (1985); *Jumpin' Jack Flash* (1986); *Burglar* (1987); *Fatal Beauty* (1987); *Clara's Heart* (1988); *The Telephone* (1988); *Homer and Eddie* (1989); *Beverly Hills Brats* (1989); *Ghost* (1990); *The Long Walk Home* (1990); *Soapdish* (1991); *Wisecracks* (doc, 1991); *The Player* (cameo, 1992); *Sarafina!* (1992); *Sister Act* (1992); *Naked in New York* (1993); *National Lampoon's Loaded Weapon I* (cameo, 1993); *Made in America* (1993); *Sister Act II: Back in the Habit* (1993).

---

## Gordon, Ruth (1896–1985)

An actress, screenwriter, and playwright, Ruth Gordon enjoyed a long and varied career. She is best remembered for her sophisticated comedy screenplays, in collaboration with her second husband, Garson Ka-

nin, whom she married in 1942, and her delightfully droll and decidedly unsophisticated comic characterizations as an elderly actress.

Born Ruth Gordon Jones, she tried to break into the legitimate theater during the 1910s. She first appeared in the movies with small roles in films, such as an early and otherwise forgotten version of *Camille* (1916). Gordon had success on the stage in the ensuing decades and was finally lured back to Hollywood in the early 1940s to play character parts in such films as *Abe Lincoln in Illinois* (1940), well cast as Mary Todd Lincoln, *Dr. Erlich's Magic Bullet* (1940), and *Edge of Darkness* (1943).

When a play she had written, *Over 21*, was turned into a movie in 1945, she decided to write directly for the screen, penning with Garson Kanin clever hits such as *Adam's Rib* (1949) and *Pat and Mike* (1952) for director George Cukor and stars Katharine Hepburn and Spencer Tracy. Both were nominated for best screenplay Oscars. She received a third nomination in that category for her drama *A Double Life* (1947).

Gordon disappeared from the screen as both an actress and a writer for more than a decade before returning for a last unlikely stab at stardom in 1965. This final run began with her Oscar-nominated work in *Inside Daisy Clover* (for best supporting actress). The following year she had a modest part in *Lord Love a Duck* (1966), but it wasn't until her startling Oscar-winning best supporting actress performance in *Rosemary's Baby* (1968) that critics and audiences began to take notice.

However, the best was yet to come. Gordon's baroque characters in the cult BLACK COMEDY hits *Where's Poppa?* (1970) and *HAROLD AND MAUDE* (1972) made her a favorite among young filmgoers. Her eccentric, liberated old lady in the latter film (she was the love interest for the young Bud CORT) was a genuinely original invention.

After playing Maude, however, there were few good roles written for actresses her age. Nonetheless, she had memorable turns in Clint Eastwood's two broad comedies, *Every Which Way but Loose* (1978) and *Any Which Way You Can* (1980). She continued appearing in films during the early 1980s, such as the hit *My Bodyguard* (1980) and the flop *Jimmy the Kid* (1982).

---

**FILMS:** *The Whirl of Life* (a, 1915); *Camille* (a, 1916); *Abe Lincoln in Illinois* (a, 1940); *Dr. Ehrlich's Magic Bullet* (a, 1940); *Two-Faced Woman* (a, 1941); *Action in the North Atlantic* (a, 1943); *Edge of Darkness* (a, 1943); *Over 21* (based on her play, 1945); *A Double Life* (sc, 1947); *Adam's Rib* (sc, 1949); *The Marrying Kind* (story, sc, 1952); *Pat and Mike* (sc, 1952); *The Actress* (sc, based on her play, *Years Ago*, (1953); *Inside Daisy Clover* (a, 1965); *Lord Love a Duck* (a, 1966); *Rosie* (adapted from her play, *A Very Rich Woman*, 1967); *Rosemary's Baby* (a, 1968); *Whatever Happened to Aunt Alice?* (a, 1969); *Where's Poppa?* (a, 1970); *Harold and Maude* (a, 1972); *The Big Bus* (a, 1976); *Every Which Way but Loose* (a, 1978); *Boardwalk* (a, 1979); *Any Which Way You Can* (a, 1980); *My Bodyguard* (a, 1980); *Jimmy the Kid* (a, 1982); *Delta Pi* (a, 1985); *Maxie* (a, 1985); *Voyage of the Rock Aliens* (a, 1985).

---

# Gould, Elliott (1938– )

A tall, shaggy-haired actor, Elliott Gould became a comedic star who personified an antiestablishment persona during the late 1960s and early 1970s. By the latter half of the 1970s, however, he had become so overexposed that his career had begun to nosedive. He has since become a character actor of some skill and note, but there was a time when he was the hottest, quirkiest, and most irreverent comic leading man in the movies.

Born Elliott Goldstein in Brooklyn, New York, his passion for performing was aided by his stage-struck mother. Committed to performing at the age of eight, he found occasional roles as cute moppets on TV and worked as a child model. Trained in every aspect of the show business arts, he broke into the legitimate stage as a dancer, eventually winning a major role in the well-received musical *I Can Get It for You Wholesale* in 1962. More noteworthy than his performance was the fact that he met and later married another player in the show, Barbra Streisand. Her performance in *Wholesale* catapulted her into the career-making role of Fanny BRICE in the stage musical *Funny Girl*, zooming past her new husband, who eventually took to managing her career instead of pursuing his own.

That situation changed in the latter half of the 1960s when their relationship unraveled. He distinguished himself in a supporting role in the period film comedy *The Night They Raided Minsky's* (1968) and followed that with several cutting-edge comedies that turned him, for a short while, into as big a star as his ex-wife. He appeared in Paul MAZURSKY's *Bob & Carol & Ted & Alice* (1969), Robert Altman's *M*A*S*H* (1970), and the protest movie *Getting Straight* (1970). There were hits and misses during the next few years, but it was a testament to the esteem in which he was held that Ingmar Bergman requested him for *The Touch* (1971); Gould was the first non-Swede to star in one of the great director's films.

Gould showed off his dancing skills in *Harry and Walter Go to New York* (1976), an amusing song and dance comedy, but by this time his career was already beginning its slide. A sad-faced actor, he has performed less often in comedies during the last fifteen years, although he sometimes shows that old comedic flair in films like *The Muppets Take Manhattan* (1984) and *The Lemon Sisters* (1989). He was quite wonderful, if pathetic, in a small dramatic role in *Bugsy* (1991).

---

**FILMS INCLUDE:** *Quick, Let's Get Married* (1964); *The Night They Raided Minsky's* (1968); *Bob & Carol & Ted & Alice* (1969); *M*A*S*H* (1970); *I Love My Wife* (1970); *Move* (1970); *Getting Straight* (1970); *The Touch* (1971); *Little Murders* (1971); *The Long Goodbye* (1973); *S*P*Y*S* (1974); *Busting* (1974); *California Split* (1974); *Who?* (1975); *Whiffs* (1975); *Nashville* (cameo, 1975); *I Will, I Will, for Now* (1976); *Mean Johnny Barrows* (1976); *Harry and Walter Go to New York* (1976); *A Bridge Too Far* (1977); *Matilda* (1978); *Capricorn One* (1978); *The Silent Partner*

(1978); *The Lady Vanishes* (1979); *Escape to Athena* (1979); *The Muppet Movie* (1979); *Falling in Love Again* (1980); *The Last Flight of Noah's Ark* (1980); *Dirty Tricks* (1981); *The Devil and Max Devlin* (1981); *Over the Brooklyn Bridge* (1983); *The Muppets Take Manhattan* (1984); *The Naked Face* (1985); *Inside Out* (1986); *Vanishing Act* (1987); *Dangerous Love* (1988); *The Telephone* (1988); *The Lemon Sisters* (1989); *Night Visitor* (1989); *Dead Men Don't Die* (1990); *Bugsy* (1991).

***The Graduate***   This landmark 1967 film set box office records, made a directorial star out of Mike NICHOLS, reestablished Anne Bancroft as a class actress, brought Katherine Ross to the attention of the public, and made Dustin Hoffman one of the biggest stars of the time. But most amazing of all, no one involved in the project, least of all the director, realized they were making a blockbuster hit that would speak for a generation.

"We had two previews of *The Graduate*," Mike Nichols told Joseph Gelmis in an interview, "and that first reaction of the audience astonished us all. I hadn't thought of it as either that funny or that rousing. I was very unnerved when they began to make noises and cheer at the end."

*The Graduate* is a seriocomic movie about middle-class alienated youth. Benjamin Braddock (Hoffman) has just graduated from college and is trying to decide what to do with his life. In the meantime, he is seduced by the wife of a family friend, Mrs. Robinson (Bancroft), only to fall in love with his lover's daughter, Elaine (Ross). In the movie's dramatic conclusion, Benjamin ignores society's expectations and pursues Elaine right up to (and just past the end of) her wedding ceremony to another man. Although Benjamin and Elaine are together at the end of the movie, Nichols clearly indicates that the two characters have no idea what they're going to do next.

Nichols was supposed to make his directorial debut with *The Graduate*, but he delayed production when he had the opportunity to direct *Who's Afraid of Virginia Woolf?* (1966). He used the extra time to rework the script with Buck HENRY, who added (among others) the famous scene when Benjamin is told in one word where his future lies: "Plastics."

The movie was not only a commercial success, earning in excess of $50 million, it was also a critical hit, earning Mike Nichols a best director Oscar. In addition, *The Graduate* was nominated for best picture. Based on the novel of the same name by Charles Webb, the film was produced by Joseph E. Levine and photographed by Robert Surtees.

**Grant, Cary (1904—1986)**   Without a doubt, Cary Grant was Hollywood's greatest light comedian. Put him in a ROMANTIC COMEDY with a half-decent script, and he'd make his dialogue sound as if it were written by a two-time Oscar winner. Blessed with an exquisitely charming voice, dashing good looks, and a rakish style, Grant was the ultimate in sophistication. Wisely, however, he always undercut his image with a comic irreverence that kept him from seeming either wimpy or snobbish. In addition to romantic comedy, Grant was the acknowledged master of SCREWBALL COMEDY, starring in the vast majority of Hollywood's best examples of the genre.

Born Archibald Leach in Bristol, England, the future actor lived in extreme poverty, scraping for a living like a character out of a Dickens novel. It has often been said that Archie Leach literally turned himself into the very image of the urbane Cary Grant as a means of obliterating any memory of his past.

While a teenager, Grant joined an acrobatic act and came to America with it in 1920. He quit the acrobats in the United States, hitting the VAUDEVILLE circuit with a mind-reading routine. He flopped and went back to England in 1923, eventually breaking into the legitimate theater in MUSICAL COMEDIES. Spotted on the London stage, he was hired for an Oscar Hammerstein musical on Broadway called *Golden Dawn*.

His stage career was soon well established. With

the advent of sound motion pictures, Grant (like so many other stage-trained actors) saw an opportunity to make big money. He went to Hollywood, managing no better than a job at Paramount feeding lines to an actress who was being screen-tested. The actress remains unknown, but the line-feeder got discovered. Grant had been right: There was big money to be made in Hollywood. His starting salary was $450 per week.

Grant's first film was a musical, *This Is the Night* (1932), in which he had a modest role. He had supporting parts in a string of films, including playing the heavy who nearly destroys Marlene Dietrich in *Blonde Venus* (1932) and Mae WEST's foil in *She Done Him Wrong* (1933) and *I'm No Angel* (1933). It was from Mae West that he said he learned how to play comedy.

In 1936 Grant suddenly began to shine at the box office. As is often the case, it was a combination of having the right script, the right chemistry between co-stars, and the right director that made an actor who had appeared in twenty films suddenly catch on with the public. The movie was the comedy/drama *Sylvia Scarlett*, his co-star was Katharine Hepburn, and the director was George CUKOR.

Grant's contract was finished with Paramount before *Sylvia Scarlett* was released. He was a free agent when he suddenly became a major star. In a unique arrangement, Grant signed a nonexclusive contract with *two* studios, Columbia and RKO, and even managed to win script approval. He was now master of his own fate, and very few stars have ever chosen their films more wisely than Cary Grant.

Grant worked with Hollywood's most inspired directors. As a consequence, the actor starred in a substantial number of top-notch comedies, most notably Howard HAWKS's wonderful screwball comedies *Bringing Up Baby* (1938), *His Girl Friday* (1940), *I Was a Male War Bride* (1949), and *Monkey Business* (1952).

Grant worked with other great directors as well, most of whom took advantage of the actor's comic gifts. George Cukor knew a good combination when he saw one and teamed Grant again with

Katharine Hepburn in *Holiday* (1938) and *The Philadelphia Story* (1940). The great comedy director Leo MCCAREY used him to perfection in *The Awful Truth* (1937). George Stevens used both Grant's heroic dash and his impeccable timing for the rousing comic adventure film *Gunga Din* (1939). And how fondly would we remember Frank CAPRA's BLACK COMEDY *Arsenic and Old Lace* (1944) if not for Grant?

When it came to drama, though, Grant was at his best in the films of Alfred Hitchcock, appearing in some of the master's best films, including *Suspicion* (1941), *Notorious* (1946), *To Catch a Thief* (1955), and *North by Northwest* (1959). Of course, Hitchcock had a dark sense of humor, himself, and Grant was a perfect hero for Hitchcock for that very reason.

The number of quality films that Grant starred in is staggering, and he was rarely long between hit movies. From the effervescent *Topper* (1937) to the social comedy *Mr. Blandings Builds His Dream House* (1948) to the generational sex comedy *The Bachelor and the Bobby-Soxer* (1947) to the military comedy *Operation Petticoat* (1959), Grant never really fell out of public favor. He remained popular from the mid-1930s right through to the mid-1960s. His last film, *Walk Don't Run* (1966), was a solid moneymaker. When Grant was offered the directorship of a large cosmetics firm, he opted to leave his movie career while he was still on top.

Very few actors have walked away from the limelight as Grant did. And even Jimmy Cagney returned to films after a twenty-year retirement. But not Grant. He was America's best-looking senior citizen, and movie fans the world over lamented his leaving the silver screen.

Somehow, in all his years in Hollywood, Grant had never received an Oscar. However, the Academy belatedly rectified that by presenting the actor with a special award "for his unique mastery of the art of screen acting." Certainly, there was hardly another actor who made comedy seem so easy.

Grant lived happily ever after in the movies far more often than he did in real life. He was married four times, most of the unions rather short. His first wife was Charlie CHAPLIN's discovery, Virginia Cherrill (1933–1935). He then married heiress Barbara Hutton (1942–1945), one of his co-stars, actress Betsy Drake (1949–1959), and, a much younger actress, Dyan Cannon (1965–1968).

FILMS: *This Is the Night* (1932); *Sinners in the Sun* (1932); *Merrily We Go to Hell* (1932); *The Devil and the Deep* (1932); *Blonde Venus* (1932); *Hot Saturday* (1932); *Madame Butterfly* (1932); *She Done Him Wrong* (1933); *The Woman Accused* (1933); *The Eagle and the Hawk* (1933); *Gambling Ship* (1933); *I'm No Angel* (1933); *Alice in Wonderland* (1933); *Thirty Day Princess* (1934); *Born to Be Bad* (1934); *Kiss and Make-Up* (1934); *Ladies Should Listen* (1934); *Enter Madame* (1935); *Wings in the Dark* (1935); *The Last Outpost* (1935); *Sylvia Scarlett* (1936); *Big Brown Eyes* (1936); *Suzy* (1936); *Wedding Present* (1936); *The Amazing Quest of Ernest Bliss* (1936); *When You're in Love* (1937); *Topper* (1937); *The Toast of New York* (1937); *The Awful Truth* (1937); *Bringing Up Baby* (1938); *Holiday* (1938); *Gunga Din* (1939); *Only Angels Have Wings* (1939); *In Name Only* (1939); *His Girl Friday* (1940); *My Favorite Wife* (1940); *The Howards of Virginia* (1940); *The Philadelphia Story* (1940); *Penny Serenade* (1941); *Suspicion* (1941); *The Talk of the Town* (1942); *Once Upon a Honeymoon* (1942); *Mr. Lucky* (1943); *Destination Tokyo* (1944); *Once Upon a Time* (1944); *None but the Lonely Heart* (1944); *Arsenic and Old Lace* (1944); *Without Reservations* (1946); *Night and Day* (1946); *Notorious* (1946); *The Bachelor and the Bobby-Soxer* (1947); *The Bishop's Wife* (1947); *Mr. Blandings Builds His Dream House* (1948); *Every Girl Should Be Married* (1948); *I Was a Male War Bride* (1949); *Crisis* (1950); *People Will Talk* (1951); *Room for One More* (1952); *Monkey Business* (1952); *Dream Wife* (1953); *To Catch a Thief* (1955); *The Pride and the Passion* (1957); *An Affair to Remember* (1957); *Kiss Them for Me* (1957); *Indiscreet* (1958); *Houseboat* (1958); *North by Northwest* (1959); *Operation Petticoat* (1959); *The Grass Is Greener* (1961); *That Touch of Mink* (1962); *Charade* (1963); *Father Goose* (1964); *Walk Don't Run* (1966).

**The Great McGinty**   The 1940 SATIRE *The Great McGinty* marked the directorial debut of Preston STURGES, who also wrote the screenplay. The film has the distinction of being the first critical and commercial success of a studio-era film that was written and directed by the same person. Sturges's triumph had the epoch-making effect of opening Hollywood's doors for other writer/directors like Billy WILDER and John Huston.

*The Great McGinty* is noteworthy for other reasons, as well. It is a surprisingly biting film that is loaded with unbridled cynicism. It is the story of a hobo who, through ever greater dishonesty and manipulation, manages to rise to high public office only to lose everything—including wife, family, power, and position—when he turns *honest*. This is *Mr. Smith Goes to Washington* turned on its head. It makes us laugh because of Sturges's witty dialogue and the tightrope-walking tone established by his direction.

The movie is also a case of lucky timing. Had Sturges made this movie one year later, after America's entry into World War II, he would have been run out of Hollywood on a rail for so bluntly presenting such deep corruption in American democracy. Instead, because it was 1940, *The Great McGinty* brought Sturges a best screenplay Oscar.

A master of social comedy, this movie started Sturges on one of the most remarkable runs of success in Hollywood history. Between 1940 and 1944 he could do no wrong, either critically or commercially. All of his comedies during this period were deeply ironic, biting, and hysterical. He found the knack for poking fun at America and Americans and made audiences laugh with the recognition of his insights, rather than recoil in horror. *The Great McGinty* may not have been the best of his films, but it was the first, and it made all of the others possible.

The film starred Brian Donlevy as the hobo and featured the beginnings of Sturges's stock company, most notably William Demarest. Also in the cast were Muriel Angelus, Akim Tamiroff, Allyn Joslyn, Louis Jean Heydt, and Arthur Hoyt.

## Grodin, Charles (1935—)

An offbeat comic actor with a subtle, deadpan delivery, Charles Grodin has easily shuttled back and forth between starring and supporting roles since the late 1960s. The key to Grodin's humor is his dry, sincere style; his characters would be the last to see anything funny in his performances.

Born in Pittsburgh, Pennsylvania, Grodin studied at the Pittsburgh Playhouse as well as at the University of Miami. He made his film debut in the little-seen *Sex and the College Girl* (1964). Grodin came to somewhat greater prominence in a supporting role in *Rosemary's Baby* (1968). His big breakthrough, however, came as the male lead in Elaine MAY's hit comedy *The Heartbreak Kid* (1972). It appeared as if Grodin were destined for comic stardom, but he took an unexpected turn, showing up instead in dramas such as *11 Harrowhouse* (1974) and *King Kong* (1976).

His career seemed to sputter in the mid-1970s until he slowly began to emerge in films as a rich comic addition in the role of a supporting player. His presence in such movies as Warren Beatty's *Heaven Can Wait* (1978) and Albert Brooks's *Real Life* (1979) added immeasurably to their success.

Having found his niche, Grodin became almost immune to criticism. Whether in poor films such as *Sunburn* (1979), *The Couch Trip* (1987), and even the megaflop *Ishtar* (1987), he has been uniformly praised and admired for finding small truths in the midst of major fiascoes. And in good films, such as *Seems Like Old Times* (1980) and *The Lonely Guy* (1984), he has been quietly brilliant, bringing an impressive gallery of silly prigs and comical neurotics to the screen. Only once has he been seriously panned in recent years, and that was for *Movers and Shakers* (1985), a SATIRE about the movie business he wrote, co-produced, and starred in, that left the critics and audiences cold.

Grodin recouped smartly from that disaster and in the late 1980s threatened to finally become a full-fledged star, thanks to his wonderfully fussy performance playing against Robert De Niro in the acclaimed hit comedy *Midnight Run* (1988). He followed that success by starring opposite a dog in the 1992 hit family comedy *Beethoven*. In *Dave* (1993), Grodin performed a hilarious turn as a small-time accountant who, overnight, fixes the national budget for a friend who's impersonating the president of the United States.

FILMS: *Sex and the College Girl* (1964); *Rosemary's Baby* (1968); *Catch-22* (1970); *The Heartbreak Kid* (1972); *11 Harrowhouse* (also sc, 1974); *King Kong* (1976); *Thieves* (1977); *Heaven Can Wait* (1978); *Real Life* (1978); *Sunburn* (1979); *It's My Turn* (1980); *Seems Like Old Times* (1980); *The Great Muppet Caper* (1981); *The Incredible Shrinking Woman* (1981); *The Lonely Guy* (1984); *The Woman in Red* (1984); *Movers and Shakers* (also p, sc, 1985); *Last Resort* (1986); *Ishtar* (1987); *The Couch Trip* (1988); *Midnight Run* (1988); *You Can't Hurry Love* (1988); *Taking Care of Business* (1990); *Clifford* (1991); *Beethoven* (1992); *Dave* (1993); *Beethoven's 2nd* (1993).

## Guttenberg, Steve (1958—)

Do moviegoers choose to see Steve Guttenberg in movies or do they merely go to comedies that he happens to be appearing in? We won't know the answer to that question until he successfully carries a movie solely on his own comic shoulders. So far, virtually all of the hit comedies in which he has appeared have been ensemble films. As a consequence, despite leading roles in an impressive list of hit comedies, his personal appeal remains in doubt. In any event, one can certainly say that he's a personable young actor with a pleasing, if somewhat bland, comic edge.

Although his easy charm belies it, Guttenberg is a seriously trained actor who received his education at the School of Performing Arts in New York City. Later, he studied with the best: John Houseman (at Juilliard), Lee Strasberg, and Uta Hagen.

After working in off-Broadway plays, Guttenberg took off for the lure of Hollywood, and in 1977 he starred in his first movie, a comedy called *The*

*Chicken Chronicles*. He worked steadily after that in movies and on TV, although little attention was paid to him until *Diner* (1982), in which he played the would-be groom who refused to marry unless his fiancée passed a sports trivia test.

Within two years, his string of hit comedies had begun with the innocuous, lowbrow *Police Academy* (1984). He went on to make three sequels, bowing out after the fourth film, although the series continued without him. In the meantime, Guttenberg was part of the large cast of the hit *Cocoon* (1985). He also starred in the adventure comedy *Short Circuit* (1986), in which he was upstaged by a robot with human feelings; it was another box office winner. That success, however, was nothing compared with the unexpected response to the sentimental hit comedy *Three Men and a Baby* (1987) and its sequel *Three Men and a Little Lady* (1990). In 1988 he appeared in yet

another sequel, *Cocoon: The Return* (1988). Another way of describing his career might be that he's had three hit films and five hit sequels.

FILMS INCLUDE: *The Chicken Chronicles* (1977); *The Boys from Brazil* (1978); *Players* (1979); *Can't Stop the Music* (1980); *Diner* (1982); *The Man Who Wasn't There* (1983); *Police Academy* (1984); *Cocoon* (1985); *Bad Medicine* (1985); *Police Academy 2: Their First Assignment* (1985); *Police Acadey 3: Back in Training* (1986); *Short Circuit* (1986); *The Bedroom Window* (1987); *Amazon Women on the Moon* (1987); *Police Academy 4: Citizens on Patrol* (also p, 1987); *Surrender* (1987); *Three Men and a Baby* (1987); *High Spirits* (1988); *Cocoon: The Return* (1988); *Don't Tell Her It's Me* (1990); *Three Men and a Little Lady* (1990).

# H

**Hackett, Buddy (1924—)** A squat, cartoonish, marbles-in-his-mouth comedian, Buddy Hackett had his greatest impact in the movies during the 1960s. Mostly known as a "blue" stand-up comedy star of nightclubs, he has, ironically, played mostly lovable comic parts in G-rated movies.

Born Leonard Hacker in Brooklyn, New York, he worked in his father's upholstery business before making a name for himself as a comedian in the Catskill Mountain resorts north of New York City. Hackett made his movie debut opposite Donald O'CONNOR in *Walking My Baby Back Home* (1953). However, despite his strong comic showing, the movie didn't do much for him; he didn't appear in another film for five years.

Hackett eventually achieved national recognition thanks to his TV guest appearances on variety and talk shows, which led to occasional comic lead roles in slight films like *All Hands on Deck* (1961) and *Everything's Ducky* (1961). He was wasted in a small supporting role in *The Music Man* (1962), but his comic talents were fully recognized by Stanley Kramer, who gave Hackett a major part in the all-star comedy classic IT'S A MAD MAD MAD MAD WORLD (1963). Nonetheless, relatively few good roles came his way after that (he's difficult to cast; a role would have to be tailored for him), and he only appeared intermittently thereafter, most amusingly in a lead role in the Disney comedy hit *The Love Bug* (1969).

---

FILMS INCLUDE: *Walking My Baby Back Home* (1953); *God's Little Acre* (1958); *All Hands on Deck* (1961); *Everything's Ducky* (1961); *The Music Man* (1962); *The Wonderful World of the Brothers Grimm* (1962); *It's a Mad Mad Mad Mad World* (1963); *Muscle Beach Party* (1964); *The Good Guys and the Bad Guys* (cameo, 1969); *The Love Bug* (1969); *Loose Shoes* (1977); *The Little Mermaid* (voice only, 1989).

---

**Hagerty, Julie (1954—)** A tall, willowy comedian, Julie Hagerty has a little-girl voice that is both her claim to fame and the albatross not just around her neck but in it. Her voice certainly keeps her from getting a wider variety of roles, although it does ensure that she will continue to appear most often in comedies.

Born in Cincinnati, Ohio, she always had her sights set on an acting career, studying for the stage even when she was a child. As an adult, Hagerty gained stage experience in New York when she joined The Production Company, a theater group founded by her brother Michael Hagerty and director Norman Rene.

Hagerty got her first significant break in 1980 when she appeared in a TV movie comedy called *The Day the Women Got Even*. In that same year, her movie career took off when she played the wide-eyed, innocent female lead in *Airplane!* Audiences were charmed by her kookie delivery, not aware that that was actually how she talked. She has been playing similar sorts of ditzy heroines and/or supporting characters ever since, with her most notable performances in Woody ALLEN's *A Midsummer Night's Sex Comedy* (1982) and Albert BROOKS's *Lost in America* (1985). In more recent years, her roles have generally

**125**

been smaller. As a consequence, she has been acting on the stage with greater frequency, both on Broadway and across the country.

---

**FILMS:** *Airplane!* (1980); *Airplane II: The Sequel* (1982); *A Midsummer Night's Sex Comedy* (1982); *Bad Medicine* (1985); *Goodbye, New York* (1985); *Lost in America* (1985); *Aria* (1987); *Beyond Therapy* (1987); *Rude Awakening* (1989); *Bloodhounds of Broadway* (1989); *Reversal of Fortune* (1990); *What About Bob?* (1991); *Noises Off* (1992).

---

**Hanks, Tom (1956–)** An actor who has built an impressive body of work in a relatively short period of time, Tom Hanks is an everyman with whom audiences can easily and readily identify. Like James Stewart and Jack LEMMON, two actors Hanks has been compared with, he is as adept at light comedy as he is at drama, but the vast majority of his work has been in the service of laughter.

Hanks, born in Concord, California, began his acting career with an internship at the Great Lakes Shakespeare Festival in Cleveland, Ohio, acting in such plays as *The Taming of the Shrew* and *The Two Gentlemen of Verona*. After brief stints on the stage in both New York and Los Angeles, he won a starring role in the ABC-TV sitcom "Bosom Buddies," which ran for two years in the early 1980s.

Hanks made his film debut in a "slice-and-dice" movie called *He Knows You're Alone* (1981), but had his first memorable role in *Splash* (1984), a surprise hit that took in more than $60 million at the ticket window. He then went on to star in a series of movies that were extremely variable in both their quality and their box office appeal. While *Bachelor Party* (1984) earned $40 million, *The Man with One Red Shoe* (1985) and *Every Time We Say Goodbye* (1986) made zilch. *Volunteers* (1985) and *The Money Pit* (1986) both found a modest cult following, but the film that genuinely got the attention of both the critics and the paying public was *Nothing in Common* (1986), which was the first movie that showed

*Popular star Tom Hanks has displayed a wide comic range, from the harsh, biting humor of* Punchline *(1988) to the sweet, romantic comedy of* Sleepless in Seattle *(1993).*
PHOTO COURTESY OF MOVIE STAR NEWS.

Hanks was capable of reaching deeper, richer emotions underneath his comic persona.

During this period of growth, Hanks often worked with other strong comic performers such as John CANDY in *Volunteers*, Jackie GLEASON in *Nothing in Common*, and Dan AYKROYD in *Dragnet* (1987). When given the opportunity to carry a major motion picture on his own shoulders, he did not disappoint. After Robert De Niro could not settle on contractual terms to play Josh Baskin in *Big* (1988), the role fell to Hanks, and it brought him both a blockbuster hit that earned more than $100 million and his first Academy Award nomination for best actor.

In that same year, he electrified the critics with

his dazzling performance as a self-destructive stand-up comedian in *Punchline*. Unfortunately, the movie was not the commercial success its producer (and co-star) Sally Field had hoped it would be. Equally disappointing was *The Burbs* (1989), which seemed to set Hanks on a surprising downward course. Neither *Turner and Hooch* (1989) nor *Joe versus the Volcano* (1990) set the world on fire, but the shockingly disastrous *Bonfire of the Vanities* (1990), for which many thought Hanks was ill-cast, nearly burned his career to a crisp.

After a change of agents and an amusing turn in the hit *A League of Their Own* (1992)—in which he delivers the longest urination scene in movie history—Hanks seemed poised to recapture his winning ways, which, in fact, he did when he starred in the ROMANTIC COMEDY hit *Sleepless in Seattle* (1993).

**FILMS:** *He Knows You're Alone* (1981); *Splash* (1984); *Bachelor Party* (1984); *The Man with One Red Shoe* (1985); *Volunteers* (1985); *Every Time We Say Goodbye* (1986); *The Money Pit* (1986); *Nothing in Common* (1986); *Dragnet* (1987); *Big* (1988); *Punchline* (1988); *The Burbs* (1989); *Turner and Hooch* (1989); *Bonfire of the Vanities* (1990); *Joe versus the Volcano* (1990); *Radio Flyer* (1992); *A League of Their Own* (1992); *Sleepless in Seattle* (1993); *Philadelphia* (1993).

**Harlow, Jean (1911–1937)** Known as "the blonde bombshell," Jean Harlow was an actress who was modern, vulgar, and wonderfully funny. Harlow brought a healthy sex appeal to the movies in much the same way that Mae WEST did (except that Harlow was far more credible). In fact, MGM considered hiring West to write for their star. However, they didn't need to; Harlow was the definitive sex goddess/comedian of the 1930s, and she didn't need Mae West's dialogue to prove it—all she had to do was slink across the silver screen.

Born Harlean Carpenter, in Kansas City, Mis-

*Discovered by Howard Hughes, Jean Harlow combined sex and comedy in just the right proportion to become a major star. The blond bombshell had a relatively short, meteoric career during the 1930s that ended with her tragic death at the age of twenty-six.* PHOTO COURTESY OF THE SIEGEL COLLECTION.

souri, she came from a middle-class family. She ran away from home to get married when she was sixteen. After the marriage failed, she went to Hollywood and worked as an extra, eventually winning a small part in *Moran of the Marines* (1928). Other bit roles followed, most notably in *The Love Parade* (1929) and Charlie CHAPLIN's *CITY LIGHTS* (1931).

Nothing came of her work until Howard Hughes got a glimpse of her. He wanted her for *Hell's Angels* (1930), his epic airplane movie that had already been two years in the making, but had to be reshot because of the advent of the talkies. Hughes, always a good bet to discover a beauty, saw her potential and signed her up to star in his film as the woman who comes between the two heroes. It's also worth noting that it was in *Hell's Angels* that she became the first to utter the time-honored cliché, "Would you be shocked if I put on something more comfortable?"

*Hell's Angels* was a big hit, partly because of the remarkable aerial display in the movie, and partly because Harlow was so sexy. Hughes had her under a long-term contract and loaned her to other studios for lead roles, notably to Warner Bros. for *Public Enemy* (1931), although she wasn't the one who received the grapefruit in her face (that was Mae Clarke). She was also loaned to Columbia, where she starred in Frank CAPRA's *Platinum Blonde* (1931), a movie clearly titled to take best advantage of her peculiar hair color.

Hughes finally sold her contract to MGM for $60,000. Harlow appeared in two MGM films without causing much of a ripple, but then came *Red Dust* (1932) with Clark Gable. The two stars ignited sexual fires, making the rather daring movie a blockbuster hit. Harlow and Gable were a hot team; they were paired together a total of five times in just six years, and all of their films were big box office draws.

After *Red Dust*, Harlow was *the* Hollywood sex goddess. Wearing low-cut gowns and sporting a blue-collar vocabulary, she got laughs in all sorts of pictures. For instance, she was a perfect foil for the purposefully stuffy cast in MGM's all-star film *Dinner at Eight* (1933), just as she was the perfect victim in the aptly titled *Bombshell* (1933).

She could play funny/tough (*Riff Raff*, 1935) as well as just plain funny (*Suzy*, 1936). Regardless of what she played, the slinky star had one hit after another. There was no reason to believe that she might not have had an extremely long career because she was only twenty-six when tragedy struck.

Harlow had been filming *Saratoga* (1937) when she fell ill and suddenly died of uremic poisoning. The movie was finished with a double and went on to become a great hit precisely because it was the sex star's last movie.

---

FILMS: *The Saturday Night Kid* (1929); *Hell's Angels* (1930); *The Secret Six* (1931); *The Public Enemy* (1931); *The Iron Man* (1931); *Goldie* (1931); *Platinum Blonde* (1931); *Three Wise Girls* (1932); *The Beast of the City* (1932); *Red-Headed Woman* (1932); *Red Dust* (1932); *Bombshell* (1933); *Hold Your Man* (1933); *Dinner at Eight* (1933); *The Girl from Missouri* (1934); *Reckless* (1935); *China Seas* (1935); *Riffraff* (1936); *Suzy* (1936); *Wife vs. Secretary* (1936); *Libeled Lady* (1936); *Personal Property* (1937); *Saratoga* (1937).

---

**Harold and Maude**  The 1972 BLACK COMEDY *Harold and Maude*, starring Bud CORT and Ruth GORDON, was among the first of what came to be known as cult movies. Dismissed by the critics, the movie was embraced by young filmgoers, who turned it into an art house hit. In addition, it was a favorite "midnight movie" as well as a constantly booked film on the revivalist theater circuit. It predated the success of *The Rocky Horror Picture Show*, the ultimate cult movie, by four years.

The story centers around the twenty-year-old Harold (Cort) who is fascinated by death. He is constantly staging mock suicides to get the attention of his mother (played drily by British actress Vivian Pickles). At a funeral, Harold meets Maude (Gordon), a seventy-nine-year-old woman who is brimming with life. Her free spirit and lust for life appeal to Harold, who falls in love with her.

Full of wacky comedy, yet grounded in vulnerability, *Harold and Maude* remains a genuinely fresh and original piece of work. It was written and produced by Colin Higgins (1941–1988), who used this film to catapult himself into mainstream Hollywood comedies, penning the screenplays for *Silver Streak* (1977), *Foul Play* (1978), *9 to 5* (1980), and *The Best Little Whorehouse in Texas* (1982) as well as directing these films. *Harold and Maude* was directed by Hal Ashby (1929–1988), his second as a director (after *The Landlord*, 1970), opening the door to bigger films for him. He followed *Harold and Maude* with *The Last Detail* (1973), *Shampoo*

(1975), *Bound for Glory* (1976), *Coming Home* (1977), and, back to his *Harold and Maude* roots, *Being There* (1979).

*Harold and Maude* also featured the acting of Cyril Cusack, Charles Tyner, and Ellen Geer. The memorable score was provided by singer/songwriter Cat Stevens.

## Hartley, Hal (1960– )

A gifted independent filmmaker, Hal Hartley emerged in the early 1990s as a screenwriter/director with a uniquely quirky, comic vision of suburban life in America. Working with many of the same cast and crew from film to film, Hartley might well be a modern, low-budget version of Preston STURGES, complete with his own satirical view of American morality.

A graduate of the film program at the State University of New York at Purchase, Hartley is living proof that university-trained directors do not come solely from NYU, USC, and UCLA. He made three highly regarded short films between 1985 and 1988 (*Kid*, *The Cartographer's Girlfriend*, and *Dogs*) before getting the opportunity to direct his first feature film, the BLACK COMEDY *The Unbelievable Truth* (1990). Shot in eleven days in 1988, it took two years to get it released; a tumultuous reception at the Toronto Film Festival in 1989 brought attention to the film, and critics did the rest. His auspicious debut was followed by a remarkably mature and polished sophomore effort, *Trust* (1991), a seriocomic love story that poked fun at the American family in ways both mischievously devious and original. It was an art house hit that led to *Simple Men* (1992), a less successful movie both critically and commercially. Nonetheless, Hartley's talent for finding humor in tragedy, and tragedy in humor, marks him as filmmaker to watch.

FILMS: *The Unbelievable Truth* (1990), *Trust* (1991), *Simple Men* (1992).

## Hawks, Howard (1896–1977)

The father of the SCREWBALL COMEDY, Howard Hawks is still the untouchable master of the genre. Unlike most other directors who tended to specialize in one or two different areas, Hawks worked in almost all of the popular categories, from gangster films to Westerns and from biblical epics to science fiction, making memorable films in all of them. However, Hawks outdid himself and the rest of Hollywood when he invented the screwball comedy with the 1934 film *TWENTIETH CENTURY*. Although he didn't make a great many comedies, his contribution to the comic arts should not be underestimated.

Born in Goshen, Indiana, Hawks was the eldest of three sons of a well-to-do paper manufacturer. He spent much of his youth in Southern California, but went to college in the East, receiving a degree in mechanical engineering from Cornell University. After serving in World War I, Hawks put his mechanical engineering to use, building his own cars and planes. His fascination with machinery brought him into the movie business.

Hawks got his start as a props man in 1918 with the Mary Pickford Company, eventually getting experience in the script and editing departments. When he came into some family money at age twenty-six, he wrote, directed, and produced his own comedy shorts. He continued building his reputation and skill, getting the opportunity to direct his first feature film for Fox in 1926, *The Road to Glory*, which was based on his story.

Hawks easily made the transition to the sound era, and rightly so; the director was fascinated with language. In fact, one of his best screwball comedies, *Ball of Fire* (1941), deals directly with the subject of slang.

Whether directing dramas or comedies, he often had actors speak their dialogue with a ferocious speed that built unique rhythms and pacing. When it came to the comedies, that speed heightened the comic effects by creating a dizzying bombardment of wisecracks that left audiences as breathless as it must have left the actors.

Hawks's themes were consistent. In his dramas, he presented heroes who were talented professionals—people who took their work very seriously and thought of their jobs as a duty to civilization. His comic heroes felt the same way about their work, but they had something far more formidable than a villain to keep them from success: In Hawks's comedies, the heroes were up against women (who were smarter and far more capable). In essence, his dramas dealt with a male-dominated society, and his comedies with a female-dominated society.

Cary Grant was the ideal Hawks comedy character because he could be overwhelmed and charming at the same time. He starred in four of Hawks's screwball comedies, *Bringing Up Baby* (1938), *His Girl Friday* (1940), *I Was a Male War Bride* (1949), and *Monkey Business* (1952).

Except for discovering Lauren Bacall and Angie Dickinson, Hawks didn't establish new stars. He was certainly never known for his fancy camera work or intricate story construction. Hawks simply planted the camera and told his stories in a straightforward manner, and his style worked. Besides his great screwball comedies, he directed such classics as *The Dawn Patrol* (1930), *Scarface* (1932), *Only Angels Have Wings* (1939), *The Big Sleep* (1946), *Red River* (1948), *Gentlemen Prefer Blondes* (1953), and *Rio Bravo* (1959).

While he rarely received writing or story credits, he almost always was deeply involved in the screenwriting process. In fact, he performed uncredited screenwriting duties on such notable films as *Underworld* (1927), *Red Dust* (1932), *Captains Courageous* (1937), *Gunga Din* (1939), and *Gone with the Wind* (1939).

Hawks never won an Oscar, although he was nominated for a best director Academy Award for *Sergeant York* (1941). He was finally given in honorary Oscar in 1975.

**FILMS:** As feature director: *The Road to Glory* (also story, 1926); *Fig Leaves* (also story, 1926); *The Cradle Snatchers* (1927); *Paid to Love* (1927); *A Girl in Every Port* (also story, 1928); *Fazil* (1928); *The Air Circus* (co-d, 1928); *Trent's Last Case* (1929); *The Dawn Patrol* (also co-sc, 1930); *The Criminal Code* (1931); *The Crowd Roars* (also story, 1932); *Scarface* (1932); *The Shame of a Nation* (also co-p, (1932); *Tiger Shark* (1932); *Today We Live* (also p, 1933); *Viva Villa!* (co-d, co-sc, credited to Jack Conway, 1933); *Twentieth Century* (also p, 1934); *Barbary Coast* (1935); *Ceiling Zero* (1936); *The Road to Glory* (1936); *Come and Get It* (co-d with William Wyler, 1936); *Bringing Up Baby* (also p, 1938); *Indianapolis Speedway* (story only); *Only Angels Have Wings* (also p, story, 1939); *His Girl Friday* (also p, 1940); *Sergeant York* (1941); *Ball of Fire* (1942); *Air Force* (1943); *Corvette K-225* (p only, 1943); *To Have and Have Not* (also p, 1944); *The Big Sleep* (also p, 1946); *Red River* (also p, 1948); *A Song Is Born* (1948); *I Was a Male War Bride* (1949); *The Thing* (p, co-sc only, 1951); *The Big Sky* (also p, 1952); *O'Henry's Full House* ("The Ransom of Red Chief" segment, 1952); *Monkey Business* (1952); *Gentlemen Prefer Blondes* (1953); *Land of the Pharaohs* (also p, 1955); *Rio Bravo* (also p, 1959); *Hatari!* (also p, 1962); *Red Line 7000* (also story, p, 1965); *El Dorado* (also p, 1967); *Rio Lobo* (also p, 1970).

## Hawn, Goldie (1945— )

Known primarily for her comic roles, Goldie Hawn has endured as a star by combining an appealing ditziness with an endearing vulnerability. Most important, while her characters may often appear to be airheads, they are almost always smarter than they seem. Her staying power can also be attributed to the fact that she is one of a relative handful of powerful female stars who has produced some of her own movies, most notably one of the biggest comedy hits of the 1980s, *Private Benjamin* (1980), which earned more than $100 million.

Born Goldie Jean Hawn in Washington, D.C., to a musically inclined family—her father was a musician and her mother a dance teacher—Hawn pursued a show business career from an early age. Although she acted on stage as early as 1961 in a Virginia Stage Company presentation of *Romeo and*

*Goldie Hawn has been an enduring comic star in the movies since 1969. She went into a commercial slump during the better part of the 1980s, but emerged in the early 1990s with a number of comic hits, including* Death Becomes Her *(1992), from which the above still is taken.*

PHOTO BY DEANA NEWCOMB, © UNIVERSAL PICTURES.

*Juliet* (she was Juliet), her passion was dancing. At eighteen she arrived in New York, worked at the World's Fair, and then danced as a go-go girl in a sleazy New Jersey strip joint. Not long after, she became a chorus girl in Las Vegas, but was so fed up with her life that she gave herself two weeks to get a break or she was going home to Maryland. She got the break, being cast in a small role in an Andy Griffith TV special. Noticed on the air by an agent, she was offered a three-week stint on the new "Laugh-In" TV show, and her career quickly took off.

Although she had a previous short run in the TV series "Good Morning World" in 1967, her early

show business persona was formed on the enormously popular "Laugh-In," where she played a goofy, childlike airhead who giggled incessantly. Audiences loved her. And so did film director Billy Wilder, who saw her on the show and thought she'd be just right for the comedy he was making, *Cactus Flower* (1969). She was cast in the movie and came away with a best supporting actress Oscar. Later, in an interview with film critic Rex Reed, she candidly admitted, "My greatest regret is that I won an Oscar before I learned how to act."

Before hitting it big in the movies with *Cactus Flower*, Hawn had a bit role in the Disney production of *The One and Only Genuine Original Family Band* (1968). She worked steadily in the movies as a comedian in such films as *There's a Girl in My Soup* (1970), *Dollars* (1971), and *Butterflies Are Free* (1972), all of which traded on Hawn's off-center kooky image. In 1974, however, she surprised filmgoers by starring in a stark drama, *The Sugarland Express*, directed by the then-unknown Steven Spielberg. The film and Hawn received a shower of praise from the critics, but her fans didn't especially want to see her as a dramatic actress.

Hawn returned to light comedy in such films as *The Girl from Petrovka* (1974), *Shampoo* (1975), in support of Warren Beatty, and *The Duchess and the Dirtwater Fox* (1976). She entered her most successful period when she joined with Chevy Chase in *Foul Play* (1978). After stumbling with *Travels with Anita* (1979), she produced and starred in *Private Benjamin* (1980), a film that garnered her a best actress Oscar nomination, while also vaulting her to the top echelon of female movie stars.

The hits kept coming. *Seems Like Old Times* (1981) reunited her with Chevy Chase, and *Best Friends* (1982) was a favorite of the critics. Subsequent efforts in the mid- to late 1980s, however, were less well received. Her production of *Swing Shift* (1984) was a box office disappointment, and *Protocol* (1984) was a pallid imitation of *Private Benjamin*. She appeared rarely on the big screen in the second half of the 1980s, starring in only two comedies, *Wildcats* (1986) and *Overboard* (1987), neither one of them stirring much interest. The latter film co-starred her longtime lover, Kurt Russell.

Most of her flops lacked co-stars of her box office stature. In her best and most successful movies, she had Peter Sellers, Chevy Chase, Burt Reynolds, and Warren Beatty. Finally, in the 1990s, she teamed up with stronger partners again and hit paydirt. First there was Mel Gibson, who helped her to her first hit in a decade with *Bird on a Wire* (1990). She flopped in two subsequent suspense dramas, but came back strong in comedy again, pairing with Steve Martin in *Housesitter* (1992) and Meryl Streep in *Death Becomes Her* (1992).

**FILMS:** *The One and Only Genuine Original Family Band* (1968); *Cactus Flower* (1969); *There's a Girl in My Soup* (1970); *$ (Dollars)* (1971); *Butterflies Are Free* (1972); *The Girl from Petrovka* (1974); *The Sugarland Express* (1974); *Shampoo* (1975); *The Duchess and the Dirtwater Fox* (1976); *Foul Play* (1978); *Travels with Anita* (1978); *Lovers and Liars* (1979); *Private Benjamin* (also p, 1980); *Seems Like Old Times* (1980); *Best Friends* (1982); *Protocol* (also p, 1984); *Swing Shift* (1984); *Wildcats* (also p, 1986); *Overboard* (1987); *Bird on a Wire* (1990); *My Blue Heaven* (p only, 1990); *Deceived* (1991); *Crisscross* (1992); *Housesitter* (1992); *Death Becomes Her* (1992).

## Hayes, George "Gabby" (1885—1969)

The epitome of the comic old codger, George "Gabby" Hayes was a fixture in Westerns for nearly thirty years. Much of that time he played the hero's grizzled old sidekick, rattling on, to fine comic effect, about what "he" would do if he ever got his hands on the bad guys.

Born in Wellsville, New York, Hayes had a modest career in VAUDEVILLE before donning spurs as a villain in silent and early sound Westerns. As he got older, however, he had a metamorphosis, and comedy became his mainstay. He was ideal as a comic

*One of the great comic sidekicks, George "Gabby" Hayes enlivened any number of Westerns with his over-the-top snarls and epithets.*  PHOTO COURTESY OF THE SIEGEL COLLECTION.

balance to William Boyd's upright Hopalong Cassidy in the mid-1930s, and Hayes continued to bring a certain outrageousness to the films of otherwise humorless heroes like Roy Rogers.

Hayes, however, was not confined to B-movie Westerns. He appeared in small roles in a number of non-Westerns, most notably the musical *Love Me Tonight* (1932) and Frank CAPRA's populist comedy *Mr. Deeds Goes to Town* (1936). More often, however, he was in big-budget Westerns, such as King Vidor's *Texas Rangers* (1936), Cecil B. De Mille's *The Plainsman* (1937), and Raoul Walsh's *Dark Command* (1940).

Hayes disappeared from the big screen for most of the 1950s due to his success on television.

**FILMS INCLUDE:** *Why Women Marry?* (1923); *The Rainbow Man* (1929); *Rose of the Rio Grande* (1931); *Love*

*Me Tonight* (1932); *Wild Horse Mesa* (1933); *In Old Santa Fe* (1934); *Lucky Texan* (1934); *Randy Rides Alone* (1934); *Tumbling Tumbleweeds* (1935); *Hopalong Cassidy* (1935); *Mr. Deeds Goes to Town* (1936); *Texas Rangers* (1936); *The Plainsman* (1937); *In Old Mexico* (1938); *The Frontiersman* (1938); *Let Freedom Ring* (1939); *Arizona Kid* (1939); *Dark Command* (1940); *The Ranger and the Lady* (1940); *Colorado* (1940); *Nevada City* (1941); *Man of Cheyenne* (1942); *In Old Oklahoma* (1943); *Tall in the Saddle* (1944); *Don't Fence Me In* (1945); *Helldorado* (1946); *Wyoming* (1947); *Albuquerque* (1948); *El Paso* (1949); *The Cariboo Trail* (1950).

## Heckerling, Amy (1954—)

In the vanguard of Hollywood's small, but growing, number of successful women writer/directors, Amy Heckerling has an impressive list of commercial hit comedies that span the last decade. She has helped open the door for more female filmmakers and has proven that there is a viable marketplace for comedies that center on women and women's concerns. For instance, her first film comedy, *Fast Times at Ridgemont High* (1982), is a young girl's coming of age story. Her biggest hits, the two *Look Who's Talking* movies (1989 and 1990), are gentle comedies about children and families.

Born in New York City, she received her moviemaking training at NYU, gaining further experience at the American Film Institute's facilities in Los Angeles. She worked as a video editor for TV before getting the chance to direct the low-budget teen comedy *Fast Times at Ridgemont High*, a movie that surprised many with its energy, originality, and sensitivity. It was a hit that helped to establish the careers of Sean Penn, Jennifer Jason Leigh, and Judge Reinhold, while also introducing Eric Stoltz, Anthony Edwards, and Nicolas Cage (under his real name, Nicolas Coppola). Heckerling showed the same knack for picking talent when she paired the effervescent Kirstie ALLEY with John Travolta (resurrect-

ing his career) in the surprise hit *Look Who's Talking* (1989), while also having the good commercial sense to use the voice of Bruce Willis for the talking baby.

---

**FILMS INCLUDE:** *Fast Times at Ridgemont High* (1982); *Johnny Dangerously* (1984); *Into the Night* (cameo only, 1985); *National Lampoon's European Vacation* (1985); *Look Who's Talking* (also sc, 1989); *Look Who's Talking, Too* (also sc, 1990); *Look Who's Talking Now!* (p only, 1993).

---

## Henry, Buck (1930—)

An actor, screenwriter, and director, Buck Henry came into his own in the mid-1960s, flourishing during the next fifteen years as a creator of slightly off-center comedies. His films generally skewered middle-class American values, although not so roughly as to keep middle-class audiences from laughing at the jokes. His skill as a writer was in adapting the works of others to the screen in a crisp, cinematic style; his original work was somewhat less impressive. A frustrated actor, Henry almost always appears in the films he's written as well as many he hasn't. A slightly built, bookish-looking man, he projects a dry, amusing personality on film.

Born Buck Henry Zuckerman in New York City, he comes by his comedy instincts honestly; he's the son of Ruth Taylor, a former Mack SENNETT comedian who was a member of Keystone's BATHING BEAUTIES. His father was a general in the U.S. Air Force who later conquered Wall Street. With show business in his blood, Henry started out as an actor, making his way to Broadway in a small role in *Life with Father* in 1946. That turned out to be the high point of his acting career for a long time. By 1960 he was still struggling, finally joining an off-Broadway improvisational group, The Premise, before finally heading off to Hollywood to try his hand at TV comedy writing.

Henry had some modest success writing jokes and skits for Steve Allen, Garry Moore, and the TV show "That Was the Week That Was." The writing that changed his life, however, came in collaboration with Mel BROOKS when they created and sold the TV sitcom "Get Smart" in 1964.

Life was looking up for Henry. That year at thirty-four he wrote and acted in his first film, *The Troublemaker*, a quirky comedy that brought him additional attention. With his next film, he hit the big time, co-scripting *The GRADUATE* (1967) and gaining a best screenplay Academy Award nomination. He also appeared in a small role in the film, as he would often do in the future.

His career grounded in critical and commercial success, Henry went on to further triumphs during the rest of the 1960s and 1970s, with screenplays for comedies such as *Candy* (1968), *Catch 22* (1970), *The Owl and the Pussycat* (1970), *What's Up, Doc?* (1972), and *Heaven Can Wait* (1978), the last of which he co-directed with Warren Beatty, sharing a best director Oscar nomination.

The 1980s and early 1990s have witnessed a sharp decline in Henry's writing. He's done less of it, and what he's done has not been anywhere near the quality of his earlier work. *First Family* (1980), *Protocol* (1984), and *I Love New York* (1987) did nothing for his reputation. On the other hand, he has been appearing in front of the camera with greater frequency during the last fifteen years, perhaps fulfilling his original need to perform. Recently, for instance, with sly humor, he played a screenwriter pitching a remake of *The Graduate* in Robert Altman's *The Player* (1992).

FILMS INCLUDE: *The Troublemaker* (a, story, sc, 1964); *The Graduate* (a, sc, 1967); *Candy* (sc, 1968); *The Secret War of Harry Frigg* (a, 1968); *Catch-22* (a, sc, 1970); *The Owl and the Pussycat* (a, sc, 1970); *Taking Off* (a, 1971); *Is There Sex After Death?* (a, 1971); *What's Up, Doc?* (sc, 1972); *The Day of the Dolphin* (sc, 1973); *The Man Who Fell to Earth* (a, 1976); *Heaven Can Wait* (a, p, co-d, 1978); *Old Boyfriends* (a, 1978); *The Nude Bomb* (based on "Get Smart" characters, 1980); *First Family* (a, sc, d, 1980); *Gloria* (a, 1980); *Eating Raoul* (a, 1982); *Protocol* (sc, 1984);

*Aria* (a, 1987); *I Love New York* (sc, 1987); *Dark Before Dawn* (a, 1988); *Rude Awakening* (a, 1989); *Tune in Tomorrow* (a, 1990); *Defending Your Life* (a, 1991); *The Lounge People* (a, 1991); *The Linguini Incident* (a, 1991); *The Player* (cameo, 1992); *Grumpy Old Men* (a, 1993).

**Henson, Jim (1936—1990)** The creator of the much-beloved Muppets, Jim Henson built a comedy empire that appealed to adults as much as it did to kids. From Kermit the Frog to Fozzie Bear and from Miss Piggy to the Cookie Monster, he created a huge gallery of characters that have educated and entertained a generation. In the process, he made several Muppet movies, all of them endearing, funny hits. He was less successful with more adult material, suffering critical and commercial failures with *The Dark Crystal* (1982) and *Labyrinth* (1986).

Born in Greenville, Mississippi, Henson became a working puppeteer while still in his teens. He had a regular puppet show segment on a local Washington, D.C., TV station long before he invented the Muppets and brought them to "Sesame Street" in 1969. While "Sesame Street" was an educational program, "The Muppet Show" (1976–1981), which was syndicated all over the world and appeared on commercial TV, was pure (and delightful) entertainment for both kids and adults. So was his "Fraggle Rock" show (1983–1987).

Henson's stunning success with the Muppets led to his first feature film, *The Muppet Movie* (1979), which happened to be a sweet and funny comedy as well as a charming musical. He made several other Muppet films in the following years as well as other projects for film and TV.

After Henson's sudden and unexpected death from pneumonia, his five children took over his empire.

FILMS: *Time Piece* (short, p, 1965); *The Muppet Movie* (a—puppeteer song, p, 1979); *An American Were-*

wolf in London (a, 1981); *The Great Muppet Caper* (a—puppeteer song, d, (1982); *The Dark Crystal* (a—puppeteer story, p, d, 1982); *The Muppets Take Manhattan* (a—puppeteer p, 1984); *Sesame Street Presents: Follow That Bird* (a, 1985); *Into the Night* (a, 1985); *Labyrinth* (story, d, 1986).

---

**Herbert, Hugh (1887—1952)**   a unique comedy talent, Hugh Herbert played eccentric characters—usually absentminded and scatterbrained types with plenty of nervous twitches. Audiences never seemed to tire of his trademark cries of "woo-woo" whenever he got excited or nervous, despite the fact that he not only played numerous supporting roles, but many leads as well. Of course, the starring roles were often in low-budget comedies, but Herbert was a longtime favorite who appeared in more than one-hundred movies between the late 1920s and the early 1950s.

Born in Binghamton, New York, Herbert made his name as a comedian in VAUDEVILLE and on the legitimate stage before embarking on a career in the movies when he was already approaching middle age. Many of his most memorable appearances were as comic relief in musicals such as *Footlight Parade* (1933), *Dames* (1934), *Gold Diggers of 1935* (1935), *Kismet* (1944), and *A Song Is Born* (1948).

Herbert had a big enough name to be included in Warner Bros. all-star *A Midsummer Night's Dream* (as Snout, 1935) and was cuckoo enough to hold his own with the rambunctious comedy of OLSEN AND JOHNSON in their hit *Hellzapoppin* (1941).

---

FILMS INCLUDE: *Husbands for Rent* (1928); *Hook, Line and Sinker* (1930); *Friends and Lovers* (1931); *Laugh and Get Rich* (1931); *Million Dollar Legs* (1932); *Footlight Parade* (1933); *Convention City* (1933); *Wonder Bar* (1934); *Dames* (1934); *Gold Diggers of 1935* (1935); *A Midsummer Night's Dream* (1935); *To Beat the Band* (1935); *We Went to College* (1936); *That Man Is Here Again* (1937); *Marry the Girl* (1937); *The Perfect Specimen* (1937); *Gold Diggers in Paris*

*"Woo-Woo," it's Hugh Herbert, who often played excitable characters who inevitably uttered that trademark sound. He had a long career as a loveable, if eccentric, supporting player.*
PHOTO COURTESY OF MOVIE STAR NEWS.

(1938); *Hollywood Hotel* (1938); *The Great Waltz* (1938); *Little Accident* (1939); *The Family Next Door* (1939); *Eternally Yours* (1939); *Slightly Tempted* (1940); *Meet the Chump* (1940); *Hellzapoppin* (1941); *Kismet* (1944); *A Song Is Born* (1948); *The Beautiful Blonde from Bashful Bend* (1949); *Havana Rose* (1951).

---

**Herman, Pee-wee (1952—)**   The actor Paul Reubens created the character of Pee-wee Herman so convincingly and thoroughly that one tends to think of them as one and the same. In his guise as a bizarre child-man, with white pancake makeup and too-tight clothes, Herman became a weird-voiced, manic, contemporary version of silent screen comedian Harry LANGDON. After two hit films as

*Pee-wee Herman was such a peculiar and original creation that he subsumed the identity of his creator, Paul Reubens. Herman's film career seemed assured with two amusing and commercially viable features, but it all came crashing down in a scandal that left him a bit player, acting in the films of friends like director Tim Burton.* PHOTO COURTESY OF MOVIE STAR NEWS.

Pee-wee Herman, however, his career was shattered by scandal.

Born Paul Reubenfield in Peekskill, New York, he grew up in Florida. In his early years in show business, he had an act called Hilarious Betty and Eddie (he was Eddie), which appeared twice on TV's "The Gong Show." Later, he was part of an improvisational comedy group called the Groundlings, out of which came the character of Pee-wee (named for his minuscule harmonica).

During the early 1980s, Reubens had small roles in film comedies. His real success, however, occurred on TV with a unique and imaginative chil-

dren's show called "Pee-wee's Playhouse." It became a hit with both children and adults and landed Herman the starring roles in two films. *Pee-wee's Big Adventure* (1985) was scripted by Reubens himself and imaginatively directed by Tim BURTON. The second film, *Big Top Pee-wee* (1988), was somewhat less successful. Nonetheless, there was no telling how far the character of Pee-wee Herman might have gone had not Reubens been arrested for indecent exposure in a Sarasota, Florida, adult movie theater, ruining his image as a performer for children. Bereft of his Pee-wee character, Reubens's career lies in shambles. His subsequent film work has been in small roles, most notably as the Penguin's father in *Batman Returns* (1992).

FILMS INCLUDE: *The Blues Brothers* (1980); *Cheech and Chong's Next Movie* (1980); *Cheech and Chong's Nice Dreams* (1981); *Pandemonium* (1981); *Meatballs, Part II* (1984); *Pee-wee's Big Adventure* (also sc, 1985); *Flight of the Navigator* (voice only, 1986); *Back to the Beach* (1987); *Big Top Pee-wee* (also p, 1988); *Buffy, the Vampire Slayer* (cameo, 1992); *Batman Returns* (1992).

## Hill, George Roy (1922–)

Although often referred to as an action director, George Roy Hill would more accurately be called a director of comedies. The majority of his films have been comedies, though some are also full of action. In 1969 he popularized what became known as the "buddy film" when he directed Paul Newman and Robert Redford in the hit comedy/Western *Butch Cassidy and the Sundance Kid.* He is also noted for being the director who brought back old-fashioned story structure to the movies after the sometimes ramshackle efforts of more avant-garde directors during the 1960s.

Born in Minneapolis, Minnesota, to a family with a background in journalism and business, Hill grew up with a passion for airplanes. That passion eventually led to his serving as a pilot during World

War II and as an instructor during the Korean War, emerging from the military with the rank of captain. His interest in aviation eventually led to the making of one of his more personal film projects, *The Great Waldo Pepper* (1975), a nostalgic movie about stunt pilots who barnstormed around the country during his youth.

Hill went to Yale University where he studied music and then to Trinity College in Dublin, Ireland, where he entered show business as an actor. He made his first professional stage appearance in a bit part in George Bernard Shaw's *The Devil's Disciple* at Dublin's Gaiety Theater in 1948.

Hooked on the stage, Hill continued his acting career in the United States until he began writing and directing for television, soon winning both a writing and a directing Emmy for "A Night to Remember" in 1954. His success on television led to directing efforts on Broadway, where he made a decidedly strong impression with his first play, *Look Homeward, Angel*, in 1957. The play won both the New York Drama Critics Circle Award and the Pulitzer Prize. He continued directing for the stage during the late 1950s and early 1960s, most notably *Period of Adjustment* in 1960. Hill made his movie directorial debut by adapting the same play to the big screen in 1962.

Hill's movie career during the 1960s was full of great peaks and valleys. As was often to be the case, his best films of the decade were the comedies, which included *The World of Henry Orient* (1964), *Thoroughly Modern Millie* (1967), and his first big blockbuster, *Butch Cassidy and the Sundance Kid* (1969), for which he received a best director Oscar nomination. The less successful films were the drama *Toys in the Attic* (1963) and the commercial and critical flop *Hawaii* (1966).

The 1970s became Hill's golden period. With the clout that came from directing *Butch Cassidy and the Sundance Kid*, he was able to make what many considered an unmakable movie, Kurt Vonnegut's surrealistic *Slaughterhouse Five* (1972). This BLACK COMEDY was well received by most critics and found a loyal, enthusiastic audience among young people. He followed that with *The Sting* (1974), the most popular movie of his career. Once again pairing Newman and Redford, this time in a slick comedy caper film, *The Sting* brought Hill a best director Oscar while also winning the best picture Academy Award. In its day, it was also the fourth biggest box office grossing movie of all time, just behind *The Godfather* (1972), *The Sound of Music* (1965), and *Gone with the Wind* (1939).

Hill continued to create seriocomic hits, although of a more modest variety. *Slap Shot* (1977) was a controversial comedy because it dealt with the violence and blood lust inherent in the game of hockey. Critics didn't know quite how to take it, but it has since become a more highly regarded film than it was during the time of its release. There was no controversy, however, about *A Little Romance* (1979), a lovely film that enjoyed a quiet success. His next movie, *The World According to Garp* (1982), received a mixed reaction from both reviewers and audiences alike. Hill has made only two films since, the straight drama *The Little Drummer Girl* (1984), which flopped, and the comedy *Funny Farm* (1988), the kind of movie he does best.

FILMS: As director, except as noted: *Walk East on Beacon* (a only, 1952); *Period of Adjustment* (1962); *Toys in the Attic* (1963); *The World of Henry Orient* (1964); *Hawaii* (1966); *Thoroughly Modern Millie* (1967); *Butch Cassidy and the Sundance Kid* (1969); *Slaughterhouse Five* (1971); *The Sting* (1973); *The Great Waldo Pepper* (also story, p, 1975); *Slap Shot* (1977); *A Little Romance* (1979); *The World According to Garp* (also p, 1982); *The Little Drummer Girl* (1984); *Funny Farm* (1988).

**Holliday, Judy (1922—1965)** A comedian who brought depth and vulnerability to the archetypal "dumb blond" role, Judy Holliday made only eleven films, but her image shined very bright during the ten short years of her Hollywood fame. Pretty in an accessible sort of way, Holliday played both prim, repressed comic heroines as well as saucy, outspoken women, leading the way in Hollywood toward a richer, more liberal view of female characters.

Born Judith Tuvim in New York City, she called herself Judy Holliday because *tuvim* means "holiday" in Hebrew. Before she made a name for herself on the stage, she operated the switchboard for Orson Welles's Mercury Theater. Holliday formed a cabaret team with Betty Comden and Adolph Green, which led to a few small roles in films during the mid-1940s. Holliday gave up on Hollywood, however, went back east, and built her career on Broadway. She hit it big in 1946 as Billie Dawn, the supposedly dumb blond in the hugely successful stage comedy *Born Yesterday*. She would eventually reprise the role on film in 1950, winning a best actress Oscar. In the meantime, however, Holliday came to the attention of film audiences in 1949 when she played the comically addled murder suspect in the hit Hepburn/Tracy film *Adam's Rib* (1949).

Despite her Academy Award, Holliday continued to work just as much on Broadway during the 1950s as she did in Hollywood. With an unusual voice, she might have been difficult to cast, but when she appeared on screen she nearly always stole the show. Her screen credits during the 1950s included a subtle and sensitive performance in the drama *The Marrying Kind* (1952), but she was best known for her comedies, the better ones among them being *Phffft* (1954), *The Solid Gold Cadillac* (1956), and the MUSICAL COMEDY *Bells Are Ringing* (1960), her last picture.

---

FILMS: *Greenwich Village* (1944); *Something for the Boys* (1944); *Winged Victory* (1944); *Adam's Rib* (1949); *Born Yesterday* (1950); *The Marrying Kind* (1952); *It Should Happen to You* (1954); *Phffft* (1954); *The Solid Gold Cadillac* (1956); *Full of Life* (1957); *Bells Are Ringing* (1960).

---

**Hood, Darla**   See OUR GANG

**Hope, Bob (1903—)**   There is a tendency to forget the enormous number of comedies Bob Hope made for the big screen because of his long television career, but he was a bona fide movie star of remarkable duration who entered the top-ten list of moneymakers in 1941 and stayed there every single year until 1953. His screen character was usually that of a fast-talking, wisecracking con man who ran scared at the first sign of trouble. He also thought he was God's gift to women and couldn't understand why he never got the girl. In other words, Bob Hope's character was a glorious fool. From his solo hits to his legendary partnership with Bing CROSBY in the famous "Road" movies, Hope fashioned a film career that made him one of Hollywood's most successful comic actors. It's no accident that he has been admired and studied for his comic timing by a great many subsequent film comedians.

Born Leslie Townes Hope in London, England, his family emigrated to America and settled in Cleveland, Ohio, when he was four. After winning several Charlie CHAPLIN impersonation contests he found the courage to try his hand at VAUDEVILLE. Starting with an act of "songs, patter, and eccentric dancing," he eventually made his way to Broadway, appearing in the hit show *Roberta* (1933).

Several other successful Broadway shows followed, and his reputation as a comic actor led to his own radio show. When Paramount decided to continue its successful series of "Big Broadcast" movies with *The Big Broadcast of 1938* (1938), it hired a slew of radio personalities, including Hope. It was his first film, and he acquitted himself well, singing with Shirley Ross the song that was to become his theme, "Thanks for the Memories."

Hope continued in movies, making several minor films until he made the hit *The Cat and the Canary* (1939), a funny horror film in which he began perfecting his special brand of comic cowardice. The 1940s was Hope's richest decade in terms of hits and quality comedies. It began with his first teaming with Bing Crosby and Dorothy Lamour in the original "Road" movie, *The Road to Singapore* (1940). There were seven "Road" movies in all, and the

Hope/Crosby team was one of the most beloved in all of film comedy because it seemed as if the two stars were having the time of their lives. In addition to the early "Road" films, Hope filled out the 1940s with such memorable comedies as *Monsieur Beaucaire* (1945) and *My Favorite Brunette* (1947). In 1949 he was voted the top box office star in the country, thanks to his hit comedy *Paleface* (1948), with Jane Russell.

By the mid-1950s, however, Hope's film comedies began to falter. Except for a few solid efforts such as *The Seven Little Foys* (1955), *Beau James* (1957), and the last of the "Road" movies with Crosby, most of Hope's movies of the latter 1950s and 1960s were rather stale. By this time he had become more of a television star than a film star. However, if Bob Hope is an American institution, then the foundation of that institution was laid in his classic comedies of the 1940s.

FILMS: *The Big Broadcast of 1938* (1938); *College Swing* (1938); *Give Me a Sailor* (1938); *The Cat and the Canary* (1939); *Never Say Die* (1939); *Some Like It Hot* (1939); *The Ghost Breakers* (1940); *Road to Singapore* (1940); *Caught in the Draft* (1941); *Louisiana Purchase* (1941); *Nothing but the Truth* (1941); *Road to Zanzibar* (1941); *My Favorite Blonde* (1942); *Road to Morocco* (1942); *Star Spangled Rhythm* (1942); *Let's Face It* (1943); *They Got Me Covered* (1943); *Welcome to Britain* (1943); *The Princess and the Pirate* (1944); *Duffy's Tavern* (1945); *Monsieur Beaucaire* (1946); *Road to Utopia* (1946); *My Favorite Brunette* (1947); *Road to Rio* (1947); *Variety Girl* (1947); *Where There's Life* (1947); *The Paleface* (1948); *The Great Lover* (1949); *Sorrowful Jones* (1949); *Fancy Pants* (1950); *The Lemon Drop Kid* (1951); *My Favorite Spy* (1951); *The Greatest Show on Earth* (1952); *Road to Bali* (1952); *Son of Paleface* (1952); *Here Come the Girls* (1953); *Off Limits* (1953); *Casanova's Big Night* (1954); *The Seven Little Foys* (1955); *The Iron Petticoat* (1956); *That Certain Feeling* (1956); *Beau James* (1957); *Paris Holiday* (also p, story, 1958); *Alias Jesse James* (also p, 1959); *The Five Pennies* (1959); *The Facts of Life* (1960); *Bachelor in Paradise* (1961); *Road to Hong Kong* (1962); *Call Me Bwana* (1963); *Critic's Choice* (1963); *A Global Affair* (1964); *I'll Take Sweden* (1965); *Boy, Did I Get a Wrong Number!* (1966); *Not with My Wife, You Don't* (1966); *The Oscar* (1966); *Eight on the Lam* (1967); *The Private Navy of Sgt. O'Farrell* (1968); *How to Commit Marriage* (also p, 1969); *Cancel My Reservation* (also p, 1972); *It's Showtime* (1976); *The Muppet Movie* (1979); *Going Hollywood: The War Years* (1988); *Entertaining the Troops* (1989).

## Horton, Edward Everett (1886–1970)

Most well known for playing comic supporting roles, usually as a fussy upper-class twit, Edward Everett Horton appeared in more than 150 films over a period of nearly fifty years. He had his greatest appeal during the 1930s and 1940s in some of Hollywood's most enduring films.

Despite his apparent British accent, Horton was born in Brooklyn, New York, the son of a *New York Times* employee. He went on the stage in 1908, eventually making his way to Hollywood in the early 1920s, where he played a number of leading roles in silent, feature-length comedies. However, he came into his own when the movies began to talk, because Horton had a uniquely memorable speaking voice.

He worked constantly in the 1930s, appearing in many of the best early comedies of the decade, among them *The Front Page* (1931), *Trouble in Paradise* (1932), and *Design for Living* (1933). He made his mark on Hollywood history, however, with his comedic support of Fred Astaire in three of the great dancer's best MUSICAL COMEDIES, *The Gay Divorcee* (1934), *Top Hat* (1935), and *Shall We Dance* (1937).

Horton's comedic gifts were exploited by many of Hollywood's best comic directors, from Ernst LUBITSCH in *The Merry Widow* (1934) and *Bluebeard's Eighth Wife* (1938) to George CUKOR in *Holiday* (1938). Even Busby BERKELEY used him to fine effect in *The Gang's All Here* (1943).

*Loveable bumbler Edward Everett Horton played comic relief par excellence, usually as an upper-class twit. He is seen here in a publicity still from* Here Comes Mr. Jordan *(1941).*
PHOTO COURTESY OF MOVIE STAR NEWS.

Horton was seen only intermittently in the movies after the late 1940s. He did, of course, make an appearance in the all-star comedy film IT's A MAD MAD MAD MAD WORLD (1963). When he wasn't in the movies, one place he could be heard was on the TV cartoon show "Rocky and Bullwinkle," for which he narrated "Fractured Fairy Tales."

FILMS INCLUDE: *A Front Page Story* (1922); *Too Much Business* (1922); *Ruggles of Red Gap* (1923); *Flapper Wives* (1924); *The Business of Love* (1925); *Marry Me* (1925); *La Boheme* (1926); *The Whole Town's Talking* (1926); *Taxi! Taxi!* (1927); *The Terror* (1928); *The Sap* (1929); *Sonny Boy* (1929); *The Hottentot* (1929); *Once a Gentleman* (1930); *Take the Heir* (1930); *The Front Page* (1931); *Reaching for the Moon* (1931); *Lonely Wives* (1931); *The Age of Love* (1931); *Smart Woman* (1931); *Kiss Me Again* (1931); *Trouble in Paradise* (1932); *Design for Living* (1933); *A Bedtime Story* (1933); *Alice in Wonderland* (as Mad Matter, 1933); *The Merry Widow* (1934); *The Gay Divorcee* (1934); *Ladies Should Listen* (1934); *The Devil Is a Woman* (1935); *His Night Out* (1935); *In Caliente* (1935); *Top Hat* (1935); *The Man in the Mirror* (1936); *Hearts Divided* (1936); *Nobody's Fool* (1936); *The Singing Kid* (1936); *Lost Horizon* (1937); *Shall We Dance* (1937); *Angel* (1937); *The Perfect Specimen* (1937); *Holiday* (1938); *Bluebeard's Eighth Wife* (1938); *Paris Honeymoon* (1939); *Here Comes Mr. Jordan* (1941); *Ziegfeld Girl* (1941); *The Magnificent Dope* (1942); *I Married an Angel* (1942); *Thank Your Lucky Stars* (1943); *The Gang's All Here* (1943); *Arsenic and Old Lace* (1944); *Lady on a Train* (1945); *Cinderella Jones* (1946); *Her Husband's Affairs* (1947); *The Story of Mankind* (1957); *Pocketful of Miracles* (1961); *It's a Mad Mad Mad Mad World* (1963); *Sex and the Single Girl* (1964); *The Perils of Pauline* (1967); *Cold Turkey* (1971).

### Hoskins, Allen Clayton "Farina"  *See* OUR GANG

### Howard, Ron (1954— )

Originally known as "Ronny" when he was a child actor in movies and on TV, Ron Howard has developed into one of Hollywood's most successful young directors, demonstrating a particularly light and easy touch with comedies. With a commercial sensibility leavened with a surprising sensitivity, he has created a string of critical and box office hits.

A native of Duncan, Oklahoma, Howard began acting at age two when he appeared on stage with his parents in a Baltimore production of *The Seven Year Itch*. The first of a handful of film appearances was in *The Journey* (1959), but he was more noticeable in *The Music Man* (1962) and at the very center of *The Courtship of Eddie's Father* (1963). He became better known as Opie on TV's long-running "Andy Griffith Show" and as Richie on "Happy Days," the latter role a reprise, of sorts, of the ordinary high school senior he played in George Lucas's hit film *American Graffiti* (1973).

As Ron Howard, a name he preferred after becoming an adult, he found himself typecast by his success in *Happy Days*. He had few roles of note until he played the young man who learned a few lessons about life from John Wayne in *The Shootist* (1976) and then starred in a low-budget but fast-paced racing movie, *Eat My Dust!* (1976). His success in the latter film gave him the opportunity to co-write, direct, and star in a similar film, *Grand Theft Auto* (1977), which turned a profit at the box office and received some admiring nods from the critics for its competence and energy.

As a director during the 1980s, Howard emerged from the low-budget, crash-and-cash films with *Night Shift* (1982), the sleeper hit of the year, which he followed with yet another surprise hit, an offbeat ROMANTIC COMEDY, *Splash* (1984). Howard then made the ambitious science fiction drama *Cocoon* (1985), winning universal praise for his sensitive direction of one of the year's biggest box office draws. It appeared as if he could do no wrong until he directed the lowbrow comedy flop *Gung Ho* (1986).

Producer and writer George Lucas had plenty of faith in Howard and invited him to direct *Willow* (1988), a big-budget fantasy film. That, too, was a disappointment at the box office and was followed by what should have been a surefire comedy with Tom HANKS, *The Burbs* (1989), that also failed to perform at the ticket windows. Howard's once shining career seemed in trouble, until he came through with a smash film that tapped into a fresh vein of comedy: baby boomers with children. The movie was *Parenthood* (1989), and it resurrected Ron Howard's flagging directorial career.

It seems, however, that Howard is determined to make big-budget spectaculars, ignoring his considerable skill with intimate comedies. So far, he seems to be doing all right, producing respectable work on *Backdraft* (1991) and following with the epic love story *Far and Away* (1992), which was quite worthy

in many respects, but failed to cover its substantial budget. Despite its size and scope, one of *Far and Away*'s best features, incidentally, was its quirky sense of humor.

---

FILMS INCLUDE: As actor: *The Journey* (1959); *The Music Man* (1962); *The Courtship of Eddie's Father* (1963); *Village of the Giants* (1965); *Smoke* (1970); *The Wild Country* (1970); *American Graffiti* (1973); *Happy Mother's Day, Love, George* (1973); *The Spikes Gang* (1974); *The First Nudie Musical* (1975); *Eat My Dust* (1976); *The Shootist* (1976); *Roger Corman: Hollywood's Wild Angel* (1978); *More American Graffiti* (1979); *Just One Step: The Great Peace March* (1988).

As producer: *Leo and Loree* (1980); *No Man's Land* (1987); *Clean and Sober* (1988); *Vibes* (1988); *Closet Land* (1991).

As director; *Grand Theft Auto* (also a, co-sc, 1977); *Night Shift* (1982); *Splash* (1984); *Cocoon* (1985); *Gung Ho* (also p, 1986); *Willow* (1988); *The Burbs* (1989); *Parenthood* (also story, 1989); *Backdraft* (1991); *Far and Away* (also p, 1992); *The Paper* (1994).

---

# Hudlin Brothers, The

Writer/director Reginald (1961–) and producer Warrington Hudlin have quietly become a vibrant, young comic filmmaking force. They burst upon the cinema scene with the boisterous, critically and commercially successful *House Party* (1990), a hip-hop hit that became one of the most financially rewarding films of its time, making more than ten times its production costs.

The two brothers were born in East St. Louis, Illinois. Reginald graduated from Harvard, while Warrington graduated from Yale. Both brothers pursued filmmaking, with Reginald making short fiction films and Warrington making documentaries, including a documentary about Spike Lee's *School Daze*. In 1978, Warrington co-founded the Black Filmmaker Foundation, which has grown

*Director Reginald Hudlin (left) and producer Warrington Hudlin (right) make a formidable young filmmaking team, having a couple of hits under their belts already, including* House Party *(1990) and* Boomerang *(1992). The brothers are seen here on the set of the latter film.*
PHOTO BY BRUCE W. TALAMON, © PARAMOUNT PICTURES.

**FILMS:** *House Party* (sc, d, p, 1990); *Bebe's Kids* (sc, p, 1992); *Boomerang* (d, p, 1992); *Posse* (cameo, 1993).

**Hughes, John (1950–)** A prolific screenwriter, director, and producer of comedies, John Hughes cornered the 1980s youth market, making entertaining movies about teenagers from their point of view. During the early 1990s he focused on making films from a still younger point of view. Hughes has also been the principal filmmaker behind the various "National Lampoon" movies of the last dozen years.

Born in Chicago, Illinois, Hughes began his show business career as a gag writer before succumbing to the lure of advertising. When his unusual sense of humor could no longer be contained, he began writing for *The National Lampoon* magazine, eventually becoming a contributing editor. His association with the magazine brought him the opportunity to pen the screenplay for *National Lampoon's Class Reunion* (1982). It was not well received by the critics, but it did well enough at the box office to successfully launch Hughes's screenwriting career.

While Hughes was only half responsible for the bomb *Nate and Hayes* (1983) (he co-wrote the screenplay), he came into his own as a screenwriter with two major critical and box office hits, *Mr. Mom* (1983) and *National Lampoon's Vacation* (1983). His subsequent crazy comedies have fared less well with the critics but have generally been commercial winners. His later hits in this area have been *National Lampoon's European Vacation* (1985), *Planes, Trains and Automobiles* (1987), which he also directed, and *The Great Outdoors* (1988).

His reputation as "the voice of the younger generation," however, has come from a whole other set of movies. They, too, have been comedies, but have been rooted in a more human experience that seems to speak to many teenage moviegoers. It is no coincidence that he has also directed and occasionally

through the years to three-thousand members. Eventually, the two brothers joined to produce music videos for Heavy D and the Boys, Channel Two, Blue Magic, The Jamaica Boys, and others.

Their low-budget success with *House Party*, which had been filmed once before by Reginald as his senior thesis at Harvard, opened Hollywood's doors for this ambitious, multi-talented team. Next, both brothers produced the black animated musical *Bebe's Kids* (1992), with Reginald providing the screenplay. Based upon characters created by Robin Harris, the film was not a success. In the same year, however, Warrington produced and Reginald directed the Eddie Murphy comedy *Boomerang* (1992), bringing to it some of the same energy, quirky secondary characters, and lively sense of humor that infused *House Party*.

produced these films, making his directorial debut, in fact, with *Sixteen Candles* (1984).

He followed that success by writing, directing, and producing *The Breakfast Club* (1985), a bold and somewhat innovative movie for the teen exploitation market that had the audacity to simply let a handful of young people speak their minds on film; it was a major hit, highlighting the talents of several young actors and helping to turn them into major teen stars, among them Molly Ringwald, Anthony Michael Hall, Judd Nelson, Emilio Estevez, and Ally Sheedy.

Hughes has written several other youth market movies, including the pleasantly silly *Weird Science* (1985) and a joyous celebration called *Ferris Bueller's Day Off* (1986). He followed those films with a new departure, *She's Having a Baby* (1988), a movie that asked his audience to face the next stage of their lives. It was neither a critical nor a commercial success, suggesting that Hughes would have to find another way to address his loyal following.

In the meantime, Hughes jumped ahead to a different clientele, making movies for families with young kids. He touched a nerve in that regard with the comedic babysitting movie *Uncle Buck* (1989). He had the good fortune to discover a child star (Macaulay Culkin) in that film, whom he elevated to the lead in *Home Alone* (1990) and *Home Alone 2: Lost in New York* (1992), a couple of monster hits that Hughes both wrote and produced.

FILMS: *National Lampoon's Class Reunion* (sc, 1982); *Mr. Mom* (sc, 1983); *Nate and Hayes* (sc, 1983); *National Lampoon's Vacation* (sc, song, 1983); *Sixteen Candles* (sc, d, 1984); *The Breakfast Club* (sc, p, d, 1985); *National Lampoon's European Vacation* (story, sc, 1985); *Weird Science* (sc, d, 1985); *Ferris Bueller's Day Off* (sc, p, d, 1986); *Pretty in Pink* (sc, p, 1986); *Planes, Trains and Automobiles* (sc, p, song, 1987); *Some Kind of Wonderful* (sc, p, 1987); *The Great Outdoors* (sc, p, 1988); *She's Having a Baby* (sc, p, d, 1988); *National Lampoon's Christmas Vacation* (sc, p, 1989); *Uncle Buck* (sc, p, d, 1989); *Home Alone*

(sc, p, 1990); *Career Opportunities* (sc, p, 1991); *Curly Sue* (sc, p, d, 1991); *Only the Lonely* (p, 1991); *Dutch* (sc, p, 1991); *Home Alone 2: Lost in New York* (p, 1992); *Dennis the Menace* (co-sc, p, 1993).

---

## Hutchins, Bobby "Wheezer"   *See* OUR GANG

## Hutton, Jim (1933–1979)

A tall, lean leading man, Jim Hutton excelled in light romantic comedies during the 1960s. From *Where the Boys Are* (1960) through *Who's Minding the Mint?* (1967), he very nearly specialized in comedies. Even one of the two Westerns he starred in during that stretch was a comedy, *The Hallelujah Trail* (1965).

Born in Binghamton, New York, Hutton was a discovery of Hollywood director Douglas Sirk, who saw the young soldier in a military stage show in Germany. Sirk gave him a modest supporting role in the drama *A Time to Love and a Time to Die* (1958). In his film debut, Hutton was listed in the credits as Dana Hutton.

Within a few films, Hutton found his way into comedies, and mostly stayed there. His career peaked with *Walk, Don't Run* (1966), in which he shared top billing with Cary GRANT. It was Grant's last film, and the great disparity in charm between the ever-suave and youthful Grant and the relatively callow Hutton could not have been put in more stark relief. When success in comedies began to elude him, he starred in big-budget action films in the late 1960s and early 1970s, after which his career took a nosedive.

His son, actor Timothy Hutton, who bears a rather striking resemblance to his father, has been a successful film actor who came into prominence with an Academy Award for best supporting actor in *Ordinary People* (1980). Sadly, he won the Oscar a year after his father's death. Timothy has been a leading man in the movies throughout the 1980s and 1990s, although not yet in a comedy.

FILMS INCLUDE: *A Time to Love and a Time to Die* (1958); *Ten Seconds to Hell* (1959); *Where the Boys Are* (1960); *The Subterraneans* (1960); *The Honeymoon Machine* (1961); *Bachelor in Paradise* (1961); *Period of Adjustment* (1962); *The Horizontal Lieutenant* (1962); *Looking for Love* (1964); *Never Too Late* (1965); *The Hallelujah Trail* (1965); *Major Dundee* (1965); *The Trouble with Angels* (1966); *Walk, Don't Run* (1966); *Who's Minding the Mint?* (1967); *The Green Berets* (1968); *Hellfighters* (1969); *Psychic Killer* (1975).

# I—J

**It Happened One Night**   A modest ROMANTIC COMEDY, *It Happened One Night* is about a spoiled, runaway heiress who falls in love with a wisecracking, down-on-his luck reporter while traveling together on a long bus ride. This 1934 film became the year's biggest hit, winning five major Oscars and changing Hollywood history.

*It Happened One Night* was directed by Frank CAPRA (Oscar), the screenplay was written by Robert Riskin (Oscar), and it starred Clark Gable (Oscar) and Claudette Colbert (Oscar). The film was produced by Columbia, and therefore Harry Cohn received the film's best picture Academy Award. It was the only film to ever win all five top Academy Awards until *One Flew Over the Cuckoo's Nest* equalled the feat in 1975.

The movie was a success for a number of reasons, the first being the strong script with natural, idiosyncratic dialogue. Second, there were genuine sparks between the macho Gable and the headstrong Colbert. Third, the film was largely shot on location, and the natural feel of the open road added immeasurably to the movie's believability. Finally, Capra's uncanny ability to tell a story with visual flair was very much in evidence, from the famous "Walls of Jericho" scene to the equally famous hitchhiking sequence.

In his splendid autobiography *Frank Capra: The Name Above the Title*, the director explained how the movie came into being. The film was based on a short story called "Night Bus" by Samuel Hopkins Adams, which Capra read in *Cosmopolitan* while sitting in a barbershop. He had Columbia buy the film rights to the story for $5,000.

As it happened, two previous "bus trip" films had been made by other studios and both had been flops. Columbia studio boss Harry Cohn ordered that the word *bus* be taken out of the title, so the name of the film was changed to *It Happened One Night*.

The biggest challenge Capra had was casting the movie. Despite his long string of hits at Columbia, the studio was still a poverty row enterprise, and inducing stars to sign on to the project proved difficult. Capra wanted to cast the role of the heiress first, but despite his previous successes, a number of actresses, including Myrna Loy, Margaret Sullavan, Miriam Hopkins, and Constance Bennett all turned him down after reading the original script.

In that first script, however, the rich heiress was just a brat and the reporter was a poor painter. Thanks to suggestions made by colleague Myles Connolly to make the two characters more sympathetic, particularly to change the painter to a reporter, Capra and Riskin rewrote the screenplay in a week.

They then decided to go after the male lead in the hope of getting a star whose presence in the cast would help them sign a formidable leading lady. In a well-known bit of Hollywood folklore, MGM owed Columbia the use of one of its stars. Capra wanted Robert Montgomery, who refused. MGM's Louis B. Mayer forced Columbia to take one of his up-and-coming actors, Clark Gable. The reason? Gable was demanding more money, and Mayer's way of showing him who was boss was to humiliate him by loaning him to lowly Columbia.

With Gable set for the film, Capra went after Claudette Colbert for the female role because she was on vacation from Paramount and could make her own deals without studio interference. To induce her to sign, she was offered twice her usual salary, which brought her $50,000 for one month's work. She was well worth the money. According to Capra:

> In the well-known hitchhiking scene in which she proves her leg is greater than Gable's thumb, she refused to pull up her dress and show her leg. We waited until the casting director sent us a chorus girl with shapely underpinnings to "double" for Colbert's. When she saw the double's leg, she said, "Get her out of here. I'll do it. That's not *my* leg!" And it sure wasn't. There are no more luscious gams in the world than Colbert's—not even Marlene's.

The film's entire budget was a mere $325,000, with a shooting schedule of four weeks. When the film opened, its initial reviews were lukewarm, at best. However, the word of mouth on the film was stupendous. Every week the crowds grew larger at theaters all over the country. Before long it was the talk of the industry, and critics went back to see the film to find out what it was they had missed the first time around.

The film's overwhelming success wrought great changes in Hollywood. Columbia not only had its first best picture Academy Award, *It Happened One Night* catapulted the studio into the ranks of the majors, never to be a poverty row outfit again. Clark Gable's supposed punishment ended up turning him into MGM's major male star, and Louis B. Mayer had to triple the actor's salary. Also from a filmmaking perspective, this movie was deeply significant. In Myles Connolly's words, as reported by Capra, "You [Capra] took the old classic four of show business—hero, heroine, villain, comedian—and cut it down to *three*, by combining hero and comedian into one person." It was an immensely important change in story and character structure that remains to this day.

Proving that lightning rarely ever strikes twice in

the same place, the film was remade in 1956 as *You Can't Run Away from It* with June Allyson and Jack LEMMON. It was not nearly as successful as the original.

**It's a Mad Mad Mad Mad World**   Directed by Stanley Kramer, this 1963 film is the one and only super all-star comedy of the sound era. The film it most resembles in that regard is TILLIE'S PUNCTURED ROMANCE (1914), the first feature-length comedy that was cast with virtually every comic star of the silent era, or at least those who worked for Mack SENNETT (which was the cream of the comedy crop). Unlike the "Big Broadcast" films and others of their ilk in the 1930s, which often featured many notable comedians, *It's A Mad Mad Mad Mad World* was cast with a full array of comic stars of every imaginable type without regard to studio affiliation (thanks to the end of the studio system).

A Sennett-inspired chase film on an epic scale, the movie was built around a search for stolen loot buried beneath the mysterious "Big W." At the film's center was Spencer Tracy, playing a detective. Essentially a dramatic actor, Tracy's presence grounded the film while all around him total craziness ensued. The search for the treasure began with Jimmy DURANTE, who literally kicks a bucket (when dying) while giving the clue to the whereabouts of the loot. Among the rest of the stellar comedy cast (in parts ranging from leads to supporting players to cameos) were Milton BERLE, Jonathan WINTERS, Sid CAESAR, Phil SILVERS, Buddy HACKETT, Mickey ROONEY, Peter FALK, Buster KEATON, Edie ADAMS, TERRY-THOMAS, Andy DEVINE, Eddie "Rochester" ANDERSON, Ben BLUE, Paul FORD, Minta DURFEE, Edward Everett HORTON, Don KNOTTS, Zasu PITTS, Arnold Stang, Jesse White, Sterling Holloway, Norman Fell, William Demarest, Dick Shawn, and many others.

One of the generous elements of the film was its recognition of comedians from the past. Whether audiences recognized them or not (and most didn't), the movie honored many all-but-forgotten silent comedy stars, ranging from Minta Durfee to Ben Blue. Unfortunately, some of those cameos weren't seen by audiences when the 154-minute film was originally released. Already a staggeringly long movie, it had been cut from its intended length of 175 minutes. Happily, the longer version is now available on video.

The film was a box office winner, although some critics carped about its relentless excess, but in that it was merely following the frenetic style of Sennett's Keystone era, to which the movie was a loving tribute.

**Jiggs and Maggie**  *See* SERIES COMEDIES

**Johnson, Chic**  *See* OLSEN AND JOHNSON

**Jones, Chuck**  *See* WARNER BROS. CARTOONS

# K

**Kahn, Madeline (1942—)** One of the leading character actress/comedians of the last two decades, Madeline Kahn is thoroughly offbeat, with an excruciatingly funny speaking voice. She always seems to arrive at a punch line (or the heart of her character) from an unexpected direction, making the laughter she creates all the richer. A two-time Oscar nominee, she was at the peak of her popularity during the 1970s when she came to the fore in several of Mel BROOKS's most inspired comedies. In addition to Brooks, she has often worked with other creative talents at the top of their comedic careers, among them Peter Bogdanovich, Neil SIMON, Jim HENSON, and Gene WILDER.

Born in Boston, Massachusetts, Kahn studied opera before embarking on a career in the theater. She sang and performed on and off Broadway, before Peter Bogdanovich cast her in a supporting role in *What's Up, Doc?* (1972). Knowing a good thing when he had one, Bogdanovich cast her again in *Paper Moon* (1973), for which she won a best supporting actress Oscar nomination; she lost to co-star Tatum O'Neal. With her zaniness exhibited for all to see in two straight hit films, it wasn't long before Mel Brooks took her under his wing and gave her some of her funniest material in *Blazing Saddles* (1974), for which she received her second best supporting actress Academy Award nomination, and *Young Frankenstein* (1974). Brooks would later use her in two more of his films, *High Anxiety* (1977) and *History of the World, Part I* (1981). In the meantime, Gene Wilder, an alumnus of the Mel Brooks school of humor, also cast Kahn in his directorial effort, *The Adventure of Sherlock Holmes' Smarter Brother* (1975). Although she is not the usual sort of actress for whom Neil Simon writes his material, she was perfect in his private eye spoof *The Cheap Detective* (1978) and was a welcome foil to Miss Piggy in Jim Henson's *The Muppet Movie* (1979) and Alan ARKIN in Marshall BRICKMAN's overlooked little gem *Simon* (1980).

Her success of the 1970s ended abruptly in the 1980s. She was in several out-and-out bombs, such as *Wholly Moses!* (1980), *City Heat* (1984), and *Clue* (1985). Even when she was in good movies, like *History of the World, Part I* and *Simon*, audiences were sparse. As a result, Kahn made fewer and fewer films during the 1980s and early 1990s. Instead, she concentrated on the stage, ultimately winning a Tony Award for best actress for her 1992–1993 performance on Broadway in *The Sisters Rosensweig*.

FILMS INCLUDE: *The Dove* (short, 1968); *What's Up, Doc?* (1972); *Paper Moon* (1973); *From the Mixed-Up Files of Mrs. Basil E. Frankweiler/The Hideaways* (1973); *Blazing Saddles* (1974); *Young Frankenstein* (1974); *At Long Last Love* (1975); *The Adventure of Sherlock Holmes' Smarter Brother* (1975); *Won Ton Ton—The Dog Who Saved Hollywood* (1976); *High Anxiety* (1977); *The Cheap Detective* (1978); *The Muppet Movie* (1979); *First Family* (1980); *Happy Birthday, Gemini* (1980); *Simon* (1980); *Wholly Moses!* (1980); *History of the World, Part I* (1981); *Yellowbeard* (1983); *Slapstick (of Another Kind)* (1984); *City Heat* (1984); *Clue* (1985); *An American Tail* (voice, 1986); *My Little Pony: The Movie* (voice only, 1986); *Betsy's Wedding* (1990).

**Kalmar and Ruby** Bert Kalmar (1884–1947) and Harry Ruby (1895–1974) were a songwriting, playwriting, and screenwriting team that penned clever tunes as well as comic entertainments. Kalmar was the lyricist, and Ruby was the composer. The duo is most closely associated with the MARX BROTHERS, for whom they wrote three of their funniest movies, one of which, *Animal Crackers* (1930), was based on the writing team's Broadway show. The other two films they created for the Marx Brothers were *Horsefeathers* (1932) and *Duck Soup* (1933). Naturally, they also wrote the famous witty songs from these films, including "Hooray for Captain Spaulding," "Whatever It Is, I'm Against It," and "All God's Chillun' Got Guns."

In addition to writing comedy scripts and music for the Marx Brothers, Kalmar and Ruby also provided Eddie CANTOR with one of his best scripts, *The Kid from Spain* (1932). The duo wrote nine Broadway shows, three of which were turned into movies, including *Animal Crackers* (which they co-wrote with George S. KAUFMAN), *The Cuckoos* (1930), and *Top Speed* (1930).

By the mid-1930s, however, the team began to lose steam. Their scripts were not quite up to their early successes, even though their music was still quite memorable in films such as *Hips, Hips, Hooray* (1934) and *Walking on Air* (1936).

Ruby went on to write the music and scripts for several other modest films without Kalmar in the mid- to late 1940s and early 1950s. After Kalmar's death in 1947, Hollywood recognized the two collaborators with *Three Little Words* (1950), a biopic in which Fred Astaire played Kalmar, and Red SKELTON portrayed Ruby. The film featured many of the team's most beloved songs.

FILMS INCLUDE: *Check and Double Check* (1930); *The Cuckoos* (1930); *Top Speed* (1930); *Animal Crackers* (1930); *The Kid from Spain* (1932); *Horsefeathers* (1932); *Duck Soup* (1933); *Kentucky Kernels* (1934); *Hip, Hips, Hooray* (1934); *Walking on Air* (1936); *Everybody Sing* (1938); *Wake Up and Dream* (1946); *Carnival in Costa Rica* (1948).

---

**Kane, Carol (1952– )** With her off-kilter cuteness, Carol Kane has evolved into an undervalued character comedian who is used as often for her uniqueness as she is for her talent. A small-boned, curly haired redhead with saucer eyes and a little girl voice, Kane has been appearing in movies for more than twenty years, reaching the apex of her career back in 1975 when she was nominated for a best actress Academy Award for her performance in *Hester Street*.

Born in Cleveland, Ohio, Kane worked in the theater as early as age fourteen. Within four years she began showing up in small roles in movies, including high-profile films like *Carnal Knowledge* (1971) and *The Last Detail* (1973). Her big break came when she landed the lead role in *Hester Street* (1975); her Oscar nomination vaulted her to prominence, but she was a hard type to cast, and good roles didn't come easy. Until that point, she wasn't particularly known for comedy, but that changed when she lightened up in *Harry and Walter Go to New York* (1976). Her zaniness was highlighted to even better effect in Gene Wilder's *The World's Greatest Lover* (1977). Although neither of those films were significant hits, her work in them suggested she might be the right actress to play Andy Kaufman's oddball wife in the TV sitcom "Taxi," a role she held from 1981 to 1983.

If the 1970s was her decade in the movies, the 1980s and beyond have been her TV years. In addition to "Taxi," Kane was a regular on "All Is Forgiven" (1986), "American Dreamer" (1990), and "Brooklyn Bridge" (1992)—not to mention being a frequent guest on "Late Night with David Letterman." It's not that she hasn't worked regularly in the movies, it's simply that she flits in and out of movies without making much of an impact. For the most part, her work in the movies, while amusingly eccentric in films like *Scrooged* (1988) and *The Lemon*

*Sisters* (1990), suggests a talent that has not had the chance to fully flower.

---

**FILMS INCLUDE:** *Is This Trip Really Necessary?* (1970); *Desperate Characters* (1971); *Carnal Knowledge* (1971); *Wedding in White* (1973); *The Last Detail* (1973); *Hester Street* (1975); *Dog Day Afternoon* (1975); *Harry and Walter Go to New York* (1976); *Valentino* (1977); *The World's Greatest Lover* (1977); *Annie Hall* (1977); *My Sister, My Love/The Mafu Cage* (1979); *When a Stranger Calls* (1979); *The Muppet Movie* (1979); *La Sabina* (1979); *Pandemonium* (1981); *The Games of Countess Dolingen of Gratz* (1981); *Norman Loves Rose* (1982); *Can She Bake a Cherry Pie?* (1983); *Over the Brooklyn Bridge* (1984); *Racing with the Moon* (1984); *The Secret Diary of Sigmund Freud* (1984); *Translyvania 6-5000* (1985); *Jumpin' Jack Flash* (1986); *Ishtar* (1987); *The Princess Bride* (1987); *Sticky Fingers* (1988); *License to Drive* (1988); *Scrooged* (1988); *Flashback* (1990); *Joe versus the Volcano* (1990); *My Blue Heaven* (1990); *The Lemon Sisters* (1990); *Addams Family Values* (1993).

---

# Kanin, Garson (1912—)

A respected screenwriter, director, playwright, and author, Garson Kanin made his greatest mark in Hollywood with a string of sophisticated comedies, many of which he penned with his wife, Ruth GORDON. All of his work reflects a high level of playfulness, energy, and intelligence.

Born in Rochester, New York, Kanin was a high school dropout who helped support his family as a musician and comedian during the early years of the Depression. Eventually, he received formal training at the American Academy of Dramatic Arts and embarked on an acting career in 1933, appearing in such Broadway plays as *Little Ol' Boy* (1933), *Boy Meets Girl* (1935), and *Star Spangled* (1936). During the mid-1930s he doubled as an assistant director for the famed Broadway director George Abbott. Not long after, Kanin began directing for the Broadway

stage, putting on such shows as *Hitch Your Wagon* (1937) and *Too Many Heroes* (1937).

Kanin received the call to Hollywood in 1938 and worked there steadily until World War II. In his first few short years in the movie business, however, he directed a steady stream of charming, funny films that predated the rise of Preston STURGES. Like Sturges, Kanin's movies—such as *The Great Man Votes* (1939), *Bachelor Mother* (1939), *My Favorite Wife* (1940), and *Tom, Dick and Harry* (1941)—were rooted in (and made fun of) social issues and conventions.

During the war, Kanin went on to produce and direct a number of highly regarded documentaries for the government, among them a collaboration with Jean Renoir, *A Salute to France* (1946), and a collaboration with Sir Carol Reed, *The True Glory* (1945), a film that won a best documentary Oscar.

At the close of World War II, Kanin returned to Broadway as a playwright. His success was almost immediate when he scored with *Born Yesterday* in 1946 (later turned into a hit film of the same name in 1950 and remade again in 1993). It was also in 1946 that he returned to writing screenplays, and in 1948 he and his wife, Ruth Gordon, co-scripted *A Double Life*, for which they shared an Academy Award nomination for best original screenplay. Among his other fine screenplays were several wonderfully adroit, sophisticated comedies for Spencer Tracy and Katharine Hepburn, most notably *Adam's Rib* (1949) and *Pat and Mike* (1952).

Since the mid-1950s, Kanin has mostly been absent from Hollywood. He directed two unsuccessful comedies in 1969, *Where It's At* and *Some Kind of a Nut*, but was otherwise involved in the theater during the late 1950s and 1960s. Although he had written books during the 1950s, he developed a moderately successful career as a writer of both fiction and nonfiction during the 1970s and 1980s, many of his books using Hollywood for their backgrounds.

---

**FILMS:** *A Man to Remember* (d, 1938); *Next Time I Marry* (d, 1938); *Bachelor Mother* (a, d, 1939); *The*

*Great Man Votes* (d, 1939); *They Made Her a Spy* (sc, 1939); *My Favorite Wife* (d, 1940); *They Knew What They Wanted* (d, 1940); *Tom, Dick and Harry* (d, 1941); *Night Shift* (short, d, 1942); *Fellow Americans* (d, 1942); *Ring of Steel* (d, 1942); *A Lady Takes a Chance* (uncred sc, 1943); *The More the Merrier* (uncred sc, 1943); *Battle Stations* (short, d, 1944); *Night Stripes* (short, d, 1944); *A Salute to France* (co-d, 1944); *The True Glory* (p, co-d, 1945); *From This Day Forward* (sc, 1946); *A Double Life* (sc, 1947); *Adam's Rib* (sc, 1949); *Born Yesterday* (based on play, 1950); *The Marrying Kind* (story, sc, 1952); *Pat and Mike* (sc, 1952); *It Should Happen to You* (story, sc, 1954); *The Girl Can't Help It* (from novella *Do Re Mi*, 1956); *High Time* (story, 1960); *The Rat Race* (sc, from own play, 1960); *The Right Approach* (based on play, *The Live Wire*, 1961); *Walk Don't Run* (uncred sc from *The More the Merrier*, 1966); *Some Kind of a Nut* (sc, d, 1969); *Where It's At* (sc, d, 1969); *Born Yesterday* (based on play, 1993).

---

**Kaufman, George S. (1889—1961)** A Pulitzer Prize—winning playwright who had very little to do with Hollywood, at least directly, George S. Kaufman is responsible nonetheless for an extraordinary number of hit comedies based on his plays. The fact is, Kaufman hated Hollywood; he thought the studio chiefs were morons and resented the low esteem in which writers were held. Even as a dabbler in movies, however, he was brilliant. He co-wrote the story of one of Eddie CANTOR's best films, *Roman Scandals* (1933); he co-wrote the screenplay (with Morrie RYSKIND) of the MARX BROTHERS' biggest hit, *A Night at the Opera* (1935); and he directed the highly praised sophisticated comedy *The Senator Was Indiscreet* (1947). All the rest of his work, however, was for the stage.

Curiously, for a man who did not like the collaborative aspects of filmmaking (he'd call it interference), he inevitably wrote his plays with collaborators. He also worked with some of the best writers of his time, including Ring Lardner, Moss Hart, Marc Connelly, Edna Ferber, KALMAR AND RUBY, and Morrie Ryskind.

While Kaufman is associated with the Marx Brothers by virtue of having written their most successful film as well as the two Broadway shows that became their first two movies, *The Cocoanuts* (1929) and *Animal Crackers* (1930), he also wrote many other hit shows that became famous comedies, including *Dinner at Eight* (1933), *Stage Door* (1937), *You Can't Take It with You* (1938), and *The Man Who Came to Dinner* (1942). There is no obvious connective style or thread to these films except that they are all devilishly funny and that none of his comic heroes will suffer fools.

Kaufman was not only a famous writer, he was also a famous lover. His name is forever linked with that of actress Mary Astor, whose graphic (and laudatory) diary entries involving the two of them came to light in a bitter 1936 divorce and child custody case between her and her physician husband.

---

**FILMS:** Adapted by others from his plays: *Dulcy* (1923); *Merton of the Movies* (1924); *Beggar on Horseback* (1925); *The Cocoanuts* (1929); *Animal Crackers* (1930); *The Royal Family of Broadway* (1931); *Dinner at Eight* (1933); *Stage Door* (1937); *You Can't Take It with You* (1938); *Dulcy* (remake, 1940); *The Man Who Came to Dinner* (1942); *Merton of the Movies* (remake, 1947); *The Solid Gold Cadillac* (1956).

Work done directly for the movies: *Roman Scandals* (co-story, 1933); *A Night at the Opera* (co-story, co-sc, 1935); *The Senator Was Indiscreet* (d, 1947).

---

**Kaye, Danny (1913—1987)** A warm, sweet-tempered, and engaging comic star for nearly twenty years, Danny Kaye made movies that were rarely as brilliant as he was. He usually played befuddled but lovable simpletons who were less than courageous, yet capable of the most hysterical forms of indirect bravery. Kaye was an inventive and lively singer; he, in fact, rose to fame thanks to his rapid-

*A multi-talented actor, comedian, singer, and dancer, Danny Kaye brought a whimsical charm to the big screen. The only fault one can find in his film career was that he was so often better than his material. He is seen here in a publicity still from one of his early starring features,* The Wonder Man *(1945).*
PHOTO COURTESY OF MOVIE STAR NEWS.

fire delivery of wonderfully idiotic songs, many of which were written by his lifelong wife, Sylvia Fine.

Born David Daniel Kaminski to a poor tailor and his wife in Brooklyn, New York the young man quit school at thirteen to enter show business. He got his start as a comic in what became known as the "Borscht Belt," an enclave of resort hotels in the Catskill Mountains north of New York City where Jews often went to vacation during the summer. From there, Kaye traveled the dying VAUDEVILLE circuit, gaining experience and trying out new material.

Spotted for the rising young comedian that he

was, Kaye made several two-reel shorts for the small independent EDUCATIONAL PICTURES, but they didn't immediately bring him fame and fortune. They were, however, later compiled into a film inaccurately titled *The Danny Kaye Story.*

After Kaye had several successes on Broadway in the late 1930s and early 1940s, Hollywood took another chance on him in the person of Samuel Goldwyn. The famous producer had once made the movies of Eddie CANTOR; he saw the same genius in the young Kaye and signed him to a film contract.

The following year, Kaye began his long and commercially successful association with Goldwyn, starring in *Up in Arms* (1944), the first of many bright and generally entertaining comedies. In all, Kaye starred in seventeen feature films; while not all of them were gems, most were hits. A number of them, thanks to Kaye, have become minor classics.

The actor's most fondly remembered movies are *Wonder Man* (1945), *The Secret Life of Walter Mitty* (1947), *The Inspector General* (1949), *Hans Christian Andersen* (1952), *Knock on Wood* (1953), *The Court Jester* (1956), and *Merry Andrew* (1958).

Kaye occasionally shared top billing with other stars, most notably Bing CROSBY in *White Christmas* (1954) and in his last feature film, the all-star drama *The Madwoman of Chaillot* (1969).

Long associated with his devotion to the world's children, Kaye was an early and inspired advocate of UNICEF. He made a serious short called *Assignment Children* for the United Nations in 1954, and in that year was also given a special Oscar for "his unique talents, his service to the Academy, the motion picture industry, and the American people."

Occupied with his highly regarded TV variety program, "The Danny Kaye Show" (1963–1967) and his continued commitment to UNICEF, his film career virtually came to a halt. He didn't seem to mind. He starred in the Broadway musical *Two by Two* in 1970 and traveled the country as a popular comic guest conductor of various city symphony orchestras. Later, he made occasional forays back into television, most memorably as Captain Hook in a new version of *Peter Pan* (1975) and in *Skokie* (1981), giving a stunning dramatic performance as a concentration camp survivor facing the nightmare of neo-Nazis marching in his home town near Chicago.

---

**FILMS:** *Dime a Dance* (short, 1937); *Cupid Takes a Holiday* (short, 1938); *Getting an Eyeful* (short, 1938); *Money or Your Life* (short, 1938); *Night Shift* (short, 1942); *The Birth of a Star* (1944); *Up in Arms* (1944); *The Wonder Man* (1945); *The Kid from Brooklyn* (1946); *The Secret Life of Walter Mitty* (1947); *A Song Is Born* (1948); *The Inspector General* (1949); *It's a Great Feeling* (1949); *On the Riviera* (1951); *Hans Christian Andersen* (1952); *Assignment Children* (1954); *Hula from Hollywood* (short, 1954); *Knock on Wood* (1954); *White Christmas* (1954); *The Court Jester* (1956); *Me and the Colonel* (1958); *Merry Andrew* (1958); *The Five Pennies* (also p, 1959); *On the Double* (1961); *The Man from the Diner's Club* (1963); *The Madwoman of Chaillot* (1969).

---

## Keaton, Buster (1895—1966)

Known as "The great stone face," Buster Keaton was the indomitable foe of fate; he was a modern everyman who locked horns with nature and machines, somehow nearly always surviving the comic disasters that came hurtling his way. Depending upon one's taste in film comedy, Buster Keaton is either the greatest movie comedian of all time or the second greatest, just behind Charlie CHAPLIN. While Chaplin's comedy was essentially theatrical, Keaton's humor was utterly cinematic. Chaplin's humor was warm, and Keaton's was cool and aloof, but both were enormously funny and richly deserving of their reputations. It was Chaplin, however, who remained famous and revered throughout most of his life, while Keaton faded from view in the early 1930s. Happily, both Keaton and his artistry were finally rediscovered before he died.

Born Joseph Francis Keaton in Piqua, Kansas, to a VAUDEVILLE family, he received his nickname from an old family friend, the famous escape artist Harry Houdini. It seems that at the age of six months, the infant Keaton fell down a long flight of stairs without so much as a scratch. Houdini apparently thought Keaton was bust-proof, and the nickname Buster stuck.

By age three, Keaton had joined his family in their vaudeville act, and "The Three Keatons" became a popular act. Young Keaton was soon the star attraction. Later, after his father began drinking heavily, making their acrobatic act terribly dangerous, the trio disbanded. Keaton went to New York to appear as a solo in *The Passing Show of 1917* at Broadway's Winter Garden Theater at a salary of $250 per week. At that time he bumped into an old vaudeville friend who was with Roscoe "Fatty" ARBUCKLE. That meeting not only changed Keaton's plans, it changed his life.

Keaton was invited to watch the filming of a comedy short at Arbuckle's studio. Mesmerized by the camera, that very day he turned down the guaranteed $250 per week vaudeville salary for just $40 per week from Arbuckle.

Keaton learned everything he could about film comedy from Arbuckle, working for the popular comedian for four years (minus a stint in the army). He first appeared on film in *The Butcher Boy* (1917). From the very beginning, his persona was the same: the unsmiling stone face. Keaton had developed his stoic expression very early on in his vaudeville career, noting that audiences laughed when he didn't smile. Nonetheless, Keaton laughed once on film in *Fatty at Coney Island* (1917).

Keaton took over Arbuckle's studio in 1921 when his rotund friend went to another company. It should also be noted that Keaton forever remained loyal to his mentor, even in the worst days of the famous Arbuckle scandal.

Just before he took over the studio, Keaton appeared in his first feature, *The Saphead* (1920), a film he didn't write or direct, but a movie whose success would soon pave the way for his own features. They came after Keaton's classic two-reelers such as *The*

*Playhouse* (1921), *The Boat* (1921), and *Cops* (1922). His movies had an absurdist quality that seems thoroughly modern today. Yet they were also enormously popular in their own time. Keaton was a huge success, ruling the comedy roost with Chaplin by the early 1920s.

Keaton shared his directorial chores with Eddie CLINE, but Cline himself graciously conceded that 90 percent of the comic inventions in their films belonged to Keaton. Their first feature together was *The Three Ages* (1923), an amusing takeoff of *Intolerance* (1916). However, Keaton really hit his stride with his second feature, *Our Hospitality* (1923). Virtually all of his silent features through 1928 were as good or better.

He presaged Woody ALLEN's *The Purple Rose of Cairo* (1985) with his *Sherlock Junior* (1924), a film in which Keaton, as a film projectionist, jumps in and out of the movie that he's projecting within the film. *The Navigator* (1924) was his biggest box office success. *The General* (1926), however, is considered his masterpiece, with one of the greatest chase scenes in all of film comedy. It was so good, in fact, that the MARX BROTHERS stole it for their climax in *Go West* (1940).

Keaton was his own boss, making movies the way he wanted to make them. Then everything suddenly fell apart. In his book, *My Wonderful World of Slapstick*, Keaton explained, "I made the worst mistake of my career. Against my better judgement I let Joe Schenck talk me into giving up my own studio to make pictures at the booming MGM lot in Culver City." The other great comics of the day, Chaplin and Harold LLOYD begged him not to do it. Not a businessman, Keaton relented under Schenck's offer of a $3,000 per week salary.

From the very beginning, MGM tried to change the way Keaton made his films. The first movie he made at his new home was *The Cameraman* (1928). It was an excellent comedy and a hit, but Keaton had to battle for every gag. He made two more comedies for MGM that were hits, including his first talkie *Free and Easy* (1930), but the quality was already falling off.

His films thereafter began to bomb. In an attempt to make him a dramatic actor, Keaton was screen-tested for the Lionel Barrymore role in *Grand Hotel* (1932). Nothing came of that, and his subsequent comedies at the studio continued to do terrible business. By this time, however, Keaton was drinking heavily, broke, and divorced (from actress Natalie Talmadge, Joe Schenck's sister-in-law). MGM fired him in 1933.

During the next two decades, Keaton only occasionally appeared in films, usually in minor roles. He supplemented his meager income as an uncredited gagman on a number of films during the 1940s. He became the forgotten genius, until Chaplin made *Limelight* in 1952, featuring Keaton in a small role. The two giants of silent comedy appearing on the screen together reminded people of an earlier greatness. It was then that the rediscovery of Keaton's artistry slowly began. In 1957, Donald O'CONNOR starred in *The Buster Keaton Story*, a movie of minor merit except that it introduced a new generation to the once-famous silent star. The movie also finally ended Keaton's perpetual poverty, the sale of his story enabled him to live comfortably for the rest of his life.

In 1959, Keaton was given a special Academy Award "for his unique talents which brought immortal comedies to the screen." Finally recognized for his contribution to film comedy, Keaton spent the rest of his years making guest appearances in movies as diverse as *IT'S A MAD MAD MAD MAD WORLD* (1963) and *How to Stuff a Wild Bikini* (1965). More important, however, in the ensuing decades Keaton's silent films (which had been found and restored during the 1950s) reached new audiences that laughed just as the old audiences had back in the 1920s. Keaton was able to see that, too, before he died.

FILMS: Shorts: *The Butcher Boy* (a, 1917); *Fatty at Coney Island* (a, 1917); *A Country Hero* (a, 1917); *His Wedding Night* (a, 1917); *Oh, Doctor!* (a, 1917); *A Reckless Romeo* (a, 1917); *The Rough House* (a, 1917); *The Bell Boy* (a, 1918); *The Cook* (a, 1918);

Good Night Nurse (a, 1918); Moonshine (a, 1918); Out West (a, 1918); Back Stage (a, 1918); The Garage (a, 1918); The Hayseed (a, 1919); Love (a, 1919); The Round Up (a, 1919); Convict 13 (a, sc, d, 1920); Neighbors (sc, d, 1920); One Week (a, sc, d, 1920); The Scarecrow (a, sc, d, 1920); The Boat (a, sc, d, 1921); The Goat (a, sc, d, 1921); Hark Luck (a, sc, d, 1921); The Haunted House (a, sc, d, 1921); The High Sign (a, sc, d, 1921); The Paleface (a, sc, d, 1921); The Playhouse (a, sc, d, 1921); The Blacksmith (a, sc, d, 1922); Cops (a, sc, d, 1922); Day Dreams (a, sc, d, 1922); The Electric House (a, sc, d, 1922); The Frozen North (a, sc, d, 1922); My Wife's Relations (a, sc, d, 1922); The Balloonatic (a, sc, d, 1923); The Love Nest (a, sc, d, 1923); The Gold Ghost (a, 1933); Allez Oop (a, 1934); Palooka from Paducha (a, 1935); One-Run Elmer (a, 1935); Hayseed Romance (a, 1935); An Old Spanish Custom (a, 1935); Tars and Stripes (a, 1935); The E-Flat Man (a, 1935); The Timid Young Man (a, 1935); Grand Slam Opera (a, co-sc, 1936); Three on a Limb (a, 1936); Blue Blazes (a, 1936); The Chemist (a, 1936); Mixed Magic (a, 1936); Jail Bait (a, 1937); Ditto (a, 1937); Love on Wheels (a, 1937); Life in Sometown USA (d only, 1938); Hollywood Handicap (d only, 1938); Streamlined Swing (d only, 1938); Pest from the West (a, 1939); Mooching Through Georgia (a, 1939); The Jones Family in Hollywood (a, co-story, 1939); The Jones Family in Quick Millions (a, co-story, 1939); Nothing but Pleasure (a, 1940); Pardon My Berth Marks (a, 1940); The Taming of the Snood (a, 1940); The Spook Speaks (a, 1940); His Ex Marks the Spot (a, 1940); So You Won't Squawk (a, 1941); She's All Mine (a, 1941); General Nuisance (a, 1941); The Triumph of Lester Snapwill (a, short 1964).

Features: The Saphead (a, p, 1920); The Three Ages (a, d, 1923); Our Hospitality (a, d, 1923); Sherlock Jr. (a, d, 1924); The Navigator (a, d, 1924); Seven Chances (a, d, 1925); Go West (a, sc, d, 1925); Battling Butler (a, d, 1926); The General (a, co-sc, d, 1926); College (a, d, 1927); Steamboat Bill, Jr. (a, d, 1928); The Cameraman (a, p, d, 1928); Split Marriage (a, p, 1929); The Hollywood Revue (a, 1929); Free and Easy (a, 1930); Parlor, Bedroom and Bath (a, p, 1931); Sidewalks of New York (a, p, 1931); The Passionate Plumber (a, p, 1932); Speak Easily (a, 1932); What! No Beer? (a, 1933); Hollywood Cavalcade (a, 1939); The Villain Still Pursued Her (a, 1940); Li'l Abner (a, 1940); Forever and a Day (a, 1943); San Diego, I Love You (a, 1944); That's the Spirit (a, 1945); That Night with You (a, 1945); God's Country (a, 1946); El Moderno Barba Azul (Mexico, a, 1946); The Loveable Cheat (a, 1949); In the Good Old Summertime (a, 1949); You're My Everything (a, 1949); Sunset Boulevard (a, 1950); Limelight (a, 1952); Around the World in 80 Days (a, 1956); The Adventures of Huckleberry Finn (a, 1960); It's a Mad Mad Mad Mad World (a, 1963); Pajama Party (a, 1964); Beach Blanket Bingo (a, 1965); How to Stuff a Wild Bikini (a, 1965); Sergeant Deadhead (a, 1965); A Funny Thing Happened on the Way to the Forum (a, 1966).

**Keaton, Diane (1946–)** Gawky, eccentric, and vulnerable, Diane Keaton emerged in the 1970s as an original comic actress. She subsequently surprised many critics with her depth of talent as a dramatic performer, but her persona, nonetheless, remains that of a quirky comedian.

Born Diane Hall to a middle-class family in Los Angeles, California, she dropped out of college to become an actress. After traveling to New York she studied at the well-known Neighborhood Playhouse. Her rise was meteoric by show business standards; after mere months of playing in stock, she won a modest role in Hair, a show that became the hottest ticket on Broadway during the 1960s. She also had the job of understudying the lead, eventually inheriting the role in 1968 after the star left the show.

As big a break as starring in Hair was, it wasn't half as big as when Woody ALLEN tapped her to be the female lead in his Broadway production of Play It Again, Sam in 1969. The two subsequently became lovers, and he later featured her in a great many of his films, writing for her many of the best female comedy roles of the 1970s.

Keaton had made her movie debut in 1970 in a

small role in *Lovers and Other Strangers*. She played a more important supporting role as Al Pacino's wife in *The Godfather* (1972), later reprising her role in the sequels *The Godfather, Part II* (1974) and *The Godfather, Part III* (1990). However, her real film fame came not from Francis Ford Coppola's hits, but from her neurotic and endearing performance in the film version of *Play It Again, Sam* (1972).

Critics and audiences loved the film and although it was clearly a Woody Allen vehicle, Keaton was singled out for considerable praise. While she starred in other non-Allen comedies during the 1970s, such as *I Will, I Will . . . For Now* (1976) and *Harry and Walter Go to New York* (1976), her early reputation was built on her co-starring leads in the Woody Allen classics *Sleeper* (1973), *Love and Death* (1975), and *Manhattan* (1979). Her most important Allen film was *ANNIE HALL* (1977), which was loosely based on Keaton's relationship with her director/lover—even to the point of giving the title character her actual last name, Hall. She won the best actress Oscar for her performance in that film, a rare win for a comic actress.

In the same year that she made *Annie Hall*, Keaton also starred in what was then her most important dramatic role, playing the lead in *Looking for Mr. Goodbar* (1977). The provocative and much-discussed film concerning sexual repression highlighted Keaton's acting versatility and likely helped her win the Academy Award.

After her amicable breakup with Woody Allen, she went on to make mostly serious movies, including *Reds* (1981), a hit romantic movie of ideas, directed by and co-starring Warren Beatty, and *Shoot the Moon* (1982), a powerful, critically acclaimed movie about divorce. The rest of the decade, and the years since, have only occasionally been kind. The rough times began with two major bombs, *The Little Drummer Girl* (1984) and *Mrs. Soffel* (1984). Keaton bounced back, though, with several highly regarded films, *Crimes of the Heart* (1986) and *Baby Boom* (1987). Unfortunately, only the latter was successful at the box office.

In the late 1980s, Keaton also made a rather bizarre directorial debut with *Heaven* (1987), compiling a mélange of interviews and film clips concerning the hereafter. Her career has since sputtered, leaving her with a thankless role as Steve MARTIN's wife in *Father of the Bride* (1991). Her recent professional reuniting with Woody Allen in *Manhattan Murder Mystery* (1993), however, suggests a possible comic renaissance in the years ahead.

---

**FILMS:** *Lovers and Other Strangers* (1970); *The Godfather* (1972); *Play It Again, Sam* (1972); *Sleeper* (1973); *The Godfather, Part II* (1974); *I Will, I Will . . . For Now* (1975); *Love and Death* (1975); *Harry and Walter Go to New York* (1976); *Annie Hall* (1977); *Looking for Mr. Goodbar* (1977); *Interiors* (1978); *Manhattan* (1979); *Reds* (1981); *Shoot the Moon* (1981); *The Little Drummer Girl* (1984); *Mrs. Soffel* (1984); *Crimes of the Heart* (1986); *Baby Boom* (1987); *Heaven* (d only, 1987); *Radio Days* (1987); *The Good Mother* (1988); *The Lemon Sisters* (1990); *The Godfather, Part III* (1990); *Father of the Bride* (1991); *Manhattan Murder Mystery* (1993); *Look Who's Talking Now!* (voice only, 1993).

---

**Keaton, Michael (1951– )** To some, Michael Keaton is Batman, already stereotyped forever. To others, he is a compelling dramatic actor. To the faithful, however, Keaton is a dynamic comic force who may stray, but who will ultimately return to his comedy roots. Many comedians are driven by emotional pain, which they mask with humor, and there isn't anyone on the current comedy scene who more boldly projects that pain than Keaton. He seems tormented to the border of insanity—or so it sometimes appears in the actor's eyes. It's no wonder that director Tim BURTON saw Keaton as his deeply troubled Batman. If comedy is an outlet for that pain, then Keaton will be back. In the meantime, though, he has built an impressive body of work that is both comedic and dramatic.

Born Michael Douglas in Pittsburgh, Pennsylvania, he was the baby in a brood of seven. He majored in speech at Kent State University in Ohio, before developing a comedy shtick (with, among others, a partner named Louis, the Dancing Chicken) and working the local Pittsburgh clubs and coffee houses. A few years later he set off for Los Angeles as a stand-up comic, had some success, and ended up on the TV sitcom "All's Fair" in 1976. It had a one-season run, as did his next TV sitcom (with Jim Belushi), "Working Stiffs" in 1979. The failure of the second show was a lucky break because it left him free to star with Henry Winkler in the Ron HOWARD-directed *Night Shift* (1980). The film was a sleeper comedy hit; it captured Keaton's dangerous, manic comic drive and also showcased him as a rising star.

Despite bumps along the way, Keaton's star has certainly risen. His second comedy, *Mr. Mom* (1983), was a smash, while *Johnny Dangerously* (1984) got smashed by the critics. He could have had the lead in Ron Howard's *Splash* (1984), but turned it down. Then he picked the wrong Howard comedy, *Gung Ho* (1985), and flopped again. Woody ALLEN fired him three weeks into the shooting of *The Purple Rose of Cairo* (1985), and Keaton went on to make a couple of films that came and went without much notice. By the late 1980s, his career was in a slide. Two films saved him: the critically acclaimed drama *Clean and Sober* (1988) and the outrageous Tim Burton comedy *Beetlejuice* (1988). Praised in both, and the latter a box office surprise hit, Keaton was off and running again—and he ran right into *Batman* (1989).

The Batman movies are essentially dark comedies, but the villains are the comedians, not Batman. Since becoming the caped crusader, Keaton has opted out of comedy, playing the psychotic stalker in *Pacific Heights* (1990) and the flawed heroic policeman in *One Good Cop* (1991). His one comedic turn was in, of all things, Shakespeare, playing (some said overplaying) Dogberry in Kenneth Branagh's *Much Ado About Nothing* (1993).

FILMS: *Night Shift* (1982); *Mr. Mom* (1983); *Johnny Dangerously* (1984); *Gung Ho* (1986); *Touch and Go* (1986); *The Squeeze* (1987); *Beetlejuice* (1988); *Clean and Sober* (1988); *Batman* (1989); *The Dream Team* (1989); *Pacific Heights* (1990); *One Good Cop* (1991); *Batman Returns* (1992); *Much Ado About Nothing* (1993); *My Life* (1993); *The Paper* (1994).

**Kelly, Patsy (1910—1981)** A comedian who had success both in short subjects and in features, Patsy Kelly was known for her way with a wisecrack, being brassy and sassy without ever being boorish. In her comedy shorts, Kelly was a dynamic, earthy force of nature. She was no less a presence in her feature film performances, but in the longer movies she was more often relegated to playing female sidekicks and comic relief characters. She was in her comic prime during the 1930s and early 1940s.

Kelly was born in and grew up in New York City where she excelled as a dancer. Discovered by Frank Fay while still a teenager, she eventually made it to Broadway as both a dancer and an actress, appearing with such big-name stars as Will ROGERS and Al Jolson. By this time, her own name was up in lights.

Hal ROACH brought Kelly out to the West Coast in 1933 to fill in for the departing Zasu PITTS in a series of comedy shorts with Thelma TODD. Todd and Kelly were an exquisite match of cool and hot, and their many shorts together were notably popular, some of the best of them being *Air Fright* (1933), *I'll Be Suing You* (1934), and *Top Flat* (1935). After Todd's mysterious death in 1935, Kelly went on to make three more shorts for Roach with two other actresses, but the magic was gone.

In the meantime, Kelly was also appearing in feature films for Roach, which usually meant comedies. She was used to good effect in such movies as *The Countess of Monte Cristo* (1934), *The Gorilla* (1939), and *Topper Returns* (1941).

She left Hollywood in 1943 to work on the stage, but by the latter 1950s she was in semiretirement. Kelly appeared from time to time, however, on the big screen, making her first appearance on film in seventeen years when she played the maid in *Please Don't Eat the Daisies* (1960). She sporadically returned to the movies in featured roles during the rest of the 1960s and 1970s in films as varied as Sam Fuller's *The Naked Kiss* (1964), *The Ghost in the Invisible Bikini* (1966), and (as a witch) *Rosemary's Baby* (1968). Her big comeback, though, came on the stage when she won a Tony Award for her performance in the 1971 revival of *No, No, Nanette* on Broadway. She rounded out her movie career with two last comedic turns in *Freaky Friday* (1977) and *North Avenue Irregulars* (1979).

---

**FILMS:** Shorts include: *Beauty and the Bus* (1933); *Backs to Nature* (1933); *Air Fright* (1933); *Babes in the Goods* (1944); *Soup and Fish* (1934); *Maid in Hollywood* (1934); *I'll Be Suing You* (1934); *Three Chumps Ahead* (1934); *One Horse Farmers* (1934); *Opened by Mistake* (1934); *Done in Oil* (1934); *Bum Voyage* (1934); *Treasure Blues* (1935); *Sing, Sister, Sing* (1935); *The Tin Man* (1935); *The Misses Stooge* (1935); *Slightly Static* (1935); *Twin Triplets* (1935); *Hot Money* (1935); *Top Flat* (1935); *All American Toothache* (1935); *Pan Handlers* (1936); *Hill Tillies* (1936); *At Sea Ashore* (1936).

Features include: *Going Hollywood* (1933); *The Countess of Monte Cristo* (1934); *The Girl from Missouri* (1934); *Go into Your Dance* (1935); *Every Night at Eight* (1935); *Page Miss Glory* (1935); *Thanks a Million* (1935); *Private Number* (1936); *Sing, Baby, Sing* (1936); *Kelly the Second* (1936); *Pigskins Parade* (1936); *Wake Up and Live* (1937); *Nobody's Baby* (1937); *Pick a Star* (1937); *Ever Since Eve* (1937); *Merrily We Live* (1938); *There Goes My Heart* (1938); *The Cowboy and the Lady* (1938); *The Gorilla* (1939); *Hit Parade of 1941* (1940); *Road Show* (1941); *Topper Returns* (1941); *Broadway Limited* (1941); *Playmates* (1941); *Sing Your Worries Away* (1942); *In Old California* (1942); *Ladies' Day* (1943); *Please Don't Eat the Daisies* (1960); *The Crowded Sky* (1960); *The Naked Kiss* (1964); *The Ghost in the Invisible Bikini* (1966); *Rosemary's Baby* (1968); *The Phynx* (1970); *Freaky Friday* (1977); *North Avenue Irregulars* (1979).

---

**Kennedy, Edgar (1890—1948)** Edgar Kennedy was the master of the *slow burn*, a comically incremental reaction to events running out of control. Kennedy would look on, with ever greater exasperation, trying (without success) to cope with some indignity until the slowly burning fuse of his patience would finally strike the black powder of his anger—and he would explode! Kennedy moved easily between comedy short subjects and features throughout his thirty-five-year career in the movies. Nonetheless, he was best known to audiences of his day because of a series of shorts he made from 1931 until his death from throat cancer in 1948. These two-reel comedies were first known as "The Average Man" films, but later came to be called "The Edgar Kennedy Series." They depicted Kennedy as society's comic victim, an everyman who struggled mightily (and usually in vain) with the commonplace, from marriage to machinery and from mothers-in-law to impossible neighbors.

Born in Monterey, California, Kennedy worked in VAUDEVILLE for only a few years before linking up with Mack SENNETT's Keystone comedians in 1914. Kennedy would eventually work with many of comedy's greats, beginning his career by playing a foil to the greatest of them all, Charlie CHAPLIN. After leaving Sennett to work for Hal ROACH, Kennedy later acted with and also occasionally directed (as E. Livingston Kennedy) the comedy team of LAUREL AND HARDY. He had particular success with Stan and Ollie, directing some of their most memorable early sound shorts, including *From Soup to Nuts* (1928) and *You're Darn Tootin'* (1928), and appearing with them in the famous *Two Tars* (1928).

A barrel-chested, balding man with a blue-collar look about him, Kennedy found plenty of comedy work in features, many of them big-budget movies. For instance, he can be seen in such "straight" hits as *San Francisco* (1936), *A Star Is Born* (1937), and *Anchors Aweigh* (1945) as well as in comedies as diverse as Howard HAWKS's SCREWBALL COMEDY *TWENTIETH CENTURY* (1934), the OLSEN AND JOHNSON gem *Crazy House* (1943), and, reunited with his old friends, the Laurel and Hardy feature *Air Raid Wardens* (1943).

---

**FILMS INCLUDE:** Shorts: *Caught in a Cabaret* (1914); *The Knockout* (1914); *The Star Boarder* (1914); *The Noise of Bombs* (1914); *The Great Vacuum Robbery* (1915); *A Game Old Knight* (1915); *His Bitter Pill* (1916); *His Hereafter* (1916); *Her Fame and Shame* (1917); *Torpedoed Love* (1917); *She Loved Him Plenty* (1918); *The Marriage Circus* (co-d only, 1925); *Cupid's Boots* (d only, 1925); *From Soup to Nuts* (d only, 1928); *You're Darn Tootin'* (d only, 1928); *A Pair of Tights* (1928); *Two Tars* (1928); *Angora Love* (1929); *Moan and Groan* (1929); *Perfect Day* (1929); *Bacon Grabbers* (1929); *Shivering Shakespeare* (1930); *Lemon Meringue* (1931); *Bon Voyage* (1932); *Mother-in-Law's Day* (1932); *The Merchant of Menace* (1933); *Good Housewrecking* (1933); *In-Laws Are Out* (1934); *Edgar Hamlet* (1935); *Happy Tho Married* (1935); *Dummy Ache* (1936); *High Beer Pressure* (1936); *Locks and Bonds* (1937); *Bad Housekeeping* (1937); *Dumb's the Word* (1937); *Edgar and Goliath* (1937); *False Roomers* (1938); *Kennedy's Castle* (1938); *Beaux and Errors* (1938); *Kennedy the Great* (1939); *Maid to Order* (1939); *Mutiny in the County* (1940); *It Happened All Night* (1941); *Heart Burn* (1942); *Hold Your Temper* (1943); *The Kitchen Cynic* (1944); *You Drive Me Crazy* (1945); *Noisy Neighbors* (1946); *Trouble or Nothing* (1946); *Do or Diet* (1947); *Television Turmoil* (1947); *No More Relatives* (1949).

Features: *Tillie's Punctured Romance* (1914); *Skirts* (1921); *The Battling Fool* (1924); *The Golden Princess* (1925); *Across the Pacific* (1926); *Going Crooked* (1926); *My Old Dutch* (1926); *The Wrong Mr. Wright* (1927); *Finger Prints* (1927); *Wedding Bill$* (1927); *Trent's Last Case* (1929); *They Had to See Paris* (1929); *Carnival Boat* (1932); *Tillie and Gus* (1933); *Duck Soup* (1933); *Twentieth Century* (1934); *All of Me* (1934); *Kid Millions* (1934); *The Bride Comes Home* (1935); *Small Town Girl* (1936); *San Francisco* (1936); *Three Men on a Horse* (1936); *A Star Is Born* (1937); *Double Wedding* (1937); *Hollywood Hotel* (1938); *It's a Wonderful World* (1939); *In Old California*

(1942); *The Falcon Strikes Back* (1943); *Crazy House* (1943); *Air Raid Wardens* (1943); *It Happened Tomorrow* (1944); *Anchors Aweigh* (1945); *Captain Tugboat Annie* (1945); *Mad Wednesday* (1947); *Heaven Only Knows* (1947); *Unfaithfully Yours* (1948); *My Dream Is Yours* (1949).

---

**Keystone Kops**  Created by Mack SENNETT and named after his Keystone Studio, the Keystone Kops were a SLAPSTICK comedy (police) force that ran rampant across movie theater screens between 1912 and 1920. Their humor was violent, fast paced, crude, and thoroughly anarchic. These bumbling, incompetent members of the constabulary were buffoons, and audiences laughed heartily at their one-and two-reel sendups of authority.

There was nothing realistic about the Keystone Kops. They were living, breathing cartoon characters who existed at a breakneck, frenetic pace, chasing supposed bad guys while crashing into every imaginable obstacle along the way. Led by Ford STERLING, who was Police Chief Teeheezal, the Keystone Kops ensemble became emblematic of silent screen comedy.

The name of the group, if not the group itself, returned to movie marquees in 1955 with the disappointing *Abbott and Costello Meet the Keystone Kops*. The film is noteworthy, at least, thanks to a cameo appearance by Mack Sennett.

**Keystone Studio**  *See* Mack SENNETT

**Kline, Kevin (1947—)**  An Errol Flynn look-alike, Kevin Kline is an accomplished stage actor who came to films in starring roles. While he made his movie debut in the starkly dramatic *Sophie's Choice* (1982), many of his subsequent films have been comedies, including his Oscar-winning performance in *A Fish Called Wanda* (1988).

*Here is a typical scene of slapstick chaos associated with the original gang that couldn't shoot (or drive) straight, the Keystone Kops.*
PHOTO COURTESY OF THE SIEGEL COLLECTION.

Born in St. Louis, Missouri, the actor has taken a circuitous route to stardom. It wasn't acting that first attracted him to performing, it was music. He studied piano, composing, and conducting at the Indiana University School of Music. Eventually, however, acting got the better of him, and he moved to New York where he received additional training at the Juilliard School of Drama.

After four years of touring with John Houseman's The Acting Company, Kline came to stage prominence in his Broadway debut, starring in the Hal Prince musical *On the Twentieth Century*. It brought him the first of his two Tony Awards. The second was for Joseph Papp's production of the musical *The Pirates of Penzance*.

One of Kline's great gifts is his versatility; he has shown comic swashbuckling exuberance in the film version of *The Pirates of Penzance* (1982), bemused whimsicality, best seen in *Soapdish* (1991), broad comedy in *I Love You to Death* (1990), sophisticated comedy in the triumphant *Dave* (1993), and both SCREWBALL COMEDY and physical comedy in *A Fish Called Wanda*. With all of that, he can still command respect as proven in films as diverse as *The Big Chill* (1993), *Cry Freedom* (1987), and *Grand Canyon* (1991).

In addition to his movie work, Kline has continued to devote himself to the stage, particularly New York's Public Theater, where he has been appointed artistic associate.

**FILMS:** *Sophie's Choice* (1982); *The Pirates of Penzance* (1982); *The Big Chill* (1983); *Silverado* (1985); *Violets Are Blue* (1986); *Cry Freedom* (1987); *A Fish Called Wanda* (1988); *The January Man* (1988); *I Love You to Death* (1990); *Soapdish* (1991); *Grand Canyon* (1991); *Chaplin* (1992); *Dave* (1993).

**Knotts, Don (1924—)** Pop-eyed and frantic Don Knotts has made a career out of playing characters who seem just an inch away from a nervous breakdown. The actor, at his comic extreme, is first cousin to a Mexican jumping bean. In a film career of more than thirty years, however, he never fully answered his "knottiest" problem: How can this amusing comic sidekick become a genuine star comedian? His shtick as the comic relief character Barney Fife on TV's "The Andy Griffith Show," while providing him with fame, was not the ideal type of character upon which to build a major career.

Born in Morgantown, West Virginia, Knotts got his start as an entertainer in the U.S. Army, appearing in a show called *Stars and Grapes*. After the service, he turned professional with a ventriloquist act. His big break came in the stage comedy *No Time for Sergeants*, in which he played a secondary role in support of Andy Griffith. When the play went before the cameras, both actors recreated their roles. Their rapport was such that Griffith asked Knotts to play Barney Fife on "The Andy Griffith Show," which premiered in 1960. Knotts went on to win three Emmys in a row for best supporting actor, staying with the series for a total of six years.

Ever the comic relief character on TV, Knotts was much the same in the movies for several years, most notably in *Move Over, Darling* (1963), but that

changed with his starring role in *The Incredible Mr. Limpet* (1963). Knotts also starred in *The Shakiest Gun in the West* (1968), *The Apple Dumpling Gang* (1974), and *The Prize Fighter* (1979). His films, both alone and (later) co-starring Tim CONWAY, have been primarily low-budget comedies for younger audiences. More recently, Knotts has been back on TV, once again in comic supporting roles.

**FILMS INCLUDE:** *No Time for Sergeants* (1958); *Wake Me When It's Over* (1960); *The Last Time I Saw Archie* (1961); *It's a Mad Mad Mad Mad World* (1963); *Move Over, Darling* (1963); *The Incredible Mr. Limpet* (1964); *The Ghost and Mr. Chicken* (1966); *The Reluctant Astronaut* (1967); *The Shakiest Gun in the West* (1968); *The Love God?* (1969); *How to Frame a Figg* (also co-story, 1971); *The Apple Dumpling Gang* (1975); *Gus* (1976); *No Deposit, No Return* (1976); *Herbie Goes to Monte Carlo* (1977); *Hot Head and Cold Feet* (1978); *The Apple Dumpling Gang Rides Again* (1979); *The Prizefighter* (1979); *The Private Eyes* (1980); *Pinocchio and the Emperor of the Night* (voice only, 1987).

**Kornman, Mary** *See* OUR GANG

**Kovacs, Ernie (1919—1962)** Looking menacing with his broad face, mustache, and inevitable big cigar, Ernie Kovacs's idea of hurting someone was to make him laugh too hard. An innovative comic talent on TV in the 1950s, he migrated to the movies in the latter half of the decade, with uneven results. He co-starred three times with Jack LEMMON, with whom he made an excellent comic partner, in *Operation Mad Ball* (1957), *Bell, Book and Candle* (1958), and *It Happened to Jane* (1959). Ultimately, however, Kovacs was more dynamic on TV because he controlled the medium. In the movies, he was merely one of the actors, although he did make a great comic villain. Had he made his own films—a direction in which he was surely heading—they might very well have been something special.

Born in Trenton, New Jersey, Kovacs was intent upon a career as a dramatic actor; he attended the American Academy of Dramatic Art in New York before gaining a small measure of fame as a radio announcer/comedian between 1942 and 1950. He was known for performing outlandish stunts live on the air, and his reputation helped land him his first TV show in 1950. He had a number of shows during the decade: "Kovacs on the Corner," "It's Time for Ernie," "Ernie in Kovacsland," "Kovacs Unlimited," and "The Ernie Kovacs Show." Every one of them offered Kovacs the opportunity to invent a comic vocabulary for the fledgling TV medium.

He met his second wife, Edie ADAMS, on the set of "Kovacs on the Corner"; they were married four years later in 1954. She sang and did comedy with him on their shows. A man who lived life far beyond the limit, Kovacs left his widow $600,000 in debt when he died in a traffic accident at forty-two.

---

**FILMS:** *Operation Mad Ball* (1957); *Bell, Book and Candle* (1958); *It Happened to Jane* (1959); *Strangers When We Meet* (1960); *Pepe* (1960); *North to Alaska* (1960); *Wake Me When It's Over* (1960); *Our Man in Havana* (1960); *Five Golden Hours* (1961); *Sail a Crooked Ship* (1962).

---

# L

## La Cava, Gregory (1892—1952)
A well-regarded director of intelligent, sophisticated comedies, Gregory La Cava shined particularly bright in the mid-1930s. He was an actor's director, eliciting career performances from his players, as well as an author's director, finding his material's perfect tone and pace. He often co-scripted the films he directed and occasionally produced them, particularly at the end of his career.

Born George Gregory La Cava in Towanda, Pennsylvania, he became a cartoonist before turning to animation work in the mid-1910s. On a frame-by-frame basis, he learned the principles of comic timing when he worked with gifted animator Walter Lantz on projects like the Katzenjammer Kids cartoons. He later used that knowledge as a writer/director of comedy shorts in the early 1920s.

La Cava made the transition to feature films in 1922, directing a number of amusing comedies. However, his rise to the top of Hollywood's directorial ranks didn't occur until he made the much admired, if controversial, political comedy *Gabriel Over the White House* (1933). From then on, he was a hot director, with such films as *The Affairs of Cellini* (1934), *She Married Her Boss* (1935), and *My Man Godfrey* (1936). The latter film brought him his first best director Academy Award nomination. The following year he received a second nomination for *Stage Door* (1937).

With *Stage Door* La Cava reached the height of his career. He made only five more films after 1937, and none of them were up to his best work of the mid-1930s.

**FILMS INCLUDE:** Features only: *His Nibbs* (1922); *Restless Wives* (1924); *The New School Teacher* (1924); *Womanhandled* (1925); *Say It Again* (1926); *So's Your Old Man* (1926); *Let's Get Married* (1926); *Paradise for Two* (also p, 1927); *Tell It to Sweeney* (also p, 1927); *Running Wild* (also co-sc, 1927); *The Gay Defender* (1927); *Feel My Pulse* (also p, 1928); *Half a Bride* (1928); *Big News* (1929); *Saturday's Children* (1929); *His First Command* (1930); *Laugh and Get Rich* (also sc, 1931); *Smart Woman* (1931); *Symphony of Six Million* (1932); *The Age of Consent* (1932); *The Half-Naked Truth* (also co-sc, 1932); *Gallant Lady* (1933); *Bed of Roses* (1933); *Gabriel Over the White House* (1933); *What Every Woman Knows* (1934); *The Affairs of Cellini* (1934); *Private Worlds* (also co-sc, 1935); *She Married Her Boss* (1935); *My Man Godfrey* (also p, 1936); *Stage Door* (1937); *Fifth Avenue Girl* (also p, 1939); *Primrose Path* (also co-sc, p, 1940); *Unfinished Business* (also p, 1941); *Lady in a Jam* (also p, 1942); *Living in a Big Way* (also story, co-sc, 1947).

## Lahr, Bert (1895—1967)
Immortality touched Bert Lahr when he donned whiskers and tail as the Cowardly Lion in *The Wizard of Oz* (1939). Apart from that career-making role, Lahr surfaced only occasionally in motion pictures, usually in supporting roles. Nonetheless, his presence was such that almost any appearance he made was memorable. With his small eyes surrounded by

heavy bags (particularly in later life), his rubbery face, and distinctive braying laugh, Lahr was a clown of the highest order.

Born Irving Lahrheim in New York City, he dropped out of school when he was fifteen to join the Seven Frolics. He enjoyed a long VAUDEVILLE and BURLESQUE career that finally brought him to the movies in 1929 when he made his first comedy short, *Faint Heart*. Over the next decade, he made just two more shorts and appeared in little more than a handful of features before winning the role of the Cowardly Lion.

Instead of cashing in on his success in *The Wizard of Oz*, Lahr did not appear again on the big screen for another three years; he was starring in *DuBarry Was a Lady* on Broadway. Surprisingly, when the play was turned into a film, Lahr was not invited to recreate his stage triumph. He did return to Hollywood, however, but he never found the kind of material that was worthy of his talents. His best film during this later period was *Rose Marie* (1954). Lahr's last film was *The Night They Raided Minsky's* (1968), a tribute to burlesque, from whence Lahr came.

---

**FILMS INCLUDE:** Features only: *Flying High* (1931); *Mr. Broadway* (1933); *Merry-Go-Round of 1938* (1937); *Love and Hisses* (1937); *Josette* (1938); *Just Around the Corner* (1938); *Zaza* (1939); *The Wizard of Oz* (1939); *Ship Ahoy* (1942); *Sing Your Worries Away* (1942); *Meet the People* (1944); *Always Leave Them Laughing* (1949); *Mr. Universe* (1951); *Rose Marie* (1954); *The Second Greatest Sex* (1955); *Ten Girls Ago* (1962); *The Night They Raided Minsky's* (1968).

---

**Lake, Arthur**   *See* SERIES COMEDIES

**Lamour, Dorothy**   *See* SERIES COMEDIES

**Landis, John (1950—)**   A daring comic sensibility turned John Landis into the hottest director in

Hollywood in the late 1970s and early 1980s. A director/screenwriter/producer (and sometimes actor), he captured, through comedy, the disaffection and alienation of young audiences, while simultaneously providing them with counterculture comic heroes for whom they could root. If his films have been less successful in the years since, it's likely because he has lost his boldness, becoming a far less adventurous filmmaker.

Born in Chicago, Illinois, Landis broke into films with the low-budget *Schlock* (1971), a clever sendup of cheap horror films, which he wrote, directed, and appeared in (wearing a gorilla suit). It was six years before he directed another movie, although he picked up a couple of acting roles in *Battle for the Planet of the Apes* (1973) and *Death Race 2000* (1975). His next assignment, however, was the link to his ultimate success. He was hired by Jim ABRAHAMS, Jerry ZUCKER, and David ZUCKER to direct their first screenplay. The film was *The Kentucky Fried Movie* (1977), which became the most financially successful independent film ever made. A hilarious parody, it had the kind of antiestablishment humor that made it easy to jump to the happily antisocial humor of his next film, *Animal House*, the sleeper hit of 1978.

Landis was on a roll; his next film was the audacious *Blues Brothers* (1980), which he also scripted. It was the most expensive comedy ever made, costing an estimated $30 million. Most film pundits thought it could never make back its money, but it did, and then some, becoming the most commercially successful comedy to date in Hollywood history. He followed with a full-blooded horror movie that also happened to be funny, *An American Werewolf in London* (1982). Landis next introduced Eddie MURPHY to movie audiences in the hit comedy *Trading Places* (1983) and made the startlingly popular video of Michael Jackson's "Thriller" (1983). A tragic helicopter accident on the set of *Twilight Zone: The Movie* (1983), which killed actor Vic Morrow, had a negative effect on the director's career.

Landis has made some good movies since, most notably the wrongly maligned *Three Amigos!* (1986), but none of his films have matched the expectations established by his earlier successes.

**FILMS:** *Schlock* (a, sc, d, 1971); *Battle for the Planet of the Apes* (a, 1973); *Death Race 2000* (a, 1975); *The Kentucky Fried Movie* (a, d, 1977); *National Lampoon's Animal House* (d, 1978); *1941* (a, 1979); *The Blues Brothers* (a, sc, d, 1980); *An American Werewolf in London* (a, sc, d, 1981); *Eating Raoul* (a, 1982); *Trading Places* (d, 1983); *Making Michael Jackson's Thriller* (short, part one, sc, p, d, 1983); *Twilight Zone: The Movie* ("Prologue" and "Back There" segments, sc, p, d, 1983); *The Muppets Take Manhattan* (a, 1984); *Into the Night* (a, d, 1985); *Spies Like Us* (d, 1985); *Clue* (story, p, 1985); *Three Amigos!* (d, 1986); *Amazon Women on the Moon* (p, d, 1987); *Coming to America* (d, 1988); *Spontaneous Combustion* (a, 1989); *Darkman* (a, 1990); *Oscar* (d, 1991); *Sleepwalkers* (a, 1992).

## Langdon, Harry (1884—1944)

A rather nonathletic actor, Harry Langdon was different from his three acrobatic and physical comic contemporaries, Charlie CHAPLIN, Buster KEATON, and Harold LLOYD. Nonetheless, Langdon was, for a short while, a compelling star who proved that physical comedy wasn't a necessary ingredient for silent screen success. In fact, during the mid-1920s, he was an enormously popular comic star. With his almost otherwordly baby face, Langdon played at a peculiar form of humor that combined his childlike looks with his adult desires. The result was funny, but it had a disturbing edge.

From a very early age, Langdon began working in the circus, VAUDEVILLE, and BURLESQUE—in short, anywhere he could earn a living in show business. As his body grew older, though, his face didn't seem to age. He looked strangely like a young child with a man's body.

When Langdon, who had a reputation as an entertainer, came to Hollywood, he was signed up by Mack SENNETT and eventually teamed with gag-writer (soon to become famous director) Frank CAPRA and director Harry Edwards. With the help of these two talented men, Langdon flourished on film.

He started with two-reelers, making his first film in 1924, *Picking Peaches*. There were, all together, twenty-five two- and three-reelers, virtually all of which were hits.

In 1926, Langdon made his first feature. He had left Sennett and had gone to Warner Bros. Wisely, he had taken Capra and Edwards with him. Three excellent full-length comedies followed: *Tramp, Tramp, Tramp* (1926) and, with Capra directing, *The Strong Man* (1927) and *Long Pants* (1927). All three were massive hits.

However, Langdon literally destroyed his own career by firing Capra and Edwards to write and direct his own movies. He made several films for Warner Bros. over the next year and a half, and each was worse than the last. By 1931 he was bankrupt.

Except for the occasional role in a feature, Langdon spent most of the 1930s and early 1940s making sound shorts of no particular distinction. His greatest contributions to film comedy during this time came as a story man and screenwriter for LAUREL AND HARDY in the latter 1930s.

For three years, Harry Langdon was the equal of the other silent comic greats. Chaplin, Keaton, and Lloyd, however, knew their own creative capabilities. Langdon did not. Yet, thanks to Langdon, one of America's greatest directors of the 1930s and 1940s, Frank Capra, received his early training. Of course, there is also the haunting legacy of that baby face in the films Langdon made from 1924 to 1927.

**FILMS:** All shorts and as actor, except as indicated: *Picking Peaches* (1924); *All Night Long* (1924); *Boobs in the Wood* (1924); *The Cat's Meow* (1924); *Feet of Mud* (1924); *The First Hundred Years* (1924); *Flickering Youth* (1924); *His Marriage Wow* (1924); *The Hansom Cabman* (1924); *His New Mamma* (1924); *Luck o' the Foolish* (1924); *Shanghaied Lovers* (1924); *The Sea Squawk* (1924); *Smile Please* (1924); *Horace Greeley, Jr.* (1925); *Lucky Stars* (1925); *Plain Clothes*

(1925); *Remember When?* (1925); *There He Goes* (1925); *The White Wing's Bride* (1925); *Fiddlesticks* (1926); *Saturday Afternoon* (1926); *Ella Cinders* (feature, 1926); *Soldier Man* (feature, 1926); *The Strong Man* (feature 1926); *Tramp Tramp, Tramp* (feature, also p, 1926); *Long Pants* (feature, 1927); *His First Flame* (feature, 1927); *Three's a Crowd* (feature, also d, 1927); *The Chaser* (feature, also d, 1928); *Heart Trouble* (feature, also d, 1928); *The Head Guy* (1929); *Hotter Than Hot* (1929); *Skirt Shy* (1929); *Sky Boy* (1929); *The Big Kick* (1930); *The Fighting Parson* (1930); *The King* (1930); *See America Thirsty* (1930); *The Shrimp* (1930); *A Soldier's Plaything* (1930); *The Big Flash* (1930); *Hallelujah, I'm a Bum* (feature, 1933); *The Hitch Hiker* (1933); *Hooks and Jabs* (1933); *Knight Duty* (1933); *Marriage Humor* (1933); *My Weakness* (1933); *On Ice* (1933); *A Roaming Romeo* (1933); *Tied for Life* (1933); *Tired Feet* (1933); *A Circus Hoodoo* (1934); *No Sleep on the Deep* (1934); *Petting Preferred* (1934); *Shivers* (1934); *Trimmed in Furs* (1934); *Atlantic Adventure* (1935); *His Bridal Sweet* (1935); *His Marriage Mixup* (1935); *I Don't Remember* (1935); *The Leathernecker* (1935); *Wise Guys* (d only, 1937); *Blockheads* (sc, story only, 1938); *A Doggone Mixup* (1938); *He Loved an Actress* (1938); *Sue My Lawyer* (also story, 1938); *There Goes My Heart* (feature, 1938); *Cold Turkey* (1939); *The Flying Deuces* (feature, sc, story only, 1939); *Goodness! A Ghost* (also sc, 1939); *Zenobia* (feature, 1939); *A Chump at Oxford* (feature, story, sc only, 1940); *Misbehaving Husbands* (feature, 1940); *Saps at Sea* (feature, story, sc only, 1940); *All American Co-Ed* (feature, 1941); *Beautiful Clothes* (1941); *Double Trouble* (feature, 1941); *Road Show* (sc only, 1941); *Carry Harry* (1942); *House of Errors* (also story, 1942); *Piano Mooner* (also story, sc, 1942); *Tireman, Spare My Tires* (1942); *What Makes Lizzy Dizzy* (1942); *A Blitz on the Fritz* (1943); *Blond and Groom* (also story, sc, 1943); *Here Comes Mr. Zerk* (1943); *Spotlight Scandals* (feature, 1943); *Block Busters* (feature, 1944); *Bride by Mistake* (feature, gagman only, 1944); *Defective Detectives* (1944); *Hot Rhythm* (feature, 1944); *Mopey Dopey* (1944); *To Heir Is Human* (1944); *Pistol Packin' Nitwits* (also story, 1945);

*Snooper Service* (1945); *Swingin' on the Rainbow* (feature, 1945).

---

**Lasser, Louise (1941—)** An offbeat comedian, Louise Lasser's stellar attributes are her peculiar, nasal, sing-song voice and an amusing physical stiffness; neither her voice nor her movements ever seem quite normal. As a result, she brings a unique and unexpected pace and timing to whatever comedy she appears in.

Born in New York City, Lasser was a political science major at Brandeis University before embarking on a show business career. She was twenty-three when she joined The Third Ear, an improvisational group created by comic Elaine MAY. Stage work followed, and so did her relationship with Woody ALLEN. She had a small role in the film *What's New Pussycat?* (1965), which Allen scripted, and she provided her voice for his hilarious spy spoof *What's Up, Tiger Lily?* (1966). In that same year, she and Allen married. Curiously, they divorced the same year as their next collaboration, *Bananas* (1971). Of all her performances, *Bananas* is by far the most impressive. She was not only Allen's perfect feminine foil, she was his comic match as a performer. Despite the end of their marriage, she has occasionally appeared in his films.

After leaving Allen, her movie career stalled. It wasn't until she starred in the TV soap opera parody "Mary Hartman, Mary Hartman" (1976–1977) that she became a major star. When the show faded, so did Lasser. Drug charges hastened her professional descent. She rebounded to the extent that she can periodically be seen in small film roles.

---

FILMS INCLUDE: *What's New Pussycat?* (1965); *What's Up Tiger Lily?* (voice only, 1966); *Bananas* (1971); *Such Good Friends* (1971); *Everything You Always Wanted to Know About Sex (But Were Afraid to Ask)* (1972); *Slither* (1973); *In God We Trust* (1979); *Stardust Memories* (uncred, 1980); *Nightmare at Shadow Woods* (1983); *Crimewave* (1985); *Rude*

*Awakening* (1989); *Sing* (1989); *Frankenhooker* (1990); *The Night We Never Met* (1993).

---

**Laurel and Hardy** Very few comedy teams have remained as consistently popular as Stan Laurel (1890–1965) and Oliver Hardy (1892–1957) with audiences both during their filmmaking years and after. There is something fundamental about their humor. In part, it comes from the team's wise choice to allow the audience to feel both superior and sympathetic to their two likable bufoonish characters. Their humor also comes from their carefully developed sense of comic chaos. Rare was the Laurel and Hardy film that didn't take the time to set a slow fuse of ever-expanding, destructive one-upmanship. It might start with the spilling of a drink, but it would likely end with the apocalyptic demolition of a house.

Thin, shy Stan Laurel and rotund, overbearing Oliver Hardy milked laughs out of their Mutt and Jeff relationship, finding a mother lode of comedy in their constant desire to better themselves. It's no accident that both comedians wore bowlers, suits and ties and referred to themselves as Mr. Laurel and Mr. Hardy. They were yuppie-wannabees well before their time. Audiences, however, were always way ahead of them, knowing full well that Stan and Ollie's schemes were doomed to failure. But just how they would fail was always open to doubt, and that's where the gags came in.

Laurel and Hardy always reacted to their failures in the same way. For instance, Laurel had his famous high-pitched, whining cry; Hardy had his perfectly timed complaint, "Here's another fine mess you've gotten us into." It was the sheer repetition of their set pieces that made them comfortably familiar while also limiting their growth. However, they were a popular team for roughly twenty years and have kept a large measure of their popularity thanks to TV, revival houses, and more recently, videotape.

Laurel and Hardy, however, weren't always a team.

Stan Laurel, who was born Arthur Stanley Jefferson in Ulverston, England, was a member, along with Charlie CHAPLIN, of Fred Karno's Company, a music hall troupe. Laurel had been Chaplin's understudy and did a fine job of imitating him. After Chaplin became a movie star, Laurel was hired in Hollywood to make a Chaplinlike short subject, *Nuts in May* (1917). It was Laurel's first appearance on film, and he was in the movie business to stay, soon working for the former cowboy star turned producer, Bronco Billy Anderson. In 1917 Laurel appeared in *Lucky Dog* with an actor named Oliver Hardy—but nothing came of it. It was much later, when both Laurel and Hardy were working for Hal ROACH, that the two comedians became a team. In the meantime, Stan Laurel made more than fifty one- and two-reelers as a single.

Although Hardy seems just as British as Laurel, the heftier member of the team was born Norvell Hardy in Atlanta, Georgia. He began his career as an extra in 1913. Because of his size, he often played villains. Also because of his size, he picked up the nickname "Babe."

In 1926, when Laurel and Hardy were under contract to Hal Roach, they played together in *Slipping Wives*, followed by a number of large-cast "Comedy All-Star" films. There was a certain chemistry in their pairing, and Hal Roach (not the two comedians) decided to turn them into a team. Under the inspired direction of Leo MCCAREY, who learned his craft making comedy shorts for Roach, the new team of Laurel and Hardy cranked out more than thirty shorts that immediately captured a loyal audience. After McCarey left to pursue his directorial career, Stan Laurel fashioned their gags and routines, becoming the main creative force in the comedy team. Much of the inventiveness of their humor is due solely to his comic imagination.

Laurel and Hardy dealt with the coming of talkies in the late 1920s rather effectively by generally ignoring it. They simply continued doing their same brand of humor, adding only the language that seemed appropriate and nothing more nor less. They made their first feature in 1931, *Pardon Us,*

*The comedy of Stan Laurel and Oliver Hardy remains popular today, as evidenced by a contemporary fan club called Sons of the Desert, named for one of the duo's best feature films.* PHOTO COURTESY OF THE SIEGEL COLLECTION.

which did moderate business. Their main work was still comedy shorts, and they hit their critical apogee in 1932 when they won an Oscar for *The Music Box*. It was the first Oscar ever given in the category of "Short Subjects, Live Action Comedy."

For several years they made both shorts and features. It is their features of this era, however, that are now best remembered, for they include their two most-loved films, *Sons of the Desert* (1933) and *Babes in Toyland* (1934). As the 1930s rolled on, so did

Laurel and Hardy, making a large number of other funny films such as *Way Out West* (1937), *Blockheads* (1938), *The Flying Deuces* (1939), and *A Chump at Oxford* (1940). The latter film was their last quality comedy.

The duo continued making movies in the 1940s, but after leaving Roach for a larger studio at the beginning of the decade, Laurel lost control of their material and their films were rather poor. Their last movie together was *Utopia* (1950), a French production that didn't serve them (or the audience) well.

Hardy had made a couple of supporting appearances in films without Laurel, specifically in *Zenobia* (1939) and *The Fighting Kentuckian* (1949).

Their close, personal relationship was such that, when Oliver Hardy died in 1957, Laurel refused to work on film again. Soon after, Hollywood finally realized that one of its treasures had passed away without proper recognition. Seeking to avoid making the same mistake twice, in 1960 Stan Laurel was presented a special Oscar for "his creative pioneering in the field of cinema comedy."

---

FILMS: As a team, shorts unless otherwise indicated: *A Lucky Dog* (1917); *Slipping Wives* (1926); *The Battle of the Century* (1927); *Call of the Cuckoos* (1927); *Do Detectives Think?* (1927); *Duck Soup* (1927); *Eve's Love Letters* (1927); *Flying Elephants* (1927); *Hats Off* (1927); *Love 'Em and Weep* (1927); *Now I'll Tell One* (1927); *Putting Pants on Philip* (1927); *Sailors, Beware!* (1927); *The Second Hundred Years* (1927); *Seeing the World* (1927); *Should Tall Men Marry?* (1927); *Sugar Daddies* (1927); *Why Girls Love Sailors* (1927); *With Love and Hisses* (1927); *Early to Bed* (1928); *The Finishing Touch* (1928); *From Soup to Nuts* (1928); *Habeas Corpus* (1928); *Leave 'Em Laughing* (1928); *Should Married Men Go Home?* (1928); *Their Purple Moment* (1928); *Two Tars* (1928); *We Faw Down* (1928); *You're Darn Tootin'* (1928); *Angora Love* (1929); *Bacon Grabbers* (1929); *Berth Marks* (1929); *Big Business* (1929); *Double Whoopee* (1929); *The Hollywood Revue of 1929* (feature, 1929); *The Hoosegow* (1929); *Liberty* (1929); *Man 'o' War* (1929); *Perfect Day* (1929); *That's My Wife* (1929); *They Go Boom* (1929); *Unaccustomed As We Are* (1929); *Wrong Again* (1929); *Another Fine Mess* (1930); *Below Zero* (1930); *Blotto* (1930); *Brats* (1930); *Hog Wild* (1930); *The Laurel and Hardy Murder Case* (1930); *The Night Owls* (1930); *The Rogue Song* (1930); *Beau Hunks* (1931); *Chicken Come Home* (1931); *The Chiselers* (1931); *Come Clean* (1931); *Helpmates* (1931); *Laughing Gravy* (1931); *On the Loose* (1931); *One Good Turn* (1931); *Our Wife* (1931); *Pardon Us* (feature, 1931); *The Stolen Jools* (feature, 1931); *Any Old Port* (1932); *The Chimp* (feature, 1932); *County Hospital* (1932); *The Music Box* (1932); *Pack Up Your Troubles* (feature, 1932); *Scram!* (1932); *Their First Mistake* (1932); *Towed in a Hole* (1932); *Busy Bodies* (1933); *The Devil's Brother* (feature, 1933); *Dirty Work* (1933); *Me and My Pal* (1933); *The Midnight Patrol* (1933); *Sons of the Desert* (feature, 1933); *Twice Two* (1933); *Wild Poses* (1933); *Babes in Toyland* (feature, 1934); *Going Bye-Bye!* (1934); *Hollywood Party* (feature, 1934); *The Live Ghost* (1934); *Oliver the Eighth* (feature, 1934); *Them Thar Hills* (1934); *The Fixer Uppers* (1935); *Heroes of the Regiment* (feature, 1935); *Thicker Than Water* (1935); *Bonnie Scotland* (feature, 1935); *Tit for Tat* (1935); *The Bohemian Girl* (feature, 1936); *On the Wrong Trek* (1936); *Our Relations* (feature, also Laurel—p, 1936); *Pick a Star* (feature, 1937); *Way Out West* (feature, also Laurel—p, 1937); *Blockheads* (feature, 1938); *Swiss Miss* (feature, 1938); *The Flying Deuces* (feature, 1939); *A Chump at Oxford* (feature, 1940); *Saps at Sea* (feature, 1940); *Great Guns* (feature, 1941); *A-Haunting We Will Go* (feature, 1942); *The Tree in a Test Tube* (1942); *Air Raid Wardens* (feature, 1943); *The Dancing Masters* (feature, 1943); *Jitterbugs* (feature, 1943); *The Big Noise* (feature, 1944); *Nothing But Trouble* (feature, 1944); *The Bullfighters* (feature, 1945); *Atoll K/Utopia* (feature, 1950); *The Golden Age of Comedy* (compilation, 1957); *The Crazy World of Laurel and Hardy* (compilation, 1964); *Laurel and Hardy's Laughing '20s* (compilation, 1965); *The Further Perils of Laurel and Hardy* (compilation, 1967); *Four Clowns* (compilation, 1969); *The Best of Laurel and Hardy* (compilation, 1971).

Oliver Hardy only: *Outwitting Dad* (1914); *Spaghetti a la Mode* (1915); *Charley's Aunt* (1915); *Paperhanger's Helper* (1915); *Mixed Flats* (1915); *Dreamy Knights* (1916); *The Serenade* (1916); *Aunt Bill* (1916); *Human Hounds* (1916); *The Heroes* (1916); *Love and Duty* (1916); *Better Halves* (1916); *Backstage* (1917); *The Villain* (1917); *The Millionaire* (1917); *The Fly Cop* (1917); *The Pest* (1917); *The Hobo* (1917); *His Day Out* (1918); *The Handyman* (1918);

The Chef (1918); Hello Trouble (1918); Playmates (1918); Mules and Mortgages (1919); Married to Order (1920); The Blizzard (1921); Little Wildcat (1922); Fortune's Mask (1922); One Stolen Night (1923); The Three Ages (1923); King of the Wild Horses (1924); The Wizard of Oz (as the Tin Man, 1925); Stop, Look and Listen (1926); Madame Mystery (1926); The Gentle Cyclone (1926); The Perfect Clown (1926); No Man's Law (1927); Fluttering Hearts (1927); Zenobia (1939); The Fighting Kentuckian (1949); Riding High (1950).

Stan Laurel only: Nuts in May (1917); The Evolution of Fashion (1917); Bears and Bad Men (1918); Do You Love Your Wife? (1918); Frauds and Frenzies (1918); Hickory Hiram (1918); Huns and Hyphens (1918); Hustling for Health (1918); It's Great to Be Crazy (1918); Just Rambling Along (1918); No Place Like Jail (1918); Phoney Photos (1918); Whose Zoo? (1918); Hoot Mon (1919); The Rent Collector (1921); The Egg (1922); Mud and Sand (1922); The Pest (1922); The Weak-End Party (1922); Collars and Cuffs (1923); Frozen Hearts (1923); Gas and Air (1923); The Handy Man (1923); Kill or Cure (1923); A Man About Town (1923); Mother's Joy (1923); Noon Whistle (1923); Oranges and Lemons (1923); Pick and Shovel (1923); Roughest Africa (1923); Save the Ship (1923); Scorching Sands (1923); Short Orders (1923); The Soilers (1923); Under Two Jags (1923); When Knights Were Cold (1923); White Wings (1923); The Whole Truth (1923); Brothers Under the Chin (1923); Detained (1924); Madam Mix-Up (1924); Monsieur Don't Care (1924); Near Dublin (1924); Postage Due (1924); Rupert of Hee-Haw (1924); Short Kilts (1924); Smithy (1924); West of Hot Dog (1924); Wide Open Spaces (1924); Zeb vs. Paprika (1924); Dr. Pyckle and Mr. Pride (1925); Enough to Do (also d, 1925); Half a Man Short (1925); Moonlight and Noses (also d, 1925); Navy Blue Days (1925); Pie-eyed (1925); The Sleuth (1925); The Snow Hawk (1925); Somewhere in Wrong (1925); Twins (1925); Unfriendly Enemies (also d, 1925); Wandering Papas (also d, 1925); Yes, Yes, Nanette (also d, 1925); Atta Boy (1926); Get 'Em Young (1926); On the Front Page (1926).

**Lemmon, Jack (1925– )** Known primarily as a comic actor, Jack Lemmon made his reputation playing the contemporary middle-class fellow who fitfully suffers society's humiliations. Rather than play nebbishy roles, Lemon's realistically grounded characters were constantly frustrated by their circumstances in life. His characters have inevitably embodied the values of the mass audience: skittish about sex, fearful of authority, and full of self-doubts. His physical appearance was also perfect for the Hollywood version of an everyman: handsome without being too good looking, and utterly average in height, weight, and build. Lemmon could well be called Hollywood's leading light comedy actor of the late 1950s and 1960s, but he has segued easily and comfortably into a greater number of dramatic roles during the second half of his long and illustrious career.

Born John Uhler Lemmon III in Boston, Massachusetts, he grew up in a family that was anything but average. His father was a wealthy businessman who owned a large doughnut company. The young Lemmon had the advantages of a prep school and a Harvard education. His first important experience as an actor came at Harvard where he became involved in the drama club.

After a stint in the navy, Lemmon began paying his dues as an actor, working on radio, off Broadway, and especially on television, where he honed his craft in more than four hundred appearances during one five-year stretch. By the time he made his movie debut opposite Judy HOLLIDAY in It Should Happen to You (1954), Lemmon was already a seasoned veteran despite his baby face and his mere twenty-nine years.

Lemmon's rise to stardom came with relative speed. His supporting performance as Ensign Pulver in only his fourth film, the hit comedy Mr. Roberts (1955), brought him an Oscar. Many other strong performances followed in films such as Operation Mad Ball (1957), Cowboy (1958), and Bell, Book and Candle (1959).

Finally, it was his association with director Billy WILDER that turned him into a major star. The first of their seven comedies together was Lemmon's breakout film *Some Like It Hot* (1959). He was not yet a household name, and his agreement to join Tony Curtis and Marilyn MONROE in the cast was a dangerous career move on his part because he spent much of his screen time dressed as a woman. His willingness to take the chance paid off in a major hit film. He was rewarded with both a best actor Academy Award nomination and the starring role in what many consider both Billy Wilder and Jack Lemmon's greatest film, *The Apartment* (1960), a seriocomic movie in which the actor showed great emotional depth in his portrayal of a man torn between his own confused desires. For the second year in a row, Lemmon received a best actor Oscar nomination.

The 1960s was Lemmon's most successful decade. Virtually every one of his films during that ten-year span was a hit. And during that long string of box office winners, the actor showed great range, starring in, among others, the bleak drama *The Days of Wine and Roses* (1962), gaining yet another Oscar nomination in the best actor category; the bawdy sex comedy *Irma La Douce* (1963); the BLACK COMEDY *The Fortune Cookie* (1966), which was also the first of his many acting collaborations with Walter MATTHAU; and the purely entertaining *The Odd Couple* (1968), which not only continued Lemmon's acting relationship with Matthau, it also launched another long and fruitful association with comic playwright and screenwriter Neil SIMON.

Lemmon had fewer hits in the 1970s as his comic persona, best suited to late 1950s and early 1960s, became passé. He was, nonetheless, able to help turn *The Out-of-Towners* (1970) and *The Prisoner of Second Avenue* (1975) into hits, thanks to two very funny Neil Simon scripts. From a commercial standpoint, he was less successful with comedies such as *The War Between Men and Women* (1972), *Avanti!* (1972), and *The Front Page* (1974). Although he received excellent reviews for his performance in the TV film *The Entertainer* (1976), he was reduced in 1977 to appearing in the all-star cast of *Airport '77*. It was also

during the 1970s that Lemmon tried his hand at directing, working behind the camera in the Walter Matthau comedy *Kotch* (1971). The film was generally well received by both the critics and the public, but Lemmon has not directed again.

Two high points in Lemmon's career during the 1970s were dramatic roles that gave the actor new stature. He won the best actor Academy Award for his performance as a desperate factory owner in *Save the Tiger* (1973) and then stole the show from Jane Fonda and Michael Douglas in *The China Syndrome* (1979), gaining his sixth Oscar nomination.

For the most part, Lemmon has continued to lean more heavily toward drama in his later years, pulling down his seventh Oscar nomination as a dying man in *Tribute* (1980), receiving his eighth Oscar bid as a concerned father in *Missing* (1982), playing a cynical priest in *Mass Appeal* (1984), and acting as a man at the end of his rope in *Glengarry Glen Ross* (1992). Two of his more comedic films during recent years, *Buddy, Buddy* (1981) and *Macaroni* (1985), were both critical and commercial flops, but he recouped smartly with Walter Matthau in *Grumpy Old Men* (1993).

---

**FILMS:** *It Should Happen to You* (1954); *Phfft* (1954); *Three for the Show* (1954); *Mister Roberts* (1955); *My Sister Eileen* (1955); *You Can't Run Away from It* (1956); *Fire Down Below* (1957); *Operation Mad Ball* (1957); *Bell, Book and Candle* (1958); *Cowboy* (1958); *It Happened to Jane* (1959); *Some Like It Hot* (1959); *The Apartment* (1960); *Pepe* (1960); *The Wackiest Ship in the Army* (1960); *Days of Wine and Roses* (1962); *The Notorious Landlady* (1962); *Irma la Douce* (1963); *Under the Yum Yum Tree* (1963); *Good Neighbor Sam* (1964); *The Great Race* (1965); *How to Murder Your Wife* (1965); *The Fortune Cookie* (1966); *Luv* (1967); *The Odd Couple* (1968); *There Comes a Day* (short, 1968); *The April Fools* (1969); *The Out-of-Towners* (1970); *Kotch* (cameo, d, 1971); *Avanti!* (1972); *The War Between Men and Women* (1972); *Save the Tiger* (1973); *The Front Page* (1974); *The Prisoner of Second Avenue* (1974); *Alex and the Gypsy* (1976); *Airport '77* (1977); *The*

*China Syndrome* (1979); *Ken Murray: Shooting Stars* (1979); *Portrait of a 60% Perfect Man* (narration, 1980); *Tribute* (also song, 1980); *Buddy Buddy* (1981); *Missing* (1982); *Mass Appeal* (1984); *Macaroni* (1985); *That's Life!* (1986); *Dad* (1989); *JFK* (1991); *The Player* (1992); *Glengarry Glen Ross* (1992); *Short Cuts* (1993); *Grumpy Old Men* (1993).

## Lewis, Jerry (1926—)

A comic actor, director, writer, and producer, Jerry Lewis is best known for his film persona of the childlike geek, which has sustained him in more than forty movies. His film career can be neatly divided into three segments: the period of the amusing Martin and Lewis movies, the brilliant solo years, and the startlingly rapid, steep decline. Most American film critics hold him in little regard, considering him an uninspired comedian who is hopelessly juvenile. On the other hand, he is exalted in Europe (particularly France) where he is seen as a modern-day Charlie CHAPLIN. His place in the Hollywood canon fairly falls somewhere between the two extremes.

Born Joseph Levitch in Newark, New Jersey, to a show business family, Lewis joined his parents' act, singing with them on stage when he was five. However, his real training came in the resort area in the Catskill Mountains north of New York City known as the "Borscht Belt," where he honed his stand-up comedy routine. He didn't have much success as a single, but then he joined with another young unknown entertainer, Dean MARTIN, to form a team in Atlantic City in 1946, and they were an overnight sensation.

Lewis was the wild man comic to Martin's crooning straight man, and the team's nightclub success led with surprising speed to a supporting role in their first film, *My Friend Irma* (1949). The movie was only mediocre, but it had a big reception at the box office, thanks to the popularity of Martin and Lewis, who were a fresher, zanier version of AB-BOTT AND COSTELLO. They were quickly rushed into a starring film of their own, *My Friend Irma*

*Jerry Lewis was one of the most consistently popular stars in Hollywood history. Including his sixteen movies with Dean Martin, Lewis had a streak of thirty-seven films in a row that turned a profit. No wonder he was laughing.*
PHOTO COURTESY OF MOVIE STAR NEWS.

*Goes West* (1950), and Martin and Lewis continued making films together until 1956, with a total of sixteen, every one of them a commercial hit. Among the better efforts were *Living It Up* (1954), *Artists and Models* (1955), and *Pardners* (1956).

When Martin quit the team, Lewis began taking greater control of his solo career. He had a hit record ("Rockabye Your Baby"—later used as a title to one of his films) and also began producing, writing, and directing his own movies. His first solo effort was *The Delicate Delinquent* (1957), a movie not unlike his films with Dean Martin. Lewis began to experiment and grow as a filmmaker, learning from director Frank TASHLIN, and in the early 1960s he wrote, directed, and produced a handful of excellent comedies, including two masterpieces, *The Ladies' Man* (1961) and *The Nutty Professor* (1963). His other fine films of that era were *The Bellboy* (1960), *The Errand Boy* (1961), and *The Patsy* (1964).

After the *The Family Jewels* (1965), an overripe film in which Lewis played seven roles, the quality of his movies dropped precipitously. Nonetheless, his comedies continued to be profitable for a short while longer, adding to a remarkable record of more than thirty-seven straight hits (a streak that includes his Martin and Lewis movies). His later films, such as *The Big Mouth* (1967) and *Which Way to the Front* (1970), were pale shadows of his early 1960s works and were part of a series of commercial flops that cost him his financing sources.

One reason commonly given for Lewis's demise as a comic film star is that he played a character who had to be young. Playing his sincere goofball as a middle-aged man became embarrassing rather than amusing. There was, therefore, something sad about Lewis's return to film comedy in the same old role in *Hardly Working* (1979).

More recently, however, Lewis has begun playing dramatic parts to great effect. His portrayal of a Johnny Carsonlike talk show host in Martin Scorsese's *The King of Comedy* (1983) and a dramatic TV movie role as the father of a dying child finally brought him good reviews from American critics.

In addition to his film work, Lewis has three times tried and failed as the host of a television series. He has also consistently worked in nightclubs. Although his film career has faded, he is universally known in America as the host and driving force of "The Jerry Lewis Telethon," which raises money to fight muscular dystrophy. Lewis and his telethon have become a television institution.

FILMS: As actor with Dean Martin: *My Friend Irma* (1949); *My Friend Irma Goes West* (1950); *At War with the Army* (1950); *Sailor Beware* (1951); *That's My Boy* (1951); *Jumping Jacks* (1952); *The Stooge* (1952); *The Caddy* (1953); *Money from Home* (1953); *Scared Stiff* (1953); *Living It Up* (1954); *Three Ring Circus* (1954); *Artists and Models* (1955); *You're Never Too Young* (1955); *Hollywood or Bust* (1956); *Pardners* (1956).

As actor, Lewis only: *Road to Bali* (cameo, 1952); *The Delicate Delinquent* (also p, 1957); *The Sad Sack* (1957); *The Geisha Boy* (also p, 1958); *Rock-a-Bye Baby* (also p, 1958); *Don't Give Up the Ship* (1959); *Visit to a Small Planet* (1959); *The Bellboy* (also sc, p, d, 1960); *Cinderfella* (also p, 1960); *Raymie* (sings title song only, 1960); *The Ladies' Man* (also story, sc, p, d, 1961); *The Errand Boy* (also sc, p, d, 1961); *It's Only Money* (1962); *It's a Mad Mad Mad Mad World* (cameo, 1963); *The Nutty Professor* (also sc, p, d, 1963); *Who's Minding the Store?* (1963); *The Patsy* (also story, sc, d, 1964); *The Disorderly Orderly* (1964); *The Family Jewels* (also sc, p, d, 1965); *Boeing Boeing* (1965); *Three on a Couch* (also p, d, 1966); *Way . . . Way Out* (1966); *The Big Mouth* (also sc, p, d, 1967); *Don't Raise the Bridge, Lower the River* (1968); *Hook, Line and Sinker* (also p, 1969); *One More Time* (d only); *Which Way to the Front?* (also p, d, 1970); *Hardly Working* (also co-sc, d, 1981); *The King of Comedy* (1983); *Cracking Up/Smorgasbord* (sc, d, 1983); *Slapstick of Another Kind* (1984); *Cookie* (1989); *Mr. Saturday Night* (1992); *Arizona Dream* (France, 1993).

## Lloyd, Christopher (1938—)

Since his movie debut as one of the asylum inmates in *One Flew over the Cuckoo's Nest* (1975), Christopher Lloyd has built a film comedy career out of playing eccentrics and crazies. Obviously, madness becomes him.

Born in Stamford, Connecticut, Lloyd studied his craft at the respected Neighborhood Playhouse in New York City. He made his professional stage debut at sixteen and continued to work in the theater throughout his twenties and most of his thirties before getting some movie and TV work.

Most of his early film roles were small; his first big break came with the recurring role of the Reverend Jim on the hit TV sitcom "Taxi." He won two Emmy awards for his work during the four years he appeared on the show.

Lloyd worked steadily in larger film roles thereafter, but with little in the way of name recognition.

*Back to the Future* changed that forever when the modest comedy zoomed to the top of the 1985 box office chart. After that, his was a name that audiences responded to on the marquee, and he had leading roles (usually villainously comic) in movies such as *Who Framed Roger Rabbit?* (1988), *The Addams Family* (1991), and *Dennis the Menace* (1993).

---

**FILMS INCLUDE:** *One Flew Over the Cuckoo's Nest* (1975); *Three Warriors* (1977); *Goin' South* (1978); *The Black Marble* (1979); *The Lady in Red* (1979); *Butch and Sundance: The Early Days* (1979); *The Onion Field* (1979); *Schizoid* (1980); *Pilgrim Farewell* (1980); *The Legend of the Lone Ranger* (1981); *The Postman Always Rings Twice* (1981); *Mr. Mom* (1983); *To Be or Not to Be* (1983); *Joy of Sex* (1984); *Miracles* (1984); *The Adventures of Buckaroo Banzai: Across the 8th Dimension* (1984); *Star Trek III: The Search for Spock* (1984); *Clue* (1985); *Back to the Future* (1985); *Track 29* (1987); *Walk Like a Man* (1987); *The Cowboy and the Ballerina* (1988); *Eight Men Out* (1988); *Who Framed Roger Rabbit?* (1988); *The Dream Team* (1989); *Why Me?* (1989); *Back to the Future II* (1989); *Back to the Future III* (1990); *DuckTales: The Movie* (1990); *Suburban Commando* (1991); *The Addams Family* (1991); *Dennis the Menace* (1993); *Addams Family Values* (1993); *Twenty Bucks* (1993).

---

# Lloyd, Harold (1893—1971)

In terms of ticket sales, Harold Lloyd was the most popular silent comedian of the 1920s, filling more seats with fans in movie theaters than either Charlie CHAPLIN or Buster KEATON. In part, Lloyd owed his success to greater productivity; he made more films than either of his rivals. His success, furthermore, had nothing to do with shallow audience values; Lloyd was a superb comic actor who created an American go-getting character with whom 1920s jazz-age audiences could easily identify. His brand of comedy was both visually inventive and physically demanding. Mostly, however, it was simply breathtaking. He became known for "stunt" comedy, doing daredevil feats that elicited screams of fear and comic delight as he teetered at the brink of disaster.

Lloyd, born in Burchard, Nebraska, was nineteen and living in San Diego, California, when a camera crew from the Edison Company arrived to shoot some location footage. Young Lloyd picked up work playing an extra and was immediately hooked on the movies.

Later, in Hollywood, he teamed up with Hal ROACH in a fledgling production company and starred in a primitive comedy one-reeler, *Just Nuts* (1915). A year later Lloyd invented a character called Lonesome Luke, whom he patterned on Charlie Chaplin. Instead of wearing baggy clothes like the tramp, Lloyd dressed his Lonesome Luke in particularly tight-fitting togs. The character was immediately popular, and Lloyd ended up making more than one hundred Lonesome Luke comedy shorts. However, Lloyd wasn't satisfied.

He had an idea for a new character whom he called Glasses. This character was the epitome of the upwardly mobile striving young American. With a seemingly mild and meek disposition, Lloyd's hero simply would not give up until he was a success. Glasses first appeared on film in a one-reeler titled *Over the Fence* (1917).

By 1918 Lloyd had dropped the Lonesome Luke character completely due to the public acceptance of his new character Glasses. (Incidentally, his trademark glasses had no lenses in them.) One-reelers gave way to two-reelers during the next few years. By this time, the only obstacle to Lloyd's growing fame was a bomb, but not the celluloid variety. In 1920 he was posing for a publicity still while leaning on a prop explosive. Except it wasn't a prop. The bomb blew up, and Lloyd spent six months in a hospital, losing two fingers (including his thumb) on his right hand. After the accident, Lloyd wore a specially constructed glove that gave no hint of the missing digits. The public had no idea that the daredevil comic was performing his stunts with a physical handicap.

*Known for his elaborate comic stunts, Harold Lloyd was more than an accomplished daredevil. His carefully constructed physical gags were second only to Keaton's, and he was actually more popular (in terms of ticket sales) than both Keaton and Chaplin during the 1920s due to his considerable productivity.*  PHOTO COURTESY OF MOVIE STAR NEWS.

Lloyd continued to expand the scope of his films. With complete artistic control of his movies, Lloyd made three-, four-, and five-reelers. By 1922 he was making full-fledged features, the first of which was *Dr. Jack*. His second feature, *Safety Last* (1923), became his most famous. In one of film comedy's grandest stunts, he was suspended from the hands of a clock on a high-rise building.

From this point on, Lloyd's humor tended to inspire awe rather than belly laughs. His breathtaking stunts (done without benefit of a stuntman) remain unequalled to this day.

The hits followed quickly after *Girl Shy* (1924), which was one of the top moneymakers of the year. *The Freshman* (1925) was his most successful movie at the box office; it was also one of the biggest grossers of the silent era, with receipts of over $2.5 million. *For Heaven's Sake* (1926), *The Kid Brother* (1927), and *Speedy* (1928) were also highly successful.

It wasn't sound that stunted Lloyd's career because he had a pleasant voice. The problem was that Glasses no longer seemed quite believable as a character once the shock of the Great Depression set in. Nonetheless, he continued making films throughout the 1930s and had modest success, although nothing like he had enjoyed during his silent comedy days. His best films of this era were *The Milky Way* (1936) and *Professor Beware* (1938), after which he retired from the screen. He made a curious comeback in 1947 in the Preston STURGES film *Mad Wednesday* (also known as *The Sin of Harold Diddlebock*), in which the plot began with the end of Lloyd's silent hit *Safety Last*.

Lloyd married his one-time leading lady from the early 1920s, Mildred Davis, and they remained together until her death in 1969. In 1952 Lloyd was given a special Oscar, honoring him as a "master comedian." It was a well-deserved tribute.

One of the reasons Lloyd is less well known today than Chaplin and Keaton is that Lloyd owned the rights to all his major works. Guarding his films from exploitation, he proved too zealous a protector, keeping them out of public display for so long that his reputation as a comic star faded into near obscurity. It wasn't until near the end of his life that he finally began allowing his movies to be shown.

FILMS INCLUDE: Shorts: *Just Nuts* (1915); *From Italy's Shores* (1915); *Willie Goes to Sea* (1915); *Lonesome Luke* (1915); *Once Every Ten Minutes* (1915); *Spitball Sadie* (1915); *Terribly Stuck Up* (1915); *Some Baby* (1915); *Fresh from the Farm* (1915); *Giving Them Fits* (1915); *Tinkering with Trouble* (1915); *Rouses Rhymes and Roughnecks* (1915); *Peculiar Patients' Pranks* (1915); *Lonesome Luke: Social Gangster* (1915); *Luke Leans to the Literary* (1916); *Luke Rolls in Luxury* (1916); *Luke Foils the Villain* (1916); *Lonesome Luke: Circus King* (1916); *Luke's Double* (1916); *Ice* (1916); *An Awful Romance* (1916); *Unfriendly Fruit* (1916); *A Matrimonial Mixup* (1916); *Caught in a Jam* (1916); *Luke Joins the Navy* (1916); *Luke and the Mermaids* (1916); *Jailed* (1916); *Luke Gladiator* (1916); *Luke's Movie Muddle* (1916); *Drama's Dreadful Deal* (1917); *Lonesome Luke: Lawyer* (1917); *Lonesome Luke on Tin Can Alley* (1917); *Lonesome Luke's Honeymoon* (1917); *Lonesome Luke: Plumber* (1917); *Stop! Luke! Listen!* (1917); *Lonesome Luke's Wild Women* (1917); *Over the Fence* (1917); *Birds of a Feather* (1917); *Lonesome Luke from London to Laramie* (1917); *Rainbow Island* (1917); *Love Laughter and Lather* (1917); *The Flirt* (1917); *Clubs Are Trump* (1917); *We Never Sleep* (1917); *Bashful* (1917); *The Big Idea* (1918); *The Lamb* (1918); *Here Come the Girls* (1918); *It's a Wild Life* (1918); *The Non-Stop Kid* (1918); *Fireman Save My Child* (1918); *The City Slicker* (1918); *Somewhere in Turkey* (1918); *Kicking the Germ out of Germany* (1918); *An Ozark Romance* (1918); *Nothing but Trouble* (1918); *Look Out Below* (1919); *A Sammy in Siberia* (1919); *Young Mr. Jazz* (1919); *Si Senor* (1919); *The Marathon* (1919); *Spring Fever* (1919); *Billy Blazes Esq.* (1919); *Just Neighbors* (1919); *Chop Suey and Co.* (1919); *The Rajah* (1919); *Soft Money* (1919); *Bumping into Broadway* (1919); *Captain Kidd's Kids* (1919); *From Hand to Mouth* (1919); *His Royal Slyness* (1919); *Haunted Spooks* (1920); *An Eastern Western* (1920); *High and Dizzy* (1920); *Get Out and Get Under* (1920); *Number Please* (1920); *Now or Never* (1921).

Extended shorts and features: *Among Those Present* (1921); *Be My Wife* (1921); *I Do* (1921); *A Sailor-Made Man* (1921); *Never Weaken* (1921); *Grandma's Boy* (1922); *Back to the Woods* (1922); *Dr. Jack* (1922); *Safety Last* (also sc, 1923); *Why Worry?* (1923); *Girl Shy* (1924); *Hot Water* (1924); *The Freshman* (1925); *For Heaven's Sake* (1926); *The Kid Brother* (1927); *Speedy* (1928); *Welcome Danger* (also p, 1929); *Feet First* (1930); *Movie Crazy* (also p, 1932); *The Cat's Paw* (1934); *The Milky Way* (1936); *Professor Beware* (also p, 1938); *A Girl, a Guy and a Gob* (p only, 1941); *My Favorite Spy* (p only, 1942); *Mad Wednesday/The Sin of Harold Diddlebock* (1947); *Harold Lloyd's World of Comedy* (compilation, 1962); *Harold Lloyd's Funny Side of Life* (compilation, 1963).

**Lombard, Carole (1908—1942)** A consummate comedian who pioneered a new sort of female star, Carole Lombard was beautiful without being brittle, and witty and feisty without losing her glamour. In other words, she was as modern an actress as Hollywood has ever produced. Lombard seemed destined for a career as a glamour queen, but she surprised everyone by proving herself an upscale version of Jean HARLOW; she could be both sexy and funny without being vulgar. Her appeal was obviously genuine because it worked not only on movie audiences, but on movie stars as well; during the 1930s, she married, in succession, William Powell and Clark Gable.

Born Jane Peters in Fort Wayne, Indiana, she was the product of a broken home. After moving to California with her mother, she made her first appearance in the movies at age twelve. She was spotted in her own backyard by director Alan Dwan, who was visiting nearby. He decided she had the ideal look for a part in *A Perfect Crime* (1921).

Lombard set out to learn her craft. When she was sixteen, she tested for the role of Georgia (the female lead) in Charlie CHAPLIN's *The Gold Rush* (1924), but she didn't get the part. The following year, however, finally brought her back into the film business with a starring role in *Marriage in Transit* (1925). In 1927 she hooked up with Mack SENNETT's studio and received a valuable two-year education in silent film comedy playing in a number of comic two-reelers.

Lombard mostly played vamps or glamorous sophisticates in the early 1930s. She had achieved a certain level of popularity in mediocre movies, but was hardly a major star. As David Shipman wrote in his book *The Great Movie Stars*, she was "noted more for her slinky blonde looks, good legs, and daring gowns than for anything else."

That all changed when she starred with John Barrymore in Howard HAWK's first SCREWBALL COMEDY, *TWENTIETH CENTURY* (1934). Barrymore was fabulous in one of his last great roles, but Lombard was the revelation. Her comic abilities were on grand display, and suddenly audiences and film studios saw a great talent behind the beauty.

Unfortunately, that talent was trapped in a number of mediocre movies over the next few years, but there were also several comedies that gave Lombard a chance to shine. *My Man Godfrey* (1936), in which she starred with ex-husband William Powell, was a standout. So was *Nothing Sacred* (1937). In that year

she was Hollywood's highest-paid star, earning $465,000.

Dramatic roles came her way along with comedies. She was winsome in *Made for Each Other* (1939) with Jimmy Stewart and wonderfully tough-minded in *They Knew What They Wanted* (1940) with Charles Laughton.

Lombard's last movie was Ernst LUBITSCH's anti-Nazi satire *To Be or Not to Be* (1942). She starred with Jack BENNY in what is now considered a classic comedy. At the time, however, it was poorly recieved by the critics.

Lombard died that same year in a tragic plane crash near Las Vegas while returning home to her husband, Clark Gable, after a successful war bond drive. The nation mourned along with Gable.

FILMS: Features: *A Perfect Crime* (1921); *Marriage in Transit* (1925); *Hearts and Spurs* (1925); *Durand of the Badlands* (1925); *The Road to Glory* (1926); *The Divine Sinner* (1928); *Power* (1928); *Me Gangster* (1928); *Show Folks* (1928); *Ned McCobb's Daughter* (1928); *High Voltage* (1929); *Big News* (1929); *The Racketeer* (1929); *The Arizona Kid* (1930); *Safety in Numbers* (1930); *Fast and Loose* (1930); *It Pays to Advertise* (1931); *Man of the World* (1931); *Ladies' Man* (1931); *Up Pops the Devil* (1931); *I Take This Woman* (1931); *No One Man* (1932); *Sinners in the Sun* (1932); *Virtue* (1932); *No More Orchids* (1932); *No Man of Her Own* (1932); *From Hell to Heaven* (1933); *Supernatural* (1933); *The Eagle and the Hawk* (1933); *Brief Moment* (1933); *White Woman* (1933); *Bolero* (1934); *We're Not Dressing* (1934); *Twentieth Century* (1934); *Now and Forever* (1934); *Lady by Choice* (1934); *The Gay Bride* (1934); *Rumba* (1935); *Hands Across the Table* (1935); *Love Before Breakfast* (1936); *The Princess Comes Across* (1936); *My Man Godfrey* (1936); *Swing High Swing Low* (1937); *Nothing Sacred* (1937); *True Confession* (1937); *Fools for Scandal* (1938); *Made for Each Other* (1939); *In Name Only* (1939); *Vigil in the Night* (1940); *They Knew What They Wanted* (1940); *Mr. and Mrs. Smith* (1941); *To Be or Not to Be* (1942).

**Long, Shelley (1949— )** Blonde, perky, and an accomplished improvisational comedian, Shelley Long reached the height of her movie popularity soon after she left her starring role in the hit TV sitcom "Cheers." Before and after that brief tenure at the top, she has played to smaller audiences in generally lesser films.

Born in Fort Wayne, Indiana, Long majored in drama at Northwestern University before becoming a TV news producer. The call of comedy beckoned, however, and she quit her job to join the Second City comedy group in Chicago. She then traveled to Hollywood, where she found work in TV movies during the late 1970s and early 1980s. Her first film appearance was in the soapy drama *A Small Circle of Friends* (1980), but comedy suited her better, as was soon shown in *Caveman* (1982) and *Night Shift* (1983), in which she had significant supporting parts.

It was the TV sitcom "Cheers," however, that turned Long into a star in 1982. However, she never gave up on the movies, playing leads in several comedies during her five years on TV, the best of them being *The Money Pit* (1985). Her first two films after leaving the show, *Outrageous Fortune* (1987), in which she co-starred with Bette MIDLER, and *Hello, Again* (1987), which she carried alone, were both successful films, although the Midler/Long duo did far better at the box office. Her next film, *Troop Beverly Hills* (1989), was a bomb, as were her feature films throughout the early 1990s.

---

FILMS INCLUDE: *A Small Circle of Friends* (1980); *Caveman* (1981); *Night Shift* (1982); *Losin' It* (1983); *Irreconcilable Differences* (1984); *The Money Pit* (1986); *Hello, Again* (1987); *Outrageous Fortune* (1987); *Troop Beverly Hills* (1989); *Don't Tell Her It's Me* (1990); *Frozen Assets* (1992).

---

**Loos, Anita (1893—1981)** One of Hollywood's wittiest and most prolific screenwriters, Anita Loos had a film career that spanned thirty years and bridged the early silents and the golden years of the studio sound era. Although best known as the author of the novel *Gentlemen Prefer Blondes*, which became the basis of a play and two movie adaptations (filmed in 1928 and 1953), Loos's fertile imagination and clever way with words would have, in any event, earned her a place in film comedy history.

Discovered by D. W. Griffith, who bought her first story idea for $15 in 1912 and turned it into *The New York Hat*, Loos went on to write scores of one- and two-reelers as well as features. She was one of the rare breed of women who worked steadily in the film business as a screenwriter. And she was certainly the most famous.

Loos had a talent for creating unusual stories and amusing subtitles. Griffith, however, was not well known for his sense of humor, so it was a happy circumstance that she was assigned to write scripts in 1916 for the relatively unknown Douglas Fairbanks. With a series of exuberant, clever comedies such as *Manhattan Madness* (1916), *The Matrimaniac* (1916), and *Wild and Woolly* (1917), Loos helped define Fairbanks's early star personality and launch his spectacular career.

Loos's success with Fairbanks gave her considerable clout in Hollywood, and with her fine working relationship with director (and later, husband) John Emerson, Loos went on to write and occasionally produce successful female-oriented films, many of them comedies, during the 1920s, such as *The Perfect Woman* (1920), *Woman's Place* (1921), and *Learning to Love* (1925).

While a great many screenwriters of the silent era were pushed aside after the arrival of sound, Loos had no trouble finding work due to her playwriting success with *Gentlemen Prefer Blondes* (which she adapted to the stage from her novel).

As she did in the 1920s, Loos fashioned most of her sound films for the female audience, writing light romantic comedies such as *Hold Your Man* (1933) and *The Biography of a Bachelor Girl* (1935). She was at her acerbic best when she wrote the screenplay for *The Women* (1939). However, like any adaptable Hollywood screenwriter, she was capable of writing melodramas too, penning *Riffraff* (1936) and the most popular film of 1936, *San Francisco*. While her last official screenplay was *I Married an Angel* in 1942, she was rediscovered by the public yet again when *Gentlemen Prefer Blondes* was remade as a musical with Jane Russell and Marilyn MONROE in 1953.

A prolific author, Loos wrote a number of nonfiction books, including two with her husband, *How to Write Photoplays* (1919) and *Breaking into the Movies* (1921). After John Emerson's death in 1956, she wrote a series of autobiographies: *A Girl Like I* (1966), *Kiss Hollywood Good-Bye* (1974), and *Cast of Thousands* (1977). She also wrote a biography of her silent screen contemporaries, *The Talmadge Girls* (1978).

**FILMS INCLUDE:** As screenwriter: *The New York Hat* (1912); *The Telephone Girl and the Lady* (1912); *The Lady and the Mouse* (1913); *The Mistake* (1913); *A Lesson in Mechanics* (1914); *Lord Chumley* (1914); *A Ten Cent Adventure* (1915); *Double Trouble* (1915); *American Aristocracy* (1916); *A Corner in Cotton* (also story, 1916); *The Deadly Glass of Beer* (1916); *His Picture in the Papers* (also story, 1916); *Intolerance* (titles, 1916); *The Matrimoniac* (1916); *The Social Secretary* (also story, 1916); *The Wharf Rat* (also story, 1916); *In Again, Out Again* (also story, 1917); *Wild and Woolly* (1917); *Come on In* (also story, p, 1918); *Goodbye, Bill* (also story, p, 1918); *Let's Get a Divorce* (1918); *Getting Mary Married* (also story, 1919); *Oh, You Women!* (also story, 1919); *The Virtuous Vamp* (also p, 1919); *The Branded Woman* (1920); *In Search of a Sinner* (adapt, p, 1920); *The Love Expert* (also story, p, 1920); *Mama's Affair* (adapt, 1921); *Polly of the Follies* (also story, p, 1922); *Red Hot Romance* (also story, p, 1922); *Dulcy* (1923); *Three Miles Out* (1924); *Learning to Love* (1925); *Publicity Madness* (story only, 1927); *Gentlemen Prefer Blondes* (from her novel, titles, 1928); *The Fall of Eve* (story only, 1929); *Blondie of the Follies* (dial only, 1932); *Hold Your Man* (also story, 1933); *The Girl from Missouri* (also story, 1934); *The Social Register* (from her own play, 1934); *Biography of a Bachelor Girl* (adapt, 1935); *Riffraff* (1935); *San Francisco* (1936); *Mama*

*Steps Out* (1937); *Saratoga* (also story, 1937); *The Women* (1939); *Susan and God* (1940); *Blossoms in the Dust* (1941); *They Met in Bombay* (1941); *When Ladies Meet* (1941); *I Married an Angel* (1942); *Gentlemen Prefer Blondes* (from her novel, 1953); *Gentlemen Marry Brunettes* (from her novel, 1955).

**Lubitsch, Ernst (1892—1947)** Very few directors during the studio era were considered giants in their own time, but Ernst Lubitsch was. He was a director/producer whose sex comedies in both the silent and sound eras set the standard for sophistication. In addition, he created the comic operetta on film, melding music, farce, and (as he did with all of his films) his signature "Lubitsch touch," which might be described as deft visual innuendos that spoke volumes about what was happening behind closed doors. According to film critic Andrew Sarris, it was the "counterpoint between sadness and gaiety that represents the Lubitsch touch."

Certainly, there was an undercurrent of melancholy that enriched and deepened Lubitsch's humor, making his films seem somehow nostalgic even when they were contemporaneous. Some of that feeling was due to the curious fact that the German director set most of his Hollywood films in European locales. However, Hollywood was definitely his home. In fact, he once said, "I've been to Paris, France, and I've been to Paris, Paramount. Paris, Paramount, is better."

Born to a well-to-do Berlin tailor, Lubitsch became enamored of the stage while an adolescent. In 1911 he became a member of Max Reinhardt's legendary Deutsches Theater, quickly establishing himself in important roles. The theater didn't pay very well and, to make extra money, he took a job with a Berlin film company in 1912. The following year he began acting in films, starring in a series of comedy shorts in which he played a stereotypical Jewish character named Meyer. The Meyer comedies proved to be quite popular, and he furthered his film education and career by both writing his own scripts and directing himself in subsequent movies.

When the Meyer shorts finally faded in popularity, Lubitsch stopped acting to direct full time, soon becoming one of Germany's leading directors by the late 1910s and early 1920s. He had several huge international hits, among them *Gypsy Blood* (1918), *The Oyster Princess* (1919), and *Deception* (1920). His reputation was such that Mary Pickford decided she had to have him direct her. Lubitsch made his American debut directing Pickford in *Rosita* (1923). The film was the first of a remarkable series of triumphs, and Lubitsch remained in Hollywood for the rest of his life.

The director soon found his comic footing, creating one silent film success after another with movies that cleverly whirled around themes of sex and money. His *The Marriage Circle* (1924) was clearly inspired by Charlie CHAPLIN's *A Woman of Paris* (1923), and there were those who thought that Lubitsch had surpassed it. As for *Lady Windemere's Fan* (1925), Andrew Sarris said that it "was an improvement over (Oscar) Wilde's original."

While many foreign directors were defeated by the coming of sound, Lubitsch thrived. For instance, his continental operettas *The Love Parade* (1929), *One Hour with You* (1932), and *The Merry Widow* (1934), all with Jeanette MacDonald and Maurice CHEVALIER, were witty souffles that advanced the emerging art of the movie musical. Furthermore, Lubitsch was just as entertaining without music, making *Trouble in Paradise* (1932) one of the cleverest, most satisfying bedroom farces that ever graced the big screen.

Lubitsch began producing his own films in the latter half of the 1930s when he became the production manager at Paramount. His new duties didn't stop him from continuing to add to his seemingly endless string of quality comedies, including *Bluebeard's Eighth Wife* (1938), *Ninotchka* (1939), *The Shop Around the Corner* (1940), and *That Uncertain Feeling* (1941).

His only major critical and commercial flop also happened to be one of his greatest films, *To Be or Not*

*to Be* (1942), a movie that starred Jack BENNY and Carole LOMBARD. There was a storm of protest against the film because Lubitsch had made an anti-Nazi farce that showed Hitler and company to be buffoons and fools rather than starkly evil men. *To Be or Not to Be* has since come to be regarded as a classic and was even remade virtually scene-for-scene with Mel BROOKS in 1983.

Lubitsch shrugged off the failure, but could not shrug off his declining health. He managed to direct just two other critical and commerical hits, *Heaven Can Wait* (1943) and *Cluny Brown* (1946), before succumbing to his sixth heart attack. He died while directing *That Lady in Ermine* (1948), a film that was completed by Otto Preminger.

In a film career spanning nearly thirty-five years, most of them in America, where he became one of the industry's most revered (and copied) directors, Lubitsch nevertheless failed to win a best director Academy Award. He had, however, been nominated for *The Patriot* (1928), *The Love Parade* (1929), and *Heaven Can Wait* (1943). Aware that he was a very sick man, the Academy moved quickly to honor him while he was still alive with a special Oscar in 1946 "for his distinguished contributions to the art of the motion picture."

---

FILMS: As director in the United States: *Rosita* (1923); *The Marriage Circle* (1924); *Three Women* (also co-story, 1924); *Forbidden Paradise* (1924); *Kiss Me Again* (1925); *Lady Windemere's Fan* (1925); *So This Is Paris* (1926); *The Student Prince* (1927); *The Patriot* (1928); *Eternal Love* (1929); *The Love Parade* (1929); *Paramount on Parade* (co-d with ten others, 1930); *Monte Carlo* (1930); *The Smiling Lieutenant* (also co-sc, 1931); *The Man I Killed/Broken Lullaby* (1932); *One Hour with You* (1932); *Trouble in Paradise* (also p, 1932); *If I Had a Million* (single episode, supervising d, 1932); *Design for Living* (1933); *The Merry Widow* (1934); *Desire* (p only, 1936); *Angel* (also p, 1937); *Bluebeard's Eighth Wife* (also p, 1938); *Ninotchka* (1939); *The Shop Around the Corner* (also p, 1940); *That Uncertain Feeling* (also p, 1941); *To Be or Not to Be* (also co-story, co-p, 1942); *Heaven Can*

*Wait* (also p, 1943); *A Royal Scandal* (p only, 1945); *Cluny Brown* (also p, 1946); *That Lady in Ermine* (also p, finished by Otto Preminger, 1948).

---

**Lynde, Paul (1926—1982)** A long-faced, comically snooty character actor, Paul Lynde appeared to look down his nose at everyone, sneering with contempt and putting down everything and everyone around him. His lines didn't have to be funny to get a laugh; his tone, body language, and voice all conveyed his humorously superior attitude.

Born in Mt. Vernon, Ohio, Lynde had early success in show business, making it to Broadway in his mid-twenties in the revue *New Faces of 1952*. He recreated his performance in the 1954 film version of the show, simply called *New Faces*. He didn't begin appearing regularly in movies until the early 1960s, when he recreated yet another of his Broadway roles for the big screen in *Bye, Bye, Birdie* (1963). By then, however, he was a recognized comic talent, showing up in supporting roles in two other film comedies, *Son of Flubber* (1963) and *Under the Yum Yum Tree* (1963).

Lynde worked steadily in Hollywood during the 1960s in what became his stock-in-trade, the prissy, smug, and wisecracking comic relief in films like *Beach Blanket Bingo* (1965) and *The Glass Bottom Boat* (1966). His distinctive voice was used several times in animated movies during the late 1960s and 1970s, although he became less visible on the big screen. He was, however, regularly seen on TV in the center square of the game show "Hollywood Squares," where he held court for a great many years.

Lynde's last movie appearance was in *The Villain* (1978), in which he played an Indian chief named Nervous Elk, a role that encapsulated the kind of goofy, over-the-top characters he played throughout his career.

---

FILMS: *New Faces* (also co-sc, 1954); *Son of Flubber* (1963); *Under the Yum Yum Tree* (1963); *Bye, Bye, Birdie* (1963); *For Those Who Think Young* (1964); *Send Me No Flowers* (1964); *Beach Blanket Bingo* (1965); *The Glass Bottom Boat* (1966); *How Sweet It Is* (1968); *Charlotte's Web* (voice only, 1973); *Journey Back to Oz* (voice only, 1974); *Hugo the Hippo* (voice only, 1976); *The Villain* (1978).

# M

**Ma and Pa Kettle** *See* Marjorie MAIN; SERIES COMEDIES

**MacLaine, Shirley (1934—)** A gifted actress, singer, and dancer, Shirley MacLaine has been a star for more than thirty years thanks largely to her success as a comedian. Whether playing the proverbial prostitute with a heart of gold (which she's done in fourteen films!) or quirky older women, the majority of her film roles have been of a comedic nature. An actress of unconventional beauty and even more unconventional attitudes, the redheaded performer has appeared in only a few musicals, but her long, leggy look has been as much of an asset to her career as her pixieish manner.

Born Shirley MacLean Beatty to a middle-class family in Richmond, Virginia, she was given dancing lessons at the age of two and a half to firm up her weak ankles. Dancing appealed to her and, aided by her amateur drama coach mother, she pursued a show business career by venturing to New York at age sixteen. It paid off, at least temporarily, when she won a chorus job in a revival of *Oklahoma*. She went home to finish high school before finally returning to New York two years later with the new stage name of Shirley MacLaine.

If the way in which she rose to fame had been made into a movie, the screenwriter would have been drummed out of Hollywood for plagiarizing the 1933 movie classic *42nd Street*. MacLaine had just gotten the job of understudying for star Carol Haney in the new musical *The Pajama Game* but, after only four days of rehearsal, MacLaine had to go

on when Haney broke her ankle. When she dropped her hat during the famous "Steam Heat" number, she reportedly swore loud enough for everyone in the theater to hear. But by the end of the show, the audience loved her; she became an overnight sensation. Hal Wallis, the famed movie producer, caught her performance and immediately signed her to a five-year movie contract.

MacLaine's film debut was an auspicious one, playing a lead role in Alfred Hitchcock's macabre comedy *The Trouble with Harry* (1955). Although the film was a commercial failure, MacLaine received good reviews. Except for a sexy and amusing performance in the Martin and Lewis comedy *Artists and Models* (1955), the young actress didn't attract much attention again until she burst forth in a riveting performance of both humor and pathos as the poor, love-starved Ginny in Vincente Minnelli's drama *Some Came Running* (1958). Her portrayal brought her the first of her five best actress Academy Award nominations.

The early 1960s were her best, most productive screen years. They were also the years when she performed in her most endearing comedies. She started off the decade singing and dancing in *Can-Can* (1960) and gave what many consider to be her best performance in the ROMANTIC COMEDY *The Apartment* (1960), for which she won her second Oscar nomination. Not long after, she stepped into the title role of *Irma La Douce* (1962), substituting for Elizabeth Taylor, and had another big comedy hit, plus her third Oscar nomination. There were other notable comedies along the way, but then came a long string of flops. Even her return to musicals in

*Sweet Charity* (1969) was a loser at the box office. She didn't star in another hit film until *Two Mules for Sister Sara* (1970), but even that was essentially a Clint Eastwood vehicle.

Although MacLaine wasn't a big box office draw in the early 1970s, her reputation was enhanced by her performance in *Desperate Characters* (1971). And she had the chance to recoup her star status when she played a mature mother tortured by her decision to trade her dancing career for marriage and family in *The Turning Point* (1977). The film was a hit, garning MacLaine yet another Oscar nomination. She ended the decade with a delicious comic supporting performance in *Being There* (1979).

*Terms of Endearment* (1983) brought MacLaine her fifth Academy Award nomination and, finally, her first best actress Oscar. Even so, she was little seen on movie screens during the following five years. During that period she was particularly active as an author, writing autobiographical books leavened with New Age insights and philosophies. She has even starred in a TV miniseries based on one of her bestsellers, *Out on a Limb*.

Beginning in the late 1980s, however, she began starring with pleasing regularity (about one film per year) in high quality movies, most recently the poignant comedy *Used People* (1992) and the affecting serio-comic *Guarding Tess* (1994).

She is the older sister of actor/director/producer Warren Beatty.

FILMS: *The Trouble with Harry* (1955); *Artists and Models* (1955); *Around the World in 80 Days* (1956); *Hot Spell* (1958); *The Matchmaker* (1958); *Some Came Running* (1958); *The Sheepman* (1958); *Ask Any Girl* (1959); *Career* (1959); *Ocean's Eleven* (cameo, 1960); *The Apartment* (1960); *Can-Can* (1960); *All in a Night's Work* (1961); *The Children's Hour* (1961); *Two Loves* (1961); *My Geisha* (1962); *Two for the Seesaw* (1962); *Irma la Douce* (1963); *John Goldfarb, Please Come Home* (1964); *What a Way to Go!* (1964); *The Yellow Rolls Royce* (1964); *Gambit* (1966); *Woman Times Seven* (1967); *The Bliss of Mrs. Blossom* (1968); *Sweet Charity* (1969); *Two Mules for*

*Sister Sara* (1970); *Desperate Characters* (1971); *The Possession of Joel Delaney* (1972); *The Year of the Woman* (1973); *The Other Half of the Sky: A China Memoir* (doc, also sc, p, d, 1974); *The Turning Point* (1977); *Being There* (1979); *A Change of Seasons* (1980); *Loving Couples* (1980); *Cannonball Run II* (1983); *Terms of Endearment* (1983); *Madame Sousatzka* (1988); *Steel Magnolias* (1989); *Postcards from the Edge* (1990); *Waiting for the Light* (1990); *Used People* (1992); *Wrestling Ernest Hemingway* (1993); *Guarding Tess* (1994).

## Main, Marjorie (1890–1975)

Relatively late in life, Marjorie Main became a character actress comedy star. Her speciality was playing rural battle-axes; she was tough as nails, and her comedy was just as pointed. An accomplished dramatic actress earlier in her career, Main is remembered today largely for her hit low-budget Ma and Pa Kettle comedy series.

Born Mary Tomlinson in Acton, Indiana, to a minister and his wife, she changed her name so that her family would not have to be ashamed of their actress daughter. She worked on the stage with a fair degree of success until she married. Main retired from acting, only to gradually return on a small scale with modest roles in the occasional movie. When her husband died in 1935, she had to find work, which she did with stunning results.

Main was a standout on Broadway in *Dead End* and *The Women*, reprising her roles in the film versions of both (1937 and 1939, respectively). She was so powerful as Humphrey Bogart's mother in the former that she was typecast for several years as a poor, grim, urban mother. It wasn't until 1940, when she was teamed with Wallace BEERY in a successful attempt to recreate the magic of his pairing with the late Marie DRESSLER, that Main's comic gifts became fully apparent. The film was *Wyoming* (1940), and it led to a number of subsequent teamings with Beery in films, including *Barnacle Bill* (1941), *Jackass Mail* (1942), *Rationing* (1944), *Bad Bascomb* (1946), and *Big Jack* (1949). In every one of them, Main and Beery are bickering, bantering, and battling, all to comic effect.

As successful as her movies with Beery were, they didn't hold a candle to the series that was spun off her character of Ma Kettle in *The Egg and I* (1947). Nine Ma and Pa Kettle movies followed between 1949 and 1957, with Percy Kilbride as Pa Kettle in most of them. The films earned an average of ten times their production costs, making them a hugely profitable enterprise.

In the meantime, Main also appeared in plenty of other films, supporting such talents as ABBOTT AND COSTELLO in *The Wistful Widow of Wagon Gap* (1947), Lucille BALL and Desi Arnaz in *The Long, Long Trailer* (1954), and even Judy Garland and Gene Kelly in *Summer Stock* (1950).

Main retired in 1957 in good health, living to the age of eighty-six before dying of cancer.

FILMS INCLUDE: *A House Divided* (1931); *Hot Saturday* (1932); *Crime without Passion* (1934); *Dead End* (1937); *Stella Dallas* (1937); *King of the Newsboys* (1938); *Boys of the Streets* (1938); *Test Pilot* (1938); *Too Hot to Handle* (1938); *Three Comrades* (1938); *Penitentiary* (1938); *Angels Wash Their Faces* (1939); *The Women* (1939); *They Shall Have Music* (1939); *Another Thin Man* (1939); *I Take This Woman* (1940); *Dark Command* (1940); *Wyoming* (1940); *Susan and God* (1940); *A Woman's Face* (1941); *The Trial of Mary Dugan* (1941); *Honky Tonk* (1941); *Barnacle Bill* (1941); *The Bugle Sounds* (1942); *Jackass Mail* (1942); *Tennessee Johnson* (1942); *We Were Dancing* (1942); *Heaven Can Wait* (1943); *Johnny Come Lately* (1943); *Gentle Annie* (1944); *Rationing* (1944); *Meet Me in St. Louis* (1944); *Murder He Says* (1945); *The Harvey Girls* (1946); *Undercurrent* (1946); *Bad Bascomb* (1946); *The Egg and I* (1947); *The Wistful Widow of Wagon Gap* (1947); *Big Jack* (1949); *Ma and Pa Kettle* (1949); *Ma and Pa Kettle Go to Town* (1950); *Summer Stock* (1950); *Mrs. O'Malley and Mr. Malone* (1950); *The Law and the Lady* (1951); *Ma and Pa Kettle Back on the Farm* (1951); *Ma and Pa Kettle at the Fair* (1952); *It's a Big Country* (1952); *The Belle of New York* (1952); *Ma and Pa Kettle on Vacation* (1953);

*Fast Company* (1953); *Rose Marie* (1954); *Ricochet Romance* (1954); *The Long, Long Trailer* (1954); *Ma and Pa Kettle at Home* (1954); *Ma and Pa Kettle at Waikiki* (1955); *The Kettles in the Ozarks* (1956); *Friendly Persuasion* (1957); *The Kettles on Old McDonald's Farm* (1957).

## Marin, Richard "Cheech" *See* CHEECH AND CHONG

## Marshall, Garry (1935—)

Before embarking on a new career as film director with a decided taste for comedy, Garry Marshall was a hugely successful writer/producer of TV sitcoms, including "The Dick Van Dyke Show" and "Happy Days." He had the golden touch with his movies as well, turning most of them into critical and commercial hits. A big, garrulous man with an amusing, Runyonesque style of speaking, he has occasionally been known to appear in the films of other directors.

Born in New York City, Marshall intended to pursue a career as a journalist, but found himself writing copy for sitcoms rather than newspapers. He had dabbled in the movies between his two hit TV series, writing and producing *How Sweet It Is* (1968) and *The Grasshopper* (1970), neither of which made a ripple. When he returned to moviemaking in 1982, he produced and directed the satiric *Young Doctors in Love*, turning in a solid hit. He also wrote and directed *The Flamingo Kid* (1984), a seriocomic period piece about a boy coming of age. *Nothing in Common* (1986) was also, in its way, a coming of age story, except it dealt with a grown man (Tom HANKS) and his dying father (Jackie GLEASON).

Marshall's only misstep in the 1980s was directing the Goldie HAWN comedy *Overboard* (1987), which immediately sank. He stayed closer to shore with *Beaches* (1988), another seriocomic story about death and dying, starring Bette MIDLER and Barbara Hershey.

All of this seemed like small potatoes when Marshall came out with what seemed, on the surface, to be a modest little ROMANTIC COMEDY called *Pretty Woman* (1990). The movie caught the imagination of the country, becoming a steamroller of a hit. It made Julia Roberts a major star, reestablished Richard Gere as a top-drawer leading man, and put Garry Marshall in the Hollywood driver's seat.

He then drove right into a brick wall with *Frankie and Johnnie* (1991), a film that looked like a "can't miss" on paper. It was based on a critically acclaimed play and starred Al Pacino and Michelle Pfeiffer, but it bombed anyway.

Since then, Marshall has made amusing cameo appearances in several films, putting more of his energy into a seriocomic play he wrote called *Wrong Turn at Lungfish*, starring George C. Scott. It opened off Broadway to mixed reviews in early 1993.

Marshall is the older brother of actress/director Penny Marshall, who came to fame as Laverne on the TV sitcom "Laverne and Shirley." Penny Marshall has become a director of note with a number of major hits to her credit, including the comedies *Jumpin' Jack Flash* (1986) and *Big* (1988) as well as the dramas *Awakenings* (1990) and *A League of Their Own* (1992).

---

**FILMS:** *How Sweet It Is* (sc, p, 1968); *Psych-Out* (a, 1968); *The Grasshopper* (sc, p, 1970); *Young Doctors in Love* (p, d, 1982); *The Flamingo Kid* (sc, d, 1984); *Lost in America* (a, 1985); *Nothing in Common* (d, 1986); *Overboard* (d, 1987); *Beaches* (d, 1988); *Pretty Woman* (d, 1990); *Frankie and Johnny* (d, 1991); *Soapdish* (a, 1991); *A League of Their Own* (a, 1992); *Hocus Pocus* (a, 1993).

---

**Martin and Lewis** See Jerry LEWIS; Dean MARTIN

**Martin, Dean (1917–)** An actor, singer, and comedian, Dean Martin has enjoyed a long movie career that can be divided into three distinct parts:

his partnership with Jerry LEWIS, his serious acting roles, and his self-spoofing period. The first two parts of Martin's career are both rich and amusing. His last and longest period, while full of comedy films, is of the least consequence.

Born Dino Crocetti in Steubenville, Ohio, the young crooner teamed up with the aspiring comedian Jerry Lewis, and together they became a nightclub sensation. They were soon rounded up for the movies, becoming the hottest comedy team in Hollywood since the heyday of ABBOTT AND COSTELLO. Lewis played the innocent, bumbling sidekick to Martin's handsome and suave man of the world.

The Martin and Lewis films, beginning with *My Friend Irma* (1949) and ending with *Hollywood or Bust* (1956), were consistently popular. They made a total of sixteen films together, with Martin singing a few numbers in each movie and setting up Lewis's humor. Their best films together include *Scared Stiff* (1953), *Artists and Models* (1955), and *Pardners* (1956).

Eventually, Lewis began to seriously overshadow Martin in their films, and the straight man wanted out. He also didn't want to work nearly as hard as Lewis did, and there was a rift between them that has never truly healed.

It was widely assumed in show business circles that Martin would quickly disappear after the breakup of the team. And it certainly seemed likely after he starred in the silly romantic comedy *Ten Thousand Bedrooms* (1957). However, Dean Martin recovered his career and his respect in the industry with a mixture of strong starring and supporting performances in *The Young Lions* (1958), *Some Came Running* (1958), *Rio Bravo* (1959), and *Bells Are Ringing* (1960).

Curiously, despite his desire to cut down his workload with Lewis, Martin appeared to be everywhere during the 1960s. His recording and TV careers blossomed (he had his own hit show—"The Dean Martin Show"—for many years), and he appeared in an average of nearly three films per year in that decade. The quality of his comedies during this period was spotty, but there were some notable bright spots, particularly the amusing *Who Was That Lady?* (1960) and *How to Save a Marriage and Ruin Your Life* (1968), and four mildly entertaining Matt Helm films that spoofed James Bond. Interspersed with the occasional Westerns and extremely rare dramas were a melange of Sinatra "rat pack" movies of varying humor, the best of them being *Ocean's Eleven* (1960). After the 1960s, Martin's interest in movies ended. His output since then has consisted of little more than a handful of films that culminated in appearances in the dreadful *Cannonball Run* (1980) and its 1983 sequel.

Despite his considerable movie output, Dean Martin's claim to fame in the area of film comedy ultimately rests with his memorable work with Jerry Lewis.

FILMS: With Jerry Lewis: *My Friend Irma* (1949); *My Friend Irma Goes West* (1950); *At War with the Army* (1950); *Sailor Beware* (1951); *That's My Boy* (1951); *Jumping Jacks* (1952); *The Stooge* (1952); *The Caddy* (1953); *Money from Home* (1953); *Scared Stiff* (1953); *Living It Up* (1954); *Three Ring Circus* (1954); *Artists and Models* (1955); *You're Never Too Young* (1955); *Hollywood or Bust* (1956); *Pardners* (1956).

Martin only: *Ten Thousand Bedrooms* (1957); *Some Came Running* (1958); *The Young Lions* (1958); *Career* (1959); *Rio Bravo* (1959); *Bells Are Ringing* (1960); *Ocean's Eleven* (1960); *Pepe* (1960); *Who Was That Lady?* (1960); *Ada* (also song, 1960); *All in a Night's Work* (1961); *Road to Hong Kong* (1962); *Sergeants 3* (1962); *Who's Got the Action?* (1962); *Come Blow Your Horn* (1963); *Four for Texas* (1963); *Toys in the Attic* (1963); *Who's Been Sleeping in My Bed?* (1963); *Kiss Me, Stupid* (1964); *Robin and the Seven Hoods* (1964); *What a Way to Go!* (1964); *Marriage on the Rocks* (1965); *The Sons of Katie Elder* (1965); *Murderers Row* (1966); *The Silencers* (1966); *Texas Across the River* (1966); *The Ambushers* (1967); *Rough Night in Jericho* (1967); *Five Card Stud* (1968); *Bandolero!* (1968); *How to Save a Marriage and Ruin Your Life* (1968); *The Wrecking Crew* (1968); *Airport* (1970); *Something Big* (1971); *Showdown* (1973); *Mr. Ricco* (1975); *Cannonball Run* (1980); *Cannonball Run II* (1983).

**Martin, Steve (1945—)** A multitalented comedian, Steve Martin has written, produced, and starred in some of the most imaginative and daring comedies of the 1980s and early 1990s. Unlike many former stand-up comedians, Martin has effectively made the leap beyond his club and concert persona to create an impressive array of comic film characters. Routinely overlooked by the Academy of Motion Picture Arts and Sciences, Martin has quietly put together a body of work that is both bracing in its intelligence and vastly entertaining in its humor.

Born in Waco, Texas, and raised in Southern California, Martin found his entry into show business through magic tricks. He lived near Knott's Berry Farm where he performed his act, adding comedy routines along the way. When he was still very young, Martin became a television comedy writer. He won an Emmy for his work on the "Smothers Brothers Comedy Hour" and later wrote for Sonny and Cher, Pat Paulsen, Glenn Campbell, and John Denver. He finally stopped writing for others and decided to perform his own material.

Martin worked as a stand-up comic during the late 1960s and most of the 1970s, coming to prominence on "The Tonight Show." He soon became a major comedy star when he made several guest host appearances on "Saturday Night Live" and (with Dan AYKROYD) created the phrase "A wild and crazy guy." He won two Grammy awards for his first two albums (which went platinum), *Let's Get Small* and *Wild and Crazy Guy*, and even had a hit novelty single, "King Tut," which sold more than 1.5 million copies. At the height of his popularity as a TV, club, and concert comic, he even had a best-selling book, *Cruel Shoes*.

Martin's first venture into film was a short he wrote and starred in called *The Absent-Minded Waiter* (1977), which was nominated for an Academy

*Seen here in the vastly underrated* Leap of Faith *(1992), Steve Martin once again proves that he is a comic talent willing to stretch and take risks. The film above will likely join his other cult favorites,* Pennies from Heaven *(1981),* The Man with Two Brains *(1983), and* The Lonely Guy *(1984).* PHOTO BY MARCIA REED, © PARAMOUNT PICTURES.

Award. After appearing in a small role in *Sgt. Pepper's Lonely Hearts Club Band* (1978), Martin moved into lead roles, co-writing and starring in *The Jerk* (1979), directed by Carl REINER, who went on to become the comedy star's frequent collaborator. *The Jerk* was a colossal hit, grossing over $100 million. It instantly established Martin as a major movie star.

Martin's next film was the innovative and striking musical comedy directed by Herbert Ross, *Pennies from Heaven* (1981). Martin learned to tap dance for the film and gave a virtuoso performance in what was a smart but overly ambitious movie. The audience disliked this film that was so startlingly different from *The Jerk*; it failed badly at the box office.

Martin quickly teamed with director Carl Reiner for two comedies, *Dead Men Don't Wear Plaid* (1982) and *The Man with Two Brains* (1983). He gave yet

another excellent performance in *The Lonely Guy* (1984), but none of them were blockbuster hits, either with the critics or with the public.

Martin finally broke out with the roundly admired and commercially successful *All of Me* (1984) in which he co-starred with Lily TOMLIN. The film marked the fourth pairing of Steve Martin and Carl Reiner. *All of Me* showcased Martin's remarkable ability as a physical comedian, and he received the best actor award from the New York Film Critics for his performance. Many thought he was wrongfully overlooked for an Oscar nomination.

He gave a stirring supporting performance as the demented dentist in the movie version of the hit off-Broadway musical *Little Shop of Horrors* (1986). After co-scripting and starring with Chevy CHASE and Martin SHORT in the poorly received *Three Amigos*

(1986), the ever-ambitious Martin was the executive producer, co-scripter, and star of the marvelously imaginative romantic comedy *Roxanne* (1987), a clever modern version of Edmond Rostand's classic story, *Cyrano de Bergerac*. The Los Angeles Film Critics honored him with their best actor citation, and the Writers Guild of America gave him their award for best screenplay based on material from another medium.

From the wonderfully silly *Dirty Rotten Scoundrels* (1988) to the sweetly comic *Father of the Bride* (1991), and from the incisively wry *L.A. Story* (1991) to the hilarious *Leap of Faith* (1992), Martin has become not only one of Hollywood's most successful comedy stars, he has also become one of the industry's most creative and audacious actors.

---

Films: *Sgt. Pepper's Lonely Hearts Club Band* (1978); *The Jerk* (also story, sc, song, 1979); *The Kids Are Alright* (1979); *The Muppet Movie* (1979); *Pennies from Heaven* (1981); *Dead Men Don't Wear Plaid* (also sc, 1982); *The Man with Two Brains* (also sc, 1983); *All of Me* (1984); *The Lonely Guy* (1984); *Movers and Shakers* (1985); *Little Shop of Horrors* (1986); *Three Amigos* (also sc, p, song, 1986); *Planes, Trains and Automobiles* (1987); *Roxanne* (also sc, p, 1987); *Dirty Rotten Scoundrels* (1988); *Parenthood* (1989); *My Blue Heaven* (1990); *L.A. Story* (also story, sc, p, 1991); *Father of the Bride* (1991); *Grand Canyon* (1991); *Housesitter* (1992); *Leap of Faith* (1992).

---

**Marx Brothers, The**  Appearing in a mere thirteen films, the Marx Brothers—Groucho, Chico, Harpo, and (in their first five movies) Zeppo—were a veritable comedy attack force, slinging a wild, anarchic style of humor at movie audiences, the likes of which film fans had never before experienced. A Marx Brothers movie was, with rare exceptions, always greater than the sum of its parts. The plots were of little consequence; what mattered was Groucho's rapid-fire puns and his ever-present leer, Chico's lamebrain Italian accent and his inven-

*Chico, Groucho, and Harpo (left to right), The Marx Brothers, minus Zeppo, who left the act after the team's fifth film, Duck Soup (1933). Notice Harpo's expression; he called the face he's making a "Gookie," named after a local character from their neighborhood who unconsciously made the same face while doing his job.*    PHOTO COURTESY OF THE SIEGEL COLLECTION.

tive piano playing, and Harpo's silent lechery and his coat that seemed to double as a Sear's warehouse. Nonetheless, there is no denying that they were the funniest, as well as the most influential, comedy team in Hollywood history. Their humor paved the way for such later film comedians as Mel BROOKS and Woody ALLEN.

Chico (1891–1961) was born Leonard Marx. His nickname came from a strong and persistent interest in "chicks." Harpo (1893–1964), born Adolph Marx, got nicknamed from his playing of the harp. Groucho (1895–1977) was born Julius Marx, picking up his nickname because of his moody, "grouchy" behavior. And, finally, Zeppo (1901–1979) was born Herbert Marx, and according to Harpo, picked up his nickname because he was always doing chin-ups like "Zippo," a popular monkey act in VAUDEVILLE. There was a fifth brother, Gummo (1893–1977), born Milton Marx, who was tagged with his nickname because he wore gumsole shoes. Gummo, however, left the act very early on and never appeared in any of the Marx Brothers' films.

Born in New York City, the boys were the children of a poor tailor, Sam Marx, and an ambitious mother, Minnie Marx, who encouraged her kids to enter show business with the considerable help of her brother, vaudeville star Al Shean, of the team of Gallagher and Shean.

The brothers' individual comic personalities evolved over a long stretch in vaudeville. In particular, Harpo's mute clown came into being when, in an act written by their Uncle Al, he was given only three lines. In the review the following day, a local critic wrote that Harpo was brilliant as a mime, but the magic was lost when he spoke. Harpo never spoke in character again (except for a sneezed "achoo" in *At the Circus*, 1939).

When they arrived on Broadway with a loosely written play called *I'll Say She Is* in 1924, the knockabout vaudevillians suddenly became the toast of Broadway. A year later, they opened in *The Cocoanuts*, a play written for them by George S. KAUFMAN and Morrie RYSKIND, with music and lyrics by legendary Irving Berlin. They made their first film during the run of that play, a privately financed picture called *Humorisk*. Made in 1925, this silent film, now lost, was never released. Meanwhile, *The Cocoanuts* had a stupendous run on Broadway, drawing audiences from 1925 to 1928. It eventually was filmed in Astoria, Queens, by day while they performed another hit play, *Animal Crackers*, at night on the Great White Way.

Paramount put the Marx Brothers under contract, releasing *The Cocoanuts* in 1929 and *Animal Crackers* in 1930. The latter film contained the song that would become Groucho's theme song, "Hooray for Captain Spaulding."

They made three more films for Paramount, moving to Hollywood to make them. And each was more outrageously funny than the one that came before. In *Monkey Business* (1931), the Brothers made a mockery of, among other things, the fledg-

ling gangster movie genre; then came their hilarious put-down of higher education, *Horse Feathers* (1932); that was followed by DUCK SOUP (1933), in which they reduced politics and the institution of war to rubble. These last two films are arguably their finest achievements.

Unfortunately, *Duck Soup* was not a rousing success at the box office, and Paramount chose not to renew the Marx Brothers' contract. At that point Zeppo quit the team to become a theatrical agent. Since then, Margaret DUMONT has usually been referred to as the fourth Marx Brother. She was always the rich dowager who somehow was taken in by Groucho's patter. Groucho often said that she rarely understood his insults (e.g., "You're fighting for this woman's honor . . . which is more than she ever did." *Duck Soup*, 1933). Dumont appeared in a total of seven of the Marx Brothers' movies.

Although Paramount no longer wanted the Marx Brothers, Irving Thalberg at MGM did. He proposed, however, that they be paid 25 percent less because Zeppo had quit and there were only three Marx Brothers left. Groucho retorted that they were twice as funny without Zeppo; Thalberg relented, and a deal was struck.

Thalberg had a plan for making the Marx Brothers far more commercially successful. It was his idea that the Brothers were actually *too funny*. He wanted them to slow down their movies by adding a love interest that would attract a female audience. And he also thought it would be a good idea for the boys to take their comic bits out on the road to hone them for their pictures.

The result of Thalberg's brainstorm was *A Night at the Opera* (1935), the most commercially successful of the Marx Brothers' movies. *A Day at the Races* (1937) was not quite as successful, but after Irving Thalberg died, MGM seemed to lose interest in the team, and their films were soon beset by sillier romantic subplots. Nonetheless, there were still wonderful moments in their movies, particularly in *At the Circus* (1939) and *Go West* (1940).

Among their other movies were the film version of the hit play *Room Service* (1938), *The Big Store*

(1941), an independent production of *A Night in Casablanca* (1946), and their last movie together and the only one in which Harpo had top billing, *Love Happy* (1949).

The Marx Brothers never made another movie together after *Love Happy*—at least as a team. They did appear in separate segments of an all-star film, *The Story of Mankind* (1957). Of the three brothers, only Groucho remained fully active in entertainment. In addition to his hit radio and TV series "You Bet Your Life" during the 1950s, he also appeared solo in several films, including the Carmen MIRANDA movie *Copacabana* (1947), *Double Dynamite* (1951) with Jane Russell, *A Girl in Every Port* (1952), and finally *Skidoo* (1968). Groucho also cowrote a screenplay with Norman Krasna for a 1937 film, *The King and the Chorus Girl*, which starred Joan BLONDELL.

---

**FILMS:** Starring Groucho, Chico, and Harpo, unless otherwise indicated: *Too Many Kisses* (Harpo only, 1925); *Humorisk* (also Zeppo, never released, lost, 1925); *The Cocoanuts* (also Zeppo, 1929); *Animal Crackers* (also Zeppo, 1930); *Monkey Business* (also Zeppo, 1931); *Horse Feathers* (also Zeppo, 1932); *Duck Soup* (also Zeppo, 1933); *A Night at the Opera* (1935); *A Day at the Races* (1937); *Room Service* (1938); *At the Circus* (1939); *Go West* (1940); *The Big Store* (1941); *Stage Door Canteen* (Harpo only, 1943); *A Night in Casablanca* (1946); *Copacabana* (Groucho only, 1947); *Love Happy* (1949); *Mr. Music* (Groucho only, 1950); *Double Dynamite* (Groucho only, 1951); *A Girl in Every Port* (Groucho only, 1952); *Will Success Spoil Rock Hunter?* (Groucho cameo, 1957); *The Story of Mankind* (1957); *Skidoo* (Groucho only, 1968).

---

**Matthau, Walter (1920—)** A late-blooming star, Walter Matthau came to prominence in the latter half of the 1960s as a sort of modern-day W. C. FIELDS. Since then, and for the better part of twenty years, he has played cranky comic characters to per-

fection. With his lived-in-looking face and body, Matthau seemed hardly a candidate for movie stardom, but thanks to an abundance of talent, the right roles, and a receptive audience, he became a top box office attraction and an Oscar-winning performer.

Born Walter Matuschanskavasky to a former Catholic priest and his Jewish wife, who had left Russia for the American promised land, Matthau grew up in poverty on New York's Lower East Side. His first taste of the theater came at age eleven when his job of selling soda in a Yiddish Theater during intermission led to his acting on stage in bit parts.

After serving in the army air force as a gunner, he used the G.I. Bill to study acting at the New School's Dramatic Workshop in New York City. With his unique face, he seemed best suited for character parts, and he played them with ever-increasing success on stage until he made his film debut in the Burt Lancaster Western *The Kentuckian* (1955). He played the villain—as he would in virtually all of his films during the next decade.

Matthau worked constantly between 1955 and 1965, appearing on Broadway, starring in a short-lived TV series, "Tallahassee 7000" in 1959, and playing bad guys in the movies, most memorably in *A Face in the Crowd* (1957), *King Creole* (1958), and *Charade* (1963). He even directed himself in a low-budget film called *Gangster Story* (1958).

A highly respected actor, Matthau merely needed the right vehicle to show off his abilities; happily, playwright/screenwriter Neil SIMON provided it, penning the role of Oscar Madison expressly for him in the Broadway play *The Odd Couple*. The critical and public response to his performance made Matthau an undisputed star, at least in New York, and when he later essayed the same role in the film version of the play in 1968, he solidified his standing as a major comic film talent. Simon has since provided a great many other excellent roles for Matthau in such films as *Plaza Suite* (1971), *The Sunshine Boys* (1975), which garnered him one of his two best actor Oscar nominations, and *California Suite* (1978).

Even before the film version of *The Odd Couple*

was made, director Billy WILDER wisely cast Matthau in his BLACK COMEDY *The Fortune Cookie* (1966). Matthau's brilliant performance as a comically sleazy lawyer brought him a best supporting actor Academy Award. He also came away with a lasting personal and professional relationship with his co-star Jack LEMMON. The two of them would work together on a total of six films, including *The Odd Couple, Kotch* (1971), in which Lemmon directed Matthau to his other best actor Oscar nomination, *The Front Page* (1974), a final reuniting with Billy Wilder as director of *Buddy, Buddy* (1981), and *Grumpy Old Men* (1993).

After having proved himself to be a master comic actor, Matthau then set out to show he could do other things as well. The transition began with *Pete 'n' Tillie* (1972), a seriocomic film that demonstrated the actor's dramatic potential. His next three films were pure action movies, all of them well reviewed and all of them hits: *Charley Varrick* (1973), *The Laughing Policeman* (1973), and *The Taking of Pelham 1, 2, 3* (1974). In yet another display of versatility, Matthau, then in his late fifties, starred in *House Calls* (1978), a light ROMANTIC COMEDY with Glenda Jackson. The film was such a hit that the two of them were brought back together for another romance in *Hopscotch* (1980). In the meantime, however, Matthau continued enchancing his W. C. Fields image by growling at children in *The Bad News Bears* (1976) and *Little Miss Marker* (1979).

Due to ill health, Matthau has appeared with less frequency in the movies during the 1980s—and also with less commercial success than in the past. Despite generally good personal notices, comedies such as *First Monday in October* (1981), *The Survivors* (1983), and *The Couch Trip* (1988) have not been hits. After a long wait, though, Matthau was finally cast in a role well suited to his image, the crotchety neighbor Mr. Wilson in *Dennis the Menace* (1993).

FILMS: *The Kentuckian* (1955); *The Indian Fighter* (1955); *Bigger Than Life* (1956); *A Face in the Crowd* (1957); *Slaughter on Tenth Avenue* (1957); *King Creole* (1958); *Onionhead* (1958); *Ride a Crooked Trail* (1958); *Voice in the Mirror* (1958); *Gangster Story* (also d, 1959); *Strangers When We Meet* (1960); *Lonely Are the Brave* (1962); *Who's Got the Action?* (1962); *Charade* (1963); *Island of Love* (1963); *Ensign Pulver* (1964); *Fail Safe* (1964); *Goodbye Charlie* (1964); *Mirage* (1965); *The Fortune Cookie* (1966); *A Guide for the Married Man* (1967); *Candy* (1968); *The Odd Couple* (1968); *The Secret Life of an American Wife* (1968); *Cactus Flower* (1969); *Hello, Dolly!* (1969); *Kotch* (19971); *A New Leaf* (1971); *Plaza Suite* (1971); *Pete 'n' Tillie* (1972); *Charley Varrick* (1973); *The Laughing Policeman* (1973); *Earthquake* (1974); *The Front Page* (1974); *The Taking of Pelham 1, 2, 3* (1974); *The Sunshine Boys* (1975); *The Bad News Bears* (1976); *Gentleman Tramp* (1976); *California Suite* (1978); *Casey's Shadow* (1979); *House Calls* (1978); *Hopscotch* (1980); *Little Miss Marker* (also p, 1980); *Portrait of a 60% Perfect Man* (1980); *Buddy, Buddy* (1981); *First Monday in October* (1981); *I Ought to Be in Pictures* (1981); *The Survivors* (1983); *Movers and Shakers* (1985); *Pirates* (1986); *The Couch Trip* (1988); *JFK* (1991); *Dennis the Menace* (1993); *Grumpy Old Men* (1993).

## May, Elaine (1932—)

One of the first women in the modern Hollywood era to write and direct major motion pictures, Elaine May is also an actress who has intermittently worked both in front of and behind the camera during the better part of the last three decades. Her best films exhibit a biting wit along with clever and knowing observations about human character.

Born Elaine Berlin in Philadelphia, Pennsylvania, to a theatrical family, she performed in several plays in which her father, Jack Berlin, of the Yiddish Theater, was also a performer. While at the University of Chicago she met Mike NICHOLS, another aspiring young actor, and the two of them formed a comedy team that proved to be enormously popular. They were a hit on the cabaret circuit during the 1950s, getting laughs with a fresh and witty brand of satire. They went their separate ways in 1961, and

May began writing and directing for the theater, although she soon found herself temporarily drawn back into performing, appearing in *Luv* (1967) and *Enter Laughing* (1967).

During the 1970s May was one of a rare breed: a female screenwriter and director. She wrote the script for *Such Good Friends* (1971) under the pen name Esther Dale, and co-wrote the smash hit *Heaven Can Wait* (1978). However, her greatest fame during the 1970s came when she wrote, directed, and starred in the hit comedy movie *A New Leaf* (1971). When she followed that success with yet another hit, *The Heartbreak Kid* (1972), where she directed her daughter, Jeannie Berlin, to a best supporting actress nomination, it appeared as if May was going to become a major new directorial force. Her next film, *Mikey and Nicky*, however, went considerably overbudget (presaging her greatest disaster), spent years being edited, and didn't arrive on movie screens until 1976. It was not a success.

May stepped in front of the cameras again in 1978 in *California Suite*, but it was her work with the script for *Heaven Can Wait* that brought her acclaim that year, garnering her a best screenplay Oscar nomination. She went on to work on the screenplay for the highly regarded *Tootsie* (1982), but did not receive a screen credit for her efforts. She was not heard from again until she directed Warren Beatty and Dustin Hoffman in the colossal flop *Ishtar* (1987), a film that went stupendously overbudget. It was ripped by the critics, and audiences simply didn't show up to see it despite the film's star power. Beatty and Hoffman took a lot of the heat, but May's reputation suffered a terrible beating. In 1990 May joined her daughter (who starred) in the cast of a delightful comedy called *In the Spirit*.

---

**FILMS:** *Enter Laughing* (a, 1967); *Bach to Bach* (a, 1967); *Luv* (a, 1967); *A New Leaf* (a, sc, d, 1971); *Such Good Friends* (sc, 1971); *The Heartbreak Kid* (d, 1972); *Mikey and Nicky* (sc, d, 1976); *California Suite* (a, 1978); *Heaven Can Wait* (co-sc, 1978); *Ishtar* (d, 1987); *In the Spirit* (a, 1990).

**Mazursky, Paul (1930—)**  A talented writer/director/producer, Paul Mazursky usually infuses his comic films with sharp, pungent observations of our times. Sometimes criticized for merely skimming the surface of current issues, he is also one of the few commercial filmmakers who regularly takes on issues of any kind.

Born Irwin Mazursky in Brooklyn, New York, he began performing while in school and, after graduation from Brooklyn College, continued to pursue his career with little success. He first appeared on film in Stanley Kubrick's *Fear and Desire* (1953) and later had a significant role in *The Blackboard Jungle* (1955). However, the real jungle was the acting world. Although he continued to find occasional roles in films and on TV throughout the 1950s and into the 1960s, he made his first important breakthrough as a writer, penning sketches for the high-quality comedy/variety TV series "The Danny Kaye Show." His writing credits helped him sell his first screenplay, written in collaboration with his early writing partner Larry Tucker, *I Love You, Alice B. Toklas!* (1968).

Given a chance to direct his own script, written with Larry Tucker, Mazursky hit a home run his first time up with his lively and timely comedy about sexual freedom, *Bob & Carol & Ted & Alice* (1969). The film didn't quite have the courage of its convictions, but it was still a shocking theme for a Hollywood comedy in the late 1960s.

Averaging a film every two years since his debut as a director, Mazursky has only seriously flopped when he made either obviously autobiographical or pretentious films. Among his either critical or box office failures were *Alex in Wonderland* (1970), *Next Stop, Greenwich Village* (1976), *Willie and Phil* (1980), *The Tempest* (1982), and *The Pickle* (1993). This is not to say that all of these films were bad—Mazursky has the uncanny ability to make even his poor films rich and interesting.

He began producing as well as writing and directing with his third film, *Blume in Love* (1973). With this movie he found his stride, establishing a cozy, intimate visual style. He followed that success with the warm and knowing, yet satisfyingly unsentimental *Harry and Tonto* (1974). His biggest success of the 1970s was the seriocomic *An Unmarried Woman* (1978) because he was the first Hollywood filmmaker to focus on the social and emotional upheaval that divorce causes for women. The film, which he produced and scripted, was nominated for best screenplay and best picture Oscars.

During the mid 1980s Mazursky excelled with his gently satirical comedy hits *Moscow on the Hudson* (1984) and *Down and Out in Beverly Hills* (1986). After stumbling with *Moon Over Parador* (1988), he came back with the unexpectedly powerful romantic drama, *Enemies, A Love Story* (1989), which brought him a best screenplay Academy Award nomination. He seemed to lose his touch in the early 1990s with the disappointing *Scenes from a Mall* (1991) and the abysmal *The Pickle* (1993), which happens to be about a movie director in crisis.

It should be noted that Mazursky is a student of the cinema. A number of his films have been based on foreign film classics. For instance, his *Willie and Phil* is an American version of François Truffaut's *Jules and Jim* (1961), while *Down and Out in Beverly Hills* is the same story that Jean Renoir told in *Boudu Saved from Drowning* (1932).

It should be further noted that the acting bug still bites the director. In addition to occasionally appearing in small roles in other directors' films such as *A Star Is Born* (1976), Mazursky lurks in small roles in many of his own films, among them *Alex in Wonderland*, *Blume in Love*, *An Unmarried Woman*, *Down and Out in Beverly Hills*, and *The Pickle*. In *Moon Over Parador*, he goes so far as to play Richard Dreyfuss's mother!

**FILMS INCLUDE:** As actor: *Fear and Desire* (a, 1953); *Blackboard Jungle* (a, 1955); *Deathwatch* (a, 1966); *I Love You, Alice B. Toklas* (a, sc, p, song, 1968).

As director, credits complete: *Bob & Carol & Ted & Alice* (a, sc, d, 1969); *Alex in Wonderland* (a, sc, d, 1970); *Blume in Love* (a, sc, p, d, 1973); *Harry and Tonto* (a, sc, p, d, 1974); *Next Stop, Greenwich Village* (sc, p, d, 1976); *A Star Is Born* (a, 1976); *An Unmarried Woman* (a, sc, p, d, 1978); *An Almost Perfect Affair* (a, 1979); *A Man, a Woman and a Bank* (a, 1979); *Willie & Phil* (a, sc, p, d, 1980); *History of the World, Part I* (a, 1981); *The Tempest* (a, sc, p, d, 1982); *Moscow on the Hudson* (a, sc, p, d, 1984); *Into the Night* (a, 1985); *Down and Out in Beverly Hills* (a, sc, p, d, 1986); *Moon Over Parador* (a, sc, p, d, 1988); *Punchline* (a, 1988); *Enemies, A Love Story* (a, sc, p, d, 1989); *Scenes from the Class Struggle in Beverly Hills* (a, 1989); *Taking Care of Business* (p, 1990); *Scenes from a Mall* (sc, p, d, 1991); *The Pickle* (a, sc, p, d, 1993).

## McCarey, Leo (1898—1969)

One of Hollywood's premier directors who reached the height of his career in the late 1930s and early 1940s, Leo McCarey found an ideal balance between comedy and sentiment, creating a string of memorable hit movies.

Born Thomas Leo McCarey in Los Angeles, California, his background was rather unusual for a director who began his career in the silent era. Many early directors had training either in mechanical fields like engineering or in the theater, but McCarey had been a lawyer—a bad one. He once told filmmaker Peter Bogdanovich that he had literally been chased out of a courtroom by one of his clients, and he kept on running until he reached Hollywood. The year was 1918, and he was so enamored of the movies that he took any film job he could get. In the early 1920s he worked as an assistant to director Tod Browning and was soon given the opportunity to direct his first feature film, *Society Secrets* (1921). Unfortunately, he wasn't quite ready to handle such a burden, and the movie was a dismal failure.

From 1923 to 1929 McCarey wrote scripts, supervised production, and directed comic short subjects at the Hal ROACH Studio, gaining expertise as a gag man and learning how to fashion cinematic comedy. Toward the end of that period he was involved in the production of LAUREL AND

HARDY's greatest early shorts, including their classic *Big Business* (1929).

McCarey took a second stab at feature film directing in 1929 with a minor film called *The Sophomore*. This time he passed muster and continued directing feature films until 1962. There was nothing special about his earliest films until he began directing star comics such as Eddie CANTOR in *The Kid from Spain* (1932), the MARX BROTHERS in *DUCK SOUP* (1933), and Mae WEST in *Belle of the Nineties* (1934). He directed a different kind of star in 1935 when he made a clever comedy with the unexpected choice of Charles Laughton as the lead in *Ruggles of Red Gap*. The film was a critical and box office hit, firmly establishing McCarey as a comedy director of note.

After a noble but failed attempt at resurrecting Harold LLOYD's career with *The Milky Way* (1936), McCarey went on to produce and direct an unflinchingly honest film about the American family and the Great Depression. The movie was *Make Way for Tomorrow* (1937), and it had surprisingly good humor despite its heart-rending story of an aging couple forced to spend their last years apart.

Beginning with *Make Way for Tomorrow*, McCarey produced every movie he directed except one, and from 1939 onward he either supplied the stories for his films or co-wrote the screenplays. For a solid decade, he had hit after hit, beginning in 1937 with the delightful SCREWBALL COMEDY starring Cary GRANT and Irene Dunne, *The Awful Truth* (1937), a movie that boldly and comically dealt with the issue of divorce. McCarey won an Academy Award as best director in 1937, ostensibly for *The Awful Truth*, but most likely because he had shown such remarkable directorial range that year.

McCarey was building to the high point of his career when he made *Love Affair* (1939), *My Favorite Wife* (1940), and *Once Upon a Honeymoon* (1942). He reached the apex when he directed *Going My Way* (1944), a warm and sentimental comedy starring Bing CROSBY. The movie was a spectacular hit and won a total of seven Academy Awards, including (for McCarey) best director, best original story, and best picture. He followed that success with the sequel, *The Bells of St. Mary's* (1945), which was also a smash hit, becoming the only sequel in Hollywood history to make more money at the box office than its predecessor.

McCarey directed only one film in the late 1940s, the moderately successful and sweet-natured *Good Sam* (1948), starring Gary Cooper. Four years later, McCarey's career took a nosedive when he made *My Son John* (1952), an incredibly heavy-handed anti-Communist film that is almost unwatchable today. Nonetheless, given the tenor of the times, McCarey received a best story Oscar nomination for that film. He found his lighter touch again with *An Affair to Remember* (1957), a remake of his 1939 film, *Love Affair*. McCarey's humor—his greatest asset—was sadly lacking in *Rally Round the Flag, Boys!* (1958), and the drama was flat in his last film, *Satan Never Sleeps* (1962).

FILMS INCLUDE: As director, partial list of shorts: *All Wet* (1924); *Bad Boy* (1925); *Innocent Husbands* (1925); *Crazy Like a Fox* (1926); *Dog Shy* (1926); *Be Your Age* (1926); *Eve's Love Letters* (1927); *We Faw Down* (1928); *Liberty* (1929); *Wrong Again* (1929).

As director, complete list of features: *Society Secrets* (1921); *The Sophomore* (1929); *Red Hot Rhythm* (also story, 1929); *Let's Go Native* (1930); *Part Time Wife* (also sc, 1930); *Wild Company* (1930); *Indiscreet* (1931); *The Kid from Spain* (1932); *Duck Soup* (1933); *Belle of the Nineties* (1934); *Six of a Kind* (1934); *Ruggles of Red Gap* (1935); *The Milky Way* (1936); *Make Way for Tomorrow* (also a, p, 1937); *The Awful Truth* (also p, 1937); *The Cowboy and the Lady* (story only, 1938); *Love Affair* (also story, p, 1939); *My Favorite Wife* (story, p, 1940); *Once Upon a Honeymoon* (also story, p, 1942); *Going My Way* (also story, p, 1944); *The Bells of St. Mary's* (also story, p, 1945); *Good Sam* (also story, p, 1948); *My Son John* (also story, sc, p, 1952); *An Affair to Remember* (also story, sc, song, 1956); *Rally Round the Flag, Boys!* (also sc, p, 1958); *Satan Never Sleeps* (also sc, p, lyrics, 1962); *Move Over Darling* (based on his story, *My Favorite Wife*, 1963).

**McCullough, Paul** *See* CLARK AND MC-CULLOUGH

**McFarland, "Spanky"** *See* OUR GANG

**McGuire, Mickey** *See* Mickey ROONEY; SERIES COMEDIES

**Midler, Bette (1945—)** A powerhouse singer, comedian, and actress, Bette Midler has a bigger-than-life personality. Outrageous, bawdy, vulgar, and talented beyond measure, she has conquered show business from film to television and from con-

certs to recordings. She's even written best-selling books. Midler is most widely known for her film work, which turned her into one of the few bona fide bankable female stars of the 1980s.

Born and raised in Honolulu, Hawaii, Midler studied drama at the University of Hawaii. George Roy HILL was shooting the sprawling epic *Hawaii* (1965) at that time and Midler was cast as an extra, playing the role of a missionary's seasick wife. The role required her to be in Los Angeles during the final shooting, and not long after she moved to New York City.

Midler made her New York stage debut in *Miss Nefertiti Regrets*, going on to play (as a replacement) the role of Tzeitel in the hit Broadway show *Fiddler on the Roof*. During the years that followed, she

*Bette Midler's aborted film career turned suddenly vibrant when she emerged as a comic actress in the mid-1980s. Giving a nod toward drama in* For the Boys *(1991), seen above, didn't create a hit, but did give her a best actress Academy Award nomination, which is something her comedies never did.* PHOTO BY FRANCOIS DUHAMEL, © 20TH CENTURY-FOX.

began singing in New York cabarets, building a loyal, ever-growing following. She performed in one-woman Broadway shows, for which she won a special Tony Award, TV specials, for which she won an Emmy Award, and she recorded hit records, for which she won three Grammy Awards. All that was left was to conquer the movies, which she did when she starred in *The Rose* (1979), scoring a hit in a film patterned loosely on the tragic life of rocker Janis Joplin. Midler's performance brought her a best actress Academy Award nomination.

Her next film, the comedy *Jinxed* (1982), was just that. Despite plenty of laughs, the movie was an unmitigated disaster, sending her film career into a tailspin. She found refuge with the Walt Disney Company's Touchstone division, which helped resurrect her career with just the right comic roles to take advantage of her awesome personality. *Down and Out in Beverly Hills* (1986), *Ruthless People* (1986), *Outrageous Fortune* (1987), and *Big Business* (1988) all did big business. This string of hits, all of which captured her robust comic gifts, turned Midler into a major film comedy draw. She went on to produce and star in *Beaches* (1988), a seriocomic hit about friendship, before finally stumbling with her remake of *Stella Dallas*, called *Stella* (1990). Her highly anticipated pairing with Woody ALLEN in Paul MAZURSKY'S *Scenes from a Mall* (1991) was also a major disappointment (although the two stars were delightful together). Her big-budget musical drama *For the Boys* (1991), which she produced, also failed to find an audience, although it did garner her a second best actress Oscar nomination. Most recently, Midler gave an amusing performance as a comically evil witch in the critically panned but commercially successful *Hocus Pocus* (1993).

---

**FILMS:** *Hawaii* (extra, 1965); *The Rose* (1979); *Divine Madness* (also sc, lyrics, 1980); *Jinxed!* (1982); *Down and Out in Beverly Hills* (1986); *Ruthless People* (1986); *Outrageous Fortune* (1987); *Beaches* (also p, songs, 1988); *Big Business* (1988); *Stella* (1990);

*Scenes from a Mall* (1991); *For the Boys* (1991); *Hocus Pocus* (1993).

---

**Miranda, Carmen (1909—1953)** Known as "The Brazilian Bombshell," Carmen Miranda was a hit virtually from the beginning of her relatively short but memorable Hollywood career. A comic caricature of Latin sensuality, she got laughs by playing way over the top, while wearing some of the most outlandish costumes this side of Barnum and Bailey.

Born Maria de Carmo Miranda de Cunha in Portugal, she moved with her family to Brazil while still a youngster. By her mid-twenties, she was a popular radio and film star well beyond her country's borders. She came to America in 1939, singing "South American Way" in the Broadway show *Streets of Paris*. The number was such a showstopper that she was asked to reprise it in a Betty Grable musical, *Down Argentine Way* (1940).

Miranda stole the movie from Grable, and American audiences went crazy over this outrageous singer with the wild costumes, fruit basket hats, platform shoes, and garish makeup. While Miranda was never the heroine of a romance (Hollywood was still too bigoted for that), she often played the friend of the love interest, giving her advice in fractured English and in song. Even though her acting ability was woefully inadequate, her sheer force of personality was enough to sustain her for the better part of a decade as a leading lady.

Her most memorable movies were *That Night in Rio* (1941) and *The Gang's All Here* (1943). The latter film was directed by the inimitable Busby BERKELEY, and though the movie is rather poor, it is without doubt the ultimate in kitsch, appreciated even then for its good-natured silliness.

The fact is her movies were rarely any good, yet they were never boring. Miranda was much too bizarre a presence to ever be dull. Musicals such as *Greenwich Village* (1944) and *Something for the Boys*

(1945) kept her before the public, but the public was becoming less interested as she suffered the inevitable end of her novelty appeal. Nonetheless, she was an amusing and offbeat co-star to Groucho Marx in *Copacabana* (1947).

Miranda appeared in just three more movies, disappearing almost as quickly from the Hollywood scene as she had come. She graced just fourteen films in America, her last being a featured role in the Martin and Lewis comedy *Scared Stiff* (1953). She died that same year of peritonitis, ending a colorful, if short, chapter in Hollywood musical comedy history.

---

**FILMS:** In the United States: *Down Argentine Way* (1940); *That Night in Rio* (1941); *Weekend in Havana* (1941); *Springtime in the Rockies* (1942); *Four Jills in a Jeep* (1943); *The Gang's All Here* (1943); *Greenwich Village* (1944); *Something for the Boys* (1944); *Doll Face* (1945); *If I'm Lucky* (1946); *Copacabana* (1947); *A Date with Judy* (1948); *Nancy Goes to Rio* (1950); *Scared Stiff* (1953).

---

## Monroe, Marilyn (1926—1962)

Hollywood's legendary sex goddess, Marilyn Monroe was the blonde bombshell who combined a voluptuous body and outrageously sexy walk with little-girl innocence and vulnerability. Early in her career many thought she was merely a sex symbol without talent, but she proved to be surprisingly versatile in everything from musicals to dramas; however, she was at her best in comedies. Her film career was relatively short—less than fifteen years—and her total number of major starring roles numbered only eleven, but in the majority of those she exhibited her considerable skills as a comedian.

Born Norma Jean Mortenson in Los Angeles, California, to the unmarried Gladys Mortensen, Monroe was raised mostly by a succession of foster parents. There was a history of mental illness in her mother's family, and Monroe's mother spent a large part of her adult life in sanitariums. At the time of Monroe's birth, her mother was working as a film cutter. She was a movie fanatic, probably naming her illegitimate daughter after her favorite movie star, Norma Talmadge.

Monroe's adolescent years were full of loneliness and trauma, including a reputed sexual attack by one of her male guardians. Finally, at sixteen, in an effort to escape to a better life, she married twenty-one-year-old Jim Dougherty. Not long after they were wed, Dougherty joined the merchant marine. They were divorced after only four years.

To help the war effort and earn extra money, Monroe began working in a defense industry plant, packing parachutes. David Conover, an army photographer, arrived at the factory to take pictures of women working in support of the armed forces overseas. His shots of Marilyn for *Yank* magazine brought her a great deal of attention, leading to a burgeoning career as a model. Her modeling agency decided to change her hair color from its natural brown to blonde.

Long interested in the movies due to her mother's involvement with the film industry, Monroe began auditioning at several studios. Her first break came when Ben Lyon, the casting director of 20th Century-Fox, saw something in her and signed her to a contract. Lyon gave her the name Marilyn, taking it from Marilyn Miller, an actress who (ironically) had died at the age of thirty-seven, a victim of poisoning. Monroe was Marilyn's mother's maiden name and she liked the way it sounded with Marilyn.

Monroe was given acting lessons at Fox and eventually cast in tiny roles in two movies, *Scudda Hoo! Scudda Hay!* (1948), in which she can only be seen in a canoe for a short moment, and *The Dangerous Years* (1948). Fox promptly dropped her option. As it happened, however, Marilyn had been keeping company with sixty-nine-year-old Joseph M. Schenck, a powerful producer at Fox with connections all over Hollywood. Schenck, as a favor to Marilyn, called the president of Columbia Pictures,

Harry Cohn, and asked him to give her a contract. Cohn signed her up, gave her the lead in a B-movie musical, *Ladies of the Chorus* (1949), and then dropped her. According to Monroe, Cohn let her go because she rebuffed his sexual advances.

In the course of trying to make a living, she posed nude for a calendar spread, earning $50 for her efforts. When she became famous and the photos resurfaced, the calendar sold more than one million copies. The publicity helped her career.

Following her brief stint at Columbia, Monroe freelanced, hoping to catch on somewhere. One of her small roles was in the last MARX BROTHERS movie, *Love Happy* (1949), significant for her career only because William Morris agent Johnny Hyde saw her in it. He became both her lover and her mentor, guiding her and getting her small but important parts in such films as *The Asphalt Jungle* (1950) and *All About Eve* (1950).

Monroe was starting to get noticeable press attention, and Hyde succeeded in garnering her a good seven-year contract at Fox in 1951 just before he died of a heart attack. Her studio continued to groom her for stardom, giving her modest roles in films such as *As Young As You Feel* (1951), *Love Nest* (1951), *Let's Make It Legal* (1951), *Clash by Night* (1951), *We're Not Married* (1952), and *Monkey Business* (1952). In most of these early films she was cast as a dumb blonde, the studio banking on her sex appeal and not her acting abilities.

Finally, in *Niagara* (1953), she had her first important major role; despite the fact that the film was mediocre, her presence turned it into a hit. Her career suddenly went into overdrive. Her next film, the musical comedy *Gentlemen Prefer Blondes* (1953), teamed her with another busty movie star, Jane Russell, and the hit movie proved that Marilyn could do more than look beautiful. She could sing in her own inimitable breathy, sexy style and dance with provocative bravado. However, the real surprise was that she was an extremely adept comedian.

Monroe made only five good movies after *Gentlemen Prefer Blondes*; *How to Marry a Millionaire* (1953) was one of them. In both films she played a sort of innocent gold digger, a variation on the dumb blonde. To varying degrees, she continued to play that part in *There's No Business Like Show Business* (1954) and the classic comedy *The Seven Year Itch* (1955). The only exception was the drama *River of No Return* (1954). In any event, all of her films were big hits, yet Marilyn was unhappy that she was not being given an opportunity to play a wider variety of roles. She walked out on her contract and went to New York to study acting with Paula and Lee Strasberg.

In 1954 she had married baseball hero Joe DiMaggio. The marriage lasted only nine months, breaking up while she worked on *The Seven Year Itch*. While in New York, Monroe met and fell in love with America's leading playwright, Arthur Miller, who became her third and last husband.

Meanwhile, Fox finally capitulated and gave Marilyn a new contract that gave her approval rights of her scripts and directors. Her next film under that contract was the dramatic hit *Bus Stop* (1956), proving Marilyn knew what she was doing. For the first time, critics who had previously scoffed at her acting ability began to change their tune.

Having proved her point, Monroe returned to her forte, making three more comedies in a row. Unfortunately, her next film was the rather weak *The Prince and the Showgirl* (1957) with Laurence Olivier. She bounced back strongly with Billy WILDER's hugely successful *Some Like It Hot* (1959). *Let's Make Love* (1960) was not a successful romantic comedy, but it became noteworthy from a gossip point of view because of her affair with co-star Yves Montand.

By this time, though, Monroe's professional behavior was becoming less and less tolerable. She was often late to arrive on the set and sometimes didn't show up at all. In addition, she was extremely difficult to direct; a number of her directors publicly complained about both her tardiness and the constant need to retake her scenes because she could not give a consistently credible performance.

Well aware of her reputation, John Huston agreed to direct her in a film that Arthur Miller had written for her, *The Misfits* (1961). It was the last movie she ever made. Because of her emotional problems and dependence on sleeping pills, the film went way over budget. It was, nonetheless, a powerful movie, and she gave an elegant performance as an ethereal child/woman. Although generally well received by the critics, it was not a winner at the box office (at least not on its initial release). A week before the movie opened, Monroe announced her divorce from Miller.

Monroe began making *Something's Got to Give* (1962), a light romantic comedy with Dean MAR-TIN, but the film was never finished. When the film fell hopelessly behind schedule due to her behavior, she was fired.

Meanwhile, through Frank Sinatra and Peter Lawford, Monroe had met and had become intimately involved with President John F. Kennedy, who then passed her like a football to his brother, U.S. Attorney General Robert F. Kennedy. She died of a drug overdose under mysterious circumstances.

---

FILMS: *Scudda Hoo! Scudda Hay!* (1948); *Dangerous Years* (1948); *Ladies of the Chorus* (1948); *Love Happy* (1950); *A Ticket to Tomahawk* (1950); *The Asphalt Jungle* (1950); *All About Eve* (1950); *Right Cross* (1950); *The Fireball* (1950); *Hometown Story* (1951); *As Young as You Feel* (1951); *Love Nest* (1951); *Let's Make It Legal* (1951); *Clash by Night* (1952); *We're Not Married* (1952); *Don't Bother to Knock* (1952); *Monkey Business* (1952); *O. Henry's Full House* (1952); *Niagara* (1953); *Gentlemen Prefer Blondes* (1953); *How to Marry a Millionaire* (1953); *River of No Return* (1954); *There's No Business Like Show Business* (19954); *The Seven Year Itch* (1955); *Bus Stop* (1956); *The Prince and the Showgirl* (1957); *Some Like It Hot* (1959); *Let's Make Love* (1960); *The Misfits* (1961).

---

## Monsieur Verdoux

Released in 1947, *Monsieur Verdoux* was Charlie CHAPLIN's most daring comedy and greatest commercial failure. Starring as the film's title character, Chaplin also wrote, directed, produced, and scored the movie. In this BLACK COMEDY, Chaplin shocked audiences with his bleak examination of morality; the movie was at least fifteen years ahead of its time.

The film revolves around the murderous intentions of Verdoux (Chaplin), who lost his job as a bank clerk during the Great Depression and now resorts to marrying and murdering rich, unattractive women for their inheritances so that he may continue to support his invalid wife and their son. It is the capitalist ideal taken to its furthest extreme; Verdoux treats his killings as a business. The comedy comes from all manner of hilarious obstacles that keep him from finishing off one of his adoring new wives (Martha RAYE in her most memorable performance).

The idea for the film was suggested to Chaplin by Orson Welles, but the execution (no pun intended) is purely Chaplinesque. Through hilarious comic invention, physical humor, and pathos, he turns the tables on his audience, asking us to identify with Verdoux, the killer, cunningly making us his accomplice in his intricate plans.

Although some have accused Chaplin of sermonizing at the end of *Monsieur Verdoux*, the dialogues Verdoux has with a reporter and then a priest are essential to the understanding of Verdoux's depth of revulsion with the world. He pointedly tells the reporter, "As a mass killer I'm an amateur . . . wars, conflict, it's all business. One murder makes a villain, millions a hero." To the priest, who begs him to confess his sins, he asks, "Who knows what sin is?"

An intelligent, complicated, and endlessly provocative film, *Monsieur Verdoux* was unlike anything American audiences had experienced. Chaplin was attacked unmercifully by the press and religious leaders. He quickly withdrew it from circulation.

Where, asked disillusioned fans, had Chaplin's lovable Little Tramp gone? There were vestiges of his famous persona in Chaplin's Jewish barber in *The Great Dictator* (1940), but in *Monsieur Verdoux*, the tramp had all but disappeared (or so it seemed). In one viscerally shocking moment, as Verdoux is led to his execution, his back to the camera, the character suddenly takes a comic little step that is unmistakeably that of the tramp. With that, it all comes clear: Verdoux and the tramp are the same—and society is about to execute him. The tramp has not disappeared, he has been sentenced to death! There is perhaps no other moment in the cinema as profoundly (and intentionally) bleak as the last moment of this brilliantly ironic masterpiece.

## Moore, Dickie   *See* OUR GANG

## Moore, Dudley (1935—)   A comedy cult favorite during the late 1960s and most of the 1970s, Dudley Moore attained stardom suddenly in 1979 in Blake EDWARD's comic masterpiece *10*. This hit was soon followed by the actor's bravura performance in the smash comedy *Arthur* (1981). Unfortunately, Moore's film career since those two blockbusters has been considerably less successful.

Music was Moore's early preoccupation. Born in London, England, he learned to play the violin at an early age, later winning an organ scholarship to Oxford's Magdalen College where he earned a Bachelor of Arts degree in music in 1957 and a degree in composition in 1958.

His first big show business break came in a university revue called *Beyond the Fringe*. It was so successful that it played on the London stage and was brought to Broadway. During the 1960s, he joined with fellow "Fringe" player Peter Cook, and the two of them became a popular, if cerebral, comedy team. They appeared in *The Wrong Box* (1966), which was Moore's first film; it was quickly followed by *Bedazzled* (1967), in which he and Cook starred. In addition, Moore co-wrote the story, composed the film's musical score, and also sang. The hip comedy became a cult classic and it still holds up very well today.

*Bedazzled* was the most enjoyable of Moore's early film roles. He continued appearing in movies, but none of them were mainstream hits. After spending a large chunk of the 1970s on the stage, Moore finally charmed the mass audience with his supporting performance in the hit Goldie HAWN and Chevy CHASE film comedy *Foul Play* (1978). The highly popular *10* turned him into a major ROMANTIC COMEDY star, earning him the nickname "Cuddly Dudley." After an inconsequential flop, *Wholly Moses* (1980), Moore scored again as the lovable drunk in *Arthur* (1981). There was a flurry of films thereafter, each of them trying to capitalize on Moore's cuteness. But *Six Weeks* (1982), *Romantic Comedy* (1983), *Lovesick* (1983), and *Unfaithfully Yours* (1984) were mediocre at best, and overly sentimental and lacking in originality at worst. For the most part, though, Moore was consistently better than his material, charming his way through films that he might have been wiser to avoid.

Moore's box office clout regained strength in 1984 when he starred in *Micki and Maude*, a clever, frenetic comedy. Unfortunately, that same year he starred in a stinker, *Best Defense* (1984), and followed it a year later with his (literally) elfish performance in the poorly received *Santa Claus: The Movie* (1985). After disappearing from movie screens for two years, he starred in *Like Father, Like Son* (1987), yet another box office loser. As always, however, he garnered sympathetic notices from critics.

Finally, in an effort to recoup his popularity, Moore agreed to produce and star in *Arthur 2: On the Rocks* (1988). The film crashed at the box office.

**FILMS:** *The Wrong Box* (1966); *Bedazzled* (also co-story, music, 1967); *Inadmissible Evidence* (music and singing only, 1967); *30 Is a Dangerous Age, Cynthia* (also co-sc, music, 1968); *The Bed Sitting Room* (1969); *Monte Carlo or Bust!/Those Daring Young Men in Their Jaunty Jalopies* (1969); *Staircase* (music only, 1969); *Alice's Adventures in Wonderland* (1972); *Pleasure at Her Majesty's* (1976); *Foul Play* (1978); *The Hound of the Baskervilles* (also sc, music, 1978); *10* (1979); *Derek and Clive Get the Horn* (also p, music, 1980); *Wholly Moses!* (1980); *Arthur* (1981); *Six Weeks* (also music, 1982); *Lovesick* (1983);

*Romantic Comedy* (1983); *Unfaithfully Yours* (1983); *Best Defense* (1984); *Micki and Maude* (1984); *Santa Claus: The Movie* (1985); *Koneko Monogatari* (1986); *Like Father, Like Son* (1987); *Arthur 2: On the Rocks* (also p, 1988); *The Adventures of Milo and Otis* (1989); *Crazy People* (1990); *Blame It on the Bellboy* (1992); *The Pickle* (cameo, 1993).

## Moranis, Rick (1954—)

A short, slightly built comic actor, Rick Moranis is known for playing nerdy, but resourceful characters. In a motion picture career that is only a decade long, Moranis has had the good fortune to have already worked with many of the most successful comic filmmakers of our time, including Ivan REITMAN, John HUGHES, and Mel BROOKS.

Born in Toronto, Canada, Moranis first came to fame as a writer/actor on the seminal TV comedy show "SCTV," for which he won a writing Emmy. One of his characters on SCTV was Bob McKenzie, one of the crazed McKenzie brothers. The two siblings became the subject of Moranis's first feature film, *Strange Brew* (1983), which the actor co-wrote and co-directed.

In many of his films that followed, Moranis usually played secondary comic creations, most notably in support of Dan AYKROYD and Bill MURRAY in *Ghostbusters* (1984) and its sequel in 1989, as well as in support of Steve MARTIN in *Parenthood* (1989). He had the lead in the musical comedy *Little Shop of Horrors* (1986), but the film was so full of star turns that he got lost in the shuffle. The movie was not a major hit.

Moranis finally became a comedy star in his own right, thanks to the hugely successful Disney family films *Honey, I Shrunk the Kids* (1989) and *Honey, I Blew Up the Kid* (1992), playing, as one would expect, a nerdy inventor.

FILMS INCLUDE: *Strange Brew* (also sc, d, 1983); *Ghostbusters* (1984); *The Wild Life* (1984); *Streets of Fire* (1984); *Brewster's Millions* (1985); *Head Office*

*The invisible star, Rick Moranis, has been a cast member in a startling number of hits belonging to a wide variety of comic styles. With all that, he's still the least heralded of comic stars.*
PHOTO BY TERRY O'NEILL, © UNIVERSAL PICTURES.

(1986); *Club Paradise* (1986); *Little Shop of Horrors* (1986); *Spaceballs* (1987); *Ghostbusters II* (1989); *Honey, I Shrunk the Kids* (1989); *Parenthood* (1989); *My Blue Heaven* (1990); *L.A. Story* (1991); *Honey, I Blew Up the Kid* (1992); *Splitting Heirs* (1993); *The Flintstones* (1994).

## Mostel, Zero (1915—1977)

A broad (and broadly built) comic actor with a blustery manner but a sweet face, Zero Mostel might have had a far more significant film career had he not been black-listed during the Communist witch-hunt in Hollywood during the early 1950s. Despite a fifteen-year hiatus from films, Mostel still managed to create a number of indelible comic portraits from the mid-1960s until his death in 1977.

Born Samuel Joel Mostel in Brooklyn, New York, he was the son of a Rabbi. Zero was a nickname he picked up as a child, and it stuck. He received his Bachelor of Arts degree in art from City College New York and briefly attended New York University, but soon drifted into the entertainment world as a stand-up comic, which led to a radio program. A Broadway show, *Keep 'Em Laughing*, showcased his comic talent, and he was signed to make his motion picture debut in *DuBarry Was a Lady* (1943), playing the dual role that Bert LAHR made famous on Broadway. It was Mostel's first and only starring role in films for the next twenty-three years. He was fired by his studio (MGM) for making leftist remarks in public. When he returned to Hollywood in the early 1950s, he came back as a supporting player, often in the role of a villain. He was quickly banished, again, blacklisted after testifying before the House UnAmerican Activities Committee in 1951. Worse, he was barred from working on Broadway as well.

Bereft of an income, Mostel turned to painting, scraping by with club work as a comic and traveling overseas to perform in England, until he was finally hired again for the American stage. By the early 1960s his professional vindication was at hand. He won three best actor Tonys during the decade: for *Rhinoceros*, *A Funny Thing Happened on the Way to the Forum*, and *Fiddler on the Roof*, the last being his most famous performance as Tevye. However, it was *A Funny Thing Happened on the Way to the Forum* that brought him back to the movies, recreating his role in the 1966 film version of the play. As for *Fiddler on the Roof*, Mostel was bitterly disappointed when he wasn't given the opportunity to reprise his role on film (it went to actor Topol).

Although Mostel worked steadily after his return to movies in the mid-1960s, very few of his films could contain his talent. His best work was as Max Bialystock in the Mel BROOKS classic, *The PRODUCERS* (1967), the serious film adaptation of *Rhinoceros* (1972), and the autobiographical role of the blacklisted performer in *The Front* (1976).

His son, Josh Mostel, is also a comic actor, performing regularly both on TV and in films in supporting roles; he has also directed for the stage.

**FILMS INCLUDE:** *DuBarry Was a Lady* (1943); *Panic in the Streets* (1950); *The Enforcer* (1951); *The Guy Who Came Back* (1951); *The Model and the Marriage Broker* (1951); *Mr. Belvedere Rings the Bell* (1951); *Sirroco* (1951); *A Funny Thing Happened on the Way to the Forum* (1966); *The Producers* (1967); *Great Catherine* (1968); *Monsieur Lecoq* (also sc, 1968); *The Great Bank Robbery* (also song, 1969); *The Angel Levine* (1970); *The Hot Rock* (1972); *Rhinoceros* (1972); *Marco* (1973); *Once Upon a Scoundrel* (1973); *Foreplay* (1974); *The Front* (1976); *Hollywood on Trial* (1976); *Journey into Fear* (1976); *Mastermind* (1976); *Watership Down* (voice only, 1978); *Best Boy* (documentary, 1979).

**Murphy, Eddie (1961—)**   On the basis of his first three films in the early 1980s, comic actor Eddie Murphy rocketed to Hollywood superstar status. A comic juggernaut, it seemed as if he was incapable of a commercial misstep. Throughout the 1980s his films garnered generally good reviews and gargantuan box office receipts. His brash, cocky humor, coupled with a disarming personal charm, brought him a legion of fans. In the face of mediocre material, however, some of those fans began to desert him in the early 1990s. His early comedic persona was often harsh and jarring, but it had much of the honesty and piercing truth of Richard PRYOR at his best, whose rein as Hollywood's leading black comedy star Murphy had usurped. Murphy's later films have begun to betray a certain meanness of spirit and self-satisfied smugness that has detracted from his appeal. Nonetheless, he remains a powerful comic force.

Murphy was born in the Bushwick section of Brooklyn, New York. His father was a New York city cop and amateur comedian who died when the future star was eight. Raised by his mother and stepfather, Murphy soon showed a flair for comedy. He began writing and performing his own routines at youth centers and local bars when he was fifteen.

*Very few comic performers command the kind of big bucks that Eddie Murphy can, but a rash of comedies grossing over $100 million does that. Two of his movies,* Beverly Hills Cop *(1984) and its 1987 sequel, are in the top-ten comedy moneymakers of all time.* PHOTO BY BRUCE W. TALAMON, © PARAMOUNT PICTURES, COURTESY OF THE TERRIE WILLIAMS AGENCY.

Hitting New York City, Murphy made it to The Comic Strip, the showcase that launched many a comedian's career.

At nineteen, Murphy landed an audition for the new cast of TV's "SATURDAY NIGHT LIVE" and was signed as a featured player for the 1980–1981 season. He was an instant hit on the show, staying with the program for four years and creating such memorable characters as the prison poet Tyrone Green, the grownup Buckwheat, the grumpy Gumby, and the TV huckster Velvet Jones.

"Saturday Night Live" had already served as a breeding ground for movie comedy stars Chevy CHASE, Dan AYKROYD, John BELUSHI, Bill MUR-RAY, and Gilda RADNER. It seemed logical for Murphy to also try his luck in the movies. His first film was *48 Hrs.* (1982), in which he co-starred with Nick Nolte. It was a smash hit, and Murphy was highly praised as a natural actor. For his second film he teamed with Dan Aykroyd in *Trading Places* (1983). It was another winner. Murphy had been protected in his first two ventures by virtue of his sharing top billing; he didn't have to carry either film on his shoulders.

That changed with his third film, the movie that established him as one of Hollywood's biggest box office draws. The film was *Beverly Hills Cop* (1984), a spectacular hit.

Murphy had generally received good reviews from the critics for his first three films. That changed after *The Golden Child* (1986) and *Beverly Hills Cop II* (1987), but it didn't keep his fans away. The direction of his career became a subject of much discourse in 1988 when two of his comedy concerts were recorded on film and edited into a motion picture that was released to theaters as *Eddie Murphy: Raw* (1988). The four-letter words were flying in that film, but so were the dollars; *Raw* became the biggest moneymaker in concert film history. Murphy followed that success with the ambitious *Coming to America* (1988), a major hit and highly regarded by critics impressed with Murphy's growth as an actor.

Some wondered if he overreached himself, however, when he wrote the screenplay, produced, and directed himself in the disappointing *Harlem Nights* (1989). The film did not have the box office success that was predicted. In one way or another, none of this next three films fared much better; *Another 48 Hrs.* (1990) was an outright bomb, *Boomerang* (1992) was widely castigated for its misogynist point of view, and *Distinguished Gentleman* (1993), while generally praised by the critics, got a surprisingly tepid response at the box office.

**FILMS:** *48 Hrs.* (1982); *Trading Places* (1983); *Best Defense* (1984); *Beverly Hills Cop* (1984); *The Golden*

*Child* (1986); *Beverly Hills Cop II* (also story, 1987); *Eddie Murphy: Raw* (also sc, song, p, 1987); *Coming to America* (also song, 1988); *Harlem Nights* (also sc, p, d, 1989); *Another 48 Hrs.* (1990); *Boomerang* (1992); *Distinguished Gentleman* (1993).

**Murray, Bill (1950–)** With a cat-that-ate-the-canary grin, Bill Murray exudes comic arrogance. His characters often take on all comers with quips, come-ons, and outright lies. Hollywood's master of the sardonic, he's the bad boy who gets away with murder because he's just so charming. It isn't that he's handsome—he has thinning hair, pockmarked skin, and a slightly lopsided face. But with a humorously taunting vocal style and a mischievous gleam in his eyes, he rarely fails in getting his laughs.

Born William Doyle-Murray in Chicago, Illinois, he did some acting while a student at Regis College before joining the Second City comedy troupe along with his brother, Brian Doyle-Murray. He had good company in the Chicago chapter of the famous improv group; among his fellow performers were John BELUSHI and Harold RAMIS.

Murray began making his mark with "The National Lampoon Radio Hour" and in the cabaret revue *The National Lampoon Show*. It wasn't until the second season of NBC-TV's "SATURDAY NIGHT LIVE" that Murray suddenly had his chance to shine. He replaced Chevy CHASE on the show in 1977 when Chase, one of the original Not Ready for Prime Time Players, took off for Hollywood. Murray soon developed several famous characters that became staples on the show: the lounge lizard singer; Todd, the nerd who gave "noogies" to Gilda RADNER's Lisa; and the name-dropping film critic on "Weekend Update." For his efforts, Murray won an Emmy Award for writing during his second season on the show. He stayed with "Saturday Night Live" until 1980, following Chase and many other alumni from the show who headed to Hollywood for movie careers.

*Bill Murray is one of the most underrated comic actors in Hollywood. His breezy, throwaway style belies the deep conviction he brings to his offbeat characters. Murray is seen here playing against type as a dangerously funny mobster opposite Robert De Niro in* Mad Dog and Glory *(1992).*
PHOTO BY RON PHILLIPS, © UNIVERSAL PICTURES.

By this time Murray had already made his starring debut in Ivan REITMAN's *Meatballs* (1979), the first of a string of comedy hits in which the director and star collaborated. They also hit comic paydirt together with *Stripes* (1981) as well as with the two *Ghostbusters* films (1984 and 1989). The *Ghostbusters* role came to him only because John Belushi, for whom it had been intended, had died of a drug overdose.

Not content to run in place, Murray has experimented and taken chances with his persona. He has played the goofy groundskeeper in *Caddyshack* (1980) as well as the impossible neurotic in *What About Bob?* (1991). He has tried his hand (disastrously) with drama, scripting and starring in the heavy-going *The Razor's Edge* (1984) as well as co-directing the comedy *Quick Change* (1990). He was brilliant as Dustin Hoffman's roommate (perhaps cheated out of a best supporting actor Academy Award nomination) in *Tootsie* (1982) and was comically menacing opposite Robert De Niro in *Mad Dog and Glory* (1993). Most recently, he gave what many consider his best performance—both acidic and vulnerable—in the hit comedy fantasy *Groundhog Day* (1993).

**FILMS:** *Shame of the Jungle* (voice only, 1975); *The Dogs* (1978); *A Bird for All Seasons* (1979); *First Love* (1979); *Meatballs* (1979); *Mr. Mike's Mondo Video* (1979); *Caddyshack* (1980); *Where the Buffalo Roam* (1980); *Loose Shoes* (1981); *Stripes* (1981); *Nothing Lasts Forever* (1982); *Tootsie* (1982); *Ghostbusters* (1984); *The Razor's Edge* (also sc, 1984); *Little Shop of Horrors* (1986); *Scrooged* (1988); *Ghostbusters II* (1989); *Quick Change* (also co-p, co-d, 1990); *What About Bob?* (1991); *Mad Dog and Glory* (1993); *Groundhog Day* (1993).

**musical comedy**  The movie musical comes in many guises, but its liveliest form derives from that distinctly American theatrical phenomenon, the musical comedy. Invented on Broadway, it was brought to the world via Hollywood. While there are exceptions, musical comedies tend to be effervescent, optimistic, and utterly intent upon entertaining.

The first talkie, *The Jazz Singer* (1927), was also Hollywood's first musical, and Al Jolson declared in that film, "You ain't heard nothin' yet." Given the crudity of the first sound films, he was right; you really hadn't heard anything yet. As early as 1929, however, the first full flowering of the musical comedy on film was occurring, courtesy of Ernst LUBITSCH's charming and risqué operettas *The Love Parade* (1929) and *Monte Carlo* (1930). Rouben Mamoulian took the form to its brilliant height with *Love Me Tonight* (1932).

In the meantime, many comedies of the 1930s were also leavened with song and dance and should be considered musical comedies, among them the films of Eddie CANTOR and even the MARX BROTHERS. In later decades, the same would be true for the likes of ABBOTT AND COSTELLO, Dean MARTIN and Jerry LEWIS, and Danny KAYE.

The glory of the genre, of course, ultimately belongs to the films and filmmakers who were devoted primarily to the musical elements first and the comedy second. Fred Astaire and Gene Kelly fit this category, as do the Busby BERKELEY spectaculars of the 1930s or the Broadway musical extravaganzas of the 1950s and early 1960s. For most people, these films are the pinnacle of musical comedy art.

Busby Berkeley breathed new life into the musical and created a dynamic visual style when he choreographed and directed the musical numbers in *Footlight Parade* (1933), *Gold Diggers of 1933* (1933), and *42nd Street* (1933). These lavish, audacious feats of kitsch have never been duplicated. For instance, the very idea of putting one hundred dancing pianos on screen (which Berkeley presented in *Gold Diggers of 1935*) was both wonderfully silly and thoroughly awe-inspiring.

Berkeley's "mass" extravaganzas, full of scores of scantily clad women creating kaledioscope effects (e.g., forming images of violins, flowers, etc.) was in contrast to the "intimate" musicals, which were characterized by the subtle, graceful, and elegant dance numbers of the Fred Astaire/Ginger Rogers musicals. They were leavened not only with the amusing byplay of the stars, but also with some of the best comic relief characters in the business, among them Edward Everett HORTON and Eric BLORE. Astaire and Rogers, in films such as *The Gay Divorcee* (1934), *Top Hat* (1935), and *Swing Time* (1936), created the yardstick by which the intimate musical comedy film would be measured.

With varying degrees of success, each studio pursued its own course in the profitable musical comedy genre. More often than not, a musical comedy performer (or performers) helped save a studio from bankruptcy. For instance, RKO avoided Chapter 11 thanks to the enormous successes of Fred Astaire and Ginger Rogers in the 1930s. Also in the 1930s, Deanna Durbin sang Universal out of near insolvency, just as Shirley Temple kept the wolf from the door at 20th Century-Fox until it developed such other popular musical comedy stars as Alice Faye and Betty Grable. Of course, not every leading musical comedy performer was a savior, but many were immeasurably important to their studio's bottom line. For example, Dick Powell warbled very profitably for Warner Bros. in innumerable musicals during the bulk of the 1930s, just as Bing CROSBY was a major musical comedy asset at Paramount.

And then there was MGM, which boasted more stars than there are in the heavens. By the late 1930s, a good many of them were musical comedy stars. The studio was rather dormant in the musical field during most of the 1930s, but finally began its emergence as a powerhouse in the genre with such films as *The Wizard of Oz* (1939) and *Babes in Arms* (1939). MGM eventually became the predominant creator of musicals in the 1940s and 1950s, many of them musical comedies. One of MGM's discoveries was Gene Kelly, whose exuberant and acrobatic style, especially in films such as *The Pirate* (1948), *On the Town* (1949), and *Singin' in the Rain* (1952), gave the musical a shot in the arm.

Astaire and Kelly, as well as such talents as Judy Garland, Mickey ROONEY, Mario Lanza, and Cyd Charisse, were all part of MGM's famous "Freed unit." Arthur Freed, a noted songwriter and producer, put together an awesome assemblage of musical talent, presiding over the creation of many of the film industry's most illustrious musicals. With the assistance of such innovative directors as Vincente Minnelli and Stanley Donen, the Freed unit produced such memorable musical comedy hits as *Ziegfeld Follies* (1946), *Till the Clouds Roll By* (1946), *Easter Parade* (1948), and *Summer Stock* (1950).

The movie industry was under siege during the 1950s, losing patrons and revenue to television. Just as Hollywood turned to epics and spectaculars to compete with the little box, the musical comedy also looked for ways to compete, ultimately becoming more adventurously sexy; hence, the casting of Marilyn MONROE in *Gentlemen Prefer Blondes* (1953). The musical comedies of the 1950s began to fade toward the end of the decade, however, the genre temporarily losing steam.

In the 1960s, the musical comedy finally collapsed under its own budgetary weight. After a spate of hugely successful Broadway musical adaptations, including the musical comedies *My Fair Lady* (1964) and *Funny Girl* (1968), film companies poured massive amounts of money into a series of very poor ones, such as *Doctor Dolittle* (1967) and *Star!* (1968), which were staggering box office failures, souring the movie industry on the entire genre.

The audience for musical comedy largely narrowed to the youth market in the 1970s, with *Grease* (1978) becoming one of the few musical comedy hits of the decade. By the mid-1980s and early 1990s, the musical comedy seemed more alive with animated characters than with real ones. *The Little Mermaid* (1989), *Beauty and the Beast* (1991), and *Aladdin* (1992), all from Disney, have, if not revitalized the musical comedy, at least reminded us of its glory.

**Myers, Mike (1963—)**  Yet another "SATURDAY NIGHT LIVE" performer to star in film comedies, Mike Myers had a gigantic hit with *Wayne's World* (1992), which was his motion picture debut. The feature-length version of his popular "Saturday Night Live" skits about two young suburban nerds with a cable-access show, *Wayne's World* opened to critical praise and took in more than $100 million. What remains to be seen is whether movie audiences will respond to Myers in other kinds of comedies. For instance, his second comedy, *So I Married an Axe Murderer* (1993), bombed at the box office.

Myers was born and raised in Toronto, Canada. The day he graduated from high school, he auditioned and was accepted into the Toronto-based Second City comedy troupe. Later, he moved to Chicago and joined that Second City team. He was introduced to the city's suburb of Aurora where Wayne Campbell, his "Saturday Night Live" creation, lives and broadcasts his cable show from his basement.

FILMS: *Wayne's World* (a, characters, co-sc, 1992); *So I Married an Axe Murderer* (a, 1993); *Wayne's World II* (a, characters, co-sc, 1993).

*So far, the only commercial success Mike Myers has had as a comic movie star has been playing Wayne Campbell in* Wayne's World *(1992), as shown above. It remains to be seen if he can, like so many other "Saturday Night Live" alumni, parlay his early movie success into a long and varied film comedy career.*

PHOTO BY SUZANNE TENNER, © PARAMOUNT PICTURES.

# N

**Network** It is rare, indeed, for a comedy to not only be funny in its own time, but to be even more horrifyingly funny years later when the very things it satirizes turn out to be true. Such is the case with *Network* (1976), Paddy CHAYEFSKY's dynamic SAT-IRE of television.

The story of a fourth TV network, whose executives are willing to do anything to get higher ratings, was written by Oscar-winning playwright/screenwriter Chayefsky, directed by Sidney Lumet, and starred a cast of dramatic, rather than comic actors. Among those who appeared in this landmark film were William Holden, Faye Dunaway, Peter Finch, Robert Duvall, Ned Beatty, Beatrice Straight, Wesley Addy, Darryl Hickman, Ken Kercheval, William Prince, and Marlene Warfield. Oscars went to Dunaway, Finch, and Straight, as well as to the film's author, Chayefsky.

Accused of writing "surreal stuff" when he penned *Network*, Chayefsky replied, "No, I still write realistic stuff. It's the world that's turned into a satire."

The casting of the crazed anchorman, the linchpin of the movie, gave the filmmakers pause. The role was actually offered to both Walter Cronkite and John Chancellor, neither of whom were actually crazy enough to take it. Ironically, Walter Cronkite's daughter did have a role in the film, playing a terrorist. When Henry Fonda, yet another icon of trust turned the role down, it fell into the lap of the very talented, but far less well known Peter Finch.

In the most famous scene in the film, the crazed anchorman exhorts his listeners to go to their windows and shout, "I'm mad as hell, and I'm not going to take it anymore." The expression entered our vocabulary, and millions know it today, even if they don't know its derivation.

## Nichols, Mike (1931—)

A contemporary director, Mike Nichols has made a number of intelligent, cutting-edge comedies. While not a full-time comedy director, much of Nichols's best work has garnered kudos from the press and laughter from the moviegoing public.

Born Michael Igor Peschkowsky in Berlin, Germany, he was seven when he emigrated with his Jewish family to the United States to avoid persecution at the hands of the Nazis. Nichols was twelve when his father died, but he managed to continue his education, eventually attending the University of Chicago thanks to a series of scholarships and a succession of jobs as varied as a janitor and a jingle contest judge.

After college, he studied acting with Lee Strasberg in New York, but he couldn't find an acting job so he returned to Chicago with as little acting experience as when he left. Back in his home town, however, he teamed up with several friends, including Barbara Harris, Paul Sills, Alan ARKIN, and Elaine MAY, and began an improvisational theater group that performed for three straight years at Chicago's Compass club.

In the late 1950s, Nichols and May formed a two-person comedy act, which culminated in a hit Broadway show in 1960, *An Evening with Mike Nichols and Elaine May*. The team broke up in the early 1960s, and Nichols eventually took a stab at directing for the theater, making his debut with Neil SIMON's *Barefoot in the Park* in 1963. The show was a smash, and Nichols directed six more stage plays, all of them major hits.

His success on Broadway was such that he was inevitably asked to direct a movie. His first was *The GRADUATE* (1967), but he delayed production on that movie when he had the opportunity to direct *Who's Afraid of Virginia Woolf?* (1966). Nichols came away with both a box office winner and a best director Oscar nomination.

*The Graduate* became an even more successful movie. It was one of the highest grossing films of the 1960s, earning in excess of $60 million. It made Dustin Hoffman a star and brought Nichols the best director Academy Award. The film was also nominated for a best picture Oscar, but lost to *In the Heat of the Night*.

With the clout that came from two hits in a row, he was given an $11 million budget to direct the movie version of Joseph Heller's *Catch-22* (1970), a novel that was generally considered unfilmable. The result was a flawed comic masterpiece. Equally ambitious was *Carnal Knowledge* (1971), a film about sexual and social relationships that showed its audience no quarter; it was a provocative and extremely controversial movie that also proved to be popular.

Despite his Hollywood success, Nichols has continued to direct for the stage, giving Whoopie GOLDBERG a career boost by putting her in a one-woman show.

When not working in the legitimate theater, Nichols has moved easily and comfortably between film comedies and dramas. Among his forays into humor have been *The Fortune* (1975), which earned a pittance; *Gilda: Live* (1980), which showcased the talents of Gilda RADNER; *Heartburn* (1986), which failed at the box office; *Biloxi Blues* (1988), an excellent adaptation of Neil Simon's autobiographical play; *Working Girl* (1988), one of the director's biggest comedy hits; and *Postcards from the Edge* (1990), which garnered good reviews, if modest business.

With the exception of *The Fortune* and *Gilda: Live*, all of Nichols's comedies have been social/cultural films that elicit laughter while exploring diverse themes.

**FILMS: As director:** *Who's Afraid of Virginia Woolf?* (1966); *Bach to Bach* (a only, 1967); *The Graduate* (1967); *Catch-22* (1970); *Carnal Knowledge* (also p, 1971); *The Day of the Dolphin* (1973); *The Fortune* (also p, 1975); *Gilda: Live* (1980); *Silkwood* (also p, 1983); *Heartburn* (also p, 1986); *The Longshot* (p only, 1986); *Biloxi Blues* (1988); *Working Girl* (1988); *Postcards from the Edge* (also p, 1990); *Regarding Henry* (also p, 1991).

## Nielsen, Leslie (1925—)

In light of his entire career, Leslie Nielsen would not necessarily be considered a comic actor, but he has blossomed (quite unexpectedly) in the last decade as a delightfully droll comedian. A rugged leading man for the better part of twenty-five years in B movies and TV, who would have thought he'd emerge late in life as a comedy star? He did just that in the hit comedy *Airplane!* (1980). There were lots of other noncomedians in that film saying the silliest things with a straight face, but there was something about Nielsen that stuck with the film's producers. They cast him again, this time in the lead of their shortlived but wonderfully goofy 1982 TV series "Police Squad." Suddenly, as Lt. Frank Drebbin, Nielsen had a comic personality that he could make his own, and he's gleefully milked it for all it's worth, becoming a movie star thanks to two (so far) hit films inspired by "Police Squad."

Born in Regina, Canada, Nielsen got his start in show business as a radio announcer and disc jockey. He worked on the stage before making his way to Hollywood and leading roles in generally inferior films, some of them even light comedies like *Tammy and the Bachelor* (1957). Only a few of Nielsen's films are noteworthy. He was one of the stars of the classic science fiction film *Forbidden Planet* (1956); he had a modest role in *Harlow* (1965), the better of the two Jean Harlow biopics (with Carroll Baker); and he appeared in the memorable disaster movie *The Poseidon Adventure* (1972). There was plenty of TV work for Nielsen through the years, as well. His face and voice were known to millions, and a fair number of steady TV watchers probably knew his name, but he was hardly a major star—until he reprised his TV role of Lt. Drebbin in *The Naked Gun: From the Files of Police Squad* (1988) and *The Naked Gun 2½: The Smell of Fear* (1991).

---

**FILMS INCLUDE:** *Ransom* (1956); *The Vagabond King* (1956); *Forbidden Planet* (1956); *The Opposite Sex* (1956); *Tammy and the Bachelor* (1957); *Hot Summer Night* (1957); *The Sheepman* (1958); *Harlow* (1965); *Dark Intruder* (1965); *Beau Geste* (1966); *The Reluctant Astronaut* (1967); *Gunfight in Abilene* (1967); *Rosie* (1967); *Dayton's Devils* (1968); *How to Commit Marriage* (1969); *Change of Mind* (1969); *The Poseidon Adventure* (1972); *Viva Knievel* (1977); *Airplane!* (1980); *Prom Night* (1980); *The Creature Wasn't Nice* (1981); *Creepshow* (1982); *Wrong Is Right* (1982); *Soul Man* (1986); *The Patriot* (1986); *Home Is Where the Heart Is* (1987); *Nightstick* (1987); *Nuts* (1987); *The Naked Gun: From the Files of Police Squad* (1988); *Repossessed* (1990); *The Naked Gun 2½: The Smell of Fear* (1991); *All I Want for Christmas* (1991); *Surf Ninjas* (1993); *Naked Gun 33⅓: The Final Insult* (1994).

---

## Normand, Mabel (1894—1930)

Often directing herself in silent movies, the pretty and lithe Mabel Normand had considerable impact on early film comedy. She was the only female equivalent to such silent screen comedy stars as Charlie CHAPLIN, Buster KEATON, Harold LLOYD, and Fatty ARBUCKLE. And she was very much their equal in popularity. Her career, however, was cut short by scandal and ill health.

Born in Boston, Massachusetts, Normand's introduction to show business came through her father who was a piano player on the VAUDEVILLE circuit. At sixteen, she landed a job at Biograph.

The studio was just beginning its renaissance under the tutelage of D. W. Griffith, but it was Mack SENNETT at Biograph who took her under his wing.

Her first billed leading role was in *The Diving Girl* (1911). Normand became a star quickly thereafter, her name often included in one-reel comedy titles such as *Mabel's Adventures* (1912), *Mabel's Strategem* (1912), *Mabel's Heroes* (1913), and *Mabel's Awful Mistake* (1913).

When Sennett left Biograph to establish his Keystone Studio in 1912, Normand followed. She became one of his biggest stars, leading casts that included Charlie Chaplin, Ford STERLING, Fatty Arbuckle, and the rest of the Keystone company. She directed and co-directed a number of her own films with excellent results.

Her comedy was very much in the Keystone tradition: knockabout, silly, enormously energetic, and extremely broad. Like her comic contemporaries, she was as much an acrobat and gymnast as she was an accomplished actress. Her starring performance in Sennett's ambitious 1914 feature TILLIE'S PUNCTURED ROMANCE proved her thespian skills, and more feature-length movies appeared to be in her future. But it didn't happen right away.

In the meantime, Normand made her most successful series of shorts with Fatty Arbuckle, the two of them appearing as a rather mismatched wife and husband in films such as *Mabel and Fatty's Wash Day* (1915), *Mabel and Fatty's Simple Life* (1915), and *Fatty and Mabel Adrift* (1916).

Her popularity was such that Sennett (who nearly married Normand on several occasions) finally created The Mabel Normand Feature Film Company in 1916. She starred in *Mickey* that same year but, inexplicably, it wasn't released until 1918. When it was finally presented to the public it was a huge hit, but more importantly it showed a multi-talented actress who could play a range of emotions. By then, however, Normand had already left Sennett's employ in frustration and had signed up with the Samuel Goldwyn Company.

Although Normand made several successful features during the next few years, such as *Molly O* (1921), her wild partying had already become legendary, and both her personal and professional lives were beginning to suffer. However, it wasn't until 1922 when her lover, director William Desmond Taylor, was murdered that her career began to seriously unravel. She was a suspect in the highly publicized killing but was never charged with the crime. That scandal was followed by the murder of a prominent millionaire by Normand's chauffeur who used a gun that newspapers claimed belonged to the actress. Audiences were no longer able to laugh at Mabel Normand after all that bad publicity and they deserted her. Just like her old partner Fatty Arbuckle, scandal had robbed her of her future.

Normand made a few more films, mostly shorts, but a combination of her high living and a worsening case of tuberculosis finally caught up with her. She died from pneumonia at thirty-six.

---

**FILMS INCLUDE:** *The Diving Girl* (1911); *Mabel's Adventures* (1912); *Mabel's Strategem* (1912); *The Fatal Chocolate* (1912); *Mabel's Heroes* (1913); *Mabel's Awful Mistake* (1913); *A Red Hot Romance* (1913); *Her New Beau* (1913); *Mabel's Dramatic Career* (1913); *Cohen Saves the Flag* (1913); *The Gusher* (1913); *Mabel's Stormy Love Affair* (1914); *Caught in a Cabaret* (also sc, d, 1914); *The Fatal Mallet* (also sc, d, 1914); *Her Friend the Bandit* (also sc, d, 1914); *Mabel at the Wheel* (also d, 1914); *Mabel's Busy Day* (also sc, d, 1914); *Tillie's Punctured Romance* (1914); *Mabel and Fatty's Wash Day* (also d, 1915); *Mabel and Fatty's Simple Life* (also d, 1915); *Fatty and Mabel Viewing the World's Fair at San Francisco* (also d, 1915); *The Little Teacher* (1915); *My Valet* (1915); *Stolen Magic* (1915); *Fatty and Mabel Adrift* (1916); *Bright Lights* (1916); *The Venus Model* (1918); *Mickey* (1918); *Peck's Bad Girl* (1918); *Dodging a Million* (1918); *Joan of Plattsburg* (1918); *A Perfect 36* (1918); *Jinx* (1919); *The Pest* (1919); *Sis Hopkins* (1919); *Upstairs* (1919); *The Slim Princess* (1920); *What Happened to Rosa?* (1920); *Molly O* (1921); *Back to the Woods* (1922); *Head Over Heels* (1922); *Oh Mabel Behave* (1922); *The Extra Girl* (1923); *Suzanna* (1923); *One Hour Married* (1926); *Raggedy Rose* (1926).

---

# O

**Oakie, Jack (1903—1978)** With his chubby body, round face, and fast-talking style, Jack Oakie made a career out of good-natured oafishness during the 1930s and early 1940s. The characters Oakie portrayed were usually dumb but friendly and always sure they were smarter than they really were. His comic speciality was the DOUBLE TAKE, which he eventually extended into a unique triple take with great effect.

Born Lewis Delaney Offield in Sedalia, Missouri, Oakie took his stage name from the state of Oklahoma where he spent most of his youth. After a stint as a clerk on Wall Street, Oakie became an actor, making his theatrical debut in the chorus of *Little Nellie Kelly* (1922). He honed his comic craft both on Broadway and in VAUDEVILLE until he arrived in Hollywood in 1928. However, the rotund Oakie hardly looked like star material, and he began his movie career in minor roles in films such as *Finders Keepers* (debut, 1928) and *The Fleet's In* (1928).

By the early 1930s, however, he had become a comic leading man, sharing top billing with W. C. FIELDS in *Million Dollar Legs* (1932). Considering the fact that he was in his thirties, it was somewhat surprising that Oakie starred in a rash of college movies such as *College Humor* (1933), *College Rhythm* (1934), and *Collegiate* (1936). His best film of the decade, though, was a ditsy ROMANTIC COMEDY called *Murder at the Vanities* (1934).

In 1940 Oakie reached the height of his career, as a supporting player in Charlie CHAPLIN's *The Great Dictator*. He played Benzini Napaloni, the dictator of Bacteria, in a hysterical takeoff of Mussolini. The role won him an Oscar nomination as best support-

ing actor and is the character for which Oakie is best remembered.

Oakie was popular in the early 1940s, but his career began to wind down after World War II. During the decade he consistently played small comic parts, along with the occasional dramatic role. He retired in 1951, only to return for brief appearances in a handful of movies, the last one being *Lover Come Back* (1962).

FILMS INCLUDE: *Finders Keepers* (1928); *Road House* (1928); *The Fleet's In* (1928); *The Dummy* (1929); *Chinatown Nights* (1929); *The Wild Party* (1929); *Street Girl* (1929); *Hard to Get* (1929); *Fast Company* (1929); *Close Harmony* (1929); *The Man I Love* (1929); *Sweetie* (1929); *The Sap from Syracuse* (1930); *Let's Go Native* (1930); *Hit the Deck* (1930); *The Social Lion* (1930); *Sea Legs* (1930); *The Gang Buster* (1931); *June Moon* (1931); *Dude Ranch* (1931); *Touchdown* (1931); *Million Dollar Legs* (1932); *Dancers in the Dark* (1932); *If I Had a Million* (1932); *Madison Square Garden* (1932); *Once in a Lifetime* (1932); *Uptown New York* (1932); *Sailor Be Good* (1933); *From Hell to Heaven* (1933); *The Eagle and the Hawk* (1933); *Too Much Harmony* (1933); *Sitting Pretty* (1933); *College Humor* (1933); *Alice in Wonderland* (1933); *Murder at the Vanities* (1934); *Looking for Trouble* (1934); *Shoot the Works* (1934); *College Rhythm* (1934); *The Call of the Wild* (1935); *The Big Broadcast of 1936* (1935); *King of Burlesque* (1936); *Colleen* (1936); *Collegiate* (1936); *Florida Special* (1936); *The Texas Rangers* (1936); *Champagne Waltz* (1937); *That Girl from Paris* (1937); *Super Sleuth* (1937); *The Toast of New York* (1937); *Hitting a New High* (1937); *Radio*

*It's hard to shine alongside the brilliant Charlie Chaplin, but that's just what Jack Oakie did in* The Great Dictator *(1940). Oakie is seen here, gesturing in that film as Benzini Napaloni of Bacteria, a wickedly effective sendup of Italy's Benito Mussolini. The role brought him a best supporting actor Academy Award nomination. In addition to the seated Chaplin, that's Henry Daniell looking on.*
PHOTO COURTESY OF MOVIE STAR NEWS.

City Revels (1938); *The Affairs of Annabel* (1938); *Thanks for Everything* (1938); *The Great Dictator* (1940); *Tin Pan Alley* (1940); *Young People* (1940); *Little Men* (1940); *The Great American Broadcast* (1941); *Navy Blues* (1941); *Rise and Shine* (1941); *Song of the Islands* (1942); *Iceland* (1942); *Hello Frisco Hello* (1943); *Wintertime* (1943); *It Happened Tomorrow* (1944); *The Merry Monahans* (1944); *Sweet and Low Down* (1944); *Bowery to Broadway* (1944); *That's the Spirit* (1945); *She Wrote the Book* (1946); *When My Baby Smiles at Me* (1948); *Thieves' Highway* (1949); *Last of the Buccaneers* (1950); *Tomahawk* (1951); *Around the World in 80 Days* (cameo, 1956); *The Wonderful Country* (1959); *The Rat Race* (1960); *Lover Come Back* (1962).

**O'Connor, Donald (1925– )** During the late 1940s and early 1950s, Donald O'Connor came into his own as a cheerful, exuberant performer. He was at his best as a musical comedy entertainer, but was rarely given the kind of material that would have enabled him to properly show off his talents. Except for his strong supporting singing and dancing role in *Singin' in the Rain* (1952), O'Connor's reputation

*Donald O'Connor (center), a song and dance man with a decidedly comic edge, reached his greatest fame during the 1950s as the star of the* Francis (The Talking Mule) *series. Here he is flanked by Richard Deacon and Julie Adams, with Francis in the foreground, in* Francis Joins the WACS *(1954).*     PHOTO COURTESY OF MOVIE STAR NEWS.

largely rests with his charming light comedy work in the Francis the Talking Mule series during the 1950s.

Born into a family of circus performers in Chicago, Illinois, O'Connor was no stranger to show business. He joined his parents and siblings when they made the transition to VAUDEVILLE, and by age eleven he had made his film debut in *Melody for Two* (1937). Except for a short return to vaudeville during the early 1940s, O'Connor worked steadily in the movies until the late 1950s.

O'Connor was not a star as a child actor, but he had his moments in such films as *Sing You Sinners* (1938), *Tom Sawyer, Detective* (1938), in which he played Huck Finn, and *Boy Trouble* (1939). During the early 1940s he starred in a number of low-budget films that featured his singing and dancing. They were not terribly popular; certainly the critics paid little attention to them. However, there were a number of small, if flawed, gems among these little films, in particular *Mister Big* (1943), *Chip Off the Old Block* (1944), and *Patrick the Great* (1945).

During the latter half of the 1940s, O'Connor's career began a slow slide that ended when he was cast as the lead playing opposite a talking mule in *Francis* (1950). It was a low-budget, nonmusical movie that caught fire at the box office. Suddenly, O'Connor was a hot actor again, and he ultimately starred in five of the last six Francis films during the early and mid-1950s (Mickey ROONEY starred in the final movie in the series). Between Francis films, O'Connor created a lasting impression in one of Hollywood's greatest musicals, *Singin' in the Rain*, creating the classic number "Make 'em Laugh." He also starred in several other musicals, including *Call Me Madam* (1953), *Walkin' My Baby Back Home* (1953), and *There's No Business Like Show Business* (1954).

He landed the title role in *The Buster Keaton Story* (1957), but the film was a critical and commercial disappointment. In retrospect, O'Connor was much too upbeat an actor to play Buster KEATON with his deadpan "stone face." In any event, he had already quit the Francis films, and by the late 1950s his movie career had come to an end. He composed symphonies and made only a handful of film appearances, among them *That Funny Feeling* (1965), *Ragtime* (1981), and *A Time to Remember* (1990). He has been more readily found on the dinner theater circuit in recent years.

FILMS: *Melody for Two* (1937); *Men with Wings* (1938); *Sing, You Sinners* (1938); *Sons of the Legion* (1938); *Tom Sawyer, Detective* (1938); *Beau Geste* (1939); *Death of a Champion* (1939); *Million Dollar Legs* (1939); *Night Work* (1939); *On Your Toes* (1939); *Unmarried* (1939); *Get Hep to Love* (1942); *Give Out, Sisters* (1942); *Private Buckaroo* (1942); *When Johnny Comes Marching Home* (1942); *It Comes Up Love* (1943); *Mister Big* (1943); *Top Man* (1943); *Bowery to Broadway* (1944); *Chip Off the Old Block* (1944); *Follow the Boys* (1944); *The Merry Monahans* (1944); *This Is the Life* (1944); *Patrick, The Great* (1945); *Something in the Wind* (1947); *Are You with It?* (1948); *Feudin', Fussin', and A-Fightin'* (1948); *Francis* (1949); *Yes, Sir, That's My Baby* (1949); *Curtain Call at Cactus Creek* (1950); *Double Crossbones* (1950); *The Milkman* (1950); *Francis Goes to the* *Races* (1951); *Francis Goes to West Point* (1952); *Singin' in the Rain* (1952); *Call Me Madam* (1953); *Francis Covers the Big Town* (1953); *I Love Melvin* (1953); *Walking My Baby Back Home* (1953); *Francis Joins the WACS* (1954); *There's No Business Like Show Business* (1954); *Francis in the Navy* (1955); *Anything Goes* (1956); *The Buster Keaton Story* (1957); *Cry for Happy* (1961); *The Wonders of Aladdin* (1961); *That Funny Feeling* (1965); *That's Entertainment* (1974); *The Big Fix* (1978); *Pandemonium* (1981); *Ragtime* (1981); *A Time to Remember* (1990).

**Olsen and Johnson**  If there was one comedy team that captured some of the "anything goes" anarchy of the MARX BROTHERS comedies of the early 1930s, it was the team of Ole Olsen and Chic Johnson. There is a manic, irrepressible quality to their humor that still seems eminently modern. The movie career of Olsen and Johnson was erratic and all too brief, but it included three hilarious movies that continue to amaze and delight with their outrageous sight gags, puns, and all-round nuttiness.

John Sigvard "Ole" Olsen (1892–1965) was born in Wabash, Indiana, the son of Norwegian immigrants. He had hoped to become a concert violinist and paid his way through Chicago's Northwestern University by playing violin in a local band. Chicago-born Harold Ogden "Chic" Johnson (1891–1962) joined the band in 1914 as a replacement pianist, and the two became fast friends. They struck off on their own as a twosome, beginning first as a musical act, but soon careening into comedy because that's where the money was in VAUDEVILLE.

They became star performers by the late 1910s and early 1920s and took their comedy on the airwaves, becoming stars of radio, as well. They even wrote songs, including the 1923 novelty hit "Oh Gee, Oh Gosh, Oh Golly, I'm in Love." Their continued success throughout the 1920s made it inevitable that they would be tapped for the movies. They made their film debut in *Oh Sailor, Behave!*

(1930) as comic relief characters. The film enabled them to show off only a small fraction of their zany antics, which was also the case with their next two films, *Fifty Million Frenchmen* (1931) and *Gold Dust Gertie* (1931).

Except for a couple of one-reel shorts and two minor comedies made at Republic, Olsen and Johnson didn't reappear in Hollywood until the early 1940s, but then they came back wackier and more wonderful than ever.

After a two-year run on Broadway with their zany stage show *Hellzapoppin*, they turned their hit comedy revue into a somewhat more conventional film that, while it didn't capture the wildness of the live performance, had laughs aplenty and energy to spare. Then it was back to Broadway for another hit show called *Sons O' Fun*. While that was not turned into a movie, the boys were brought back to Hollywood to make *Crazy House* (1943), which might well be their funniest film. If it isn't their funniest, then their next film, *Ghost Catchers* (1944), would have to take the prize. Full of lunatic sight gags and nonstop one-liners, this movie, a comic takeoff on ghost films, suggests recent genre spoofs like *Airplane!*, *Loaded Weapon I*, and *Hot Shots*.

The comedy team made one more Hollywood film, *See My Lawyer* (1945), but their role was too small to make the film work. They would not be seen on film again until they made a cameo appearance in a little-seen short subject called *It's a Tough Life* (1957). In the meanwhile, they toured, played clubs, and continued working, only slowing down a short while before Chic Johnson's death in 1962. His longtime partner, Ole Olsen, died three years later.

---

FILMS: *Oh Sailor, Behave!* (1930); *Fifty Million Frenchmen* (1931); *Gold Dust Gertie* (1931); *Hollywood on Parade, A-2* (short, 1932); *Hollywood on Parade, B-13* (short, 1934); *Country Gentlemen* (1937); *All Over Town* (1937); *Hellzapoppin* (1941); *Crazy House* (1943); *Ghost Catchers* (1944); *See My Lawyer* (1945); *It's a Tough Life* (short, 1957).

---

**Our Gang** An ever-changing comedy team comprised of small children, Our Gang began making films in 1922 and continued to do so until 1944. Created by Hal ROACH, very little happened in an Our Gang comedy short; the appeal of the films was based on the characters rather than gags or elaborate chases. The cast changes (as kids grew too old to be cute) also helped reinvigorate the series.

There are two theories behind the creation of the long-running and much-beloved Our Gang group. The first, offered by Hal Roach, was that it was a natural extension of his success with the "Sunshine Sammy" comedies (1921–1922) starring Ernie Morrison, which dealt with the comic adventures of a precocious little child named Sammy. Others believe Our Gang came into being largely due to the unprecedented public interest in Jackie Coogan, the child star of Charlie CHAPLIN's *The Kid* (1921).

Whatever the reason, Hal Roach put together a group of children and began filming one-reel comedies that detailed their antics. The children were chosen by Roach based on their physical appearance rather than their acting ability. Among the first child actors in Our Gang were Joe Cobb, Mary Kornman, Mickey Daniels, Jackie David, Jackie Condon, Farina (Allen Clayton Hoskins), and Pete, the dog with the painted black circle around his right eye.

After sound came in, new cast members were added, including child actors Jackie Cooper, Dickie Moore, and Scotty Beckett, all of whom would later become stars in their own right. They didn't stay with the group for very long, but George Emmett "Spanky" McFarland, Carl "Alfalfa" Switzer, Darla Hood, and Matthew "Stymie" Beard did, forming the core of the group during its golden period in the 1930s. They were supported by Norman "Chubby" Chaney and Bobby "Wheezer" Hutchins. Pete, the dog, was the only constant.

In 1936, an Our Gang comedy, *Bored of Education*, won an Academy Award as the best short of the year. Roach decided to capitalize on the group's popularity by making its one and only feature film that same year, *General Spanky*.

*Our Gang went through a great many cast changes during its two decades of existence, but to audiences, reared on their antics as "The Little Rascals" on TV, they are epitomized by these two young fellows, freckle-faced Carl "Alfalfa" Switzer (left) and pudgy George Emmett "Spanky" McFarland (right).*
PHOTO COURTESY OF THE SIEGEL COLLECTION.

The Our Gang comedies had been distributed by MGM, and in 1938 Hal Roach sold the rights to continue the series to his distributor. MGM churned out the shorts for another six years.

In 1955 Roach sold one hundred of his pre-1938 sound shorts to TV, reintroducing them to a new generation of viewers as "The Little Rascals" (MGM still held the rights to the name "Our Gang").

A new Our Gang movie, called *The Little Rascals*, is tentatively slated for release in the second half of 1994.

---

FILMS INCLUDE: Selected sound shorts: *Free Eats* (1932); *Spanky* (1932); *Bedtime Worries* (1933); *Forgotten Babies* (1933); *For Pete's Sake* (1934); *Honkey Donkey* (1934); *Teacher's Beau* (1935); *Bored of Education* (1936); *Rushin' Ballet* (1937); *Fishy Tales* (1937); *Practical Jokers* (1938); *Captain Spanky's Showboat* (1939); *The Big Premiere* (1940); *Robot Wrecks* (1941); *Going to Press* (1942).
Feature: *General Spanky* (1936).

---

**Oz, Frank (1944—)** A master puppeteer, Frank Oz is also an accomplished actor (though his face is rarely seen on film) and a director with a considerable flair for comedy. Having once collaborated long and well with Jim HENSON, Oz found yet another talent for whom he has an affinity, Steve MARTIN. The director and actor have made three films together: *Little Shop of Horrors* (1986), *Dirty Rotten Scoundrels* (1988), and *Housesitter* (1992). He seems to do well with folks who have a "SATURDAY NIGHT LIVE" background; in addition to Martin, Oz has directed Bill MURRAY in the hit movie *What About Bob?* (1991).

Born Frank Oznowicz in England, he began developing his reputation for talent on TV's "Sesame

*The multi-talented Frank Oz created the Muppets Miss Piggy and Fozzy Bear as well as pulled the strings as the director of films like* Dirty Rotten Scoundrels *(1988) and* What About Bob? *(1991). He is seen here directing yet another hit comedy,* Housesitter *(1992), starring Steve Martin and Goldie Hawn.*
PHOTO BY KERRY HAYES, © UNIVERSAL PICTURES.

Street" and "The Muppet Show." A widely re-spected puppeteer, he created the characters of Miss Piggy and Fozzy Bear, among others, while also providing them with their voices. He received far more attention, however, when it was revealed that he performed the character of Yoda in *The Empire Strikes Back* (1980) and *The Return of the Jedi* (1983). Other small acting roles also came his way, most notably in *The Blues Brothers* (1980), *An American Werewolf in London* (1981), and *Trading Places* (1983).

Anxious to grow and expand as an artist, Oz co-directed (with Jim Henson) *The Dark Crystal* (1982). Based on that experience, Henson turned over the directorial reigns completely to Oz for *The Muppets Take Manhattan* (1984), a film that Oz also scripted. Producer Steven Spielberg gave Oz the opportunity to direct *Little Shop of Horrors*. Despite the poor box office performance of the film, it was well received by critics, and its well-crafted comedy opened the door for Oz's subsequent triumphs.

FILMS INCLUDE: *The Blues Brothers* (a, 1980); *The Empire Strikes Back* (a, 1980); *An American Werewolf in London* (a, 1981); *The Great Muppet Caper* (a, p, 1981); *The Dark Crystal* (a, co-d, 1982); *Return of the Jedi* (a, 1983); *Trading Places* (a, 1983); *The Muppets Take Manhattan* (a, sc, d, 1984); *Sesame Street Presents: Follow That Bird* (a, 1985); *Spies Like Us* (a, 1985); *Labyrinth* (a, 1986); *Little Shop of Horrors* (d, 1986); *Dirty Rotten Scoundrels* (d, 1988); *What About Bob?* (d, 1991); *Housesitter* (d, 1992).

# P

**Pangborn, Franklin (1893—1958)** In a long career as a comic supporting player, often as hotel clerks, waiters, and bureaucrats, Franklin Pangborn was Hollywood's premier supercilious fussbudget. He could always be counted on to look down his nose (grimacing haughtily) at the hero or heroine, while neatly spinning a few lines of comically derogatory dialogue. Although he appeared in scores of films throughout the 1930s and 1940s, many of them major hits, he is best remembered as W. C. FIELDS's humorous antagonist in *The Bank Dick* (1940) and *Never Give a Sucker an Even Break* (1941) as well as for his consistently funny work as a member of Preston STURGES's comic stock company during the early 1940s.

Born in Newark, New Jersey, Pangborn came from a well-to-do family that frowned upon his show business aspirations. He did well, despite their disapproval, becoming a respected stage actor, often in (believe it or not) villainous roles. The future Mr. Prissy of the movies actually played the evil Messala in the theatrical production of *Ben Hur*—and got raves from the critics.

As a stage actor in Los Angeles, Pangborn dabbled in the movies during the silent era. It wasn't until talkies arrived, however, that audiences began discovering his talent for getting laughs. He starred in two-reel comedies for several years, which led to modest supporting roles in major features such as the all-star *International House* (1933), Ernest LU-BITSCH's *Design for Living* (1933), and Frank CAPRA's *Mr. Deeds Goes to Town* (1936). It was his comically snooty character in *My Man Godfrey* (1936), though, that finally established his comic persona. He played that kind of character until the end of the 1940s, when he stopped making movies.

Film's loss was TV's gain. Pangborn starred in his own TV series called "Myrt and Marge." He returned to the movies just one last time, in 1957, for a small role in the all-star *The Story of Mankind*.

FILMS INCLUDE: *Getting Gertie's Garter* (1927); *The Cradle Snatchers* (1927); *The Night Bride* (1927); *A Blonde for a Night* (1928); *My Friend from India* (1928); *The Sap* (1929); *Lady of the Pavements* (1929); *Not So Dumb* (1930); *International House* (1933); *Design for Living* (1933); *Flying Down to Rio* (1933); *Cockeyed Cavaliers* (1934); *College Rhythm* (1934); *Mr. Deeds Goes to Town* (1936); *My Man Godfrey* (1936); *It Happened in Hollywood* (1937); *Stage Door* (1937); *A Star Is Born* (1937); *Bluebeard's Eighth Wife* (1938); *Vivacious Lady* (1938); *Carefree* (1938); *Just Around the Corner* (1938); *Topper Takes a Trip* (1939); *Fifth Avenue Girl* (1939); *Christmas in July* (1940); *The Bank Dick* (1940); *Sullivan's Travels* (1941); *Never Give a Sucker an Even Break* (1941); *The Palm Beach Story* (1942); *Now, Voyager* (1942); *Crazy House* (1943); *Hail the Conquering Hero* (1944); *The Great Moment* (1944); *The Horn Blows at Midnight* (1945); *Two Guys from Milwaukee* (1946); *Mad Wednesday* (1947); *My Dream Is Yours* (1949); *The Story of Mankind* (1957).

**parody films** During the last couple of decades, parodies of famous films and film genres have proliferated. Mel BROOKS began the modern trend with

*Movie parodies have become increasingly popular on the big screen; there are at least three released per year. Among the more successful in this happily derivative subgenre have been* Hot Shots *(1991) and its sequel, shown above,* Hot Shots! Part Deux *(1993), both starring Charlie Sheen.*
PHOTO BY BRUCE BIRMELIN, © 20TH CENTURY-FOX.

the Western parody *Blazing Saddles* (1974) and the horror spoof *Young Frankenstein* (1974). It was also Brooks who established the unwritten rule of such parodies: anything for a laugh!

Brooks got the parody ball rolling, but others stepped up to keep it rolling. *Airplane!* (1980), by Jim ABRAHAMS, David ZUCKER, and Jerry ZUCKER, sent the parody form flying (literally) in what many consider to be the funniest genre sendup in Hollywood history. The threesome, together and individually, have continued to make fun of recent hit films

with a parody of *Top Gun* (1986) called *Hot Shots* (1991), a parody of the *Rambo* films called *Hot Shots, Part Deux* (1993), and cop sendups *Naked Gun* (1988) and *Naked Gun 2½* (1991). Other filmmakers have also gotten into the act, with films like the *Lethal Weapon* parody *Loaded Weapon I* (1993).

The concept of parodying popular movies is not new; it actually goes back to the silent era. Cross-eyed comic Ben TURPIN, for instance, had his greatest success during the 1920s spoofing current hit films. Turpin's hilarious takeoff on Rudolph Valentino's *The Sheik* (1921) was called *The Shriek of Araby* (1923).

Turpin wasn't the only successful parodist; even little Shirley Temple, before she became a child star in sentimental musicals, scored a hit as a three-year-old in "Baby Burlesks," a series of one-reel sendups of famous features in the early 1930s.

The fact that parody has made a comeback in the last twenty years speaks volumes about our love affair with the movies. The intensity with which we identify with certain movies and their conventions is the wellspring of the parodist's humor. If we didn't care, we wouldn't get the jokes.

**Pendleton, Austin (1940—)** An effective and memorable comic supporting actor in films since 1968, Austin Pendleton has emerged as a highly respected director for the stage. Slightly built, wearing glasses, he has a scholarly look about him. In later years, he has taken to a more disheveled appearance, like a nerd gone wild. With a whiny, singsong quality to his voice, he often seems like a very intelligent child-man.

To a large degree, Pendleton has plied his acting trade in contemporary films, with large budgets, name stars, and hot directors. Like the characters he usually plays, the films he appears in are generally smart and sophisticated, such as *Catch-22* (1970), *Starting Over* (1979), *Simon* (1980), *Mr. and Mrs. Bridge* (1990), and *Searching for Bobby Fischer* (1993). Even when the films tend to be lowbrow, like *The Great Smokey Roadblock* (1976) and *First Family*

(1980), he can be counted upon to be playing an upscale buffoon. In most of his films, his roles are rather small.

---

**FILMS INCLUDE:** *Skidoo* (1968); *Catch-22* (1970); *Every Little Crook and Nanny* (1972); *What's Up, Doc?* (1972); *The Thief Who Came to Dinner* (1973); *The Front Page* (1974); *The Great Smokey Roadblock* (1976); *The Muppet Movie* (1979); *Starting Over* (1979); *Simon* (1980); *First Family* (1980); *Talk to Me* (1982); *My Man Adam* (1985); *Short Circuit* (1986); *Off Beat* (1986); *Hello Again* (1987); *Mr. and Mrs. Bridge* (1990); *My Cousin Vinny* (1992); *Searching for Bobby Fischer* (1993); *Guarding Tess* (1994).

---

## Perelman, S. J. (1904—1979)

A popular literary humorist who wrote short stories, novels, and plays, S. J. Perelman also wrote a significant number of screenplays. Although he shared an Oscar for best screenplay adaptation for *Around the World in 80 Days* (1956), the Hollywood work with which he is most associated is the MARX BROTHERS films *Monkey Business* (1931) and *Horse Feathers* (1932).

Born Sidney Joseph Perelman in Brooklyn, New York, he was a graduate of Brown University. On the strength of his first book, a hit comic trifle published in 1929 called *Dawn Ginsbergh's Revenge*, he was hired to help out with the two Marx Brothers scripts. Perelman's acerbic, witty style meshed well with Groucho's—perhaps too well. Many years later, Groucho would bristle when Perelman was given credit for writing lines that Groucho said were his own. In any event, Perelman worked on and off in Hollywood, almost always in collaboration with one writer or another, including his wife, Laura, who happened to be a sibling of novelist Nathanael West.

Few of Perelman's scripts after his two for the Marx Brothers were of any special note. His particular dry, intellectual wordplays were really best suited for Groucho, and few actors could make it work for

them. One of his best later films wasn't an original screenplay, but rather another writer's 1948 adaptation of his stage show, *A Touch of Venus*.

---

**FILMS INCLUDE:** *Monkey Business* (1931); *Horse Feathers* (1932); *Sitting Pretty* (1933); *Florida Special* (1936); *Early to Bed* (1936); *Boy Trouble* (1939); *Ambush* (1939); *The Golden Fleecing* (1940); *One Touch of Venus* (based on play, 1948); *Around the World in 80 Days* (1956).

---

**pie in the face** The first pie thrown for comic effect was in *A Noise from the Deep* (1913), a Mack SENNETT film made at the Keystone Studio. Departing from the script, Mabel NORMAND threw a pie in Fatty ARBUCKLE's face, creating a comic bit of business that has become a hallowed institution in SLAPSTICK film comedy.

It is generally accepted that the custard pie was the dessert of choice for throwing in actors' faces. In fact, the custard pies used in silent comedies weren't made of custard at all. They were blackberry pies, which showed up better in black and white films. Genuine custard pies came into vogue later.

The pie in the face made the transition from the silent era to talkies rather well, finding use in 1930s films starring LAUREL AND HARDY and the THREE STOOGES. In more recent decades, pies have been tossed in movies such as *Beach Party* (1963), *The Great Race* (1964), and *Blind Date* (1987).

---

## Pitts, ZaSu (1898—1963)

During the sound era, ZaSu Pitts had a long and prosperous career as a scatterbrained cuckoo, playing comic relief in major feature films. At the same time, she also co-starred in a great many low-budget comedy shorts and features. To the surprise of many who only know her talkie work, she was also one of Hollywood's most intensely dramatic actresses during the silent era.

ZaSu was given her memorable name at birth in Parsons, Kansas; it was created by combining the last two letters of *Eliza* and the first two letters of *Susan*, her father's sisters.

Pitts had the good fortune to break into the movie business in a Mary Pickford film, *The Little Princess* (1917). Audiences took to her and she worked steadily thereafter in a variety of genres, including adventures, comedies, and romances. Her claim to fame during the silent era, however, was her association with Erich von Stroheim in two of his most ambitious, artful films, *Greed* (1924) and *The Wedding March* (1928). Known for serious drama, she had also starred as the female lead in the silent version of *All Quiet on the Western Front* (1930), but she was replaced by Beryl Mercer for the sound version.

Pitts appeared in supporting roles in a number of serious movies, such as *Bad Sister* (1931) and *Back Street* (1932), but her forte during the rest of her career was comedy. She played ditsy characters in films such as Ernst LUBITSCH's *Monte Carlo* (1930), *Love, Honor, and Oh Baby!* (1933), *Mrs. Wiggs of the Cabbage Patch* (1934), *Ruggles of Red Gap* (1935), *52nd Street* (1937), and *So's Your Aunt Emma* (1942).

During the 1930s Pitts worked with comedian Thelma TODD in a successful series of comedy shorts and played the comic love interest to Slim SUMMERVILLE in a rash of B-movie comedies.

In the late 1940s she surprised audiences with her restrained character performance in *Life with Father* (1947), but she went on to appear in just a handful of films during the 1950s and early 1960s. She occupied herself instead with television, appearing in support of Gale Storm in her series "Oh, Susanna" between 1956 and 1959. Pitts's last movie appearance was in the all-star comedy film IT'S A MAD MAD MAD MAD WORLD (1963).

---

FILMS INCLUDE: *The Little Princess* (1917); *A Modern Musketeer* (1917); *Rebecca of Sunnybrook Farm* (1917); *Poor Relations* (1919); *Better Times* (1919); *The Other Half* (1919); *Bright Skies* (1920); *Patsy* (1921); *Is Matrimony a Failure?* (1922); *For the Defense* (1922); *Poor Men's Wives* (1923); *Tea, with a Kick* (1923); *Three Wise Fools* (1923); *Greed* (1924); *The Goldfish* (1924); *Daughters of Today* (1924); *Triumph* (1924); *Changing Husbands* (1924); *The Legend of Hollywood* (1924); *The Fast Set* (1924); *A Woman's Faith* (1925); *Wages for Wives* (1925); *Pretty Ladies* (1925); *Lazybones* (1925); *Thunder Mountain* (1925); *Monte Carlo* (1926); *Mannequin* (1926); *Early to Wed* (1926); *Sunny Side Up* (1926); *Her Big Night* (1926); *Casey at the Bat* (1927); *Buck Privates* (1928); *The Wedding March* (1928); *Sins of the Fathers* (1928); *Wife Savers* (1928); *The Dummy* (1929); *Twin Beds* (1929); *Paris* (1929); *This Thing Called Love* (1929); *Oh Yeah!* (1929); *No No Nanette* (1930); *All Quiet on the Western Front* (silent version only, 1930); *Honey* (1930); *Monte Carlo* (1930); *The Lottery Bride* (1930); *River's End* (1930); *Finn and Hattie* (1931); *Bad Sister* (1931); *Seed* (1931); *Beyond Victory* (1931); *The Guardsman* (1931); *The Unexpected Father* (1932); *Make Me a Star* (1932); *Back Street* (1932); *Destry Rides Again* (1932); *Blondie of the Follies* (1932); *Once in a Lifetime* (1932); *They Just Had to Get Married* (1933); *Aggie Appleby, Maker of Men* (1933); *Out All Night* (1933); *Professional Sweetheart* (1933); *Meet the Baron* (1933); *Her First Mate* (1933); *Love Honor and Oh Baby!* (1933); *Mr. Skitch* (1933); *Love Birds* (1934); *The Meanest Gal in Town* (1934); *Three on a Honeymoon* (1934); *Dames* (1934); *Private Scandal* (1934); *Sing and Like It* (1934); *Their Big Moment* (1934); *Mrs. Wiggs of the Cabbage Patch* (1934); *The Gay Bride* (1934); *Ruggles of Red Gap* (1935); *Spring Tonic* (1935); *Hot Tip* (1935); *Going Highbrow* (1935); *Mad Holiday* (1936); *The Plot Thickens* (1936); *13 Hours by Air* (1936); *Forty Naughty Girls* (1937); *52nd Street* (1937); *Eternally Yours* (1939); *Naughty but Nice* (1939); *Mickey the Kid* (1939); *Nurse Edith Cavell* (1939); *It All Came True* (1940); *No No Nanette* (remake, 1940); *Mexican Spitfire's Baby* (1941); *Miss Polly* (1941); *Broadway Limited* (1941); *So's Your Aunt Emma* (1942); *Tish* (1942); *Mexican Spitfire at Sea* (1942); *Let's Face It* (1943); *Breakfast in Hollywood* (1945); *Life with Father* (1947); *The Perfect Marriage* (1947); *Francis* (1950); *The Denver and the Rio Grande* (1952); *Francis Joins the WACS* (1954); *This Could Be the Night* (1957); *Teenage Millionaire*

(1961); *The Thrill of it All* (1963); *It's a Mad Mad Mad Mad World* (1963).

---

**political humor** It is generally assumed that political comedies are the equivalent of box office cyanide. Not true. Like any other movie, if a political comedy can tap into the deeply felt attitudes of an audience, it can come up a winner.

In 1933 the worst year of the Great Depression, there were two political comedies: the fantasy *Gabriel Over the White House* (1933) and the Marx Brothers' classic DUCK SOUP (1933). The former is a wild and wooly tale of a crook who becomes president, only to undergo a transformation, turning into a virtual messiah who attempts to save the world. That was the hopeful comedy. *Duck Soup* was the anarchic vision of politics simply gone (comically) mad. Neither of these movies was a hit at the time of its release.

Later in the decade, *Mr. Smith Goes to Washington* (1939) exposed corruption in the U.S. Senate. Official Washington was outraged at the suggestion that such a thing was possible. Of course, the moviegoing public knew better and flocked to see the Frank CAPRA film.

A darker version of *Gabriel Over the White House* was Preston STURGES' *The GREAT MCGINTY* (1940). Once again, a crook rises in politics to a very high position, only to turn to goodness. In this case, however, his one honest moment brings his doom. Audiences responded to the comedy because it was dead on, capturing the corruption of the system while being acutely observant of human character.

With war already burning across Europe, times were turbulent in 1940. Some films, like *The Great McGinty*, looked to the shortcomings of American institutions, while others looked across the sea. Charlie CHAPLIN did the latter with his brilliant sendup of fascism in general, and Hitler in particular, in *The Great Dictator* (1940). The movie was also the first in which Chaplin spoke and was one of the biggest hits of the year. Chaplin wasn't the only one

making fun of Hitler, either. Moe Howard, of the THREE STOOGES, often played a bumbling Hitler in short comedies during the war.

From the end of World War II until the early 1960s, political comedies virtually disappeared. The red scare of the late 1940s and early 1950s put the fear of Joe McCarthy into many a filmmaker and distributor. Why risk a political comedy when it could so easily be misconstrued as an attack on the government? At the beginning of that era, Frank Capra returned to political comedy with *State of the Union* (1948), which was as much about a husband and wife as it was about politics. The same could be said for *Kisses for My President* (1964), which came at the end of that era and in the same year as the film that finally opened the door in a big way to political comedy: DR. STRANGELOVE (1964). This bleak BLACK COMEDY found its audience in young filmgoers who feared for their safety and their lives. Nuclear war never seemed more possible than during the 1962 Cuban Missile Crisis, and *Dr. Strangelove or: How I Learned to Stop Worrying and Love the Bomb* tapped into that fear with comic gusto.

Political comedies that don't tap into viewers' concerns tend not to work. The political trappings aren't enough to sustain a comedy unless there is some satiric meat when one is chewing on the political bone. For instance, *First Family* (1980), a silly comedy with a terrific cast, was left adrift in a TV sitcom-style film because it wasn't about anything except its jokes. On the other hand, two recent political comedies, *Bob Roberts* (1992) and *Dave* (1993), both hit paydirt because they struck a nerve in the audience. Written and directed by and starring Tim Robbins, *Bob Roberts* worked because it was such a richly detailed SATIRE of a right-wing political campaign, and liberals hadn't ever seen anything like it, except in their worst nightmares. As for *Dave*, it was a modern version of *Mr. Smith Goes to Washington*, acknowledging the deep corruption of the system, but suggesting that average people could still overcome it. In this instance, especially, the political comedy zeroed in on what many resent in government, made fun of it at every turn, and then provided viewers with a credible comic ordinary hero.

## Pollard, Harry "Snub" (1886–1962)

An ordinary-looking man in every other way during his silent screen heyday, Harry "Snub" Pollard sported a huge, drooping, Fu Manchu mustache. As did so many silent screen comics, Pollard had a doleful appearance. He played put-upon husbands and misunderstood workers who eventually got out of jams through one sort of comic invention or another. A modest star of two-reel comedies during the late 1910s and the better part of the 1920s, Pollard was already fading in popularity when talkies came in. Nonetheless, he managed to hang on in the sound era right through to his death in 1962, although after the 1930s, he appeared mostly in bit parts.

Born Harold Frazer in Melbourne, Australia, Pollard received his early show business training in VAUDEVILLE down under. He came to the United States with a singing group called the Pollard Light Opera Company. The group got considerably lighter when Pollard quit them to join the movie business.

Pollard can be seen in a few of Charlie CHAPLIN's early shorts, but his first serious success as a comedian came as a supporting player in Harold LLOYD's

*He of the drooping mustache, "Snub" Pollard was a star of two-reel comedies during the latter half of the silent era. He is seen here in the short* California or Bust *(1923).* PHOTO COURTESY OF THE SIEGEL COLLECTION.

Lonesome Luke series between 1915 and 1919. Producer Hal ROACH liked what he saw in Pollard and gave him his own series, which ran until the mid-1920s when the comic star left to go out on his own. Unfortunately, he flopped, and his career never fully recovered.

Pollard did little of comic note during the thirty-odd years he worked in talkies, yet he was clearly admired by those with whom he had worked or who appreciated the silent screen art. Among those who gave him work in his later years were Preston STURGES in *The Beautiful Blonde from Bashful Bend* (1949), Jerry LEWIS in *Rock-a-Bye Baby* (1958) and *The Errand Boy* (1961), and Frank CAPRA in *Pocketful of Miracles* (1961). Perhaps most memorably, and poignantly, he can be seen playing the violin, along with Buster KEATON at the piano, in the famous music hall performance scene at the end of Chaplin's *Limelight* (1951).

FILMS INCLUDE: Shorts: *Lonesome Luke: Gangster* (1915); *Luke Laughs Last* (1916); *The Flirt* (1917); *Bliss* (1917); *The Big Idea* (1918); *The Lamb* (1918); *Captain Kidd's Kids* (1919); *His Royal Slyness* (1919); *All at Sea* (1919); *It's a Hard Life* (1919); *Tough Luck* (1919); *Looking for Trouble* (1919); *How Dry I Am* (1919); *The Dippy Dentist* (1920); *Getting His Goat* (1920); *Red Hot Hottentots* (1920); *Don't Weaken* (1920); *Insulting the Sultan* (1920); *A London Bobby* (1920); *Money to Burn* (1920); *The Hustler* (1921); *The High Rollers* (1921); *The Morning After* (1921); *Hocus-Pocus* (1921); *His Best Girl* (1921); *Law and Order* (1921); *Big Game* (1921); *Down and Out* (1922); *Pardon Me* (1922); *In the Movies* (1922); *Stage Struck* (1922); *The Dumb Bell* (1922); *Nearly Rich* (1922); *Hook, Line and Sinker* (1922); *The Courtship of Miles Sandwich* (1923); *It's a Gift* (1923); *A Tough Winter* (1923); *Jack Frost* (1923); *California or Bust* (1923); *The Mystery Man* (1923); *Why Marry?* (1924); *The Big Idea* (1924); *Are Husbands Human?* (1925); *The Doughboy* (also p, 1926); *The Yokel* (also p, 1926); *The Bum's Rush* (also p, 1927).

Features: *Ex-Flame* (1930); *East Lynne* (1931); *The Purchase Price* (1932); *Cockeyed Cavaliers* (1934);

*Stingaree* (1934); *The Gentleman from Louisiana* (1936); *White Legion* (1936); *Arizona Days* (1937); *Riders of the Rockies* (1937); *Frontier Town* (1938); *The Perils of Pauline* (1947); *The Crooked Way* (1949); *The Beautiful Blonde from Bashful Bend* (1949); *Limelight* (1951); *Man of a Thousand Faces* (1957); *Rock-a-Bye Baby* (1958); *Who Was That Lady?* (1960); *Pocketful of Miracles* (1961); *The Errand Boy* (1961).

**Pollard, Michael J. (1939—)** Small and goofy-looking, with a Silly Putty face, Michael J. Pollard plays characters that can be endearingly naive and raucously funny at the same time. Pollard came to fame as C. W. Moss, the comically inept getaway driver in *Bonnie and Clyde* (1967). He was nominated for a best supporting actor Academy Award for the role. For a brief time he rode the crest of his celebrity with leading roles in offbeat films like *Little Fauss and Big Halsy* (1970) and *Dirty Little Billy* (1972). When fans didn't line up to see him, he soon fell back to supporting and featured parts, often playing characters who are either a little larcenous, a little murderous, or just plain nuts.

Born Michael J. Pollack in Passaic, New Jersey, he studied his craft at The Actors Studio. Pollard worked on the stage, but found work early on in the movies, making his film debut in a small role in *Hemingway's Adventures of a Young Man* (1962). He knocked around Hollywood for five years before his breakthrough in *Bonnie and Clyde*, finding his most rewarding work during that period in the Roger Corman film *The Wild Angels* (1966).

He was in a couple of comedies, *Enter Laughing* (1966) and *Caprice* (1967), before his run at fame, but he played comedy, or at least for a comic effect, in most of his films during the 1970s and beyond. For instance, he is quite slimy and funny in the otherwise full-tilt action movie *Split Second* (1992).

FILMS INCLUDE: *Hemingway's Adventures of a Young Man* (1962); *The Stripper* (1963); *Summer Magic*

*Michael J. Pollard reached his greatest level of fame during the late 1960s and early 1970s, but he has continued to work to comic effect (and with considerable frequency) during the late 1980s and early 1990s in quirky featured roles.*

PHOTO COURTESY OF MOVIE STAR NEWS.

(1963); *The Wild Angels* (1966); *Enter Laughing* (1966); *Caprice* (1967); *Bonnie and Clyde* (1967); *Hannibal Brooks* (1968); *Jigsaw* (1968); *Little Fauss and Big Halsy* (1970); *The Legend of Frenchie King* (1971); *Dirty Little Billy* (1972); *Vengeance Is Mine* (1976); *Between the Lines* (1977); *Melvin and Howard* (1980); *America* (1982); *Heated Vengeance* (1985); *The American Way* (1986); *The Patriot* (1986); *Riders of the Storm* (1987); *American Gothic* (1987); *Roxanne* (1987); *Scrooged* (1988); *Next of Kin* (1989); *Fast Food* (1989); *Season of Fear* (1989); *Sleepaway Camp III: Teenage Wasteland* (1989); *Tango and Cash* (1989); *Night Visitor* (1989); *Enid Is Sleeping* (1990); *I Come in Peace* (1990); *Dick Tracy* (1990); *The Art of Dying* (1991); *Split Second* (1992); *Skeeter* (1992); *Motorama* (1992).

**Porky Pig**   *See* WARNER BROS. CARTOONS

**pratfall**   Nearly a lost art, *pratfall* is the comic term for landing on one's hind quarters without injury. There was hardly a silent comedian who didn't perform pratfalls. Before the coming of sound, physical humor was especially highly prized, and its practioners, such as Charlie CHAPLIN, Buster KEATON, and Fatty ARBUCKLE, were among those who took pratfalls with the greatest comical grace.

Viewed today as lowbrow humor, most modernday comic actors shy away from such antics, although Chevy CHASE has been known to take a pratfall every now and then.

**Prentiss, Paula (1939—)**   In the 1960s, Paula Prentiss was at her apex as a screwball comedian. She possessed presence, beauty, and a quick-witted intelligence. Famed SCREWBALL COMEDY director Howard HAWKS had seen her potential and cast her in *Man's Favorite Sport?* (1964). Prentiss's career never fully blossomed, however. Her popular period consisted of generally light ROMANTIC COMEDIES like *Bachelor in Paradise* (1962) and *The Horizontal Lieutenant* (1963).

Born Paula Ragusa in San Antonio, Texas, Prentiss went to college at Northwestern University, but barely had time to frame a diploma before she was making her film debut in *Where the Boys Are* (1961). Films of the same nature—aimed at the teen market—followed, but by the middle of the decade, she worked her way into larger films such as *The World of Henry Orient* (1964) and the John Wayne movie *In Harm's Way* (1965). Her career should have taken off when she appeared in a leading role in the biggest comedy hit in Hollywood history, *What's New, Pussycat?* (1965). However, a desire to work with her husband, actor Richard BENJAMIN, led them both to put aside their movie careers to work side by side in the sophisticated TV sitcom "He and She." Critically acclaimed, the show hit the airwaves in 1967; the Nielsen families didn't care who liked it, and the show never made it to 1968.

Later, Prentiss and Benjamin would work together in films many times, with roles in *Catch-22*

(1970), *Saturday the 14th* (1981), and *Packin' It In* (1982). Besides her work with Benjamin, she was in a number of hit films during the 1970s, but the attention always seemed to fall on someone else in the production, or else the quality movie was somehow missed (or avoided) by the public. Among her better films were *Born to Win* (1971), *Last of the Red Hot Lovers* (1972), *The Parallax View* (1974), and *The Stepford Wives* (1975).

---

**FILMS INCLUDE:** *Where the Boys Are* (1961); *The Honeymoon Machine* (1962); *Bachelor in Paradise* (1962); *The Horizontal Lieutenant* (1963); *Man's Favorite Sport?* (1964); *Looking for Love* (1964); *The World of Henry Orient* (1964); *In Harm's Way* (1965); *What's New Pussycat?* (1965); *Catch-22* (1970); *Move* (1970); *Born to Win* (1971); *Last of the Red Hot Lovers* (1972); *Crazy Joe* (1973); *The Parallax View* (1974); *The Stepford Wives* (1975); *The Black Marble* (1980); *Buddy, Buddy* (1981); *Saturday the 14th* (1981); *Packin' It In* (1982).

---

**The Producers** The first feature-length film from Mel BROOKS was *The Producers*, the 1968 movie that introduced him as a formidable comedy writer and director. It was also the wildly irreverent film that boasted the classic bad-taste musical production number "Springtime for Hitler," which also happened to be the original title of the film.

Brooks, who had tried his hand unsuccessfully as a playwright, had his revenge on the theater in this much-beloved cult favorite. *The Producers* tells the tale of a down-and-out theatrical producer, Max Bialystock (Zero MOSTEL), who convinces a timid accountant, Leo Bloom (Gene WILDER), to join him in a scam to sell investors 25,000 percent of a play. When the play fails, they intend to keep all the money. Of course, the play *has* to fail for them to get away with their scheme, so to ensure that result, Bialystock and Bloom go to extraordinary comic lengths to make sure that their production will be a bust—they buy the worst play imaginable, hire the

most pretentious director, and then hire a bizarre, aging hippie as their star. Of course, audiences go wild for the show and turn it into a hit. Our comic heroes go to jail where, naturally, they're last seen putting on a prison play and overselling their stock in it.

The movie was fresh and original, but not altogether successful when it was first released. Critics were divided, but word of mouth from laughter-convulsed fans eventually turned *The Producers* into a moneymaker. More credibility for the film came in the form of a best supporting actor Academy Award nomination for Gene Wilder. It was really a co-starring role, but he was nothing short of brilliant in it. It was this film that turned Wilder into a comic star. Brooks won a best original screenplay Oscar for his hilarious script.

The principal players in *The Producers* were Zero Mostel, Gene Wilder, Kenneth Mars, Dick Shawn, Lee Meredith, Christopher Hewett, Andreas Voustinas, Estelle Windwood, Renee Taylor, and William Hickey.

Without question, this film offered Dick Shawn, as the star of the play within the movie, the best role of his film career. If Gene Wilder and Zero Mostel hadn't been so funny, Shawn would have totally stolen the movie. As it is, he only stole the scenes he was in. As for Brooks, he didn't appear in the film (one of the rare times that would ever happen in one of his comedies), but his voice can be heard, as it was dubbed into the "Springtime for Hitler" musical extravaganza.

**Pryor, Richard (1940–)** Projecting a comic machismo while at the same time showing abject fear, Richard Pryor was the leading black comic actor of the late 1970s and early 1980s. During his time at the top he eventually wrote, directed, produced, and starred in films, although rarely performing all of those functions at one time.

Born in Peoria, Illinois, and raised by his grandmother, who ran a brothel, Pryor rose to fame as a nightclub and TV comic during the 1960s. He parlayed that success into a number of small movie roles in films such as *The Busy Body* (1968), *You've Got to Walk It Like You Talk It or You'll Lose That Beat* (1971), and *Dynamite Chicken* (1972). He had played mostly comic turns in his early films, but when he played the more serious supporting role of Piano Man in the biography of Billie Holiday, *Lady Sings the Blues* (1972), Pryor was honored with a best supporting actor Oscar nomination.

Pryor appeared in the highly regarded documentary *Wattstax* (1973), supported Sidney Poitier and Bill COSBY in the hit *Uptown Saturday Night* (1974), and showed his screenwriting ability by co-scripting (with Mel BROOKS) *Blazing Saddles* (1974) before finally hitting it big as a star in his own right in the second half of the 1970s. His breakthrough film was *The Bingo Long Travelling All-Stars and Motor Kings* (1976). In that same year, he began his long and mutually rewarding relationship with fellow comic actor Gene WILDER. The first of their four films together, *Silver Streak* (1976), was a major comedy hit. They hit it big again with *Stir Crazy* (1980). The duo tried to resurrect the magic twice more with *See No Evil, Hear No Evil* (1989) and *Another You* (1991) with considerably less success.

During the late 1970s and early 1980s, however, Pryor was on a roll, garnering critical and box office success with films like *Blue Collar* (1978), *Richard Pryor—Live in Concert* (1979), and *Richard Pryor Live on the Sunset Strip* (1982).

Pryor was among the biggest box office draws in Hollywood until he accidentally set himself on fire in a drug-related accident. Badly burned, Pryor set about to reclaim his health and career. He did well with the former, but had mixed results with the latter. Movies such as *Bustin' Loose* (1981), which he co-produced and wrote the story for, and *Some Kind of Hero* (1982) were solid successes. Then he faltered with two major bombs in a row, *The Toy* (1982) and *Superman III* (1983), the latter film paying him a cool $4 million, a testament to his drawing power.

Pryor's box office appeal remained strong enough to allow him to bring to the screen an autobiographical film he starred in, co-scripted, directed, and produced, *Jo Jo Dancer, Your Life Is Calling* (1986). The film received mixed reviews from the critics, but brought him renewed attention as a serious filmmaker. In recent years, however, his films lacked the inspired satiric anger and energy of his best work of the late 1970s, and he settled for making minor comedies such as *Critical Condition* (1987) and *Moving* (1988). During filming of the former he discovered he had multiple sclerosis. The acceleration of the disease, along with a series of heart attacks, has left the once fierce comedian in considerably poor health.

---

**FILMS:** *The Busy Body* (1967); *Wild in the Streets* (1968); *The Phynx* (1970); *You've Got to Walk It Like You Talk It or You'll Lose That Beat* (1971); *Dynamite Chicken* (1972); *Lady Sings the Blues* (1972); *Wattstax* (1972); *Hit* (1973); *The Mack* (1973); *Some Call It Loving* (1973); *Blazing Saddles* (sc only, 1974); *Uptown Saturday Night* (1974); *Adios Amigo* (1976); *The Bingo Long Traveling All-Stars and Motor Kings* (1976); *Car Wash* (1976); *Silver Streak* (1976); *Greased Lightning* (1977); *Which Way Is Up?* (1977); *Blue Collar* (1978); *California Suite* (1978); *The Wiz* (1978); *The Muppet Movie* (1979); *Richard Pryor— Live in Concert* (also sc, 1979); *In God We Trust* (1980); *Stir Crazy* (1980); *Wholly Moses!* (1980); *Bustin' Loose* (also story, p, 1981); *Richard Pryor Live on the Sunset Strip* (also sc, p, 1982); *Some Kind of Hero* (1982); *The Toy* (1982); *Richard Pryor Here and Now* (also sc, d, 1983); *Superman III* (1983); *Brewster's Millions* (1985); *Richard Pryor Live and Smokin'* (also sc, 1985); *Jo Jo Dancer, Your Life Is Calling* (also sc, p, d, 1986); *Critical Condition* (1987); *Moving* (1988); *Harlem Nights* (1989); *See No Evil, Hear No Evil* (1989); *Another You* (1991).

# R

**Radner, Gilda (1947—1989)** A gifted comedian, Gilda Radner was one of the original Not Ready For Prime Time Players on "SATURDAY NIGHT LIVE" who went to Hollywood to pursue a movie career. Cute rather than pretty, Radner had a sweet face and an impish quality, but she was also a very fine comic actress who, unfortunately, did not have enough time to make her mark; she became ill with ovarian cancer and, after a long and public fight with the disease, died in 1989.

Radner was married to actor/director Gene WILDER from 1984 until her death, and the two of them appeared in three films together: *Hanky Panky* (1982), *The Woman in Red* (1984), and *Haunted Honeymoon* (1986). None of them were big box office draws, although *The Woman in Red* (a remake of the French *Pardon Mon Affaire*) was the best of the mediocre lot. The film that perhaps best captures her spirit is her concert film *Gilda Live* (1980).

Before Radner's death, she published her autobiography, *It's Always Something*, the ironic title taken from her "Saturday Night Live" character Rosanne Rosannadanna's famous catchphrase.

---

**FILMS:** *Mr. Mike's Mondo Video* (1979); *First Family* (1980); *Gilda Live* (1980); *Hanky Panky* (1982); *It Came from Hollywood* (1982); *The Woman in Red* (1984); *Movers and Shakers* (1985); *Haunted Honeymoon* (1986).

---

**Ramis, Harold (1944— )** Although he has written, directed, and sometimes produced and acted in many of the most popular comedies since the late 1970s, Harold Ramis remains surprisingly little known among filmgoers. He should be as heralded as Ivan REITMAN, with whom he has often collaborated, because he has been a veritable hit machine after co-scripting the first $100 million box office comedy hit *National Lampoon's Animal House* (1978). If he has worked well with Ivan Reitman behind the camera, he has worked best with Bill MURRAY in front of the camera. Murray has starred in six of Ramis's films, including his most accomplished to date, the warm, intelligent, and creative *Groundhog Day* (1993). Prolific and surprisingly consistent, Ramis's films are sophomoric humor at its best.

Born in Chicago, Illinois, he got his start in comedy as the jokes editor of *Playboy* magazine. In 1969, he joined Chicago's Second City improvisational theater troupe, soon moving on to write and perform in *The National Lampoon Show* in New York. Beginning in 1976, Ramis was the head writer as well as a regular performer on "SCTV."

While *Animal House* gave Ramis his entrée into the movies, it was *Caddyshack* (1980) that proved his directorial flair. Unlike most other writer/directors, however, Ramis doesn't always direct his own material. He has written some of his most successful scripts for other directors, most notably Ivan Reitman, who directed his two *Ghostbusters* scripts into megahits (1984 and 1989). On the other hand, he has also directed films that he has not written, most notable among them *National Lampoon's Vacation* (1983).

Ramis has always had the urge to perform, but he has not developed a following despite an attractive, pleasing manner. In addition to supporting roles in his own films, he was hired strictly for his acting for *Baby Boom* (1987) and *Stealing Home* (1988).

---

FILMS INCLUDE: *National Lampoon's Animal House* (co-sc, 1978); *Meatballs* (sc, 1979); *Caddyshack* (sc, d, 1980); *Heavy Metal* (a, 1981); *Stripes* (a, co-sc, 1981); *National Lampoon's Vacation* (d, 1983); *Ghostbusters* (a, co-sc, 1984); *Armed and Dangerous* (story, sc, p, 1986); *Back to School* (sc, p, 1986); *Club Paradise* (sc, d, 1986); *Baby Boom* (a, 1987); *Stealing Home* (a, 1988); *Caddyshack II* (sc, 1988); *Ghostbusters II* (a, co-sc, 1989); *Groundhog Day* (a, co-sc, co-p, d, 1993).

---

**Randall, Tony (1920–)** A light comedy star in the movies during the late 1950s and 1960s, Tony Randall occasionally had leads, but usually played major supporting characters. His most memorable roles were in the three Rock Hudson/Doris DAY comedies *Pillow Talk* (1959), *Lover Come Back* (1961), and *Send Me No Flowers* (1964). Adept at playing both mordant types and excitable, bubbly characters, Randall has proven himself a versatile comic performer. Although he will likely be remembered for his brilliantly funny Felix Unger in the long-running TV sitcom "The Odd Couple" (1970–1975), Randall's exquisite comic performances in *Will Success Spoil Rock Hunter?* (1957) and *The Seven Faces of Dr. Lao* (1964) should not be forgotten.

Born Leonard Rosenberg in Tulsa, Oklahoma, he went to Northwestern University before becoming a radio and stage actor. Much of his movie career has been sandwiched around his exploits on TV. His first exposure on television was in the TV series "One Man's Family" (1949–1952). He went on to co-star in "Mr. Peepers" (1952–1955), in which he more readily showed the TV public his flair for comedy.

Randall didn't make the jump from TV to movies, but rather from Broadway to Hollywood. He was one of the stars of the hit Broadway show *Oh, Men! Oh, Women!*, reprising his role in the film version of the show in 1957. This led to more film work, including starring alongside Jayne Mansfield in the clever and immensely popular *Will Success Spoil Rock Hunter?* Had Randall continued making more films, his movie career might have been more substantial. Instead, he returned to Broadway for a year and a half before making another movie.

Randall worked steadily in Hollywood during most of the 1960s, scoring in a few other hits, but he was already in his mid-forties by the time he made *The Alphabet Murders* (1966), and he might have rightly felt that the best he could hope for in the future were ever fewer and smaller supporting roles. Thus, he turned to television, where he starred in three successive TV sitcoms: "The Odd Couple," "The Tony Randall Show" (1976–1977), and "Love, Sidney" (1981–1982). He only occasionally showed up in movies during the 1980s and 1990s, devoting himself with ever-greater energy to his pet project, the National Actors Theater in New York City, of which he is the founder (and occasional star).

---

FILMS INCLUDE: *Oh Men! Oh Women!* (1957); *No Down Payment* (1957); *Will Success Spoil Rock Hunter?* (1957); *The Mating Game* (1959); *Pillow Talk* (1959); *The Adventures of Huckleberry Finn* (1960); *Let's Make Love* (1960); *Lover Come Back* (1961); *Boys' Night Out* (1962); *Island of Love* (1963); *Robin and the Seven Hoods* (cameo, 1964); *The Brass Bottle* (1964); *Send Me No Flowers* (1964); *The Seven Faces of Dr. Lao* (1964); *Fluffy* (1965); *The Alphabet Murders* (1966); *Bang! Bang! You're Dad/Our Man in Marrakesh* (1966); *Hello Down There* (1969); *Everything You Always Wanted to Know About Sex but Were Afraid to Ask* (1972); *Scavenger Hunt* (1979); *Foolin' Around* (1980); *The King of Comedy* (1983); *My Little Pony: The Movie* (voice only, 1986); *That's Adequate* (1989); *Gremlins 2: The New Batch* (voice only, 1990); *Fatal Instinct* (1993).

---

**Raye, Martha (1908–)** If Betty Hutton was "The Blond Bombshell," Martha Raye was "The Brunette Blast." She roared through her roles like a freight train, with a decibel level to match. She was known for her big mouth, both literally and figuratively. Her film career took place mostly in the late 1930s and early 1940s, during which she usually played awesomely overpowering women who somehow comically managed to collar the hero by film's end. Her humor was as broad as she was; Raye was not the most subtle of actresses.

Born Margaret Teresa Yvonne O'Reed, she was the daughter of two VAUDEVILLE entertainers who happened to be in Butte, Montana, when she came into the world. She joined the act by the time she was three. Later she would say, "I didn't have to work until I was three. But after that, I never stopped." Raye was telling the truth. She worked the vaudeville circuits as a singer and comedian before making it to Broadway in the late 1920s. Although hardly a beauty, her boundless comic energy made her seem a natural for comic supporting roles. At first, however, MGM thought of turning her into a two-reel comedy star. She made her first appearance on film in a short subject called *A Nite in a Nite Club* (1934); she didn't become a star of anything. Two years later, however, Paramount signed her up and she stayed with that studio for fifteen feature films over a period of just five years. Those films form the bulk of her career.

In the 1940s she appeared in better movies, but in smaller roles, usually in support of other comedians like ABBOTT AND COSTELLO in *Keep 'Em Flying* (1941), OLSEN AND JOHNSON in *Hellzapoppin* (1941), and, to her everlasting glory, in Charlie CHAPLIN's masterpiece, MONSIEUR VERDOUX (1947).

Raye has appeared in just four films since the end of the 1940s, most notably *Jumbo* (1962). She made her living with nightclub performances, stagework, TV appearances, and as a spokesperson for a denture cleanser, describing herself as "The Big Mouth."

Martha Raye was given a special Academy Award in 1969 for entertaining American armed forces overseas. She had done so with great fervor during World War II, the Korean War, and the Vietnam War.

FILMS: Features: *Rhythm on the Range* (1936); *College Holiday* (1936); *The Big Broadcast of 1937* (1936); *Hideaway Girl* (1936); *Mountain Music* (1937); *Double or Nothing* (1937); *Artists and Models* (1937); *Waikiki Wedding* (1937); *Give Me a Sailor* (1938); *College Swing* (1938); *The Big Broadcast of 1938* (1938); *Tropic Holiday* (1938); *Never Say Die* (1939); *$1,000 Touchdown* (1939); *The Farmer's Daughter* (1940); *The Boys from Syracuse* (1940); *Keep 'Em Flying* (1941); *Navy Blues* (1941); *Hellzapoppin* (1941); *Pin Up Girl* (1944); *Four Jills in a Jeep* (1944); *Monsieur Verdoux* (1947); *Jumbo* (1962); *The Phynx* (cameo, 1970); *Pufnstuf* (voice only, 1970); *The Concorde: Airport '79* (1979).

**Reiner, Carl (1922—)**  Although he has acted in TV and films, it has been his writing and directing that has earned Carl Reiner his considerable reputation as a consistently funny and entertaining filmmaker. He has worked so successfully in both TV and film, however, that it is hard to say where he has had his greatest impact. Nonetheless, this versatile actor, writer, and director has put his stamp on modern film comedy, particularly in the late 1960s and early 1970s when he directed the cult classic *Where's Poppa?* (1970) and again in the late 1970s and early 1980s when he directed Steve MARTIN in the stand-up comic's first four movies.

Born to a Bronx, New York, watchmaker, Reiner went to work as a machinist's helper at age sixteen before enrolling in the Work Projects Administration Dramatic Workshop. At eighteen, he got his first acting job at the Rochester Summer Theater.

When World War II broke out, Reiner enlisted in the Army Signal Corps and was soon transferred to Maurice Evans's Special Services Unit, which toured the South Pacific entertaining GIs. A fellow soldier in that division was writer/comedian Howard Morris, who later introduced him to Sid CAESAR.

Reiner worked as a writer on Caesar's landmark

TV comedy program "Your Show of Shows," later teaming with fellow writer Mel BROOKS in the creation of the 2,000-Year-Old Man records that won three Grammy nominations and became a top-selling comedy album. Reiner next created, wrote, produced, and occasionally acted in the long-running TV sitcom hit "The Dick Van Dyke Show."

Even while he was working in the television medium, Reiner ventured into movies, working first as an actor during the early 1960s in films such as *Happy Anniversary* (1959), *The Gazebo* (1960), and *Gidget Goes Hawaiian* (1961). Probably his most well-known role as an actor was in *The Russians Are Coming! The Russians Are Coming!* (1966). It was also during the 1960s that Reiner began to write, as well as act, for the big screen in movies such as *The Thrill of It All* (1963) and *The Art of Love* (1965).

In the late 1960s, Reiner made the leap to film directing, beginning with *Enter Laughing* (1967), a movie based on his autobiographical novel, which he also turned into a play. He made two more movies, a nostalgic recreation of the silent film era, *The Comic* (1969), and the ferociously funny and irreverent *Where's Poppa?*. Both movies have become cult classics, particularly the latter film, but neither did well at the box office during their initial releases. He didn't direct another movie until he made the hit *Oh, God!* (1977), starring George BURNS.

Reiner then co-scripted and directed what became one of Hollywood's all-time biggest comedy hits, Steve Martin's first feature, *The Jerk* (1979), which took in more than $100 million. Reiner and Martin made such a good team that they worked together three more times in *Dead Men Don't Wear Plaid* (1982), *The Man with Two Brains* (1983), and *All of Me* (1984). He directed John Candy with nearly equal aplomb in the mildly successful *Summer Rental* (1985). Since the mid-1980s, however, Reiner has had less success on the big screen, disappointing with such films as *Summer School* (1987) and *Sibling Rivalry* (1990).

Among his other productions, Reiner also produced a son who is fast becoming another important director, Rob REINER.

**FILMS:** *Happy Anniversary* (a, 1959); *The Gazebo* (a, 1960); *Gidget Goes Hawaiian* (a, 1961); *It's a Mad Mad Mad Mad World* (a, 1963); *The Thrill of It All* (story, sc, 1963); *The Art of Love* (a, sc, 1965); *Alice of Wonderland in Paris* (voice only, 1966); *Don't Worry, We'll Think of a Title* (cameo, 1966); *Enter Laughing* (sc, based on novel, p, d, 1966); *The Russians Are Coming! The Russians Are Coming!* (a, 1966); *A Guide for the Married Man* (a, 1967); *The Comic* (sc, p, d, 1969); *Generation* (a, 1969); *Where's Poppa* (d, 1970); *Ten from Your Show of Shows* (a, compilation, 1973); *Oh, God!* (a, d, 1977); *The End* (a, 1978); *The One and Only* (d, 1978); *The Jerk* (a, d, 1979); *Dead Men Don't Wear Plaid* (a, sc, d, 1982); *The Man with Two Brains* (sc, d, 1983); *All of Me* (d, 1984); *Summer Rental* (d, 1985); *Summer School* (d, 1987); *Bert Rigby, You're a Fool* (sc, d, 1989); *Sibling Rivalry* (d, 1990); *Spirit of '76* (a, 1990); *Fatal Instinct* (d, cameo, 1993).

**Reiner, Rob (1945— )** The son of multi-talented Carl REINER, Rob Reiner has carved a considerable niche for himself, first as a comic actor and, since the mid-1980s, as a formidable director of both comedies and dramas.

Born in New York City, Reiner made brief acting appearances in two of his father's films, *Enter Laughing* (1966) and *Where's Poppa?* (1970). It was TV, however, not film, where Reiner burst forth as an actor. He became famous on the small screen by portraying Mike "Meathead" Stivic on TV's "All in the Family" (1971–1978). He did some film acting during the 1970s as well, but it was his switch to directing that vaulted him to a new level of respect in the industry.

His first directorial effort was the rock documentary spoof, *This Is Spinal Tap* (1984), which proved both a critical and box office success. He continued with a string of comedy hits that included *The Sure Thing* (1985), *The Princess Bride* (1987), and *When Harry Met Sally* (1989).

In recent years, he has veered away from directing comedies, even as he has made acting appearances in the comedies of other directors. His dramas, *Stand by Me* (1986), *Misery* (1990), and *A Few Good Men* (1992) have all been substantial hits.

---

FILMS INCLUDE: *Enter Laughing* (a, 1966); *Halls of Anger* (a, 1970); *Where's Poppa?* (a, 1970); *Summertree* (a, 1971); *How Come Nobody's on Our Side?* (a, 1975); *Fire Sale* (a, 1977); *This Is Spinal Tap* (d, a, sc, music, 1984); *The Sure Thing* (d, 1985); *Stand By Me* (d, 1986); *The Princess Bride* (d, p, 1987); *Throw Momma from the Train* (a, 1987); *When Harry Met Sally* (d, p, 1989); *Misery* (d, p, 1990); *Postcards from the Edge* (a, 1990); *Spirit of '76* (a, 1990); *Regarding Henry* (a, 1991); *A Few Good Men* (d, p, 1992); *Sleepless in Seattle* (a, 1993).

---

## Reitman, Ivan (1946—)

From humble beginnings in shlock horror films in Canada, Ivan Reitman has developed since the late 1970s into Hollywood's premier comedy producer/director. An excellent judge of talent as well as having a reliable sense of public taste, Reitman has been responsible for a considerable number of comedy hits. These include *National Lampoon's Animal House* (1978), both blockbuster *Ghostbusters* movies (1984 and 1989), and the ambitious and sophisticated political comedy *Dave* (1993).

Born in Czechoslovakia, Reitman moved with his family to Canada when he was four. His early experience came in TV production and stage work. Drawn to the movies and the availability of public funding in Canada for the cinema, Reitman began producing films in 1971, making mostly low-budget horror films, including two with the young director David Cronenberg, *They Came from Within* (1975) and *Rabid* (1977). There was no reason to believe Reitman had a particular gift for comedy; one might have naturally assumed he was more inclinced toward horror or psychological suspense. Nonetheless, one year after producing *Rabid*, he produced a small film with a relatively unknown cast that became the biggest comedy box office hit of its time, taking in more than $100 million; the film was *National Lampoon's Animal House*.

The Hollywood door opened wide for Reitman, and he dashed right through it, directing Bill MURRAY to two hits in a row, *Meatballs* (1979) and *Stripes* (1981). Continuing his association with Murray, as well as with gifted comedy screenwriter Harold RAMIS, Reitman went on to direct *Ghostbusters*, a comedy that outdistanced *Animal House* at the box office and became a cinema sensation. He became such a hot comedy director that even non-comic icons wanted to make comedies with him; Robert Redford starred in his next film, *Legal Eagles* (1986).

Reitman's special gift might well be casting; he had the good sense to pair Danny DeVITO with Arnold Schwarzenneger in *Twins* (1988), although he did stumble with a similar sort of pairing of Sylvester Stallone and Estelle Getty in *Stop or My Mom Will Shoot* (1991), a film he produced but did not direct. Nonetheless, he has an exceptionally high percentage of hits versus misses. In that sense, Reitman is the Steven Spielberg of Hollywood comedy.

---

FILMS INCLUDE: *Foxy Lady* (music, ed, p, d, 1971); *Cannibal Girls* (p, d, 1972); *They Came from Within* (music, p, 1975); *Death Weekend* (music, p, 1977); *Rabid* (music, p, 1977); *National Lampoon's Animal House* (p, 1978); *Meatballs* (d, 1979); *Heavy Metal* (p, 1981); *Stripes* (p, d, 1981); *Spacehunter: Adventures in the Forbidden Zone* (p, 1983); *Ghostbusters* (p, d, 1984); *Legal Eagles* (story, p, d, 1986); *Big Shots* (p, 1987); *Casual Sex?* (p, 1988); *Feds* (p, 1988); *Twins* (p, d, 1988); *Ghostbusters II* (p, d, 1989); *Kindergarten Cop* (p, d, 1990); *Stop or My Mom Will Shoot* (p, 1991); *Beethoven* (p, 1992); *Dave* (p, d, 1993); *Beethoven's 2nd* (p, 1993).

---

## Reubens, Paul   See Pee-wee HERMAN

## Riskin, Robert (1897—1955)

A screenwriter with comically adventurous ideas and a strong flair for witty dialogue, Robert Riskin was the most valued scriptwriter at Columbia Pictures throughout the 1930s. He frequently worked closely with director Frank CAPRA.

Born in New York City, Riskin began writing in his teens, becoming a successful playwright in his twenties. He was brought out to Hollywood to try his hand at screenwriting after two of his plays were turned into films, *Illicit* (1931) and *Miracle Woman* (1931), the latter a Capra-directed movie.

Capra called Riskin in to write the dialogue for *Platinum Blonde* (1931), and they went on to work together in many of Capra's biggest hits, including *American Madness* (1932), *Lady for a Day* (1933), *Broadway Bill* (1934), *Mr. Deeds Goes to Town* (1936), *Lost Horizon* (1937), *You Can't Take It with You* (1938), and *Meet John Doe* (1941). Every one of the above films was a hit, but their greatest achievement together was IT HAPPENED ONE NIGHT (1934), which swept the Academy Awards, bringing Riskin a best screenplay Oscar.

While Riskin's best work was with Capra, he also wrote strong screenplays for others, including *The Whole Town's Talking* (1935) for John Ford and *The Real Glory* (1939) for Henry Hathaway. He also wrote and directed one of his own scripts, making *When You're in Love* (1937) with only modest success.

Riskin and Capra went their different ways in the early 1940s and never worked together again; neither of them had quite the success alone that they had when they were a team. Curiously, Capra's greatest achievement in his post-Riskin era was *It's a Wonderful Life* (1946), a film that owed much to the structure of Riskin's *American Madness* script. By the same token, Riskin's best screenplay of the post-Capra era was *Magic Town* (1947), which happened to be a distinctly Capraesque story.

Riskin slowed down considerably in the late 1940s and early 1950s, making few films of distinction. Several of his scripts, however, were the basis of films made after his death, including a remake of *It Happened One Night*, called *You Can't Run Away from It* (1956), and Frank Capra's remake of Riskin's own *Lady for a Day*, which was retitled *A Pocketful of Miracles* (1961).

---

FILMS: *Illicit* (based on play, 1931); *Many a Slip* (based on play, 1931); *Arizona* (sc, 1931); *Men Are Like That* (sc, 1931); *Men in Her Life* (sc, 1931); *The Miracle Woman* (based on play, 1931); *American Madness* (story, 1932); *The Big Timer* (story, sc, 1932); *Virtue* (sc, 1932); *The Night Club Lady* (sc, 1932); *Ex-Lady* (story, 1933); *Ann Carver's Profession* (story, sc, 1933); *Lady for a Day* (sc, 1933); *It Happened One Night* (sc, 1934); *Broadway Bill* (sc, 1934); *Carnival* (story, sc, 1935); *The Whole Town's Talking* (sc, 1935); *Mr. Deeds Goes to Town* (sc, 1936); *When You're in Love* (sc, d, 1937); *Lost Horizon* (sc, 1937); *You Can't Take It with You* (sc, 1938); *The Real Glory* (assoc. p, 1939); *They Shall Have Music* (assoc. p, 1939); *Meet John Doe* (sc, 1941); *The Thin Man Goes Home* (story, sc, 1944); *Magic Town* (story, sc, p, 1947); *Mister 880* (sc, 1950); *Riding High* (sc, 1950); *Half Angel* (sc, 1951); *Here Comes the Groom* (story, 1951); *You Can't Run Away from It* (based on *It Happened One Night*, 1956); *Pocketful of Miracles* (based on *Lady for a Day*, 1961).

---

## Ritter, John (1948— )

With a boyish face, a warm personality, and a modest gift for physical humor, John Ritter is an expert in light comedy. Ritter has enjoyed far more success on TV than in films, but his occasional forays into motion picture comedy have not been entirely in vain. He scored well in Peter Bogdanovich's *Nickleodeon* (1976), only to appear in comedies during the following five years with indifferent success. His biggest hit came a number of years later when he starred in Blake EDWARDS's amusing sex comedy *Skin Deep* (1989).

Born in Los Angeles, California, Ritter is the youngest son of country-western singing star Tex Ritter. He went to the University of Southern Cali-

*Moses!* (1980); *They All Laughed* (1981); *Real Men* (1987); *Skin Deep* (1989); *Problem Child* (1990); *Problem Child 2* (1991); *Noises Off* (1992).

*Known primarily as a TV star, John Ritter has quietly amassed a modest but memorable body of work as a feature film comedy star, most notably in* Skin Deep *(1989). He is seen here in* Problem Child 2 *(1991) with Michael Oliver.*

PHOTO BY ROBERT DE STOLFE, © UNIVERSAL PICTURES.

fornia to study psychology, but changed his major two years later to theater arts when the acting bug struck.

Following graduation, he immediately began working in summer stock. After a number of movie appearances in the early 1970s, Ritter hit the big time in 1977 when he co-starred in the hugely popular TV sitcom "Three's Company." He later had another comedy series, "Hooperman," in 1987.

Active in TV movies during the 1980s, Ritter has only recently begun to return to the big screen with any degree of regularity. His most recent films include *Problem Child* (1990) and the Bogdanovich FARCE *Noises Off* (1992).

**FILMS:** *The Barefoot Executive* (1970); *Scandalous John* (1971); *The Other* (1972); *The Stone Killer* (1973); *Nickleodeon* (1976); *Breakfast in Bed* (1977); *Americathon* (1979); *Hero at Large* (1980); *Wholly*

**Ritz Brothers, The** A comedy team with a distinct brand of nuttiness, the Ritz Brothers entertained audiences for six decades, most of that in live performances. Their time in Hollywood was relatively brief, with their best work on the big screen taking place in the late 1930s.

Born in Newark, New Jersey, to Austrian immigrant parents whose last name was Joachim, Al (1901–1965), Jimmy (1903–1985), and Harry (1906–1986) changed their name to Ritz, choosing it (as legend has it) from a laundry truck that zoomed by when their agent insisted that as The Joachim Brothers they would never make the big time.

Older brother Al got his start in show business first, winning an amateur contest at age ten. He was just fifteen when he had a bit part in a silent film. All three brothers worked up dance routines, but chose to work alone until their fourth brother, George (who didn't perform with them), pulled them together into an act and initially managed them, getting the boys their first bookings. By this point, it was the mid-1920s, and from modest beginnings they quickly earned a reputation with their "Collegians" routine, a sketch that involved both dancing and comedy. Before long, they were VAUDEVILLE headliners, working in the *Earl Carroll Vanities* on Broadway.

In 1934 they made their first film together, a short called *Hotel Anchovy*. Its success led to a contract with 20th Century-Fox, the studio for which the Ritz Brothers would make most of their best films. They started out as comic relief in a number of Alice Faye MUSICAL COMEDIES, among them *Sing, Baby, Sing* (1936) and *On the Avenue* (1937). The public responded, even if the critics did not, and soon they were given their own films to carry, beginning with *Life Begins at College* (1937) and culminating with

*The irrespressible Ritz Brothers, Jimmy, Harry, and Al (left to right), never achieved much in the way of critical acclaim, but they provided plenty of comedy in any number of otherwise lamentable movies.*   PHOTO COURTESY OF THE SIEGEL COLLECTION.

their best movie, the musical comedy spoof *The Three Musketeers* (1939).

Unhappy with their treatment at Fox, the Ritz Brothers moved to Universal in the early 1940s. The change was not for the best. They made four low-budget comedies that were, at best, mediocre. They fled Hollywood and did not return again until the mid-1970s, when surviving brothers Harry and Jimmy were featured in *Blazing Stewardesses* (1975) and *Won Ton Ton—The Dog Who Saved Hollywood* (1975). Harry Ritz, whom Mel BROOKS once called "The funniest man alive," made his last film

appearance in a cameo role in Brooks's *Silent Movie* (1976).

FILMS: *The Avenging Trail* (Al only, 1918); *Hotel Anchovy* (short, 1934); *Broadway Highlights #6* (short, 1936); *Sing, Baby, Sing* (1936); *One in a Million* (1937); *On the Avenue* (1937); *You Can't Have Everything* (1937); *Life Begins at College* (1937); *The Goldwyn Follies* (1938); *Kentucky Moonshine* (1938); *Straight, Place, and Show* (1938); *The Three Musketeers* (1939); *The Gorilla* (1939); *Pack Up Your Troubles* (1939); *Argentine Nights* (1940); *Behind the*

*Eight Ball* (1942); *Hi'Ya, Chum* (1943); *Screen Snap-shots #5* (short, 1943); *Screen Snapshots #8* (short, 1943); *Never a Dull Moment* (1943); *Blazing Stewardesses* (Harry and Jimmy only, 1975); *Won Ton Ton—The Dog Who Saved Hollywood* (Harry and Jimmy only, 1976); *Silent Movie* (Harry only, 1976).

**Roach, Hal (1882—1992)** One of the great names in film comedy, Hal Roach worked as a screenwriter, director, and producer with many of the most beloved comic actors in Hollywood history, among them Harold LLOYD, LAUREL AND HARDY, and OUR GANG.

Hal Roach and Mack SENNETT were the two giants of comedy production during the silent era, but only Roach prospered beyond the coming of sound. The Hal Roach Studio depended less on SLAPSTICK and broad FARCE (unlike Sennett) and more on character humor. As American audiences became less fascinated with stunts and more interested in people, Sennett's brand of humor became passé, and Roach's became the norm.

Born in Elmira, New York, Roach was an adventurer who saw a good deal of life as a young man. He skinned mules, prospected for gold in Alaska, and traveled almost everywhere. When fate dropped him in Hollywood in 1912, he worked as an extra and stuntman. It was during this early apprenticeship that he met Harold Lloyd, who was no further along in his film career than Roach. They eventually struck up a partnership that led to Roach's producing and often directing a series of one- and two-reel comedies starring Lloyd as Lonesome Luke. The movies were immediately popular and became the springboard for their future successes.

Lloyd, of course, eventually went off on his own, and Roach continued to develop new comedy talents for his growing studio. In the 1920s, Roach hit paydirt with Our Gang and Laurel and Hardy. He also had comedy talents such as Harry "Snub" POLLARD, Charlie CHASE, and Edgar KENNEDY under

contract. Remarkably, Roach not only oversaw production on all of his films, but he also often co-wrote and directed an enormous number of his studio's films.

In the 1930s, Roach was rewarded for his work in comedy when Laurel and Hardy won an Oscar for their short *The Music Box* (1932). He received a best short film nomination for *Tit for Tat* (1935) and took another Oscar home for the Our Gang short *Bored of Education* (1936). Before he was through, Roach pulled down two more best short film Academy Award nominations for *There Goes My Heart* (1938) and *Flying with Music* (1942).

Not content to merely make comedy shorts, Roach branched out in the 1930s to make comedy features as well. Laurel and Hardy led the way with *Rogue Song* (1930) and *Pardon Us* (1931). He eventually even made an Our Gang feature (their only one) in 1936, *General Spanky*.

Roach had no distribution of his own and depended upon MGM to disseminate his movies. In 1938, as he moved out of shorts to concentrate solely on feature films, he sold his Our Gang rights to MGM.

In the late 1930s, he moved to feature films, producing movies as varied as the comedy *Topper Takes a Trip* (1939) and the highly acclaimed version of John Steinbeck's *Of Mice and Men* (1939). During World War II, he served as a filmmaker for the army. When the war was over—ever the adventurer—Roach left movie production to investigate the fledgling medium of TV.

Finally, in the late 1950s, The Hal Roach Studio closed its doors for good. However, the grand old comedy producer wasn't quite finished making the world laugh. In 1967 he produced a compilation film called *The Crazy World of Laurel and Hardy*. After all, Roach had put Stan Laurel and Oliver Hardy together as a team; it was only fitting that he should put them together one last time. In 1983, at age 101, Roach was given a special Academy Award "in recognition of his distinguished contributions to the motion picture art form."

**FILMS INCLUDE:** *Just Nuts* (p, d, 1915); *Lonesome Luke* (p, d, 1915); *Lonesome Luke: Social Gangster* (p, d, 1915); *Lonesome Luke's Movie Muddle* (p, d, 1916); *Luke's Double* (p, d, 1916); *Lonesome Luke on Tin Can Alley* (p, d, 1917); *All Aboard* (p, d, 1917); *The Flirt* (p, d, 1917); *Fireman Save My Child* (p, d, 1918); *Pipe the Whiskers* (p, d, 1918); *Captain Kidd's Kids* (p, d, 1919); *Bumping into Broadway* (p, d, 1919); *His Royal Slyness* (p, d, 1919); *From Hand to Mouth* (p, d, 1919); *Haunted Spooks* (p, d, 1920); *High and Dizzy* (p, d, 1920); *An Eastern Westerner* (p, d, 1920); *Get Out and Get Under* (p, d, 1920); *Number Please* (p, d, 1920); *Now or Never* (p, d, 1921); *A Sailor-Made Man* (story, p, 1921); *Doctor Jack* (story, p, 1922); *Grandma's Boy* (story, p, 1922); *Our Gang* (p, 1922); *Safety Last* (story, sc, p, 1923); *The Call of the Wild* (p, 1923); *Uncensored Movies* (p, 1923); *The Battling Orioles* (story, p, 1924); *All Wet* (p, 1924); *The King of Wild Horses* (story, p, 1924); *The White Sheik* (sc, p, d, 1924); *Bad Boy* (p, 1925); *Innocent Husbands* (p, 1925); *45 Minutes from Hollywood* (p, 1926); *Mighty Like a Moose* (p, 1926); *Slipping Wives* (p, 1927); *Putting Pants on Philip* (p, 1927); *The Battle of the Century* (story, p, 1927); *Leave 'Em Laughing* (story, p, 1928); *Two Tars* (p, 1928); *Early to Bed* (p, 1928); *Big Business* (p, 1929); *Double Whoopee* (p, 1929); *Perfect Day* (co-story, p, 1929); *Brats* (co-story, p, 1930); *The Laurel and Hardy Murder Case* (p, 1930); *Another Fine Mess* (p, 1930); *Pardon Us* (p, 1931); *Our Wife* (p, 1931); *Helpmates* (p, 1932); *Their First Mistake* (p, 1932); *The Music Box* (p, 1932); *Pack Up Our Troubles* (p, 1932); *Fra Diavolo/The Devil's Brother* (p, co-d, 1933); *Sons of the Desert* (p, 1933); *Busy Bodies* (p, 1933); *Babes in Toyland* (p, 1934); *Tit for Tat* (p, 1935); *General Spanky* (p, 1936); *Bored of Education* (p, 1936); *Our Relations* (p, 1936); *Way Out West* (p, 1937); *Topper* (p, 1937); *Merrily We Live* (p, 1938); *Swiss Miss* (p, 1938); *Blockheads* (p, 1938); *There Goes My Heart* (p, 1938); *Of Mice and Men* (p, 1939); *Captain Fury* (p, d, 1939); *The Housekeeper's Daughter* (p, d, 1939); *Topper Takes a Trip* (p, 1939); *Zenobia* (p, 1939); *One Million B.C.* (p, co-d, 1940); *A Chump at Oxford* (p, 1940); *Saps at Sea* (p, 1940); *Road Show* (p, 1941); *Miss Polly* (p, 1941); *Niagara Falls* (p, 1941); *Topper Returns* (p, 1941); *Tanks a Mil-lion* (p, 1941); *Brooklyn Orchid* (p, 1942); *Flying with Music* (p, 1942); *The Devil with Hitler* (co-p, 1944); *One Million Years B.C.* (remake, assoc. p, 1966); *The Crazy World of Laurel and Hardy* (compilation, 1967).

**Road Movies**  *See* Bing CROSBY; Bob HOPE; SERIES COMEDIES

**Roberts, Tony (1939—)**  A light comedy leading man, Tony Roberts is best known to film audiences for his performances in six Woody ALLEN movies, often playing Allen's laid-back best friend. With his clipped speech and bemused, wiseacre style, Roberts can often seem a cool, somewhat aloof character, a trait that has kept him from becoming a bigger star in films.

Born David Anthony Roberts in New York City, he studied drama at Northwestern University, making his way as a stage actor, which he continues to do. He was most visible on the big screen, in better films, during the 1970s and early 1980s. His performance as Diane KEATON's husband obsessed with business (and phone numbers) in *Play It Again, Sam* (1972) brought him critical attention and led not only to more work with Allen, but to more varied film work as well. For instance, he was seen the following years in two major movies, *Serpico* (1973) and *The Taking of Pelham 1, 2, 3* (1974). By and large, he has done his best work in Allen's films, with special mention for his performances in *Annie Hall* (1977) and *A Midsummer Night's Sex Comedy* (1982).

**FILMS INCLUDE:** *Beach Girls and the Monster* (1965); *$1,000,000 Duck* (1971); *Star Spangled Girl* (1971); *Play It Again, Sam* (1972); *Serpico* (1973); *The Taking of Pelham 1, 2, 3* (1974); *Annie Hall* (1977); *Opening Night* (1977); *Just Tell Me What You Want* (1980); *Stardust Memories* (1980); *A Midsummer Night's Sex Comedy* (1982); *Amityville III: The Demon* (1983); *Key Exchange* (1985); *Seize the Day* (1986); *Hannah* *and Her Sisters* (1986); *Radio Days* (1987); *18 Again!* (1988); *Switch* (1991); *Popcorn* (1991).

---

**Rogers, Will (1879—1935)** The uncle everyone wished they had, Will Rogers was loved for his folksy wit, his wisdom, and his charm. His career as a screen humorist was short, and probably only serious movie fans can name more than two or three of his films (if that many). Nonetheless, the image of the man has endured, as evidenced by a smash Broadway musical in the early 1990s called *The Will Rogers Follies*.

Born William Penn Adair Rogers in Colagah, Indian Territory (which later became the state of Oklahoma), of reputedly Irish and Cherokee ancestry, he learned his roping and riding tricks very early in life. Those tricks served him in good stead when he joined a wild West show in Johannesburg, South Africa, after delivering mules to the British there during the Boer War.

Rogers continued working in wild West shows until he made his way to New York and took a stab at VAUDEVILLE. At that time his act consisted of nothing more than his rope tricks; he had yet to speak on stage. It wasn't until he got a laugh ad-libbing a joke to cover a failed trick that he suddenly became a humorist.

Over the next several years Rogers began making amusing comments on politics, politicians, and human nature. By 1912, he had become a well-known vaudevillian and was able to make the leap to Broadway. Five years later, he was a star attraction in Ziegfeld's Follies.

The movies beckoned in 1918, and Rogers made his first film, *Laughing Bill Hyde* for Samuel Goldwyn. The movie did reasonably well, and it seemed as if Will Rogers was about to become a silent screen star. However, after twelve more features between 1918 and early 1922, the rope-twirling star had failed to find an audience. His appeal was in what he said and how he said it, and silent films simply couldn't project his personality.

*Will Rogers was a beloved American entertainer who also happened to be a movie star. Only a few of his film comedies hold up to scrutiny today, but his image as a man of wit and wisdom has never dimmed.* PHOTO COURTESY OF THE SIEGEL COLLECTION.

Neither Hollywood nor Rogers was willing to give up, however. He made *One Glorious Day* (1922) for Paramount and an independent version of *The Headless Horseman* (1922). He even produced, wrote, and directed three films that same year and then went broke.

Except for two silent features in 1927, Rogers's only other film experience during the silent era was in a series of a dozen shorts he made for Hal ROACH in the mid-1920s that weren't terribly successful either.

Although his film career appeared to be a bust, Rogers's popularity continued to grow thanks to his humor columns in the newspapers. He had also written two successful books. With the coming of sound, Hollywood gave Rogers another chance with *They Had to See Paris* (1929), and he was a hit.

From then on his film career never seriously faltered. He was an ordinary American who managed to ridicule and satirize without offending. His movies, coupled with his radio performances and newspaper columns, made him a commanding popular figure of considerable stature. His support of Franklin Delano Roosevelt was generally credited with helping FDR win the presidency in 1932. Rogers had been offered the nomination for governor of Oklahoma but declined it. (He did, however, serve as the honorary mayor of Beverly Hills.)

Although his movies were almost all formula affairs, they were immensely successful, making Rogers the second most popular film star in 1933 (after Marie DRESSLER) and the top draw in 1934.

Rogers made a total of twenty sound films, but only a mere handful hold up reasonably well today. His best were *A Connecticut Yankee* (1931), *State Fair* (1934), *Judge Priest* (1934), and *Steamboat 'Round the Bend* (1935). The latter two were directed by John Ford. Rogers died in a plane crash in Alaska in 1935.

---

FILMS INCLUDE: *Laughing Bill Hyde* (1918); *Almost a Husband* (1919); *Jubilo* (1919); *Cupid the Cowpuncher* (1920); *Honest Hutch* (1920); *Jes' Call Me Jim* (1920); *Boys Will Be Boys* (1921); *Guile of Women* (1921); *Doubling for Romeo* (1921); *An Unwilling Hero* (1921); *One Glorious Day* (1922); *The Headless Horseman* (1922); *Fruits of the Faith* (short, 1923); *Two Wagons Both Covered* (short, 1924); *A Texas Steer* (1927); *They Had to See Paris* (1929); *Happy Days* (1929); *So This Is London* (1930); *Lightnin'* (1930); *Ambassador Bill* (1931); *Young as You Feel* (1931); *A Connecticut Yankee* (1931); *Business and Pleasure* (1932); *Too Busy to Work* (1932); *Down to Earth* (1932); *State Fair* (1933); *Mr. Skitch* (1933); *Doctor Bull* (1933); *David Harum* (1934); *Handy Andy* (1934); *Judge Priest* (1934); *The Country Chairman* (1935); *Doubting Thomas* (1935); *Steamboat 'Round the Bend* (1935); *Life Begins at Forty* (1935); *In Old Kentucky* (1935).

---

**romantic comedy** In its simplest form, a romantic comedy is the "boy meets girl, boy loses girl, boy gets girl" formula played for laughs. In other words, it's the same three-part formula one might have in a romantic drama such as *An Affair to Remember* (1957), except this formula is loaded with comic twists and turns. *Sleepless in Seattle* (1993) separated its lovers by a continent, confused the trendy dessert tiramisu with a sex act, and had its protagonists, Tom HANKS and Meg RYAN, partially reenact scenes from *An Affair to Remember*, inviting the audience (if not the characters) in on the joke.

The difference between a straight romantic movie and a romantic comedy is essentially the difference between asking the audience to take the story seriously and letting them know that what they're witnessing is a plausible but far-fetched tale full of coincidences, near misses, and comic business that is hardly likely to happen in real life. Romantic drama, as a consequence, often ends sadly (that's where the "three-hanky" description comes from, as does the appellation, "a weepie"). One cries at the end of *An Affair to Remember*, while one rejoices at the end of *Sleepless in Seattle*, witnessing the ending in the latter film that we wished for the characters in the former.

Finally, a romantic comedy must end, as all comedies do, with a marriage (or a reasonable facsimile thereof). Walking hand-in-hand as in the ending of *Sleepless in Seattle* will do, but so will the ending of *The GRADUATE* (1967), which literally ends with a wedding, except not between the hero and heroine. Of course, the hero runs off with the bride at the film's end, providing the audience, at the very last moment, with shock, but also laughter—and the definition of romantic comedy.

**Rooney, Mickey (1920—)** If there ever were an actor born to perform, it was Mickey Rooney. A prodigiously talented actor, he began his career as a child star before becoming one of Hollywood's most popular and amusing teenagers, a role he was able to play well into his twenties because of his short stature and baby face. His career as an adult actor has been uneven, at best, but he continues to appear on film, becoming Hollywood's last working link to the silent comedy era.

Born Joe Yule, Jr., in Brooklyn, New York, he was the son of a VAUDEVILLE couple. He began performing at fifteen months old in his parents' act, making his film debut at age six in a silent short, *Not to Be Trusted* (1926). The following year he took the name of Mickey McGuire, the same moniker as the comic strip character he played in a long-running series of comedy shorts made between 1927 and 1933. In 1932, when he began to appear in films other than the Mickey McGuire ones, he changed his name to Mickey Rooney.

Rooney played small roles in films such as *The Big Cage* (1933) and *The Chief* (1933), bouncing around from studio to studio until MGM finally signed him to a long-term contract in 1935. He was promptly loaned out to Warner Bros., where he made a lasting impression as Puck in *A Midsummer Night's Dream* (1935). He was in three films supporting child star Freddie Bartholomew, and his brash personality was the perfect antidote to the young English actor's reserve. After *Little Lord Fauntleroy* (1936), *The Devil Is a Sissy* (1936), and *Captains Courageous* (1937), Rooney began to emerge as a star as Bartholomew peaked and began to fade.

In 1937 MGM produced a B movie called *A Family Affair*, the first of the Andy Hardy films in which Rooney starred as the affable teenager in an archetypal American family. The film was a surprise hit and was followed by fifteen more lightly comic Andy Hardy films.

When Judy Garland was featured in *Love Finds Andy Hardy* (1938), Rooney found his perfect female counterpart. The two MGM teenagers starred together in a total of three of Rooney's Andy Hardy films, but more notably in a series of charming musical comedies, including *Babes in Arms* (1939), *Strike Up the Band* (1940), *Babes on Broadway* (1941), and *Girl Crazy* (1943).

At the same time that Rooney was playing light comedy in the Andy Hardy films and singing and dancing in musicals, he was also playing heavy dramatic roles in films such as *Boy's Town* (1938) and

*Young Tom Edison* (1940). It was eminently clear that Rooney was an immensely talented young man with a remarkable acting range. The public could hardly get enough of him. He appeared in anywhere from three to eight films per year during the latter 1930s and early 1940s, becoming the recipient of a special Academy Award, along with another teenage star, Deanna Durbin, for his "significant contribution in bringing to the screen the spirit and personification of youth and as a juvenile player setting a high standard of ability and achievement." He reached the apex of his career in 1939 when he became the nation's top box office draw, a title he held for three straight years.

After starring with Elizabeth Taylor in *National Velvet* (1944), Rooney joined the army. It was hard for audiences to accept the young, baby-faced actor as Andy Hardy on his return from the service, and *Love Laughs at Andy Hardy* (1946) was a commercial flop. So were the rest of his movies during the late 1940s. By 1949 MGM bought out his contract, and Rooney was on his own, setting up an independent film company that produced a string of box office and critical failures throughout the early part of the new decade, eventually forcing him to declare bankruptcy.

Although Rooney worked in nightclubs and on TV, he continued making films, usually B movies without much distinction. Then he established himself in three important character roles: as a soldier in *The Bold and the Brave* (1956), for which he was nominated for an Oscar as best supporting actor; as a tough sergeant in the service comedy *Operation Mad Ball* (1957); and as a vicious gangster in the title role of *Baby Face Nelson* (1957). MGM temporarily brought Rooney back into the family fold, starring him in the last Andy Hardy film, *Andy Hardy Comes Home* (1958). It was a bomb and a career mistake for the actor.

Rooney was nothing if he wasn't irrepressible; he continued to find work in a variety of poor films until he once again played a comedy relief role as Audrey Hepburn's Japanese neighbor in *Breakfast at Tiffany's* (1961), nearly stealing the movie. From comedy to drama, he was once again riveting in a supporting role in *Requiem for a Heavyweight* (1962), but the actor couldn't parlay his good reviews into starring roles. In addition to a stream of appearances in minor films throughout the 1960s, he managed to create some memorable moments in a few bigger budget comedies such as IT'S A MAD MAD MAD MAD WORLD (1963) and *The Comic* (1969).

Rooney's comeback picture, *The Black Stallion*, was the surprise hit film of 1979. Many thought he deserved an Oscar nomination as best supporting actor. Despite his success in the movie, Hollywood didn't come calling in a big way. He has appeared in only the occasional, schlock movie during the 1980s and early 1990s. In any event, 1979 was certainly a big year for the actor; he hit it big on Broadway in the revival of *Sugar Babies* and soon after found an outlet for his dramatic talents on television, starring in several powerful TV movies, including his Emmy-winning performance in the title role of *Bill* (1981).

Although Rooney reached the peak of his fame in the late 1930s and early 1940s, he has never been long out of the limelight. Married eight times, most memorably to Ava Gardner (1942–1943), he has made and lost a fortune, tinkered in the business world, and conquered the stage, the nightclub circuit, and TV. In 1983, Rooney received a special Oscar for fifty years of versatility as a performer.

---

**FILMS:** Features only: *Orchids and Ermine* (1927); *My Pal the King* (1932); *Information Kid* (1932); *The Beast of the City* (1932); *Sin's Pay Day* (1932); *High Speed* (1932); *The Life of Jimmy Dolan* (1933); *Broadway to Hollywood* (1933); *The Big Cage* (1933); *The Big Chance* (1933); *The World Changes* (1933); *The Chief* (1933); *Beloved* (1934); *Love Birds* (1934); *Manhattan Melodrama* (1934); *I Like It That Way* (1934); *Chained* (1934); *Blind Date* (1934); *Hide-Out* (1934); *Half a Sinner* (1934); *Death on a Diamond* (1934); *Upper World* (1934); *Reckless* (1935); *A Midsummer Night's Dream* (1935); *Down the Stretch* (1935); *The County Chairman* (1935); *The Healer* (1935); *Ah Wilderness* (1935); *Little Lord Fauntleroy* (1936); *The Devil Is a Sissy* (1936); *Riff Raff* (1936); *A Family Affair* (1937); *Captains Courageous* (1937); *The Hoosier Schoolboy* (1937); *Slave Ship* (1937); *Live, Love, and Learn* (1937); *You're Only Young Once* (1937); *Thoroughbreds Don't Cry* (1937); *Love Is a Headache* (1938); *Judge Hardy's Children* (1938); *Lord Jeff* (1938); *Hold That Kiss* (1938); *Love Finds Andy Hardy* (1938); *Boys Town* (1938); *Stablemates* (1938); *Out West with the Hardys* (1938); *The Hardys Ride High* (1939); *The Adventures of Huckleberry Finn* (1939); *Andy Hardy Gets Spring Fever* (1939); *Babes in Arms* (1939); *Judge Hardy and Son* (1939); *Andy Hardy Meets Debutante* (1940); *Young Tom Edison* (1940); *Strike Up the Band* (1940); *Andy Hardy's Private Secretary* (1941); *Men of Boys Town* (1941); *Life Begins for Andy Hardy* (1941); *The Courtship of Andy Hardy* (1942); *Babes on Broadway* (1942); *Andy Hardy's Double Life* (1942); *A Yank at Eton* (1942); *The Human Comedy* (1943); *Girl Crazy* (1943); *Thousands Cheer* (1943); *Andy Hardy's Blond Trouble* (1944); *National Velvet* (1944); *Love Laughs at Andy Hardy* (1947); *Killer McCoy* (1947); *Summer Holiday* (1948); *Words and Music* (1948); *The Big Wheel* (1949); *Quicksand* (1950); *The Fireball* (1950); *He's a Cockeyed Wonder* (1950); *My True Story* (d only, 1951); *The Strip* (1951); *My Outlaw Brother* (1951); *Sound Off* (1952); *All Ashore* (1953); *A Slight Case of Larceny* (1953); *Off Limits* (1953); *The Atomic Kid* (1954); *Drive a Crooked Road* (1954); *The Bridges at Toko-Ri* (1955); *The Twinkle in God's Eye* (1955); *The Bold and the Brave* (1956); *Francis in the Haunted House* (1956); *Magnificent Roughnecks* (1956); *Operation Mad Ball* (1957); *Baby Face Nelson* (1957); *A Nice Little Bank That Should Be Robbed* (1958); *Andy Hardy Comes Home* (1958); *The Last Mile* (1959); *The Big Operator* (1959); *The Private Lives of Adam and Eve* (also co-d, 1960); *Platinum High School* (1960); *King of the Roaring Twenties* (1961); *Breakfast at Tiffany's* (1961); *Requiem for a Heavyweight* (1962); *It's a Mad Mad Mad Mad World* (1963); *The Secret Invasion* (1964); *How to Stuff a Wild Bikini* (1965); *24 Hours to Kill* (1965); *Ambush Bay* (1966); *Skidoo* (1968); *The Extraordinary Seaman* (1969); *The Comic* (1969); *80 Steps to Jonah* (1969); *The Cockeyed Cow-*

boys of Calico County (1970); The Manipulator (1971); Richard (1972); Pulp (1972); That's Entertainment (1974); Journey Back to Oz (voice only, 1974); Ace of Hearts (1974); Rachel's Man (1975); Find the Lady (1976); The Domino Principle (1977); Pete's Dragon (1977); The Magic of Lassie (1978); The Black Stallion (1979); An Arabian Adventure (1979); Find the Lady (1979); The Fox and the Hound (1981); The Care Bears Movie (voice only, 1985); Lightning: The White Stallion (1986); Rudolph and Frosty's Christmas in July (1986); Erik the Viking (1989); Little Nemo: Adventures in Slumberland (Japan, voice only, 1990); My Heroes Have Always Been Cowboys (1991); Silent Night, Deadly Night 5: The Toy Maker (1992).

## Rosenbloom, "Slapsie" Maxie (1903—1976)

At the top of the boxing world from 1930 to 1934 when he was the light heavyweight champion of the world, "Slapsie" Maxie Rosenbloom stayed in the Hollywood ring for a long bout, as well, playing comical supporting roles from the 1930s to the 1960s. Most of his appearances, however, took place in the latter half of the 1930s and in the early 1940s.

Born Max Rosenbloom in New York City, the fighter received his nickname from none other than author Damon Runyon, who called him "Slapsie" because he kept his opponents off stride with a unique slapping motion with his gloves.

If ever there was a Runyonesque character, Rosenbloom was it. A reform school graduate, he had 289 professional fights, not counting all the street brawls that came before. Drawn to show business, Rosenbloom was helped along by several celebrity fight fans, among them George Raft and Carole LOMBARD. The latter got him a role in her film Nothing Sacred (1937).

He appeared in an odd variety of films, including the tongue-in-cheek gangster comedy The Amazing Dr. Clitterhouse (1938); ABBOTT AND COSTELLO's Abbott and Costello Meet the Keystone Kops (1955); the major comedy release starring Bob HOPE, The Loui-

siana Purchase (1941); and the low-budget comedy horror film, The Boogie Man Will Get You (1942). Even as late as 1951, the former boxer managed to grab the title role in Skipalong Rosenbloom (1951).

Rosenbloom's last film was the cleverly titled Don't Worry, We'll Think of a Title (1966). In his later years, after his Los Angeles nightclub failed, the effects of so many blows to the head from so many fights finally took their toll. He died after spending years in a nursing home, suffering the debilitating effects of Paget's Disease. Before he died, however, he was elected into the Boxing Hall of Fame.

FILMS INCLUDE: Mr. Broadway (1933); Muss 'Em Up (1936); Kelly the Second (1936); Nothing Sacred (1937); The Amazing Dr. Clitterhouse (1938); The Kid Comes Back (1938); Mr. Moto's Gamble (1938); Naughty But Nice (1939); The Kid from Kokomo (1939); 20,000 Men a Year (1939); Public Deb #1 (1940); Ringside Maisie (1941); Louisiana Purchase (1941); The Boogie Man Will Get You (1942); Three of a Kind (1944); Irish Eyes Are Smiling (1944); Follow the Boys (1944); Crazy Knights (1944); Men in Her Diary (1945); Hazard (1948); Skipalong Rosenbloom (1951); Mr. Universe (1951); Abbott and Costello Meet the Keystone Kops (1955); Hollywood or Bust (1956); The Beat Generation (1959); Don't Worry, We'll Think of a Title (1966).

## Ruby, Harry  See KALMAR AND RUBY

## Ruggles, Charlie (1886—1970)

More often than not, Charlie Ruggles played that nice, well-bred man with the little mustache who always seemed to be in trouble with his wife. If he wasn't in dutch with his wife, then it was his employer who had it in for him. Ruggles was much loved by audiences for his portrayals of ordinary guys in a film career that spanned more than fifty years.

Born in Los Angeles, California, he was a successful stage actor in New York before making his way back home and into the movies. Although he began acting sporadically in films as early as 1915, his little-man-against-the-world persona didn't take shape until 1932 when his segment of the anthology film *If I Had a Million* touched a common nerve. In that movie he played a timid clerk in a china shop who had to pay for every piece of statuary he broke; in his nervous fear, he broke plenty. When he won $1 million in the lottery, however, he stormed into his place of employment and systematically broke everything—no doubt to the cheers of movie audiences everywhere. His wife in the film, played by Mary Boland, went on to play his complaining spouse in eleven other movies.

Ruggles began impressing audiences as a comic actor in *Charley's Aunt* (1930) as well as Ernst LUBITSCH's *Smiling Lieutenant* (1931), *One Hour with You* (1932), and *Trouble in Paradise* (1932). His reputation grew with films such as *Love Me Tonight* (1932), *Alice in Wonderland* (as the March Hare, 1933), *Six of a Kind* (1934), *Ruggles of Red Gap* (1935), *Bringing Up Baby* (1938), and *It Happened on Fifth Avenue* (1947).

Ruggles left the movies in the late 1940s to star in his own TV series, "The Ruggles" (1949–1952). Unlike *Ruggles of Red Gap*, the title of which was only coincidentally the same as his own name, the TV show was built around Ruggles and a fictional wife. He stayed with the fledgling TV medium for another long-running series that began in 1953, "The World of Mr. Sweeney," which was loosely based on a 1934 film in which Ruggles had starred. In the early 1960s, his pleasing voice could be heard as the narrator of "Aesop's Fables" on the animated TV series "The Rocky and Bullwinkle Show" (1961–1962). When Ruggles returned to the big screen, he played amusing supporting roles, several of them in light Disney comedies such as *The Parent Trap* (1961) and *Son of Flubber* (1963).

Charlie Ruggles was the brother of director Wesley Ruggles (1889–1972), who also had a substantial Hollywood career. Wesley went to Hollywood at about the same time as his brother, becoming one of the KEYSTONE KOPS in 1914. As

an actor, he had roles in a number of Charlie CHAPLIN comedies during the 1910s. As a director, he made comedies as often as other types of films. He made a number of well-regarded movies, among them, Mae WEST's *I'm No Angel* (1933).

---

**FILMS INCLUDE:** *Peer Gynt* (1915); *Gentlemen of the Press* (1929); *The Battle of Paris* (1929); *Young Man of Manhattan* (1930); *Her Wedding Night* (1930); *Charley's Aunt* (1930); *Honor Among Lovers* (1931); *The Smiling Lieutenant* (1931); *Husband's Holiday* (1931); *The Girl Habit* (1931); *Love Me Tonight* (1932); *One Hour with You* (1932); *Make Me a Star* (1932); *Trouble in Paradise* (1932); *If I Had a Million* (1932); *Madame Butterfly* (1932); *Alice in Wonderland* (1933); *Murders in the Zoo* (1933); *Mama Loves Papa* (1933); *Friends of Mr. Sweeney* (1934); *Six of a Kind* (1934); *Ruggles of Red Gap* (1935); *No More Ladies* (1935); *The Big Broadcast of 1936* (1935); *People Will Talk* (1935); *Early to Bed* (1936); *Anything Goes* (1936); *Wives Never Know* (1936); *Turn Off the Moon* (1937); *Mind Your Own Business* (1937); *Bringing Up Baby* (1938); *Service de Luxe* (1938); *Night Work* (1939); *Boy Trouble* (1939); *No Time for Comedy* (1940); *The Farmer's Daughter* (1940); *Model Wife* (1941); *Honeymoon for Three* (1941); *Invisible Woman* (1941); *The Perfect Snob* (1941); *Friendly Enemies* (1942); *Our Hearts Were Young and Gay* (1944); *Incendiary Blonde* (1945); *A Stolen Life* (1946); *My Brother Talks to Horses* (1946); *It Happened on Fifth Avenue* (1947); *Give My Regards to Broadway* (1948); *Look for the Silver Lining* (1949); *The Pleasure of His Company* (1961); *All in a Night's Work* (1961); *The Parent Trap* (1961); *Son of Flubber* (1963); *Papa's Delicate Condition* (1963); *I'd Rather Be Rich* (1964); *Follow Me Boys!* (1966); *The Ugly Dachshund* (1966).

---

## Russell, Rosalind (1908—1976)

A talented and popular actress, Rosalind Russell did much of her best, most memorable work in comedies. A versatile actress, she performed on screen in more than fifty films, the bulk of them in the 1930s and 1940s; she was usually better than her material. While there are relatively few films in which she appeared that have weathered the test of time, Russell was an important actress because she proved that attractive and desirable female characters could also be smart, resourceful, and witty. If Joan Crawford portrayed career women who suffered for their choices, Rosalind Russell portrayed them as healthy, confident, and fun-loving.

Born to a wealthy family in Waterbury, Connecticut, Russell had the advantages of a good education at Marymount College and the American Academy of Dramatic Arts before beginning her acting career. She first appeared on the stage in the late 1920s, gaining valuable experience before heeding the call to Hollywood. Her debut on film was in a major supporting role in *Evelyn Prentice* (1934). After nearly a dozen mediocre movies, she made her critical breakthrough playing the unlikable title role in the hit *Craig's Wife* (1936). With her stock rising, she was given better scripts, making the most of them by starring in such strong dramatic films as *Night Must Fall* (1937) and *The Citadel* (1938).

Russell's first serious turn in sophisticated comedy was playing one of the three major roles in the all-star, all-female *The Women* (1939). More comedies followed, such as *His Girl Friday* (1940), in which she proved to be the quintessential screwball comedian. After more comedy hits, such as *No Time for Comedy* (1940), she brought her wonderfully brittle comedic style to *My Sister Eileen* (1942), for which she received a best actress Oscar nomination.

She played a different kind of sister in *Sister Kenny* (1946), a biopic about the nurse who helped discover the cure for polio. It brought her a second Oscar nomination and precipitated her plunge into more dramatic fare. The following year she garnered her third Oscar nomination for her work in *Mourning Becomes Electra* (1947). However, her subsequent movies during the late 1940s and early 1950s were neither notable nor successful, except for *Picnic* (1955), by which time she was playing second leads.

In 1958 Russell made a comeback in the title role

of *Auntie Mame*, winning her fourth and last best actress Academy Award nomination. Despite her success, she didn't appear on film again until 1962 when she blitzed the nation's movie screen with three films, the most memorable being *Gypsy*.

Russell appeared in only a handful of movies during the rest of her career, usually playing strong supporting roles in light comic films such as *The Trouble with Angels* (1966), *Rosie!* (1968), and *Where Angels Go, Trouble Follows* (1968). Her last theatrical film was the unfortunate *Mrs. Pollifax—Spy* (1971), an embarrassing movie that Russell also scripted under a pen name. She then turned to television, starring in a TV movie titled *The Crooked Hearts* (1972). That same year, Russell became one of the few actors, and only the second woman, to be honored by the Academy with the Jean Hersholt Humanitarian Award.

---

**FILMS:** *Evelyn Prentice* (1934); *Forsaking All Others* (1934); *The President Vanishes* (1934); *The Night Is Young* (1935); *West Point of the Air* (1935); *The Casino Murder Case* (1935); *Reckless* (1935); *China Seas* (1935); *Rendezvous* (1935); *It Had to Happen* (1936); *Trouble for Two* (1936); *Under Two Flags* (1936); *Craig's Wife* (1936); *Live, Love, and Learn* (1937); *Night Must Fall* (1937); *Man Proof* (1938); *Four's a Crowd* (1938); *The Citadel* (1938); *Fast and Loose* (1939); *The Women* (1939); *His Girl Friday* (1940); *No Time for Comedy* (1940); *Hired Wife* (1940); *This Thing Called Love* (1941); *Design for Scandal* (1941); *They Met in Bombay* (1941); *The Feminine Touch* (1941); *My Sister Eileen* (1942); *Take a Letter, Darling* (1942); *Flight for Fredom* (1943); *What a Woman* (1943); *She Wouldn't Say Yes* (1944); *Roughly Speaking* (1944); *Sister Kenny* (1946); *The Guilt of Janet Ames* (1947); *Mourning Becomes Electra* (1947); *The Velvet Touch* (1948); *Tell It to the Judge* (1949); *A Woman of Distinction* (1950); *Never Wave at a WAC* (1953); *The Girl Rush* (1955); *Picnic* (1956); *The Unguarded Moment* (story only, 1956); *Auntie Mame* (1958); *A Majority of One* (1962); *Gypsy* (1962); *Five Finger Exercise* (1962); *The Trouble with Angels* (1966); *Oh Dad, Poor Dad, Mama's Hung You in the*

*Closet and I'm Feeling So Sad* (1967); *Rosie!* (1967); *Where Angels Go, Trouble Follows* (1968); *Mrs. Pollifax—Spy* (1971).

## Ryan, Meg (1962—)

A blonde actress who is more adorable than beautiful, Meg Ryan has a little girl smile that makes her instantly accessible; it's one of the many comic tools she has at her disposal. After appearing in eight films during the 1980s, she suddenly vaulted into prominence in 1989 as a star comedian in *When Harry Met Sally*. If her status fell into doubt in the uneven years that followed, she confirmed her romantic comic appeal in the surprise summer hit, *Sleepless in Seattle* (1993).

Born in Fairfield, Connecticut, she was a journalism major at New York University before making the committment to acting. She made her movie debut as Candice Bergen's daughter in *Rich and Famous* (1981) and then worked steadily, often in significant roles, in films as varied as *Amityville 3-D* (1983) and *Top Gun* (1986). While Ryan appeared (with future husband Dennis Quaid) in the Martin SHORT comedy *Innerspace* (1987), her own comic talents did not fully blossom on screen until she starred with Billy CRYSTAL in *When Harry Met Sally*, directed by Rob REINER. Her famous faked orgasm scene in the deli from that film has already become a classic.

Two of her next three films were ROMANTIC COMEDIES, *Joe versus the Volcano* (1990) and *Prelude to a Kiss* (1992), but despite their abundant good qualities, both were box office disappointments. There was nothing disappointing, however, about *Sleepless in Seattle* (1993); directed by Nora EPHRON, the film reestablished Ryan's credentials as a fine comedian.

FILMS: *Rich and Famous* (1981); *Amityville 3-D* (1983); *Armed and Dangerous* (1986); *Top Gun* (1986); *Innerspace* (1987); *Promised Land* (1987); *D.O.A.* (1988); *The Presidio* (1988); *When Harry Met Sally* (1989); *Joe versus the Volcano* (1990); *The Doors*

*Meg Ryan is the romantic comedy heroine of our time, evoking a sexy, slightly offbeat accessibility. She became a comic star in* When Harry Met Sally *(1989) and confirmed that stardom with* Sleepless in Seattle *(1993). She is seen here with Alec Baldwin in a film that should have been a romantic comedy hit,* Prelude to a Kiss *(1992), but wasn't.*
PHOTO BY DON SMETZER, © 20TH CENTURY-FOX.

(1991); *Prelude to a Kiss* (1992); *Sleepless in Seattle* (1993); *Flesh and Bone* (1993).

## Ryskind, Morrie (1895—1985)

A playwright and screenwriter best known for his work for the MARX BROTHERS, Morrie Ryskind wrote *The Cocoanuts* (1929), *Animal Crackers* (1930), *A Night at the Opera* (1935), and *Room Service* (1938). Unlike George S. KAUFMAN, with whom he frequently collaborated, Ryskind had no trouble adapting to Hollywood. His work stood behind the success of such films as the hit SCREWBALL COMEDY *My Man Godfrey* (1936) and the hit sophisticated comedy *Stage Door* (1937).

Born in Brooklyn, New York, Ryskind was the co-winner (along with George S. Kaufman and Ira Gershwin) of the first Pulitzer Prize ever awarded to a Broadway musical, winning the coveted award in 1932 for *Of Thee I Sing*. During the Communist witch-hunt years of the late 1940s and early 1950s, when confronted with his Socialist past, Ryskind recanted it and eventually joined the ultra right-wing John Birch Society. By this time, however, his Hollywood career was essentially over, having had its greatest flowering during the 1930s and early 1940s.

---

**FILMS INCLUDE:** *The Cocoanuts* (co-play basis, sc, 1929); *Animal Crackers* (co-play basis, sc, 1930); *Palmy Days* (sc, 1931); *A Night at the Opera* (co-sc, 1935); *Anything Goes* (sc, 1935); *Ceiling Zero* (1935); *My Man Godfrey* (sc, 1936); *Stage Door* (sc, 1937); *Room Service* (sc, 1938); *Man About Town* (story, sc, 1939); *Louisiana Purchase* (based on play, 1941); *Penny Serenade* (sc, 1941); *Claudia* (sc, 1943); *Where Do We Go from Here?* (story, sc, 1945); *My Man Godfrey* (based on screenplay, 1957).

---

# S

**Saks, Gene (1921– )**   Actor and director Gene Saks is fully committed to works of comedy, particularly to the works of playwright Neil SIMON, with whom he is most closely associated. Although he started out as an actor, Saks's thespian skills are incidental to his career; he doesn't act in the films he directs, and when he does appear in front of a camera, it is usually in a modest role.

Born in New York City, Saks attended Cornell University before embarking on a full-time acting career. Progress came slowly; he did manage to get roles on and off Broadway as well as on TV, but his was hardly a well-known name. By the early 1960s it was clear Saks was never going to make the big time as an actor. He switched gears, eventually directing Broadway shows before providing the same skill and expertise to film directing with his winning work on Neil Simon's *Barefoot in the Park* (1967). Most of the films he has directed since have been adaptations of stage plays, usually those of Neil Simon, including *The Odd Couple* (1968), *Last of the Red Hot Lovers* (1972), and *Brighton Beach Memoirs* (1986).

---

**FILMS INCLUDE:** *A Thousand Clowns* (a, 1965); *Barefoot in the Park* (d, 1967); *The Odd Couple* (d, 1968); *Cactus Flower* (d, 1969); *Last of the Red Hot Lovers* (d, 1972); *Mame* (d, 1974); *The Prisoner of Second Avenue* (a, 1974); *The One and Only* (a, 1978); *Lovesick* (a, 1983); *The Goodbye People* (a, 1984); *Brighton Beach Memoirs* (d, 1986); *Funny* (a, 1988); *Tchin-Tchin* (d, 1991).

---

**satire**   Playwright George S. KAUFMAN once described satire as that which closes on Saturday night. In other words, the intelligent use of wit and irony to cut fools and folly down to size has rarely been an audience pleaser among those seeking simple entertainment. What has been true of the theater has also been true of the movies. There have been relatively few out-and-out film satires made, and many of those that were made were not box office winners.

If Hollywood has had little stomach for satirizing society at large, it has found gold in satirizing itself. In the silent era, comedian Ben TURPIN rose to fame with outlandish two-reel satires of famous movies. In more recent times, *Airplane!* (1980), which made a hilarious mockery of every aviation film cliché, started a new trend that satirizes not just a single film, but entire genres. Movies such as *Top Secret!* (1984), satirizing spy movies, and *Hot Shots* (1991) and *Hot Shots, Part Deux* (1993), poking fun at action films, have found a happy niche in the movie marketplace.

Serious satire found its way into the Hollywood mainstream in the early 1930s when America was in the grip of the Great Depression. There was certainly plenty to satirize in those bleak days, and Frank CAPRA was among the first to capitalize on audience discontent with *American Madness* (1932). Later in that decade, *Nothing Sacred* (1937) poked fun at American gullibility. However, nobody satirized American society or institutions better during the 1930s than the MARX BROTHERS, who attacked everything from higher education in *Horse Feathers* (1932) to government and war in *DUCK SOUP* (1933).

The leading movie satirist of the 1940s was unquestionably writer/director Preston STURGES, whose hit comedies made fun of such topics as politics in *THE GREAT MCGINTY* (1940), for which Sturges won a best original screenplay Oscar; marriage in *The Palm Beach Story* (1942); and small town American values in *The Miracle of Morgan's Creek* (1944).

Hollywood took itself very seriously during the late 1940s and 1950s, producing very few satires during those years. The postwar era and early cold war years were filled with such angst that most comedies, as an antidote, tended to be extremely light. Even when the remake of *Nothing Sacred* was turned into a film in 1954, it was designed as an innocuous vehicle for Dean MARTIN and Jerry LEWIS and renamed *Living It Up*. The one major exception during this period was Charlie CHAPLIN's *MONSIEUR VERDOUX* (1947), a film so bleak in its harsh humor, satirizing religion and justice, that it brought cries of outrage, and many theaters refused to run it.

The tumultuous 1960s brought back the satire with surprising box office strength. The rise of the counterculture and the movement of the movies toward a younger, baby boomer audience gave films more of an opportunity to be outrageous. Among the filmmakers who responded were Stanley Kubrick, whose *DR. STRANGELOVE* (1964) satirized the military mind and dealt with the threat of nuclear destruction with pungent BLACK COMEDY. Later in the decade, *The President's Analyst* (1967) took potshots at everything from the government to the phone company with hilarious results.

The leading film satirist of the 1970s was screenwriter Paddy CHAYEFSKY, whose angry comedies were noted for both their humor and their truth. His screenplays for the hits *The Hospital* (1971) and *NETWORK* (1976) were winners, both bringing him Oscars for best screenplay. Other notable satires during this decade were the powerful *Catch-22* (1970), *Little Murders* (1971), and the mild *Fun with Dick and Jane* (1977).

The self-indulgent 1980s should have been rich ground for satirist filmmakers, but the pickings were surprisingly lean among mainstream directors. Satire bubbled up with a vengeance, however, from the underground cinema, most notably in the person of writer/director John WATERS, who made such iconoclastic social satires as *Polyester* (1981) and *Hairspray* (1988).

More recently, *Hero* (1992), a big-budget film starring Dustin Hoffman and satirizing journalism and society's image of heroism, once again proved George Kaufman's dictum correct. *Hero* died on Saturday night—and every other night of the week—failing at the box office despite (or perhaps because of) its piercing satirical edge.

## "Saturday Night Live"

The long-running TV comedy show "Saturday Night Live" has spawned more film comedy stars than any other single source other than VAUDEVILLE. Created and produced by Lorne Michaels, the show hit the airwaves on NBC-TV in 1975. It was an immediate sensation, gathering rave reviews, a pile of Emmys, and a loyal audience. The incredible talent of its initial troupe of performers, the famous Not Ready for Prime Time Players, so many of whom graduated to Hollywood stardom, established the TV show as a jump-off point to the movies and has remained so through the years.

The list of cast members who have gone on to star in film comedies is a who's who of contemporary comic movie stars and includes Dan AYKROYD, John BELUSHI, Chevy CHASE, Gilda RADNER, Eddie MURPHY, Bill MURRAY, Billy CRYSTAL, Martin SHORT, Mike MYERS, and Albert BROOKS. Many other alumni from the program appear in films in smaller roles. Often, current cast members show up in movies without ever leaving their regular gig.

The show has even spawned a number of hit movies that were based on characters and sketches that were once broadcast on the show. For instance, *The Blues Brothers* (1980), starring Dan Aykroyd and John Belushi, was based on a series of "Saturday

*Not since vaudeville has the movie industry had a single source of comic talent as bountiful as the long-running "Saturday Night Live" TV show. Its producer, Lorne Michaels (right, with sunglasses) is seen here on the set of* Wayne's World *(1992), the hit spin-off comedy he also produced.*   PHOTO BY SUZANNE TENNER, © PARAMOUNT PICTURES.

Night Live" performances by the twosome in their guises of Elwood and Jake. Aykroyd and Jane Curtin teamed up to turn their popular Conehead sketches of the late 1970s into the recent feature-length comedy *The Coneheads* (1993). Mike Myers and Dana Carvey also joined to turn out *Wayne's World* (1992), a huge hit based on characters created for the show.

**Schlesinger, Leon**   *See* WARNER BROS. CARTOONS

**screwball comedy**   If FARCES are known for their improbable plots, then screwball comedies (or crazy comedies, as they are also known) are marked by improbable characters. The genre received its name after a baseball pitch known as a "screwball," which breaks in the opposite direction of the traditional curveball. In other words, a screwball comedy is filled with characters who act differently than you might first expect, which explains why so many of these movies are set in high society where one can be eccentric without being a candidate for the looney bin. Another characteristic of screwball comedies is the breakneck speed with which characters speak to one another, often delivering their lines in overlapping dialogue; the language in a screwball comedy can be just as dizzy as the characters.

The father of the screwball comedy was director Howard HAWKS, who perfected and popularized the genre. Hawks gave birth to the screwball com-

with *The Awful Truth* (1937), and George CUKOR with *Holiday* (1938). They were all shining examples of the genre during its prime.

Except for Hawks's efforts, the screwball comedy faded away in subsequent decades, although one could make a case that a number of the Martin and Lewis films of the 1950s were modified crazy comedies on the basis of Jerry LEWIS's exceedingly bizarre characterizations. It seemed as if the screwball comedy was a thing of the past, however, until Peter Bogdanovich made a conscious effort to revive it with *What's Up Doc?* (1972), a film that owes a great deal of its energy and structure to *Bringing Up Baby*.

In recent years there have been films that flirt with the concept of the screwball comedy, such as Hawks devotee Jonathan Demme's two romps *Something Wild* (1986) and *Married to the Mob* (1988), but the pure form seems rooted forever in a madcap 1930s sensibility.

## Segal, George (1934—)

A mischievous grin combined with exquisite comic timing brought George Segal great success as a light ROMANTIC COMEDY star in the 1970s. An actor who might be described as the middle-class Cary GRANT or a latter-day Jack LEMMON, he has been in movies since 1961.

Born in New York City and educated at Columbia University, Segal was just as interested in a music career as he was in acting. Among the many groups he formed were Bruno Lynch and His Imperial Jazz Band and, while in the army, Corporal Bruno's Sad Sack Six. He later worked for The Circle in the Square theater as a janitor, ticket taker, usher, and, finally, understudy in the hope of getting a chance to act. He finally made his theatrical debut in Molière's *Don Juan* for a different theater company. It played one night and closed.

Segal continued to find acting opportunities in such plays as *The Iceman Cometh*, *Antony and Cleopatra*, and *Leave It to Jane*. However, he received his most important training when he became one of

*No one was better at screwball comedy than Cary Grant, seen here literally dressed for work in the Howard Hawks production of* I Was a Male War Bride *(1949).*

PHOTO COURTESY OF MOVIE STAR NEWS.

edy with *TWENTIETH CENTURY* (1934), a hilarious film peopled with such wild characters that it seemed as if there were hardly a sane person in the cast. He went on to make the most famous screwball comedies in Hollywood history, namely *Bringing Up Baby* (1938), *His Girl Friday* (1940), which was a reworked version of *The Front Page*, *Ball of Fire* (1942), *I Was a Male War Bride* (1949), and *Monkey Business* (1952).

Hawks was the premier director of screwball comedies, but not the only one. Among other directors who dabbled in the genre were Gregory La Cava, with *My Man Godfrey* (1936), Leo MCCAREY

the original cast members of the long-running comic improv show *The Premise*.

Segal made his film debut in a small role in *The Young Doctors* (1961). Throughout the rest of the early 1960s he shuttled between the theater, TV, and movies, appearing in modest roles in such dramatic films as *Act One* (1963) and *The New Interns* (1964). His career began to pick up substantially in the mid-1960s when he scored a hit as the lead in *King Rat* (1965), a part that was turned down by both Paul Newman and Steve McQueen. He joined an all-star cast in *Ship of Fools* (1965), played Biff in the televised Lee J. Cobb version of *Death of a Salesman* in 1966, and received a best supporting actor Oscar nomination for his role in *Who's Afraid of Virginia Woolf?* (1966).

He seemed well on his way to stardom as a dramatic actor and, indeed, did star in a number of interesting and relatively good movies during the rest of the 1960s, but he didn't quite take off. Films such as *The Quiller Memorandum* (1966), *The St. Valentine's Day Massacre* (1967), *The Southern Star* (1969), and *Bridge at Remagen* (1969) were, more often than not, mediocre or poor performers at the ticket window despite their many worthy attributes.

During the 1970s, however, Segal found his niche as the contemporary everyman, struggling, with comic effect, to deal with many of the foibles and fundamental issues of modern society. He showed his seriocomic range in the highly regarded *Loving* (1970), nearly stole the hit comedy *The Owl and the Pussycat* (1970) from his powerful co-star, Barbra Streisand, and gave a tour de force performance in the cult favorite *Where's Poppa?* (1970). Finally, in 1973, he hit his full commercial stride with several box office winners, the sophisticated romantic comedy, *A Touch of Class* (1973), Paul MAZURSKY's poignantly funny *Blume in Love* (1973), and Robert Altman's manic *California Split* (1974).

While his material was considerably less interesting in the latter half of the 1970s, Segal did manage a couple of winning films that dealt humorously with middle-class values, *Fun with Dick and Jane* (1977) and *The Last Married Couple in America* (1979).

The 1980s were less kind to Segal. He has not been in many movies, and those he has starred in have not often been hits, as evidenced by the poor reception to *Carbon Copy* (1981). Like many a film star in decline, he has taken to appearing quite often in television movies such as *The Cold Room* (1984). He began starring in 1987 in "Murphy's Law," his own TV series. Lately he seems to have comfortably settled into supporting roles in films such as *For the Boys* (1991).

**FILMS:** *The Young Doctors* (1961); *Act One* (1963); *Invitation to a Gunfighter* (1964); *The New Interns* (1964); *King Rat* (1965); *Ship of Fools* (1965); *Lost Command* (1966); *The Quiller Memorandum* (1966); *Who's Afraid of Virginia Woolf?* (1966); *The St. Valentine's Day Massacre* (1967); *Bye Bye Braverman* (1968); *No Way to Treat a Lady* (1968); *The Southern Star* (1969); *The Bridge at Remagen* (1969); *Loving* (1970); *The Owl and the Pussycat* (1970); *Where's Poppa?* (1970); *Born to Win* (also p, 1971); *The Hot Rock* (1972); *Blume in Love* (1973); *A Touch of Class* (1973); *California Split* (1974); *The Terminal Man* (1974); *The Black Bird* (also p, 1975); *Russian Roulette* (1975); *The Duchess and the Dirtwater Fox* (1976); *Fun with Dick and Jane* (1976); *Rollercoaster* (1977); *Who Is Killing the Great Chefs of Europe?* (1978); *Lost and Found* (1979); *The Last Married Couple in America* (1980); *Carbon Copy* (1981); *Killing 'Em Softly* (1981); *Not My Kid* (1985); *Stick* (1985); *Many Happy Returns* (1986); *All's Fair* (1989); *Look Who's Talking* (1989); *The Endless Game* (1990); *For the Boys* (1991); *Me Myself and I* (1992).

**Seidelman, Susan (1952—)** Despite disappointing box office returns and mixed critical reaction on her later films, Susan Seidelman is one of the most promising female comedy directors in Hollywood. Her low-budget first feature, *Smithereens* (1982), brought her to public attention, and her first comedy, *Desperately Seeking Susan* (1984), was a bona fide hit. Her films since then, like the two that preceded them, have been very much from a woman's point of view, offering a freshly original satiric perspective on love and relationships, among other things.

Seidelman grew up in a New Jersey suburb outside Philadelphia, Pennsylvania. Graduating from the New York University Film School with a number of award-winning satiric student films to her credit, she spent less than $100,000 to make *Smithereens*. An art house hit, the movie was hardly a comedy, but its theme of a woman in search of an identity came through in a more comic vein in her second film, *Desperately Seeking Susan*. Her third movie, the ambitious comedy *Making Mr. Right* (1987), deserved a better fate than it received at the hands of many critics and a surprisingly disinterested audience. A satire about a woman's desire to program her idea of a perfect man into a robot, it was a well-done, delightfully original film. *Cookie* (1989), scripted by Nora EPHRON, also had its comic charms, but didn't light any fires among moviegoers. *She-Devil* (1990) was the movie that really set her back; with Meryl Streep and Roseanne Barr, the film had high expectations that were dashed by critical and box office disaster.

---

FILMS: *Smithereens* (story, ed, p, d, 1982); *Desperately Seeking Susan* (d, 1984); *Making Mr. Right* (p, d, 1987); *Cookie* (p, d, 1989); *She-Devil* (p, d, 1990); *Yesterday* (d, 1992).

---

# Sellers, Peter (1925—1980)  Both a talented
SLAPSTICK artist and a gifted impersonator, Peter Sellers enjoyed a comic screen career for thirty years. Unlike most comedy stars who have made their mark by becoming a recognizable comic character, this British comic actor became an international star on the basis of playing a remarkably wide variety of comic roles.

Born Richard Henry Sellers in Southsea, England, to a show business family, he began working on stage with his parents when he was a child. He continued playing in English music halls throughout his adolescence and then had a tour of duty with the Royal Air Force entertaining the troops. After World War II, he came to a modest level of fame as a member of the popular madcap BBC radio program "The Goon Show," which later inspired the creation of "Monty Python's Flying Circus." On the basis of being one of the "goons," Sellers embarked on a movie career, appearing in his first feature film in 1951, *Penny Points to Paradise* (1951).

Sellers's film career was steady if unspectacular during most of the 1950s, with solid supporting performances in such British movies as *The Ladykillers* (1955) and *Man in a Cocked Hat* (1959), but he began to come into his own as a star both in England and America with *The Mouse That Roared* (1959), when he played three roles in the hit comedy about a tiny country that declares war on the United States to get foreign aid.

His film career had extreme ups and downs during the next twenty years. Far too often he starred in mediocre movies, but when he had good material—particularly during the late 1960s (largely in Hollywood productions)—Sellers was a delight to watch. His best performances during that high point were in DR. STRANGELOVE (1964), for which he received a best actor Academy Award nomination, *The World of Henry Orient* (1964), *What's New Pussycat?* (1965), *The Wrong Box* (1966), *After the Fox* (1966), *The BoBo* (1967), *I Love You, Alice B. Toklas* (1968), and *The Party* (1968).

Sellers's portrayal of Inspector Clouseau, the role for which he became most famous, also began in the mid-1960s with *The Pink Panther* (1964) and was followed by *A Shot in the Dark* (1964). The role was resurrected in 1975 with *The Return of the Pink Panther* (1975), *The Pink Panther Strikes Again* (1976), and *Revenge of the Pink Panther* (1978). The Pink Panther films, all directed by Blake EDWARDS, saved Sellers's floundering career in the mid-1970s after his starring roles in such poor movies as *Where Does It Hurt?* (1972) and *The Blockhouse* (1973).

His revival in the latter 1970s gave him the opportunity to play what many consider his greatest role, the TV-watching hero of *Being There* (1979). His work in the film was recognized by his peers when they nominated him for his second best actor Academy Award. *Being There* would have made a great exit film for the comic actor, but a couple of mediocre comedies followed before his untimely death. Worse, outtakes from his Pink Panther movies found their way to the screen in 1982 in the form of *Trail of the Pink Panther* (1982), a travesty of a film that did not honor his memory.

---

**FILMS:** *Penny Points to Paradise* (1951); *Down Among the Z Men* (1952); *Orders Are Orders* (1954); *John and Julie* (1955); *The Ladykillers* (1955); *The Smallest Show on Earth* (1957); *The Naked Truth* (1957); *Tom Thumb* (1958); *Up the Creek!* (1958); *Man in the Cocked Cat* (1959); *The Battle of the Sexes* (1959); *I'm All Right, Jack* (1959); *The Mouse That Roared* (1959); *The Millionairess* (1960); *Two-Way Stretch* (1960); *Never Let Go* (1960); *Mr. Topaze* (also d, 1961); *Lolita* (1962); *Waltz of the Toreadors* (1962); *Trial and Error* (1962); *The Road to Hong Kong* (cameo, 1962); *Only Two Can Play* (1962); *The Wrong Arm of the Law* (1962); *Heaven's Above!* (1963); *Dr. Strangelove or: How I Learned to Stop Worrying and Love the Bomb* (1964); *The Pink Panther* (1964); *A Shot in the Dark* (1964); *The World of Henry Orient* (1964); *What's New, Pussycat?* (1965); *After the Fox* (also song, 1966); *The Wrong Box* (1966); *The BoBo* (1967); *Casino Royale* (1967); *Woman Times Seven* (1967); *I Love You, Alice B. Toklas* (1968); *The Party* (1968); *Hoffman* (1970); *A Day at the Beach* (1970); *The Magic Christian* (also sc, 1970); *There's a Girl in My Soup* (1970); *Alice's Adventures in Wonderland* (1972); *Where Does It Hurt?* (1972); *The Blockhouse* (1973); *Ghost in the Noonday Sun* (1973); *The Optimists* (1973); *The Great McGonagall* (1974); *The Return of the Pink Panther* (1975); *Undercovers Hero* (1975); *Murder by Death* (1976); *The Pink Panther Strikes Again* (1976); *Revenge of the Pink Panther* (1978); *Being There* (1979); *The Prisoner of Zenda* (1979); *The Fiendish Plot of Dr. Fu Manchu* (1980); *Trail of the Pink Panther* (1982).

**Semon, Larry (1889—1928)** In the early 1920s, Larry Semon was among the most popular of comic stars, just a notch below the great Buster KEATON and Charlie CHAPLIN. Unlike their characters, however, Semon's was a grotesque; he accentuated his unattractive features to make himself appear as ugly as possible. In addition, he walked like a marionette, in a weird herky-jerky fashion. Ultimately, his character was so unnatural that audience identification was impossible. Nonetheless, other comics of the day thought very highly of Semon's ability to construct a gag or a stunt. Unfortunately, Semon's humor was limited to chases and stunts that were strung together in a hodgepodge. What was lacking was any sort of interrelationship between the humor, the story, and the characters. It's no wonder, therefore, that Semon's films have not weathered the test of time.

Semon, born in West Point, Mississippi, grew up with a knowledge of show business; his father was the magician, Zera the Great. After working as a cartoonist for a New York newspaper, Semon began writing and directing one- and two-reel comedies for Vitagraph in 1916. Not long after, he started putting himself in his own films such as *Spooks and Spasms* (1917). He became immensely popular playing a bizarre version of a young, romantic lead who pursued the girl. The humor, of course, came from this freaky looking man acting as if he were a macho, Valentino-type character.

After his success in shorts, Semon began making features. He often wrote, directed, and starred in his films, but he was infamous for requiring lavish budgets that could not be sustained by the profits from his movies. Nonetheless, his best feature film, *Kid Speed* (1924), was made during these otherwise declining years. Semon also played the scarecrow in a silent version of *The Wizard of Oz* (1925), a film he directed as well as co-scripted.

When his comedy career went bust in 1927 with the commercial failure of *Spuds*, a film he produced as well as directed, wrote, and starred in, he turned to dramatic acting, appearing in Joseph von Sternberg's excellent early gangster film *Underworld*

(1927). It was not enough to save Semon's film career. In relatively quick succession during 1928, he went bankrupt, suffered a mental breakdown, and died of pneumonia. Larry Semon is the silent comedian that time forgot.

---

FILMS INCLUDE: *A Villainous Villain* (d, 1916); *Love and Loot* (d, 1916); *Footlights and Fakers* (d, 1917); *Boasts and Boldness* (a, d, 1917); *Spooks and Spasms* (a, d, 1917); *Rough Toughs and Roof Tops* (a, sc, d, 1917); *Spies and Spills* (a, d, 1918); *Babes and Boobs* (a, d, 1918); *Passing the Buck* (a, sc, d, 1919); *The Simple Life* (a, d, 1919); *The Stagehand* (a, co-d, 1920); *The Fall Guy* (a, co-d, 1921); *The Show* (a, co-d, 1922); *The Sleuth* (a, co-d, 1922); *No Wedding Bells* (a, d, 1923); *Midnight Cabaret* (a, d, 1923); *The Girl in the Limousine* (a, d, 1924); *The Perfect Clown* (a, 1925); *The Wizard of Oz* (a, co-sc, d, 1925); *Stop, Look, and Listen* (a, co-sc, p, d, 1926); *Spuds* (a, sc, p, d, 1927); *Underworld* (a, 1927).

---

## Sennett, Mack (1880—1960)

As director, producer, and film executive, Mack Sennett was the first to make comedy a sole preoccupation, building Keystone into Hollywood's earliest, most successful speciality studio. Known as the father of SLAPSTICK film comedy, Sennett made movies that created a healthy tradition of irreverence; nothing—certainly not authority—was immune from his good-natured jabs. His frenetic comedies served as a training ground for many of the silent era's greatest comic stars, among them Charlie CHAPLIN, Mabel NORMAND, Fatty ARBUCKLE, Ford STERLING, Edgar KENNEDY, Harry LANGDON, Ben TURPIN, and, in her early career, even Gloria Swanson. And, of course, there were the KEYSTONE KOPS.

Sennett's comedies weren't clever so much as they were outrageous. His films were solidly based on well-timed but unpredictable physical comedy; crashing buildings, comic chases, and pie-throwing were constant features. Although lacking in subtlety, his movies were bold and fresh in their wild aban-don. If his movies ultimately fell into a formula that limited his most talented performers, the energy that drove his best work also drove audiences into hysterics.

Born Mikall Sinnott of Irish parentage in the French-Canadian province of Quebec, he grew to be a sturdy young man who worked with his hands as a laborer; his only apparent talent was a strong and deep singing voice. When he was seventeen, not long after his family moved to New England, he happened to meet Marie DRESSLER and charmed her into giving him a letter of introduction to the theatrical impresario David Belasco. The letter worked insofar as he got to meet Belasco, but it didn't result in a job. Undaunted, Mikall (by then Michael, and eventually Mack) decided to try his luck in BURLESQUE, making his debut in 1902 playing the rear end of a horse, an inauspicious yet somehow appropriate beginning for the future iconoclast who took such fierce delight in poking fun at society's customs and institutions.

Sennett was not a terribly successful performer but he persevered, eventually joining the Biograph company in 1908 as a comic film actor. He appeared in movies during the next several years, often as a minor star, but his on-camera histrionics did not lead to a long acting tenure. Happily, Sennett had begun writing his own scripts at Biograph and was soon directing them under the tutelage of cinema pioneer D. W. Griffith.

By 1912 Sennett was a major director of comedies (Griffith cared little for comedy and happily relegated such films to his eager protégé) and had already established the style and content of his knockabout FARCES with such Biograph players as Mabel Normand and Ford Sterling. He left Biograph to establish Keystone later that year with two former bookies who provided the financing, and many of his comedy stars went with him.

Sennett's first Keystone film was *Cohen Collects a Debt* (1912), which picked up right where he left off at Biograph; the film was inventive and full of motion and mayhem. It was no coincidence that the first pie thrown in an actor's face was thrown in a

Keystone comedy. Another of Sennett's most memorable inventions was the Keystone Kops, a goofy crew of policemen who somehow always managed to catch their man (or woman) at the end, but only after innumerable hysterical blunders and misadventures.

The raucous physical humor of the Keystone comedies delighted the mass audience, but so did the Keystone BATHING BEAUTIES, who represented the other side of Sennett's wonderfully vulgar imagination. He was wise enough to know that pretty girls in skimpy (for their day) bathing suits would sell tickets, and he provided his bathing beauties with just enough comic business to make the films risqué rather than salacious.

Sennett often provided the ideas for his comedies, although he made little use of scripts. He would send his crew and comics off to an actual event (car races, parades, etc.) and have them film scenes "on location"; later he would figure out how to meld these scenes into a story and fill in the transitions. Invariably, however, his movies ended with a comic chase, a topsy-turvy rendition of what Sennett had learned about editing and pacing from D. W. Griffith.

Sennett was in the forefront when the film industry moved toward consolidation. In 1915 he joined the other two giants of the silent screen, his mentor D. W. Griffith and Thomas H. Ince, to form a new studio called Triangle. The venture was not a success, and Sennett pulled out of the arrangement in 1917—but at a cost. He had to give up the name Keystone. It was a symbolic loss, but it also marked the beginning of the end of Sennett's reign as the king of comedy.

Under the new corporate name, Mack Sennett Comedies, he continued making movies with many of his established stars, but he made shorts almost exclusively. Although he had pioneered comedy features with success when he made TILLIE'S PUNCTURED ROMANCE (1914), he was ultimately more comfortable with the shorter form. Given his mastery of physical comedy rather than story structure or character development, it was, perhaps, wise for

Sennett to avoid making many features. Nonetheless, slapstick was becoming passé during the 1920s, and audiences began to favor the more sophisticated comedy of character that could be found in Hal ROACH's comedies such as OUR GANG, LAUREL AND HARDY, and others.

Sennett had also begun presenting more polished, less anarchic movies, but by then he had already lost many of his best stars, including his one-time fiancée, Mabel Normand. (His relationship with Normand was the basis of the critically acclaimed 1974 Broadway musical *Mack and Mabel*, with Robert Preston as Sennett and Bernadette Peters as Normand.) His last great star during the silent era was Harry Langdon, certainly a comic of character, but unfortunately his career was short-lived. In any event, the talkies literally sounded the death knell for Sennett's brand of fast-paced humor. During the early sound years, action and chases were subordinated to a static camera and clever repartee.

Sennett continued making shorts during the first half of the 1930s, producing, among other films, W. C. FIELDS's most cherished two-reelers *The Dentist* (1932), *The Fatal Glass of Beer* (1933), *The Pharmacist* (1933), and *The Barber Shop* (1933). By 1935, however, Sennett's long and wondrous career in Hollywood was over. Slapstick had become a low-brow art form left to the likes of the THREE STOOGES and was no longer appreciated by the masses as an original form of film comedy.

Sennett retired from making movies. In 1937 he received a special Academy Award that honored "the master of fun."

---

FILMS INCLUDE: As actor only: *The Song of the Shirt* (1908); *Balked at the Altar* (1908); *Mr. Jones at the Ball* (1908); *The Curtain Pole* (1909); *The Lonely Villa* (also co-sc, 1909); *The Way of a Man* (1909); *Pippa Passes* (1909); *The Gibson Goddess* (1909); *Nursing a Viper* (1909); *In Old California* (1910); *The Dancing Girl of Butte* (1910); *All on Account of the Milk* (1910); *The Newlyweds* (1910); *An Affair of Hearts* (1910); *The Call to Arms* (1910); *The Italian Barber*

(1911); *The Last Drop of Water* (1911); *Hollywood Cavalcade* (1939).

As director: *The Lucky Toothache* (also a, sc, 1910); *The Masher* (also a, sc, 1910); *Cupid's Joke* (also a, 1911); *The Country Lovers* (also a, 1911); *Too Many Burglars* (also a, 1911); *Their First Divorce* (also a, 1911); *The Joke on the Joker* (1912); *Pants and Pansies* (1912); *The Fatal Chocolate* (also a, 1912); *Neighbors* (1912); *Willie Becomes an Artist* (1912); *The Tourists* (also a, 1912).

As director/producer: *The Water Nymph* (1912); *Cohen Collects a Debt* (1912); *Stolen Glory* (1912); *At Coney Island* (also a, 1912); *Mabel's Lovers* (1912); *Brown's Seance* (1912); *The Drummer's Vacation* (1912); *A Red Hot Romance* (1913); *Those Good Old Days* (1913); *A Game of Poker* (1913); *A Fishy Affair* (1913); *The Bangville Police* (1913); *Algy on the Force* (1913); *Mabel's Awful Mistake* (also a, 1913); *The Speed Queen* (1913); *The Waiters' Picnic* (1913); *Safe in Jail* (1913); *The Tale of a Black Eye* (1913); *Cohen's Outing* (1913); *The Firebugs* (1913); *Mabel's New Hero* (1913); *Schintz the Tailor* (1913); *Two Old Tars* (1913); *Cohen Saves the Flag* (1913); *Mabel at the Wheel* (co-d, 1914); *Love and Dynamite* (1914); *Tango Tangles* (1914); *Bathing Beauty* (1914); *Twenty Minutes of Love* (1914); *He Loved the Ladies* (1914); *Tillie's Punctured Romance* (1914); *For Better—But Worse* (also a, 1915); *Those College Girls* (1915); *My Valet* (also a, sc, 1915); *Stolen Magic* (also a, sc, 1915); *A Movie Star* (p only, 1916); *Bright Lights* (p only, 1916); *The Moonshiners* (p only, 1916); *Teddy at the Throttle* (p only, 1917); *A Clever Dummy* (p only, 1917); *The Pullman Bride* (p only, 1917); *Mickey* (p only, 1918); *Sleuths* (p only, 1918); *The Foolish Age* (p only, 1919); *Yankee Doodle in Berlin* (p only, 1919); *Uncle Tom without a Cabin* (p only, 1919); *Down on the Farm* (p only, 1920); *Married Life* (p only, 1920); *Love, Honor, and Behave* (p only, 1920); *Home Talent* (also sc, co-d, 1921); *The Crossroads of New York* (story, sc, p, only, 1922); *The Shriek of Araby* (story, sc, p only, 1923); *The Extra Girl* (story, p only, 1923); *Picking Peaches* (p only, 1924); *The Halfback of Notre Dame* (p only, 1924); *Boobs in the Woods* (p only, 1925); *The Marriage Circus* (p only, 1925); *Lucky Stars* (p only, 1925); *Hoboken to Hollywood* (p only, 1926); *The Prodigal Bridegroom* (p only, 1926); *Should Sleepwalkers Marry?* (p only, 1927); *Fiddlesticks* (p only, 1927); *Love in a Police Station* (p only, 1927); *The Goodbye Kiss* (p only, 1928); *The Campus Carmen* (p only, 1928); *Whirls and Girls* (1929); *Girl Crazy* (1929); *The Golfers* (1929); *A Hollywood Star* (1929); *Clancy at the Bat* (1929); *The Big Palooka* (1929); *Sugar Plum Papa* (1930); *Bulls and Bears* (1930); *Fat Wives for Thin* (1930); *The Chumps* (1930); *Hello Television* (p only, 1930); *Midnight Daddies* (1930); *Divorced Sweethearts* (1930); *Dance Hall Marge* (1931); *A Poor Fish* (1931); *Monkey Business in Africa* (1931); *Movie Town* (also a, 1931); *One More Chance* (1931); *Speed* (1931); *The Candid Camera* (p only, 1932); *The Dentist* (p only, 1932); *Hypnotized* (also co-story, 1932); *The Fatal Glass of Beer* (p only, 1933); *The Pharmacist* (p only, 1933); *The Barber Shop* (p only, 1933); *Flicker Fever* (also sc, 1934); *Just Another Murder Story* (also story, 1934); *Way Up Thar* (1935); *The Timid Young Man* (1935).

---

**series comedies** "Nothing succeeds like success" might be the credo for the many long-running film series comedies that have graced the big screen. Like any business enterprise, Hollywood has sought out a popular product that it could sell over and over again, cutting down the risk of failure. Therefore, finding a comic formula to which the public repeatedly responds has always been a highly desirable, as well as especially profitable, direction for film producers.

Moviemakers have approached series comedies from several different angles. For instance, some have been established by relying on already well-known names from other media, such as comic strip characters; hence the immediate recognition and appeal of the Blondie series. That particularly successful series lasted twelve years (1938–1950) and consisted of twenty-eight movies. It starred the perfectly cast Penny Singleton as Blondie and Arthur Lake as Dagwood Bumstead. Earlier than that,

Mickey ROONEY starred in a long-running (1927–1933) series of comedy short subjects based on the popular Mickey McGuire comic strip character; there were approximately fifty of those produced.

Later, of course, Rooney starred in one of the most popular of all comedy series, the Andy Hardy films. There were a total of sixteen movies in the series, which began in 1937 with *A Family Affair* and ended in 1958 with *Andy Hardy Comes Home*. In this instance, as in many others, the original movie wasn't intended as the first of a series, but proved so popular that it made good commercial sense to keep going back to the well (until it finally dried up). Among the other series that began innocently enough as one-shots were the Maisie films (ten in all, between 1939 and 1947), starring Ann SOTHERN, and the Ma and Pa Kettle movies, which were spawned from the popular reaction to the secondary leads in *The Egg and I* (1947). The latter series, starring Marjorie MAIN and Percy Kilbride began in 1949 with *Ma and Pa Kettle* and ended, eight films later, with *The Kettles on Old MacDonald's Farm* (1957).

Some series were high concept/low comedy entries, such as Francis, the Talking Mule, a series that lasted for seven movies between 1949 and 1956. Donald O'CONNOR starred in six of them, and Chill Wills supplied the voice of the mule. Other series were designed to appeal to specific age groups. The youth-oriented Henry Aldrich series (1939–1944) ran through eleven movies. Seven Beach Party films in the early 1960s, starring Frankie Avalon and Annette Funicello, were also pitched directly to the youth audience.

The most successful series were built around the chemistry between the actors. No wonder, then, that the Road movies starring Bing CROSBY, Bob HOPE, and Dorothy Lamour were so popular. There were seven films in the series, beginning with *Road to Singapore* (1940) and ending with *Road to Hong Kong* (1962). Unlike most other series, this one was spread over a twenty-two-year period, while most others tended to come out of the studios on a regular schedule like automobiles on an assembly line.

Other long-running comedy series included the Cohens and the Kellys, the Mexican Spitfire films, the Mr. Belvedere films, the Topper movies, and the Jiggs and Maggie series (which happened to star Mickey Rooney's father, Joe Yule).

One would have thought that series comedies would have ended after the advent of TV, but this hasn't been the case. The movies may not come as fast or as often as in the old days, but they keep on coming, just the same. Witness the three *Back to the Future* films starring Michael J. FOX, the *National Lampoon Vacation* films, and the *Police Academy* series.

## Shawn, Wallace (1943—)

An actor, screenwriter, and playwright, Wallace Shawn is a genuinely distinctive talent. He is a squirrely sort of actor; short, pudgy, and balding, he cuts a comic figure, which is accentuated by the combination of a supercilious intellectual demeanor and a minor speech impediment. Shawn is one of those actors who is funny as soon as he arrives on screen. Although he often plays comically pompous characters, his appearance belies his artistic depth. He co-wrote and co-starred in the art house hit *My Dinner with Andre* (1981) and is the author of a number of highly regarded plays, including *Aunt Dan and Lemon* and *The Fever*.

Born in New York City, Shawn came from a highly respected literary family. He was educated at both Harvard and Oxford. This unlikely actor made one of the most memorable supporting role debuts in recent decades. His character, Jeremiah, was extolled to the heavens by Diane KEATON throughout much of Woody ALLEN's *Manhattan* (1979), only to have Allen and the audience finally see him, discovering the startlingly comic gap between Keaton's description and Shawn's turtlish appearance. For years, he was "Jeremiah" to movie fans who didn't know his real name.

Shawn has gone on to appear in supporting roles with considerable regularity in movies throughout the 1980s and into the 1990s. Among his other noteworthy films are *Simon* (1980), *Lovesick* (1983), and *The Princess Bride* (1987).

---

**FILMS INCLUDE:** *Manhattan* (1979); *All That Jazz* (1979); *Starting Over* (1979); *Atlantic City* (1980); *Simon* (1980); *A Little Sex* (1981); *My Dinner with Andre* (also sc, 1981); *The First Time* (1982); *Lovesick* (1983); *Deal of the Century* (1983); *Strange Invaders* (1983); *Saigon: Year of the Cat* (1983); *Crackers* (1984); *The Hotel New Hampshire* (1984); *The Bostonians* (1984); *Micki and Maude* (1984); *Heaven Help Us* (1985); *Head Office* (1986); *The Bedroom Window* (1987); *Prick Up Your Ears* (1987); *Nice Girls Don't Explode* (1987); *The Princess Bride* (1987); *Radio Days* (1987); *The Moderns* (1988); *Scenes from the Class Struggle in Beverly Hills* (1989); *She's Out of Control* (1989); *We're No Angels* (1989); *Shadows and Fog* (1992); *Meteor Man* (1993).

---

*Martin Short has the bright-eyed innocence of Danny Kaye and the mischeviousness of Harpo Marx. He is a genuine comic talent who has not yet fully come to flower in the movies. He is seen here in a close-up from* Pure Luck *(1991) that captures his boyish charm.* PHOTO BY JACK ROWAND, © UNIVERSAL PICTURES.

**Short, Martin (1951—)** A cute and lovable clown, Martin Short has played leads and increasingly major supporting roles in film comedies since the late 1970s. He is a versatile character actor who plays excitable, nervous types.

Born and raised in Hamilton, Ontario, Canada, he went on to study social work at McMaster, his local university. There he met Eugene Levy and Dave Thomas, who would later become his co-stars on Canada's famous "SCTV." The two actors had a profound influence on Short, urging him to pursue his interest in show business. He listened to them, making his professional acting debut in a Toronto production of *Godspell*. More acting and singing stints followed, eventually leading to success on Canadian TV. He first appeared on a TV series called "The Associates" (1979–1980) and then on the show "I'm a Big Girl Now" (1980–1981). After that Short fully hit his stride on the "SCTV Comedy Network" (1982–1984), winning an Emmy and a Nelly (the Canadian equivalent of the Emmy) for his comedy writing. "SATURDAY NIGHT LIVE" was the next stop (1984– 1985). Like so many others who were groomed for stardom on the late night TV show, he then took off for Hollywood to seek his fortune in feature films.

Short's earlier two films, *Lost and Found* (1979) and *The Outsider* (1979), did nothing for him. The big difference with his next was that Lorne Michaels, the "Saturday Night Live" producer, suggested him for a role in a spoof of a silent era Western. He was hired to ride and get laughs along with Steve MARTIN and Bill MURRAY. Although *The Three Amigos!* (1986) was given short shrift by the critics, audiences liked it. A rash of starring roles followed, most memorably in *Innerspace* (1987), but his other films didn't fly.

By the early 1990s, Short seemed destined for supporting roles, giving, for instance, a comic shot in the arm to *Father of the Bride* (1991) as a hysterically ridiculous caterer. Instead of settling for that route, however, he surprised many by turning to Broadway and starring in a musical adaptation of Neil SIMON's *The Goodbye Girl*. Most people didn't know he could sing, and he wowed critics and crowds alike, gaining a Tony Award nomination for his work on the show.

---

**FILMS:** *Lost and Found* (1979); *The Outsider* (1979); *The Canadian Conspiracy* (1986); *Three Amigos!* (1986); *Cross My Heart* (1987); *Innerspace* (1987); *Three Fugitives* (1989); *The Big Picture* (unbilled, 1989); *Pure Luck* (1991); *Father of the Bride* (1991); *Captain Ron* (1992); *We're Back* (voice only, 1993); *The Pebble and the Penguin* (voice, 1993); *Clifford* (1994).

---

**Silvers, Phil (1911–1985)** With his oddly shaped face, black-framed glasses, and machine-gun delivery, Phil Silvers dominated his movie scenes with a comic ferocity equalled by few others. Although he starred in the film version of his hit Broadway show *Top Banana* (1954), in truth Phil Silvers spent much of his movie career playing second bananas. A bigger star on TV during the 1950s than he ever was in the movies, Silvers nonetheless appeared in a great many films during the first half of the 1940s and then had a renaissance, of sorts, in films during the mid-1960s.

He was born Philip Silversmith, the last of eight children to a Russian Jewish immigrant family that had settled in Brooklyn, New York. He entered show business as a singer when he was thirteen. He had dropped out of school, getting his education instead in BURLESQUE houses and in VAUDEVILLE. He finally made his breakthrough to the legitimate stage in a 1939 show called *Yokel Boy*.

Silvers went to Hollywood in 1940 and left five years later, not quite having made a name for himself, mostly because he was usually cast as the hero's best friend rather than as the hero. Nonetheless, he

*That "cat that ate the canary" grin is pure Phil Silvers. He was a burlesque and vaudeville comic with a fast-talking line of patter who sandwiched a movie career around his greatest achievement, the Sergeant Bilko character he created for TV in the 1950s.* PHOTO COURTESY OF MOVIE STAR NEWS.

can be seen giving a number of good performances in some very fine films, among them *Tom, Dick and Harry* (1941), *Roxie Hart* (1942), *Four Jills in a Jeep* (1944), and *Cover Girl* (1944).

Silvers came into his own on the stage, rather than in films. He won a Tony Award for *High Button Shoes* and then another for *Top Banana*. It was his success on the stage that led to his greatest triumph, the brilliant TV comedy, "You'll Never Get Rich," which was later known as "The Phil Silvers Show," although most people referred to the program simply by the name of Silvers's character, Bilko. The service comedy about Sergeant Bilko's comically conniving attempts to strike it rich ran from 1955 to 1959, stopping only because Silvers was exhausted from the heavy demands of the show.

A comedy icon thanks to Bilko, Silvers had an easier time of it in the movies during the 1960s. After joining the comedy elite in IT's A MAD MAD MAD MAD WORLD (1963), he took a lead role in the film version of *A Funny Thing Happened on the Way to the Forum* (1966). He had another hit with *Buona Sera, Mrs. Campbell* (1968). In both films he played characters similar to Bilko.

He worked both on the stage and in the movies during the early 1970s, muting his hard edge in Disney's *The Boatniks* (1970). Failing health reduced him to occasional cameo roles after that.

---

FILMS INCLUDE: *The Hit Parade of 1941* (1940); *Tom, Dick and Harry* (1941); *The Penalty* (1941); *Lady Be Good* (1941); *Ice-Capades* (1941); *You're in the Army Now* (1941); *Roxie Hart* (1942); *All Through the Night* (1942); *Footlight Serenade* (1942); *Just Off Broadway* (1942); *My Gal Sal* (1942); *Coney Island* (1943); *A Lady Takes a Chance* (1943); *Four Jills in a Jeep* (1944); *Cover Girl* (1944); *Where Do We Go from Here?* (1945); *Diamond Horseshoe* (1945); *A Thousand and One Nights* (1945); *Summer Stock* (1950); *Top Banana* (1954); *Lucky Me* (1954); *Forty Pounds of Trouble* (1963); *It's a Mad Mad Mad Mad World* (1963); *A Funny Thing Happened on the Way to the Forum* (1966); *A Guide for the Married Man* (1967); *Follow That Camel* (UK, 1967); *Buona Sera, Mrs. Campbell* (1968); *The Boatniks* (1970); *The Strongest Man in the World* (1975); *Won Ton Ton—The Dog Who Saved Hollywood* (1976); *The Chicken Chronicles* (1977); *The Cheap Detective* (1978); *Racquet* (1979); *The Happy Hooker Goes to Hollywood* (1979).

---

# Simon, Neil (1927—)
He is America's most successful playwright, and virtually all of Neil Simon's work has been comedies. Of his more than twenty plays, most have been turned into movies, many of them boasting a screenplay also by Simon. In addition, he has penned more than ten original screenplays, many of them major commercial and critical hits. His comic speciality is a strong mix of sharp one-liners and richly wrought characters. The old complaint about Simon was that his humor was glib and that he would inevitably go for the joke rather than the heart. In recent years, he has dampened those charges with a series of autobiographical plays and movies that have evoked tears and laughter.

Born Marvin Neil Simon in the Bronx, New York, he later picked up the nickname of "Doc" because he was such a good comic surgeon, often saving the work of others with his perceptive revisions. Simon honed his skills writing for television programs such as "The Tallulah Bankhead Show" in 1951, "The Sid Caeser Show" in 1956–1957, and "The Phil Silvers Show" during 1958–1959. He left television in 1961 when he had his first hit play on Broadway, *Come Blow Your Horn*, a comedy that found its way to the movies in 1963.

Simon continued writing plays, but broke directly into the movie business when he wrote the original screenplay for the Peter SELLERS comedy *After the Fox* (1966). The critical and commercial success of that film opened the doors for him to write the screenplays for many of his previous hit plays, such as *Barefoot in the Park* (1967) and *The Odd Couple* (1968).

While keeping up his prodigious output for Broadway, Simon alternated between adapting his own work for the screen and writing original screenplays. Among his best film adaptations have been *Plaza Suite* (1971), *Last of the Red Hot Lovers* (1972), *The Prisoner of Second Avenue* (1975), *The Sunshine Boys* (1975), *Chapter Two* (1979), *Brighton Beach Memoirs* (1986), and *Biloxi Blues* (1988). On one rare occasion he also adapted the work of another author, writing the screenplay for the Steve MARTIN film *The Lonely Guy* (1984).

Among Simon's best original works for the screen have been *Murder by Death* (1976) and *The Goodbye*

*Girl* (1977). By and large, however, his original screenplays have not been as satisfying as his adaptations. Neither have they been as successful at the box office. Rare is the Neil Simon flop, but *Max Dugan Returns* (1982), *The Slugger's Wife* (1985), and *The Marrying Man* (1991) are some of the exceptions.

While his first play, *Come Blow Your Horn*, was somewhat autobiographical, he eschewed the personal for nearly two decades until he wrote *Chapter Two*. The story dealt (in fictionalized form) with his coming to terms with the death of his first wife and marriage to his second wife, actress Marsha Mason (who played herself in the film). He subsequently wrote a highly acclaimed trilogy for the theater, all three plays becoming films, *Brighton Beach Memoirs*, *Biloxi Blues*, and *Broadway Bround*, the last of which is the only work Simon has adapted as a TV movie. All three stories detailed, in turn, his growing up, army life, and beginnings as a writer. These plays, and especially his autobiographical, Pulitzer Prize-winning play (and film) *Lost in Yonkers* (1993), have brought a compelling warmth to his sometimes brittle humor.

FILMS: *Come Blow Your Horn* (based on play, 1963); *After the Fox* (story, sc, 1966); *Barefoot in the Park* (based on play, sc, p, 1967); *The Odd Couple* (based on play, sc, 1968); *Sweet Charity* (based on play, libretto, 1969); *The Out-of-Towners* (based on play, sc, 1970); *Plaza Suite* (based on play, sc, 1971); *Star Spangled Girl* (based on play, 1972); *The Heartbreak Kid* (sc, 1972); *Last of the Red Hot Lovers* (based on play, sc, 1972); *The Prisoner of Second Avenue* (based on play, sc, 1974); *The Sunshine Boys* (based on play, sc, 1975); *Murder by Death* (sc, 1976); *The Goodbye Girl* (sc, 1977); *California Suite* (based on play, sc, 1978); *The Cheap Detective* (sc, 1978); *Chapter Two* (based on play, sc, 1979); *Seems Like Old Times* (sc, 1980); *I Ought to Be in Pictures* (based on play, sc, p, 1981); *Only When I Laugh* (based on play, sc, p, 1981); *Max Dugan Returns* (sc, p, 1982); *The Lonely Guy* (sc, 1984); *The Slugger's Wife* (sc, 1985); *Brighton Beach Memoirs* (based on play, sc, 1986);

*Biloxi Blues* (based on play, sc, 1988); *The Marrying Man* (sc, p, 1991); *Lost in Yonkers* (based on play, sc, 1993).

## Singleton, Penny  *See* SERIES COMEDIES

## Skelton, Red (1910—)
One of the few sound era comedians who might have also been a successful silent screen clown, Red Skelton was a first-rate mime who excelled at physical comedy. He also had a rubbery face to go with his lanky body. Skelton had his greatest success in the movies during the latter half of the 1940s, before finding even greater fame on TV during the 1950s and 1960s.

Born Richard Bernard Skelton, he was the son of a circus clown. His father died before he was born, and Skelton lived a childhood of punishing poverty. When he was ten, he ran away from home. Making his way through the bowels of show business, he worked in circuses, VAUDEVILLE, and BURLESQUE, fashioning himself as a comic. In reality, he was an anonymous entertainer—until he came up with his surefire "doughnut dunking" routine, which established him as a hot new comedian.

When Skelton reached the pinnacle of vaudeville success, playing the Paramount Theater in New York City, he segued into radio and finally films. He made his movie debut in *Having Wonderful Time* (1938), but it took him a while to establish his comic persona, mostly because MGM didn't know how to best take advantage of his talent. And what a talent he was; he gave a brilliant comic performance in *Ziegfeld Follies* (1946), an anthology movie that featured Skelton doing his famous "Guzzler's Gin" commercial.

Bouncing back and forth between comic relief roles in big-budget films and starring roles in lesser projects, Skelton managed a fair degree of popularity during the 1940s, but hardly the kind of following that belonged to the likes of Bob HOPE or Danny KAYE. In the mid-1940s the great Buster

KEATON, by then a faded and nearly forgotten man, took Skelton under his wing, offering him advice on how to best develop his talents. Keaton urged him to stress his abilities as a physical comic, and Skelton listened. The result was a series of slick SLAPSTICK hit films in the latter half of the 1940s, including *The Fuller Brush Man* (1948), *A Southern Yankee* (1948), and *The Yellow Cab Man* (1950), that lifted the comic actor to a new level of stardom.

In 1953 Skelton turned his attention to television, beginning a remarkable run of twenty years as a TV superstar. It was on TV that he further developed his pantomime skills with characters such as Freddie the Freeloader and Clem Kadidlehopper.

If his professional life had reached an all-time high, his personal life had turned grim, indeed. His nine-year-old son, Richard, Jr., died of leukemia, and his second wife had tried to commit suicide. Skelton, himself, became far more maudlin on his TV show before it finally ended its long and successful run. In later years, Skelton became known as a painter, specializing in clowns.

---

FILMS: Shorts: *Seein' Red* (1939); *Broadway Buckaroo* (1939); *Radio Bugs* (voice only, 1944); *Luckiest Guy in the World* (voice only, 1946).

Features: *Having Wonderful Time* (1938); *Flight Command* (1941); *Whistling in the Dark* (1941); *The People vs. Dr. Kildare* (1941); *Lady Be Good* (1941); *Dr. Kildare's Wedding Day* (1941); *Maisie Gets Her Man* (1942); *Ship Ahoy* (1942); *Whistling in Dixie* (1942); *Panama Hattie* (1942); *DuBarry Was a Lady* (1943); *I Dood It* (1943); *Thousands Cheer* (1943); *Whistling in Brooklyn* (1943); *Bathing Beauty* (1944); *Ziegfeld Follies* (1946); *The Show-Off* (1946); *Merton of the Movies* (1947); *A Southern Yankee* (1948); *The Fuller Brush Man* (1948); *Neptune's Daughter* (1949); *The Yellow Cab Man* (1950); *Three Little Words* (1950); *Watch the Birdie* (1950); *The Fuller Brush Girl* (cameo, 1950); *Duchess of Idaho* (cameo, 1950); *Texas Carnival* (1951); *Excuse My Dust* (1951); *Lovely to Look At* (1952); *Half a Hero* (1953); *The Clown* (1953); *Susan Slept Here* (cameo, 1954); *The Great Diamond Robbery* (1954); *Around the World in 80 Days* (cameo, 1956); *Public Pigeon Number One* (1957); *Ocean's Eleven* (cameo, 1960); *Those Magnificent Men in Their Flying Machines* (UK, 1965).

---

**slapstick**    The derivation of the term that defines this kind of comedy was taken from the name of a paddle—a slapstick—that was once used in knockabout FARCES to whack the actors; it made a loud, comic noise.

Slapstick is usually considered a lowbrow form of physical humor that depends upon pain and humiliation for its laughter; the archetypal slapstick gags have their victim falling on a banana peel or being hit in the face with a pie. In general, slapstick depends heavily upon chases, PRATFALLS, seemingly dangerous comic collisions, practical jokes, and otherwise turbulent, "roughhouse" antics.

Because film began as entertainment for the poor and uneducated, the lowbrow appeal of slapstick originally made it the king of Hollywood comedy. Another reason for the appeal of slapstick during the silent era was simply because physical comedy was virtually the only way to make people laugh in the absence of sound. All of the great silent comics, as well as the lesser ones, built their art out of rudimentary slapstick. Mack SENNETT's KEYSTONE KOPS and his other comedians practiced slapstick in its most extreme form. Charlie CHAPLIN, Buster KEATON, Harold LLOYD, and Harry LANGDON, among others, all eventually practiced a more inventive style of slapstick, adding a human element that gave their comedy depth and their characters resonance.

Slapstick became a less pure comedy form during the sound era as verbal humor became possible. Comedians such as LAUREL AND HARDY, the THREE STOOGES, and ABBOTT AND COSTELLO still depended heavily on slapstick for their humor. The Three Stooges, in particular, relied on hitting and slapping each other in ever more elaborate fashion to get their laughs. Even more verbal comics, however, such as W. C. FIELDS, Eddie CANTOR, and even the MARX BROTHERS relied on a certain amount of slapstick to enliven their comedy.

As a major comic force in Hollywood, slapstick seemingly reached its end with Danny KAYE's gentle physical humor and Jerry LEWIS's raucous bumbling. It seemed as if slapstick reached its apotheosis in Stanley Kramer's epic *IT'S A MAD MAD MAD MAD WORLD* (1963). However, later comic talents such as Mel BROOKS and Woody ALLEN, while appearing to be too sophisticated for such comedy, have cleverly wrought a great many laughs with slapstick humor, the most obvious example being Brooks's movie *Silent Comedy* (1976).

Recently, Chevy CHASE and Kevin KLINE have brought a touch of physical humor to the movies. A younger generation of actors is discovering the joys of slapstick, as evidenced by Johnny Depp's much-admired performance in *Benny and Joon* (1993), in which he plays a contemporary character who acts as if he's in a silent comedy. Finally, however, the last great practitioner of the art of slapstick in Hollywood isn't a star, but a director. Blake EDWARDS appears to be keeping the tradition alive single-handedly in his Pink Panther series, as well as in many of his other recent films, most notably *Blind Date* (1987) and *Skin Deep* (1989).

**Sothern, Ann (1909–)** A vivacious actress who played light comedy with a brassy edge, Ann Sothern had an image as tough as nails. She was mostly a B-movie star who had success in Hollywood over a period of twenty years before becoming a major TV comedy star during the 1950s.

Born Harriette Lake in Valley City, North Dakota, she was a classically trained singer, the prize student of her own mother. An attractive petite blonde, Sothern had a brief fling with the movies (using her real name) at the beginning of the sound era. She showed off her voice in a small bit in the musical *The Show of Shows* (1929) and appeared in several other movies, but nothing came of that effort.

Instead of hanging around the fringes of Holly-

wood, she went east, rapidly making a name for herself on Broadway. By 1933 she was back on the West Coast (this time, as Ann Sothern), becoming a B-movie lead in mostly light comic romances at Columbia Pictures and RKO.

Although Sothern never became a major movie star, her career took a significant turn for the better when she signed with MGM in 1939. She began a popular series of adventure comedies, playing a tough showgirl named Maisie who was all brass except for her heart of gold. There were ten Maisie features made between 1939 and 1947, all of them B movies. They were generally successful and helped focus public attention on Sothern, who often had to carry these otherwise thinly plotted vehicles with her wit, energy, and sassy charm.

Happily for Sothern, MGM gave her other roles as well during these years, enabling her to show off her musical talents in films like *Lady Be Good* (1941) and *Panama Hattie* (1942). Although she wasn't known for her serious acting, she proved herself more than capable in films like *A Letter to Three Wives* (1949).

By the early 1950s, however, her film career was noticeably slowing down. Taking a chance, she bolted for television. Her first show, "Private Secretary" (1953–1957) was a hit, as was her follow-up sitcom "The Ann Sothern Show" (1958–1961). In both cases, she played a character who owed more than a passing debt to Maisie.

In the decades that followed, Sothern made occasional appearances in films, TV, and on the stage. Her most recent movie performance was more than simply memorable. She garnered an Academy Award nomination for best supporting actress for her effervescent work in *The Whales of August* (1987), outshining the likes of Bette Davis and Lillian Gish. Also in the film was Sothern's actress daughter (with actor Robert Sterling), Tisha Sterling.

FILMS INCLUDE: *The Show of Shows* (1929); *Doughboys* (1930); *Let's Fall in Love* (1933); *Broadway Through a Keyhole* (1933); *Blind Date* (1934); *The*

Hell Cat (1934); Kid Millions (1934); The Girl Friend (1935); Grand Exit (1935); Folies Berg`ere (1935); Hooray for Love (1935); Don't Gamble with Love (1936); You May Be Next (1936); My American Wife (1936); The Smartest Girl in Town (1936); Walking on Air (1936); Dangerous Number (1937); Supersleuth (1937); Danger: Love at Work (1937); She's Got Everything (1937); There Goes the Groom (1937); There Goes My Girl (1937); Trade Winds (1939); Hotel for Women (1939); Joe and Ethel Turp Call on the President (1939); Fast and Furious (1939); Maisie (1939); Brother Orchid (1940); Dulcy (1940); Congo Maisie (1940); Lady Be Good (1941); Maisie Was a Lady (1941); Maisie Gets Her Man (1942); Panama Hattie (1942); Thousands Cheer (1943); Cry Havoc (1943); Three Hearts for Julia (1943); Maisie Goes to Reno (1944); Up Goes Maisie (1946); Undercover Maisie (1947); April Showers (1948); Lords and Music (1948); The Judge Steps Out (1949); A Letter to Three Wives (1949); Nancy Goes to Rio (1950); Shadow on the Wall (1950); The Blue Gardenia (1953); The Best Man (1964); Lady in a Cage (1964); Sylvia (1965); Chubasco (1968); The Killing Kind (1973); Golden Needles (1974); Crazy Mama (1975); The Manitou (1977); The Little Dragons (1980); The Whales of August (1987).

## Sterling, Ford (1883—1939)

A memorable comic heavy, Ford Sterling is best remembered as Chief Teheezal, head policeman of the famous KEYSTONE KOPS. A SLAPSTICK star whose best work was done largely for Mack SENNETT, Sterling's appearance was noteworthy for his heavy, dark eyebrows, miniscule goatee, and thin, rubbery legs.

Born George Ford Stitch in LaCrosse, Wisconsin, the young lad joined the circus as a teenager where he became known as "Keno, the Boy Clown." He was twenty-eight and a mildly successful veteran of both VAUDEVILLE and the legitimate theater when he joined Mack Sennett's comedy group at Biograph in 1911, appearing that year in Abe Gets Even with Father. It was not long after,

however, that Sennett left Biograph to form Keystone, and Sterling went with him, making history in a variety of fast-paced, adventurous slapstick comedies.

Sterling occasionally directed his own one- and two-reel comedies. He also often acted in the Keystone ensemble, which included Mabel NORMAND and Fatty ARBUCKLE. At the height of his popularity during the teens, he had his own series of shorts, the Sterling Comedies. Perhaps Ford Sterling's greatest contribution to film comedy was his shoes—although not when they were on his feet. While at Keystone, Charlie CHAPLIN borrowed several items from different performers to create his classic tramp outfit. Among those items borrowed were Sterling's enormous shoes, which Chaplin wore on the wrong feet.

After leaving Sennett in 1921, Sterling continued acting with uneven success. The age of slapstick humor had passed its peak. Nonetheless, he worked steadily throughout the 1920s and made the transition into sound films, appearing in a small number of early 1930s films including Alice in Wonderland (1933), in which he played the White King. His last film was Black Sheep (1935). This physical comedian, who was so adept at impossible twirls, suffered the loss of a leg due to an accident in the 1930s and died not long after.

FILMS INCLUDE: Abe Gets Even with Father (1911); The Flirting Husband (1912); The Ambitious Butler (1912); Cohen Collects a Debt (1912); A Bear Escape (1912); The Beating He Needed (1912); The Deacon's Troubles (1912); Hide and Seek (1913); The Gusher (1913); The Firebugs (1913); Zuzu the Band Leader (1913); That Ragtime Band (1913); On His Wedding Day (1913); Hide and Seek (1913); The New Conductor (1913); Safe in Jail (1913); Between Showers (1914); Love and Dynamite (1914); Raffles (1914); In the Clutches of the Gang (1914); Gentleman Burglar (1914); Courthouse Crooks (1915); Only a Messenger Boy (1915); The Hunt (also co-d, 1915); Our Dare Devil Chief (1915); His Father's Footsteps (also co-d, 1915); His Pride and Shame (also co-d, 1916); His Wild

*Oats* (also co-d, 1916); *His Lying Heart* (d, 1916); *The Manicurist* (also d, 1916); *Stars and Bars* (also d, 1917); *Her Torpedoed Love* (1917); *Pinched in the Finish* (1917); *Beware of Boarders* (1918); *Her Screen Idol* (1918); *Yankee Doodle in Berlin* (1919); *Hearts and Flowers* (1919); *Love, Honor, and Behave* (1920); *Married Life* (1920); *Don't Weaken* (1920); *An Unhappy Finish* (1921); *Oh Mabel Behave* (also co-d, 1922); *The Brass Bottle* (1923); *The Spoilers* (1923); *Galloping Fish* (1924); *He Who Gets Slapped* (1924); *So Big* (1924); *Steppin' Out* (1925); *The Trouble with Wives* (1925); *Daddy's Gone A-Hunting* (1925); *Miss Brewster's Millions* (1926); *Good and Naughty* (1926); *The American Venus* (1926); *The Road to Glory* (1926); *The Show-Off* (1926); *Everybody's Acting* (1926); *Casey at the Bat* (1927); *For the Love of Mike* (1927); *Gentlemen Prefer Blondes* (1928); *Oh Kay!* (1928); *Wife Savers* (1928); *Sally* (1929); *The Fall of Eve* (1929); *Showgirls in Hollywood* (1930); *Kismet* (1930); *Her Majesty Love* (1931); *Alice in Wonderland* (1933); *Black Sheep* (1935).

*Although movie fans have only recently put face to name, Daniel Stern's comic talents have been appreciated by his colleagues for quite some time. Now, in addition to acting, he has emerged as a comic director with* Rookie of the Year *(1993). Stern gave himself a featured role in the film that stars Thomas Ian Nicholas; both are seen above.*

PHOTO BY MICHAEL P. WEINSTEIN, © 20TH CENTURY-FOX.

**Stern, Daniel (1957—)**  To the casual movie fan, Daniel Stern is a fresh new face in the comedy firmament. Thanks to the two *Home Alone* movies (1990 and 1992) and his co-starring role with Billy CRYSTAL in *City Slickers* (1991), he has suddenly come to the fore as a comic actor. He's even directed his first film, *Rookie of the Year* (1993), playing a goofy featured role in the production as well. However, the fact is that Stern has been giving strong comic performances in films for years, going all the way back to the sleeper hit of 1979, *Breaking Away*, the movie in which he made his motion picture debut. Since then, the tall, attractive actor has played in a wide variety of generally upscale films, usually in comedies and often as the buddy of the hero.

Born in Bethesda, Maryland, Stern broke into the movies early; he was only twenty-two when he co-starred in *Breaking Away* as one of the hero's friends. He's been in at least one movie every year since 1979, and many of them highly regarded, such as *Starting Over* (1979), *I'm Dancing as Fast as I Can* (1981), *Diner* (1982), *The Milagro Beanfield War* (1988), and two Woody ALLEN movies, *Stardust Memories* (1980) and *Hannah and Her Sisters* (1986). With all of that, it was probably Stern's TV work that set the stage for his later movie success. He received a great deal of attention as the narrator of the charming and popular coming-of-age TV show "The Wonder Years" (1988–1993). In addition, he directed ten of the show's episodes.

FILMS INCLUDE: *Breaking Away* (1979); *Starting Over* (1979); *One-Trick Pony* (1980); *It's My Turn* (1980); *A Small Circle of Friends* (1980); *Stardust Memories* (1980); *I'm Dancing as Fast as I Can* (1981); *Honky Tonk Freeway* (1981); *Diner* (1982); *Get Crazy* (1983); *Blue Thunder* (1983); *C.H.U.D.* (1984); *Key Exchange* (1985); *The Boss' Wife* (1986); *Hannah and Her Sisters* (1986); *Born in East L.A.* (1987); *The Milagro Beanfield War* (1988); *D.O.A.* (1988); *Leviathan* (1989); *Friends, Lovers and Lunatics* (1989); *Little*

*Monsters* (1989); *Coupe De Ville* (1990); *Home Alone* (1990); *My Blue Heaven* (1990); *City Slickers* (1991); *Home Alone 2: Lost in New York* (1992); *Rookie of the Year* (also d, 1993).

---

**Sturges, Preston (1898—1959)** The first screenwriter of the sound era to also become a director, Preston Sturges led the way for other writer/directors who soon followed. Sturges was *the* comedy writer/director of the 1940s despite the fact that all of his best work was done in the first half of the decade. His rise as a comedy director was as meteoric as his fall, but the films he made during his blazing time in the sun are among the most idiosyncratic and romantically goofy comedies Hollywood has ever produced. As a full-service filmmaker, his scripts sparked with snappy repartee, and he directed those scripts with a frantic, almost breathless pace that never let up. His humor was cynical, sometimes savage, SATIRE that usually undercut Hollywood conventions and expectations. If he sometimes lacked the courage of his convictions and often gave his audiences illogical happy endings, the mighty leaps that brought those surprising, rose-colored climaxes were so ingenious that they, too, brought laughter and delight.

Born Edmond P. Biden in Chicago to an extremely wealthy family, he was largely educated abroad in France, Switzerland, and Germany. Both before and after serving a volunteer stint as a flyer in the Army Air Corps during World War I, he worked for his mother's cosmetics company. In that capacity, he invented a kissproof lipstick. Like Howard Hughes, Sturges was a tinkerer, inventor, and airplane nut. And, like Hughes, he was drawn to the movies—but not right away.

While recuperating from an operation to remove his appendix, this twentieth-century Renaissance man wrote several plays, one of which became the 1929 Broadway hit comedy *Strictly Dishonorable*. It later turned up in two movie versions, the first in 1931 and the second in 1951. He followed his play to Hollywood, where his quick wit and colorful language were ideal for the movies. He was soon writing dialogue for such films as *The Big Pond* (1930), later progressing to original screenplays for films including *The Power and the Glory* (1933), *Diamond Jim* (1935), *Easy Living* (1937), and *Remember the Night* (1940).

Unhappy with the way his screenplays were being directed, however, he appealed to Paramount to let him direct his own work. Until then, the studios had developed a strict division between writers and directors. Paramount, however, had traditionally been one of the more liberal studios, and Sturges was given his chance.

Sturges's debut as a writer/director was THE GREAT MCGINTY (1940), the sleeper hit of the year. It satirized American politics by presenting a hobo turned governor, who made it to the top through graft and corruption, only to fall from grace when he turned honest. It was Frank CAPRA gone haywire, and audiences and the critics loved it. Sturges received a best screenplay Oscar for his iconoclastic effort.

Sturges followed that auspicious beginning with a stunning, unbroken string of six more witty and piercing comedy hits. All of them poked fun at some aspect of society: advertising and American gullibility in *Christmas in July* (1940); intellectual snobbery in *The Lady Eve* (1941); Hollywood pretentiousness in *Sullivan's Travels* (1941); marriage and sex in *The Palm Beach Story* (1942); small-town Americana and sex in *The Miracle of Morgan's Creek* (1944); and both mother and hero worship in *Hail the Conquering Hero* (1944). These last two films marked the peak of his career—both, in the same year, garnered best screenplay Oscar nominations.

Sturges's films were identifiable not only by their rapid-fire verbal style and clever content, but also by his choice of actors. There was an informal Sturges stock company of performers who consistently showed up in his movies, most notably Franklin PANGBORN, William Demarest, Jimmy CONLIN, Edgar KENNEDY, and Eric BLORE.

As quickly as he emerged on the directorial scene,

Sturges submerged even faster. After the uncharacteristic *The Great Moment* (1944), he joined forces with the man he was so much like, Howard Hughes. It was an understandable but fatal mistake. The association proved unworkable, and Sturges limped through the next few years writing, directing, and producing movies that lacked the spark of his previous work. The best of those films was the ambitious but flawed *Mad Wednesday* (also known as *The Sin of Harold Diddlebock*, 1947), a movie designed to resurrect the comedy career of silent screen great Harold LLOYD. It was a flop. Then came *Unfaithfully Yours* (1948) and *The Beautiful Blonde from Bashful Bend* (1949), neither of them major Sturges efforts, although the former was a modest hit (remade in 1984 with Dudley Moore in the Rex Harrison role).

Sturges had had enough of Hughes by the end of the 1940s and went to Europe, where he eventually made his last movie, the pallid *The French They Are a Funny Race* (1956).

FILMS: *The Big Pond* (dial, 1930); *Fast and Loose* (add dial, 1930); *Strictly Dishonorable* (from his play, 1931); *Child of Manhattan* (from his play, 1933); *The Power and the Glory* (story, sc, 1933); *Thirty Day Princess* (sc, 1933); *We Live Again* (sc, 1934); *Diamond Jim* (sc, 1935); *The Good Fairy* (sc, 1935); *One Rainy Afternoon* (song, 1936); *Easy Living* (sc, 1937); *Hotel Haywire* (story, sc, 1937); *If I Were King* (sc, 1938); *Port of Seven Seas* (sc, 1938); *Never Say Die* (sc, 1939); *Remember the Night* (sc, 1940); *The Great McGinty* (sc, d, 1940); *Christmas in July* (sc, p, d, 1940); *The Lady Eve* (sc, d, 1941); *Sullivan's Travels* (sc, d, 1941); *The Palm Beach Story* (sc, d, 1942); *Star Spangled Rhythm* (a, 1942); *The Miracle of Morgan's Creek* (sc, d, 1944); *Hail the Conquering Hero* (sc, d, 1944); *The Great Moment* (sc, d, 1944); *I'll Be Yours* (sc, 1947); *Mad Wednesday/The Sin of Harold Diddlebock* (sc, p, d, 1947); *Unfaithfully Yours* (story, sc, p, d, 1948); *The Beautiful Blonde From Bashful Bend* (sc, p, d, 1949); *Strictly Dishonorable* (from his play, 1951); *The French They Are a Funny Race* (France, sc, d, 1956); *The Birds and the Bees* (sc, 1956); *Paris Holiday* (a, 1958); *Rock-a-Bye Baby* (based on *The Miracle of Morgan's Creek*, 1958); *Unfaithfully Yours* (from sc, 1984).

## Summerville, Slim (1892—1946)

A lanky, homely looking comic actor, Slim Summerville usually played country bumpkins. With a long face, long nose, and large ears, he looked odd enough for a Fellini movie, but in the absence of Fellini in the 1910s, Mack SENNETT would have to do. He gave Summerville the opportunity to become a member of the KEYSTONE KOPS as well as appear in dozens of other two-reelers playing rustic fools. Summerville gave up acting in the 1920s to direct two-reel comedies, but returned during the sound era, mostly in feature-length comedies. The most memorable of these were nine low-budget laughers co-starring ZaSu PITTS, including *Her First Mate* (1933).

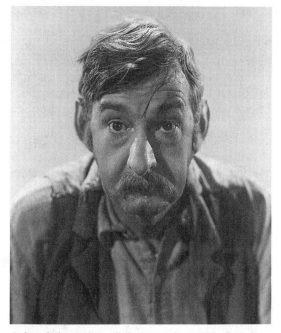

*Sad-eyed Slim Summerville had a comedy career that lasted more than thirty years, taking him from the Keystone Kops well into the sound era.*
PHOTO COURTESY OF THE SIEGEL COLLECTION.

Born George J. Sommerville in Canada, he eventually ran away from home while in his teens. He ended up in Hollywood in 1913 and found a good use for his quirky looks: He hired on as an extra in comedies. Comedian Edgar KENNEDY got Sommerville his first break, sending him over to Sennett's Keystone studio with the advice of moving out of the extra ranks.

Summerville stayed with Sennett from 1914 to 1918, where he enjoyed a fair degree of popularity, although he was never a genuine star. As a director in the 1920s, he worked at some of the lesser studios, making comedy shorts of no special distinction. He is best remembered today for his comic supporting and occasional leading performances in more than seventy-five films during the sound era, from his dramatic portrayal of Tjaden in *All Quiet on the Western Front* (1930) to his stellar comedy in *Love, Honor and Oh! Baby* (1933).

FILMS INCLUDE: Shorts and features: *Mabel's Busy Day* (1914); *The Knockout* (1914); *Laughing Gas* (1914); *Cursed by His Beauty* (1914); *Dough and Dynamite* (1914); *Ambrose's First Falsehood* (1914); *Tillie's Punctured Romance* (1914); *Their Social Splash* (1915); *Beating Hearts and Carpets* (1915); *Her Winning Punch* (1915); *The Home Breakers* (1915); *Her Painted Hero* (1915); *The Great Vacuum Robbery* (1915); *Those College Girls* (1915); *Those Bitter Sweets* (1915); *His Bread and Butter* (1916); *The Three Slims* (1916); *His Busted Trust* (1916); *Roping Her Romeo* (1917); *Villa of the Movies* (1917); *The Dog Catcher's Love* (1917); *Her Fame and Shame* (1917); *The Kitchen Lady* (1918); *Skirts* (1921); *The Texas Streaks* (1926); *The Beloved Rogue* (1927); *Riding for Fame* (also co-sc, 1928); *One Hysterical Night* (1929); *Strong Boy* (1929); *All Quiet on the Western Front* (1930); *Troopers Three* (1930); *The Spoilers* (1930); *See America Thirst* (1930); *Bad Sister* (1931); *The Front Page* (1931); *The Unexpected Father* (1932); *Tom Brown of Culver* (1932); *Air Mail* (1932); *They Just Had to Get Married* (1933); *Her First Mate* (1933); *Love, Honor and Oh! Baby* (1933); *Their Big Moment* (1934); *Love Birds* (1934); *The Farmer Takes a Wife* (1935); *Way Down East* (1935); *Love Begins at 40* (1935); *Captain January* (1936); *White Fang* (1936); *Pepper* (1936); *The Country Doctor* (1936); *Love Is News* (1937); *The Road Back* (1937); *Off to the Races* (1937); *Rebecca of Sunnybrook Farm* (1938); *Kentucky Moonshine* (1938); *Jesse James* (1939); *Gold Rush Maisie* (1940); *Western Union* (1941); *I'm from Arkansas* (1944); *The Hoodlum Saint* (1946).

## Swain, Mack (1876–1935)

The archetypal silent screen comic bad guy, Mack Swain was a three-hundred-pound behemoth who towered over his little comic costars—therein lay the root of his comedy. He rarely played mean-spirited villains; more often he simply acted out of natural, understandable instincts that just happened to be in conflict with the needs of the heroes and heroines of his films. His claim to fame is his long association with Charlie CHAPLIN. Swain appeared as Chaplin's nemesis both in his early silent films and during his brilliant period of maturation in the early 1920s, including in his classic *The Gold Rush* (1925).

Born in Salt Lake City, Utah, Swain had already had a more than twenty-year career in show business, working in everything from minstrel shows to the Broadway stage. He came to the movies in late 1913, immediately becoming a vital member of Mack SENNETT's Keystone crew. His earliest assignments were to play threatening comic support for Charlie Chaplin and Mabel NORMAND, but soon after he and Chester CONKLIN were teamed in their own Keystone series, usually referred to as the Ambrose and Walrus films. Swain played the lumbering, amiable Ambrose; Conklin played the conniving Walrus. An early incarnation of ABBOTT AND COSTELLO, the Ambrose and Walrus shorts were successful for a time, but the series petered out by the end of the decade, as did Swain's career.

Charlie Chaplin came to the rescue, hiring Swain to play his comic foil in *The Idle Class* (1921), *Pay Day* (1922), and *The Pilgrim* (1923). Swain's crowning achievement also came thanks to Chaplin. He cast his old Keystone friend as Big Jim McKay in *The Gold Rush*, ultimately immortalizing Swain as the ravenous prospector who imagines that the Little Tramp is a chicken and tries to eat him.

*The Gold Rush* showed that Swain still had the goods as a comic actor, and he worked steadily thereafter throughout the silent era, but fell back mostly to comedy shorts during the early sound era.

FILMS INCLUDE: *A Busy Day* (1914); *The Knockout* (1914); *Caught in a Cabaret* (1914); *Mabel's Married Life* (1914); *Getting Acquainted* (1914); *His Prehistoric Past* (1914); *Laughing Gas* (1914); *Tillie's Punctured Romance* (1914); *Ambrose's First Falsehood* (1914); *Ambrose's Sour Grapes* (1915); *Ambrose's Fury* (1915); *The Battle of Ambrose and Walrus* (1915); *Love, Speed and Thrills* (1915); *The Home Breakers* (1915); *Our Dare Devil Chief* (1915); *Vampire Ambrose* (1916); *A Modern Enoch Arden* (1916); *By Stork Delivery* (1916); *A Movie Star* (1916); *His Bitter Pill* (1916); *The Danger Girl* (1916); *Thirst* (1917); *His Naughty Thought* (1917); *His Pullman Bride* (1917); *The Idle Class* (1921); *Pay Day* (1922); *The Pilgrim* (1923); *The Gold Rush* (1925); *The Torrent* (1926); *Kiki* (1926); *Hands Up!* (1926); *Sea Horses* (1926); *Footloose Widows* (1926); *The Shamrock and the Rose* (1927); *The Beloved Rogue* (1927); *Finnegan's Ball* (1927); *Mockery* (1927); *Tillie's Punctured Romance* (remake, 1928); *Gentlemen Prefer Blondes* (1928); *Caught in the Fog* (1928); *The Last Warning* (1929); *The Cohens and Kellys in Atlantic City* (1929); *The Sea Bat* (1930); *Redemption* (1930); *Finn and Hattie* (1931); *Midnight Patrol* (1932).

**Switzer, Carl "Alfalfa"**   *See* OUR GANG

# T

**Tashlin, Frank (1913—1972)** A specialist in comedy, Frank Tashlin directed almost all of the major comedians of his era, including Bob HOPE, Red SKELTON, the MARX BROTHERS, Dean MARTIN and Jerry LEWIS, Danny KAYE, and even Doris DAY. A former cartoonist, he exhibited a unique ability to turn human characters into seeming cartoon caricatures. A writer/director, Tashlin is most closely associated with Jerry Lewis, whom he directed in a great many hits.

Like so many visual artists, Tashlin was not a success in school, which he quit at age thirteen. He had no special career until he stumbled into the film business as a cartoonist in 1930, working on Paul Terry's Aesop's Film Fables series. He knocked about for another fifteen years with jobs ranging from gag man for Hal ROACH to story editor for Walt DISNEY. He even left the film business for four years to write his own comic strip. In the mid-1940s he began writing comedy screenplays with a strong dash of whimsy, such as *One Touch of Venus* (1948), *The Paleface* (1948), *The Fuller Brush Man* (1948), and *Love Happy* (1949).

After having written scripts for comedians such as Bob Hope and Red Skelton, he then was given the opportunity to direct them in his scripts as well. His films were successful, and his career reached its height during the latter half of the 1950s and the early 1960s. He wrote, directed, and produced the classic *Will Success Spoil Rock Hunter?* (1957). He also wrote and directed a string of highly successful Jerry Lewis solo films, among them *The Geisha Boy* (1958), *Cinderfella* (1960), and *The Disorderly Orderly* (1964).

Either comedy changed or Tashlin lost his touch, but in the mid-1960s his films seemed exceedingly tired and lacking in his usual verve. He directed a couple of late Doris Day vehicles, *The Glass Bottom Boat* (1966) and *Caprice* (1967), without much flair, and his last film was the innocuous Bob Hope comedy *The Private Navy of Sgt. O'Farrell* (1968).

Tashlin died four years later, largely forgotten in the United States, but hailed as an important comic director by French critics who appreciated his work with Jerry Lewis, their idol.

FILMS: *Delightfully Dangerous* (co-story, 1945); *Variety Girl* (story, sc, 1947); *The Fuller Brush Man* (sc, 1948); *One Touch of Venus* (sc, 1948); *The Paleface* (sc, 1948); *Love Happy* (sc, 1949); *Mss Grant Takes Richmond* (sc, 1949); *The Fuller Brush Girl* (sc, 1950); *The Good Humor Man* (sc, 1950); *Kill the Umpire* (story, sc, 1950); *The First Time* (sc, d, 1952); *Son of Paleface* (sc, d, 1952); *Marry Me Again* (sc, d, 1954); *Susan Slept Here* (sc, d, 1954); *Artists and Models* (sc, d, 1955); *The Lieutenant Wore Skirts* (d, sc, 1955); *The Scarlet Hour* (story, sc, 1955); *The Girl Can't Help It* (sc, p, d, 1956); *Hollywood or Bust* (d, 1956); *Will Success Spoil Rock Hunter* (story, sc, p, d, 1957); *The Geisha Boy* (sc, d, 1958); *Rock-a-Bye Baby* (sc, d, 1958); *Say One for Me* (p, d, 1959); *Cinderfella* (sc, d, 1960); *Bachelor Flat* (sc, d, 1961); *It's Only Money* (d, 1962); *The Man from the Diner's Club* (d, 1963); *Who's Minding the Store?* (sc, d, 1963); *The Disorderly Orderly* (sc, d, 1964); *The Alphabet Murders* (d, 1966); *The Glass Bottom Boat* (d, 1966); *Caprice* (sc, d, 1967); *The Private Navy of Sgt. O'Farrell* (sc, d,

1968); *The Shakiest Gun in the West* (based on *The Paleface*, 1968).

---

**Terry-Thomas (1911–1990)** Playing either comic villains or heroic twits, Terry-Thomas was the epitome of an upper-crust Englishman. The mustachioed, gap-toothed comedian was one of Britain's leading film comedians. Although he appeared in films from the 1930s to the late 1970s, his most productive period lasted from the mid-1950s to the late 1960s. Unlike those of most British comedians, Terry-Thomas's films received wide distribution in the United States, and he eventually appeared in a considerable number of Hollywood comedies.

Born Thomas Terry Hoar Stevens in Finchley, England, to a wealthy family, he made an early mark in the 1930s as a radio comic. His career interrupted by World War II, he returned to show business in the latter half of the 1940s, becoming a popular radio and TV comedian. He had appeared in films as early as the mid-1930s and then again in the late 1940s, but he didn't take with the public. That changed, finally, in the mid-1950s with hits such as *Private's Progress* (1955). By the end of the decade, he was an international star with a string of hit comedies that included *Too Many Crooks* (1959), *Man in a Cocked Hat* (1959), *I'm All Right Jack* (1959), and *School for Scoundrels* (1960).

Terry-Thomas arrived in Hollywood soon thereafter and made enough of an impact to be included in the all-star comedy film *IT'S A MAD MAD MAD MAD WORLD* (1963). He also scored well in *How to Murder Your Wife* (1965), *Those Magnificent Men in Their Flying Machines* (1965), and *A Guide for the Married Man* (1967). However, by the time he appeared in the Jerry LEWIS movie *Don't Raise the Bridge, Lower the River* (1968), his career had begun its downslide. Nonetheless, there were sparks of the old Terry-Thomas in films throughout the 1970s, most notably in *The Abominable Doctor Phibes* (1971).

**FILMS INCLUDE:** *This'll Make You Whistle* (1936); *It's Love Again* (1936); *Rhythm in the Air* (1936); *Rhythm Racketeer* (1937); *Under Your Hat* (1940); *For Freedom* (1940); *The Brass Monkey* (1947); *A Date with a Dream* (1948); *Helter Skelter* (1949); *The Green Man* (1956); *Private's Progress* (1956); *Blue Murder at St. Trinian's* (1957); *The Naked Truth* (1957); *Your Past Is Showing* (1957); *Lucky Jim* (1957); *Happy Is the Bride* (1958); *Tom Thumb* (1958); *Man in a Cocked Hat* (1959); *Too Many Crooks* (1959); *I'm All Right, Jack* (1959); *School for Scoundrels* (1960); *Make Mine Mink* (1960); *A Matter of Who* (1961); *The Wonderful World of the Brothers Grimm* (1962); *Kill or Cure* (1962); *Bachelor Flat* (1962); *It's a Mad Mad Mad Mad World* (1963); *How to Murder Your Wife* (1965); *Strange Bedfellows* (1965); *Those Magnificent Men in Their Flying Machines* (1965); *Munster, Go Home* (1966); *Our Man in Marrakesh* (1966); *A Guide for the Married Man* (1967); *The Karate Killers* (1967); *Arabella* (1967); *The Perils of Pauline* (1967); *Don't Raise the Bridge, Lower the River* (1968); *Where Were You When the Lights Went Out?* (1968); *How Sweet It Is* (1968); *2,000 Years Later* (1969); *Those Daring Young Men in Their Jaunty Jalopies/Monte Carlo or Bust!* (1969); *The Abominable Doctor Phibes* (1971); *Doctor Phibes Rises Again* (1972); *Robin Hood* (1973); *The Vault of Horror* (1973); *Who Stole the Shah's Jewels?* (1974); *Side by Side* (1975); *The Bawdy Adventures of Tom Jones* (1976); *The Mysterious House of Dr. C* (1976); *Spanish Fly* (1976); *The Last Remake of Beau Gest* (1977); *The Hound of the Baskervilles* (1977).

---

**Three Stooges, The** The humor of the Three Stooges was lowbrow SLAPSTICK, often tasteless, violent, and repetitive, but it was also liberatingly funny. There is no middle ground when it comes to the Stooges—people either love them or hate them. To those who love them, they possess an almost cartoonlike nuttiness that lifts their best work to the level of inspired lunacy. The Three Stooges made

*The Three Stooges had the longest running comedy series in Hollywood history, making a total of 190 comedy shorts at Columbia Pictures from 1934 to 1958. Although Moe (left) and Larry (right) were the constants in the team, it was Curly (center) who best defined their humor.*
PHOTO COURTESY OF THE SIEGEL COLLECTION.

190 two-reelers between 1934 and 1958 at Columbia Pictures, setting a record for the longest-running comedy series in Hollywood history. The reason for their longevity at Columbia had less to do with their popularity than with the superstition of studio head Harry Cohn. They were kept on because Cohn reportedly thought of the comedy team as his good luck charm; they had come to the studio the year that Columbia hit the big time with Frank CAPRA's *IT HAPPENED ONE NIGHT* (1934), and the movie mogul insisted on keeping them around. When Cohn died in 1958, The Three Stooges lost their patron saint; they were let go after completing their last short, *Sappy Bullfighters* (1958).

Originally a VAUDEVILLE act created in 1923 and billed as Ted Healy and His Stooges, the group consisted of star Ted Healy and just two Stooges, brothers Moe Howard, born Moses Harry Horowitz (1897–1975), and Shemp Howard, born Samuel Horowitz (1895–1955). Larry Fine, born Lawrence Feinberg (1902–1975), joined the act five years later in 1928, bringing the total number of Stooges to three.

Their first appearance in the movies was with Healy in the feature-length motion picture *Soup to Nuts* (1930), in which they were billed as The Rackateers. Shemp left the act after their film appearance to begin a long and successful solo career. He was replaced by Moe and Shemp's kid brother, Curly Howard, born Jerome Horowitz (1903–1952).

After several more years of knocking around in vaudeville and appearing in movies with Healy, the Stooges decided to break away. They took their act over to Columbia, where they refined their peculiar chemistry as a comedy team. Moe was the leader, the know-nothing know-it-all who ordered the other two around, hitting, poking, and slapping his brethren at seemingly every turn. Larry was the innocent with the "porcupine" hairdo, the sweet Stooge who just wanted to get along. Curly was the wild man, the spark that fired the team's engine. He was pure id and ego wrapped up in a fat, bald package full of manic energy.

Moe, Larry, and Curly made their stunning debut (sans Healy) as The Three Stooges in *Woman Haters* (1934), a musical with the dialogue delivered in rhyming couplets. They went on to churn out an average of eight shorts per year throughout the 1930s and the first half of the 1940s, doing most of their best work during that period. In fact, they were nominated for an Oscar for *Men in Black* (1934), but were beaten by Disney's *Three Little Pigs*. They retorted the following year with *Three Little Pigskins* (1935). Among their other classic shorts were *Hoi Polloi* (1935), *Violent Is the Word for Curly* (1938), *Calling all Curs* (1939), and *You Natzy Spy* (1940), in which Moe looked amazingly like Hitler.

After Curly suffered a stroke in 1946, the call went out to brother Shemp to return to the team. He did so with modest results, but the group was never the same without Curly. When Shemp died in 1955, Joe Besser filled in, and was then replaced by Joe DeRita, who shaved his head and called himself Curly-Joe. The team went steadily downhill.

It seemed their career was over when Columbia let them go, but a curious thing happened. The studio unloaded to television all of the Three

Stooges shorts featuring Curly. A whole new audience of kids discovered the trio and went crazy for them. In the twilight of their lives, The Three Stooges were hotter than they had ever been in their entire careers. Their faces appeared on lunch boxes and they cashed in with personal appearances and a series of terrible feature films, among them *Have Rocket, Will Travel* (1958) and *The Three Stooges Meet Hercules* (1961). They simply weren't the same Stooges who made those lunatic shorts back in the 1930s and 1940s. Without Curly, or even Shemp, and feeling their age, Moe, Larry, and the none-too-talented Curly-Joe continued to lumber through featured appearances in movies such as *Four for Texas* (1963), but they finally wore out. Larry Fine's stroke in 1971 effectively shut down the act. Moe died the same year as his dear friend and partner, Larry, in 1975.

---

FILMS INCLUDE: Shorts with Curly: *Nertsery Rhymes* (1933); *Beer and Pretzels* (1933); *Hello Pop!* (1933); *Plane Nuts* (1933); *Hollywood on Parade* (1933); *Screen Snapshots* (1933); *The Big Idea* (1934); *Woman Haters* (1934); *Punch Drunks* (1934); *Men in Black* (1934); *Three Little Pigskins* (1934); *Horses' Collars* (1935); *Restless Knights* (1935); *Pop Goes the Easel* (1935); *Uncivil Warriors* (1935); *Pardon My Scotch* (1935); *Hoi Polloi* (1935); *Three Little Beers* (1935); *Ants in the Pantry* (1936); *Movie Maniacs* (1936); *Half-Shot Shooters* (1936); *Disorder in the Court* (1936); *A Pain in the Pullman* (1936); *False Alarms* (1936); *Whoops I'm an Indian* (1936); *Slippery Silks* (1936); *Grips, Grunts and Groans* (1937); *Dizzy Doctors* (1937); *Three Dumb Clucks* (1937); *Back to the Woods* (1937); *Goofs and Saddles* (1937); *Cash and Carry* (1937); *Playing the Ponies* (1937); *The Sitter-Downers* (1937); *Termites of 1938* (1938); *Wee Wee Monsieur* (1938); *Tassel in the Air* (1938); *Flat Foot Stooges* (1938); *Healthy, Wealthy and Dumb* (1938); *Violent Is The Word for Curly* (1938); *Three Missing Links* (1938); *Mutts to You* (1938); *Three Little Sew and Sews* (1939); *We Want Our Mummy* (1939); *A-Ducking They Did Go* (1939); *Yes, We Have No Bonanza* (1939); *Saved by the Belle* (1939); *Calling All Curs* (1939); *Oily to Bed, Oily to Rise* (1939); *Three Sappy People* (1939); *You Natzy Spy* (1940); *Rockin' Through the Rockies* (1940); *A-Plumbing We Will Go* (1940); *Nutty but Nice* (1940); *How High Is Up?* (1940); *From Nurse to Worse* (1940); *No Census, No Feeling* (1940); *Cookoo Cavaliers* (1940); *Boobs in Arms* (1940); *So Long, Mr. Chumps* (1941); *Dutiful but Dumb* (1941); *All the World's a Stooge* (1941); *I'll Never Heil Again* (1941); *An Ache in Every Stake* (1941); *In the Sweet Pie and Pie* (1941); *Some More of Samoa* (1941); *Loco Boy Makes Good* (1942); *Cactus Makes Perfect* (1942); *What's the Matador?* (1942); *Matri-Phoney* (1942); *Three Smart Saps* (1942); *Even as I.O.U.* (1942); *Sock-a-Bye Baby* (1942); *They Stooge to Conga* (1943); *Dizzy Detectives* (1943); *Spook Louder* (1943); *Back from the Front* (1943); *Three Little Twirps* (1943); *Higher Than a Kite* (1943); *I Can Hardly Wait* (1943); *Dizzy Pilots* (1943); *Phony Express* (1943); *A Gem of a Jam* (1943); *Crash Goes the Hash* (1944); *Busy Buddies* (1944); *The Yoke's on Me* (1944); *Idle Roomers* (1944); *Gents without Cents* (1944); *No Dough, Boys* (1944); *Three Pests in a Mess* (1945); *Booby Dupes* (1945); *Idiots Deluxe* (1945); *If a Body Meets a Body* (1945); *Micro-Phonies* (1945); *Beer Barrel Polecats* (1946); *A Bird in the Head* (1946); *Uncivil Warbirds* (1946); *Three Troubledoers* (1946); *Monkey Businessmen* (1946); *Three Loan Wolves* (1946); *G.I. Wanna Home* (1946); *Rhythm and Weep* (1946); *Three Little Pirates* (1946); *Half Wits' Holiday* (1947).

Shorts with Shemp: *Fright Night* (1947); *Out West* (1947); *Hold that Lion* (1947); *Brideless Groom* (1947); *Sing a Song of Six Pants* (1947); *All Gummed Up* (1947); *Shivering Sherlocks* (1948); *Pardon My Clutch* (1948); *Squareheads of the Round Table* (1948); *Fiddlers Three* (1948); *The Hot Scots* (1948); *Heavenly Daze* (1948); *I'm a Monkey's Uncle* (1948); *Mummy's Dummies* (1948); *A Crime on Their Hands* (1948); *The Ghost Talks* (1949); *Who Done It?* (1949); *Hocus Pocus* (1949); *Fuelin' Around* (1949); *Malice in the Palace* (1949); *Vagabond Loafers* (1949); *Dunked in the Deep* (1949); *Punchy Cowpunchers* (1950); *Hugs and Mugs* (1950); *Dopey Dicks* (1950); *Love at First Bite* (1950); *Self-Made Maids* (1950); *Three*

*Hams on Rye* (1950); *Studio Stoops* (1950); *Slap-happy Sleuths* (1950); *A Snitch in Time* (1950); *Three Arabian Nuts* (1951); *Baby Sitters' Jitters* (1951); *Don't Throw That Knife* (1951); *Scrambled Brains* (1951); *Merry Mavericks* (1951); *The Tooth Will Out* (1951); *Hula-La-La* (1951); *Pest Man Wins* (1951); *A Missed Fortune* (1952); *Listen, Judge* (1952); *Corny Casanovas* (1952); *He Cooked His Goose* (1952); *Gents in a Jam* (1952); *Three Dark Horses* (1952); *Cuckoo on a Choo Choo* (1952); *Up in Daisy's Penthouse* (1953); *Booty and the Beast* (1953); *Loose Loot* (1953); *Tricky Dicks* (1953); *Spooks* (1953); *Pardon My Backfire* (1953); *Rip, Sew and Stitch* (1953); *Bubble Trouble* (1953); *Goof on the Roof* (1953); *Income Tax Sappy* (1954); *Musty Musketeers* (1954); *Pals and Gals* (1954); *Knutzy Knights* (1954); *Shot in the Frontier* (1954); *Scotched in Scotland* (1954); *Fling in the Ring* (1955); *Of Cash and Hash* (1955); *Gypped in the Penthouse* (1955); *Bedlam in Paradise* (1955); *Stone Age Romeos* (1955); *Wham Bam Slam* (1955); *Hot Ice* (1955); *Blunder Boys* (1955); *Husbands Beware* (1956); *Creeps* (1956); *Flagpole Jitters* (1956); *For Crimin' Out Loud* (1956); *Rumpus in a Harem* (1956); *Hot Stuff* (1956); *Scheming Schemers* (1956); *Commotion on the Ocean* (1956).

Shorts with Joe Besser: *Hoofs and Goofs* (1957); *Muscle Up a Little Closer* (1957); *A Merry Mix-Up* (1957); *Space Ship Sappy* (1957); *Guns-a-Poppin'* (1957); *Horsing Around* (1957); *Rusty Romeos* (1957); *Outer Space Jitters* (1957); *Quiz Whiz* (1958); *Fifi Blows Her Top* (1958); *Pies and Guys* (1958); *Sweet and Hot* (1958); *Flying Saucer Daffy* (1958); *Oils Well That Ends Well* (1958); *Triple Crossed* (1959); *Sappy Bullfighters* (1959).

Features: *Soup to Nuts* (1930); *Turn Back the Clock* (1933); *Meet the Baron* (1933); *Dancing Lady* (1933); *Myrt and Marge* (1934); *Fugitive Lovers* (1934); *Hollywood Party* (1934); *The Captain Hates the Sea* (1934); *Start Cheering* (1938); *Time Out for Rhythm* (1941); *My Sister Eileen* (1942); *Rockin' In the Rockies* (1945); *Swing Parade of 1946* (1946); *Gold Raiders* (1951); *Have Rocket, Will Travel* (1959); *Stop! Look! and Laugh* (1960); *Snow White and The Three Stooges* (1961); *The Three Stooges Meet Hercules* (1962); *The Three Stooges in Orbit* (1962); *The Three Stooges Go Around the World in a Daze* (1963); *It's a Mad Mad Mad Mad World* (1963); *Four for Texas* (1963); *The Outlaws Is Coming* (1965).

---

**Tillie's Punctured Romance**  Made in 1914 by Mack SENNETT at his Keystone Studio, *Tillie's Punctured Romance* was the first feature-length comedy ever made, coming out at six reels. (Previously, most comedies were one- and two-reelers.) The film is far more important for its historical value than it is for its aesthetic contribution to the art of comedy. The fact is, *Tillie's Punctured Romance* is not a very funny movie. It was, however, enormously popular.

The film featured Marie DRESSLER, then a famous stage actress, as Tillie. Making her movie debut, Dressler found herself in a film adapted from her own Broadway hit *Tillie's Nightmare*. Her co-star, at less than half her ample size, was Charlie CHAPLIN, who did not portray his Little Tramp character in this film. A flagship picture for Sennett, he employed virtually every name comic actor on the Keystone lot, which in 1914 was the premier fun factory in Hollywood.

Besides being the first comic feature, it was also the first comedy all-star film. In addition to Dressler and Chaplin, the movie featured Mabel NORMAND, Chester CONKLIN, Mack SWAIN, Minta DURFEE, Charley CHASE, Phyllis Allen, Al St.John, Charles Bennett, Hank Mann, and the KEYSTONE KOPS. Sennett produced and directed the movie, taking no chances with this all-important project.

*Tillie's Punctured Romance* told the story of a dowdy country girl who becomes the heir to a fortune. Chaplin, playing a debonair swindler, tries to cheat her out of her inheritance, only to be foiled by film's end. Naturally, as this was a Keystone film, the finale featured an elaborate comic chase sequence.

The movie proved such a hit that Dressler became

a very popular movie actress and even starred in a couple of sequels, *Tillie's Tomato Surprise* (1915) and *Tillie Wakes Up* (1917). In 1928 *Tillie's Punctured Romance* was remade as a sound film.

## Todd, Thelma (1905—1935)

The beautiful and talented Thelma Todd starred in two-reel and feature comedies, making her mark in the first half of the 1930s. She is probably best remembered as the College Widow in the MARX BROTHERS romp *Horse Feathers* (1932), but she worked with virtually every major comic talent of her time, from Buster KEATON to Jimmy DURANTE. She left a lasting legacy of thirty-eight comedy shorts, which she made between 1931 and 1935 with two different comedians, ZaSu PITTS and Patsy KELLY.

Born in Lawrence, Massachusetts, Todd worked as a part-time model, putting herself through college. After graduation, she became a teacher, but worked only for a short time. She won the Miss Massachusetts beauty contest, which prompted a Paramount talent scout to sign her to a contract. After receiving a short acting course in New York, she was given small roles in silent films in 1926, just before the advent of the talkies. Her career moved along swiftly; by 1927 she was starring opposite Gary Cooper in *Nevada* (1927).

The talkies did not prove an obstacle to her career; Todd possessed a sexy, vibrant voice that was perfectly suited to the new technology. Nonetheless, her career stalled short of instant stardom. Hal ROACH stepped in at this point, adding her to his stable of comedy stars, among them Charley CHASE, LAUREL AND HARDY, and Harry LANGDON, all of whom she eventually worked with. Later, he teamed her with ZaSu Pitts with the intention of turning the two of them into the female equivalent of Laurel and Hardy. Todd and Pitts were amusing together, and their films were quite popular. When Pitts left the Roach studio, Todd was then teamed with Patsy Kelly, who proved an even better partner. Their humor was bright, sassy, and energetic. They combined a little bit of SLAPSTICK with

what today is known as situation comedy. For her part, Todd was quick with a quip and deliciously sexy without losing any of her humor.

Even as she appeared in short subjects, Todd continued to appear in features, usually in comic roles but sometimes in dramas as well. But at the age of thirty, as she was headed for the top, Todd died suddenly under decidedly mysterious circumstances. She was found in her car, a victim of carbon monoxide poisoning. There was no note and no known reason why she might have taken her life. While her death was ruled a suicide, rumors of murder circulated throughout Hollywood. In recent years, a biography titled *Hot Toddy* attempted to solve the riddle of her death while illuminating her brief life.

FILMS INCLUDE: Features: *God Gave Me Twenty Cents* (1926); *Fascinating Youth* (1926); *Rubber Heels* (1927); *Nevada* (1927); *The Gay Defender* (1927); *Seven Footprints to Satan* (1928); *The Noose* (1928); *Heart to Heart* (1928); *Vamping Venus* (1928); *The Crash* (1928); *The Haunted House* (1928); *Naughty Baby* (1929); *Careers* (1929); *The House of Horror* (1929); *Command Performance* (1930); *Follow Thru* (1930); *Swanee River* (1931); *The Hot Heiress* (1931); *Aloha* (1931); *The Maltese Falcon* (1931); *Corsair* (1931); *Monkey Business* (1931); *This Is the Night* (1932); *Horse Feathers* (1932); *Klondike* (1932); *Call Her Savage* (1932); *Speak Easily* (1932); *Cheating Blondes* (1933); *Son of Sailor* (1933); *Sitting Pretty* (1933); *You Made Me Love You* (1933); *Counsellor-at-Law* (1933); *Hips, Hips, Hooray* (1934); *Bottoms Up* (1934); *Cockeyed Cavaliers* (1934); *Palooka* (1934); *Take the Stand* (1934); *Lightning Strikes Twice* (1935); *Two for Tonight* (1935); *The Bohemian Girl* (1936).

Shorts with ZaSu Pitts: *Let's Do Things* (1931); *Catch As Catch Can* (1931); *The Pajama Party* (1931); *War Mamas* (1931); *Seal Skins* (1932); *On the Loose* (1932); *Red Noses* (1932); *Strictly Unreliable* (1932); *The Old Bull* (1932); *Show Business* (1932); *Alum and Eve* (1932); *The Soilers* (1932); *Sneak Easily* (1933); *Asleep in the Feet* (1933); *Maids a la Mode* (1933);

*Bargain of the Century* (1933); *One Track Minds* (1933).

Shorts with Patsy Kelly: *Beauty and the Bus* (1933); *Backs to Nature* (1933); *Air Fright* (1933); *Babes in the Goods* (1934); *Soup and Fish* (1934); *Maid in Hollywood* (1934); *I'll Be Suing You* (1934); *Three Chumps Ahead* (1934); *One Horse Farmers* (1934); *Opened by Mistake* (1934); *Done in Oil* (1934); *Bum Voyage* (1934); *Treasure Blues* (1935); *Sing, Sister, Sing* (1935); *The Tin Man* (1935); *The Misses Stooge* (1935); *Slightly Static* (1935); *Twin Triplets* (1935); *Hot Money* (1935); *Top Flat* (1935); *All American Toothache* (1935).

*A gifted comic actress, Lily Tomlin hasn't appeared in nearly as many movies as her fans would like, but she has made an impact, nonetheless, in films such as* 9 to 5 *(1980),* All of Me *(1984), and* Big Business *(1988). She is seen here with Charles Grodin in* The Incredible Shrinking Woman *(1981).* PHOTO © UNIVERSAL PICTURES.

## Tomlin, Lily (1939—)

An extremely gifted actress and comedian, Lily Tomlin is an incisive, intelligent performer who has had more success on TV and on the stage (in her two one-woman shows) than she has had in the movies. Unlike most comedy stars, she doesn't project a particular comic personality, but rather an entire rainbow of personalities. For instance, none of her film heroines share any sort of similar characteristics; that's high praise for her acting skills, but that's also what has contributed to a rather small (if intensely loyal) fan base.

Born Mary Jean Tomlin in Detroit, Michigan, she dropped out of college, concentrating on becoming a cabaret artist. At about this time she met Jane Wagner, a writer, director, and producer who has been Tomlin's collaborator and friend throughout virtually all of her professional life.

Tomlin arrived in New York in 1966 and began performing on the coffee house circuit, eventually gaining her first national attention as a regular on TV's "The Garry Moore Show." That job didn't last long, as Moore went off the air in 1967.

She returned to cabaret work until she became a regular performer in 1969 on the hit TV show "Rowan and Martin's Laugh-In." She quickly became a star on the popular program thanks to her brilliant comic characterizations of Edith Ann, the devilish five-year-old, and Ernestine, the snorting switchboard operator who seemed to talk through her nose.

Tomlin left the show in 1972, making comedy records and winning Emmys for her TV specials in the years that followed. Eventually, the movies finally snared her, and she made quite a splash with her film debut in Robert Altman's highly acclaimed *Nashville* (1975). Tomlin co-wrote one of the two songs she sang in the film and won critical raves for her powerful dramatic performance. She also won over her peers, who gave her a best supporting actress Academy Award nomination.

Tomlin was not quick to follow up with another film. Two years later, however, she and Art CARNEY teamed up in a comic mystery, *The Late Show* (1977), a film that did them both proud, even if nobody went to see it. Jane Wagner directed her in the drama *Moment by Moment* (1978); it also flopped. Her ensemble work in *Nine to Five* (1980), however, was strong, and the film was a huge success. Asked to carry a film on her own, she starred in *The*

*Incredible Shrinking Woman* (1981), a movie that allowed her to show off her considerable versatility. The critics liked her, but the audiences shrunk right along with her.

Her next film, and among her best, was *All of Me* (1984), a sharply amusing movie about the differences between men and women. The film's praise, however, went largely to Steve MARTIN, who gave a virtuoso performance. The results were the same in *Big Business* (1988); her co-star, Bette MIDLER, stole the film. Since then, Tomlin has concentrated on her work for the theater, making only occasional supporting appearances in movies. An exception was the disappointing 1991 film version of her highly praised stage show *The Search for Signs of Intelligent Life in the Universe*, written by Jane Wagner. Their previous stage collaboration had led to the hit one-woman show "Appearing Nitely" in 1977.

---

FILMS: *Nashville* (also songs, 1975); *The Late Show* (1977); *Moment by Moment* (1978); *9 to 5* (1980); *The Incredible Shrinking Woman* (1981); *All of Me* (1984); *Lily Tomlin* (1986); *Big Business* (1988); *The Search for Signs of Intelligent Life in the Universe* (1991); *Shadows and Fog* (1992); *The Player* (1992); *Short Cuts* (1993).

---

## Townsend, Robert (1957—)

A multi-talented filmmaker, Robert Townsend has written, directed, and starred in three very different kinds of comedies as a means of exploring the black experience in America. His first effort, *Hollywood Shuffle* (1987), which he also produced, brought him to public attention not only because it humorously laid bare the problems African Americans have in breaking into the movies, but also because he financed the $100,000 film himself, largely on credit card debt.

Born in Chicago, Illinois, Townsend started in show business at sixteen with the Experimental Black Actors Guild and then moved on to work with Chicago's Second City Comedy troupe. After

moving to New York, he studied with Stella Adler and began appearing in off-Broadway shows as well as mounting a stand-up comedy routine.

After landing a small role in the New York film production of Paul MAZURSKY's *Willie and Phil* (1980), Townsend headed to Los Angeles to pursue more film roles, one of which was a significant part in *A Soldier's Story* (1984). He worked fairly steadily after that, getting small roles in films like *Streets of Fire* (1984) and *Ratboy* (1986), but he also saw how limited his options were as a black actor in Hollywood. That was the genesis of *Hollywood Shuffle*. The success of that film led to an offer to direct the comedy concert film *Eddie Murphy Raw* (1987) as well as to larger acting roles in films such as *The Mighty Quinn* (1989).

Townsend's next directorial effort, *The Five Heartbeats* (1991), which he also wrote, was a serio-comic musical that had been highly anticipated. Townsend had a significant budget this time and made the most of it—or, rather, too much of it. The film was far too long, dragging out its touching and uplifting story of a group of singers who simply couldn't stay together long enough to hit the big time. The movie disappeared rather quickly. *Meteor Man* (1993), while flawed, was kindly received by critics for its high-spirited, often inspired, comic riffs and its uplifting message.

---

FILMS INCLUDE: *Willie and Phil* (a, 1980); *A Soldier's Story* (a, 1984); *Streets of Fire* (a, 1984); *American Flyers* (a, 1985); *Odd Jobs* (a, 1986); *Ratboy* (a, 1986); *Hollywood Shuffle* (a, sc, p, d, 1987); *Eddie Murphy Raw* (d, 1987); *The Mighty Quinn* (a, 1989); *That's Adequate* (a, 1989); *The Five Heartbeats* (a, sc, d, 1991); *Meteor Man* (a, sc, d, 1993).

---

## Turpin, Ben (1874—1940)

Goony-looking, cross-eyed Ben Turpin was a comedy star of the silent era. His fame was such in the early 1920s that he insured his eyes with Lloyds of London in case they might uncross. Turpin's SLAPSTICK style of humor reached its apex when he made a series of short parodies of famous films. With his malleable body and bizarrely funny faces, he never played realistic comic characters in the fashion of a Charlie CHAPLIN, Buster KEATON, or Harold LLOYD. Instead, Turpin was a human cartoon character who made audiences laugh by virtue of his inspired silliness.

After working the BURLESQUE houses as a comic, Turpin made an early attempt at film comedy in 1907 at the Essanay studio. Two years later he gave up on the new movie industry, hit the VAUDEVILLE circuit, and had his first real success when he created the Happy Hooligan character. Film beckoned again in 1914, and he struggled for several years to create a comic identity. The best he could do was to play second fiddle in a number of Charlie Chaplin shorts.

After joining Mack SENNETT's Keystone Studio in 1917, Turpin finally emerged as a wonderfully adept parodist in one- and two-reel films such as *The Shriek of Araby* (1923), *Three and a Half Weeks* (1924), and *The Reel Virginian* (1924). He played hilarious versions of Valentino, Von Stroheim, Tom Mix, and a great many other stars of the day.

When talkies arrived, Turpin began appearing in feature-length comedies but only as a minor supporting player. He was seen, for instance, in Ernst LUBITSCH's *The Love Parade* (1929) and (memorably) provided the legs in the W. C. FIELDS film *Million Dollar Legs* (1932). Turpin did not act often in the 1930s, but when he did he was a fond reminder of a simpler form of silent film humor. His last film was in support of LAUREL AND HARDY in *Saps at Sea* (1940).

FILMS INCLUDE: *Mr. Flip* (1909); *Evans Links with Sweedie* (1914); *His New Job* (1915); *A Night Out* (1915); *Carmen* (1916); *The Wicked City* (1916); *Hired and Fired* (1916); *A Studio Stampede* (1917); *A Clever Dummy* (1917); *Roping Her Romeo* (1917); *She Loved Him Plenty* (1918); *The Battle Royal* (1918); *Cupid's Day Off* (1919); *Yankee Doodle in Berlin* (1919); *Uncle Tom without the Cabin* (1919); *Sleuths* (1919); *Down on the Farm* (1920); *Married Life* (1920); *Love and Doughnuts* (1921); *A Small Town Idol* (1921); *Bright Eyes* (1922); *Home Made Movies* (1922); *The Shriek of Araby* (1923); *The Daredevil* (1923); *Hollywood* (1923); *The Reel Virginian* (1924); *Romeo and Juliet* (1924); *Three and a Half Weeks* (1924); *The Marriage Circus* (1925); *Hogan's Alley* (1925); *A Prodigal Bridegroom* (1926); *Steel Preferred* (1926); *A Harem Knight* (1926); *Pride of Pikeville* (1927); *A Hollywood Hero* (1927); *Love's Languid Cure* (1927); *The College Hero* (1927); *The Wife's Relations* (1928); *The Show of Shows* (1929); *The Love Parade* (1930); *Cracked Nuts* (1931); *Million Dollar Legs* (1932); *Hollywood Cavalcade* (1939); *Saps at Sea* (1940).

**Twentieth Century**  The 1934 movie *Twentieth Century*, directed by Howard HAWKS and starring Carole LOMBARD and John Barrymore, was the first SCREWBALL COMEDY. The film is noteworthy beyond its historical significance; it happens to be enormously funny. It's also the film that fully established Lombard as a brilliant comedian, while giving the otherwise fading Barrymore his greatest comic role.

Named after the train that ran between New York and Chicago, the film tells the madcap story of two incredibly egocentric people who spend a good portion of the film on that train. Lombard plays Lily Garland, a famous actress who was once plucked out of obscurity and turned into a star by Oscar Jaffe, a theatrical producer/director played by Barrymore. Director and star had become lovers, but Garland, stifled by her mentor, escapes him to become an even bigger star on her own. Facing financial ruin, Jaffe plots to get her back for his next play. And so the battle begins, the two titanic forces go to war, each of them insulting, manipulating, and lying to each other, even as we can see (if they can't) that the two of them are a perfect pair—like kerosene and matches.

The script by Ben Hecht and Charles MacArthur crackles with devastating put-downs. In addition to

the snappy dialogue and the scintillating performances, it's the uncompromising nature of the film
that gives it its comic bite, distinguishing it from
other comedies, except for the handful made by
Hawks. There is no sentimental turning point; these
crazed characters are just who they seem to be. They
are so consumed with themselves, so unaware of
their own selfishness, that they ultimately become
comic fools of a very high order. What redeems
them is that Jaffe and Garland really do love and
need each other, not for a conventional relationship,
but to continue their bickering.

*Twentieth Century* was turned into a hit Broadway
musical in 1978 called *On the Twentieth Century*.

# U—V

**UPA (United Productions of America)** Due to a bitter strike against the Walt Disney Company in the early 1940s, a group of animators set up their own shop in 1943 and named it United Productions of America (UPA). The new studio was low on resources but high on talent. Instead of the lush animation of Disney's films, UPA's cartoons tended toward a spare, simple style, coupled with a some-what more sophisticated comic content. The studio's biggest winners were the *Mr. Magoo* and *Gerald McBoing Boing* cartoon series.

**Van Dyke, Dick (1925—)** The shame of Dick Van Dyke's movie career is that it didn't start earlier. He was nearly forty when he made his movie debut, recreating his stage success in *Bye, Bye Birdie* (1963). More than an issue of age, however, was the age itself. Van Dyke was the kind of warm, endearing, and versatile performer who would have thrived in movies during the 1940s and 1950s. Instead, he caught the tail end of that era, creating hits in films like *Mary Poppins* (1964) and *Fitzwilly* (1967) that owed more to the past than they did to the future of Hollywood comedy. He might have been right for a comedy directed by a Frank TASHLIN, but not a Paul MAZURSKY. Despite his fame and obvious talent, displayed so well in the classic TV sitcom "The Dick Van Dyke Show" (1961–1966), he did not find the success appropriate for his comedic skills. Except for a few scattered films that came later, his movie career was over by the end of the 1960s.

Born in West Plains, Missouri, Van Dyke got his first taste of show business in the army during World War II when he worked as a radio announcer. After the war and a failed business venture, he teamed up with Phil Erickson to create "The Merry Mutes" nightclub routine. He worked steadily during the 1950s in clubs, TV, and stage before making his big breakthrough in the Broadway show *Bye, Bye Birdie*. The year was 1960; it was the start of his one great decade. His TV series brought him three Emmy Awards in three successive seasons (1964–1966), but he chose to leave the program to pursue his film career full-time. In retrospect, it was a bad decision. He had shown how multi-talented he was in *Mary Poppins*, had stolen *The Art of Love* (1965), had scored a big commercial hit with *Lt. Robinson Crusoe, USN* (1966), but once he was off TV his career began to quickly erode. Making movies largely for Disney, a studio that was in steep decline at the time, didn't help. His last hit was in *Chitty, Chitty, Bang, Bang* (1968), a poor man's *Mary Poppins*. He gave a rich, detailed, and effective performance in Carl REINER's *The Comic* (1969), a film loosely based on Stan Laurel's silent screen experiences, but audiences weren't interested.

Van Dyke returned to television with two different shows, but could not recreate his 1960s success. He has starred every now and then in TV movies.

His brother, Jerry Van Dyke, is also a comic actor who has had modest success on TV.

**FILMS INCLUDE:** *Bye, Bye Birdie* (1963); *What a Way to Go!* (1964); *Mary Poppins* (1964); *The Art of Love* (1965); *Lt. Robinson Crusoe, USN* (1966); *Fitzwilly* (1967); *Divorce, American Style* (1967); *Never a Dull Moment* (1968); *Chitty, Chitty, Bang, Bang* (1968);

*Some Kind of a Nut* (1969); *The Comic* (1969); *Cold Turkey* (1971); *The Runner Stumbles* (1979); *Dick Tracy* (1990).

---

**vaudeville**    American vaudeville came out of the British music hall tradition and became Hollywood's source for a vast number of comic performers. Vaudeville was a primary outlet for live acts during the late nineteenth century and the first four decades of the twentieth, reaching its height of popularity between the turn of the century and the advent of talkies in 1927. Virtually every silent comedy actor and an enormous number of comedy stars learned their craft in vaudeville, among them Buster KEATON, BURNS AND ALLEN, the MARX BROTHERS, ABBOTT AND COSTELLO, and OLSEN AND JOHNSON. The list is long and impressive.

Vaudeville's doom was sealed when Warner Bros. and others began making sound shorts of all the great comedy acts. In those days, a performer could make a career out of one famous routine. Once that routine was committed to film, however, it was seen by huge audiences over a short period of time, rendering it obsolete. Also, the acts could be seen far cheaper in a movie theater than in a vaudeville house. In essence, talkies killed vaudeville, although the death was slow in coming.

A vaudeville show consisted of between eight and ten acts that included comedy, music, and acrobatics. The acts were booked individually by management, creating a show of usually two hours long. While BURLESQUE was strictly for adults, vaudeville provided entertainment for the whole family. During the heyday of live acts, there were vaudeville venues everywhere, from small towns to big cities. The closest equivalent of vaudeville today are the comedy clubs that have proliferated in virtually every city across the country.

# W

**Warner Bros. cartoons** Under the banner of Looney Tunes and Merrie Melodies, Warner Bros. produced the hippest, cleverest, and most amusing of the animated shorts made by Hollywood. While Warner Bros. never matched Walt DISNEY's product in relation to animation excellence, the comic sensibility of the former was consistently more sophisticated than its larger rival. The Warner Bros. animation unit boasted a zany cast of characters, including Bugs Bunny, Daffy Duck, Porky Pig, Elmer Fudd, Foghorn Leghorn, Tweety Pie, Sylvester the Cat, Pepe LePew, Wile E. Coyote, Road Runner, and Speedy Gonzales.

Under the stewardship of Leon Schlesinger, Warner Bros. began making cartoons in 1930. These early black and white films were called Looney Tunes to compete with Disney's popular Silly Symphonies. According to Douglas Gomery in *The Hollywood Studio System*, another reason the cartoon series had a musical title was based on the fact that "Warners insisted that each cartoon should include music from a current Warners feature film."

Throughout the early 1930s, the animation unit struggled to make a reputation without much success. It wasn't until Schlesinger launched Merrie Melodies, a color cartoon series in 1934, that the Warners cartoons began to catch on. More importantly, though, Schlesinger hired new talent such as Tex AVERY, Bob Clampett, Friz Freleng, Frank TASHLIN, and Chuck Jones, who developed the famous Warners cast of cartoon characters. It began to take shape in 1936 when Porky Pig made his debut and became the first animated star on the Warners lot.

Bugs Bunny, the carrot-chomping, wise-guy rabbit, was created soon after, taking his name from Bugs Hardaway, the man who originally sketched him. The unnamed character was simply referred to as "Bugs' Bunny" in the early development stage, and the name simply took hold (minus the apostrophe). While Bugs was the best-known character among the Warner Bros. animated stars, Daffy Duck offered an inspired insanity and remains a sentimental favorite of a great many fans.

Two of the most influential animators at Warners during their heyday were Friz Freleng and Chuck Jones, who helped create the frenetic action, violence, and goofy humor that became a hallmark of their studio. The pair often produced and directed the Warner Bros. cartoons, while many of the best of these animated shorts were written by Michael Maltese. From 1937 until his death in 1989, Mel Blanc provided the voices of the Warners cartoon characters. (Ironically the man whose voice proclaimed Bugs Bunny's most famous line, "What's Up, Doc?," was allergic to carrots.)

Warner Bros. cartoons reached their creative height in the 1940s. By the middle of the decade both Looney Tunes and Merrie Melodies were made in color. During the 1950s, Warners continued to make cartoons, which appeared first in movie theaters and then on television where they have continued to thrive to this day.

Unfortunately, the Warner Bros. animation unit was disbanded in 1969, but there have been Warner Bros. cartoon specials on TV throughout the years. Bugs and Daffy have recently been reborn in movie shorts by a new crew of young animators, with Mel Blanc, Jr., providing the voices.

The ultimate recognition of Warner Bros. animated shorts occurred in 1987 when the cartoons were added to the permanent collection of the Museum of Modern Art in New York City.

---

**CARTOONS INCLUDE:** *Elmer's Candid Camera* (1940); *Bugs Bunny and the Three Bears* (1944); *Hare Conditioned* (1945); *Sam, the Pirate* (1946); *Tweety Pie and Sylvester* (1947); *Mississippi Hare* (1947); *Bugs Bunny Rides Again* (1948); *Frigid Hare* (1949); *Canary Row* (1951); *The Rabbit of Seville* (1951); *Duck Amuck* (1953); *Captain Hareblower* (1954); *Speedy Gonzalez* (1955); *Nightmare Hare* (1955); *Robin Hood Daffy* (1957); *The Abominable Snow Rabbit* (1961).

---

## Waters, John (1946—)

For most of his career as a director, screenwriter, and producer—and sometime editor, cinematographer, and actor—John Waters has delighted in bad taste, repulsive images, and an in-your-face sense of humor. In a remarkable movie career spanning more than two decades, Waters has been pushing at the boundaries of satiric filmmaking, creating a comic art that is as disturbing as it is outrageous.

Born in Baltimore, Maryland, where he has since set all of his films, Waters is the progeny of a wealthy family. He began making amateur movies when he was a teenager, but even those films, with titles like *Eat Your Makeup*, suggested the dark comedy that was to come. His earliest commerical ventures were made on what might charitably be called a shoestring. They were successful enough to raise the paltry sum of $10,000 to make his third movie and breakthrough film, the comically disgusting *Pink Flamingos* (1972). The movie was a surprise hit, playing midnight showings in major cities all across the country and finding its way into college campus screenings as well. Featuring Waters's stock company performer DIVINE, *Pink Flamingos*, all audacity, shock, and outrage, put Waters on the movie map.

While some might say his subsequent films have been uneven, what's far more striking is how consistent they have been. Alternating between hits and flops, Waters has remained true to his vision of the world, even as he has slowly become more mainstream. It's hard to say, however, if Waters' films are becoming more like Hollywood's, or if Hollywood's are becoming more like Waters'.

---

**FILMS:** *Mondo Trasho* (ed, ph, sc, p, d, 1970); *Multiple Maniacs* (d, 1971); *Pink Flamingos* (ed, ph, sc, p, d, 1972); *Female Trouble* (ph, sc, p, d, 1975); *Desperate Living* (ph, sc, p, d, 1977); *Polyester* (sc, p, d, 1981); *Something Wild* (a, 1986); *Hairspray* (a, sc, p, d, 1988); *Homer and Eddie* (a, 1989); *Cry-Baby* (sc, d, 1990); *Divine* (sc, p, d, 1990); *Homer and Eddie* (a only, 1990); *Serial Mom* (sc, p, d, 1994).

---

## West, Mae (1892—1980)

With a combination of outrageous hip swinging, outlandish double entendres, and an out-and-out disregard of prudery, Mae West both shocked and delighted film audiences with her comically sexy sensibility. Looking more like a female impersonater than a sex symbol, she was easily the greatest female comedian in the sound era. She managed that feat despite a remarkably modest number of movies. In her most famous films, she not only starred, but also wrote her scripts (or, at the very least, her dialogue). Many of her risqué quips have become legend, such as, "Is that a gun you're carrying or are you just glad to see me?"

The daughter of a prominent heavyweight prize fighter, West was brought up in the public eye—and she clearly reveled in it. At age six she was appearing in stock in her hometown of Brooklyn, New York. After that, she went into VAUDEVILLE, billed as "The Baby Vamp," eventually becoming the originator of the shimmy dance.

In 1926 West starred on Broadway in a play she had written, produced, and directed. It was titled *Sex*, and it caused an uproar. People either clamored for tickets or clamored that West should be thrown

*Come up 'n' see me sometime —*
*Mae West*

*In 1935, Mae West was the highest paid woman in America. Of the legendary comic actress, it's fair to say, as she did herself, "When I'm good, I'm very good, but when I'm bad, I'm better."*     PHOTO COURTESY OF THE SIEGEL COLLECTION.

in jail for public indeceny. In the end, the latter group won their point and the impresario/star was thrown in jail for ten days on a charge of obscenity.

It was the best publicity West could have hoped for. After two less successful ventures, she opened on Broadway in 1928 with a huge hit, *Diamond Lil.* There were two more plays after that—one of which brought her back to court on obscenity charges, but this time she beat the rap.

In the early 1930s, with the Depression in full swing, Hollywood studios were willing to try anything to get people into their theaters. One of the more desperate studios was Paramount. George Raft wanted Mae West for his film, *Night After Night* (1932), and the studio decided to hire her as a sup-

porting player. She refused the part, however, until she was allowed to write her own dialogue.

Paramount was never sorry. She became a film star the very moment she made her initial screen entrance. A hat check girl cried out, "Goodness, what beautiful diamonds." Mae West cooed in return, "Goodness had nothing to do with it, dearie." Many years later George Raft wrote, "In this picture [*Night After Night*], Mae West stole everything but the cameras."

Her next film was based on her play *Diamond Lil,* except Paramount changed the title because the show had such a salacious reputation. Instead, they called it *She Done Him Wrong* (1933), and this time West was billed as the star. It was a major hit, as was the next, *I'm No Angel* (1933). The latter film brought $3 million to Paramount's coffers, making it one of the biggest hits of the year and helping to keep the studio solvent. As an added bonus, both films featured Cary GRANT, aiding his own rise to superstardom.

It was in part because of Mae West's notoriety that the Hays Office strengthened its production code. As a result, her next movie, originally titled *It Ain't No Sin*, was given the more innocuous name *Belle of the Nineties* (1934). However, West was more clever than her keepers, and despite censor-required script changes her double entendres still elicited shocked laughter from her fans.

By 1935, with three hit movies in a row, West became the hightest paid woman in America. After a modest success that same year with *Goin' to Town*, she scored another hit with *Klondike Annie* (1936). It was generally downhill after that, both in film content and in audience acceptance. *Go West Young Man* (1937) and *Every Day's a Holiday* (1938) were rather boring—thanks to the Hays Office—and offered none of West's usual clever innuendos.

Paramount didn't renew her contract, and that led to one of the screen's most interesting pairings, as Mae West and W. C. FIELDS co-starred in *My Little Chickadee* (1939) at Universal. Unfortunately, both West and Fields wrote their own scripts, and the result was pure chaos since neither one of them would fully compromise. Nonetheless, seeing them both on screen together is a treat.

West didn't make another film until 1943 when she starred in an independent feature, *The Heat's On*. By then, however, she was merely passé and not the appreciated institution that she is today.

She was active in the 1940s and most of the 1950s on Broadway, on tour, and in nightclubs. Then, however, West appeared to go into relative seclusion. That didn't mean, she wasn't in demand. She was approached for the role of Norma Desmond in *Sunset Boulevard* (1950) as well as either leads or important featured parts in such movies as *The First Traveling Saleslady* (1956), *Pal Joey* (1957), and *The Art of Love* (1964). It wasn't until 1970, however, that

West finally returned to the screen, looking amazingly well preserved at the age of seventy-eight in *Myra Breckinridge*. The movie was an unmitigated bomb, but West was the best thing in the film—and she wrote her own dialogue.

In 1978, she surprised Hollywood (and everyone else) by starring in a movie based on one of her plays, *Sextette*. The movie was uneven at best. Although it featured an all-star supporting cast, the film's real appeal was as a curiosity piece. Apparently, however, there weren't many people interested in seeing an eighty-five-year-old woman make funny sexual remarks.

At the end of her life West was seen as a living caricature. That fact seemed to disturb a great many people, but it needn't have. Mae West had *always* been a caricature of sexuality; that was the key to her enormous success as a comedian.

---

FILMS: *Night After Night* (1932); *I'm No Angel* (also story, sc, 1933); *She Done Him Wrong* (also from play *Diamond Lil*, 1933); *Belle of the Nineties* (also story, sc, 1934); *Goin' to Town* (also sc, 1935); *Go West, Young Man* (also sc, 1936); *Klondike Annie* (also sc, 1936); *Every Day's a Holiday* (also sc, 1938); *My Little Chickadee* (also co-sc, 1940); *The Heat's On* (1943); *Myra Breckinridge* (also co-dial, 1970); *Sextette* (also from play, 1978).

---

**Wheeler, Bert**   *See* WHEELER AND WOOLSEY

**Wheeler and Woolsey**   A popular comedy team during the 1930s, Wheeler and Woolsey are surprisingly little known today. True, the critics of their day had little use for the team, but when they were at their best, Wheeler and Woolsey possessed a delightful off-kilter charm. Boyish-faced Wheeler, and cigar-chomping, bespectacled Woolsey were often better than the movies they appeared in. Working steadily in generally low-budget films,

*Bert Wheeler (right) and Robert Woolsey (left, with glasses) are seen here with Thelma Todd, who co-starred with them in two of their best comedies,* Cockeyed Cavaliers *(1934) and* Hips, Hips, Hooray *(1934). Wheeler and Woolsey were consistently popular with audiences during the 1930s, until Woolsey's death in 1938.*     PHOTO COURTESY OF THE SIEGEL COLLECTION.

they almost consistently turned a profit at the box office. There is no telling how much better known they would be today had Woolsey not died of a kidney ailment at forty-nine during the height of their success.

Bert Wheeler (1895–1968), born Albert Jerome Wheeler in Paterson, New Jersey, was a successful comic stage performer long before he teamed with Woolsey. His original partner was his first wife, Betty Wheeler, with whom he developed a headlining act that lasted eleven years.

Robert Woolsey (1889–1938), born in Oakland, California, had intended upon becoming a jockey, but his career in horse racing took a tumble when he was thrown from a horse in 1907. He eventually turned to acting, becoming a star comic performer on Broadway during the 1920s.

It was the great Florenz Ziegfeld who put Wheeler and Woolsey together in his stage production of *Rio Rita* in 1928—and a comedy team was born. They reprised their roles in the 1929 film version of the show. They were the valued comic relief in that early sound film, but they didn't play second banana for long. As early as 1930 they starred

in their own films, beginning with *Half Shot at Sunrise.*

In the vast majority of their films, Wheeler and Woolsey were cast with the same leading lady, Dorothy Lee. She was a pretty, if rawly talented, young woman who served as more than decoration but less than a full partner. One might call her a cute version of Margaret DUMONT, at least insofar as she regularly provided the straight lines.

When they had talented people behind the camera, Wheeler and Woolsey responded in kind, most notably in *Diplomaniacs* (1933), written by Joseph L. Mankiewicz and Henry Myers; *Hips, Hips, Hooray* (1934) and *Cockeyed Cavaliers* (1934), both directed by Mark Sandrich; and *Kentucky Kernels* (1934) and *Nitwits* (1935), both directed by George Stevens.

Woolsey was already ill, but agreed to make *High Flyers* (1937). When it was finished, he was bedridden for more than a year before dying in 1938. Wheeler continued on in show business, making a couple of films, but mostly working in VAUDEVILLE and on the stage. He also appeared on the "Brave Eagle" TV series during the 1950s.

---

FILMS: As a team: *Rio Rita* (1929); *The Cuckoos* (1930); *Dixiana* (1930); *Half Shot at Sunrise* (1930); *Hook, Line and Sinker* (1930); *Cracked Nuts* (1931); *The Stolen Jools* (1931); *Caught Plastered* (1931); *Oh, Oh, Cleopatra* (1931); *Peach O'Reno* (1931); *Girl Crazy* (1932); *Hollywood on Parade* (1932); *Hold 'Em Jail* (1932); *So This Is Africa* (1933); *Diplomaniacs* (1933); *Cockeyed Cavaliers* (1934); *Signing 'Em Up* (1934); *Hips, Hips, Hooray* (1934); *Kentucky Kernels* (1934); *The Nitwits* (1935); *The Rainmakers* (1935); *Silly Billies* (1936); *Mummy's Boys* (1936); *On Again, Off Again* (1937); *High Flyers* (1937).

Wheeler alone: *Small Timers* (short, 1929); *Too Many Cooks* (1931); *Hollywood Handicap* (short, 1932); *A Night at the Biltmore Bowl* (short, 1935); *Sunday Night at the Trocadero* (short, 1937); *Cowboy Quarterback* (1939); *Las Vegas Nights* (1941); *Innocently Guilty* (short, 1950); *The Awful Sleuth* (short, 1951).

Woolsey alone: *Everything's Rosie* (1931); *Hollywood on Parade* (short, 1933).

---

**Wilder, Billy (1906—)**  By no means strictly a creator of comedies, Billy Wilder nonetheless made his greatest mark in Hollywood with pungent films laced with cynical humor and a bleakly comic view of human nature. A writer, director, and producer, the iconoclastic Wilder walked a fine line between art and commerce, managing to make movies that were both unsettling yet surprisingly potent at the box office.

Born Samuel Wilder in Vienna, Austria, he was called "Billy" by his mother, who loved all things American and understood it to be a popular name in this country. He came from a successful upper middle-class Jewish family and originally studied for a career in the law. After just one year of legal studies, though, he decided to become a journalist, eventually becoming a reporter for a major Berlin newspaper.

Wilder debuted as a screenwriter as one of five talented young men who collaborated on the documentary *Menschen am Sonntag/People on Sunday* (1929), co-writing the script with future Hollywood screenwriter Curt Siodmak. The film created quite a stir at the time of its release, and Wilder went on to write a number of other screenplays and provide stories for the German film company, UFA, including the highly successful *Emil and the Detectives* (1931).

Hitler's rise to power in Germany in 1933 was Wilder's cue to flee. His first stop before coming to America was in Paris where he co-wrote and co-directed his first film, *Mauvaise Graine* (1933), starring seventeen-year-old Danielle Darrieux. He would not direct a movie again until 1942.

After sweating out a difficult entry into the United States in a Mexicali consul's office in Mexico, Wilder arrived in America in 1933 broke, with little facility for the English language, yet hoping to succeed in the film mecca of Hollywood. He learned English from listening to baseball games on the radio and going to the movies. In the meantime,

he sold a story idea that became *Adorable* (1933) and went on to sell both his stories and scripts (usually written in collaboration) as he began to build a modest reputation.

Wilder's career suddenly went full throttle in 1938 when he began his brilliant twelve-year collaboration with screenwriter Charles Brackett. They began with the cleverly dark Ernst LUBITSCH comedy *Bluebeard's Eighth Wife* (1938) and then wrote such other grand comic entertainments as *Midnight* (1939), *Ninotchka* (1939), and *Ball of Fire* (1941).

Thanks to the likes of Preston STURGES and John Huston, who had opened the door for screenwriter/directors in the early 1940s, Wilder directed the comedy hit *The Major and the Minor* (1942), which he had co-authored with Brackett. During the rest of their collaborations, Wilder directed, Brackett produced, and the two of them largely turned away from comedy to write a number of hard-hitting and provocative movies that have since become classics, among them *Double Indemnity* (1944), *The Lost Weekend* (1945), for which Wilder won his first best director Oscar, *A Foreign Affair* (1948), and *Sunset Boulevard* (1950).

*Sunset Boulevard* was the last collaboration between Wilder and Brackett. Wilder always seemed to work best when he wrote in collaboration, and some of his memorable work was yet to come when he joined with I. A. L. DIAMOND to pen the screenplay for the adventurous comedy *Some Like It Hot* (1959). A critical and commercial hit, it was followed by what many consider to be Wilder's crowning achievement, *The Apartment* (1960), which won Wilder his third and last best director Oscar, an Oscar for his screenplay, and his only best picture Academy Award. Emboldened, he followed with even harsher comedies, including *One, Two, Three* (1961), *Irma La Douce* (1963), *Kiss Me, Stupid* (1964), and *The Fortune Cookie* (1966).

Wilder collaborated with Diamond on the rest of his films, including his later work that received little critical and commercial acceptance, including *Fedora* (1979) and their last film together, *Buddy, Buddy* (1981), which was also Wilder's last movie to date.

Wilder was honored by the Academy of Motion Picture Arts and Scienes with an impressive twenty Oscar nominations—twelve for his screenplay collaborations and eight for best director. He won a total of six Oscars altogether. In recognition of his achievements in a Hollywood career that began in 1933, the governors of the Academy bestowed the prestigious Irving Thalberg Memorial Award upon Wilder in 1988.

---

FILMS INCLUDE: U.S. credits only: *Adorable* (co-story, 1933); *One Exciting Adventure* (co-story, 1934); *Music in the Air* (sc, 1934); *Lottery Lover* (sc, 1935); *Champagne Waltz* (co-story, 1937); *Bluebeard's Eighth Wife* (sc, 1938); *Midnight* (sc, 1939); *What a Life* (sc, 1939); *Ninotchka* (sc, 1939); *Rhythm on the River* (co-story, 1940); *Arise, My Love* (sc, 1940); *Hold Back the Dawn* (sc, 1941); *Ball of Fire* (story, co-sc, 1941); *The Major and the Minor* (co-sc, d, 1942); *Five Graves to Cairo* (co-sc, 1943); *Double Indemnity* (co-sc, 1944); *The Lost Weekend* (co-sc, 1945); *The Emperor Waltz* (co-sc, d, 1948); *A Foreign Affair* (co-sc, d, 1948); *A Song Is Born* (based on *Ball of Fire*, 1948); *Sunset Boulevard* (co-sc, d, 1950); *Ace in the Hole/ The Big Carnival* (co-sc, d, p, 1951); *Stalag 17* (co-sc, d, p, 1953); *Sabrina* (co-sc, d, p, 1954); *The Seven Year Itch* (co-sc, d, p, 1955); *The Spirit of St. Louis* (co-sc, d, 1957); *Love in the Afternoon* (co-sc, d, p, 1957); *Witness for the Prosecution* (co-sc, d, 1958); *Some Like It Hot* (co-sc, d, p, 1959); *The Apartment* (co-sc, d, p, 1960); *One, Two, Three* (co-sc, d, p, 1961); *Irma la Douce* (co-sc, d, p, 1963); *Kiss Me, Stupid* (co-sc, d, p, 1964); *The Fortune Cookie* (co-sc, d, p, 1966); *The Private Life of Sherlock Holmes* (co-sc, d, p, 1970); *Avanti!* (co-sc, d, p, 1970); *The Front Page* (co-sc, d, 1974); *Fedora* (Germany/France, co-sc, d, p, 1978); *Portrait of a 60% Perfect Man* (a, 1980); *Buddy, Buddy* (sc, d, 1981); *The Exiles* (a, 1989).

---

# Wilder, Gene (1935—) 

Blessed with an endearing charm, an innocent face, and excellent comic timing, Gene Wilder has endured as a comedy star since the late 1960s. In addition to acting, Wilder has also ventured into screenwriting, directing, and producing comedies. As an actor, Wilder has displayed a personal style that is very much in the Danny KAYE tradition. Like Kaye, Wilder has specialized in playing nervous, inhibited characters who are forced by circumstance to get involved in outlandish comic activities. He has often been at his best when buoyed by the talents of others. In particular, Wilder has benefitted greatly from working in Mel BROOKS's stock company of players as well as collaborating with Richard PRYOR.

Wilder was born Jerry Silberman in Milwaukee, Wisconsin, to a Russian immigrant father who became a wealthy manufacturer. Wilder's interest in acting was fanned at the University of Iowa, and he pursued his studies after graduation by traveling to England to study at the prestigious Old Vic Theatre School. If he learned nothing else, he learned how to fence while in England, using that skill to earn his living as a fencing instructor when he returned to the United States.

Wilder continued his theater studies at The Actors Studio while gaining experience first on off Broadway and later on Broadway. Still, he was a virtual unknown until he made a splash in his serio-comic movie debut as a nervous undertaker in *Bonnie and Clyde* (1967). It was a small but memorable part that led to his starring role as Leo Bloom opposite Zero MOSTEL's Max Bialystock in Mel Brooks's cult favorite, *The PRODUCERS* (1968). Wilder's persona was established in this film, and he was nominated for a best actor Academy Award for his performance. Despite the fact that *The Producers* was not an immediate box office hit, it successfully launched Wilder's career.

Wilder went on to display his comic charm in films such as *Quackser Fortune Has a Cousin in the Bronx* (1970) and *Willy Wonka and the Chocolate Factory* (1971). His humor took a more bizarre turn under the direction of Woody ALLEN in the hilarious "Daisy" segment of *Everything You Always Wanted to Know About Sex (But Were Afraid to Ask)*

(1972) when he played a psychiatrist who fell in love with a sheep.

Mel Brooks finally turned Wilder into a major star in the back-to-back hits *Blazing Saddles* (1974) and *Young Frankenstein* (1974). Wilder also received credit for co-writing the screenplay of the latter film, gaining a best screenplay Oscar nomination and further enhancing his image as a creative performer.

Emboldened by the experience of having been directed by two comic actors, Wilder took the plunge and wrote, directed, and starred in his own film, *The Adventure of Sherlock Holmes' Smarter Brother* (1975). He went on to write, direct, produce, and star in *The World's Greatest Lover* (1977) as well as write, direct, and star in his segment of the anthology film *Sunday Lovers* (1981). He also directed *The Woman in Red* (1984) and *Haunted Honeymoon* (1986), both of which co-starred his wife, comedian Gilda RADNER.

While his directorial efforts have met with mixed results both with the critics and with film fans, he remained a hot property thanks to his sterling performances in collaboration with comedian Richard Pryor in the hit films *Silver Streak* (1976) and *Stir Crazy* (1980). He was also well received playing a Polish rabbi in the offbeat comedy Western *The Frisco Kid* (1979), but flopped in *Hanky Panky* (1982).

During the latter half of the 1980s Wilder dropped out of filmmaking to care for Radner, who had developed ovarian cancer. After her tragic death in 1989, he eventually returned to active filmmaking, teaming up again with Richard Pryor for two films that were not on a par with their previous work.

FILMS INCLUDE: *Bonnie and Clyde* (1967); *The Producers* (1967); *Quackser Fortune Has a Cousin in the Bronx* (1970); *Start the Revolution without Me* (1970); *Willy Wonka and the Chocolate Factory* (1971); *Everything You Always Wanted To Know About Sex (But Were Afraid to Ask)* (1972); *Rhinoceros* (1972); *Blazing Saddles* (1974); *The Little Prince* (1974); *Young Frankenstein* (also sc, 1974); *The Adventures of Sherlock Holmes' Smarter Brother* (also sc, d, 1975); *Silver Streak* (1976); *The World's Greatest Lover* (also sc, p, d, song, 1977); *The Frisco Kid* (1979); *Stir Crazy* (also song, 1980); *Sunday Lovers* (U.S. segment, also sc, d, 1980); *Hanky Panky* (1982); *The Woman in Red* (also sc, d, 1984); *Haunted Honeymoon* (also sc, p, d, 1986); *Hello Actors Studio* (1987); *See No Evil, Hear No Evil* (also sc, 1989); *Funny About Love* (1990); *Another You* (1991).

## Williams, Robin (1952—)

A uniquely gifted comic actor, Robin Williams came out of stand-up comedy and TV fame to become one of the hottest movie stars of the last decade. He has been nominated for a best actor Oscar a stunning three times for *Good Morning, Vietnam* (1987), *Dead Poets Society* (1989), and *The Fisher King* (1991). In his best roles, Williams's natural comic talents blend with the characters he plays, melding into a credible whole. However, it isn't easy finding roles that allow for characters to launch into mercurial, nonstop, and inspired comic riffs (with quicksilver changes of mood, voice, and style). When he gets such roles, though, he gives performances that cannot be duplicated by any other actor.

Born in Chicago, Illinois, Williams was the son of an automobile executive. He grew up in California, getting his higher education at Claremont Men's College where he studied political science. It was the art of performance that intrigued him, however, so he went on to study acting at the College of Marin in Kentfield, California. Becoming more serious about a career in show business, he finally left the West Coast for New York to study drama for three years at Juilliard.

Clearly, Williams wanted to be an actor, but his obvious skills lent themselves to stand-up comedy. He moved back to California and conquered the club scene, first in San Francisco and then in Los Angeles. He was already a hot comic in 1976 when he was cast in the aborted revival of TV's "Rowan and Martin's Laugh-In." Williams would have been a natural for the show had it taken off. Instead, he went back to such venues as the Comedy Store, packing them in, until he made a guest appearance in an episode of the sitcom "Happy Days," playing a goofy alien named Mork, from the planet Ork. He caused such a sensation with his hyperkinetic style of comedy that a new sitcom, "Mork and Mindy" (1978–1982), was built around his personality and talent.

The top-rated TV show made Williams a national figure, and he parlayed that into a career in the movies. The transition, however, was not an easy one. He had appeared in one film, the amusingly titled anthology movie *Can I Do It . . . Til I Need Glasses?* (1979), but the film barely used him, and it bombed. His first important film was *Popeye* (1980), in which he played the live-action version of the cartoon title character. The casting could not have been more brilliant. Williams was a natural for Popeye, just as Shelly Duvall was born to play Olive Oyl. The film, directed by Robert Altman, did not fare well with the critics and was not the hit most expected, although it did make money. Just the same, the movie was not much of a boost to Williams' career.

*The World According to Garp* (1982) took advantage of Williams's background as a student wrestler, but not his comic brilliance. After surviving *Survivors* (1983), he finally found a role that suited him, as the confused Russian who defects to the United States in *Moscow on the Hudson* (1984). The Paul MAZURSKY comedy managed to capture Williams's zaniness while also keeping him in character. Many thought the actor should have been nominated for an Oscar, but perhaps it was enough that he finally had a hit.

With ever greater frequency, Williams came through with other critical and commercial winners, having his strongest surge at the end of the 1980s and in the early 1990s. In addition to the films for which he received Oscar nominations, he was suitably subdued and effective in the drama *Awakenings* (1990); electric in *Cadillac Man* (1990); warm

and comically credible in *Hook* (1991), despite the daunting overproduction of the Spielberg film; and riotously funny as the voice of the Genie in *Aladdin* (1992).

His only recent misstep was the starring role in Barry Levinson's bomb *Toys* (1992), which may ultimately become more famous for Williams's eccentric and totally original advertising trailer. He quickly bounced back with a major hit, performing in drag in *Mrs. Doubtfire* (1993).

---

**FILMS:** *Can I Do It . . . Til I Need Glasses?* (1979); *Popeye* (1980); *The World According to Garp* (1982); *The Survivors* (1983); *Moscow on the Hudson* (1984); *The Best of Times* (1986); *Club Paradise* (1986); *Seize the Day* (1986); *Dear America* (1987); *Good Morning, Vietnam* (1987); *The Adventures of Baron Munchausen* (1988); *Dead Poets Society* (1989); *Cadillac Man* (1990); *Awakenings* (1990); *The Fisher King* (1991); *Hook* (1991); *Shakes the Clown* (1991); *Dead Again* (1991); *Ferngully: The Last Rainforest* (voice only, 1992); *Aladdin* (voice only, 1992); *Toys* (1992); *Mrs. Doubtfire* (1993).

---

**Winters, Jonathan (1925– )** There is no doubt that Jonathan Winters is one of the great improvisational comedians of our time, but his particular talent for invention doesn't translate well to film. As an actor, Winters lacks subtlety; his comic impersonations are usually broad and over the top. In the right roles, however, playing characters intended to be bigger than life, he can be devastatingly funny. With a large, round head and dark, darting eyes, he creates an unmistakable presence on screen, one that was put to good use mostly in the 1960s.

Born in Dayton, Ohio, Winters broke into show business on the radio, later showing his talents for improv on television, where he gained his reputation. When he first appeared in motion pictures, it seemed as if Winters might become a star, but the public never fully warmed to him, even if it appreciated his comic genius. Winters appeared in a rash of films in the mid- to late 1960s, such as *The Loved One* (1965), in which many consider he gave his best performance, *The Russians Are Coming! The Russians Are Coming!* (1965), and *Oh Dad, Poor Dad—Mama's Hung You in the Closet and I'm Feeling So Sad* (1967). After the 1960s, he was little seen on the big screen, but he was much on display on television (which, frankly, better suited his style of humor).

---

**FILMS INCLUDE:** *It's a Mad Mad Mad Mad World* (1963); *The Loved One* (1965); *The Russians Are Coming! The Russians Are Coming!* (1966); *Penelope* (1966); *Oh Dad, Poor Dad—Mama's Hung You in the Closet and I'm Feeling So Sad* (1967); *Eight on the Lam* (1967); *Viva, Max!* (1969); *The Fish That Saved Pittsburgh* (1979); *The Longshot* (1985); *Say Yes* (1986); *Moon Over Parador* (1988).

---

**Woolsey, Robert**   *See* WHEELER AND WOOLSEY

**Wynn, Ed (1886—1966)**   Known as "The Perfect Fool" because he was such an exemplary clown, Ed Wynn had a long, varied, and extremely successful career in show business, making only a surprisingly modest impact in the movies, and then only at the end of his life. With his trademark lisp, grandfatherly laugh, and bemused expressions, he was the ultimate avuncular comic presence in his later years on film. He might have had an entirely different movie career had he not turned down the role of the Wizard in *The Wizard of Oz* (1939).

Born Isaiah Edwin Leopold in Philadelphia, Pennsylvania, he took his middle name and broke it in half to create his stage name. He put that name to use early and often. The son of a family in the hat-making business, he ran away from home when he was fifteen to become an actor. This first attempt at

a show business career flopped when the theater company he ran off with went belly up in Maine. He returned home for a short while before taking off again, this time heading directly for New York. Virtually overnight, Wynn became a VAUDEVILLE comedy sensation.

Wynn had a string of topflight careers. He was a Broadway star in the Ziegfeld Follies during the 1910s until he was banned on Broadway (by producers) after leading a successful actors' strike in 1919. He then wrote, produced, and starred in his own hit shows in the 1920s. He became a famous radio personality (the Texaco Fire Chief) in the 1930s and then went on to win TV's first best actor Emmy Award in the late 1940s. Wynn proved himself a powerful dramatic actor in the late 1950s with a best supporting actor Oscar nomination for *The Diary of Anne Frank* (1959) and had a late-blooming career as an endearing comic supporting actor, mostly in Disney films such as *Mary Poppins* (1964), until his death in 1966.

Ed Wynn's son, Keenan Wynn (1916–1986), was the one who got his father into the movies in the late 1950s. Keenan was an all-purpose actor who played character parts. Among his comedies were *Ziegfeld Follies* (1946), *The Absent-Minded Professor* (with his father, 1961), DR. STRANGELOVE (1964), and *Herbie Rides Again* (1974). He wrote an autobiography entitled *Ed Wynn's Son* in 1960.

---

**FILMS:** *Rubber Heels* (1927); *Follow the Leader* (1930); *The Chief* (1933); *Stage Door Canteen* (1943); *The Great Man* (1957); *Marjorie Morningstar* (1958); *The Diary of Anne Frank* (1959); *Cinderfella* (1960); *The Absent-Minded Professor* (1961); *Babes in Toyland* (1961); *Son of Flubber* (1963); *The Patsy* (cameo, 1964); *Those Calloways* (1964); *Mary Poppins* (1964); *That Darn Cat* (1965); *Dear Brigitte* (1965); *The Greatest Story Ever Told* (1965); *The Gnome-Mobile* (1967).

---

# Y–Z

**Yosemite Sam**   *See* WARNER BROS. CARTOONS

**Yule, Joe**   *See* SERIES COMEDIES

**Zemeckis, Robert (1952—)**   Among the most successful of the young director/screenwriters in Hollywood, Robert Zemeckis had an unbroken directorial string of six hit comedies that began in 1984 with *Romancing the Stone*. His success has come from a combination of quirky inventiveness in his scripts, excellent casting, and fast-paced, adventurous direction.

Born in Chicago, Illinois, Zemeckis studied film at the University of Southern California. There he met his future long-time collaborator, Bob Gale, with whom he has regularly co-written his films (Gale has also doubled as a producer of many of Zemeckis's later movies).

Zemeckis's first feature was the nostalgic *I Wanna Hold Your Hand* (1978), a little character comedy about a bunch of kids in 1964 trying to get tickets to see the Beatles live on "The Ed Sullivan Show." The most telling aspect of this film, however, was the executive producer's credit: It belonged to Steven Spielberg, who had taken a liking to Zemeckis and had become his mentor.

Spielberg's 1979 bomb *1941* was based on a story and screenplay both co-written by Zemeckis. Then Zemeckis co-wrote and directed *Used Cars* (1980), yet another disappointment. It appeared as if Spielberg had misplaced his faith. With his next film,

Robert Zemeckis has directed nothing but hit comedies since making Romancing the Stone *(1984)*. He is perhaps best known for having directed all three Back to the Future *movies. He is seen here on the set of one of his more recent comedy hits,* Death Becomes Her *(1992)*.

*Romancing the Stone*, Zemeckis finally hit his stride. This ROMANTIC COMEDY, starring Michael Douglas and Kathleen Turner, turned out to be a box office winner.

Zemeckis had another hit with the release of

**293**

his next movie, *Back to the Future* (1985). This unheralded, modest comedy starring Michael J. Fox, a TV actor who until then had not shown any movie star power, took off like the souped-up car in the film, zooming to staggering box office heights. *Back to the Future* turned Fox into a movie star, garnered Zemeckis and Gale an Academy Award nomination for best screenplay, and spawned two commercially successful sequels in 1989 and 1990.

After the success of the first *Back to the Future* movie, Zemeckis and Spielberg teamed up again, this time on the brightly original and thoroughly entertaining *Who Framed Roger Rabbit?* (1988). A technological marvel that seamlessly combined live action and animation, the movie was also funny, sexy, and a gargantuan hit, both critically and commercially. Its success helped pave the way for the great ANIMATION revival of the late 1980s and 1990s.

His most recent directorial triumph was *Death Becomes Her* (1992), a BLACK COMEDY that depended heavily upon technology for its desired effects. The movie was more successful commercially than critically.

FILMS: *I Wanna Hold Your Hand* (co-sc, d, 1978); *1941* (co-story, co-sc, 1979); *Used Cars* (co-sc, d, 1980); *Romancing the Stone* (d, 1984); *Back to the Future* (co-sc, d, 1985); *Who Framed Roger Rabbit?* (d, 1988); *Back to the Future II* (co-story, based on characters, d, 1989); *Back to the Future III* (co-story, based on characters, d, 1990); *Trespass* (co-sc, p, 1992); *Death Becomes Her* (co-sc, d, 1992); *The Public Eye* (p, 1992).

## Zieff, Howard (1943—)

A light comedy director, Howard Zieff specializes in finding humor in character rather than in jokes. Rooted in reality, his heroes and heroines make us laugh because they react with comic plausibility to the sometimes unusual events that go bump in the movies. Zieff has been directing films since 1973, but not with any great frequency; he has made only eight movies in his first two decades of filmmaking. Nonetheless, he has directed several excellent comedies, including Goldie HAWN's biggest hit, *Private Benjamin* (1980).

Born in Chicago, Illinois, Zieff studied photography at the Los Angeles Art Center before becoming a hot director of TV commercials. In the days before music videos, snappy commercials could open doors to film directing, and Zieff made the move to the movies with a highly regarded little comedy called *Slither* (1973). His second film was a real charmer, *Hearts of the West* (1975), a period piece set in the early days of moviemaking. In a film that recalled COMEDY COUPLES such as Spencer Tracy and Katharine Hepburn, Zieff directed a delightful ROMANTIC COMEDY called *House Calls* (1978) that starred Walter MATTHAU and Glenda Jackson. The movie was so successful the two stars were paired again (but without Zieff) in a less succesful comic battle of the sexes.

Zieff's greatest achievement to date was *Private Benjamin*. The film was critically praised and commercially successful far beyond anyone's wildest dreams. It earned more than $100 million at the box office and turned Goldie Hawn into a superstar. Since then, however, Zieff's career has been surprisingly quiet. He remade the Preston STURGES comedy *Unfaithfully Yours* (1983), coming up second best in the comparison, and then disappeared from directing for six years before returning with the uneven Michael KEATON comedy *The Dream Team* (1989). Finally, however, he came through with the touching seriocomic *My Girl* (1991), probably best remembered as the movie in which the character played by Macauley Culkin dies. Directed with restraint and peopled with quirky, yet compelling, characters, the movie harkened back to the kind of film that Zieff does best, such as *Hearts of the West*.

**FILMS:** *Slither* (1973); *Hearts of the West* (1975); *House Calls* (1978); *The Main Event* (1979); *Private Benjamin* (1980); *Unfaithfully Yours* (1983); *The Dream Team* (1989); *My Girl* (1991); *My Girl 2* (1994).

**Zucker, David (1947– )** A director, producer, screenwriter, and very occasional actor, David Zucker, younger brother Jerry ZUCKER, and friend Jim ABRAHAMS, picked up where Mel BROOKS left off as a parodist of motion picture genres. A filmmaker since 1977, Zucker has helped (with his collaborators) to extend the boundaries of PARODY FILMS by directing his actors to play everything totally straight, no matter how silly or outrageous the dialogue and action. Zucker and company have, as a consequence, raised the art of deadpan humor to its comical zenith.

Born in Milwaukee, Wisconsin, David Zucker studied film at the University of Wisconsin at Madison, where he and his brother befriended soulmate Jim Abrahams. They formed a storefront theatrical company called the Kentucky Fried Theater. Later, they moved their theater to Los Angeles where, in 1977, the threesome wrote and appeared in their first film, *The Kentucky Fried Movie*. Directed by John LANDIS, and comprised of satirical skits and blackouts, the film became the most profitable independent feature of its day.

The success of *The Kentucky Fried Movie* opened the door for them to make a bigger-budget spoof. Their next film became what many consider their funniest, *Airplane!* (1980), a parody of every imaginable aviation movie cliché. It was a huge hit, and it propelled the threesome, who had written, produced, and directed it, to do the same with their next film, *Top Secret!* (1984), a spoof of spy movies. They changed direction to make a more conventional film; the result was the BLACK COMEDY *Ruthless People* (1986), a movie they did not write, but did direct.

Earlier in the 1980s, the two Zuckers and Abrahams had created a short-lived TV series, a wacky comedy called "Police Squad!" (1981) that came and went rather quickly. Despite its abbreviated broadcast life, the series had a devout following. Sensing that they could turn the series into a full-blown movie parody, the three collaborators wrote and produced *The Naked Gun: From the Files of Police Squad!* (1988). The only difference between this and all of their previous projects was that David Zucker directed it alone. It was the start of a slow dissolution of their unique partnership.

The first Naked Gun movie proved such a monstrous hit that David Zucker returned to the scene of the crime for a popular sequel, *The Naked Gun 2½: The Smell of Fear* (1991). He wrote and directed this one without his two partners, who participated only so far as to co-produce. In the meantime, brother Jerry was surprising everyone with his hit mainstream ROMANTIC COMEDY thriller *Ghost* (1990).

As for David Zucker, he lent his prestige as a producer to a failed attempt at a MARX BROTHERS-like comedy called *Brain Donors* (1992).

**FILMS:** *The Kentucky Fried Movie* (a, co-sc, 1977); *Airplane!* (a, co-sc, co-p, co-d, 1980); *Top Secret!* (co-sc, co-p, co-d, 1984); *Ruthless People* (co-d, 1986); *The Naked Gun: From the Files of Police Squad!* (co-sc, co-p, d, 1988); *The Naked Gun 2½: The Smell of Fear* (co-sc, co-p, d, 1991); *Brain Donors* (co-p, 1992); *Naked Gun 33⅓: The Final Insult* (co-sc, p, 1994).

**Zucker, Jerry (1950– )** Like his older brother David ZUCKER and long-time friend Jim ABRAHAMS, Jerry Zucker is a director, producer, screenwriter, and (occasionally) actor. A filmmaker since 1977, he has worked within a framework unique to the motion picture business: a three-way collaboration that has included equal credits for writing, producing, and directing the funniest PARODY FILMS of the 1980s. Recently, with his solo direction of the hit ROMANTIC COMEDY thriller

*Ghost* (1990), Jerry has established himself as a mainstream filmmaker. It was his first work fully independent of David Zucker and Jim Abrahams, fortelling a potentially brilliant future for the youngest of the original threesome.

Jerry was born in Milwaukee, Wisconsin, and attended the University of Wisconsin at Madison, where he studied film.

**FILMS:** *The Kentucky Fried Movie* (a, co-sc, 1977); *Airplane!* (a, co-sc, co-p, co-d, 1980); *Top Secret!* (co-sc, co-p, co-d, 1984); *Ruthless People* (co-d, 1986); *The Naked Gun: From the Files of Police Squad!* (co-sc, co-p, 1988); *Ghost* (d, 1990); *The Naked Gun 2½: The Smell of Fear* (co-p, 1991); *Naked Gun 33⅓: The Final Insult* (p, 1994).

# Comedy Oscar Winners

The common wisdom is that, if you want to win an Academy Award, don't make a comedy; the Oscar voters shy away from the funny stuff. The following list of comedy Oscar Winners proves that adage all too true—up to a point. There are relatively few comedy winners in the top four award categories (best picture, best actor, best actress, and best director), but the situation loosens up for comic supporting players and screenwriters.

Please note that the definition of *comedy* is rather elastic. Certainly Whoopi Goldberg's performance in *Ghost* was a comedic one even if the film was not a comedy per se; we included her in our list. Conversely, we included the Oscar-winning performances of Peter Finch and Faye Dunaway from *Network* even though their performances—especially Finch's—were so stark because the film, itself, is a comedy of volcanic proportion.

Also note that we included only the top categories in this list of Oscar winners. We have limited ourselves to the acting, directing, writing, and best picture awards, along with noting the special Oscars that went to comic performers, because in most cases those were the only Oscars the performers ever received.

| 1927–1928 | Comedy direction (the only year this award was given): Lewis Milestone for *Two Arabian Knights*. |
| | Special Oscar: Charlie Chaplin for *The Circus*. |
| 1928–1929 | No comedies received awards. |
| 1929–1930 | No comedies received awards. |
| 1930–1931 | Best actress: Marie Dressler in *Min and Bill*. |
| | Best director: Norman Taurog for *Skippy*. |
| 1931–1932 | Special Oscar: Walt Disney for creating Mickey Mouse. |
| 1932–1933 | No comedies received awards. |
| 1934 | Best picture: *It Happened One Night*. |
| | Best actor: Clark Gable in *It Happened One Night*. |
| | Best actress: Claudette Colbert in *It Happened One Night*. |
| | Best director: Frank Capra for *It Happened One Night*. |
| | Best screenplay (adapt): Robert Riskin for *It Happened One Night*. |
| 1935 | No comedies received awards. |
| 1936 | Best director: Frank Capra for *Mr. Deeds Goes to Town*. |
| 1937 | Best director: Leo McCarey for *The Awful Truth*. |
| | Special Oscar: Mack Sennett for his contribution to film comedy. |
| | Special Oscar: Edgar Bergen for creating Charlie McCarthy. |
| 1938 | Best picture: *You Can't Take it with You*. |
| | Best director: Frank Capra for *You Can't Take it with You*. |
| | Best screenplay (adapt): Ian Dalrymple, Cecil Lewis, and W. P. Lipscomb for *Pygmalion*. |
| | Special Oscars: Deanna Durbin and Mickey Rooney. |

1939    Best writing (original story): Lewis R. Foster for *Mr. Smith Goes to Washington*.

1940    Best actor: James Stewart in *The Philadelphia Story*.

Best screenplay (original): Preston Sturges for *The Great McGinty*.

Best screenplay (adapt): Donald Ogden Stewart for *The Philadelphia Story*.

1941    Best writing (original story): Harry Segall for *Here Comes Mr. Jordan*.

1942    Best screenplay (original): Michael Kanin and Ring Lardner, Jr., for *Woman of the Year*.

1943    Best supporting actor: Charles Coburn in *The More the Merrier*.

Best screenplay (original): Norman Krasna for *Princess O'Rourke*.

1944    Special Oscar: Bob Hope, for his service to the Academy.

1945    No comedies received awards.

1946    Special Oscar: Ernst Lubitsch for his distinguished contributions to the art of the motion picture.

1947    Best screenplay (original): Sidney Sheldon for *The Bachelor and the Bobby-Soxer*.

1948    No comedies received awards.

1949    No comedies received awards.

1950    Best picture: *All About Eve*.

Best actress: Judy Holliday in *Born Yesterday*.

Best supporting actor: George Sanders in *All About Eve*.

Best supporting actress: Josephine Hull in *Harvey*.

Best director: Joseph L. Mankiewicz for *All About Eve*.

Best screenplay (adapt): Joseph L. Mankiewicz for *All About Eve*.

1951    No comedies received awards.

1952    Best screenplay (original): T. E. B. Clarke for *The Lavender Hill Mob*.

Special Oscar: Harold Lloyd, the master comedian.

Special Oscar: Bob Hope, for his contribution to the laughter of the world.

1953    Special Oscar: Pete Smith for his "Pete Smith Specialties" series.

1954    Special Oscar: Danny Kaye, for his unique talents.

1955    Best supporting actor: Jack Lemmon for *Mr. Roberts*.

1956    Special Oscar: Eddie Cantor, for distinguished service to the film industry.

1957    Best screenplay (original): George Wells for *Designing Woman*.

1958    Special Oscar: Maurice Chevalier, for his contributions to the world of entertainment.

1959    Best screenplay (original): Russell Rouse, Clarence Greene, Stanley Shapiro, and Maurice Richlin for *Pillow Talk*.

Special Oscar: Buster Keaton, for his unique talents.

1960    Best picture: *The Apartment*.

Best director: Billy Wilder for *The Apartment*.

Best screenplay (original): I. A. L. Diamond and Billy Wilder for *The Apartment*.

Special Oscar: Stan Laurel, for his creative pioneering in the field of cinema comedy.

1961    No comedies received awards.

1962    Best screenplay (original): Ennio de Concini, Alfredo Giannetti, and Pietro Germi for *Divorce, Italian Style*.

1963    Best picture: *Tom Jones*.

Best director: Tony Richardson for *Tom Jones*.

Best screenplay (adapt): John Osborne for *Tom Jones*.

1964    Best actress: Julie Andrews in *Mary Poppins*.

Best supporting actor: Peter Ustinov in *Topkapi*.

Best screenplay (original): S. H. Barnett, Peter Stone, and Frank Tarloff for *Father Goose*.

1965    Best actor: Lee Marvin for *Cat Ballou*.

Best supporting actor: Martin Balsam in *A Thousand Clowns*.

Special Oscar: Bob Hope, for unique and distinguished service to the industry.

1966    Best supporting actor: Walter Matthau in *The Fortune Cookie*.

1967    Best director: Mike Nichols for *The Graduate*.

1968    Best screenplay (original): Mel Brooks for *The Producers*.

1969    Best supporting actress: Goldie Hawn in *Cactus Flower*.

Best screenplay (original): William Goldman for *Butch Cassidy and the Sundance Kid*.

Special Oscar: Cary Grant, for his unique mastery of the art of screen acting.

1970    Best screenplay (adapt): Ring Lardner, Jr., for *M\*A\*S\*H*.

1971    Best screenplay (original): Paddy Chayefsky for *The Hospital*.

Special Oscar: Charlie Chaplin, for the incalculable effect he had in making motion pictures the art form of this century.

1972    Best supporting actress: Eileen Heckart in *Butterflies Are Free*.

1973    Best picture: *The Sting*.

Best actress: Glenda Jackson in *A Touch of Class*.

Best supporting actress: Tatum O'Neal in *Paper Moon*.

Best director: George Roy Hill for *The Sting*.

Best screenplay: David S. Ward for *The Sting*.

Special Oscar: Groucho Marx, in recognition of his brilliant creativity and for the unequalled achievements of The Marx Brothers.

1974    Best actor: Art Carney in *Harry and Tonto*.

Special Oscar: Howard Hawks, a master American filmmaker.

1975    Best supporting actor: George Burns in *The Sunshine Boys*.

Best supporting actress: Lee Grant in *Shampoo*.

1976    Best actor: Peter Finch in *Network*.

Best actress: Faye Dunaway in *Network*.

Best supporting actress: Beatrice Straight in *Network*.

Best screenplay (original): Paddy Chayefsky for *Network*.

1977    Best picture: *Annie Hall*.

Best actor: Richard Dreyfuss in *The Goodbye Girl*.

Best actress: Diane Keaton in *Annie Hall*.

Best director: Woody Allen for *Annie Hall*.

Best screenplay (original): Woody Allen and Marshall Brickman for *Annie Hall*.

1978    Best supporting actress: Maggie Smith in *California Suite*.

Special Oscar: Walter Lantz, for bringing joy and laughter to every part of the world through his unique animated motion pictures.

1979    Best supporting actor: Melvyn Douglas in *Being There*.

1980    No comedies received awards.

1981    Best supporting actor: John Gielgud in *Arthur*.

1982    Best supporting actress: Jessica Lange in *Tootsie*.

Special Oscar: Mickey Rooney, for fifty years of versatility in a variety of memorable film performances.

1983 Special Oscar: Hal Roach, in recognition of his unparalleled record of distinguished contributions to the motion picture art form.

1984 No comedies received awards.

1985 Best supporting actress: Anjelica Huston in *Prizzi's Honor*.

1986 Best supporting actor: Michael Caine in *Hannah and Her Sisters*.
Best supporting actress: Diane Wiest in *Hannah and Her Sisters*.
Best screenplay (original): Woody Allen for *Hannah and Her Sisters*.

1987 Best actress: Cher in *Moonstruck*.
Best supporting actress: Olympia Dukakis in *Moonstruck*.
Best screenplay (original): John Patrick Shanley for *Moonstruck*.

1988 Best supporting actor: Kevin Kline in *A Fish Called Wanda*.

1989 No comedies received awards.

1990 Best supporting actress: Whoopi Goldberg in *Ghost*.

1991 Best supporting actor: Jack Palance in *City Slickers*.

1992 Best supporting actress: Marisa Tomei in *My Cousin Vinny*.

# Best Comedy of the Year, 1927—1993

As you can see from the previous list of comedy Oscar winners, comedies have often gotten short shrift from the Academy of Motion Picture Arts and Sciences. We'd like to make up for that by choosing the movies *we* believe are the best comedy pictures of the year, for every year since 1927.

The envelope, please . . .

1927: *Long Pants*
1928: *The Cameraman*
1929: *The Love Parade*
1930: *Animal Crackers*
1931: *City Lights*
1932: *Trouble in Paradise*
1933: *Duck Soup*
1934: *Twentieth Century*
1935: *A Night at the Opera*
1936: *Modern Times*
1937: *The Awful Truth*
1938: *Holiday*
1939: *Ninotchka*
1940: *The Great Dictator*
1941: *Ball of Fire*
1942: *To Be or Not to Be*
1943: *The More the Merrier*

1944: *Hail the Conquering Hero*
1945: *Anchors Aweigh*
1946: *It's a Wonderful Life*
1947: *Monsieur Verdoux*
1948: *Abbott and Costello Meet Frankenstein*
1949: *I Was a Male War Bride*
1950: *All About Eve*
1951: *People Will Talk*
1952: *Limelight*
1953: *The Band Wagon*
1954: *Beat the Devil*
1955: *Artists and Models*
1956: *The Court Jester*

1957: *Will Success Spoil Rock Hunter?*
1958: *This Happy Feeling*
1959: *Some Like It Hot*
1960: *The Apartment*
1961: *The Ladies' Man*
1962: *Lolita*
1963: *The Nutty Professor*
1964: *Dr. Strangelove*
1965: *A Thousand Clowns*
1966: *The Fortune Cookie*
1967: *The Graduate*
1968: *The Producers*
1969: *Take the Money and Run*
1970: *Putney Swope*
1971: A tie—*Bananas* and *The Projectionist*
1972: *Play It Again, Sam*

1973: *Sleeper*
1974: *Blazing Saddles*
1975: *Love and Death*
1976: *Network*
1977: *Annie Hall*
1978: *An Unmarried Woman*
1979: *Being There*
1980: *Simon*
1981: *S.O.B.*
1982: *Tootsie*
1983: *King of Comedy*
1984: *All of Me*
1985: *The Purple Rose of Cairo*
1986: *Three Amigos!*
1987: *Broadcast News*
1988: *Working Girl*
1989: *When Harry Met Sally*
1990: *The Freshman*
1991: *Naked Gun 2½: The Smell of Fear*
1992: *Husbands and Wives*
1993: *Groundhog Day*

# Selected Bibliography

We are deeply indebted to the authors listed below whose work we drew upon in the creation of our volume. Note that many of the books we used in our research have been published both in hardcover and in paperback, often on both sides of the Atlantic, and in any number of printings. The publishers and dates of publication listed below are for the books we actually used. In other words, if we drew upon the 1993 paperback version of a title rather than the 1992 hardcover version, we list the former rather than the latter. In addition to books, we also found valuable information in magazines and newspapers too numerous to mention. We thank all of the writers, reporters, and interviewers whose work has influenced ours.

Adamson, Joe. *Groucho, Harpo, Chico, and Sometimes, Zeppo*. New York: Simon and Schuster, 1973.

Alpert, Hollis, and Andrew Sarris, eds. *Film 68–69*. New York: Simon and Schuster, 1969.

Anderson, Janice. *History of Movie Comedy*. New York: Exeter Books, 1985.

Astor, Mary. *A Life on Film*. New York: Delacorte Press, 1967.

Aylesworth, Thomas G. *Broadway to Hollywood*. New York: Gallery Books, 1975.

Bailey, Adrian. *Walt Disney's World of Fantasy*. New York: Everest House, 1982.

Baker, Fred, and Ross Firestone, eds. *Movie People*. New York: Douglas Book Corporation, 1972.

Barry Iris. *D. W. Griffith*. New York: The Museum of Modern Art, 1965.

Baxter, John. *Hollywood in the Thirties*. New York: Paperback Library, 1970.

———. *Hollywood in the Sixties*. San Diego: A. S. Barnes & Co., 1972.

Bazin, Andre. *What Is Cinema?* Berkeley: University of California Press, 1967.

———. *What Is Cinema? Volume II*. Berkeley: University of California Press, 1971.

Bego, Mark. *Rock Hudson*. New York: Signet, 1986.

Behlmer, Rudy, ed. *Inside Warner Bros. (1935–1951)*. New York: Simon and Schuster, 1987.

Behlmer, Rudy, and Tony Thomas. *Hollywood's Hollywood*. Secaucus, NJ: The Citadel Press, 1975.

Bellone, Julius, ed. *Renaissance of the Film*. New York: The Macmillan Co., 1970.

Bergan, Ronald. *The United Artists Story*. New York: Crown Publishers, 1986.

Bernard, Jami. *First Films*. New York: Citadel Press, 1993.

Best, Marc. *Those Endearing Young Charms*. San Diego: A. S. Barnes & Co., 1971.

Black, Jonathan. *Streisand*. New York: Leisure Books, 1975.

Blesh, Rudi. *Keaton*. New York: The Macmillan Company, 1966.

Bogdanovich, Peter. *Pieces of Time*. New York: Arbor House, 1973.

Bogle, Donald. *Blacks in American Films and Television*. New York: Garland Publishing, 1988.

Bookbinder, Robert. *The Films of Bing Crosby*. Secaucus, NJ: The Citadel Press, 1977.

———. *The Films of the Seventies*. Secaucus, NJ: The Citadel Press, 1982.

Brode, Douglas. *The Films of the Sixties*. Secaucus, NJ: The Citadel Press, 1980.

Brownlow, Kevin. *The Parade's Gone By*. New York: Alfred A. Knopf, 1968.

Burns, George. *Living It Up*. New York: Berkley Publishing, 1979.

Cagney, James. *Cagney by Cagney*. New York: Pocket Books, 1977.

Capra, Frank. *Frank Capra: The Name Above the Title*. New York: The Macmillan Company, 1971.

Carey, Gary. *Katharine Hepburn, A Hollywood Yankee*. New York: St. Martin's Press, 1983.

Ceplair, Larry, and Steven Englund. *The Inquisition in Hollywood*. New York: Anchor Press/Doubleday, 1980.

Chaplin, Charles. *My Autobiography*. New York: Pocket Books, 1966.

Clark, Randall, ed. *Dictionary of Literary Biography, Volume 44: American Screenwriters, Second Series*. Detroit: Gale Research Co., 1986.

Cohen, Daniel. *Musicals*. New York: Gallery Books, 1984.

Cohen, Daniel, and Susan Cohen. *Encyclopedia of Movie Stars*. New York: Gallery Books, 1985.

Considine, Shaun. *Barbra Streisand*. New York: Delacorte Press, 1985.

Cooke, Alistair. *Douglas Fairbanks*. New York: Museum of Modern Art, 1940.

Coursodon, Jean-Pierre, and Pierre Sauvage. *American Directors: Volume I*. New York: McGraw-Hill, 1983.

Coursodon, Jean-Pierre. *American Directors: Volume II*. New York: McGraw-Hill, 1983.

Cross, Robin. *The Big Book of B Movies*. New York: St. Martin's Press, 1981.

Denby, David, ed. *Film 70–71*. New York: Simon and Schuster, 1971.

———. *Film 71–72*. New York: Simon and Schuster, 1972.

Deschner, Donald. *The Complete Films of Spencer Tracy*. Secaucus, NJ: The Citadel Press, 1968.

Dick, Bernard F. *Billy Wilder*. Boston: Twayne Publishers, 1980.

Dickos, Andrew. *Intrepid Laughter: Preston Sturges and the Movies*. Metuchen, NJ: The Scarecrow Press, 1985.

Eames, John Douglas. *The MGM Story*. New York: Crown Publishers, 1976.

———. *The Paramount Story*. New York: Crown, 1985.

Edelson, Edward. *Great Kids of the Movies*. New York: Doubleday & Co., 1979.

———. *Great Animals of the Movies*. New York: Doubleday & Co., 1980.

Edmonds, I. G., and Reiko Mimura. *Paramount Pictures*. San Diego: A. S. Barnes & Co., 1980.

Edwards, Anne. *Judy Garland*. New York: Pocket Books, 1975.

Estrin, Allen. *The Hollywood Professionals, Volume 6: Capra, Cukor, Brown*. San Diego: A. S. Barnes & Co., 1980.

Everson, William K. *The Bad Guys*. Secaucus, NJ: The Citadel Press, 1964.

———. *The Pictorial History of the Western Film*. Secaucus, NJ: The Citadel Press, 1971.

———. *The Detective in Film*. Secaucus, NJ: The Citadel Press, 1972.

———. *Classics of the Horror Film*. Secaucus, NJ: The Citadel Press, 1974.

———. *American Silent Film*. New York: Oxford University Press, 1978.

Feuer, Jane. *The Hollywood Musical*. Bloomington, IN: Indiana University Press, 1982.

Fields, Ronald J. *W. C. Fields: A Life on Film*. New York: St. Martin's Press, 1984.

Franklin, Joe. *Classics of the Silent Screen*. Secaucus, NJ: The Citadel Press, 1959.

Freedland, Michael. *Fred Astaire*. New York: Grosset & Dunlap, 1977.

Friedwald, Will, and Jerry Beck. *The Warner Brothers Cartoons*. Metuchen, NJ: The Scarecrow Press, 1981.

Gehring, Wes D. *Screwball Comedy*. Westport, CT: Greenwood Press, 1986.

Gelb, Alan. *The Doris Day Scrapbook*. New York: Grosset & Dunlap, 1977.

Gelmis, Joseph. *The Film Director as Superstar*. New York: Anchor Press, 1970.

Giannetti, Louis. *Masters of the American Cinema*. Englewood Cliffs, NJ: Prentice-Hall, 1981.

———. *Understanding Movies*. 4th ed. Englewood Cliffs, NJ: Prentice-Hall, 1987.

Gomery, Douglas. *The Hollywood Studio System*. New York: Macmillan Publishers Ltd., 1986.

Goodman, Ezra. *The Fifty Year Decline and Fall of Hollywood*. New York: Simon and Schuster, 1961.

Graham, Sheilah. *Hollywood Revisited*. New York: St. Martin's Press, 1985.

Green, Abel, and Joe Laurie, Jr. *Show Biz: From Vaude to Video*. New York: Henry Holt and Company, 1951.

Griffith, Richard, and Arthur Mayer. *The Movies*. New York: Simon and Schuster, 1970.

Gussow, Mel. *Don't Say Yes Until I Finish Talking*. New York: Pocket Books, 1972.

Hecht, Ben. *A Child of the Century*. New York: Signet, 1955.

Higham, Charles, and Joel Greenberg. *Hollywood in the Forties*. New York: Paperback Library, 1970.

———. *The Celluloid Muse, Hollywood Directors Speak*. New York: Signet, 1972.

Hopper, Hedda, and James Brough. *The Whole Truth and Nothing But.* New York: Doubleday & Co., 1963.

Horton, Andrew. *The Films of George Roy Hill.* New York: Columbia University Press, 1984.

Hutchinson, Tom. *Marilyn Monroe.* New York: Exeter Books, 1983.

Jacobs, Lewis. *The Emergence of Film Art.* New York: Hopkinson and Blake, 1969.

Jewell, Richard B., with Vernon Herbin. *The RKO Story.* New York: Arlington House, 1982.

Kael, Pauline. *I Lost It at the Movies.* New York: Bantam Books, 1966.

———. *Going Steady.* New York: Bantam Books, 1971.

———. *Kiss Kiss, Bang Bang.* New York: Bantam Books, 1971.

Katz, Ephraim. *The Film Encyclopedia.* New York: Perigee, 1982.

Kauffmann, Stanley. *A World on Film.* New York: Delta, 1966.

Keaton, Buster, with Charles Samuels. *My Wonderful World of Slapstick.* New York: Doubleday & Co., 1960.

Knight, Arthur. *The Liveliest Art.* New York: Mentor Books, 1957.

Kobal, John. *People Will Talk.* New York: Alfred A. Knopf, 1985.

Konigsberg, Ira. *The Complete Film Dictionary.* New York: New American Library, 1987.

Kuhns, William. *Movies in America.* Dayton, OH: Pflaum/Standard, 1972.

Lahue, Kalton C. *Mack Sennett's Keystone.* San Diego: A. S. Barnes & Co., 1971.

Lahue, Kalton C., and Terry Brewer. *Kops and Custards.* Norman, OK: University of Oklahoma Press, 1968.

Lambert, Gavin. *On Cukor.* New York: G. P. Putnam's Sons, 1972.

Lax, Eric. *On Being Funny: Woody Allen & Comedy.* New York: Manor Books, 1977.

Lehman, Peter, and William Luhr. *Blake Edwards.* Athens, OH: Ohio University Press, 1981.

Lenburg, Jeff. *Dustin Hoffman.* New York: Zebra Books, 1983.

Lenne, Gerard. *Sex on the Screen.* New York: St. Martin's Press, 1985.

London, Rose. *Cinema of Mystery.* New York: Bounty Books, 1975.

Macgowan, Kenneth. *Behind the Screen.* New York: Delta, 1965.

Madsen, Axel. *Billy Wilder.* Bloomington, IN: University of Indiana Press, 1969.

Maltin, Leonard. *Of Mice and Magic.* New York: McGraw-Hill, 1980.

———. *Movie and Video Guide, 1993.* New York: Plume, 1992.

Martin, Mick, and Marsha Porter. *Video Movie Guide 1993.* New York: Ballantine Books, 1992.

Marx, Arthur. *Everybody Loves Somebody Sometime.* New York: Hawthorn Books, 1974.

———. *Red Skelton.* New York: E. P. Dutton, 1979.

———. *The Nine Lives of Mickey Rooney.* New York: Berkley Publishing, 1988.

Marx, Groucho. *Groucho and Me.* New York: Manor Books, 1973.

Marx, Groucho, and Richard J. Anobile. *The Marx Bros. Scrapbook.* New York: Darien House, 1973.

Marx, Harpo, with Rowland Barber. *Harpo Speaks!* New York: Freeway Press, 1974.

Marx, Samuel. *Mayer and Thalberg: The Make-Believe Saints.* New York: Random House, 1975.

Mast, Gerald. *The Comic Mind.* Indianapolis, IN: The Bobbs-Merrill Company, 1973.

Mast, Gerald, and Marshall Cohen, eds. *Film Theory and Criticism.* New York: Oxford University Press, 1974.

Maynard, Richard A. *The Black Man on Film: Racial Stereotyping.* Hasbrouck Heights, NJ: Hayden Book Company, 1974.

McBride, Joseph, ed. *Focus on Howard Hawks.* Englewood Cliffs, NJ: Prentice-Hall, 1972.

———. *Film Makers on Film Making, Volume One.* Los Angeles: J. P. Tarcher, 1983.

———. *Film Makers on Film Making, Volume Two.* Los Angeles: J. P. Tarcher, 1983.

McDonald, Archie P., ed. *Shooting Stars.* Bloomington, IN: Indiana University Press, 1987.

McGilligan, Patrick. *Robert Altman: Jumping Off the Cliffs.* New York: St. Martin's Press, 1989.

McLaughlin, Robert. *Broadway and Hollywood.* Arno Press, 1974.

Monaco, James. *American Film Now.* New York: Signet, 1979.

Monaco, James, and the editors of Baseline. *The Encyclopedia of Film.* New York: Perigee, 1991.

Mordden, Ethan. *The Hollywood Musical.* New York: St. Martin's Press, 1981.

Morella, Joe, and Edward Z. Epstein. *Paulette*. New York: St. Martin's Press, 1985.

Morgenstern, Joseph, and Stefan Kanfer, eds. *Film 69–70*. New York: Simon and Schuster, 1970.

Naha, Ed. *The Films of Roger Corman*. New York: Arco Publishing, 1982.

Neibaur, James L. *Movie Comedians*. Jefferson, NC: McFarland & Company, 1986.

Norman, Barry. *The Hollywood Greats*. New York: Franklin Watts, 1980.

O'Leary, Liam. *The Silent Cinema*. New York: E. P. Dutton, 1970.

Parish, James Robert, and William T. Leonard. *The Funsters*. New York: Arlington House, 1979.

Pate, Janet. *The Book of Spies and Secret Agents*. New York: Gallery Press, 1978.

Peary, Danny. *Cult Movies*. New York: Delta, 1981.

Peary, Gerald, and Danny Peary, eds. *The American Animated Cartoon*. New York: E. P. Dutton, 1980.

Phillips, Gene D. *The Movie Makers*. Chicago: Nelson-Hall Company, 1973.

Pickard, Roy. *The Oscar Movies From A–Z*. New York: Taplinger Publishing Co., 1977.

———. *Shirley MacLaine*. New York: Hippocrene Books, 1985.

Pitts, Michael R. *Famous Movie Detectives*. Metuchen, NJ: The Scarecrow Press, 1979.

———. *Hollywood and American History*. Jefferson, NC: McFarland & Company, 1984.

Platt, Frank C., ed. *Great Stars of Hollywood's Golden Age*. New York: New American Library, 1966.

Poague, Leland A. *The Hollywood Professionals, Volume 7: Billy Wilder, Leo McCarey*. San Diego: A. S. Barnes & Co., 1980.

Quinlan, David. *Quinlan's Illustrated Directory of Film Comedy Actors*. New York: Henry Holt, 1992.

Quirk, Lawrence J. *The Films of Warren Beatty*. Secaucus, NJ: The Citadel Press, 1979.

———. *The Complete Films of William Powell*. Secaucus, NJ: The Citadel Press, 1986.

Randall, Richard S. *Censorship of the Movies*. Madison, WI: University of Wisconsin Press, 1968.

Reed, Rex. *Travolta to Keaton*. New York: William Morrow and Co., 1979.

Reilly, Adam. *Harold Lloyd*. New York: Macmillan Publishing Co., 1977.

Ricci, Mark, and Michael Conway. *The Complete Films of Marilyn Monroe*. Secaucus, NJ: The Citadel Press, 1964.

Robinson, David. *Buster Keaton*. Bloomington, IN: Indiana University Press, 1969.

Rothel, David. *The Singing Cowboys*. San Diego: A. S. Barnes & Co., 1978.

Rubenstein, Leonard. *The Great Spy Films*. Secaucus, NJ: The Citadel Press, 1979.

Sarris, Andrew. *The American Cinema*. New York: E. P. Dutton, 1968.

Schatz, Thomas. *Hollywood Genres: Formulas, Filmmaking, and the Studio System*. Philadelphia: Temple University Press, 1981.

Schelly, William. *Harry Langdon*. Metuchen, NJ: The Scarecrow Press, 1982.

Scheuer, Steven H. *Movies on TV and Videocassette, 1993–1994*. New York: Bantam Books, 1992.

Schickel, Richard. *The Disney Version*. New York: Simon and Schuster, 1968.

Schuth, H. Wayne. *Mike Nichols*. Boston: Twayne Publishers, 1978.

Searles, Baird. *Films of Science Fiction and Fantasy*. New York: Harry N. Abrams, 1988.

Sellers, Michael, with Sara and Victoria Sellers. *P.S. I Love You: An Intimate Portrait of Peter Sellers*. New York: Berkley Publishing, 1983.

Sennett, Ted. *Great Movie Directors*. New York: Harry N. Abrams, 1986.

Sherman, Eric, and Martin Rubin. *The Director's Event*. New York: Signet, 1972.

Shipman, David. *The Great Movie Stars*. New York: Bonanza Books, 1970.

Siegel, Scott, and Barbara Siegel. *The Encyclopedia of Hollywood*. New York: Avon Books, 1991.

Simon, John. *Private Screenings*. New York: Macmillan, 1967.

Skretvedt, Randy. *Laurel and Hardy*. Moonstone Press, 1987.

Smith, Ron. *Comic Support*. New York: Citadel Press, 1993.

Sova, Dawn B. *Eddie Murphy*. New York: Zebra Books, 1985.

Spoto, Donald. *Stanley Kramer: Film Maker*. New York: G. P. Putnam's Sons, 1978.

Thomas, Bob. *King Cohn*. New York: Bantam Books, 1968.

———. *Thalberg: Life and Legend*. New York: Doubleday & Co., 1969.

———. *Selznick*. New York: Pocket Books, 1972.

———. *Astaire*. New York: St. Martin's Press, 1984.

Thomas, Tony. *Howard Hughes in Hollywood*. Secaucus, NJ: The Citadel Press, 1985.

Tozzi, Romano. *Spencer Tracy*. New York: Galahad Books, 1973.

Tyler, Parker. *Chaplin: Last of the Clowns*. New York: Horizon Press, 1972.

Walker, Alexander. *Sex in the Movies*. Baltimore: Penguin Books, 1968.

Walker, John. *Halliwell's Filmgoer's and Video Viewer's Companion*. 10th ed. New York: HarperCollins, 1993.

Wallace, Irving, Amy Wallace, David Wallechinsky, and Sylvia Wallace. *The Intimate Sex Lives of Famous People*. New York: Dell, 1982.

Warner, Jack L., and Dean Jennings. *My First Hundred Years in Hollywood*. New York: Random House, 1965.

Warren, Doug, and James Cagney. *James Cagney: The Authorized Biography*. New York: St. Martin's Press, 1983.

Warshow, Robert. *The Immediate Experience*. New York: Anchor Books, 1964.

Weinberg, Herman G. *The Lubitsch Touch*. Mineola, NY: Dover Publications, 1977.

West, Mae. *Goodness Had Nothing to Do with It*. Englewood Cliffs, NJ: Prentice-Hall, 1960.

Wilde, Larry. *The Great Comedians*. Secaucus, NJ: The Citadel Press, 1973.

Wiley, Mason, and Damien Bona. *Inside Oscar*. New York: Ballantine Books, 1988.

Willis, Donald C. *The Films of Frank Capra*. Metuchen, NJ: Scarecrow Press, 1974.

Wilson, Robert, ed. *The Film Criticism of Otis Ferguson*. Philadelphia: Temple University Press, 1971.

Wood, Robin. *Howard Hawks*. New York: Doubleday and Co., 1968.

Yacowar, Maurice. *Loser Take All: The Comic Art of Woody Allen*. New York: Frederick Ungar Publishing Co., 1980.

———. *Method in Madness*. New York: St. Martin's Press, 1981.

Zimmerman, Paul D., and Burt Goldblatt. *The Marx Brothers at the Movies*. New York: Signet, 1970.

Zukor, Adolph. *The Public Is Never Wrong*. New York: G. P. Putnam's Sons, 1953.

# Index

This index is intended as a supplement to the A-to-Z organization of the book. Therefore, people and films that have their own entries do not appear in the index, except where they occur in other entries.

# About the Authors

Barbara and Scott Siegel are the authors of forty-four books, six of which have been bestsellers. Their books have been published in Europe, Asia, and Australia, and many of their works have been excerpted and serialized in national publications. They are also the authors of three short stories that have each appeared in anthologies that made the New York Times bestseller list.

The Siegels, who write on a wide variety of subjects, are most recently known for their books on popular culture. They are, for instance, the authors of *The Encyclopedia of Hollywood*, which Jeff Strickler of the *Minneapolis Star-Tribune* called "Remarkable! One of the most impressive film reference books I've seen. It's destined to become one of the most useful and most used Hollywood reference texts." Among their other recent books are a number of celebrity biographies, including a book about Jack Nicholson. Also, a brand new edition of their popular reference book, *The Celebrity Phone Book*, will soon be published. It lists the names, addresses, and phone numbers of 4,250 famous people. The previous edition went through four printings.

In addition to writing books, Barbara and Scott are movie, cabaret, and theater critics, and their reviews and commentary broadcast via the Siegel Entertainment Syndicate on radio stations across the U.S. and Canada. Their "New York/New York" column appears weekly in the show business publication, *Drama-Logue*, for which they also interview celebrities and regularly write film criticism. The Siegels introduce films for the Cinema Club of the New York chapter of the National Academy of Television Arts and Sciences, as well as program and direct the Summer Film Festival at a major college in New York City.

The authors, who are often invited to speak at universities, schools, and writers conferences, also own the Siegel & Siegel Ltd. literary agency, which represents a great many talented and popular clients.

In their list of priorities, Barbara and Scott put movies ahead of most everything, except each other.